Business Analysis: Microsoft® Excel 2010

Conrad Carlberg

800 E. 96th Street
Indianapolis, Indiana 46240

Co

Business Analysis: Microsoft® Excel 2010

International Standard Book Number-10: 0-7897-4317-5
International Standard Book Number-13: 978-0-7897-4317-6

Library of Congress Cataloging-in-Publication Data

Carlberg, Conrad George
Business analysis, Microsoft Excel 2010 / Conrad Carlberg.
p. cm.
ISBN 978-0-7897-4317-6
1. Corporations—Finance. 2. Corporations—Finance—Computer programs. 3. Business planning—Computer programs. 4. Microsoft Excel (Computer file) I. Title.
HG4026.C254 2010
005.54—dc22
2010017029

Printed in the United States of America

First Printing: June 2010

Trademarks

All terms mentioned in this book that are known to be trademarks or service marks have been appropriately capitalized. Que Publishing cannot attest to the accuracy of this information. Use of a term in this book should not be regarded as affecting the validity of any trademark or service mark. Intuit and QuickBooks are registered trademarks of Intuit, Inc."

Warning and Disclaimer

Every effort has been made to make this book as complete and as accurate as possible, but no warranty or fitness is implied. The information provided is on an "as is" basis. The author and the publisher shall have neither liability nor responsibility to any person or entity with respect to any loss or damages arising from the information contained in this book.

Bulk Sales

Que Publishing offers excellent discounts on this book when ordered in quantity for bulk purchases or special sales. For more information, please contact

U.S. Corporate and Government Sales
1-800-382-3419
corpsales@pearsontechgroup.com

For sales outside of the United States, please contact

International Sales 1-317-428-3341
international@pearsontechgroup.com

Associate Editor
Greg Wiegand

Acquisitions Editor
Loretta Yates

Development Editor
Sondra Scott

Technical Editor
P.K.Hari Hara Subramanian

Managing Editor
Sandra Schroeder

Project Editor
Mandie Frank

Copy Editor
Gill Editorial Services

Indexer
Lisa Stumpf

Production
Mark Shirar

Designer
Anne Jones

Contents

PART II FINANCIAL PLANNING AND CONTROL

PART IV SALES AND MARKETING

About the Author

Conrad Carlberg is president of Network Control Systems, Inc., a software-development and consulting firm that specializes in statistical and database applications, and Beyond the Ledgers, a joint venture that develops and markets software coupling Excel to QuickBooks™. He holds a Ph.D. in statistics and is a many-time recipient of Microsoft's Most Valuable Professional Award. He lives near San Diego.

Dedication

For Tabben.

Acknowledgments

I want to express my appreciation and gratitude to Loretta Yates and Mandie Frank of Que Publishing for shepherding this book through the mysterious, labyrinthine publishing process. And to technical editor Hari Subramanian and development editor Sondra Scott for curbing me when necessary.

Karen Gill's copy edit was superlative.

It's always a pleasure to see one's work validated. For example, I couldn't have been more delighted to see Richard Scoville's glowing review of this book's first edition in *PC World*. And the visibility afforded this book by the McCombs School of Business, at the University of Texas at Austin, was completely unexpected.

We Want to Hear from You!

As the reader of this book, you are our most important critic and commentator. We value your opinion and want to know what we're doing right, what we could do better, what areas you'd like to see us publish in, and any other words of wisdom you're willing to pass our way.

As an associate publisher for Que Publishing, I welcome your comments. You can email or write me directly to let me know what you did or didn't like about this book—as well as what we can do to make our books better.

Please note that I cannot help you with technical problems related to the topic of this book. We do have a User Services group, however, where I will forward specific technical questions related to the book.

When you write, please be sure to include this book's title and author as well as your name, email address, and phone number. I will carefully review your comments and share them with the author and editors who worked on the book.

Email: feedback@quepublishing.com

Mail: Greg Wiegand
Associate Publisher
Que Publishing
800 East 96th Street
Indianapolis, IN 46240 USA

For more information about this book or another Que Publishing title, visit our website at www.quepublishing.com. Type the ISBN (excluding hyphens) or the title of a book in the Search field to find the page you're looking for.

INTRODUCTION

IN THIS INTRODUCTION

The book you just opened is different from most others on Excel that you might have seen. That's because it focuses on a topic that is deeply important to us all: money.

The novelist Rex Stout once wrote, facetiously, "The science of accounting has two main branches, first addition, and second subtraction." I kept that in mind when I was casting about for the book's theme. I wanted to write a book that would show people how to maximize profit, the result of combining those two branches.

Profit, of course, is not revenue. I can't teach you how to create revenue—that's more a matter for the heart, not the head—nor would I want to offer you MBA or CPA material. I did set out to write a book that any person engaged in any level of business could use as a refresher, from basic financial documents such as general ledgers and income statements, to the operational methods such as statistical process control, to the procedures such as business case analysis that underlie investment decisions.

I also wanted to structure this book around the most popular and sophisticated numeric analysis program available: Microsoft Excel. Therefore, each chapter in *Business Analysis: Microsoft® Excel 2010* provides information about a different business task or procedure and discusses how best to apply Excel in that situation.

This book references many Excel functions and capabilities that you might already use in your daily business activities. You might also find discussions of tools that you have never used or that you might never have considered using in the context of business analysis.

After all, no one can be completely familiar with every option in an application as extensive as Excel. Several Internet newsgroups frequented by Excel users answer technical questions. Years ago, a user asked how to enter a number in a worksheet cell so that Excel would treat the number as text. (This is quite a basic operation.) Surprisingly, the question was posted by one of the most experienced, best-known, and creative Excel consultants in the country. I thought that it was a put-on and responded appropriately, but it turned out that the question was genuine.

So we all have gaps in our knowledge. The purpose here is to help fill in some of the gaps that might have entered your knowledge base since your last course in business or since you first learned how to use a worksheet.

Business Analysis: Microsoft® Excel 2010 uses case studies—that is, situations that are typical of decisions or problems that you might face on any given workday. These case studies first discuss the problem itself: why it's a problem and how a solution can contribute to a company's profitability. Then the case studies demonstrate at least one possible solution that uses Excel as a tool. The intent is for you to mentally put yourself in the situation described, work through it, and then apply or adapt the solution to an actual situation that you face.

Taking It on Faith

Since the second edition of this book was published, the financial markets have sustained some severe shocks. Enron, which had been ranked seventh in the Fortune 500, entered bankruptcy, its CEO entered prison, and $60 billion in stock and $2 billion in pensions vanished. An old and highly respected accounting firm, Arthur Andersen, was found guilty of obstruction of justice in the Enron case. Although the Supreme Court later overturned the finding, "Uncle Artie's" staff fell from 28,000 to 200. And, by no means last, WorldCom revealed that it had improperly booked $3.8 billion in expenses—then, one month later, it filed for bankruptcy. Other familiar names that gained unwanted notoriety: Global Crossing, Tyco, and Adelphia.

The basis for all this corporate malfeasance was the cooking of the books. Transactions were kept off the financial reports, and earnings and losses were misstated, in efforts to paint a pretty picture and pump up the stock price.

After publication of this book's third edition, the United States suffered the worst and longest financial slowdown since the Depression of the 1930s. The recession of 2008–2009 had many causes, but the catalysts were pretty clear. Mortgage lenders extended home loans to people who couldn't afford them—at least, not when home prices stopped rising or variable rate loans adjusted up. Investment banks started to package and sell derivative instruments such as collateralized debt obligations and credit default swaps. The former hid bad mortgages among the good. The latter constituted a form of unregulated insurance that did not have sufficient reserve funds to survive a market bottom.

To some degree, the system works on trust. As investors, creditors, customers, and employees, all of us rely on financial reports such as income statements to make decisions about our lives. We rely on independent assessments of the risks assumed by investment firms such as Madoff Investment Securities and funding agencies such as Fannie Mae to guide our investment decisions. When the dollar amounts that are used to calculate those figures are seriously misrepresented, we can make seriously bad decisions.

Nothing here or anywhere else can fully protect you from people who keep bad news off the books. You have to be as close to things as Sherron Watkins, the Enron vice president, to see what's really going on in time to phone the cops. Even the Securities and Exchange Commission somehow overlooked the improbability of the 72 consecutive months of profitable returns reported by Madoff's company. So it might seem pointless to pay attention to income statements, balance sheets, and other reports of a company's financial status. But it's not pointless.

In the third edition of this book, I wrote this:

> The vast majority of North American businesses are generally honest, and if they sometimes skate, it's not by a really indecent margin. If you want to adopt a cynical viewpoint, consider that the incentives to misrecord financials are all wrong for small and midsize businesses. It's in large businesses where the temptations are really huge, and—at least, since 2002—that's where the scrutiny is greatest.

I was wrong, obviously. Greater scrutiny, earlier on, might have at least mitigated the reckless behaviors that took down Bear-Stearns, Merrill-Lynch, Lehman Brothers, IndyMac Bank, and so on. None of these could be considered "small" or "midsize" businesses, but they escaped the light of day that might have reined in their excesses until it was too late.

Nevertheless, it's still not "...pointless to pay attention to income statements, balance sheets, and other reports of a company's financial status." Plenty of analysts paid attention to those reports, directed their own assets accordingly, and blew whistles.

Alas, no one seems to have been listening.

Renamed and Improved Functions in Excel 2010

Business Analysis with Microsoft Excel has never been intended as a version book—that is, it has never been issued as a new edition every time Microsoft issues a new version of Excel. You are reading the book's fourth edition, yet Excel has had seven separate releases (not counting service releases) since this book was first published.

The third edition took the Excel 2007 user interface, most recognizable by the Ribbon, into account in describing how to carry out various analyses in Excel. The current edition does the same, but it describes your actions first using the Ribbon, and then describes them assuming that you're using the menu structure from Excel 1997–2003.

The most recent version, Excel 2010, has a variety of functions with new names, which are mainly existing functions whose capabilities have been divided among new functions. Most are statistical functions pertaining to the unit normal distribution, the t distribution, the F distribution and so on.

For example, the existing `TDIST` function returns a one- or a two-tailed test, depending on how the user sets one of its arguments. Which tail of the distribution can be specified by subtraction, because the distribution is symmetric.

The new functions divide the capabilities among three different functions: `T.DIST` (one-tail, left), `T.DIST.RT` (one-tail, right), and `T.DIST.2T` (two-tail). The capabilities were always there, but Excel 2010 assigns them specifically instead of relying on arguments and arithmetic manipulation such as `1 - TDIST(2.07, 15, 2)`.

This book takes account of the new functions and uses them where appropriate. There are three issues to bear in mind, discussed next.

Compatibility

Excel 2010 continues to recognize the functions that are being replaced; in fact, they are referred to as "compatibility functions." This means that Excel 2010 will recognize, say, the `TDIST` function in a workbook that you create in an earlier version such as Excel 2000.

It also means that you can continue to use the existing compatibility functions in new workbooks that you create using Excel 2010. Assuming that Microsoft intends to sunset the compatibility functions eventually, you have a window during which you can gradually switch to the new function set.

Excel 2010 has an auto-complete feature for functions. You can see it in action in Figure I.1.

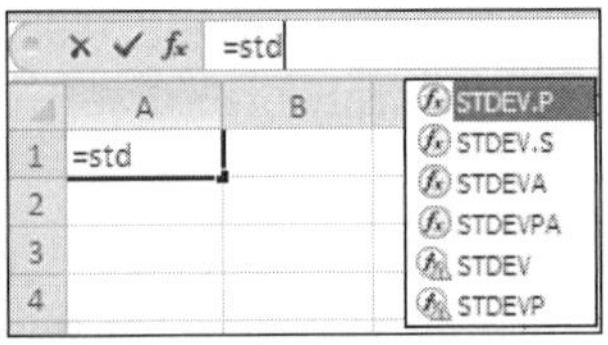

Figure I.1
The compatibility functions appear at the bottom of the list box.

Two compatibility functions are `STDEV` and `STDEVP`. When you type an equal sign and the first few letters in the function name, a list of functions that start with those letters appears. Click one of them to auto-complete the function, up to and including the opening parenthesis.

Notice in Figure I.1 that the compatibility functions appear at the bottom of the list. This is a reminder to the user that Microsoft is beginning to deprecate their use, and you should instead try to use `STDEV.P` or `STDEV.S`.

Consistency

Consistency functions is the term that, at least during the beta period for Excel 2010, Microsoft is using for the new functions. The rationale is as follows.

Prior to 2010, some functions such as `STDEV` had two versions. For example, `STDEV` is intended for use when the numbers you give it to work with are a sample from a population of values. In contrast, STDEVP is intended for use when the numbers you provide it *are* the population.

Microsoft regards the final *P* in the function name STDEVP to be inconsistent; after all, there's no final *S* in STDEV, even though it's intended to be used on a sample of data.

So, to make the names consistent, Excel 2010 has two "consistency functions" that calculate standard deviations: STDEV.S and STDEV.P. The consistency arises because both functions use the same naming pattern: the *name* of the function (STDEV) followed by a period and a *descriptor* (S or P) that identifies how you're expected to use it: on a Sample or on a Population.

This new naming scheme applies principally to statistical functions, and to the reference distribution functions in particular. (The distinction between the cumulative distribution function (CDF) and the probability density function (PDF) continues to be handled by the function arguments.)

The descriptors that Microsoft will use in the new names for old functions are as follows:

- DIST—This descriptor is attached to a function that returns a particular distribution such as the normal curve. It calls for the area under the curve to the *left* of the user-supplied value (CDF); alternatively, it can return the height of the curve at that point (PDF).
- DIST.RT—This descriptor calls for the area under a curve to the *right* of a user-supplied value.
- DIST.2T—This descriptor returns the area under the curve to the right of one value and to the left of the complementary value (often its negative). That is, it returns the probability associated with a two-tailed test.
- INV—This descriptor returns what Excel terms the *inverse* of the distribution. Students of elementary-to-intermediate statistics will probably think of this as the criterion value for a statistical test: for example, the value that Student's t-statistic must exceed to be regarded as statistically significant at some level.
- S—As discussed earlier, this descriptor returns a statistic for a sample of observations.
- P—Also as noted earlier, this descriptor returns a statistic for a population of observations.

Of course, the changes to Excel's function set go well beyond the calculation of standard deviations. There are changes to other statistical functions, a few of which include these:

- VAR is now VAR.S
- VARP is now VAR.P
- BETADIST is now BETA.DIST
- BETAINV is now BETA.INV

How This Book Is Organized

You can look in the table of contents or the index of *Business Analysis with Microsoft Excel, Fourth Edition* whenever you encounter an unfamiliar or obscure situation and read about how to solve it with the analysis tools in Excel. To make it easier to find related situations, this book is divided into four parts:

- **Part I, "Analyzing Financial Statements"**—This part discusses fundamental financial concepts and tools such as income statements, balance sheets, cash flow, and ratio analysis.
- **Part II, "Financial Planning and Control"**—This part covers budgeting methods such as pro formas, forecasting trends, and quality-control procedures, including process measurement and defect analysis.
- **Part III, "Investment Decisions"**—You'll find business case analysis and profit planning in this part. It covers strategies for structuring and testing business cases, as well as ways to quantify and manage the degree of risk involved in entering a new line of business. Also included is a chapter on fixed assets, which normally account for the greatest portion of a company's capital investment.
- **Part IV, "Sales and Marketing"**—Sales and marketing analysis, costing and pricing, and margin analysis are covered here. Since the publication of the original edition of this book, many businesses have placed their financial and operational records in true relational databases and in applications intended specifically for accounting. Therefore, this edition includes a chapter that explains the most effective ways to import data into Excel directly from databases, from accounting report files and from websites. Another chapter focuses on moving the data the opposite direction, from Excel into a database.

There's also a glossary that briefly defines important terms.

As I mentioned earlier, it's important that you be able to dip into this book to find particular topics and to use the information without necessarily reviewing everything that came before. Therefore, certain tips and recommendations on using Excel are (briefly) repeated from time to time. And in each chapter you will find full, step-by-step descriptions of how to accomplish a given task using Excel.

Two Special Skills: Named Ranges and Array Formulas

Have you ever had to interpret someone else's worksheet? Or have you ever had to use a worksheet that you constructed months or perhaps years ago, and then been completely unable to figure out what you had in mind when you constructed it? You probably have and, if so, you know what a headache it can be.

The principal difficulty with many otherwise useful worksheets is that their authors don't document them. Consider this worksheet formula:

```
=IF(AND(B12<30000,A12<5),C14*D14*.05,C14*D14*.075)
```

It could take a couple of minutes to figure out what that formula is up to, even if you know the worksheet's basic purpose. However, it would take you only a few seconds if the author had used this formula instead:

```
=IF(AND(YearToDateSales<30000,Tenure<5),Units*Price*LowCommission,
Units*Price*HighCommission)
```

It's not too difficult to infer what this formula says:

> If this person's sales during this year are less than $30,000, and this person was hired fewer than five years ago, return the sales amount times the lower commission; otherwise, return the sales amount times the higher commission.

To help make your work self-documenting, in many instances, you should give names to Excel worksheet cells, ranges, and constants. You can then use those names in your formulas and functions so that you can see it's multiplying sales dollars by a commission, not simply one relatively anonymous cell by another. Because you'll find this approach taken throughout the book, it's reviewed here.

Assigning Names

To name a *cell* or *range*, begin by selecting it on the worksheet. Click the Ribbon's Formulas tab and click the Define Name drop-down in the Defined Names group. Choose Define Name in the drop-down list and type the name you want to use in the Name box. You can also specify the name's scope as sheet-level or book-level (see Chapter 2, "Balance Sheet: Current Assets," for more information on that distinction.) If you're using a version of Excel that precedes Excel 2007, choose Insert, Name, Define, and type the name you want to use in the Names in Workbook edit box; then click OK.

Or use this quicker method: After you have selected the cell or range, click in the Name box (immediately above the column header for column A and left of the drop-down arrow), type the name, and press Enter.

To name a *constant* such as `LowCommission`, click the Define Name dropdown (or choose Insert, Name, Define), and type the name of the constant in the Names in Workbook edit box. Then, in the Refers To edit box, type the value that you want to assign to the constant and click OK. (You can't use the Name box to define a constant directly.)

A side benefit of using names instead of cell or range addresses is that you can paste names into formulas as you are creating them. After you have started typing a formula, click the Ribbon's Formulas tab and select the Use in Formula drop-down from the Defined Names group. Then click the name you want in the drop-down list. (In earlier versions, you can choose Insert, Name, Paste and select the name you want to use from the Paste Name list box.) This approach saves you keystrokes and helps prevent misspellings. Also, you don't have to recall existing names: They're right there in the list box.

When you choose a name for a range or a constant, consider using both uppercase and lowercase letters: for example, `TotalLiabilities`. Mixing uppercase and lowercase makes the name easier to read. (Compare to `totalliabilities`.) You should probably avoid using all uppercase letters. Excel's worksheet function names (for example, `SUM` and `AVERAGE`) use all uppercase letters, and you don't want to define a name that could be confused with a function.

Blank spaces and certain special characters, such as the percent symbol, aren't allowed in names. Some people like to use an underscore in place of a space, preferring `Total_Liabilities` over `TotalLiabilities`.

Using Array Formulas

Many of the formulas described in this book are a special type of Excel formula called an *array formula*. An array formula contains an array of values or a reference to an array of worksheet cells, as shown here:

```
=SUM(IF(MOD(ROW(SheetRange),2)=0,SheetRange))
```

This sums the values in the worksheet range named `SheetRange` if they are in an even-numbered row. The formula requires a special keyboard sequence to enter it correctly. On a computer running Windows, the sequence is Ctrl+Shift+Enter—that is, simultaneously hold down the Ctrl and Shift keys as you press Enter.

You can tell that Excel has interpreted your formula as an array formula if you see curly braces (sometimes termed *French braces*) around it in the formula bar. For example, the formula shown previously appears in the formula bar like this:

```
{=SUM(IF(MOD(ROW(SheetRange),2)=0,SheetRange))}
```

Don't type the braces yourself. If you do, Excel interprets the formula as text.

These are termed array formulas because they have within them arrays that you don't usually see and that Excel doesn't normally expect. For example, if expanded, the previous formula would show an array of the row numbers in `SheetRange`. Excel doesn't normally expect that you'll present an *array* of values as conditions in an `IF` function (Excel normally expects a single value as an IF condition), so you signal that's what you've done by using the Ctrl+Shift+Enter keyboard sequence.

You can explore the inner workings of array formulas by using the Evaluate Formula tool in Excel 2002 or later.. Click the Ribbon's Formulas tab and choose Evaluate Formula in the Formula Auditing group. In earlier versions, begin by choosing Tools, Formula Auditing, Evaluate Formula.

Conventions Used in This Book

Business Analysis with Microsoft Excel, Fourth Edition uses a few typeface, terminology, and formatting conventions to emphasize special information:

- A sequence like this:

  Ctrl+Enter

  means that you should hold down the Ctrl key as you press Enter.
- When you should select a sequence of options from an Excel Ribbon group, you will see this:

  Click the Data tab, then choose What-If Analysis, Goal Seek.

  This means that you should first click the Ribbon's Data tab, then the What-If Analysis dropdown, and then click on Goal Seek in the dropdown menu. The sequences for Excel 2003 and earlier, with no Ribbon, are analogous and are usually specified in the text.
- Data or formulas that you enter in an Excel worksheet cell are shown like this:
  `=SUM(CumulativeNetIncome)/ProductLife`
- New terms, or information that needs special emphasis, are shown in *italic*.
- Information about performing a task more efficiently or alternative ways to go about a task appear in tips. Tips are set apart from the main text like this:

> **TIP** To copy the selected cells, press Ctrl+C.

- Information that is related to the current topic but that might not apply to it directly is shown like this:

> **NOTE** There is one distinct IRR for each change in sign in a series of cash flows.

Working with Income Statements

1

In many ways, operating a business is like playing a game—a serious one, of course—and keeping track of your business is similar to studying games such as baseball. Serious baseball fans know hundreds of statistics, such as batting averages and strikeouts. Similarly, if you are serious about your business, you need to be able to measure and understand the numbers that describe how your company operates. Accounting in general and financial statements in particular provide the scorecards.

This chapter is no treatise on accounting and finance, but it does describe tools that you can use to better understand the financial aspects of operating your business. Plenty of textbooks cover the generally accepted procedures of accounting and finance. This chapter highlights and demonstrates some practical techniques used in those procedures.

IN THIS CHAPTER

Keeping Score

Accounting translates the actions that take place in the business world into a set of numbers that you can use to make informed decisions. Accounting captures information on how well a company operates, the many obstacles that it needs to overcome, and its prospects for the future.

Accounting rules enable you to compare your company with other companies and other industries and to make year-to-year comparisons for your own company. For example, it's against the rules to change your method of depreciation without full disclosure of the effects of the change on the company's financial statements. Depreciation amounts affect a company's reported profit; if you could change your depreciation method whenever you felt like it, you could change your reported profit when it was expedient to do so. In that event it would be impossible for those who might invest in your business or who might loan it money to have confidence in the validity of your financials. Having rules and following them makes it possible to conduct business. (As we've seen during the early 2000s, having rules and failing to follow them eventually catches up with everyone—not only the miscreants.)

It's important to be able to make comparisons with other companies when you want to seek additional funds for expansion, such as by borrowing or by inviting capital investment. Following the rules can open opportunities to succeed and to receive equal treatment in a rugged marketplace. But you don't need to be a CPA to use accounting for solid decision making. It can be as simple as subtracting your expenses from your revenues to determine your profits.

Accounting quantifies the everyday world of buying and selling. Would you buy something for more than you could sell it? Of course not—but many companies do exactly that every year. The collapse of an energy trading giant, of many of the dot-com startups, and of the telecommunications and investment banking conglomerates can be traced to that very mistake. Too often, businesses look at only the up-front costs and ignore the related, hidden, and opportunity costs. It's trite to say so, but things get trite by being true: The devil is in the details, but finance and accounting can help you maintain control.

Choosing the Right Perspective

We all tend to think of accounting as an exact science that is fully governed by rational rules, but the numbers generated are actually only best estimates. Although the rules, procedures, and methods make the numbers appear to be objective facts, they are far from absolute—especially if someone has been cooking the books.

The analysis techniques that this book describes can't prevent the excesses that U.S. business witnessed in the early 2000s. But they can help expose the corrupt practices that can't stand the light of day. The system depends on the good faith of those running it: The review of the deceptive accounting practices shone a light on the corruption that brought down Enron and subsequently companies such as Bear Stearns.

The numbers represent how well the managers are running the business. Balance sheets and income statements are not commandments; they are guides, and different users have different purposes for them.

Defining Two Purposes for Accounting

This book (along with just about any book that discusses it at all) classifies accounting according to who's using the information:

- **Management accounting** provides information to decision makers inside the company. If you want to bring a new product to market, you assess the product's potential by analyzing cost, price, market demand, and competition. You make judgments about the product—whether to introduce it, how to manage it, whether it has run its course—on the basis of the financial and operational data you have available.

- **Financial accounting** provides financial information to the company's decision makers, as well as to those outside the company, such as investors, creditors, and governments. Suppose that you wanted to raise funds by making your company a public corporation and issuing shares of stock to the investment community. Potential investors would require detailed financial accounting information (and the law would require you to make it available). An investor wants to know that a set of accepted standards was used to create the information. Otherwise, there is no way for that investor to make an informed choice.

When you decide whether to introduce a new product or make any other management decision, you use a more flexible analytic framework than when you are trying to raise capital in the investment community. You often need room to maneuver, and management accounting provides you with that room.

For example, you might want to use the last-in, first-out (LIFO) method of valuing inventory if your objective is to set sales policies. The LIFO method is the best way to measure net income, taking current prices and costs into account. But the FIFO (first-in, first-out) method provides a better estimate of assets on the balance sheet. So management accounting allows you the flexibility of choosing your method of valuation, depending on the purpose you have in mind.

→ For more information about valuing inventory, see Chapter 3, "Valuing Inventories for the Balance Sheet."

Both aspects of accounting are necessary tools, and this book discusses financial accounting from time to time. However, the principal focus is on making information as useful as possible for internal decision making.

To use accounting information for routine decision making, you don't need to explore in depth the nuances and technicalities of the accounting profession. But if you understand this information well enough to use it on a routine basis, you will be much better prepared to use your accountant's time wisely when a delicate decision is required.

Using the Income Statement

The income statement is a powerful tool for decision making. It portrays the flow of money and the relationship of revenues to expenses over a period of time. It tells us how much money was made in an accounting period such as a year. The terms *profit*, *net income*, and *earnings* are commonly, interchangeably, and somewhat loosely used to state the bottom line.

The income statement provides a starting point in the analysis of a business. The popular press frequently reports earnings and nothing more: "Today U.S. Widgets reported quarterly income of $240 million." This is positive (unless the marketplace expected it to report $480 million), but there is more to the story.

Choosing a Reporting Method

The measurement of net income is an attempt to match the value generated by a business (its *revenues*) with the resources it consumes (its *expenses*). The sentence "In fiscal year 2010, we sold $200 million of product and services, at a cost of $175 million, for a profit of $25 million," quantifies the operation of the business over a one-year period. The business now has a track record, a place to begin the analysis of its operations.

However, more detail is needed to measure and report income in a generally accepted fashion. Accountants use a series of conventions that strengthen the validity of the income statement. If you read an income statement that you believe to have been prepared using these conventions, you generally have greater faith that the information is valid and credible. Perhaps the company is worth investing in or lending money to.

There is no one way to structure an income statement. Your choice depends on how you intend to use the statement and what picture you want to present. The key is that the information be useful in support of decision making. Your audience could be potential investors, creditors, or internal (sometimes external) managers.

Figures 1.1 to 1.4 show some examples of commonly used income statement formats.

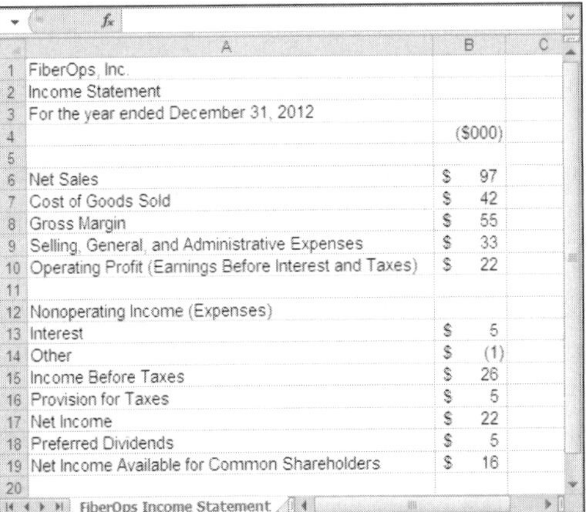

	A	B	
1	FiberOps, Inc.		
2	Income Statement		
3	For the year ended December 31, 2012		
4			($000)
5			
6	Net Sales	$	97
7	Cost of Goods Sold	$	42
8	Gross Margin	$	55
9	Selling, General, and Administrative Expenses	$	33
10	Operating Profit (Earnings Before Interest and Taxes)	$	22
11			
12	Nonoperating Income (Expenses)		
13	Interest	$	5
14	Other	$	(1)
15	Income Before Taxes	$	26
16	Provision for Taxes	$	5
17	Net Income	$	22
18	Preferred Dividends	$	5
19	Net Income Available for Common Shareholders	$	16
20			

FiberOps Income Statement

Figure 1.1
An income statement format suitable for external reporting usually omits details such as inventory levels but includes all categories that affect net income.

CASE STUDY: DOCUMENTATION FOR A BANK LOAN

Your company wants to take out a bank loan for the purchase of new factory equipment. As the company's chief operating officer, you oversee the day-to-day activities. You also stay focused on topics such as the amount of your variable costs relative to your revenue, and what your profit margins are on a product-by-product basis.

When it evaluates your company's loan application, the bank has only a secondary interest in those matters, but it is keenly interested in your sales volume, your gross profit, and your operating profit. You could use a format such as the one shown in Figure 1.1 for the income statement that accompanies your loan application.

Figure 1.1 shows a typical layout of an income statement used for external reporting purposes. Notice that there are apparent math errors in the report, in rows 17 and 19. These can appear when a currency format obscures significant digits. When, for purposes of space and simplicity, you divide actual figures by, say, 1,000 and indicate by a column header that the entries are in $1,000s, *consider* using Excel's `ROUND()` function. For example:

```
=ROUND(4690/1000,0)
```

Had this been used in cell B16 of Figure 1.1 instead of the actual entry of `4.69` (which the cell format displays as `$5`), the result of the calculation in cell B17 would have been shown as `$21` instead of `$22`.

I put the word "consider" in italic just now because the `ROUND` function can create as many problems as it solves. To continue this example, if you used `ROUND` in cell B16 of Figure 1.1, cell B17 would indeed show `$21` instead of `$22`. But then cell B19 would show `$16` when its true value is `$15`. In general, you must choose between two alternatives in this sort of situation:

- Bite the bullet and choose to show exact figures instead of rounded or truncated values. The downside is that your financials can appear cluttered and more difficult to comprehend.
- Use the `ROUND` function (or one of its close cousins, `ROUNDUP` and `ROUNDDOWN`) to get an integer or to otherwise limit the number of decimals in a value. The downside is that in the course of solving one apparent math error, you might induce another.

CAUTION

You can also select the Precision as Displayed check box, but this is a risky procedure. Doing this permanently changes a value stored as `4.69` to its displayed appearance, which might be `5`. This is seldom a good idea. However, if you must do so, you can click the File tab, select Options, and then click Advanced. Scroll down to the When Calculating This Workbook section and select the Set Precision As Displayed check box. To locate that checkbox in versions of Excel prior to Office 2007, choose Tools, Options and click the Calculation tab.

Just as there are many uses for income statements, there are many ways to structure income statements. The same firm might modify and adjust its report of income and costs based on the purpose it has in mind; as a result, the income statements need to reflect different sets of requirements.

Cells in Excel

If you're new to Excel, you might find the preceding discussion about math errors and rounding and Precision as Displayed mysterious and obscure. There is something about Excel (actually, about any worksheet application) that is absolutely fundamental but often goes unsaid: There is an important difference between what is in a cell and what the cell displays. Furthermore, a cell can contain either a value or a formula that results in a value.

Suppose that you open a new workbook, select cell A1 on Sheet1, type the number `2.51`, and press Enter. You see 2.51 in the cell, and you also see 2.51 in the Formula box. (That's the box just above the column headers and just to the right of the *fx* symbol.) In this case, what you see in the cell is what the cell contains.

Now click the Home tab on the Ribbon, and click twice the Decrease Decimal button in the Number group. You now see the number 3 in cell A1, but you still see 2.51 in the Formula box. The reason is that when you click the Decrease Decimal button, you alter the cell's appearance—its number format, in this example—but not the value stored in the cell. And when you decrease the number of visible decimals to zero, Excel responds by rounding the display to the nearest integer.

> **NOTE** If you're wondering why you get a 3 instead of a 2 when you decrease the decimals displayed for the value 2.51, you're thinking along the right lines. Microsoft could have chosen either to round the display of 2.51 to 3 or to truncate the display from 2.51 to 2. But rounding is less wrong than truncation, twice as often.

If you now use cell A1 as part of a formula in another cell, that formula uses the value in A1 regardless of the format you've chosen to use for A1. For example, suppose you enter this formula:

```
=5 - A1
```

in cell A2. That formula would result in the value 2.49 (that is, 5 – 2.51). It would not result in the value 2, as it would if it subtracted 3 from 5. Changing a cell's number format lets you alter its *apparent* value but not its *actual* value. In short: What you see isn't necessarily what you get.

Now suppose that instead of entering `2.51` in cell A1, you started by entering this formula in A1:

```
=3 - .49
```

You still see 2.51 in the cell, but now the Formula box shows the formula. You can take this as one of the rare instances of *always* in Excel: The Formula box always shows a visible cell's contents. The cell *usually* shows the value, whether the cell contains an actual value or a formula. (The exception is when you set an Excel option to show formulas, not their results, in cells.)

With the formula instead of the value in the cell, you can still use the Decrease Decimal button to cause the cell to show 3 instead of 2.51. So in a case like this, you might not see the cell's value *anywhere*; the Formula box shows the formula, and the cell shows the formula's result as modified by the number format.

As this section said at the outset, if you're new to Excel, these distinctions probably seem mysterious and obscure. But they quickly become second nature. That said, we can return to the issue of the design of income statements in Excel.

CASE STUDY: INVENTORY CONTROL IN A MERCHANDISING FIRM

You are in charge of purchasing products for resale by a retail store. To hold down inventory carrying costs and avoid the use of cash until absolutely necessary, you have instituted Just in Time inventory procedures. If these procedures are working as you designed, your inventory levels at the end of the year should be about the same as—or, ideally, lower than—the levels at the start of the year and should align with the turnover of the products your business sells. For your management purposes, you might arrange to obtain an income statement similar to the one shown in Figure1.2.

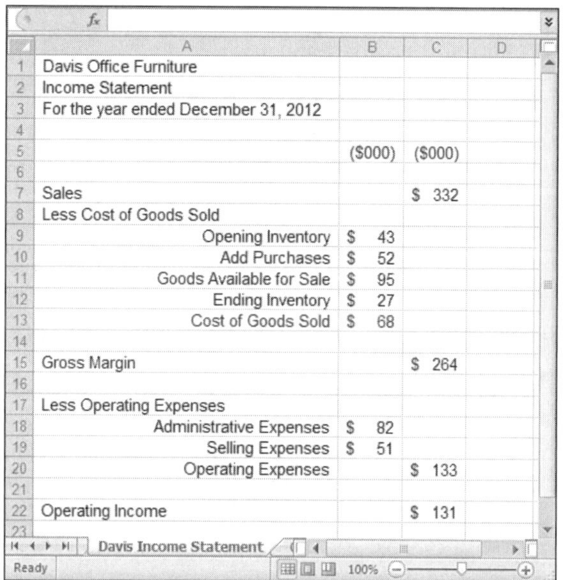

	A	B	C
1	Davis Office Furniture		
2	Income Statement		
3	For the year ended December 31, 2012		
4			
5		($000)	($000)
6			
7	Sales		$ 332
8	Less Cost of Goods Sold		
9	Opening Inventory	$ 43	
10	Add Purchases	$ 52	
11	Goods Available for Sale	$ 95	
12	Ending Inventory	$ 27	
13	Cost of Goods Sold	$ 68	
14			
15	Gross Margin		$ 264
16			
17	Less Operating Expenses		
18	Administrative Expenses	$ 82	
19	Selling Expenses	$ 51	
20	Operating Expenses		$ 133
21			
22	Operating Income		$ 131

Figure 1.2
An income statement format suitable for certain management purposes in a merchandising firm might exclude dividend information but provide details on inventory levels.

A manufacturing firm might use a different format for an income statement (see Figure 1.3). The major difference between the structure of the manufacturing firm's income statement and that of the merchandising firm is in the cost of goods sold. For the manufacturer, the cost of goods manufactured is added to the opening inventory. For the merchandiser, purchases from suppliers are added to the opening inventory. The manufacturer is likely to have various cost subcategories within the cost of goods manufactured, such as raw materials, factory overhead, and labor costs; these are often detailed in a supplement to the income statement. These subcategories do not appear in the merchandiser's income statement; the cost of purchases is seldom broken down further.

One special type of income statement supports the management of the business from the perspective of specific products and expenses. The amount of detail in the income statement should be tailored to the manager's data requirements. Figure 1.4 shows an example.

This income statement excludes items such as interest and amortization, and a manager can use it to analyze everyday operations. It provides a more targeted view of revenue and

Figure 1.3
An income statement for a manufacturing firm, formatted for planning purposes, often includes detailed information about the cost of goods manufactured in a supplement.

	A	B	C
1	Clark Manufacturing, Inc.		
2	Income Statement		
3	For the year ended December 31, 2012		
4			
5		($000)	($000)
6			
7	Sales		$ 223
8	Less Cost of Goods Sold		
9	Opening Finished Goods Inventory	$ 58	
10	Cost of Goods Manufactured (see Supplement)	$ 127	
11	Goods Available for Sale	$ 185	
12	Ending Finished Goods Inventory	$ 62	
13	Cost of Goods Sold	$ 123	
14			
15	Gross Margin		$ 100
16			
17	Less Operating Expenses		
18	Administrative Expenses	$ 34	
19	Selling Expenses	$ 20	
20	Operating Expenses		$ 54
21			
22	Operating Income		$ 46

Clark Income Statement

Figure 1.4
An income statement format that is used for the management of revenues and expenses shows how funds were acquired and spent.

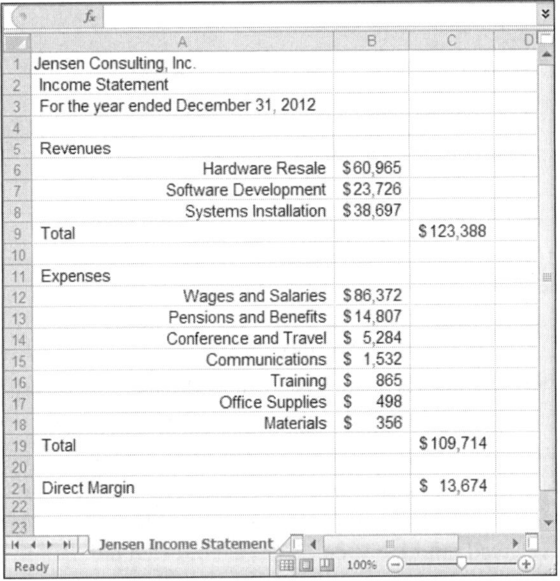

	A	B	C
1	Jensen Consulting, Inc.		
2	Income Statement		
3	For the year ended December 31, 2012		
4			
5	Revenues		
6	Hardware Resale	$60,965	
7	Software Development	$23,726	
8	Systems Installation	$38,697	
9	Total		$123,388
10			
11	Expenses		
12	Wages and Salaries	$86,372	
13	Pensions and Benefits	$14,807	
14	Conference and Travel	$ 5,284	
15	Communications	$ 1,532	
16	Training	$ 865	
17	Office Supplies	$ 498	
18	Materials	$ 356	
19	Total		$109,714
20			
21	Direct Margin		$ 13,674

Jensen Income Statement

expense and is an example of the type of income statement a manager needs to guide a department.

Ideally, you should tailor the income statement to a format that you and your managers can use routinely. You can expand the level of detail shown in Figures 1.1 to 1.4 to include the data that you need most often. Here, both judgment and creativity become critical. A simple reformat of data or an added detail line item can enrich your insight into the way your business operates.

For example, you could drive the behavior of your management team by means of a link between your bonus systems and a customized income statement. Suppose that you want to get your sales force to concentrate on developing new accounts. Your income statement might show revenue figures for sales both to existing accounts and to new business, and it might include cost figures for bonuses paid for new business. This could help prod the sales force to concentrate on the more difficult process of new business sales.

As Figures 1.1 to 1.4 imply, there are many possible ways to structure an income statement. Each one reflects a different set of circumstances, defined by the business's specific situation. There are guidelines, but there is also flexibility within those guidelines to tailor a statement to your particular needs. Your business and the way you want to use the data set the direction for the type of income statement to use.

Measuring the Operating and Nonoperating Segments

An income statement records the flow of resources over time. Operating income measures the extent to which revenues generated during the accounting period exceeded the expenses incurred in producing the revenues. This measure tells whether the firm's core operating business made money.

NOTE

It's useful to distinguish *operating* income, the difference between revenues and expenses, from *net* income, which takes the additional effect of taxes, interest, and other charges into account.

Income statements commonly divide this resource flow into operating and nonoperating segments. The operating segment represents what occurred on a day-to-day basis to generate income. The nonoperating segment represents the assets that the firm might have financed, the tax impacts of being in business, and extraordinary occurrences such as the one-time sale of a major company asset.

When you analyze a business, it is important to keep the two segments separate. If you were considering the expansion of your own business, you might first ask yourself whether the firm made money and whether you can fund an expansion with the profits. Your focus would be on the numbers produced by your normal, everyday business operations; you would not want to base your decision on the effect of a one-time, unique event. You would take that event into consideration, but you would not rely on its effect in your forecast of future earnings.

An income statement's operating segment represents the results of the company's major, ongoing activities, and the nonoperating segment represents all the company's secondary or ancillary activities. The company needs to understand both segments to grasp the total picture and know how best to prepare for its future.

Moving from the General Journal to the Income Statement

In the past, it's been typical for a business to record its daily transactions in a general journal. This record keeps track of every individual transaction in every account, such as cash investments, cash paid, accounts receivable, accounts payable, and so on.

In more recent years, the availability of relatively inexpensive accounting software has changed all that. As recently as the 1990s, for example, an accounting package for a small business could easily cost $10,000 and provide much more functionality than was needed. In 2010, a business can buy adequate accounting software for a few hundred dollars or less.

One result is that we're now entering information about product sold, sales price, sales tax, customer name, income account, and asset account into a specially designed window instead of in a ruled journal. The days of green eyeshades and sleeve garters are gone for good. (Nevertheless, and although it's usually hidden from view, all that sales and expense information is still going into a general journal that your accounting software maintains.)

Your business might involve a few high-value transactions during an accounting period, and if so you might prefer to forego the benefits of specialized accounting software. Even if the direct cost of the software is trivial, there's still a learning curve. In that case, you might want to exercise the greater control that's available to you in a generalized worksheet environment such as Excel's. And then you'll want to know more about journals, information of the sort discussed here.

Or, if you have decided to invest in accounting software, it will be easier for you to understand what's going on inside the black box if you have a glance at the remaining material in this chapter and in Chapter 2, "Balance Sheet: Current Assets." One of the reasons that some accountants love for their clients to use QuickBooks, for example, is that there's so much more opportunity for them to make more money correcting their clients' mistakes.

Getting the General Journal into Excel

Many different software programs are available to help you record and store information about your business transactions. Some programs provide the user with conveniences such as a predefined chart of accounts and automatic linkages between journals, ledgers, and other reports. Therefore, many people prefer to use software other than Excel to gather information on individual transactions. (A chart of accounts is simply a list that associates account names and purposes with numbers that identify the account. For example, you might decide to identify the liability account named `Accounts Payable` with the number 2000.) For a very small business, Excel is a sensible choice of platform for entering, storing, and retrieving information about individual transactions. (Normally, for these purposes, Excel is less powerful and flexible than a true database such as Oracle or, on a smaller scale, Microsoft Access. But the differences in power and flexibility are virtually meaningless when a relatively small amount of data is involved.)

But keep in mind that Excel is not designed as a specialized, full-featured accounting package. If you choose Excel to handle your accounting, you have to build many features from scratch, including your own categories for transactions, the double entry of individual transactions, and so on. Excel is much better suited to summarizing and analyzing the transaction data that you get from some other source—often, single-purpose accounting software.

After you have imported the data into Excel, you can manipulate it to meet your requirements, including anything from category subtotals to statistical analysis. Few accounting packages directly support the detailed financial analysis of accounting data, but most provide an export feature that creates data files that Excel can open.

On the other hand, if you enter and store individual transactions using software other than Excel, you might occasionally have difficulty importing files into Excel. Although most such programs have an option that enables you to export data in ASCII (text) format, the arrangement of the exported data might not be ideal for import into Excel. Other accounting packages can export directly into Excel, but then the worksheet that the accounting package creates might have features that you could do without.

For example, some programs export each part of a record onto a different line of the ASCII file: one line for the account number, another line for the account name, another line for the transaction amount, and so on. However, most of Excel's data and charting tools work best with a list (or, since Excel 2007, table) layout: different records in different rows and different fields in different columns. To take advantage of this layout, you would need to do some preliminary work with the accounting package's export file.

NOTE

Attractive alternatives include the use of Structured Query Language (SQL, pronounced *ess cue ell or sequel*) tools, ActiveX Data Objects (ADO), and Data Access Objects. If the accounting software that handles your transactions conforms to certain standards, you can arrange to import the data into Excel in a form that is ready for use in reports such as income statements and balance sheets.

→ You can find additional information on the tools mentioned in the previous Note in Chapter 17, "Importing Business Data into Excel."

Certainly, you can import ASCII files into an Excel worksheet quite easily by clicking the File tab, clicking Open, and then choosing Text Files from the drop-down to the right of the File edit box (prior to 2007, start by choosing File, Open).

However, after you have imported the information, you might find it necessary to move the account name and the transaction amount onto the same line as the account number. If you have many records to import, this cutting and pasting can become tedious, and you should consider recording and then running an Excel macro to do the rearrangement for you.

As another example of the issues involved with importing, QuickBooks applies Excel's Text format to certain cells in exported reports, such as its income statements. To do so is unnecessary, because Excel's General format recognizes and displays both text and numeric values properly. The Text format is both unnecessary and annoying; if you want to put a formula in a cell that's formatted as Text, you first must reformat the cell to General or to one of

Excel's numeric formats. Otherwise, Excel interprets your formula as text and won't calculate it.

In other words, there are some real conveniences and advantages to using an accounting package, even for a very small business. But be aware that the subsequent use of Excel's powerful financial analysis capabilities on the accounting data often requires that you do some preliminary work with the exported figures.

Understanding Absolute, Relative, and Mixed References

The user of a popular accounting package writes, "I click Export Report and select Export to a New Excel Spreadsheet. The export itself works fine, but then if I copy a column and paste it into my existing financial report spreadsheet, the formulas change and are incorrect."

The problem is that the accounting package being used provides formulas that refer to cells in a way that can change, depending on where the formulas are placed—and that's just what happens when the user pastes a column into an existing financial report spreadsheet. In this particular case, the accounting package was the source of the error, but there are plenty of other causes for this kind of problem—including other Excel users, people you thought were your friends.

To avoid this sort of problem, you need to be familiar with how Excel handles your data—particularly how it refers to worksheet cells. Three different kinds of cell references are used: absolute, relative, and mixed.

Consider this formula:

```
=SUM($A$1:$B$2)
```

Entered into a cell in a worksheet, the formula returns the total of the values in cells A1, A2, B1, and B2. The range of cell addresses between the parentheses implies a rectangle of cells. The first address (here, `$A$1`) identifies the rectangle's upper-left corner, and the second address (`$B$2`) identifies its lower-right corner. The colon, called the *range operator*, tells Excel to include all the other cells that are in the rectangle: in this case, A2 and B1.

Suppose that you entered the formula `=SUM($A$1:$B$2)` in cell C3. If you then copied the formula and pasted it into cell Q15, or cell AA100, or cell XFD1048576, it would still refer to that same range of cells, `$A$1:$B$2`. It's an *absolute* reference—made absolute by the dollar signs that precede the column letters and row numbers.

In contrast, suppose you entered this formula into cell C3:

```
=SUM(A1:B2)
```

It has no dollar signs. It's a *relative* reference—relative to whatever cell was active when you created the reference. In this example, that's cell C3. If you now copy and paste the formula into cell D3 (same row, one column to the right), the formula adjusts accordingly and becomes this:

```
=SUM(B1:C2)
```

Using words instead of cell addresses: Paste the copied formula one column to the right of where you originally entered it, and the relative reference responds by adjusting its columns in the same direction and distance: `A` becomes `B`, and `B` becomes `C`.

Similarly, if you copied it from cell C3 and pasted it into cell C4, it would become this:

```
=SUM(A2:B3)
```

Copy the formula down one row, and the row numbers in the relative reference adjust: `1` becomes `2`, and `2` becomes `3`.

Another way of thinking about this is that the original formula pointed to a rectangle of cells that starts two columns left and two rows up from the cell in which it was entered. When it's copied and pasted into a different cell, the formula still points to cells starting two columns left and two rows up. This behavior is characteristic of relative references.

A third type of reference is the *mixed* reference, in which either the column or the row—but not both—is anchored by means of the dollar sign. For example:

```
=SUM($A1:$A2)
```

If you enter this formula into cell A3, you can copy and paste it to a cell in any other column, and it will still depend on values in column A; the dollar signs anchor it to that column. But if you copy it from cell A3 into any other row, the rows in the reference will adjust accordingly. So if you copied the formula from cell A3 into cell B4, the formula in B4 would be this:

```
=SUM($A2:$A3)
```

The dollar sign before the column letter anchors the formula to that column. The dollar sign's absence before the row number allows the reference to adjust if you move it up or down. The analogous effect occurs with another sort of mixed reference:

```
=SUM(A$2:A$3)
```

which provides an anchor to rows 2 and 3 but allows the column reference to shift.

NOTE The same is true with range names. By default, Excel makes absolute the cell or range of cells that a range name refers to. But you can edit that reference via Define Name, making the reference mixed or relative. See the Introduction for a brief discussion of range names.

Getting the Journal Data to the Ledger

Whether you enter the general journal data directly into Excel or import it from another software application, the next step is usually to collect the transactions in their proper accounts within the general ledger. Figure 1.5 shows an example of entries in a general journal, and Figure 1.6 shows how you can collect these entries in the general ledger.

For ease in collecting the general journal entries into the general ledger, four range names are defined on the general journal sheet shown in Figure 1.5: `EntryDate` ($A$5:$A$26),

	A	B	C	D	E
1		General Journal			
2		Account Titles and	Account		
3		Explanation	Number	Debit	Credit
4					
5	6/1/11	Office Equipment	22	$ 686	
6	6/1/11	Accounts Payable	30		$ 686
7		Purchase of Laser Printer			
8					
9	6/3/11	Office Lease	21	$1,187	
10	6/3/11	Cash	1		$1,187
11		Office Rent, June			
12					
13	6/7/11	Accounts Receivable	40	$ 717	
14	6/7/11	Sales	60		$ 717
15		Sold 1 Model VM3262			
16					
17	6/9/11	Telephone Expense	23	$ 85	
18	6/9/11	Accounts Payable	30		$ 85
19		May phone bill			
20					
21	6/10/11	Salaries	50	$3,458	
22	6/10/11	Cash	1		$3,458
23		Jones and Smith for May			
24					
25	6/13/11	Subscriptions	29	$ 10	
26	6/13/11	Cash	1		$ 10
27		Courier, 3 months			

JournalDebits 686.24 — General Journal — Average: $1,024 Count: 6 Sum: $6,144 100%

Figure 1.5
General journal entries record individual transactions in chronological order as debits and credits.

`AccountNumber` ($C$5:$C$26), `JournalDebits` ($D$5:$D$26), and `JournalCredits` ($E$5:$E$26).

Two additional names are defined in the General Ledger shown in Figure 1.6: `LedgerDate`, `a name defined by an absolute reference`, refers to cell $A$4. `GLAccount` (short for general ledger account) refers to a cell in column D.

{=SUM(IF(MONTH(EntryDate)=MONTH(LedgerDate),1,0)*IF(AccountNumber=GLAccount,1,0)*JournalCredits)}

	A	B	C	D	E	F
1			General Ledger			
2						
3	Date		Account	Account	Debit	Credit
4	Jun-11		Name	Number		
5						
6			Cash	1	$ -	$4,656
7						
8			Office Lease	21	$1,187	$ -
9						
10			Office Equipment	22	$ 686	$ -
11						
12			Telehone Expense	23	$ 85	$ -
13						
14			Subscriptions	29	$ 10	$ -
15						
16			Accounts payable	30	$ -	$ 772
17						
18			Accounts receivable	40	$ 717	$ -
19						
20			Salaries	50	$3,458	$ -
21						
22			Sales	60	$ -	$ 717
23						
24					$6,144	$6,144

General Ledger — Ready 100%

Figure 1.6
General ledger entries accumulate individual transactions from the general journal into specific accounts.

Suppose that the active cell is in row 6—say, E6. If you now click the Formulas tab and click Define Name in the Defined Names group, you can then type `GLAccount` in the Name box. In the Refers To box, type this formula:

```
=$D6
```

This mixed reference means that you can type this formula

```
=GLAccount
```

into any column and any row. Because its column is fixed and its row is relative, the latter formula returns whatever value is in the row where the formula is entered, in column D.

> **NOTE** However, entering the `=GLAccount` in the column that it points to causes a circular reference, just as though you entered `=D4` into cell D4.

The effect of this referencing on how the names work is explained in more detail later in this section.

On the General Ledger worksheet, the following array formula in its Debit column accumulates the appropriate entries from the General Journal:

```
=SUM(IF(MONTH(EntryDate)=MONTH(LedgerDate),1,0)*IF(AccountNumber =
   GLAccount,1,0)*JournalDebits)
```

This array formula accumulates the appropriate credits:

```
=SUM(IF(MONTH(EntryDate)=MONTH(LedgerDate),1,0)*IF(AccountNumber =
   GLAccount,1,0)*JournalCredits)
```

> **NOTE** The two General Journal formulas just shown must be entered as *array formulas*. After typing the formula, simultaneously hold down Ctrl+Shift and press Enter. In the formula bar, you will see a pair of curly braces around the formula. This indicates that Excel has accepted the formula as an array formula. Do not enter the braces yourself from the keyboard, or Excel will interpret the formula as text.

The formulas instruct Excel to do the following:

1. `IF(MONTH(EntryDate)=MONTH(LedgerDate),1,0)`: Evaluate each entry in the General Journal's `EntryDate` column. If the month of that date equals the date for the General Ledger, return `1`; otherwise, return `0`.
2. `IF(AccountNumber = GLAccount,1,0)`: Evaluate each entry in the General Journal's `AccountNumber` column. If the account number is the same as the account number for the current General Ledger account, return `1`; otherwise, return `0`.
3. Multiply the result of step 1 by step 2. Only when both conditions are true will this step return a `1`; otherwise, it will return `0`.

4. Multiply the result of step 3 by the General Journal's entries in the `JournalDebits` range (or its `JournalCredits` range, in the second of the previous two formulas). When both the date condition and the account condition are `true`, the result is the debit (or the credit); otherwise, the result is `0`.
5. Return the sum of step 4 as applied to all the journal entries: specifically, a debit or credit if the entry passes both the date and the account conditions, and `0` otherwise.

Be sure that you understand the following aspects of the names used in these formulas:

No Provision for Different Workbooks

The range names assume that both the general journal and the general ledger worksheets belong to the same workbook. If the general journal belonged to a workbook named, say, `General Journal.xls`, the definitions of the names in the formulas would have to be qualified by references to that workbook. For example:

```
='C:\Financials\[General Journal.xls]JournalSheet'!JournalDebits
```

Both Absolute and Mixed References Are Used

Consider the definitions of the names `LedgerDate` and `GLAccount`. `LedgerDate` refers to cell $A$4: Because this is an absolute reference (note the two dollar signs), `LedgerDate` returns the same value, regardless of the location of the cell where it is entered.

`GLAccount`, on the other hand, refers to the cell in column D and in the row where the formula that uses the `GLAccount` name is located. Entered in E6, then, `GLAccount` refers to D6; entered in F16, `GLAccount` refers to D16. This is a mixed reference: Only the column is fixed, and the row changes depending on where the reference to `GLAccount` is entered.

Therefore, this formula, if entered in cell F6 and shown in Figure 1.6, uses the value 1 (in cell D6) for `GLAccount`:

```
=SUM(IF(MONTH(EntryDate)=MONTH(LedgerDate),1,0)*IF(AccountNumber =
   GLAccount,1,0)*JournalCredits)
```

But if the formula is entered into cell F8, it uses the value 21 (in cell D8). Because the name `GLAccount` refers to the mixed reference $D and whatever row the name is used in, the name itself acts as a mixed reference.

> **NOTE** This is also an instance of an implicit intersection. See Chapter 11, "Examining a Business Case: Investment," for a discussion of what an implicit intersection is and how it can make your life easier.

The effect of the mixed reference in this case is to anchor the reference to column D because of the dollar sign before the column letter and to allow the row to adjust because of the absence of a dollar sign before the row number.

By using these formulas, all the individual transactions from the General Journal are accumulated into the General Ledger, according to the account that they have been posted to and according to the correct date for the current General Ledger entry.

TIP

If you're familiar with Excel's pivot tables, you might wonder why you would not use one to summarize data from the general journal into a general ledger. You can do so if you arrange the general journal data as a three-column list: one column containing the name of the account, one column identifying the transaction as a debit or a credit, and the third column containing the amount. Now, if you use that list as the source data for a pivot table, with the account name as the `Row` field, the type of transaction (debit or credit) as the `Column` field, and the amount as the `Data` field, your pivot table will emulate a general ledger.

Getting the Ledger Data to the Income Statement

You can use a similar approach to accumulate the information in the general ledger into your income statement.

Suppose you have decided to number all fixed administrative expense accounts using five-digit account numbers beginning with 63. Health insurance might be account number 63310, vehicle insurance 63320, interest expense 63400 and so on. If you name the range in the general ledger that contains the account numbers as `LedgerAccounts`, the range containing the credits as `LedgerCredits`, and the range containing the debits as `LedgerDebits`, this array formula totals the differences between general ledger credits and general ledger debits for accounts numbered 63000 to 63999:

```
=SUM(IF(LEFT(LedgerAccounts,2)="63",LedgerCredits-LedgerDebits,0))
```

(Remember to enter the formula as an array formula. Use Ctrl+Shift and then press Enter.)

The array formula first evaluates the elements in the range named `LedgerAccounts` and strips off the two leftmost characters in each account number. Then, if those two characters equal `63` (as they will if the account number is between 63000 and 63999, inclusive), the formula returns the sum of the difference between the accounts' debits and credits.

You could use the formula to return the entry in your income statement that pertains to fixed administrative expenses. Similarly, if your chart of accounts assigned all account categories pertaining to fixed production expenses to five-digit numbers beginning with 64, you would use this:

```
=SUM(IF(LEFT(LedgerAccounts,2)="64",LedgerCredits-LedgerDebits,0))
```

You can accumulate most of the entries on an income statement in a similar way, working from the general journal to the general ledger to the income statement. Two types of entries in particular—entries such as accounts payable and prepaid expenses that involve accrual, and assets that are subject to depreciation—usually require special attention. Both affect the timing of your company's earnings. Accrual accounting is discussed in the next section.

> **TIP**
>
> The procedures suggested in this chapter work most easily if you maintain your general journal, general ledger, and income statement in the same workbook. However, Excel does not permit you to use the same name more than once in the same workbook unless you qualify it with a sheet name. So you cannot create two instances of a range named `Debits`, for example—once as a name that refers to the general journal and once as a name that refers to the general ledger—in the same workbook. One option is to use names such as `GeneralJournal!Debits`, where `GeneralJournal` is the name of a worksheet. (This is the attribute that you set when you define a name's *scope* in Excel 2007 or 2010.) Another option, used in the previous examples, is to use the name `JournalDebits` to distinguish that range from `LedgerDebits`.

➔ Depreciation is covered in the discussion of fixed assets in Chapter 16, "Fixed Assets."

It's worth mentioning again that true double entry accounting applications take care of all this data management for you. Following are the reasons to handle it yourself in Excel:

- Having a business that requires relatively few transactions per accounting period
- Exercising the greatest amount of flexibility possible over the way the business's books are managed
- Getting a fundamental understanding of the actions that an accounting package takes but that it doesn't demonstrate for the user

Managing the Financial Analyses with Accrual Accounting

Accrual accounting involves two steps: identifying the revenues for a given period and matching the associated costs, such as the cost of goods sold and sales commissions, to those revenues. This is called the *matching principle* and is a basic concept used throughout the accounting process.

The notion of matching revenue to costs incurred to produce the revenue might seem obvious, but it has some subtle implications. Suppose that you purchase license plates for a company vehicle. You pay $400 for the plates in January. You write off the full $400 in January. (That is, you show it as a cost that you incurred fully during that month.) You produce revenue or otherwise conduct business by using your vehicle during January and for the next 11 months.

In this case, you have overstated your cost of doing business in January, understated it from February through December, and failed to match the subsequent revenues with the initial expenditure. Accrual accounting allows you to spread the cost of the plates over (in this case) the full 12 months and to match the revenues the vehicle helps produce to the cost outlay for the license plates.

Revenue is not the same as cash received, and expense is not the same as cash spent. You normally recognize revenue when the effort required to generate the sale is substantially complete and there is reasonable certainty that you will receive payment. The accountant views the timing of the actual cash receipts, or the actual cash outlay, as only a technicality.

NOTE

Small businesses often use another approach, termed the *cash method*, instead of the accrual method. Under the cash method, the business records revenue when the cash is received and records costs or expenses when the cash is spent. Although the cash method is a less accurate means of associating revenues with costs and expenses, small businesses sometimes forego the extra accuracy of the accrual method for the extra simplicity of the cash method. Most single-purpose accounting software allows you to specify whether you want it to treat transactions according to the accrual method or the cash method.

For credit sales, the accrual principle means that you recognize the revenue at the time of the sale, not necessarily when the customer makes payment. Suppose that you use your credit card to buy a new set of golf clubs at your local sporting goods store. The store recognizes the revenue when you sign the credit slip, but it does not receive cash until your credit card company sends it payment. The time between recognition of revenue and cash payment can be significant. The fact that a company is profitable is not a guarantee that its cash flow will be sufficient to keep it solvent.

If a company's management is to properly understand the relationship between the company's *revenues* and its *costs* over a given period, it needs to see income statements. Balance sheets are necessary for management to understand the relationship between the company's *assets* and its *liabilities*—its worth—at a given point in time.

➜ You will find additional coverage on balance sheets in the following chapters:

Chapter 2, "Balance Sheet: Current Assets"

Chapter 3, "Valuing Inventories for the Balance Sheet"

Chapter 4, "Summarizing Transactions: From the Journals to the Balance Sheet"

Cash flow statements enable management to assess the company's solvency. In other words, these statements show whether sufficient working capital exists and will exist to continue business operations.

➜ Cash flow statements are covered in detail in Chapter 5, "Working Capital and Cash Flow Analysis."

These three types of statements—income statements, balance sheets, and cash flow statements—are intimately related, even though they serve different purposes and provide different perspectives on a company's overall financial position. These relationships are determined largely by the principle of matching costs to revenues in the income statement via accrual.

For example, increases in revenues cause increases in the owner's equity on the credit side of the balance sheet, and increases in accrued expenses cause decreases in owner's equity on the debit side of the balance sheet.

Actual cash receipts and outlays, shown on cash flow statements, summarize the effects of increases and decreases in revenues and expenses on the amount of the company's working capital.

Cash flows might or might not reflect the accrual of revenues and expenses. For example, something you buy in March might help you produce revenue for the rest of the calendar year, but the entire purchase is recorded in March. This highlights the need for adjusting entries, which help distribute the initial outlay across several accounting periods. When your company acquires an asset such as an insurance policy, you might or might not use up that asset to create revenue during the particular accounting period when you bought it.

CASE STUDY: ADJUSTING ENTRIES

Martin Consulting is a small business that provides assistance to its customers in assessing the quality of ground water. Figure 1.7 shows several examples of how Martin Consulting uses adjusting entries to record transactions via accrual.

Martin begins by getting a trial balance. This process involves totaling the balances of accounts with debit balances and then doing the same for accounts with credit balances. When the two totals agree, the ledger is in balance. See columns B and C in Figure 1.7.

At the end of July, Martin Consulting prepared the worksheet shown in Figure 1.7 as the basis for its income statement and balance sheet. The rest of this section details the steps that Martin takes to move from the basic worksheet to the financial reports for the month.

On July 1, an errors-and-omissions insurance policy was purchased in full to provide protection against faulty advice that might be given to the company's clients. The policy will remain in effect for 12 months. The cost of this policy is debited to an asset account in row 5, column B of the worksheet. When the worksheet is prepared at the end of the month, 1/12 of the value of the policy has expired; that value now becomes an expense incurred during the month of July. Row 5, column E contains $57 as an adjusting credit entry, reflecting that 1/12 of the policy's asset value has expired. Row 5, column F shows the remaining value of the asset, or $627. The adjusting debit entry appears in row 17, column D.

Notice how the cost of the insurance policy is handled. The full policy premium, $684, was actually paid during July from the company's checking account. The checking account's balance at the end of July is therefore $684 less than it would have been otherwise. Balancing that cost is the presence of a new asset: a 12-month insurance policy valued at $684 as of 7/1/2012.

Figure 1.7
Adjusting entries help to accrue revenues and expenses in the proper period.

	A	B	C	D	E	F	G
1	Martin Consulting worksheet, 7/31/2012	Trial Balance		Adjustments		Adjusted Trial Balance	
2		Debit	Credit	Debit	Credit	Debit	Credit
3	Cash	$32,650				$ 32,650	$ -
4	Accounts Receivable	$ 3,472				$ 3,472	$ -
5	Unexpired Insurance	$ 684			$ 57	$ 627	$ -
6	Supplies	$ 592			$ 136	$ 456	$ -
7	Office Equipment	$ 3,470				$ 3,470	$ -
8	Office Equipment: Accumulated Depreciation		$ 1,157		$ 96	$ -	$ 1,253
9	Accounts Payable		$ 4,223			$ -	$ 4,223
10	Unearned Consulting Fees		$ 1,280	$ 160		$ -	$ 1,120
11	Salaries Payable				$ 465	$ -	$ 465
12	Chris Martin, Capital		$31,884			$ -	$ 31,884
13	Analysis Fees		$ 6,250			$ -	$ 6,250
14	Advertising	$ 145				$ 145	$ -
15	Salaries	$ 3,600		$ 465		$ 4,065	$ -
16	Communications	$ 181				$ 181	$ -
17	Insurance expense			$ 57		$ 57	$ -
18	Supplies consumed			$ 136		$ 136	$ -
19	Consulting Fees Earned				$ 160	$ -	$ 160
20	Depreciation Expense: Office Equipment			$ 96		$ 96	$ -
21							
22	Total	$44,794	$44,794	$ 914	$ 914	$ 45,355	$ 45,355

Martin Trial Balance

Ready

By the end of July, 1/12 of the policy's value has expired. That decrease in the value of the asset is recorded in two places:

- As an adjustment to the value of the asset in row 5 of the worksheet. The adjusted value is copied to the balance sheet, where it appears as part of the company's current value.
- As an expense recorded in row 17. This expense is recorded for the month of July, even though the actual cash outlay for the insurance in July was $684. This is the mechanism that is used to match the timing of the expense with the timing of the revenue it helped to produce.

During the same period, Martin Consulting uses $136 worth of office supplies to help produce its revenue. Another adjusting entry of $136 appears in row 6, column E, reflecting the decrease in the value of the original office supplies asset of $592, and applied against that amount in row 6, column F to show its remaining value of $456 at the end of the month. The adjusting debit entry appears in row 18, column D.

The rationale for these adjusting entries is pretty clear. On July 1, the company owned 12 months of insurance coverage, and it owned 11 months' worth of coverage on July 31. Similarly, it owned $592 in office supplies on July 1 and $456 on July 31. These amounts are directly measurable, and Martin Consulting can easily enter, as adjusting debits and credits, the portions that expire or are used as expenses during the month of July.

But office equipment is another matter. At the beginning of July, the company owned equipment originally valued at $3,470 (see row 7, column B). How much of that $3,470 was used up in the production of the month's revenues? The equipment is still there: The computer is still creating worksheets, the photocopier is still making copies, the telephone is still ringing. Yet some value was taken from the equipment to generate revenue.

Depreciation is the means used to account for the fact that the equipment provided value to the process of revenue generation. In contrast to ticking off another month that has expired on an insurance policy or counting the number of mailing envelopes that were addressed and sent, Martin must estimate the value of the office equipment "used" during the month of July. He does so by means of depreciation.

Using Straight-Line Depreciation

Martin can use one of several methods to calculate the depreciation for a month (or for a quarter or for a year).

➜ Depreciation methods, and the way Excel handles them, are covered in detail in Chapter 16, "Fixed Assets."

Suppose that Martin uses the straight-line method of depreciation. The assumption is that the office equipment has a useful life of three years and will have no value after that. Then, for each month that passes during the three-year equipment lifetime, the value of the equipment declines by 1/36 of its original value—that is, the equipment depreciates each month by 1/36, or $96. The adjusting credit entry is in row 8, column E, and the adjusting debit entry is shown in row 20, column D.

By estimating the amount of monthly depreciation, Martin can calculate an office equipment expense for the month. This makes it possible to associate the expense with the revenue and to obtain a clearer picture of the month's income. Again, the matching principal holds that revenues should be matched with the expenses that helped to produce them.

You use adjusting entries not only with expenses, but also with revenues. Suppose that toward the end of July, Martin signed an agreement and accepted cash payment to perform eight hours of consulting at $160 per hour. The full amount of `$1,280` is credited to an asset account called Unearned Consulting Fees. Before the end of the month, Martin performed one of the eight contracted hours. Actually doing that work converts some of the unearned fees to an earned status. Adjusting entries, in row 10, column D, and row 19, column E, show that `$160` of the unearned fee has been converted to earned status during July.

The four adjusting entries for supplies and depreciation previously described have to do with activities that both begin and end during an accounting period. For example, the use of an estimated $136 in office supplies took place between July 1 and July 31. An adjusting entry can also record an activity that spans accounting periods. Suppose that Martin prepared an assistant's salary check, in payment for the previous two weeks, one week before the end of the month. The assistant then accrued one week of salary from July 25 through July 31. To show that this accrued salary is an expense attributable to July instead of August, Martin makes an adjusting entry in row 15, column D. To show that it is a liability that will be met subsequently (probably in August), it is also entered as a liability credit in row 11, column E.

Preparing the Trial Balance

Excel makes it simple to accumulate the trial balance and the adjusting entries into an adjusted trial balance. The actual formulas used in columns F and G of Figure 1.7 (the adjusted debit and credit balances) are discussed in detail in the "Getting an Adjusted Trial Balance" section in Chapter 5, "Working Capital and Cash Flow Analysis." For now, be aware of the following:

- Each adjusted *debit* entry is based on this formula, which is subsequently adjusted to suppress negative amounts:

```
=(TrialDebits-TrialCredits)+(AdjustDebits-AdjustCredits)
```

- Each adjusted *credit* entry is based on this formula, also adjusted to suppress negative amounts:

```
=(TrialCredits-TrialDebits)+(AdjustCredits-AdjustDebits)
```

The totals of the adjusting entries appear in Figure 1.7, in row 22, columns D and E. The totals of the adjusted entries appear in Figure 1.7, in row 22, columns F and G. The equality of the debit and credit totals shows that the entries are in balance.

TIP

Excel provides several underline formats, including Single Accounting and Double Accounting. These are often used for, respectively, subtotals and totals. To access these formats, click the Ribbon's Home tab and then select Format in the Cells group. Select Format Cells from the menu, click the Font tab, and then select the Underline combo box. In versions of Excel prior to 2007, use Format, Cells, and select the Font tab. Then use the Underline combo box to select the type of underline you want.

Moving Information into an Income Statement

Finally, it's time to move this information to an income statement and a balance sheet (see Figure 1.8).

Rows 3 through 12 represent asset and liability accounts. They are copied from the adjusted trial balance to the balance sheet columns. Rows 13 through 20 represent revenue and expense accounts and are copied to the `Income Statement` columns. Then, in row 21 of columns H and K, the debits and credits are totaled. Notice that they are no longer in balance, nor should they be. The company's revenues for July exceeded its expenses, and the difference is its operating income. To arrive at this figure, subtract the total expenses of `$4,680` in cell H21 from the total revenues in cell I21. The result, `$1,730`, appears in cell H22 and is the operating income for the month of July. Adding that to the total expenses of `$4,680` results in `$6,410`, which is in balance with the total revenues for the month.

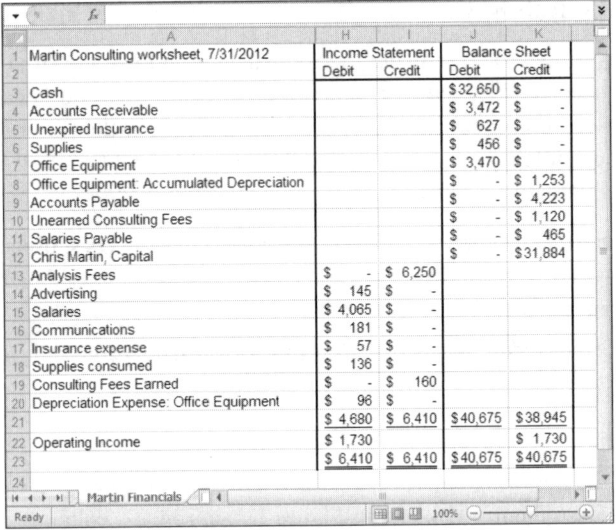

Martin Consulting worksheet, 7/31/2012	Income Statement		Balance Sheet	
	Debit	Credit	Debit	Credit
Cash			$32,650	$ -
Accounts Receivable			$ 3,472	$ -
Unexpired Insurance			$ 627	$ -
Supplies			$ 456	$ -
Office Equipment			$ 3,470	$ -
Office Equipment: Accumulated Depreciation			$ -	$ 1,253
Accounts Payable			$ -	$ 4,223
Unearned Consulting Fees			$ -	$ 1,120
Salaries Payable			$ -	$ 465
Chris Martin, Capital			$ -	$31,884
Analysis Fees	$ -	$ 6,250		
Advertising	$ 145	$ -		
Salaries	$ 4,065	$ -		
Communications	$ 181	$ -		
Insurance expense	$ 57	$ -		
Supplies consumed	$ 136	$ -		
Consulting Fees Earned	$ -	$ 160		
Depreciation Expense: Office Equipment	$ 96	$ -		
	$ 4,680	$ 6,410	$40,675	$38,945
Operating Income	$ 1,730			$ 1,730
	$ 6,410	$ 6,410	$40,675	$40,675

Figure 1.8
Entries are copied from the adjusted trial balance columns to `Income Statement` and `Balance Sheet` columns.

You use a similar process to obtain the information for the balance sheet. Notice that this final step, copying information from the adjusted trial balance to the income statement and balance sheet, is merely a matter of separating the revenue and expense data from the asset and liability data. Revenues and expenses go to the income statement; assets and liabilities go to the balance sheet.

Organizing with Traditional Versus Contribution Approaches

The traditional approach to organizing income statements focuses on the functions that a business performs, such as production, administration, and sales. This functional method of classifying costs does not allow for the examination of cost behavior. Traditional income statements are not set up to describe the cost drivers of the business.

There are no subcategories to analyze, or to use to manage costs, within each classification. Costs are grouped without indicating whether they are fixed, variable, inherent, or some other classification. When an income statement classifies results by means of administrative structures, it is difficult to analyze the statement, to use it to make decisions, and to offer recommendations. The statement might be just fine for the purposes of financial accounting, but virtually useless for the purposes of management accounting.

In contrast, the contribution format classifies results by the sources and uses of the company's resources and therefore helps to answer many additional questions. For example:

- What are the variable selling expenses for a given product?
- How much of our total costs are fixed costs?
- New equipment will increase our fixed costs because it must be depreciated. Will the equipment reduce our variable costs enough to result in lower *total* costs?

A manager needs more specific information than is available in the traditional income statement to answer questions such as these.

This is not at all to say that there is no place for the traditional format. Almost certainly, you would use a traditional format if you were applying for a business loan, considering the sale of your business, or preparing for an initial public stock offering. The traditional format is fine for those purposes, and it's widely recognized.

The contribution format is not designed for public consumption. It is intended mainly for internal purposes and is used by management for day-to-day, operational decisions. Consider the example shown in Figure 1.9.

Figure 1.9
The contribution format of an income statement focuses on data helpful for operational decisions.

	A	B	C
1	Discount Computer Products, Inc.		
2	Income Statement		
3	For the year ended December 31, 2012		
4		($000)	($000)
5	Sales		$ 323
6			
7	Less variable expenses:		
8	Variable production	$ 87	
9	Variable administrative	$ 8	
10	Variable selling	$ 38	
11	Variable expenses		$ 133
12			
13	Contribution margin		$ 190
14			
15	Less fixed expenses		
16	Fixed production	$ 41	
17	Fixed administrative	$ 23	
18	Fixed selling	$ 21	
19	Fixed expenses		$ 85
20			
21	Operating Income		$ 105
22			

Discount Income Statement

Ready 100%

In Figure 1.9, variable expenses are deducted from sales to derive what is known as a *contribution margin*.

➜ See Chapter 20, "Pricing and Costing," for more information on contribution margins.

Note that a contribution margin is the result of subtracting variable expenses from revenues. You can use the contribution margin to meet fixed expenses and to contribute toward company profit.

You need this sort of analysis if you are to make informed business decisions about products. For example, Figure 1.9 shows that Discount Computer's largest cost category is Variable Production expenses. A *variable expense* is one that changes depending on the number of units sold. The more computer products this firm sells, the larger its variable production expense.

The contribution format used by the income statement in Figure 1.9 directs a manager's attention to the costs involved in producing products. Without this data, the manager who wants to cut costs might focus on reducing fixed production costs when it's the variable costs that need attention.

The contribution approach is useful in making decisions about product profitability, product pricing, marketing channels, and many situational decisions. It enables you to understand the contribution that each product brings to the bottom line and how much to variable costs. It helps you to better understand the cost drivers of your business.

A company's business decisions focus on cost reduction, productivity, and (if the company has the stamina for it) quality management. To sharpen that focus, it is necessary to understand the structure of the costs that reduce your profitability. You will see more on this matter in future chapters.

Summary

In this chapter, you looked into various formats and purposes for income statements. They can be structured differently, depending on their audience and which management functions they support.

You saw how to use absolute, relative, and mixed references in Excel to return results that are independent of, fully dependent on, or partly dependent on their placement on the worksheet.

You learned ways to use Excel to maintain a general journal of transactions, and you learned how to roll those transactions into a general ledger and an income statement. In practice, you may leave these tasks to your accounting application. But by looking at the process in the context of an Excel worksheet, you'll have a much stronger grasp of what your application is doing behind the scenes.

You also read about accrual accounting and the matching principle, under which costs are associated with the revenues that they help to produce.

The income statement is fundamental to understanding the way your business operates. It has various uses and a virtually unlimited number of possible formats. The statement structure and format that you choose depend on both your audience and your purpose for a particular income statement.

Balance Sheet: Current Assets

2

IN THIS CHAPTER

The balance sheet complements the income statement, discussed in Chapter 1, "Working with Income Statements." You need both reports to keep track of your company's financial status. A balance sheet contains two primary sections:

- *Assets* states the balances in the company's asset accounts on a given date.
- *Liabilities and Equity* states the balances in the company's liability and its equity accounts on the same date.

These two sections must be in *balance*; that is, the total of the company's assets must equal the total of its liabilities and its equity. (You'll sometimes see this termed Owner's Equity or Stockholders' Equity.)

The income statement shows how much money a company made and how much it spent during a given period. The balance sheet summarizes the company's financial position at the end of that period. Whether that period is a month, a quarter, or a year, it tells you the value of the company's assets. It also describes the various classifications of liabilities, such as Accounts Payable, Debt, and Equity, that have claims against the company's assets.

For example, suppose that your company has inventory in stock worth $5,000. That's an asset: You can, and presumably intend to, convert it into cash by selling it to your customers. Now suppose that your company acquired that inventory partly with $2,500 in cash and the remainder on credit.

Those amounts are claims against the company's assets. The company has assumed $2,500 in accounts payable, which is the portion of the purchase made on credit. The remaining $2,500 worth of inventory belongs to owner's equity, which is the portion of the company's total assets owned by its investors. Owner's equity is grouped with liabilities such as accounts payable because it represents whatever difference exists between the assets and liabilities.

By showing the $5,000 worth of inventory both in assets and in liabilities, the balance sheet keeps the company's holdings and obligations in balance. If this were all there was to a balance sheet, it wouldn't be of much interest—but, as you will see later in this book, the balance sheet is the starting point for a variety of analyses. Using Excel to analyze the balance sheet can give you insight into how a company is run, how well it manages its resources, and how it creates profit.

First, though, it's necessary to build the balance sheet. This chapter, along with Chapters 3, "Valuing Inventories for the Balance Sheet," and 4, "Summarizing Transactions: From the Journals to the Balance Sheet," describes that process.

Designing the Balance Sheet

In contrast to the income statement discussed in Chapter 1, the balance sheet usually follows a fairly rigid format. Figure 2.1 shows a typical example.

Figure 2.1
The balance sheet for Bell Books, Inc., December 2011, demonstrates that its total assets equal the total of its liabilities and its owner's equity.

	A	B	C	D
1	Bell Books, Inc.	Balance Sheet, December 31, 2011		
2	**Assets**			
3	*Current Assets*			
4	Cash		$ 54,706	
5	Accounts Receivable		$ 17,724	
6	Less: Doubtful Accounts	$ 738		
7	Unexpired Insurance		$ 5,720	
8	Inventory, 12/1/2011		$ 21,820	
9	Office Supplies		$ 2,668	
10	Total Current Assets		$ 101,900	
11				
12	*Fixed Assets*			
13	Building and Land		$ 232,865	
14	Equipment		$ 14,363	
15	Total Fixed Assets		$ 247,228	
16				
17	Total Assets		$ 349,128	
18				
19	**Liabilities and Owner's Equity**			
20	Accounts Payable		$ 15,626	
21	Notes Payable		$ 25,000	
22	Owner's Equity		$ 308,502	
23				
24	Total Liabilities		$ 349,128	
25				

Balance Sheet
Ready 100%

The first section of the balance sheet describes the company's assets. The second section of the balance sheet summarizes the company's liabilities and owner's equity.

Understanding Balance Sheet Accounts

The Current Assets classification is normally composed of cash, accounts receivable, prepaid expenses, and inventory.

➜ Because managing inventory can require special valuation methods, this book discusses inventory separately, in Chapter 3. This chapter discusses the other current asset classifications.

The Fixed Assets category normally includes items such as land, buildings, and equipment. The difference between current assets and fixed assets is that current assets can be converted into cash fairly quickly—usually, within a year—in the course of the business's normal operations.

So if your company owns the building where it conducts its business, located on land that it also owns, you would regard both the building and the land as fixed assets. Even if you could sell them in a week, doing so would interfere with your normal business operations. In contrast, if your real estate company owns a building and land but conducts no business there, it might be appropriate to treat them as current assets.

In the same way, liabilities are classified as current and long-term. A *current liability* is a debt that a business must pay within the same time period it uses to define its current assets: Again, this is usually a year or less. An example is a bank loan that must be repaid within 12 months. An example of a long-term liability is, say, a 10-year note used to acquire your place of business.

Understanding Debit and Credit Entries

Figure 2.1 shows a balance sheet for a book retailer, Bell Books, Inc. Figure 2.2 shows the cash worksheet that supports some sections of Bell Books' balance sheet.

Figure 2.2
The cash worksheet records cash outlays as credits and cash receipts as debits.

C13 =AcctsReceivable!D13

	A	B	C	D	E
1	Date	Explanation	Debit	Credit	Balance
2	11/30/11	Closing balance, November			$ 29,344
3	12/1/11	Purchase medical insurance policy		$6,864	$ 22,480
4	12/1/11	Purchase of office supplies		$3,194	$ 19,286
5	12/4/11	Cash Receipts	$ 4,690		$ 23,976
6	12/4/11	Check for returns to supplier	$ 91		$ 24,067
7	12/7/11	Cash Receipts	$ 1,006		$ 25,073
8	12/11/11	Cash Receipts	$ 8,207		$ 33,280
9	12/14/11	Cash Receipts	$ 9,592		$ 42,872
10	12/14/11	Purchase of books from Neal Publishing		$6,023	$ 36,849
11	12/14/11	Purchase of books from Lenny Distributing		$8,474	$ 28,375
12	12/18/11	Cash Receipts	$ 4,663		$ 33,038
13	12/18/11	Accounts Receivable payment for November	$ 17,951		$ 50,989
14	12/21/11	Cash Receipts	$ 5,514		$ 56,503
15	12/23/11	Cash Receipts	$ 3,791		$ 60,294
16	12/27/11	Telephone bill, November		$1,835	$ 58,459
17	12/27/11	Cash Receipts	$ 9,050		$ 67,509
18	12/27/11	Purchase of books from Neal Publishing		$6,440	$ 61,069
19	12/29/11	Salary check, Rodgers		$2,950	$ 58,119
20	12/29/11	Salary check, Rouse		$2,761	$ 55,358
21	12/29/11	Salary check, Tafoya		$4,377	$ 50,981
22	12/29/11	Advertising bill, November		$3,116	$ 47,865
23	12/30/11	Cash Receipts	$ 6,841		$ 54,706

Cash transactions
Ready 100%

Notice that deposits to Bell Books' cash account worksheet are labeled Debits, and withdrawals from the account are labeled Credits. If it's been a while since you looked closely at an accounting statement, you might wonder why deposits go under Debits and withdrawals go under Credits. It's largely a matter of convention.

When you show account activity in a worksheet, you normally have two columns: one to record increases in the account balance and one to record decreases. (This format is referred to as a *T-account* because a horizontal line drawn beneath the column headers and a vertical line drawn between the columns themselves together resemble a *T*.)

In the context of your business's accounts, the words *debit* and *credit* do not have the same connotations that they have in everyday usage—for example, a debt versus an asset. Instead, these terms simply refer to the left (Debit) and right (Credit) columns of a T-account. Accountants have four fundamental rules for entering amounts in these columns:

- If the account is an asset account, record an increase in the account balance in the left (Debit) column.
- If the account is an asset account, record a decrease in the account balance in the right (Credit) column.
- If the account is a liability or equity account, record an increase in the right (Credit) column.
- If the account is a liability or equity account, record a decrease in the left (Debit) column.

What about revenue accounts and expense accounts? The rules for these accounts stem logically from the rules for asset accounts and liability/equity accounts, as follows:

- Revenue increases equity and so, when you record the revenue, you record the transaction as a credit to the revenue account, just as the increase in equity is recorded as a credit.
- When you acquire the revenue, you deposit it to an asset account, where it is recorded as a debit—increases in assets are recorded as debits, as noted earlier. This debit entry complements the revenue credit.
- Expenses decrease equity. So, when you record an expense transaction, you record it as a debit to the expense account, just as a decrease in equity is recorded as a debit.
- When you pay the expense, doing so decreases an asset account—typically a bank account. Decreases in assets are recorded as credits, so you record the transaction as a credit to the asset account, again as noted earlier. This credit entry complements the expense debit.

According to these rules, deposits to a cash account are recorded in the account's left, or Debit, column: cash is an asset account, and a deposit increases its balance. Similarly, because writing a check reduces the cash account's balance, the amount of the check is recorded in the right, or Credit, column. Keep in mind that, in this context, *debit* just means left column and *credit* just means right column.

Getting a Current Asset Cash Balance

In the balance sheet shown previously in Figure 2.1, the cash classification of the Current Assets section contains this formula:

```
=NovemberEndCashBalance+SUM(DecemberCashDebits)-SUM(DecemberCashCredits)
```

The names in this formula refer to ranges in the cash worksheet shown previously in Figure 2.2. The names of the ranges are as follows:

- NovemberEndCashBalance, which refers to cell E2. This amount is the closing cash balance at the end of November, the previous month.
- DecemberCashDebits, which refers to cells C3:C23. This range contains all the deposits to Bell Books' corporate checking account that were made during December.
- DecemberCashCredits, which refers to cells D3:D23. This range contains all the withdrawals from Bell Books' corporate checking account that were made during December.

2

Cell E2, named NovemberEndCashBalance, contains the value $29,344. Cell E3 contains this formula:

```
=E2+C3-D3
```

Each entry in the cash worksheet is either a debit or a credit: No entries contain both a debit and a credit. The formula in cell E3, therefore, either adds the prior balance (cell E2) to a debit figure in column C or subtracts a credit figure in column D from the prior balance.

The formula is copied from cell E3 and is pasted into the range E4:E23. The process of copying and pasting the formula adjusts its relative cell references, so each balance depends on the prior balance as well as on the current debit or credit. Cell E23 contains the *ending* balance for the month of December, and this balance will be used as the *beginning* cash balance when it comes time to create the cash worksheet for January.

It would be possible—maybe even preferable—to create the name DecemberEndCashBalance to represent cell E23 of Figure 2.2. Then the cash classification in Figure 2.1 could contain this formula:

```
=DecemberEndCashBalance
```

As the worksheets are constructed, the ending cash balance for December is calculated twice: once on the cash worksheet and once on the balance sheet. This is done partly for illustration and partly to make the calculations explicit. See the "Getting a Cash Balance for Multiple Cash Accounts" section later in this chapter for information on how the calculation is done on the balance sheet.

Using Sheet-Level Names

Before continuing with Bell Books' cash accounts, it's useful to review an enhancement to the *workbook-level* names that this chapter has used so far.

The Introduction explained how to define a name that refers to a constant or to a range of cells. When a range name doesn't include the name of a worksheet, it's a workbook-level name; formulas entered anywhere in the workbook can use it. If you defined the workbook-level name FICA as referring to cell $A$1 on `Sheet1`, you could enter this formula on any worksheet:

```
=FICA * C2
```

It would return the value in cell $A$1 of `Sheet1` times whatever value is in cell C2 of the worksheet that contains the formula. The *scope* of the workbook-level name is the entire workbook: Any worksheet in the workbook can use a workbook-level name. A workbook-level name can be defined once only in a workbook. You cannot define the workbook-level name `Adjustments` once to refer to C1:C20 on `Sheet1`, and once to refer to D1:D30 on `Sheet2`.

The worksheets shown in Figures 2.3 and 2.4 use *sheet-level* names. The worksheet in Figure 2.3 contains these sheet-level names:

Figure 2.3
The cash worksheet for the First National account shows all operating expenses except those involving suppliers.

C2 =StartBalance+SUM(Debits)-SUM(Credits)

	A	B	C	D	E
1					
2		First National ending balance, December	$2,747		
3					
4	Date	Explanation	Debit	Credit	Balance
5	11/30/11	Closing balance, November			$27,844
6	12/1/11	Purchase medical insurance policy		$6,864	$20,980
7	12/1/11	Purchase of office supplies		$3,194	$17,786
8	12/27/11	Telephone bill, November		$1,835	$15,951
9	12/29/11	Salary check, Rodgers		$2,950	$13,001
10	12/29/11	Salary check, Rouse		$2,761	$10,240
11	12/29/11	Salary check, Tafoya		$4,377	$ 5,863
12	12/29/11	Advertising bill, November		$3,116	$ 2,747
13					

FirstNational
Ready 100%

Figure 2.4
The cash worksheet for the Second National account shows all cash receipts and those transactions that involve suppliers.

C2 =StartBalance+SUM(Debits)-SUM(Credits)

	A	B	C	D	E
1					
2		Second National ending balance, December	$51,959		
3					
4	Date	Explanation	Debit	Credit	Balance
5	11/30/11	Closing balance, November			$ 1,500
6	12/4/11	Cash Receipts	$ 4,690		$ 6,190
7	12/4/11	Check for returns to supplier	$ 91		$ 6,281
8	12/7/11	Cash Receipts	$ 1,006		$ 7,287
9	12/11/11	Cash Receipts	$ 8,207		$15,494
10	12/14/11	Cash Receipts	$ 9,592		$25,086
11	12/14/11	Purchase of books from Neal Publishing		$6,023	$19,063
12	12/14/11	Purchase of books from Lenney Distributing		$8,474	$10,589
13	12/18/11	Cash Receipts	$ 4,663		$15,252
14	12/18/11	Accounts Receivable payment for October	$17,951		$33,203
15	12/21/11	Cash Receipts	$ 5,514		$38,717
16	12/23/11	Cash Receipts	$ 3,791		$42,508
17	12/27/11	Cash Receipts	$ 9,050		$51,558
18	12/27/11	Purchase of books from Neal Publishing		$6,440	$45,118
19	12/30/11	Cash Receipts	$ 6,841		$51,959
20					

SecondNational
Ready 100%

- The name `FirstNational!Debits` refers to the range `FirstNational!$C$6:$C$12`.
- The name `FirstNational!Credits` refers to the range `FirstNational!$D$6:$D$12`.
- The name `FirstNational!StartBalance` refers to the cell `FirstNational!$E$5`.

NOTE Don't worry that the formulas in the formula boxes in Figures 2.3 and 2.4 don't specify the names of the worksheets. You'll see the reason shortly.

Notice three aspects of these worksheet-level range names:

- The name itself (for example, `Debits`) is preceded, or *qualified*, by the name of the worksheet (here, `FirstNational`), and the two are separated by an exclamation point: `FirstNational!Debits`.
- The range (for example, $C$6:$C$12) is also qualified by the name of the worksheet; again, the two are separated by an exclamation point. So, the name `FirstNational!Debits` represents `FirstNational!$C$6:$C$12`.
- When the name appears in a formula *on its home sheet*, the use of the worksheet name is optional—and in practice you seldom use it there. On the `FirstNational` sheet, you could use either `FirstNational!Debits` or `Debits`. On a different worksheet, the use of the worksheet name is required. On the `SecondNational` sheet, you would need to use `FirstNational!Debits` if you wanted to refer to the `Debits` range that's found on the sheet named `FirstNational`.

2

Defining the names in this way makes them *sheet-level* names—that is, the name refers specifically to the sheet where the range exists. Using sheet-level names has some consequences:

- Unless it is qualified by the name of the sheet where it exists, the sheet-level name is not accessible from any other sheet in the workbook. Suppose that you have defined the sheet-level name `JanuaryResults!Revenues`. If a worksheet named, say, `AnnualRollup`, is active, you cannot use this formula to get the total of January's revenues:

  ```
  =SUM(Revenues)
  ```

  You would have to use this on the `AnnualRollup` sheet:

  ```
  =SUM(JanuaryResults!Revenues)
  ```

- However, on the worksheet where the sheet-level names are defined, you can use the sheet-level name without qualifying it; the name is understood to belong to the active worksheet. If the worksheet named `JanuaryResults` is active, you can use this formula to return the sum of the values in the range that the sheet-level name `JanuaryResults!Revenues` refers to:

  ```
  =SUM(Revenues)
  ```

Sheet-level names are extremely useful. Suppose that you have a workbook with a different worksheet for each month of the year—`JanuaryResults`, `FebruaryResults`, `MarchResults`, and so on. If you define sheet-level names such as `JanuaryResults!Revenues` and `FebruaryResults!Revenues`, you can use this formula (or one like it) on each of those worksheets:

```
=SUM(Revenues)
```

Then you will know that it returns the sum of the range that's named `Revenues` *for that worksheet only*. January's revenues are separated from February's and from those on all other worksheets.

Getting a Cash Balance for Multiple Cash Accounts

It would be unusual for a company of any size to maintain only one bank account. More often, companies use several bank accounts, often for different purposes. In this case, a 3D reference could be useful because you generally want a different worksheet for each cash account. You would use the 3D reference to sum the balance of the account on each worksheet.

Suppose that Bell Books uses an account at the First National Bank to handle all cash transactions *except* cash receipts and purchases from inventory suppliers that are paid for with cash. Figure 2.3 shows these transactions for the month of December.

Cell C2 in Figure 2.3 contains this formula:

```
=StartBalance+SUM(Debits)-SUM(Credits)
```

It returns the balance in the First National account at the end of December. Why does the formula as written return the balance for the First National account rather than some other account? Because the formula is entered on the worksheet where the sheet-level names `Debits` and `Credits` are defined. Therefore, if the names are sheet-level, the references *must* be to named ranges on the sheet where the formula is entered.

Suppose further that Bell Books uses an account at the Second National Bank to handle all cash receipts and purchases from inventory suppliers. Figure 2.4 shows those transactions for the month of December.

The worksheet in Figure 2.4 contains these sheet-level names:

- The name `SecondNational!Debits` refers to the range `SecondNational!$C$6:$C$19`.
- The name `SecondNational!Credits` refers to the range `SecondNational!$D$6:$D$19`.
- The name `SecondNational!StartBalance` refers to the cell `SecondNational!$E$5`.

Cell C2 in Figure 2.4 contains this formula:

```
=StartBalance+SUM(Debits)-SUM(Credits)
```

It is identical to the formula in cell C2 of Figure 2.3. But because of the use of sheet-level names, `Debits` in Figure 2.4 refers specifically to the name `Debits` on the worksheet named `SecondNational`. Similarly, `Debits` in Figure 2.3 refers specifically to the name `Debits` on the worksheet named `FirstNational`. The arguments to the `SUM` functions, therefore, represent different ranges, so they normally return different results.

As another example, if you were to activate the `FirstNational` worksheet and then scroll through the entries in the formula bar's Name box, you would see the names `StartBalance`,

`Credits`, and `Debits`. These range names would not be qualified by their sheet names because the sheet where they exist is active.

Although this preliminary work with names might seem like overkill, it helps make your workbook formulas more self-documenting and makes things much easier in the long run. For example, notice that the ending balance for each bank account in Figures 2.3 and 2.4 is in cell C2 of each sheet. This enables you to create a 3D reference in the workbook that crosses multiple sheets. Start by arranging the sheet tabs so that the worksheets you want to include in the 3D reference are adjacent. With, say, cell A1 selected, follow these steps:

1. Click the Formulas tab and click Define Name in the Defined Names group. Or, in Excel versions prior to 2007, choose Insert, Name, Define.
2. In the Name edit box, type `CashBalance`. Leave the Workbook selection in place as the name's scope.
3. In the Refers To edit box, select whatever reference is currently there by dragging across it with the mouse pointer. You can press Delete if you want, or simply allow the next step to replace the current entry.
4. Click the sheet tab named `FirstNational`, hold down the Shift key, and then click the sheet tab named `SecondNational`. Both tabs are selected, and the Refers To edit box now contains `=FirstNational:SecondNational!$A$1`.
5. The active sheet is the one whose tab you first clicked. In this example, that sheet is named `FirstNational`. Click cell C2, which contains the ending balance for December.
6. Click OK.

You now have a 3D name. `CashBalance` refers to cell C2 in the worksheets named `FirstNational` and `SecondNational`. Finally, you are in a position to use all these sheet-level and 3D names. In the balance sheet worksheet, cell C4 of Figure 2.1, you can enter this formula:

```
=SUM(CashBalance)
```

This returns the sum of all the cells that make up the 3D name `CashBalance`. In this case, the formula adds the value in cell C2 of the `FirstNational` worksheet (`$2,747`) to the value in cell C2 of the `SecondNational` worksheet (`$51,959`) to return the value `$54,706`. This is the total of Bell Books' current asset for its cash accounts.

TIP 3D names do not appear in the Name box.

A quick review:

1. The sheet-level names `Debits`, `Credits`, and `BeginningBalance` are defined on each worksheet that contains a cash account.

2. A cell that occupies the same position in each cash account worksheet—in this example, cell C2—contains this formula:

   ```
   =StartBalance+SUM(Debits)-SUM(Credits)
   ```

   It returns the ending balance for the cash account contained in that worksheet.
3. A 3D name is created. It refers to the same cell in each worksheet that has a cash account ending balance. This is the balance created in step 2. The 3D range is given a name such as `CashBalance`.
4. On the balance sheet, this formula returns the sum of the cells in the workbook that make up the `CashBalance` range:

   ```
   =SUM(CashBalance)
   ```


Handling Restricted Cash Accounts

Because cash is the most liquid of current assets (and, therefore, the most current), it's easy to think of all cash accounts as current assets. This is not necessarily true. Some of your cash accounts might be restricted, either in how you use them or in when you can access them.

Suppose that your company builds houses. A new customer approaches you, asking you to build a custom house to particular specifications. You estimate that it will take about 18 months to complete the work, and you ask the customer to pay you a substantial amount of the cost at the beginning of the project. You ask for the payment to make sure that the customer will not just walk away before paying you the total amount.

You and the customer agree to put this preliminary payment in an escrow account. Neither party may access the account before construction is complete. Although this account contains cash, it is not available to pay current liabilities, according to the agreement with your customer, and you should not include it in a balance sheet as a current asset. Instead, you might include it as unearned revenue in an other assets category on the balance sheet.

Consider another example. You might find some attractive interest rates on cash accounts that are denominated in a foreign currency, or you might gamble that the value of the U.S. dollar will fall in relation to another currency. Having no operational use for the funds, you invest $10,000 in a foreign savings account with a term of two years. Because you cannot withdraw these funds before two years have passed, you cannot use them to pay current liabilities. Again, you would represent this investment as an asset on the balance sheet, but in a classification other than current assets.

Getting a Current Asset Accounts Receivable Balance

Credit sales are a fact of life. If you are in a retail business with any real competition, you almost certainly have to accept credit cards as a method of payment, or you risk losing business to your competitors. If you sell your products to other businesses, you have to deal with the fact that they, too, want to use their assets efficiently. One way they do that is to leverage a good credit history to acquire even more goods on credit.

NOTE

This situation may be changing. As this is written in early 2010, the state of U.S. credit markets is in flux. Banks have reduced the credit limits of even long-time credit customers for unsecured debt, and simultaneously have raised interest rates. These actions are beginning to have an effect on the borrowing behavior of business customers, who are reducing the amount of leverage they employ. Nevertheless, the concepts discussed here are valid and will remain so as long as credit transactions continue to take place.

➜ See Chapter 14, "Planning Profits," for information on financial and operating leverage.

The result is that you must temporarily show these credit sales as funds that you expect to receive sometime in the future. The matching principle, which was discussed in Chapter 1, applies here: It requires that you match revenues from one time period to the expenses you incur in producing those revenues. Because you have not yet received cash payment for these credit sales, you have to record them as funds to be received—thus the term *accounts receivable*. Figure 2.5 shows an example of accounts receivable for Bell Books.

Notice that the ending balance for Accounts Receivable, shown in cell E23 of Figure 2.5, is identical to the Accounts Receivable balance shown in Bell Books' balance sheet (refer to Figure 2.1).

Bell Books records new credit sales in the Debit column of the Accounts Receivable account. This follows the rule for recording increases to asset accounts: You record those increases in the asset account's Debit column.

In Figure 2.5, Accounts Receivable records a credit entry of `$17,951` in cell D13, which represents a payment to Bell Books by its credit card processing firm. This is according to the rule for recording decreases to asset accounts: You record decreases in the asset account's Credit column. The amount of `$17,951` also appears in Figure 2.2, showing that Bell Books' cash account balance has increased by the amount of the deposit of the check into the bank.

That payment reduces the (debit) balance of Accounts Receivable for December and increases the (debit) balance of Cash by an identical amount. Notice that this transaction has no net effect on Total Assets. It simply shifts the asset from Accounts Receivable to Cash, to reflect the fact that you have finally received payment for credit purchases that occurred in November.

Allowing for Doubtful Accounts

Unfortunately, not all credit purchases result in eventual, actual cash payment. The longer a customer's account goes unpaid, the more doubtful it is that the customer will ever make good on the debt. Some business customers go bankrupt subsequent to making a purchase on credit, some implode when their smoke-and-mirrors accounting practices catch up with them, and others simply disappear. Recognized credit cards, such as MasterCard or

Figure 2.5
The accounts receivable worksheet for Bell Books details the credit sales made during December 2011.

	A	B	C	D	E
1	Date	Accounts Receivable: Explanation	Debit	Credit	Balance
2					
3	11/30/11	Closing balance, November			$ 18,827
4	12/1/11	Credit sales	$1,127		$ 19,954
5	12/1/11	Credit sales	$1,258		$ 21,212
6	12/4/11	Credit sales	$ 497		$ 21,709
7	12/4/11	Credit sales	$ 288		$ 21,997
8	12/7/11	Credit sales	$ 187		$ 22,184
9	12/11/11	Credit sales	$ 977		$ 23,161
10	12/14/11	Credit sales	$1,236		$ 24,397
11	12/14/11	Credit sales	$ 454		$ 24,851
12	12/14/11	Credit sales	$ 855		$ 25,706
13	12/18/11	Payment from service bureau, 11/11 charges		$17,951	$ 7,755
14	12/21/11	Credit sales	$ 882		$ 8,637
15	12/23/11	Credit sales	$ 789		$ 9,426
16	12/27/11	Credit sales	$1,337		$ 10,763
17	12/27/11	Credit sales	$ 392		$ 11,155
18	12/27/11	Credit sales	$ 856		$ 12,011
19	12/29/11	Credit sales	$1,291		$ 13,302
20	12/29/11	Credit sales	$1,418		$ 14,720
21	12/29/11	Credit sales	$ 390		$ 15,110
22	12/29/11	Credit sales	$1,337		$ 16,447
23	12/30/11	Credit sales	$1,277		$ 17,724

AcctsReceivable

American Express, help to minimize this risk. In most cases, if you accept cards like these as payment for a product or service, you can count on receiving payment from the credit card company.

In return for accepting the risk of fraudulent chargebacks and nonpayment (and for associated services), the credit card company charges you some percentage of the credit purchases from your business. For every $100 worth of sales, you might receive $98 from the credit card company. Many firms view this avoidance of risk as an additional benefit of accepting credit cards as payment. (And if they're smart, those firms get their paying customers to pick up the 1% or 2% tab for the deadbeats.)

Many businesses also extend credit terms directly to regular customers and clients instead of (or in addition to) extending credit via an intermediary such as a credit card firm. In these cases, the business assumes the risk that it will never receive payment. Of course, the business avoids paying a service charge to a credit card processing firm in cases like these.

When you take on the risk of nonpayment, you have to expect that some customers will never pay you. Then the matching principle requires you to estimate the amount of credit sales during a given period that you'll never collect on. Estimating losses due to uncollectible accounts reduces the profit you record for the period during which you made the sales.

Two basic approaches are used in estimating the amount of credit sales that will become uncollectible: the *aging approach* and the *percentage of sales approach*. Both depend on historic estimates of the percentage of credit sales that you will eventually have to write off.

Using the Aging Approach to Estimating Uncollectibles

The aging approach depends on an analysis of the aging of credit sales (see Figure 2.6).

Figure 2.6
The `PastDue` worksheet details individual accounts receivable for Bell Books that are past due as of December 31, 2011.

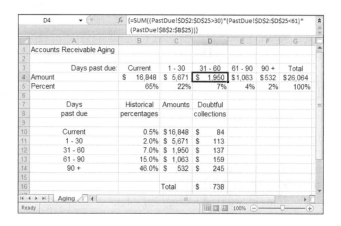

D2 =MAX(0,$G$1-30-C2)

Account number	Amount due	Date of sale	Days past due		Closing Date:	12/31/11
2490	$ 655.83	11/28/11	3			
1291	$ 732.90	11/21/11	10			
5378	$ 139.47	11/20/11	11			
1528	$ 144.22	11/17/11	14			
7585	$ 84.63	11/10/11	21			
5706	$ 894.14	11/10/11	21			
1281	$ 129.29	11/10/11	21			
7165	$ 1,101.34	11/6/11	25			
1379	$ 926.40	11/5/11	26			
6235	$ 862.78	11/1/11	30			
5482	$ 54.43	10/29/11	33			
3253	$ 505.72	10/26/11	36			
2065	$ 453.73	10/24/11	38			
3157	$ 514.75	10/17/11	45			
8798	$ 157.49	10/16/11	46			
6495	$ 96.91	10/15/11	47			
8945	$ 79.18	10/12/11	50			
4552	$ 87.79	10/3/11	59			
6838	$ 116.00	9/18/11	74			
8705	$ 156.23	9/18/11	74			
1843	$ 137.56	9/7/11	85			
8186	$ 120.82	9/6/11	86			
2824	$ 532.39	9/4/11	88			
461	$ 532.00	8/25/11	98			

PastDue

Ready 100%

The worksheet shown in Figure 2.6 details the purchases made by individual accounts, the sales amount, the date of sale, and the number of days past due for each purchase. This formula returns the number of days that an account is past due, in cell D2 of Figure 2.6:

```
=MAX(0,$G$1-30-C2)
```

Bell Books extends a 30-day grace period to its customers; then it considers an unpaid account past due. The formula uses the closing date for the balance sheet (`12/31/11`), subtracts the 30-day grace period, and then subtracts the date of the sale (the date value in cell C2). This results in the number of days past due for that sale. The formula is surrounded by the `MAX` function to prevent it from returning a negative value if the date of sale was within 30 days of the closing date—in that case, `MAX` returns a zero.

The worksheet shown in Figure 2.7 summarizes this information.

Figure 2.7
The aging approach to analysis of accounts receivable for Bell Books, December 31, 2011, summarizes the amount receivable according to the length of time the payment is past due.

D4 {=SUM((PastDue!$D$2:$D$25>30)*(PastDue!$D$2:$D$25<61)*(PastDue!$B$2:$B$25))}

Accounts Receivable Aging						
Days past due:	Current	1 - 30	31 - 60	61 - 90	90 +	Total
Amount	$ 16,848	$ 5,671	$ 1,950	$1,063	$532	$26,064
Percent	65%	22%	7%	4%	2%	100%
Days past due	Historical percentages	Amounts	Doubtful collections			
Current	0.5%	$16,848	$ 84			
1 - 30	2.0%	$ 5,671	$ 113			
31 - 60	7.0%	$ 1,950	$ 137			
61 - 90	15.0%	$ 1,063	$ 159			
90 +	46.0%	$ 532	$ 245			
		Total	$ 738			

Aging

Ready 100%

> **NOTE** Does it seem strange to subtract a number from a date? Excel keeps track of dates by means of a serial number system. By default, January 1, 1900, is serial number 1; January 2, 1900, is serial number 2; and so on. The DATE function accepts a year, month, and day as its arguments and returns the serial number for that date. Even though a cell's format causes it to display, say, 12/31/2011, the actual value in the cell is the date's serial number. Therefore, the formula in cell D2 of Figure 2.6 works out to this:
>
> ```
> =40908-30-40875
> ```


The amount of $16,848 in cell B4 of Figure 2.7 is the total of all credit sales in accounts receivable that are current as of December 31, 2011. The formula that sums the values in DecemberARDebits (cells C4:C23 in Figure 2.5) is this:

```
=SUM(DecemberARDebits)
```

The value in cell C4, $5,671, is returned by this array formula:

```
=SUM((PastDue!$D$2:$D$25<31)*(PastDue!$B$2:$B$25))
```

(Figure 2.6 shows the worksheet named PastDue.) This array formula examines the values in the range $D$2:$D$25 and returns an array of TRUE (if the value is less than 31) or FALSE (if the value is not less than 31). Excel converts these TRUE and FALSE values to 1s and 0s and then multiplies the 1s and 0s by the corresponding dollar amounts in the range $B$2:$B$25. Finally, Excel sums the results of the multiplication, to return the value of $5,671.

Similarly, the value in cell D4, $1,950, is returned by this array formula:

```
=SUM((PastDue!$D$2:$D$25<30)*(PastDue!$D$2:$D$25>61)*(PastDue!$B$2:$B$25))
```

The only differences between the array formulas in C4 and D4 are that, in D4, the following are true:

- The first comparison causes the SUM function to include only the accounts in which the number of days past due is greater than 30.
- A second comparison causes the SUM function to include accounts in which the number of days past due is less than 61.

For example, the array formula in D4 interprets the account shown on row 12 in Figure 2.6 as follows:

- TRUE for the first condition because 33 days past due is greater than 30
- TRUE for the second condition because 33 days past due is less than 61
- $54.43 for the third term

Excel interprets this item in the array formula, TRUE * TRUE * $54.43, as 1 * 1 * $54.43. Finally, the SUM function adds all the values (either the actual sale amount or 0, depending on whether both conditions are true for a given sale).

The percentage values shown in row 5 of Figure 2.7 can be useful as a means of evaluating the store's credit policies. If they stray too far from percentages that management considers acceptable for a given aging period, the store might have to tighten its criteria for extending credit.

In Figure 2.7, cells B10:B14 contain historical information about the percentage of accounts that have become uncollectible after a given period of time. Bell Books' past experience has shown that half of 1% of all current credit sales go unpaid, 2% of credit sales from 1 to 30 days are past due, and so on. These percentages are multiplied by the dollar amounts in each aging category. The results of these calculations are shown in cells D10:D14.

Their sum, `$738`, appears both in cell D16 of Figure 2.7 and in cell B6 of Figure 2.1. This is the amount that Bell Books estimates as uncollectible accounts receivable as of December 31, 2011, the date of the balance sheet.

The values that you see in cells C10:C14 in Figure 2.7 are identical to those in cells B4:F4. The C10:C14 range contains this array formula:

```
=TRANSPOSE(B4:F4)
```

You need to select the entire range C10:C14 before entering the array formula by means of Ctrl+Shift+Enter. The `TRANSPOSE` function changes the orientation of a range of cells by 90 degrees. It is often used in matrix algebra but is also helpful in cases like this one. When the underlying data in the `AcctsReceivable` sheet or the `PastDue` sheet changes, the formulas in B4:F4 also change; therefore, so do the values in C10:C14. You can also transpose a range by means of Paste Special, but be careful if you paste formulas and the source range's formulas link to other cells. You might not get what you expect.

Using the Percentage of Sales Approach to Estimating Uncollectibles

A simpler method of estimating uncollectible accounts receivable depends on historical information about the ratio of uncollected dollars to sales dollars. If you know that some percentage of sales eventually becomes uncollectible, you can simply multiply that percentage by your sales dollars for a given period.

CAUTION

If you decide to use this method, it's best to calculate the historic percentage of uncollectibles as a function of credit sales. This is because, apart from bounced checks, a cash sale never becomes uncollectible, so it doesn't help to include cash sales in the calculation. Furthermore, the relationship between the total credit sales and total cash sales in a given period might be substantially different from their relationship during the basis period. In that case, using a ratio of uncollected amounts to total sales is apt to seriously misestimate the amounts that you will never collect.

The aging approach is usually more accurate than the percentage of sales approach because it forces you to focus on the actual length of time that individual accounts are past due. The sad fact is that the longer an account is past due, the less likely it is that you will ever receive payment.

Additionally, the process of focusing on specific aging periods enables you to evaluate your policies for granting credit. For these reasons, the aging approach is usually recommended for estimating an allowance for doubtful accounts.

Getting a Prepaid Expenses Balance

The entries to the balance sheet that this chapter has discussed so far—cash and accounts receivable—are both driven by transactions that occur during the period covered by the balance sheet. Another category of current assets covers the portion of a business's resources that it uses up during more than one accounting period. Transactions that occur during the period in question might or might not change the value of these assets, and they usually require that you make an *adjusting entry* similar to those discussed in Chapter 1 in the section titled "Case Study: Adjusting Entries."

For example, suppose that your business uses a postage meter. From time to time, you take the meter to the post office and write a check for a few hundred dollars, and a clerk increases the amount of postage shown in the meter by that amount.

In effect, what you have done is *prepay* a few months of expenses by decreasing the value of one current asset—cash. If you were to prepare an income statement and a balance sheet at the end of each month, you would show the amount of metered postage that you actually used during that month as an operating expense on the income statement. The postage remaining in the meter at the end of the month is still an asset—one that you need to account for on the balance sheet.

In this way, you can associate the postage that you actually use during the month—the operating expense—with the revenues that the expense helped to generate. Doing so results in a more accurate estimate of your profit for that period. Similarly, on the balance sheet, you can accurately estimate the (admittedly, small) contribution that the postage remaining in the meter makes to your company's assets.

During the months that you are using the postage in the meter, no transaction occurs that triggers an entry in a postage journal, which would eventually show up in an income statement or balance sheet. It would be unusual to record in a journal every time you use the postage meter; it would be overkill. But the use of the postage has to be accounted for somewhere, and that's usually done with an adjusting entry at the end of each accounting period.

→ The process of making adjusting entries is discussed in more detail in Chapter 5, "Working Capital and Cash Flow Analysis," which covers adjusted trial balances.

Your business might incur many types of prepaid expenses, but nearly every company must deal with two at some point: supplies and insurance.

Although the purchase of office supplies is, formally, a prepaid expense, most businesses don't bother with recording it as such in their financial statements. They believe that it's too much trouble to perform a physical count of office supplies at the end of every accounting period to determine the value of supplies used during that period. A large corporation might treat supplies as a prepaid expense in its financial statements. However, it is likely to use an estimate of the supplies used during the period in question rather than taking a formal inventory of all the pencils, paper clips, and staples in its possession.

Insurance is another matter. It is relatively easy to quantify the amount of insurance coverage that expires during a period of time, and its value is usually considerably higher than that of office supplies. The brief example that follows clarifies the treatment of insurance as a current asset.

Dealing with Insurance as a Prepaid Expense

Imagine that Bell Books purchases a medical insurance policy for its employees on December 1, 2011. The policy will remain in force for six months, during which the company enjoys the benefits that the insurance provides. Therefore, Bell Books can consider the cost of the policy a prepaid expense: an asset whose value declines over time and might require adjusting of entries at the end of each accounting period. Bell Books records the purchase of the policy in its general journal, as shown in Figure 2.8.

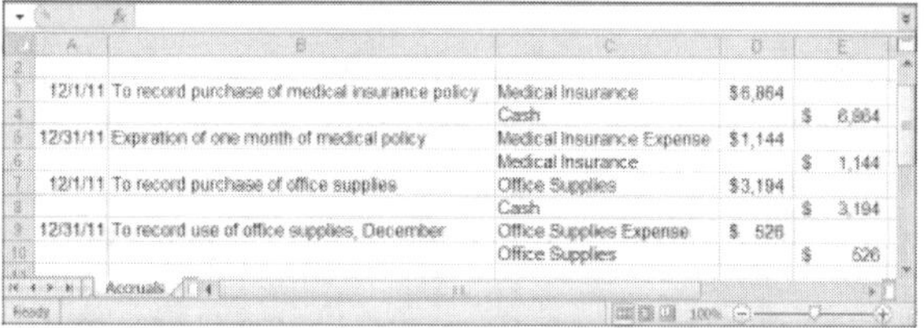

A	B	C	D	E
12/1/11	To record purchase of medical insurance policy	Medical Insurance	$6,864	
		Cash		$ 6,864
12/31/11	Expiration of one month of medical policy	Medical Insurance Expense	$1,144	
		Medical Insurance		$ 1,144
12/1/11	To record purchase of office supplies	Office Supplies	$3,194	
		Cash		$ 3,194
12/31/11	To record use of office supplies, December	Office Supplies Expense	$ 526	
		Office Supplies		$ 526

Figure 2.8
Both the original purchase of an asset such as insurance and its periodic expiration are recorded as journal entries.

Medical Insurance is an asset account. After purchasing the policy, the company has an additional asset in the form of insurance for its employees. According to the rules on debit entries and credit entries for asset accounts, an increase in the asset account's balance is recorded as a debit. Therefore, the amount of coverage provided by the policy appears in both the general journal and the ledger's Medical Insurance asset account as a debit, as shown in Figure 2.9.

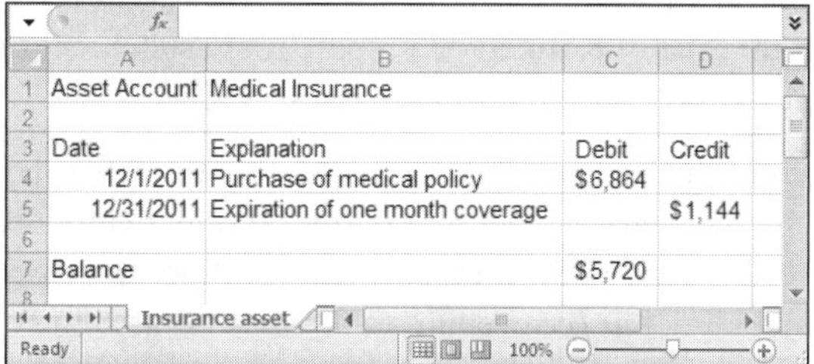

A	B	C	D
Asset Account	Medical Insurance		
Date	Explanation	Debit	Credit
12/1/2011	Purchase of medical policy	$6,864	
12/31/2011	Expiration of one month coverage		$1,144
Balance		$5,720	

Figure 2.9
The journal entries for the purchase and partial expiration of the Medical Insurance policy are also recorded as asset account ledger entries.

After one month of coverage, on December 31, 1/6 of the policy has expired, and the value of the asset therefore declines by 1/6. Again, the rules for debits and credits in asset accounts state that a decline in the value of an asset is recorded as a credit. Therefore, on December 31, Bell Books makes credit entries in its general journal and its general ledger Medical Insurance accounts. These entries reflect the expiration of 1/6 of the value of the policy. (Refer to Figures 2.8 and 2.9.)

Because this is a prepaid expense, you should also record the expiration of the one month of coverage in an expense account. An expense results in a decrease in owner's equity, and, according to the debit and credit rules, a decrease in a liability or equity account is recorded as a debit. Therefore, the expense incurred as a result of the expiration of one month of insurance coverage is recorded as a debit to the Medical Insurance account, as shown in Figure 2.10.

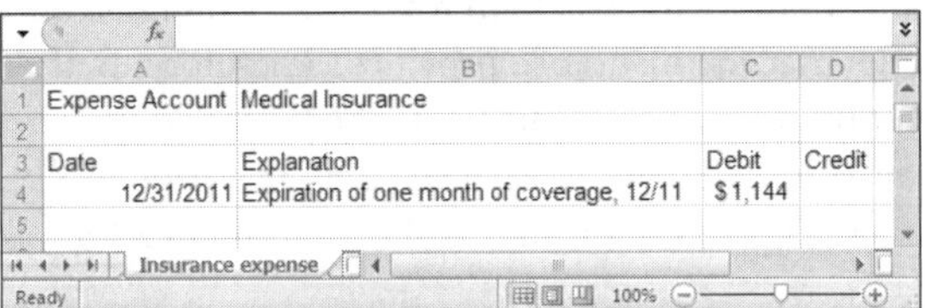

	A	B	C	D
1	Expense Account	Medical Insurance		
2				
3	Date	Explanation	Debit	Credit
4	12/31/2011	Expiration of one month of coverage, 12/11	$1,144	
5				

Figure 2.10
Debiting the Medical Insurance expense account ledger entry offsets the credit to the Medical Insurance asset account.

The prepaid expense has an effect in one more place: the prepaid expenses asset category on the balance sheet. At the end of the first month of coverage, the value of the policy has dropped by $1,144. During the remaining 5 months of coverage provided by the policy, this prepaid expense balance will continue to decline at $1,144 per month.

Getting a Current Asset Balance

Because a company's inventory is a current asset, some of the mechanics of moving inventory asset amounts among various accounts as the balance sheet is being prepared are discussed in this section.

➜ See Chapter 3, "Valuing Inventories for the Balance Sheet," for a detailed discussion about the valuing of inventories.

At the end of an accounting period, when you are preparing an income statement and a balance sheet, you usually bring the balances of the various revenue and expense accounts to zero. The reason is that the next time you prepare these statements, you want them to reflect the activity that has taken place during the next period.

A starting value of zero in the revenue and expense accounts enables you to accurately determine the profit that you earn during that period. If dollar amounts from an earlier period remain in those accounts, you won't be able to subtract the correct amount of expenses from the correct amount of revenues to arrive at an accurate earnings estimate.

The next three steps define the process of bringing the revenue and expense accounts to zero, which is also called *closing the accounts*:

1. For revenue accounts, which normally carry credit balances, make an offsetting debit entry to bring its balance to zero. For expense accounts, which normally carry debit balances, make an offsetting credit entry to close them.
2. Make these closing entries in a special, temporary account in the general journal, termed an income summary. The revenue account's debit entry is offset by a credit to the income summary. The expense account's credit entry is offset by a debit to the income summary. The difference between the sum of the revenue entries and the sum of the expense entries represents the earnings for the period due to operations. The effect is to reset the revenue and expense accounts to zero in preparation for the next period and to move their balances temporarily to the income summary account.
3. Close the temporary income summary account with a debit entry in the amount of its balance, and enter the same amount as a credit to retained earnings or, as is done in this chapter's example, directly to owner's equity.

The result of this process is that the next period can begin with zero amounts in the revenue and expense accounts. It also places the earnings from the current period (whether positive or negative) in the appropriate balance sheet account.

The procedure for asset and liability accounts is different from the procedure for revenue and expense accounts. The dollar amounts in asset and liability accounts change over time, as resources grow and debts are paid. To arrange for an asset account to have a zero balance at the beginning of an accounting period would be to say that the company's assets somehow vanished at the end of the earlier period. Instead, you want to properly attribute the *change* in the asset or liability balance, often to an equity account.

One such asset account is inventory. If your business produces products or resells them to retailers or consumers, you have inventory to account for. (If your business provides only services for its customers, you might well carry no inventory.)

Understanding the Inventory Flow

At the beginning of a period, you normally have some amount of goods in your inventory. During the period, you might purchase additional goods from your suppliers, and that increases the inventory. At the same time, you sell items from the inventory to your customers, and that decreases your inventory. The result of these activities is your ending inventory: beginning inventory, plus purchases, minus the goods used in the sales that you make to your customers.

These basic relationships can get complicated. You might have an arrangement with your suppliers that allows you to return to them, for any reason and for credit, some of the goods you purchase from them. It might be that some goods are damaged or otherwise unacceptable. And there is always theft (euphemistically, *shrinkage*) to deal with.

The terms of your purchase might call for discounts if you make payment within a specified period. To account for this sort of thing, you sometimes need to use adjusting entries or special accounts. But they do not materially change the basic flow of starting inventory, through purchases and sales, to ending inventory—which becomes the starting inventory for the next accounting period.

NOTE By rearranging this equation, you can arrive at the cost of goods sold (COGS). This is an important element in determining your company's gross profit, which is defined as sales minus COGS. One way to calculate COGS is with this equation:

```
COGS = Beginning Inventory + Purchases - Ending Inventory
```

In other words, the cost of goods available for sale is the sum of the beginning inventory and any purchases that were made. The difference between the cost of goods available for sale and the ending inventory is the cost of the goods that you actually sold to your customers. Bear in mind that this is only one way to calculate COGS. Other methods calculate a COGS amount for each sale and total those amounts for the accounting period.

Closing the Inventory Account

At the end of the period, a company often gets a physical count of the ending inventory. Then the company uses one of the valuation methods described in the next chapter, and the resulting value is used in the current assets section of the balance sheet (see Figure 2.11).

Figure 2.11 contains seven sections, indicated by their bold borders. These sections could be maintained in separate Excel worksheets, but to conserve space, they are shown here on one sheet.

The first section, labeled Inventory, shows the amount of inventory at the beginning of the period (`$21,820`) and the ending balance (`$25,760`). Under a periodic inventory system (see Chapter 3 for details), no changes are made to the inventory account during the period; purchases are recorded in their own account and COGS may be calculated at the end of the period. A closing entry, equal to the starting inventory value, is made in the account's Credit column, shown as it appears in the ledger in cell D4 and in the journal in cell H3. This amount is also entered as a debit in the general journal's income summary account (cell G2). A physical inventory is taken and the resulting value is entered as a debit (`$25,760` in cell C5) to establish the beginning inventory for the next period. The ending inventory is also credited to the journal's income summary in cell H7.

Thus, the *difference* between the beginning and the ending inventory enters the income summary account as the combination of the starting value, a debit, and the ending value, a credit. If the inventory asset increases during the period, the income summary account will be larger than it otherwise would. The opposite is also true, of course.

Purchases made to inventory during the period are also closed out by a credit entry in the ledger (cell D11) and transferred to the income summary with a credit entry (cell H11).

Closing the Revenue and Expense Accounts

Earlier, this chapter mentioned that at the end of the accounting period, the revenue and expense accounts are left with a zero balance, but asset and liability accounts such as inventory are not. For example, the sales account is given a zero balance at the end of one period and therefore at the beginning of the next. Its ending balance is entered twice at closing: once as a debit to the ledger account, to close it, and once as a credit in the income summary account. The debit in the income summary begins the process of moving revenue out of its ledger account and into the balance sheet.

In Figure 2.11, the formula used in cell D7 to calculate sales is an array formula:

```
=SUM(IF(SecondNational!B5:B19="Cash Receipts",SecondNational!C5:C19,0))+
  SUM(IF(AcctsReceivable!B3:B23="Credit Sales", AcctsReceivable!C3:C23,0))
```

This array formula looks to the worksheet named `SecondNational` to find any values in cells B5:B19 that match the value `Cash Receipts`. For any matching values, the formula sums the corresponding dollar amounts in cells C5:C19 (refer to Figure 2.4).

The same process is used with the credit sales recorded in the `Accounts Receivable` worksheet, and the results of the two `SUM` functions are totaled to give the full amount of sales for the month. In practice, just as here, you keep these two accounts separate and add their closing balances together for the purpose of the income summary account.

The three sections in Figure 2.11, labeled Advertising, Communications, and Salaries, each represent expenses incurred during the current period. The details of the activity in each account during the period have been omitted; only the ending balance and the closing entry are shown.

The closing entries in the ledger accounts also appear in the general journal's temporary income summary account. Note that the values in cells D14, D17, and D20 are identical to the values in cells H12:H14 in the figure.

Notice also the value of `$34,226` in cell H15 of Figure 2.11. It is the result of subtracting the period's expenses (purchasing, advertising, communications, and salaries) from the period's sales revenue `($70,202)`.

Figure 2.11
Closing accounts at the end of a period takes revenue and expense accounts to a zero value but normally leaves a value in asset and liability accounts.

D7 {=SUM(IF(SecondNational!B5:B19="Cash Receipts",SecondNational!C5:C19,0))+SUM(IF(AcctsReceivable!B3:B23="Credit Sales", AcctsReceivable!C3:C23,0))}

	B	C	D	F	G	H
1	*Ledger Accounts:*	Debits	Credits	*General Journal:*	Debits	Credits
2	**Inventory**			Income summary	$ 21,820	
3	Starting inventory (12/1/2011)	$ 21,820		Starting inventory (12/1/2011)		$ 21,820
4	To close starting inventory		$ 21,820	To close starting inventory		
5	Beginning balance (1/1/2012)	$ 25,760				
6	**Sales**			Inventory (12/31/2011)	$ 25,760	
7	Ending balance (12/31)		$ 70,202	Income summary		$ 25,760
8	To close	$ 70,202		Establish ending inventory		
9	**Purchases**					
10	December purchases	$ 20,937		Sales	$ 70,202	
11	To close		$ 20,937	Purchases		$ 20,937
12	**Advertising**			Advertising		$ 3,116
13	Ending balance (12/31)	$ 3,116		Communications		$ 1,835
14	To close		$ 3,116	Salaries		$ 10,088
15	**Communications**			Income summary		$ 34,226
16	Ending balance (12/31)	$ 1,835		To close revenue and expense accounts		
17	To close		$ 1,835			
18	**Salaries**			Income Summary	$ 38,166	
19	Ending balance (12/31)	$ 10,088		Owner's Equity		$ 38,166
20	To close		$ 10,088			

Account closings

Ready

Cell G18 contains this formula:

```
=H15+(H7-G2)
```

It adds the difference between the ending inventory and the beginning inventory to the income summary. This total amount, `$38,166`, represents the change in equity for the period: sales minus operating expenses plus the change in the inventory valuation. Because the value of inventory grew during the period, it increases the amount that is added to owner's equity. Had the inventory value dropped, its effect would have been to reduce the amount added to owner's equity.

Summary

In this chapter, you have seen some of the preliminary aspects of balance sheets: their uses, design, current asset components, and relationships to underlying accounts. Changes over time in these accounts cause changes in your company's worth and, thus, in its balance sheet. However, revenue and expense accounts are treated differently at the end of an accounting period than are asset and liability accounts.

Although this book doesn't teach accountancy, some accounting terminology is needed to discuss the measurement of profit. And some discussion of rules used in double-entry accounting—such as recording an increase in an expense account as a debit entry—is needed if you are to measure your profits in a way that others can understand.

Potential investors, creditors, and accountants will insist that you follow accepted principles and practices in your financial statements. This chapter has introduced some of these concepts; more are covered in subsequent chapters, but only to the extent necessary to help you create your financial statements.

Because the valuation of inventory is a somewhat complicated topic, Chapter 3 covers it in detail. Choosing the appropriate method for valuing the items in your business's inventory is essential if you are to estimate the worth of your business properly. The measurement of your profits also depends on your choice of valuation method. After looking into the topic of inventory valuation, this book returns to the balance sheet with a consideration of liabilities and owner's equity.

Valuing Inventories for the Balance Sheet

3

Particularly for a business that manufactures or resells tangible goods, the size of the company's inventory exerts a powerful influence on its profitability. The inventory of goods is often the company's major current asset and, therefore, contributes heavily to the company's worth. Further, the cost of goods sold (COGS) depends on the value of the stock that is marketed, so inventory also figures into the company's gross profit and its net income.

In part because inventory is so important to a company's worth and profitability, you have several methods and approaches available to value inventory. Because you are expected to be consistent from year to year in your inventory valuation and accounting methods, it's important to make rational choices early. Using Excel's tools and capabilities properly can help you with these choices.

This chapter describes the different methods used to assign a value to your inventory and the different ways you can account for it. You will see that the way you assign a value to your inventory affects both your profitability and your business's worth.

There are two broad considerations in this context: the timing of the computation of the cost of products, and the way that costs flow from starting to ending inventory. The timing is defined by whether a perpetual or a periodic system is used. Both systems are described in the next section.

The cost flow can be managed using any of these methods:

- Specific identification
- First-in first-out (FIFO)
- Last-in first out (LIFO)
- One of two types of average cost: weighted average and moving average

IN THIS CHAPTER

Each of these methods is discussed in the following sections.

Understanding Perpetual and Periodic Inventory Systems

Businesses that deal in goods that carry a high value usually have an easier time tracking their inventories than do businesses that sell commodities. A boat dealer, for example, tends to have fewer, and more expensive, units in stock than does an office supply store. Other things being equal, it's easier for the boat dealer to do a physical count of the number of boats in inventory than for the office supplier to count the number of reams of three-hole-punched photocopy paper in stock.

This simple fact of business life has implications for how the business accounts for its inventory. Regardless of whether you have thousands of inexpensive items to count or just a few costly ones, taking a physical inventory can serve two important purposes:

- **Verifying stock levels**—You may have a sophisticated stock tracking system that knows the precise quantity sold of any given product every business day. But it can't account for typographical errors that occur when you record new purchases. Nor does a tracking system capture the shrinkage that occurs when an employee gets a little self-indulgent with your stock of yellow stickies. A periodic physical inventory corrects inaccuracies in your data systems.
- **Determining current inventory values and COGS**—One way to calculate the COGS is to subtract the inventory on hand at the end of an accounting period from the sum of the starting inventory and new purchases. The difference is an estimate of the value of the goods sold, which you can subtract from your revenues to arrive at your gross profit. You will have much more confidence in that value if it is based on a recent physical inventory.

Granted, then, that the process of taking a physical inventory is important, and it can be burdensome. When should a business manager do it? As implied at the beginning of this section, you might do it daily—and thus update your books with a current inventory valuation—if your inventory is relatively small, with high unit costs. Or you might do it only monthly or even quarterly if you stock many different products—ones that perhaps carry relatively low unit costs.

Modern inventory management systems, even those used by inexpensive accounting packages, automatically adjust inventory levels whenever a sale is recorded or additional products enter your stock. These applications almost mandate a perpetual inventory system. That makes it important to remember that the automated system doesn't take the place of doing a physical inventory from time to time. If you don't, sooner or later your company is going to misreport its profits and its assets.

Perpetual Inventory Systems

The boat dealer can determine the COGS and the value of the ending inventory on a daily basis. It is simply a matter of counting the number of units sold, shown on the sales receipts, and multiplying that number by the cost of each unit.

Similarly, the boat dealer can value the ending inventory by performing a physical count of the boats in stock at the end of the day and multiplying by their unit costs. It's really quite simple. For example, five 24-foot sailboats at $10,000 each plus four 28-foot sailboats at $16,000 each result in a $114,000 asset valuation.

This approach is termed a *perpetual inventory* system, so named because it is both possible and feasible to directly determine the inventory on any given day—or even at any time of day.

Figure 3.1 shows an example of how a company's inventory of a particular product is evaluated, using a perpetual inventory system.

Figure 3.1
The inventory asset value is recalculated with each purchase and each sale.

J12 | fx =H12*I12

	A	B	C	D	E	F	G	H	I	J	K
1			Purchases			Sales			On Hand		
2	Date	Units	Unit Cost	Extended Cost	Units	Unit Cost	Extended Cost	Units	Unit Cost	Extended Cost	
3											
4	1/1/11	60	$ 4.00	$ 240.00				60	$ 4.00	$ 240.00	
5											
6	1/19/11				45	$ 4.00	$ 180.00	15	$ 4.00	$ 60.00	
7											
8	2/2/11	90	$ 4.00	$ 360.00				105	$ 4.00	$ 420.00	
9											
10	2/16/11				10	$ 4.00	$ 40.00	95	$ 4.00	$ 380.00	
11											
12	3/2/11	30	$ 4.00	$ 120.00				125	$ 4.00	$ 500.00	
13											
14											

Figure 3.1 shows a perpetual system with a cost flow that's about as simple as it gets. The unit costs do not change over time (see columns C, F, and I), and it is fluctuation in unit costs that can make it difficult to select an inventory valuation method.

Columns D, G, and J in Figure 3.1 contain something called *extended cost*. This is inventory management jargon for the total dollars paid for a product: so, cell D4 shows that the company paid $240.00 for an initial purchase of 60 units at a unit cost of $4.00. Similarly, cell G6 shows that the company sold $180.00 worth of product on 1/19/11: 45 units that cost the company $4.00 each.

Cells J4 and J6 show the results of the initial purchase and the first sale: the total asset value for the product is first established at $240.00 as a result of the initial purchase, and then it drops to $60.00 when $180.00 worth is sold. Two subsequent purchases and a sale leave the inventory value for this product at $500.00 as of 3/2/11, as shown in cell J12.

The pertinent aspect of the analysis shown in Figure 3.1 is that the effect of each purchase and each sale is shown as of the date on which the transaction occurred. The total asset value and the COGS are both calculated in response to each transaction.

In contrast, a periodic inventory system—discussed in the next section—calculates the COGS and, usually, the current asset value only at the end of an accounting period.

Figure 3.2 introduces the complications that occur when the unit cost of a product varies over time.

Figure 3.2
This layout keeps the acquisition costs for different purchases separate.

K16 =J14+J15+J16

	Purchases			Sales			On Hand			
Date	Units	Unit Cost	Extended Cost	Units	Unit Cost	Extended Cost	Units	Unit Cost	Extended Cost	Asset Value
1/1/11	60	$ 4.00	$ 240.00				60	$ 4.00	$ 240.00	$ 240.00
1/19/11				45	$ 4.00	$ 180.00	15	$ 4.00	$ 60.00	$ 60.00
2/2/11	90	$ 4.20	$ 378.00				15	$ 4.00	$ 60.00	
							90	$ 4.20	$ 378.00	$ 438.00
2/16/11				10	$ 4.00	$ 40.00	5	$ 4.00	$ 20.00	
							90	$ 4.20	$ 378.00	$ 398.00
3/2/11	30	$ 4.40	$ 132.00				5	$ 4.00	$ 20.00	
							90	$ 4.20	$ 378.00	
							30	$ 4.40	$ 132.00	$ 530.00

In Figure 3.2, the unit cost of the product goes from $4.00 on 1/1/11 to $4.20 on 2/2/11, and to $4.40 on 3/2/11. That means that on 2/2/11, the company has a mix of differently priced units in stock: 15 units that cost $4.00 each and 90 that cost $4.20 each. The company is still using a perpetual inventory system, because the effects of each transaction on the inventory are calculated immediately.

The company is probably using the valuation method called *FIFO*. Notice that just prior to the sale that occurs on 2/16/11, the company had 105 units in stock: 15 that cost $4.00 each and 90 that cost $4.20 each. On 2/16/11, the company sells 10 units, the count of units on hand drops by 10, and the 10 units shown as sold are among the units that cost $4.00.

Therefore, on 2/16/11 the asset value drops by $40.00 and the COGS is taken to be $40.00. Using FIFO, the company *assumes* that the units sold were the first ones to enter the inventory. The first units that were still available just prior to the sale on 2/16/11 cost $4.00 each, and the asset value and the COGS are adjusted accordingly.

NOTE

Notice that the ending inventory value for this product is $530.00 in Figure 3.2, which is $30.00 more than the $500.00 ending value shown in Figure 3.1. This difference is due solely to the unit cost increases from $4.00 to $4.20 on 2/2/11, and to $4.40 on 3/2/11, in Figure 3.2.

Periodic Inventory Systems

Using traditional methods of tracking inventory, the office supply dealer would have great difficulty managing by means of a perpetual inventory system. If a physical inventory was taken daily, there would be thousands of units to count, both in the sales records and on the shelves and storerooms at the end of the business day. Furthermore, the office supply dealer typically has many categories of merchandise and several brands within each category. This is far too much information to track by hand in a perpetual inventory system.

NOTE

In recent years, point-of-sale terminals and electronic recordkeeping have put a perpetual inventory system within the reach of many businesses. Still, these systems are not yet universal, and there are problems such as systems integration when multiple locations must be tracked. Therefore, the alternative to a perpetual system, the periodic inventory system, remains in widespread use.

Under a *periodic inventory system*, a business conducts a physical count of the items in inventory at the end of an accounting period—typically, at the end of the month or the quarter. The count of each product is multiplied by that product's cost to determine the asset value for that product. And the total value of each product is summed to get the value of the total inventory.

The total value of all products in stock at the end of the period has several uses. The two principal purposes are to quantify the value of the starting inventory for the next period and to determine the COGS during the period.

At the start of an accounting period, a business normally has units in stock: its starting inventory. During the period, the business normally acquires more units. The sum of the starting inventory and purchases made during the period is the *cost of goods available for sale*:

Cost of Goods Available for Sale = Starting Inventory + Purchases

With this information and with knowledge of the value of the ending inventory, the company can calculate its COGS:

COGS = Cost of Goods Available for Sale – Ending Inventory

For example, suppose that a company could not record its sales on a daily basis and chose to put in place a periodic system. Its inventory analysis and its figures for COGS and gross profit would be the same under either system. However, the number of units sold would be determined not by the sales receipts but by subtracting the ending inventory, determined by physical count, from the starting inventory, plus any purchases made during the period.

Refer to Figure 3.2. If you entered this formula in some blank cell on that worksheet:

```
=SUM(D4:D14)-K16
```

you'd get $220.00 as the result. That's just the sum of the initial and subsequent purchases less the ending inventory amount. Therefore, it's the COGS from 1/1/11 through 3/2/11, which might account for the company's entire first quarter results for this product.

You could get the same result by using this formula:

```
=SUM(G3:G16)
```

which sums the COGS for each sales transaction directly. But if your approach to inventory tracking does not automatically enter purchase and sales information for every pertinent transaction, you might be better off with a periodic system: Do a physical inventory at the end of the period, and arrive at the COGS for the period by means of subtraction.

So far, I've dealt with the question of getting the ending inventory amount by smugly saying, "Do a physical inventory." Eventually, individual units have to be counted, of course, but that begs the question of what you do with those counts to get a dollar value. That's the topic of the next section.

Valuing Inventories

3

The basic principle of inventory valuation is that the value of a unit of inventory is its cost. For example, if your company purchases products at a wholesale cost and resells them to consumers at a retail price, the value of your inventory of goods is determined by the amount you pay to acquire the products—not by the amount you expect to sell them for.

The inventory itself consists of whatever you have purchased and that you expect to sell in the course of your normal business operations. So inventory would not include the equipment you use or the building that you purchased for office space. Although you might resell it, you wouldn't expect to do so as part of normal business operations.

On the other hand, if your company manufactures goods, the situation can be more complicated, but the basic principle still applies: Costs establish values. Manufacturers typically have three categories of inventory: raw materials, work in process, and finished goods. You value each category differently. The value of the raw materials is simply their acquisition cost. The value of works in process is the cost of the raw materials plus any labor costs involved in processing them. And the value of finished goods consists of the material cost plus all the labor costs involved in bringing the product to completion—including factory overhead.

Valuation Methods Summarized

There are three families of methods in general use to establish the value of inventory. They are briefly summarized here; later sections discuss each in more detail.

Specific Identification

This method assigns the actual cost of acquiring and processing each inventory unit to that specific unit. Normally, companies that resell relatively few but relatively costly products use specific identification. If your business sells expensive jewelry or fine art, you find it fairly easy to attach a specific acquisition cost to each unit. But if your company sells jewelry equipment or art supplies, you find it difficult to do so; it is much harder to keep track of the amount you paid for each of 100 turquoise stones or paintbrushes.

NOTE

In practice, a company that sells a few expensive products *tends* to use a perpetual system, because it's fairly easy to do frequent physical inventories. The less expensive accounting applications such as QuickBooks do not generally do a good job of supporting the specific identification method: they tend to be geared toward an average cost method.

Average Cost

This method is deceptively simple to define. The average cost per unit of a product is just the total of your payments to suppliers of the product, divided by the number of units you purchased. The actual unit cost usually varies, due to changes in your supplier's pricing over time and to your choice of suppliers.

Therefore, average cost is, in a sense, less accurate than the specific identification of a particular unit: it's an estimate based on a history of purchases, not a particular value specifically assigned to a particular item. But average cost is often feasible when specific identification is not.

→ The section "Using Average Cost," later in this chapter, discusses in more detail the two main ways to calculate average cost.

FIFO and LIFO

Both FIFO and LIFO make assumptions about when you acquired a unit of inventory and about when you sell it. FIFO assumes that the unit you just sold was part of the earliest purchase that was still in stock—and that tells you its cost. LIFO assumes that the unit you just sold was one of those you purchased most recently—and *that* tells you its cost.

Because your acquisition costs normally change over time, your COGS also changes. Both your profitability and your total assets depend on whether you bought a unit for $50 last year and sell it for $75 today (you're probably using FIFO), or whether you bought an identical unit for $60 this morning and sell it for $75 this afternoon (you're probably using LIFO).

CAUTION

Choosing to use either LIFO or FIFO in the preparation of your tax returns and other formal financial statements is something you should discuss with your accountant. In particular, the use of LIFO has been a matter of some controversy for years.

Some companies use FIFO or LIFO in the preparation of management reports to guide decisions regarding the profitability of different product lines. You're free, of course, to use any method you think more informative when the intent is to use it as a management tool. A small business that retails fresh seafood might use the plain vanilla average cost method for its tax returns. Because of the volatility of the wholesale price of fish, that company also might use FIFO to determine that it already has quite enough monkfish on hand.

The remaining sections in this chapter discuss each of these methods in detail.

Using Specific Identification

As mentioned previously, it's relatively easy to use specific identification to value your inventory if you have relatively few units to value. And as a practical matter, this often means that those items are quite costly: A business that has just a few items to sell must either sell them at a substantial profit or close down for lack of cash.

In recent years, however, technology such as point-of-sale terminals at retail stores, the imprinting of serial numbers on many different types of goods, and the widespread use of powerful databases has changed things—in the retail industry, at least. It is now much more feasible to track each unit from its acceptance into inventory through its eventual sale.

Although specific identification is probably the most intuitively satisfying of the valuation methods, you'll see that it's often better to choose another method—particularly from the profitability standpoint. Consider the case of a retail store that sells electronic equipment.

CASE STUDY: EVANS ELECTRONICS

Evans Electronics, a retail store newly located in a shopping mall, sells personal computers, data communications equipment, and peripherals such as printers and disk drives. The store has installed a small database, using Microsoft Access as the database management system. This database enables the sales staff to record the serial number and product code of every item that the store sells. Although Evans uses one method of inventory valuation, its owner wants to know the result of each valuation method for a particular accounting period, in preparation for a meeting with her accountant regarding inventory matters.

Using a Database System to Maintain Inventory Information

The database system also maintains information about inventories. It records the date that a unit of stock was purchased, its cost, and its product code. This information is saved in a database table whose structure is shown in Figure 3.3.

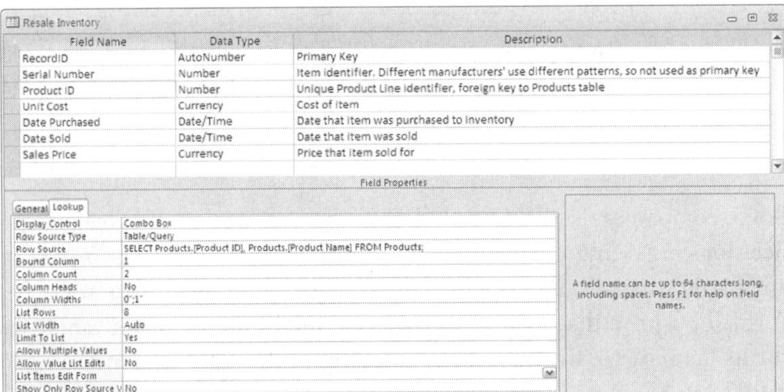

Figure 3.3
By specifying a table lookup for a row source, you can display (for example) descriptive text instead of nondescriptive identification numbers.

The database also contains several predefined queries. You can use queries to perform several different kinds of tasks, such as editing data, and adding or deleting records. But one of queries' main functions is to select data from tables, then move it to external files, display it on users' monitors, and make the data available to other applications. Some queries return data from the database on a record-by-record basis, and other queries summarize the data by groups.

Chapter 17, "Importing Business Data into Excel," goes into these matters in much more detail than this chapter does. For now, take the following information as background on the topic of inventory valuation via databases:

- You can arrange to have the most current data from a database, or from an inventory management application, moved into an Excel workbook whenever you open the workbook or whenever you call for it. It's entirely possible but not necessary to use a database designed using Microsoft Access or SQL Server.
- The information that is retrieved into Excel can come directly from tables in the database or indirectly via queries that extract data from the tables. Using queries is usually the right approach when you need to get data from more than one table at once. You can also arrange for the data to be exported by means of a report. Popular applications such as QuickBooks can convert their built-in reports to the Excel worksheet format.
- If the information is returned by queries, you can also arrange for runtime criteria. Don't be intimidated by the terminology—those are just words. Put differently, you can specify conditions such as beginning and ending dates or types of product that take effect when the query extracts the data from the tables. This approach enables you to design and reuse the basic structure of a query, such as the tables involved and the fields you want to see. Then, each time you use it, you can specify a different range of dates, type of product, and so on.

3

Using a predefined query, Evans Electronics extracts data from its database into the Excel worksheet. Figure 3.4 displays both summary information on the starting inventory as of April 1, 2010, and quantities purchased during the month.

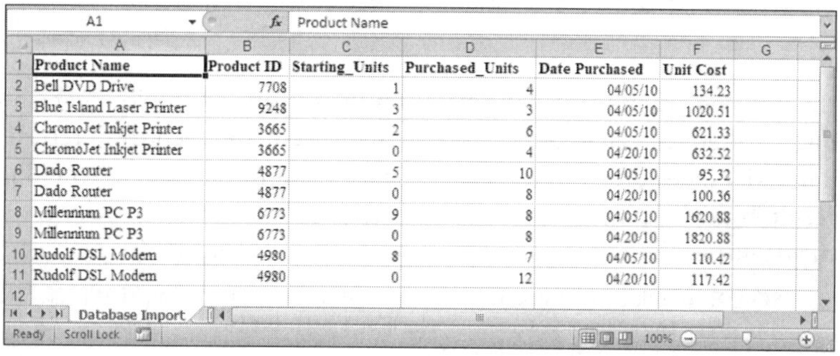

Figure 3.4
Evans Electronics' starting inventory and quantities purchased during April 2010 form the basis for valuation at the end of the period.

A1 | Product Name

	A	B	C	D	E	F	G
1	Product Name	Product ID	Starting_Units	Purchased_Units	Date Purchased	Unit Cost	
2	Bell DVD Drive	7708	1	4	04/05/10	134.23	
3	Blue Island Laser Printer	9248	3	3	04/05/10	1020.51	
4	ChromoJet Inkjet Printer	3665	2	6	04/05/10	621.33	
5	ChromoJet Inkjet Printer	3665	0	4	04/20/10	632.52	
6	Dado Router	4877	5	10	04/05/10	95.32	
7	Dado Router	4877	0	8	04/20/10	100.36	
8	Millennium PC P3	6773	9	8	04/05/10	1620.88	
9	Millennium PC P3	6773	0	8	04/20/10	1820.88	
10	Rudolf DSL Modem	4980	8	7	04/05/10	110.42	
11	Rudolf DSL Modem	4980	0	12	04/20/10	117.42	
12							

Database Import

Ready | Scroll Lock | 100%

The store's supplier raised its prices during April 2010: Notice that identical products have entered the inventory at different times and at different costs. For example, Evans acquired 7 DSL modems on April 5, 2010, at a unit cost of $110.42, and another 12 units of the same modem on April 20, 2010, at a unit cost of $117.42.

When it is time to close the books at the end of each month, the information on products sold is copied from the database to an Excel worksheet, as in Figure 3.5.

Figure 3.5
The record of product sales for April 2010 shows that some units that were sold had different acquisition costs.

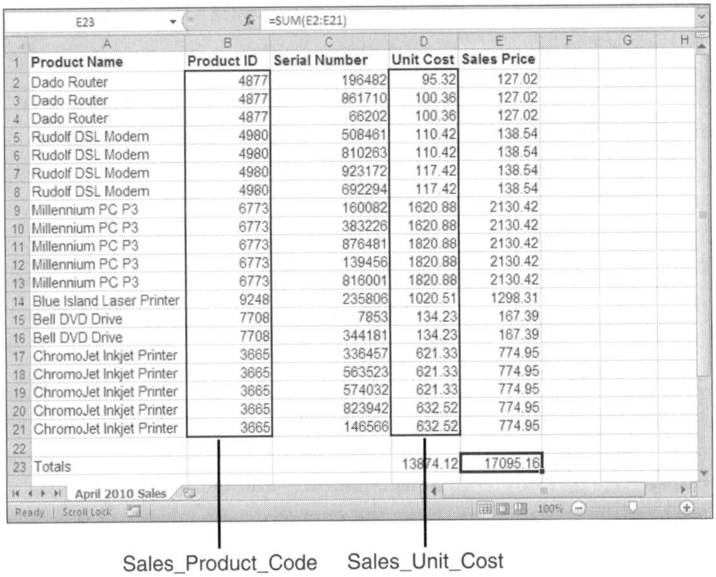

E23 =SUM(E2:E21)

	A	B	C	D	E
1	Product Name	Product ID	Serial Number	Unit Cost	Sales Price
2	Dado Router	4877	196482	95.32	127.02
3	Dado Router	4877	861710	100.36	127.02
4	Dado Router	4877	66202	100.36	127.02
5	Rudolf DSL Modem	4980	508461	110.42	138.54
6	Rudolf DSL Modem	4980	810263	110.42	138.54
7	Rudolf DSL Modem	4980	923172	117.42	138.54
8	Rudolf DSL Modem	4980	692294	117.42	138.54
9	Millennium PC P3	6773	160082	1620.88	2130.42
10	Millennium PC P3	6773	383226	1620.88	2130.42
11	Millennium PC P3	6773	876481	1820.88	2130.42
12	Millennium PC P3	6773	139456	1820.88	2130.42
13	Millennium PC P3	6773	816001	1820.88	2130.42
14	Blue Island Laser Printer	9248	235806	1020.51	1298.31
15	Bell DVD Drive	7708	7853	134.23	167.39
16	Bell DVD Drive	7708	344181	134.23	167.39
17	ChromoJet Inkjet Printer	3665	336457	621.33	774.95
18	ChromoJet Inkjet Printer	3665	563523	621.33	774.95
19	ChromoJet Inkjet Printer	3665	574032	621.33	774.95
20	ChromoJet Inkjet Printer	3665	823942	632.52	774.95
21	ChromoJet Inkjet Printer	3665	146566	632.52	774.95
22					
23	Totals			13874.12	17095.16

April 2010 Sales

Sales_Product_Code Sales_Unit_Cost

Setting Up the Database Queries

You usually set up queries in Microsoft Access by means of a graphical user interface (GUI).

> **NOTE** You can also set up the queries from within Excel, again using a GUI, if you installed Microsoft Query from your Office installation disc. You often set up queries both in Excel and in the database so that they work together to accomplish a single task.

By dragging around tables and fields on the screen, you indicate which fields you want the query to return. You establish criteria that specify the records to return in the same way. The GUI hides the Torquemada-like machinations that go on behind the scenes and that result in the Structured Query Language (SQL) code that actually extracts the data from the database. For example, here's the code that returns the Evans Electronics sales for April:

```
SELECT Products.[Product Name], Products.[Product ID],
[Resale Inventory].[Serial Number], [Resale Inventory].[Unit Cost],
[Resale Inventory].[Sales Price]
FROM [Resale Inventory] LEFT JOIN Products ON
[Resale Inventory].[Product ID] = Products.[Product ID]
```

```
WHERE ((([Resale Inventory].[Date Sold])
Between #4/1/2010# And #4/30/2010#))
ORDER BY [Resale Inventory].[Serial Number];
```

This code is actually fairly easy to understand. Here's a brief walkthrough:

- The `SELECT` statement identifies the tables and fields that are involved in the query. Here, one table is named `Products` and the other is named `Resale Inventory`. The fields from each table follow the table name. So, for example, the code says to select the `Product Name` field from the `Products` table. (Names that have embedded blanks, such as `Product Name`, are enclosed in square brackets.)
- In the `FROM` statement, the relationship (or *join*, in database jargon) between the two tables is specified. A record from `Products` is related to a record in `Resale Inventory` when they share the same Product ID.
- The `WHERE` statement specifies any criteria that the query is to apply. In this example, the criterion returns only those records with a `Date Sold` value between April 1, 2010, and April 30, 2010.
- The `ORDER BY` statement calls for the records to be returned in ascending Serial Number order.

3

When the queries have been set up (Chapter 17 provides more information on the process), you're ready to bring the data into Excel either for the first time or as a subsequent refresh.

NOTE

To refresh the data, begin by selecting any cell in the table. Click the Ribbon's Data tab and then click Refresh All in the Connections group. In Excel versions prior to 2007, choose Refresh Data from Excel's Data menu.

Recording Product Sales with Specific Identification

Figure 3.5 shows the worksheet for sales during April, retrieved from the database. Because the specific identification method is being used, each row contains information on the Product ID and Serial Number of each unit sold. Together, the Product ID and Serial Number uniquely identify a particular unit. Because the sales database can uniquely identify a particular unit, the database can also report Evans Electronics' cost of acquiring that specific unit. The cost data is passed to Excel when you run the query.

Although the unit costs for some products are different, Evans Electronics sold each unit of a given product at the same price. As a new business, Evans Electronics made a tactical decision not to increase its sales prices during the first month of operation. Clearly, the company's decision to absorb the supplier's price increase rather than to pass it on to its own customers reduces its profitability. This is not an unusual decision. However, the fact that the inventory contains identical units acquired at different costs has consequences both for the store's gross profit and for the balance sheet's asset valuation.

Using the specific identification method of valuation, Evans Electronics can analyze its inventory for the month of April, as shown in Figure 3.6.

Inventory_Unit_Cost

B17 => ='April 2010 Sales'!E23-'April Inventory Close'!B16

	A	B	C	D	E	F	G	H	I
1		Product	Unit	Starting	Purchased	Cost of Goods	Units	Ending Inventory	
2	Product Name	ID	Cost	Units	Units	Available for Sale	Sold	Units	Costs
3	Bell DVD Drive	7708	134.23	1	4	671.15	2	3	402.69
4	Blue Island Laser Printer	9248	1020.51	3	3	6123.06	1	5	5102.55
5	ChromoJet Inkjet Printer	3665	621.33	2	6	4970.64	3	5	3106.65
6	ChromoJet Inkjet Printer	3665	632.52	0	4	2530.08	2	2	1265.04
7	Dado Router	4877	95.32	5	10	1429.8	1	14	1334.48
8	Dado Router	4877	100.36	0	8	802.88	2	6	602.16
9	Millennium PC P3	6773	1620.88	9	8	27554.96	2	15	24313.2
10	Millennium PC P3	6773	1820.88	0	8	14567.04	3	5	9104.4
11	Rudolf DSL Modem	4980	110.42	8	7	1656.3	2	13	1435.46
12	Rudolf DSL Modem	4980	117.42	0	12	1409.04	2	10	1174.2
13									
14	Totals			28	70	$61,714.95	20	78	$47,840.83
15									
16	Cost of goods sold:	$13,874.12							
17	Gross profit:	$3,221.04							
18									

April Inventory Close

Inventory_Products_Code Purchase_Units

Figure 3.6
By matching product codes and costs to the sales database, Evans Electronics can tell how many units of each product were sold.

These columns in Figure 3.6 require some comment:

- The columns for Product Name, Product ID, and Unit Cost contain the unique combinations of the variables from the worksheet in Figure 3.5. For example, there are only two possible combinations of Product ID and Unit Cost for the Dado Router.
- Columns D and E come directly from the database query. The number of units in April's starting inventory can also be obtained from the ending units in the March inventory summary.
- The extended cost of each item available for sale, in column F, is the unit cost multiplied by the sum of the starting number of units and the purchased units.
- The critical portion of Figure 3.6 is in column G, Units Sold. It counts the number of units sold, for a given product, that were acquired at a given cost.

Cell G8 contains this array formula. (G8 is just an example; cells G3:G7 and G9:G12 contain similar formulas.)

```
=SUM((B8=Sales_Product_Code)*(C8=Sales_Unit_Cost))
```

The array formula returns `2` as its result. Two Dado routers that were purchased for $100.36 each were sold during April. To understand how this formula works, examine its components.

The range named `Sales_Product_Code` occupies cells B2:B21 in Figure 3.5. This fragment of the array formula

```
B8=Sales_Product_Code
```

evaluates to this:

```
{TRUE;TRUE;TRUE;FALSE;FALSE; . . . ;FALSE}
```

It returns an array of values that are TRUE or FALSE. The logical value depends on whether the value in B8 equals any values in the Sales_Product_Code range. In this case, the first three values in the array are TRUE. That is because the value of 4877 in cell B8 in Figure 3.6 equals the first three elements in Sales_Product_Code. (See cells B2:B4 in Figure 3.5.)

This fragment of the array formula

```
C8=Sales_Unit_Cost
```

evaluates to this:

```
{FALSE;TRUE;TRUE;FALSE;FALSE; . . . ;FALSE}
```

It operates in much the same way. The range named Sales_Unit_Cost occupies cells D2:D21 in Figure 3.5. The fragment also returns an array of logical TRUE or FALSE values, depending on whether the unit cost in C8 of Figure 3.6, $100.36, equals any unit costs in the Sales_Unit_Cost range. In this case, only the second and third values are TRUE. (See cells D3:D4 in Figure 3.5.)

TIP

You can see the arrays of TRUE or FALSE values—indeed, the results of any portion of an Excel formula—by highlighting a fragment in the formula bar and pressing the F9 key. When you have finished, be sure to press Esc; otherwise, the results replace the original fragment.

Excel 2002 and later versions offer a tool that accomplishes much the same end as the F9 key: Formula Evaluation. Select a cell that contains a formula, click the Formulas tab, and then click Evaluate Formula in the Formula Auditing group. (In earlier versions of Excel, select Tools, Formula Auditing, Evaluate Formula) In the Evaluate Formula window, click the Evaluate button repeatedly to watch expressions resolve into intermediate values and finally to the result you see on the worksheet. This tool is a little less flexible but much more convenient than using the F9 key.

Using Excel to Derive the Inventory Value

Excel can perform arithmetic operations on logical values. The rules are that TRUE*TRUE = 1, TRUE*FALSE = 0, and FALSE*FALSE = 0. So this fragment, which multiplies the first array of logical values times the second

```
(B8=Sales_Product_Code)*(C8=Sales_Unit_Cost)
```

evaluates to this:

```
{0;1;1;0;0;0;0;0;0;0;0;0;0;0;0;0;0;0;0;0}
```

It returns an array of 1s and 0s. The first array contains TRUE in its first three elements, and the second array contains TRUE in its second and third elements; the remaining elements in each array are FALSE. So the result of this multiplication is an array whose second and third elements are 1s and the remaining elements are 0s.

Finally, the full formula returns the sum of the array of 1s and 0s:

```
=SUM((B8=Sales_Product_Code)*(C8=Sales_Unit_Cost))
```

In this case, that sum equals 2: the number sold of products whose product code is 4877 *and* whose unit cost is $100.36.

The array formula just discussed is copied and pasted into each of the cells in the range G3:G12 in Figure 3.6. The references to the product code and unit cost adjust accordingly; they are relative references so, for example, the reference to cell B8 changes to B9 when cell G8 is copied and pasted into cell G9.

However, the range names do not adjust. In this example, both Sales_Product_Code and Sales_Unit_Cost are defined using absolute references and do not adjust in response to a copy and paste.

Therefore, the formulas compare the product code and unit cost entered in each row from 3 to 12 with named ranges whose addresses do not adjust. The result is a count of each unit that was sold during April and acquired at a given unit cost.

The number of units in the ending inventory for April (column H in Figure 3.6) is just the result of subtracting the units sold from the units in starting inventory, plus the units that were purchased. And the cost for each product at a given unit cost (column I in Figure 3.6) is the result of multiplying the number of units in the ending inventory by the associated unit cost.

Evans can now arrive at a COGS during the month of April of $13,874.12. She does so by obtaining the total cost of the goods available for sale ($61,714.95) and subtracting from that figure the total cost of the ending inventory ($47,840.83).

Therefore, the company's income statement for April would show a gross profit of $3,221.04, the result of subtracting the COGS from its total sales revenue of $17,095.16 (refer to cell E23 in Figure 3.5). Its balance sheet for April would show ending inventory assets of $47,840.83.

Using Average Cost

Suppose that as just discussed, Evans Electronics has in its starting inventory products that cost different amounts but are otherwise identical. What if the inventory management situation weren't so tidy and the store had no means of knowing which specific item it sold? That is, suppose that when it sells a Millennium PC P3 computer, Evans Electronics does not know whether it is a unit that was purchased from the supplier for $1,620.88 or for $1,820.88. Quite possibly, as this section shows, Evans Electronics doesn't *need* to know.

In a situation like that, companies often use the *average cost* method of valuing inventory. You might use this method even if you had some means of recognizing whether a computer cost you $1,620.88 or $1,820.88. In that case you *could* use the specific identification method, even though it usually entails additional cost to track specific items. In addition to greater administrative costs, if you use specific identification, your gross profit on a sale depends in part on which of several computers your customer happened to take off the shelf—computers that you acquired at different costs but that are otherwise identical.

In this sort of situation, you don't want your gross profit to depend on which one of several identical cartons the customer happens to pick up. The average cost method recognizes this: it assigns an *average* cost to each unit of inventory—an average that takes into account all the unit costs you spent to acquire your stock of a particular product. Figure 3.7 illustrates the average cost method as Evans Electronics might use it.

Figure 3.7
Evans Electronics' starting and ending inventory for April 2010 with the average cost method returns different results than with specific identification.

G4 {=SUM((A4=Sales_Product_Code)*1)}

	A	B	C	D	E	F	G	H	I
1			Purchases		Goods Available for Sale			Ending Inventory	
2	Product	Starting	Units	Average	Total	Average	Units	Units	Costs
3	ID	Costs		Cost	Cost	Cost	Sold		
4	7708	$ 134.23	4	$ 134.23	$ 671.15	$ 134.23	2	3	$ 402.69
5	9248	$ 3,061.53	3	$ 1,020.51	$ 6,123.06	$ 1,020.51	1	5	$ 5,102.55
6	3665	$ 1,242.66	10	$ 625.81	$ 7,500.72	$ 625.06	5	7	$ 4,375.42
7	4877	$ 476.60	18	$ 97.56	$ 2,232.68	$ 97.07	3	20	$ 1,941.46
8	6773	$ 14,587.92	16	$ 1,720.88	$ 42,122.00	$ 1,684.88	5	20	$ 33,697.60
9	4980	$ 883.36	19	$ 114.84	$ 3,065.34	$ 113.53	4	23	$ 2,611.22
10									
11		Cost of goods sold		$ 13,584.01					
12		Gross profit		$ 3,511.15					
13									

Average Cost Method

Figure 3.4 shows 10 combinations of Product ID by unit cost, to arrive at an inventory value based on specific identification. In contrast, Figure 3.7 shows 6 Product IDs, each with just one unit cost. The average cost method calculates a single average cost for each product code, so there is no need to represent the different actual costs that might apply in each product code on the inventory summary.

Column B of Figure 3.7 multiplies the starting inventory for each product by its unit cost, getting that data from the worksheet shown in Figure 3.4. This represents the cost of the company's inventory at the beginning of April.

Column C of Figure 3.7 shows the count of each Product ID purchased during the month of April. Cell C4, for example, compares the product code in cell A4 with the range named `Inventory_Products_Code`, found in B3:B12 of Figure 3.6. Cell C4 calculates the count of product 7708 using this array formula:

```
=SUM(IF(A4=Inventory_Products_Code,Purchase_Units,0))
```

Notice that there is only one array of logical values in the formula, so no multiplication of arrays is involved as there is using specific identification. The fragment

```
A4=Inventory_Products_Code
```

returns this array of `TRUE/FALSE` values:

```
{TRUE;FALSE;FALSE;FALSE;FALSE;FALSE;FALSE;FALSE;FALSE;FALSE}
```

In words, the value `7708` in cell A4 equals the first, and only the first, value in the range named `Inventory_Products_Code`.

3

Surrounding this fragment with the IF function and the reference to Purchase_Units (the Purchase_Units range is in cells E3:E12 of Figure 3.6) causes Excel to return the number of units purchased if the product code equals 7708:

```
IF({TRUE;FALSE;FALSE;FALSE;FALSE;FALSE;FALSE;FALSE;FALSE;FALSE},Purchase_
Units,0)
```

It returns this numeric array:

```
{4;0;0;0;0;0;0;0;0;0}
```

Finally, using this array as the argument to the SUM function returns 4, the total of the values in the array. The array formula is copied from cell C4 and pasted into cells C5:C9 to complete the count of the inventory purchases.

Column D in Figure 3.7 shows the average cost for each product purchased during the month. It begins with cell D4, which contains this array formula:

```
=SUM(IF(A4=Inventory_Products_Code,Inventory_Unit_Cost*Purchase_Units))/C4
```

Here, Inventory_Unit_Cost refers to cells C3:C12 of Figure 3.6. Again, this fragment

```
A4=Inventory_Products_Code
```

returns this array of logical values, which act as the criteria for the IF function:

```
{TRUE;FALSE;FALSE;FALSE;FALSE;FALSE;FALSE;FALSE;FALSE;FALSE}
```

When the criterion is TRUE, Excel returns the product of the unit cost and the number of units; otherwise, Excel returns FALSE. That is, this fragment

```
IF(A4=Inventory_Products_Code,Inventory_Unit_Cost*Purchase_Units)
```

returns this:

```
{536.92;FALSE;FALSE;FALSE;FALSE;FALSE;FALSE;FALSE;FALSE;FALSE}
```

The first value in the array, 536.92, is the result of multiplying the unit cost of the product by the number of units purchased: 134.23 × 4. The total of the array is returned by the SUM function. The FALSE values are treated as zeros, so the total is 536.92. Dividing that sum by the value in C4, or 4, results in 134.23, the value shown in cell D4 of Figure 3.7.

All that tells you is that the average cost of units that were bought for $134.23 is $134.23—in this particular case, a trivial outcome. It was discussed simply to illustrate the mechanics of the array formula. Now consider how it works when you actually have units of a product that you bought for two different prices. Here's the formula in cell D6 of Figure 3.7:

```
=SUM(IF(A6=Inventory_Products_Code,Inventory_Unit_Cost*Purchase_Units))/C6
```

The formula is identical to the formula in D4 that was just discussed, except that it refers to the Product ID in cell A6 and the number of units purchased in cell C6. In this case, the TRUE/FALSE array returns these values:

```
{FALSE;FALSE;TRUE;TRUE;FALSE;FALSE;FALSE;FALSE;FALSE;FALSE}
```

So the Product ID found in cell A6, 3665, is found in the third and fourth positions (corresponding to the TRUE values in the array) of the range named Inventory_Products_Code. When those array values are TRUE, the IF function says to return the product of the unit cost times the number of units purchased. The result of that is this:

```
{FALSE;FALSE;3727.98;2530.08;FALSE;FALSE;FALSE;FALSE;FALSE;FALSE}
```

The third value, `3727.98`, is the result of multiplying the unit cost of $621.33 by 6, the number of units purchased at that cost (see cells C5 and E5 in Figure 3.6). These are the six units of product 3665 that were purchased for the earlier, lower price of $621.33 each.

The fourth value in the array, `2530.08`, comes about by multiplying the unit cost of $632.52 by 4, the number of units purchased at that cost (see cells C6 and E6 in Figure 3.6). These are the four units of product 3665 that were purchased for the later, higher price of $632.52.

The `SUM` function adds `3727.98` and `2530.08`, treating the `FALSE` values in the array as zeros. Finally, this sum of 6258.06 is divided by `10`, the total number of units purchased for that Product ID, which is the value in cell C6. The resulting average cost, $625.81, appears in cell D6 of Figure 3.7.

Notice that this is a *weighted* average: Each of the two unit costs ($621.33 and $632.52) is weighted by multiplying it by the number of units purchased at that cost. So six units at $621.33 cost `$3727.98`, the third value in the array shown previously. Four units at `$632.52` cost `$2530.08`, the second value in the array. $3,727.98 plus $2,530.08, or $6,258.06, is the total cost of the purchases of this product. Dividing by the total number of purchased units, 10, yields an average cost of `$625.81` for this product, shown in cell D6 of Figure 3.7.

3

> **NOTE** The method just described is one of two popular methods, both approved under Generally Accepted Accounting Principles (GAAP) and International Financial Reporting Standards (IFRS), for calculating average cost. The approach that is illustrated in this section is termed a weighted average, as noted in the prior paragraph. But that's due more to a quirk of the standard formula than to any intrinsic characteristic of the method. You could, after all, add up the cost of all 10 units and divide by 10 to get the same result. Nevertheless, this method is usually termed the *weighted average* method. The usual alternative, the *moving average* method, is discussed in the next section.

Then each product's total cost is placed into E4:E9 by adding the total starting cost to the total cost of the purchased products. The result is the total cost of the goods available for sale: starting costs plus purchase costs.

Column F in Figure 3.7 contains the average cost of the goods available for sale, on a unit basis. In cell F9, that average cost is calculated by this array formula:

```
=E9/(SUM(IF(A9=Inventory_Products_Code,Start_Units))+C9)
```

This array formula starts with a reference to E9, which contains the total costs for all units of product 4980. It divides that total cost by the total number of units in stock—the starting units plus the units purchased during the accounting period.

The array formula gets the starting units using this fragment:

```
IF(A9=Inventory_Products_Code,Start_Units)
```

That is, if the value in A9, or 4980, equals a value in the Inventory_Products_Code range, return the associated value in the Start_Units range. (Start_Units is D3:D12 of Figure 3.6.) Simplified, the formula now looks like this:

```
=3065.34/((SUM(8;0)+C9)
```

or:

```
=3065.34/(8+19)
```

or

```
113.53.
```

Column G contains the number of units sold for each product code. The formulas in column G are considerably simpler than the corresponding calculations for the specific identification method. In this case, a single average unit cost is associated with each product code, and the number of units sold can be retrieved by this formula, used in cell G6 of Figure 3.7:

```
=SUM((A6=Sales_Product_Code)*1)
```

3

The range named Sales_Product_Code is shown in Figure 3.5, cells B2:B21. The following fragment returns an array of TRUE/FALSE values:

```
A6=Sales_Product_Code
```

To convert the TRUEs and FALSEs to 1s and 0s, it's necessary to multiply them by 1. Then the 1s and 0s are summed to determine the number of units sold.

Column H, the ending inventory in units, is obtained by subtracting the units sold from the starting inventory and then adding the units purchased. You get the figures in column I, the total cost of each product line in the ending inventory, by multiplying the number of units in the ending inventory by their average unit cost.

Calculating COGS

The COGS is the total cost of the starting inventory plus the cost of purchases, minus that of the ending inventory, just as it is using specific identification. However, the value of the COGS differs according to the method used. Under specific identification, the COGS is $13,874.12, whereas under average cost, it is $13,584.01—this is $290.11 less.

That is because the average cost method results in a different unit cost than does specific identification. Under average cost, the actual amount paid for each particular unit sold is unknown—and it's also irrelevant to COGS because the average cost is used in place of the actual amount paid.

The difference of $290.11 in COGS (between the average cost method and the specific identification method) is small in this illustration because there are roughly the same numbers of units carrying different average costs in the starting inventory. The difference would be larger if the starting inventory had 1 Millennium PC P3 computer at a cost of $1,620.88 and 15 at a cost of $1,820.88.

Under the average cost method, the company's income statement for April would show a gross profit of $3,511.15, the result of subtracting the COGS (the total cost of the goods available for sale minus the total cost of the ending inventory) from its total sales revenue of $17,095.16. Its balance sheet for April would show inventory assets of $48,130.94. Thus, both its gross profit and its inventory assets are $290.11 more than with specific identification.

NOTE Note that this result is not a general rule about the relationship between the two valuation methods. The use of average cost could cause a gross profit either greater or less than specific identification, and the same is true of asset valuation. Both the direction and the size of the difference between the two methods depend on the difference in the number of units in the inventory that carry different actual unit costs. In fact, if the numbers of units are equal, the two methods return the same result.

Using the Moving Average Method

There's another way of calculating average inventory cost, often called the *moving average* method. This method gives you an average cost for a product, but it's helpful to think of that figure as the average cost of the stock you have on hand.

Various accounting applications such as QuickBooks take advantage of the computing capacity and speed that have become generally available since the 1980s. One result is the ability to recalculate an average cost every time a transaction occurs that affects a product's quantity on hand and its valuation.

Figure 3.8 shows an example of moving average costing.

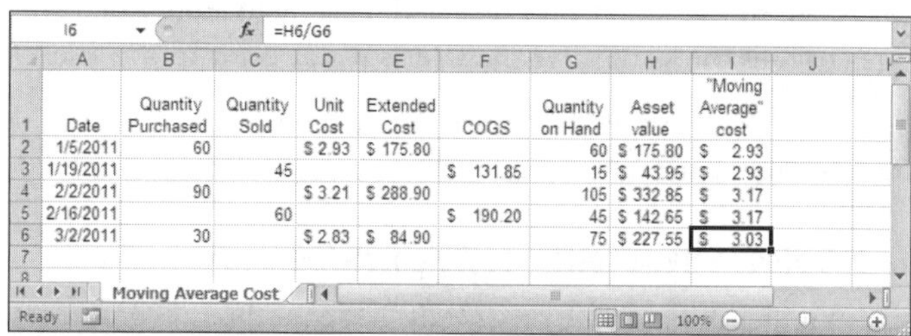

I6 =H6/G6

	A	B	C	D	E	F	G	H	I
1	Date	Quantity Purchased	Quantity Sold	Unit Cost	Extended Cost	COGS	Quantity on Hand	Asset value	"Moving Average" cost
2	1/5/2011	60		$ 2.93	$ 175.80		60	$ 175.80	$ 2.93
3	1/19/2011		45			$ 131.85	15	$ 43.95	$ 2.93
4	2/2/2011	90		$ 3.21	$ 288.90		105	$ 332.85	$ 3.17
5	2/16/2011		60			$ 190.20	45	$ 142.65	$ 3.17
6	3/2/2011	30		$ 2.83	$ 84.90		75	$ 227.55	$ 3.03

Moving Average Cost

Figure 3.8
Any average cost method returns a different average cost when the unit acquisition cost changes.

On any date, the moving average cost is the result of dividing the *current asset value* by the *quantity on hand*. In Figure 3.8, for example, the average cost of $3.17 in cell I4 is the result of dividing the asset value of $332.85 in cell H4 by the quantity on hand of 105 in cell G4.

Contrast this with the weighted average approach, which divides the *total purchase cost* by the *total quantity purchased*. Figure 3.9 shows the data from Figure 3.8, using the weighted average method instead of the moving average method.

Compare Figures 3.8 and 3.9, and notice that on and following 2/2/2011, the two methods yield different average costs.

Figure 3.9
No average cost method changes the average cost when a sale occurs.

I6 =SUM(E$2:E6)/SUM(B$2:B6)

	A	B	C	D	E	F	G	H	I
1	Date	Quantity Purchased	Quantity Sold	Unit Cost	Extended Cost	COGS	Quantity on Hand	Asset value	"Weighted Average" cost
2	1/5/2011	60		$ 2.93	$ 175.80		60	$ 175.80	$ 2.93
3	1/19/2011		45			$ 131.85	15	$ 43.95	$ 2.93
4	2/2/2011	90		$ 3.21	$ 288.90		105	$ 332.85	$ 3.10
5	2/16/2011		60			$ 185.88	45	$ 146.97	$ 3.10
6	3/2/2011	30		$ 2.83	$ 84.90		75	$ 231.87	$ 3.05

Weighted Average Cost

Identical Average Costs at the Outset

As of 1/5/2011, the quantity purchased and the quantity on hand are identical. So are the extended cost and the asset value. Therefore, dividing the total purchase cost by the quantity purchased (weighted average) yields the same result as dividing the asset value by the quantity on hand (moving average): $2.93, as shown in cell I2 of both Figure 3.8 and Figure 3.9.

3

Sales Have No Immediate Effect on Average Costs

As of 1/19/2011, the average cost under both methods is still the same, $2.93—see cell I3 in both Figure 3.8 and Figure 3.9. Sales of product do not immediately affect average costs.

The formula for weighted averages uses only the total purchase dollars and the total quantity purchased, neither of which changes when you sell some number of the product.

In moving averages, a sale reduces both the asset value and the quantity on hand by the same proportion, so the ratio of the asset value to the quantity on hand—in other words, the average cost—is the same after the sale as it was prior to the sale.

Although sales have no immediate effect on the moving average cost, they do have a subsequent effect, as shown next.

Sales Affect Moving Average Costs, Not Weighted Average Costs

As shown in Figures 3.8 and 3.9, on 2/2/2011 the methods begin to return different values for average cost. The values are different both within each method and between the two methods. The weighted average method returns a higher average cost ($3.10 in cell I4) than it did earlier ($2.93 in cell I3) because the purchase on 2/2/2011 is at a higher unit cost than the earlier purchase on 1/5/2011. This cost increase pulls up the weighted average cost.

The moving average also responds to the higher unit cost for the purchase on 2/2/2011, but its divisor is quantity on hand, not quantity purchased. The quantity on hand of 105 (cell G4 in Figure 3.8) consists of 15 remaining units purchased at $2.93 each (cell G3), and 90 purchased at $3.21 (cell B4), so the moving average cost responds more to the higher cost than does the weighted average. Because the weighted average uses quantity purchased as the divisor, it responds to the entire 60 units purchased at the lower price, not only to the 15 units still in stock. Therefore, the weighted average is not pulled up as far as the moving average is.

This is a general characteristic of the weighted average method as compared to the moving average method; the moving average results in more volatile average costs.

NOTE This is the reason that it's helpful to think of the moving average cost as the average cost of the stock on hand. It is affected both by purchases to inventory and, eventually, by sales from inventory. Weighted average cost is affected solely by purchases.

Calculating the Moving Average and Weighted Average

If you have access to the right data layout, it's easy to calculate the moving average. Figure 3.10 shows how it's done and verifies the calculations.

Figure 3.10
An inventory report from an accounting package, exported to Excel.

L4 =K4/I4

	A	B	C	D	E	F	G	H	I	J	K	L	M
1					Type	Date	Qty	Cost	On Hand	Avg Cost	Asset Value		
2		Inventory											
3			Ethernet Cable										
4					Item Receipt	01/05/2011	60.00	175.80	60.00	2.93	175.80	$ 2.93	
5					Sales Receipt	01/19/2011	-45.00		15.00	2.93	43.95	$ 2.93	
6					Item Receipt	02/02/2011	90.00	288.90	105.00	3.17	332.85	$ 3.17	
7					Sales Receipt	02/16/2011	-60.00		45.00	3.17	142.65	$ 3.17	
8					Item Receipt	03/02/2011	30.00	84.90	75.00	3.03	227.55	$ 3.03	
9			Total Ethernet Cable						75.00		227.55		
10													

Moving Average Cost

Ready 100%

With the layout shown in Figure 3.10, it's easy to calculate the moving average. The information from the accounting package appears in cells A1:K9. Just enter this formula into cell L4:

```
=K4/I4
```

Then, copy and paste the formula into cells L5:L8. When you do, you'll note that the results of the divisions equal the values for Average Cost as reported by the application that created the inventory report.

Without the assistance of an accounting application, you can create the report yourself if you're storing some information in a database or an Excel workbook. You can't do without these fields:

- **Type of transaction**—A purchase to inventory or a sale from inventory. This field is not strictly necessary, but it can help you interpret the results.
- **Date of transaction**—You need this principally to make sure that the transactions are listed in chronological order, earliest to most recent.
- **Quantity bought or sold**—These can be shown in separate columns, as in Figures 3.8 and 3.9, or as positive and negative values, as in Figure 3.10.
- **Extended cost (shown as "Cost" in Figure 3.10) in purchase transactions**—The extended cost is the total spent to acquire the product in a given purchase transaction.

If you have these fields, you can easily fill in columns I through K in Figure 3.10. Take these steps:

1. To get the *quantity on hand*, enter this formula in cell I4:

   ```
   =G4
   ```

2. If you're using one column to record quantities purchased and sold, as column G in Figure 3.10, enter this formula in cell I5:

   ```
   =I4+G5
   ```

3. Copy and paste the formula in cell I5 as far down as the inventory history for the product appears.
4. To get the (moving) average cost, enter this formula in cell J4:

   ```
   =K4/I4
   ```

5. Copy cell J4 and paste it down through the end of your transactions. Each formula temporarily returns the value zero, because column K has not yet been populated.
6. To populate column K, enter this formula in cell K4:

   ```
   =H4
   ```

7. Enter this formula in cell K5:

   ```
   =IF(H5<>0,K4+H5,K4+G5*J4)
   ```

8. Copy cell K5 and paste it through the end of the transactions. Doing so will resolve all the zero values initially shown for average cost.

> **NOTE** Step 2 in the above list assumes that you're using one column to record both purchase and sales quantities. If you're using a structure such as that in Figures 3.8 and 3.9, adjust the formula so that it adds values in the purchases column and subtracts values in the sales column.

Understanding the Asset Value Formula

The formula just given in step 7 for the asset value in Figure 3.10 has two aspects that deserve your attention. The first is relatively straightforward:

The formula looks to see whether there is a nonzero value in cell H5 (more generally, in column H). Column H contains the extended cost of a purchase to inventory, so if it is nonzero, the transaction is a purchase. In that case, the inventory asset value is the sum of the prior asset value plus the current purchase: K4 plus H5. As applied here, Excel's `IF` function returns the sum of K4 and H5 when the extended purchase cost is not zero.

Otherwise, if H5 is zero, the transaction cannot be a purchase and (in this moderately simplified example) must be a sale. In that case, find the product of G5 and J4. That's the quantity sold times the prior average cost—in other words, the COGS. To get the current asset value, combine the COGS with the prior asset value in column K.

The second aspect of the formula is fundamental to the notion of a perpetual inventory system. This fragment of the formula shown in step 7

```
G5*J4
```

calculates the COGS for a sales transaction. Using the layout shown in Figure 3.8, it multiplies the quantity sold (in cell G5) by the average cost immediately prior to the sale (in cell J4). To get the COGS for an entire accounting period, you would total the COGS for each sale made during the period.

Contrast that with the COGS using a periodic inventory system, under which the COGS *for a period* is determined by subtracting the inventory value at the end of the period from the cost of goods available for sale during the period.

In other words, both the moving average cost method and the weighted average cost method are appropriate for perpetual inventory systems. Each method adjusts the inventory asset account every time stock is purchased and every time it's sold. But no valuation method can track inventory loss and shrinkage without help, so it's important to carry out occasional physical inventories if you use a periodic system.

Using FIFO

FIFO is a method of valuing inventory that, like specific identification, uses the actual cost of a unit of inventory. Unlike specific identification (but like average cost), FIFO makes an assumption about the cost of the unit that is actually sold.

The average cost method assumes that the cost of a unit is the weighted average of the costs of all such units that have ever been bought (weighted average) or that are on hand (moving average). In contrast, FIFO assumes that the first unit sold during the accounting period has a cost equal to that of the first unit purchased to the starting inventory—thus, first in to inventory, first out of inventory.

Understanding the FIFO Process

When, for the first time during April, a customer purchases a Dado router from Evans Electronics, it is not known whether the supplier charged Evans $95.32 or $100.36 for that specific router. The FIFO method assumes, though, that the router's cost is the same as that of the router remaining in stock that was purchased earliest: $95.32 (see cell F6 in Figure 3.4). Figure 3.11 illustrates the FIFO valuation method.

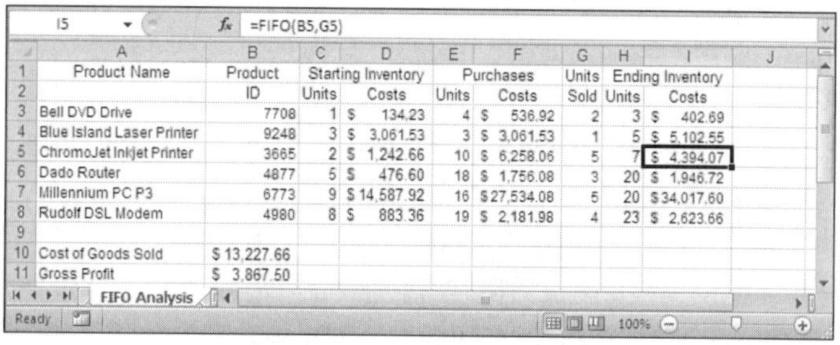

Figure 3.11
Using FIFO, Evans Electronics assumes that the cost of a unit sold is the cost of the unit that entered its inventory the earliest.

I5 =FIFO(B5,G5)

	A	B	C	D	E	F	G	H	I	J
1	Product Name	Product	Starting Inventory		Purchases		Units	Ending Inventory		
2		ID	Units	Costs	Units	Costs	Sold	Units	Costs	
3	Bell DVD Drive	7708	1	$ 134.23	4	$ 536.92	2	3	$ 402.69	
4	Blue Island Laser Printer	9248	3	$ 3,061.53	3	$ 3,061.53	1	5	$ 5,102.55	
5	ChromoJet Inkjet Printer	3665	2	$ 1,242.66	10	$ 6,258.06	5	7	$ 4,394.07	
6	Dado Router	4877	5	$ 476.60	18	$ 1,756.08	3	20	$ 1,946.72	
7	Millennium PC P3	6773	9	$ 14,587.92	16	$ 27,534.08	5	20	$ 34,017.60	
8	Rudolf DSL Modem	4980	8	$ 883.36	19	$ 2,181.98	4	23	$ 2,623.66	
9										
10	Cost of Goods Sold	$ 13,227.66								
11	Gross Profit	$ 3,867.50								

FIFO Analysis

Ready 100%

The value of the ending inventory, shown in column I in Figure 3.11, is determined by means of a user-defined function (UDF) named FIFO. (Any Excel user can write a UDF; all it takes is some knowledge of Visual Basic or, even better, Visual Basic for Applications.) This function is called in cell I5 of Figure 3.11 with this entry:

```
=FIFO(B5,G5)
```

Its arguments, cells B5 and G5, contain the particular Product ID being analyzed and the number of units of that product that were sold.

Refer to Figure 3.6. The worksheet shown there contains four named ranges that the FIFO function uses:

- `Inventory_Product_Code` refers to the range B3:B12. It contains the identifier that distinguishes, say, a router from a laser printer. Although this range uniquely identifies a product, it does not uniquely identify a product at a particular cost.
- `Start_Units` refers to the range D3:D12. It contains data on the number of units of each product code *at a particular unit cost* that are in the inventory at the beginning of the period.
- `Purchase_Units` refers to the range E3:E12. It shows how many units were purchased to the inventory during the period—again, at a particular unit cost.
- `Inventory_Unit_Cost` refers to the range C3:C12. This is the cost of each product that was acquired from the supplier at a particular time.

The FIFO UDF uses the ranges shown in Figure 3.6, but the FIFO function is entered on the worksheet shown in Figure 3.11. The reason is that we want to know the inventory value on a product-by-product basis, without regard to when the product was acquired. So the results of the function belong on a worksheet such as in Figure 3.11, where each record is a separate product in a separate row. But FIFO needs to know how many products were acquired in a particular sequence at particular prices, so the function uses data as shown in Figure 3.6, which distinguishes between different purchases of the same product.

The FIFO function is written in Visual Basic for Applications (VBA) code; see Figure 3.12.

Figure 3.12
This VBA code calculates the value of ending inventory using the FIFO method. The UDF works as described next.

(General) | FIFO

```
Function FIFO(Product_Code As String, Units_To_Remove As Long) As Currency
Dim Start_Count As Range, Start_Cost As Range
Dim Start_Product As Range, Purchase_Units As Range
Dim Counter As Integer, Remaining_Units As Long

FIFO = 0

Set Start_Count = Range("Start_Units")
Set Start_Cost = Range("Inventory_Unit_Cost")
Set Start_Product = Range("Inventory_Products_Code")
Set Purchase_Units = Range("Purchase_Units")

For Counter = 1 To Start_Count.Rows.Count
   If Product_Code = Start_Product(Counter, 1) Then
      Remaining_Units = Application.WorksheetFunction.Max(0, _
         Start_Count(Counter, 1) + Purchase_Units(Counter, 1) - Units_To_Remove)
      FIFO = FIFO + Start_Cost(Counter, 1) * Remaining_Units
      Units_To_Remove = Units_To_Remove - (Start_Count(Counter, 1) + _
         Purchase_Units(Counter, 1) - Remaining_Units)
   End If
Next Counter

End Function
```

Developing the UDF's Inputs

The first line of code declares the function by giving it the name FIFO:

```
Function FIFO(Product_Code As String, Units_To_Remove As Long) As Currency
```

It specifies that its arguments are a text (String) value and a long integer (Long) value, and that it is to return a Currency data type. Used in cell I5 of Figure 3.11, the argument Product_Code represents the value in cell B5, and the argument Units_To_Remove represents the value in cell G5.

The function's next three statements declare several variables, four of which are *object* variables:

```
Dim Start_Count As Range, Start_Cost As Range
Dim Start_Product As Range, Purchase_Units As Range
Dim Counter As Integer, Remaining_Units As Long
```

Object variables represent Excel objects, such as cells, ranges of cells, worksheets, toolbars, and so on. The four object variables used here are declared as the Range type, so they can represent ranges of cells on the worksheet. (They can also represent single cells, which are a special case of Range objects.)

- Start_Count is an object variable that represents a range of worksheet cells. The FIFO UDF uses Start_Count to represent the worksheet range that contains the number of units of each product that are in the starting inventory.
- Start_Cost is an object variable. It represents the workbook range that contains the unit cost of each product.
- Start_Product is an object variable. It represents the workbook range that contains the product codes in the starting inventory.
- Purchase_Units is an object variable. It represents the workbook range that contains the number of units of each product purchased during the month.
- Counter is an Integer variable. It controls a loop in the FIFO UDF that examines each product in the starting inventory to see whether it should contribute to the product's valuation in the ending inventory.
- Remaining_Units, a Long variable, determines how many inventory units are left in inventory after the units sold have been subtracted. A variable with a Long data type can take on integer values with much greater maximum and minimum values than a variable with an Integer data type.

NOTE

A Long variable is an Integer variable that can accommodate values as large as plus or minus 2,147,483,647. It requires slightly more memory than an Integer variable. The tiny premium in additional memory is often worth the variable's extra capacity. Integer variables cannot take on values greater than 32,767. Therefore, it's sometimes best to declare variables that index a worksheet's rows as Long instead of Integer. A worksheet contains 1,048,576, or 2^{20}, rows (prior to Excel 2007, 65,536 or 2^{16} rows).

The executable code begins with this statement, which initializes the value of FIFO:

```
FIFO = 0
```

The next four statements associate each object variable with the proper range in the workbook:

```
Set Start_Count = Range("Start_Units")
Set Start_Cost = Range("Inventory_Unit_Cost")
Set Start_Product = Range("Inventory_Products_Code")
Set Purchase_Units = Range("Purchase_Units")
```

The first of the four statements, for example, specifies that Start_Count represents the workbook range named Start_Units. Each of the ranges could be named in the workbook by clicking the Formulas tab and then clicking Define Name in the Defined Names group (prior to Excel 2007, by means of Insert, Name, Define).

3

Looping Through the Products

The Long variable Units_To_Remove is the second argument to the FIFO function: In this example, it is the value in cell G5 in Figure 3.11. Because G5 contains the value 5, Units_To_Remove starts life with the value of 5.

FIFO's For loop contains the meat of the function:

```
For Counter = 1 To Start_Count.Rows.Count
  If Product_Code = Start_Product(Counter, 1) Then
     Remaining_Units = Application.WorksheetFunction.Max(0, _
        Start_Count(Counter, 1) + Purchase_Units(Counter, 1) - Units_To_Remove)
     FIFO = FIFO + Start_Cost(Counter, 1) * Remaining_Units
     Units_To_Remove = Units_To_Remove - (Start_Count(Counter, 1) + _
        Purchase_Units(Counter, 1) - Remaining_Units)
  End If
Next Counter
```

The For and the Next statements cycle the loop through all the rows of the Start_Count range—that is, the loop executes once for each row in the range that is represented by the Start_Count variable. Start_Count represents the range named Start_Units, which is contained in cells D3:D12 of Figure 3.6. That range has 10 rows, so the loop will execute 10 times as its control variable, Counter, progresses from 1 to 10.

Within the loop, the If . . . End If block tests whether the value of Product_Code passed to the function equals the current value of the Start_Product range. If it does, the statements within the If block are executed; otherwise, the For loop continues to the next value of Counter and, thus, to the next value in the Start_Product range.

For example, suppose that Product_Code is equal to 3665, as it is when the value in cell B5 of Figure 3.11 is passed to FIFO's first argument. The third time that the loop executes, Counter equals 3. Then this expression represents the third row of the first (and only) column of the Start_Product range:

```
Start_Product(Counter, 1)
```

That range is cells B3:B12 in Figure 3.6. The third row in that range contains 3665. Therefore, Product_Code equals Start_Product(Counter, 1), and the statements within the If . . . End If block are executed.

In contrast, Counter equals 5 during the fifth time that the loop executes. Product_Code still equals 3665. Nothing that occurs in the loop changes that value. But now, this expression refers to the fifth row of the range B3:B12 in Figure 3.6:

```
Start_Product(Counter, 1)
```

That cell contains the value 4877. Now Product_Code no longer equals Start_Product(Counter, 1). The statements within the If . . . End If block are skipped, the Next statement increments the Counter variable to 6, and the loop continues.

So as the data appears in Figure 3.6, and given that we pass the value 3665 to the FIFO function, the statements in the If . . . End If block are executed when Counter equals 3 and when Counter equals 4. Follow the logical flow of the statements in the If block:

```
Remaining_Units = Application.WorksheetFunction.Max(0, _
   Start_Count(Counter, 1) + Purchase_Units(Counter, 1) - Units_To_Remove)
```

Application.WorksheetFunction.Max invokes Excel's worksheet function MAX(). Therefore, this statement returns the larger of 0 or the result of adding the number of units in the starting inventory plus the number of units purchased, minus the current number of Units_To_Remove. This usage of the Max worksheet function prevents Remaining_Units from taking on a negative value if the number of units sold is greater than the number of units in the available inventory at a given unit cost.

When Counter equals 3, the number of starting units equals 2, and the number of purchased units equals 6 (see Figure 3.6, cells D5 and E5). Units_To_Remove was passed to the FIFO function as an argument with the value 5 (that is, the number of units sold) before the loop began. So Remaining_Units equals 2 + 6 – 5, or 3. This is the number of units remaining in inventory at a given cost after accounting for the number that were sold.

Accumulating Costs into FIFO

FIFO starts life with a value of zero, and nothing happens to change that during the first two trips through the loop because the Product_Code test fails. (Used in cell I5 of Figure 3.11, Product_Code is 3665, and the first two values tested are 7708 and 9248 in cells B3 and B4 of Figure 3.6). So when Counter is set equal to 3, FIFO's value is still zero. At this point in the example, though, the code is working with the product that it's looking for, the one with the Product ID of 3665. So it's time to add the cost of its units in stock to FIFO.

```
FIFO = FIFO + Start_Cost(Counter, 1) * Remaining_Units
```

The previous assignment statement increments FIFO by the product of the unit cost times the number of units remaining in inventory. Start_Cost(Counter, 1) equals 621.33 when Counter equals 3 (see cell C5 of Figure 3.6). Remaining_Units equals 3, due to the first statement in the If block, so FIFO's value is incremented from 0 to 621.33 × 3, or 1863.99.

```
Units_To_Remove = Units_To_Remove - (Start_Count(Counter, 1) + _
   Purchase_Units(Counter, 1) - Remaining_Units)
```

Before this statement executes, `Units_To_Remove` equals `5` (that's the value in cell G5 of Figure 3.11 that's passed as an argument to the function). `Start_Count(Counter, 1)` equals `2`, `Purchase_Units(Counter, 1)` equals `6`, and `RemainingUnits` still equals `3`. The statement resolves to this:

```
Units_To_Remove = 5-(2+6-3)=5-5=0
```

The `If . . . End If` block is now complete. The `Next` statement increments the value of `Counter` to `4`. The `If` statement is tested again, and it passes the test because the fourth value in `Start_Product` is still `3665`—that's because the inventory has at least two instances of the same Product ID acquired on different dates. Execute the statements in the `If . . . End If` block once again, with `Counter` equal to `4`:

```
Remaining_Units = Application.WorksheetFunction.Max(0, _
Start_Count(Counter, 1) + Purchase_Units(Counter, 1) - Units_To_Remove)
```

Currently, the value of `Units_To_Remove` is `0`, so `Remaining_Units` is set equal to the value of the fourth row of `Start_Count` plus the fourth row of `Purchase_Units`. Those values are `0` and `4` (see cells D6 and E6 of Figure 3.6), so `Remaining_Units` equals `4`.

```
FIFO = FIFO + Start_Cost(Counter, 1) * Remaining_Units
```

`FIFO` currently equals `1863.99`. To that value is added the product of the fourth row of `Start_Cost` and `Remaining_Units`. `Start_Cost(4,1)` equals `632.52` (see Figure 3.6, cell C6). `Remaining_Units` equals `4`, so `FIFO` is set equal to 1,863.99 + 632.52 × 4, or `4394.07`.

Because there are only two instances of `3665` in `Start_Product`, the `If . . . End If` block will not execute again, and the final value of `FIFO` is `4394.07`. This is the value returned to cell I5 in Figure 3.11.

Reviewing the FIFO Process

Conceptually, the `FIFO` function has worked as follows: It looks for every instance of Product ID 3665 in the inventory. It subtracts the number of units sold from the first instance of 3665 and adds to the value of `FIFO` the number of units remaining times their unit cost. In accordance with `FIFO`'s basic assumption, the units sold are considered to be the first units to enter the inventory. The number of units sold is subtracted from the first units that `FIFO` encounters in its loop through the starting inventory.

You might find it a useful exercise to go through this same step-by-step progression by setting the number of units sold to a value greater than the first row of `Start_Count` plus the first row of `Purchase_Units` for a given product. For example, try setting the value in cell G6 of Figure 3.11 to `17`. Doing so would cause `FIFO` to account for all the units of the Dado router, Product ID 4877, in the inventory that cost `$95.32`, plus two of the units that cost $100.36, resulting in an ending inventory value for Product ID 4877 of `$602.16`. In particular, watch what happens to `Remaining_Units` and `Units_To_Remove` as `Counter` changes from `5` to `6`.

The COGS shown in Figure 3.11 is the difference between the total cost of the starting inventory and that of the ending inventory, just as it is using specific identification and average cost. Under the average cost method, the COGS is $13,584.01, about $350 more than under the FIFO method ($13,227.66). This is because the average cost method uses the weighted average of all units in the starting inventory to calculate the COGS. In contrast, FIFO uses the costs of, say, the three units that entered the starting inventory first to calculate the COGS. In this case, the cost of the units purchased earlier is lower than that of the units purchased later. Keep in mind that the earlier costs are used, even though the actual, physical units that were sold might have entered the available inventory last.

Under FIFO, Evans Electronics' income statement for April would show a gross profit of $3,867.50, the result of subtracting the COGS from its total sales revenue of $17,095.16. Its balance sheet for April would show inventory assets of $48,487.29. So both its gross profit and its inventory assets are about $350 more than with the average cost method.

Again, this is not a general rule about the relationship between the two valuation methods. FIFO's effect is different according to whether supplier prices are rising or falling over time. If supplier prices are rising, FIFO returns a lower COGS on the income statement and a greater valuation of ending inventory on the balance sheet. This is because, when prices rise, units acquired earlier cost less than units acquired later, and FIFO assumes that the COGS is a function of the cost of goods acquired earlier.

In contrast, neither the specific identification nor the average cost method is sensitive to the timing of a purchase to starting inventory.

NOTE

If you have a practical application for the `FIFO` function provided here, bear in mind that you need four worksheet ranges with the names specified in the function. (Of course, you can change those names in the function and in the workbook, if you want.) The records in those ranges must begin with the earliest acquired and end with the most recently acquired.

Using LIFO

LIFO works in much the same way as FIFO. The difference is that the cost of a unit sold is assumed to be the cost of units that entered the inventory most recently, instead of the cost of the units that entered the starting inventory earliest.

Just as with FIFO, the effect of LIFO depends on whether your supplier costs are rising or falling—although LIFO's effect is the reverse of FIFO's. Under LIFO, if your unit costs are rising, your COGS will rise, your gross profit will be smaller, and your balance sheet assets will be smaller (because the cost of the units in ending inventory will be assigned the lower, earlier values). If your unit costs are falling, however, your COGS will be lower and your gross profit will be larger, as will your balance sheet assets. Therefore, your choice of a valuation method impacts your company's reported income (and, indirectly, its income taxes), as well as its worth as reported on the balance sheet.

Figure 3.13 illustrates the use of LIFO for Evans Electronics.

Figure 3.13
The LIFO method values inventory under the assumption that the most recently acquired goods are sold first; equivalently, the goods acquired earliest remain in inventory at the end of the period.

I3 =LIFO(B3,G3)

	A	B	C	D	E	F	G	H	I
1	Product Name	Product	Starting Inventory		Purchases		Units	Ending Inventory	
2		ID	Units	Costs	Units	Costs	Sold	Units	Costs
3	Bell DVD Drive	7708	1	$ 134.23	4	$ 536.92	2	3	$ 402.69
4	Blue Island Laser Printe	9248	3	$ 3,061.53	3	$ 3,061.53	1	5	$ 5,102.55
5	ChromoJet Inkjet Printe	3665	2	$ 1,242.66	10	$ 6,258.06	5	7	$ 4,349.31
6	Dado Router	4877	5	$ 476.60	18	$ 1,756.08	3	20	$ 1,931.60
7	Millennium PC P3	6773	9	$ 14,587.92	16	$27,534.08	5	20	$ 33,017.60
8	Rudolf DSL Modem	4980	8	$ 883.36	19	$ 2,181.98	4	23	$ 2,595.66
9									
10	Cost of Goods Sold	$ 14,315.54							
11	Gross Profit	$ 2,779.62							
12									

LIFO Analysis

All the information in Figure 3.13 is the same as in Figure 3.11, except for the values of the ending inventory, the total COGS and the gross profit. The value of the ending inventory is determined by means of a UDF named `LIFO`. This function is called in cell I3 of Figure 3.13 with this entry and is copied from I3 into I4:I8:

```
=LIFO(B3,G3)
```

The only difference between the entries in column I of Figure 3.11 and those in column I of Figure 3.13 is the call to `LIFO` instead of to `FIFO`. Figure 3.14 shows the VBA code for the user-defined `LIFO` function.

Figure 3.14
This VBA code calculates the value of ending inventory using the LIFO method.

(General) LIFO

```
Function LIFO(Product_Code As String, Units_To_Remove As Long) As Currency
Dim Start_Count As Range, Start_Cost As Range
Dim Start_Product As Range, Purchase_Units As Range
Dim Counter As Integer, Remaining_Units As Long

LIFO = 0

Set Start_Count = Range("Start_Units")
Set Start_Cost = Range("Inventory_Unit_Cost")
Set Start_Product = Range("Inventory_Products_Code")
Set Purchase_Units = Range("Purchase_Units")

For Counter = Start_Count.Rows.Count To 1 Step -1
   If Product_Code = Start_Product(Counter, 1) Then
      Remaining_Units = Application.WorksheetFunction.Max(0, _
         Start_Count(Counter, 1) + Purchase_Units(Counter, 1) - Units_To_Remove)
      LIFO = LIFO + Start_Cost(Counter, 1) * Remaining_Units
      Units_To_Remove = Units_To_Remove - (Start_Count(Counter, 1) + _
         Purchase_Units(Counter, 1) - Remaining_Units)
   End If
Next Counter

End Function
```

Three small differences exist between the `FIFO` and `LIFO` UDFs. First, the line that names the function and its arguments refers to `LIFO` instead of `FIFO`.

Second, in `LIFO`, the loop that controls the progression through the starting inventory starts at the bottom of those ranges instead of at the top:

```
For Counter = StartCount.Rows.Count To 1 Step -1
```

So instead of progressing from 1 to 10, `Counter` might progress from 10 to 1 in increments of –1. Because the ranges that describe the starting inventory are sorted, top to bottom, in earlier to later order, the more recent entries are examined first, and the units that have been sold are removed from the most recent additions to the starting inventory.

Therefore, items remaining in inventory at the end of the period are assigned the cost of those that entered the inventory first. This is in accordance with the LIFO approach.

Third, the statement that assigns a value to the name of the function refers to `LIFO` instead of to `FIFO`. For example:

```
LIFO = LIFO + Start_Cost(Counter, 1) * Remaining_Units
```

Notice in Figure 3.13 that the COGS is $14,315.54. Using the FIFO method, the COGS is $13,227.66 (see Figure 3.11). Therefore, choosing to use LIFO instead of FIFO increases the COGS by $1,087.88. That is because, in this case, the costs of goods were increasing over time.

Comparing the Four Valuation Methods

As you might expect, each valuation method discussed in this chapter has both advantages and drawbacks, which are discussed in the following sections.

Specification Identification

Specific identification is the most intuitively satisfying method because it adjusts the ending inventory value according to the actual cost of the specific items that were sold during the period. It avoids the average cost method's assumption that, at any given time, all otherwise identical units bear the same acquisition cost, and it avoids the assumptions made by FIFO and LIFO that the unit that was sold was purchased at a particular time. However, specific identification enables the (possibly undesirable) manipulation of COGS, gross profit, and asset valuation. The person who chooses the actual unit that is provided to the customer controls the value of the unit that is leaving the inventory. Your company might not want its financial results to be under the direct control of a person who removes an item from stock.

This would probably not constitute a problem if your business were, for example, the retail sale of custom jewelry. In that case, each item in your inventory might be unique, and the removal of a unit from inventory would be left to the marketplace, not to a member of your staff.

Furthermore, if a company has thousands of units in its inventory, specific identification makes recordkeeping virtually unmanageable, unless a database that tracks serial numbers is in place.

Average Cost

The *average cost* method treats each otherwise identical item in the inventory as though it had the same cost, regardless of how much it cost to bring it into inventory. This method makes no assumption about when an item was acquired, as LIFO and FIFO do.

Furthermore, the item's assigned cost is not affected by the choice of which physical unit to deliver to the customer, as is the case with specific identification.

But consider the effect of rising or falling supplier prices. If your costs of acquisition are changing substantially or quickly, the current replacement cost of your inventory is changing to the same degree. Average cost combines the cost of older but functionally identical units with the cost of newer units. This can cause you to under- or overvalue your inventory. And it can cause inaccurate pricing decisions if you base your selling price as a fixed percentage of your cost.

On the other hand, if you manage your inventories according to Just In Time principles (see "Calculating Turns Ratios" later in this chapter), their levels will tend to be small relative to the amounts that you buy into stock and sell from stock. In that case, the current costs of acquisition will enter the average cost equation with a greater weight and provide quite an accurate valuation.

NOTE

It's worth noting again that there are two average cost methods: weighted average and moving average. The weighted average uses information about all the units purchased, whereas the moving average uses information only about units that are currently on hand. Therefore, the moving average cost can bounce around much more than the weighted average cost.

FIFO

The *FIFO* method values the ending inventory according to the cost of the units that were more recently acquired. Therefore, the valuation of the inventory assets on the balance sheet tends to more closely reflect their current replacement cost. As a result, the value of the business on its balance sheet tends to be more accurate.

On the other hand, the time lag between the acquisition of older units and the sale of the merchandise is greater than the lag between the acquisition of the newer units and the sale of the merchandise. Therefore, from the standpoint of the income statement, FIFO is less accurate than LIFO. This is because the measurement of the gross profit is based on the revenues that derive from current market conditions and the costs that derive from earlier market conditions.

LIFO

The *LIFO* method values the units sold during the period at the cost of the units that were most recently acquired. Therefore, the calculation of the gross profit is in closer accord with current market conditions, resulting in a more accurate income statement.

However, LIFO values the inventory at the end of the period according to the costs of the units that were acquired earliest. This can cause a misestimate of the current value of the inventory assets for the purpose of reporting the worth of the business on its balance sheet.

NOTE Because of changes in tax laws, changes in market conditions such as rising and falling costs, and occasional changes in accounting standards, no one can offer broad-brush advice about which method of inventory valuation is best, even for a given company. Use the knowledge you have gained about inventory valuation to select the appropriate method in consultation with your accountant or tax lawyer, and implement that method in your daily operations.

Handling Purchase Discounts

It often happens that a supplier offers a discount from cost in return for quick payment for goods. This purchase discount is not applied to the valuation of the inventory, but is recorded in a Purchase Discounts account. In turn, the entries in the Purchase Discounts account are used to adjust the income statement's Purchases account.

NOTE Some companies handle purchase discounts as adjustments to their inventory accounts. However, because this complicates the process of valuing the inventory, most companies use the approach outlined here.

Is it to your advantage to pay a supplier promptly and thus obtain a purchase discount? As you might expect, that depends on the amount of the discount as well as the payment deadline.

Suppose that Evans Electronics orders two PCs from its supplier. The supplier offers Evans a $30 discount if payment is made within 30 days. Payment must be made within 60 days (see Figure 3.15).

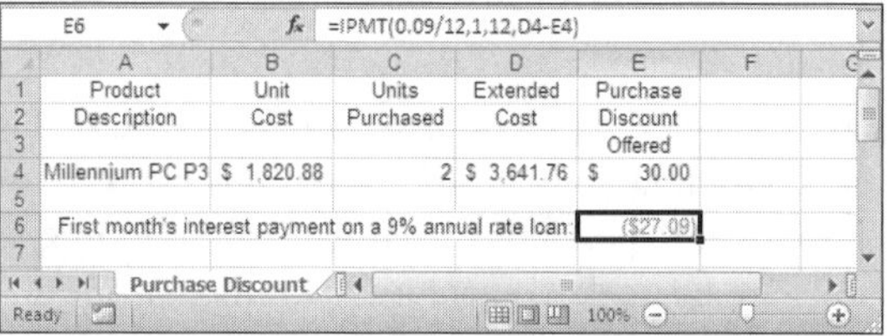

E6 =IPMT(0.09/12,1,12,D4-E4)

	A	B	C	D	E
1	Product	Unit	Units	Extended	Purchase
2	Description	Cost	Purchased	Cost	Discount
3					Offered
4	Millennium PC P3	$ 1,820.88	2	$ 3,641.76	$ 30.00
5					
6	First month's interest payment on a 9% annual rate loan:				($27.09)
7					

Purchase Discount

Figure 3.15
Analyzing a purchase discount as though it were interest on a loan can help you decide whether to take the discount.

The extended cost (that is, the number of units times the unit cost) for the two PCs is $3,641.76. Evans' choices are to pay $3,611.76 (the extended cost minus the purchase discount) within 30 days or to pay the full extended cost within 60 days. Declining the discount is, in concept at least, equivalent to borrowing $3,611.76 for the 30 days between the discount deadline and the payment deadline. The interest to be paid on this hypothetical loan can be compared to the $30 discount that the supplier offers. Evans knows it is possible to obtain a bank loan at 9% annual interest. By entering the following formula, as shown in cell E6 of Figure 3.15, Evans can compare the purchase discount to the cost of the money:

```
=IPMT(0.09/12,1,12,(D4-E4))
```

The first month's interest on a bank loan would be $27.09, as shown (as a negative value) in cell E6 of Figure 3.15. Therefore, it is to Evans' advantage to make payment before (but not long before) the discount deadline because the discount obtained exceeds the cost of money for the same period.

This worksheet function, `IPMT` (interest payment), takes four required arguments:

- **The interest rate per period**—In the example, the annual interest rate is .09, or 9%. Because the payment period is monthly, the interest rate is .09/12, or 0.75%.
- **The period for which the payment amount is desired**—In the example, `1` is used to return the first month's interest payment for a 12-month loan.
- **The number of payment periods in the loan**—For monthly payments on a one-year loan, the example uses `12`.
- **The principal amount of the loan**—The example uses the result of (D4 – E4), or `$3,611.76`, as this argument.

3

NOTE

In Excel's annuity functions, including `IPMT`, the result of the function and any argument to the function are positive if they indicate cash received and negative if they indicate cash paid out. Because this example analyzes a loan, the function's fourth argument is entered as a positive value. Because Evans Electronics would pay out $27.31 in interest for the first month, the function returns a negative value.

Calculating Turns Ratios

A *turns ratio* is a measure of how often inventory is depleted—that is, how frequently it turns over. Calculating turns ratios helps you understand how well you are managing your inventory.

The longer that units are in inventory, the longer your assets are tied up in stock and, thus, unavailable for other uses. Holding units in stock often involves carrying costs: the costs involved in storing the goods and, possibly, the costs involved in financing their purchase. And during the time units are in stock, you are not earning a profit on them unless you are holding them in the expectation that their replacement value will increase.

CAUTION

The latter effect, termed *inventory profits*, is something you should discuss with an accountant.

Therefore, many companies want to use Just In Time (JIT) inventory methods. The notion is that you do not want to tie up assets in inventory until the goods are actually needed for operational or resale purposes. The turns ratio is one measure of your ability to keep your inventory as low as possible and still meet operational and sales demands.

The turns ratio is expressed in terms of a time period, usually a year. For example, an annual turns ratio of 4.5 means that the inventory turns over 4.5 times per year. This means that sales have been brisk enough and inventories low enough that it is necessary to replenish the stock 4.5 times in a 12-month period.

You can calculate a turns ratio in terms of either units or costs (see Figure 3.16).

Figure 3.16
You can use actual units sold to calculate turns ratios or use average inventory levels to estimate turns ratios.

G14 =E14/F14

	A	B	C	D	E	F	G	H
1			3/31/2010	4/30/2010				
2	Product Description	Product ID	Quantity	Quantity	Units		Turns	
3			on Hand	on Hand	Sold		Ratio	
4	Bell DVD Drive	7708	4	2	2		6.0	
5	Blue Island Laser Printer	9248	3	2	1		4.0	
6	ChromoJet Inkjet Printer	3665	6	4	2		4.0	
7	Dado Router	4877	10	5	5		6.0	
8	Millennium PC P3	6773	8	6	2		3.0	
9	Rudolf DSL Modem	4980	7	3	4		6.9	
10								
11			3/31/2010	3/31/2011	Units	Average	Annual	
12	Product Description	Product ID	Quantity	Quantity	Sold	Inventory	Turns	
13			on Hand	on Hand	2010 - 2011		Ratio	
14	Bell DVD Drive	7708	4	2	18	3	6.0	
15	Blue Island Laser Printer	9248	3	2	21	2.5	8.4	
16	ChromoJet Inkjet Printer	3665	6	4	42	5	8.4	
17	Dado Router	4877	10	5	64	7.5	8.5	
18	Millennium PC P3	6773	8	6	48	7	6.9	
19	Rudolf DSL Modem	4980	7	3	53	5	10.6	
20								

Stock Turns Ratios

Ready 100%

Rows 4 to 9 in Figure 3.16 show a snapshot calculation of the turns ratios achieved by each product during the month. No purchases to inventory were made between March 31, 2010, and April 30, 2010.

The turns ratio for product code 4877 is shown as `6.0` in cell G7. The formula in G7 is shown here:

```
=E7/C7*12
```

This is the number of units sold during the month divided by the number on hand at the beginning of the month, multiplied by 12 to annualize the ratio. A ratio of 6.0 means that the inventory would have to be replenished six times during the year. Notice that five units were sold during the month. At this rate, the stock for this product would have to be replenished every two months, or six times (that is, its turns ratio) during the year.

Rows 14 to 19 illustrate a convenient way to examine the turns ratios for a full year. This represents a look back to March 31, 2010 from March 31, 2011. The quantities on hand at the beginning and end of the year are shown in C14:D19. The units sold, E14:E19, are obtained from the sales records for the year. The average inventory, F14:F19, is estimated by averaging the quantity on hand at the beginning of the year and the quantity on hand at the end of the year. Finally, the annual turns ratio is the number of units sold divided by the average inventory.

On a broader scale, it is also possible to calculate a turns ratio for an entire stock rather than on a product-by-product basis (see Figure 3.17).

TIP

Turns ratios in the range of 4 to 6 are normally regarded as quite good; the inventory is being managed well. A turns ratio of less than 1, indicating that it takes more than a year to turn over the stock, is terrible.

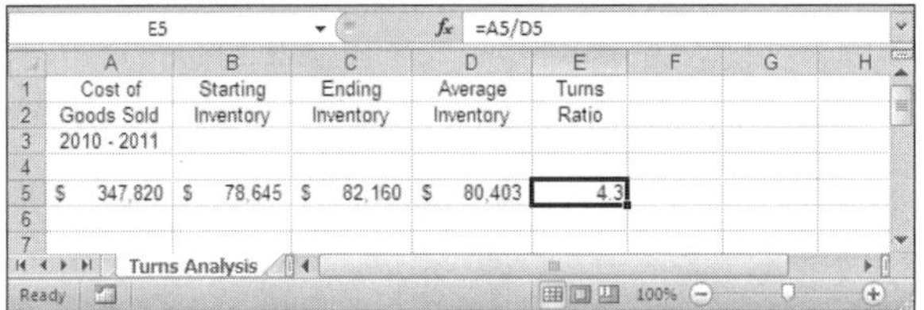

Figure 3.17
A turns ratio can be calculated for an entire inventory, regardless of product-by-product differences.

3

Figure 3.17 shows the COGS, the starting inventory, and the ending inventory for the 12-month period. The average inventory is again the average of the starting and ending values. The turns ratio is the COGS divided by the average inventory.

NOTE

Note that a company's choice of method to value its inventory (specific identification, average cost, FIFO, or LIFO) impacts its turns ratios when they are based on cost data rather than units. Particularly using LIFO or FIFO, the total inventory valuation can be based on different costs at the beginning of the year than at the end of the year.

Normally, a purchasing manager is interested in the turns ratios on a product-by-product basis. These can help guide purchasing decisions and the minimum and maximum units that should be on hand at any given time.

An overall look at a company's turns ratio, such as shown in Figure 3.17, is often of greater interest to a principal in the company or to an outside investor or creditor. Product-by-product turns ratios tend to be of little interest to people who want an overall view of how a business manages its inventories, but they are of great interest to the people responsible for managing them.

Summary

In this chapter, you examined four methods of valuing inventory and how to use them with Excel. Their effects on both the income statement (via the gross profit calculation) and the balance sheet (via the amount of company assets in ending inventory) were discussed. You saw how user-defined functions, such as LIFO and FIFO, can automate worksheet tasks in general. You also learned how to use different sorts of turns ratios to evaluate how well a company manages its assets.

The next chapter turns from a focus on a company's assets to a focus on its liabilities.

Summarizing Transactions: From the Journals to the Balance Sheet

4

IN THIS CHAPTER

Chapter 3, "Valuing Inventories for the Balance Sheet," covered the topic of inventory valuation in detail. The various methods discussed there are needed to fill in the current assets section of the balance sheet. This chapter focuses on recording transactions in journals, cataloging transactions in ledgers, and summarizing the information in the balance sheet.

Following is the basic structure of a balance sheet:

- The Assets section consists of the company's current assets (typically including cash, accounts receivable, inventory, and prepaid expenses) and its fixed assets. This section also contains any other assets that do not fit neatly within the current and fixed classifications.
- The Liabilities and Owner's Equity section consists of the company's current and long-term liabilities; it also includes the owner's equity as described next. Typically, these include accounts payable, short- and tong-term notes payable, and a few other types of liabilities that vary according to a company's line of business.
- The difference between the company's assets and its liabilities is the *equity*—that portion of the company's worth that belongs to its owner or owners.

The first three chapters of this book introduced some fundamental concepts, such as accounts, revenues, assets, debits, and credits. They also discussed some of the functional relationships among these concepts.

This chapter introduces ways that you can use Excel to establish the structural relationships among accounts, journals, and ledgers. It describes how to manage the flow of information about revenue, expenses, and profit by using Excel workbooks, worksheets, and Visual Basic for Applications (VBA) code.

Why This Chapter Is Here

I dithered for some time before deciding to include this chapter in the current edition of this book. Since the time that I first wrote it, in the mid-1990s, accounting software for personal computers has become much more popular in the marketplace. The user interfaces have evolved from arcane and puzzling to smooth and friendly. The cost of the accounting software has plummeted, and in some cases the software is offered by publishers as a loss leader for more profitable products.

I had to ask myself, in that environment for business computing, if it made sense to retain this chapter. It talks about special journals and subsidiary ledgers and how transactions move through them to appear, in the aggregate, on income statements and balance sheets.

Unless you're someone who wants to use Excel to maintain the accounting records of a small business, you have little need for that sort of information. For example, special journals are tools that make *manual* accounting easier. They help categorize transactions into useful groupings that enable the accounting process to roll up the debits and credits into the right ledgers and then into the proper accounts on the balance sheet and income statement.

But specialized accounting software has no need of structures such as special journals. Computers are intrinsically stupid, but they're also fast and accurate. So accounting software for personal computers tends to dispense with manual tools such as special journals and even deemphasizes the three traditional ledger divisions (general, accounts receivable, and accounts payable). The results still exist, of course, but the process of moving from the individual transactions to the financial summaries has been streamlined to take advantage of the computer's speed and accuracy.

So why would you care about what this chapter discusses? I spent quite some time thinking about how I could use my allotted page count talking about topics that are more interesting than the role of subsidiary ledgers in the management of your business.

I finally decided to keep this chapter, albeit with some major changes from previous editions. I had three basic reasons for that decision:

- People still talk about journals and ledgers, and the general journal certainly hasn't gone away.
- Perhaps you are building your own accounting application using Excel. I did—and I'd hate to think that I'm alone in the Excel universe.
- The chapter's topic provides an ideal context for introducing concepts and tools concerning VBA—tools that you can learn to apply in thousands of other situations.

If none of those reasons grabs you, for goodness sake move on. I think you'll like Chapter 5, "Working Capital and Cash Flow Analysis."

Understanding Journals

The basic flow of information for business transactions follows this sequence of events:

1. A business transaction occurs—usually, a sale or a purchase.
2. Information about the transaction is recorded in a *journal*. The journal usually records the information about the transactions in chronological order. For example, one record might contain data on a sale that took place on March 1, the second record might describe a purchase that was made on March 2, the third record might have data on a payment that was made on March 3, and so on.
3. Information about the transactions is copied (or *posted*) from the journal to a *ledger*. This ledger has a different section for each account, such as accounts receivable or notes payable. Within each section, information is usually recorded chronologically. The main difference between the journal and the ledger is that the ledger categorizes the information from the journal into specific accounts, whereas the journal records the information chronologically—transactions involving several different accounts would be adjacent if they occurred on the same date.
4. Information in the ledger is summarized to obtain a total for each account at the end of an accounting period. These totals are used to prepare financial statements such as the income statement and the balance sheet.

See Figure 4.1 for an example of a general journal.

Why qualify the term *journal* with the word *general*? Because keeping only one journal and one ledger gets cumbersome. Notice in Figure 4.1 that only three transactions are shown in the general journal. These transactions pertain to three relatively infrequent events: the return of some merchandise from a customer, the return of some inventory to a supplier, and the purchase of office equipment. All the remaining transactions during June are kept together in special journals.

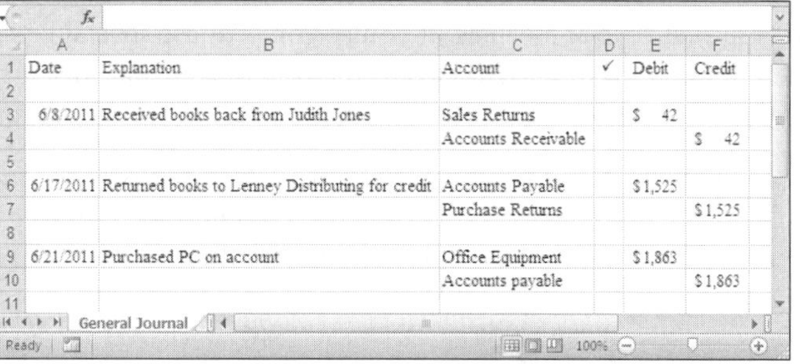

	A	B	C	D	E	F
1	Date	Explanation	Account	✓	Debit	Credit
2						
3	6/8/2011	Received books back from Judith Jones	Sales Returns		$ 42	
4			Accounts Receivable			$ 42
5						
6	6/17/2011	Returned books to Lenney Distributing for credit	Accounts Payable		$1,525	
7			Purchase Returns			$1,525
8						
9	6/21/2011	Purchased PC on account	Office Equipment		$1,863	
10			Accounts payable			$1,863
11						

Figure 4.1
Use the general journal as a catchall for transactions that don't belong in special journals.

If you had only one journal, the task of posting information from the journal to the ledger could become too time-consuming. Furthermore, using only one journal makes finding information about a specific sale or payment more tedious, even if you use Excel's lookup functions. However, computer applications whose sole purpose is accounting largely do away with this problem, and with special journals as well.

Understanding Special Journals

Companies sometimes use *special journals*, which are places to record information about particular types of transactions. The most frequently occurring transactions tend to be sales to customers and payments to creditors. Also, many companies do business with their customers and suppliers on both a cash basis and a credit basis. These frequent transactions create the need for four special journals—two for payments and two for receipts, two for cash and two for credit:

- A *cash receipts journal* contains information about payments that you receive from customers. These payments could take the form of currency, such as when a customer hands you $20 to purchase an item, or a check, such as when you receive payment for an earlier credit purchase. It might also contain information about other cash receipts, such as capital investments in the company.
- A *cash payments journal* contains information about payments that you make to creditors and suppliers. Normally, these payments are checks that you write, but they could also be payments made using currency. This journal also contains information about operating expenses that you pay in cash, such as salaries or office rent.
- A *sales journal* contains information about credit sales that you make. Together with sales information in the cash receipts journal, the sales journal accounts for all sales that your business makes.
- A *purchases journal* contains information about credit purchases that you make from your suppliers. Together with cash purchase information in the cash payments journal, the purchases journal accounts for all purchases that your business makes from suppliers.

Various other types of transactions exist that aren't recorded in these special journals—they are recorded in the general journal, which acts as a catchall for miscellaneous transactions.

Your own business might have a category of transactions that occur frequently but do not fit well into these four special journals. If you're going to use special journals at all, you should choose the ones that make sense for your line of business; any structure that has special journals for the most frequently occurring types of transactions will do.

For example, suppose that you run a car rental agency. You probably don't purchase cars from suppliers very often, but you might regularly send your cars to garages and body shops for maintenance. In that case, you might use a special repairs and maintenance journal instead of a special purchases journal.

Structuring the Special Sales Journal

The structure of your special journals depends on the journal's purpose and the information you intend to keep in it. Figure 4.2 shows an example of a special sales journal.

Figure 4.2
The special sales journal for Bell Books records credit purchases by its customers.

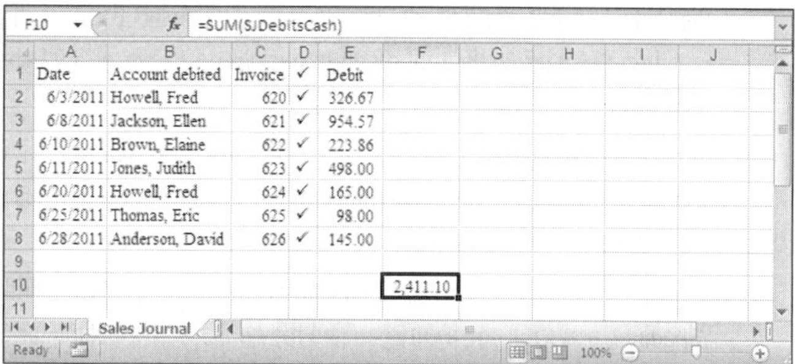
F10 =SUM(SJDebitsCash)

	A	B	C	D	E	F
1	Date	Account debited	Invoice	✓	Debit	
2	6/3/2011	Howell, Fred	620	✓	326.67	
3	6/8/2011	Jackson, Ellen	621	✓	954.57	
4	6/10/2011	Brown, Elaine	622	✓	223.86	
5	6/11/2011	Jones, Judith	623	✓	498.00	
6	6/20/2011	Howell, Fred	624	✓	165.00	
7	6/25/2011	Thomas, Eric	625	✓	98.00	
8	6/28/2011	Anderson, David	626	✓	145.00	
9						
10						2,411.10
11						

Sales Journal

Notice these key elements of the sales journal:

- Each account has a different customer name (for example, Fred Howell, Ellen Jackson, and so on). These accounts are summarized in the accounts receivable ledger so that Bell Books can keep track of whether a customer owes money on an account (and, if so, how much).See the "Creating Subsidiary Ledgers" section later in this chapter for more information on the accounts receivables ledger.
- Each customer account in the sales journal is an individual account receivable—an asset account—therefore, the transaction amount is recorded in the sales journal as a debit. (Recall that asset accounts and expense accounts record increases as debits.)
- A sales journal usually contains several transactions, and a particular customer often shows up more than once. For example, Figure 4.2 shows that Fred Howell has made two purchases during June. But the journal itself does not summarize his account. Customer account summaries are found in the accounts receivable ledger.
- Unlike the general journal shown in Figure 4.1, the special sales journal has no column titled Credit. The reason is that the offsetting credit amounts are accumulated in the general ledger's sales account.
- The check marks in Column D, shown in Figure 4.2, indicate that a particular transaction has been posted from the sales journal to the sales account in the general ledger.

Finding and Using Special Symbols

You can show a variety of special characters in Excel by choosing a particular font. These characters can represent the entire cell entry or only a portion of the entry. For example, to show the check marks in Figure 4.2, the cells were formatted using the Wingdings font. When a cell is formatted with this font, entering the formula `=CHAR(252)` causes Excel to display a check mark.

To find a particular symbol, you can enter a numeric series from 0 to 255 in, say, cells A1:A256 of a worksheet. To do so, click the Home tab, select Fill from the Editing group, and click Series.. In versions prior to Excel 2007, use Edit, Fill, Series.

With the numbers 0 through 255 in column A, enter this formula in cell B1:

```
=CHAR(A1)
```

Then copy and paste from B1 into the range B2:B256. Select B1:B256, click the Home tab, and select Symbol from the Font drop-down box in the Font group. In versions prior to Excel 2007, choose Format, Cells.

Then, using the Font tab, assign the range a font such as Symbol. Look through the B1:B256 range to see whether it contains the symbol you want. When you find it, use the combination of the value, the CHAR function, and the font to display the symbol. You can assign different fonts to different characters in a text entry by highlighting the character in the formula box and continuing exactly as you would to format a full cell.

Another approach is to click the Ribbon's Insert tab and select Symbol from the Text menu. Select a font, such as Wingdings, and scroll down until you find the symbol you're looking for. Click it and then click Insert. If you're using Excel 2002 or 2003, start by choosing Symbol from the Insert menu.

Your choice of method is just a matter of personal preference. Therefore, choose the one that makes it easier for you to find a given symbol.

Structuring the Special Purchases Journal

The purpose of the special purchases journal differs from that of the special sales journal, and it's structured a little differently. Figure 4.3 shows Bell Books' special purchases journal.

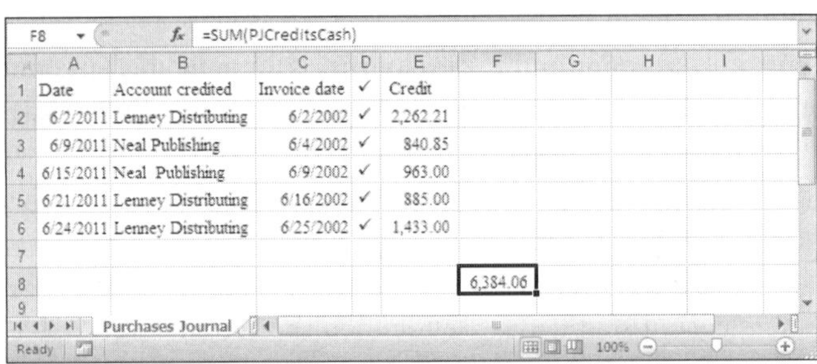

F8 =SUM(PJCreditsCash)

	A	B	C	D	E	F
1	Date	Account credited	Invoice date	✓	Credit	
2	6/2/2011	Lenney Distributing	6/2/2002	✓	2,262.21	
3	6/9/2011	Neal Publishing	6/4/2002	✓	840.85	
4	6/15/2011	Neal Publishing	6/9/2002	✓	963.00	
5	6/21/2011	Lenney Distributing	6/16/2002	✓	885.00	
6	6/24/2011	Lenney Distributing	6/25/2002	✓	1,433.00	
7						
8						6,384.06
9						

Purchases Journal

Figure 4.3
The special purchases journal for Bell Books records credit purchases from its suppliers.

For tracking purposes, the sales journal uses the invoice *number* in column C. In contrast, the purchases journal uses the *date* of the supplier's invoice; this helps Bell Books track the length of time a payable invoice has been outstanding. Of course, if you want, you can also show the supplier's invoice number in the purchases journal. Doing so will help you keep your records straight if you have a supplier who might send you more than one invoice with the same date.

Another difference between the sales and purchases journals is that the purchases journal shows the amount of the purchase as a credit, whereas the sales journal shows the amount of a sale as a debit. The purchases are posted to accounts payable, a liability account that records the company's noncash purchases, so an increase in its balance is recorded as a credit. The sales are posted to accounts receivable, an asset account that records the company's noncash sales, so balance increases are recorded as debits.

Again, there is no debit column in the purchases journal because all entries in this journal are noncash purchases. The offsetting debit entry is found in the accounts payable ledger.

Structuring the Cash Receipts Journal

The two special journals named `Sales` and `Purchases` account for all of Bell Books' noncash transactions. It's still necessary to account for the cash receipt and cash payment transactions. Figure 4.4 shows the special cash receipts journal.

Figure 4.4
Normally, a cash account is debited for cash payments.

C15 =SUM(CRJDebitsCash)

		Debits			Credits				
			Other Accounts				Accounts	Sales	Other
		Cash			Account		Receivable		Accounts
Date	Explanation	Amount	Account	Amount	Credited	✓	Amount	Amount	Amount
6/1/2011	Add'l investment	$ 52,000.00			J. Bell, Capital				$ 52,000.00
6/6/2011	Retail sales	$ 76.68						$ 76.68	
6/7/2011	Retail sales	$ 124.89						$ 124.89	
6/8/2011	Invoice dated 6/3	$ 326.67			Howell, Fred	✓	$ 326.67		
6/12/2011	Sale of 3rd floor	$ 18,000.00	Notes Rcvble	$ 6,000.00	Building				$ 24,000.00
6/12/2011	Invoice dated 6/8	$ 954.57			Jackson, Ellen	✓	$ 954.57		
6/19/2011	Invoice dated 6/15	$ 223.86			Brown, Elaine	✓	$ 223.86		
6/25/2011	Retail sales	$ 87.43						$ 87.43	
6/29/2011	Bank loan	$ 13,000.00			Notes Payable				$ 13,000.00
		$84,794.10		$6,000.00			$ 1,505.10	$ 289.00	$ 89,000.00

Cash Receipts Journal

The structure of the cash receipts journal is quite different from the structure of the sales and purchases journals. As explained previously, all transactions entered in the sales journal are credit transactions that are posted to one ledger account: the sales account. Similarly, all transactions in the purchases journal, also credit transactions, are posted to the purchases ledger account. However, you might want to post cash transactions, both receipts and payments, to one of several accounts. The structure of the cash receipts and cash payments journals builds in the additional flexibility required.

Usually, a transaction in the cash receipts journal is posted to the cash ledger account. The total ($84,794.10) of all the individual transactions that appears in column C of Figure 4.4 is posted to the cash account in the general ledger. For example, the owner of Bell Books invests an additional $52,000 in the company on June 1 (see cell C5 of Figure 4.4). This investment comes in the form of cash and, consequently, is posted—as part of the total cash receipts in column C—as a debit here. It also appears as a debit in the general ledger's cash account. (See the "Creating the General Ledger" section later in this chapter for more information about the general ledger.)

Notice that on June 12, Bell Books sold the third floor of its building to another company for $24,000. (It's a small building.) Bell Books received $18,000 of the $24,000 in cash and accepted a note receivable from the buyer for the remaining $6,000. (See cells C9 and E9 of Figure 4.4.) The $6,000 *could* have been entered in the general journal instead of in the cash receipts journal; however, it's convenient to keep the two portions of the transaction together so that you can see the entire transaction in one place.

This transaction illustrates the purpose of the columns titled Other Accounts, shown in columns D and E of the worksheet in Figure 4.4. Column D contains the name of the ledger account where the transaction will be posted, and column E contains the debit amount that will be posted there.

The amounts in the Debits section of the cash receipts journal are posted to the general ledger as follows:

- The *total* of the receipts in column C, $84,794.10, is shown in cell C15 of Figure 4.4. It is posted as one total value to the general ledger's cash account. (Again, see the "Creating the General Ledger" section later in this chapter for more information about the general ledger.)
- The *individual amounts* of any receipts in column E are posted in the general ledger to the accounts that are named in column D. In Figure 4.4, that's just one account: notes receivable (abbreviated in the figure as Notes Rcvble).

Figure 4.4 also shows the Credits section of the cash receipts journal, which has a structure similar to its Debits section. Two main ledger accounts are credited when transactions are posted from the cash receipts journal: accounts receivable (column I) and sales (column J).

For example, Bell Books received a check on June 8 from Fred Howell as payment for an invoice dated June 3. The transaction is shown in row 8 of the cash receipts journal, in Figure 4.4, as follows:

1. An entry for the amount of the check is made in cell C8, indicating that the general ledger account `Cash` is to be debited by $326.67.
2. An entry showing the account that is to be credited is made in cell G8: Fred Howell's account will be credited by $326.67. That's an account receivable, thus an asset, so a reduction in its balance due to a payment is recorded as a credit in the next step.
3. An entry showing the amount of the check is made in cell I8, indicating that the ledger account named `Accounts Receivable` is to be credited by $326.67.
4. When the amount of $326.67 is actually posted to accounts receivable, a check mark is entered in cell H8 to indicate that the posting has been made.

The posting of $326.67 as a debit to `Cash` and as a credit to accounts receivable shows that the amount is moved *into* `Cash` *from* accounts receivable at the point that the payment is received.

Entering Sales in Cash and Sales Ledgers

As another example, when a customer pays $76.68 by check on June 6 (see row 6 in Figure 4.4), that amount is entered into cell C6 to show that the account named `Cash` is to be debited by $76.68. The same figure is entered into cell J6 to show that the account named `Sales` is to be credited by $76.68.

The reason for entering the sale amount of $76.68 in both the cash and the sales ledger accounts is due to a concept that this book has assumed but not yet made explicit: *double-entry* accounting. Every business transaction must be entered as both a debit and a credit, and the debits and credits must be made in different accounts. The double-entry method has various benefits, one of which is that the sum of all debit entries in the ledger should equal the sum of all credit entries. If the two sums are not equal, you know that the business's accounts are not in balance and an error has been made somewhere.

For example, consider the transaction shown in row 13 of Figure 4.4. On June 29, Bell Books took out a bank loan for $13,000. In exchange for the loan papers, the bank wrote a check to Bell Books for $13,000, and the company deposited it in a checking account. Therefore, Bell Books' cash assets have increased by $13,000. But the company has not suddenly become $13,000 richer by depositing a check; eventually, it will need to repay the loan. Therefore, the company's liabilities have also increased by $13,000, which is documented by increasing the account named `Notes Payable` by $13,000.

The net effect, of course, is that the company's worth remains the same because loans aren't profits. In contrast, when Bell Books sells a book to a customer for cash, four events occur:

1. Its cash account (an asset account) is debited.
2. Its sales account (a revenue account) is credited.
3. Its inventory account (an asset account) is eventually credited.
4. Its cost of goods sold account (a revenue account) is eventually debited.

If the amount involved in 1 and 2 is greater than the amount involved in 3 and 4, the company makes a profit. Buy low and sell high.

Finally, notice that column H, in the Credits section of the cash receipts journal, indicates with a check mark whether a receipt of funds has been posted. The only entries in this journal that are ever marked as posted are payments to accounts receivable. The reason is that accounts receivable maintains detailed information about specific accounts (for example, Fred Howell's account, Ellen Jackson's account, and so on). Therefore, when it receives funds for a specific customer account, Bell Books posts the amount to that account.

In contrast, the company can post a total amount for cash sales to the general ledger's sales account. In that account, there's no particular reason to maintain information about who bought an item from Bell Books for cash.

NOTE Of course, there are plenty of marketing, regulatory, and legal reasons to collect and track that sort of cash transaction data. A nonprofit, for example, must record individual cash donations to support its donors' tax deductions. But there is no particular reason having solely to do with financial accounting that would cause you to record the name of the kid who just bought a skate key from your five-and-dime. (Especially because five-and-dimes aren't around any longer to sell the skate keys that aren't being made.)

Structuring the Cash Payments Journal

The sales journal and the purchases journal collect information about noncash transactions, and the cash receipts journal collects information about cash paid to the company.

Figure 4.5
Normally, the cash account is credited for cash payments.

D15 =SUM(CPJCreditsCash)

			Credits			Debits				
				Other Accounts				Accounts Payable	Purchases Amount	Other Accounts
			Cash			Account				
Date	Check	Explanation	Amount	Account	Amount	Debited	✓	Amount		Amount
6/1/2011	2416	Phone, May	$ 324.66			Phone Expense				$324.66
6/2/2011	2417	Bookmarks	$ 255.55						$255.55	
6/8/2011	2418	Invoice, 6/2	$ 2,262.21			Lenney Distributing	✓	$2,262.21		
6/17/2011	2420	Paid salaries	$ 5,252.20			Salaries				$5,252.20
6/26/2011	2421	Invoice, 6/16	$ 840.85			Neal Publishing	✓	$840.85		
6/27/2011	2422	Books	$ 525.13						$525.13	
6/28/2011	2423	Books	$ 872.66						$872.66	
6/29/2011	2424	Ad in News	$ 95.09			Advertising				$95.09
6/29/2011	2425	Insurance (3 yrs.)	$ 990.95			Unexpired Insurance				$990.95
			$ 11,419.30					$ 3,103.06	$ 1,653.34	$ 6,662.90

Cash Payments Journal

Unfortunately, the company must also pay out cash, and those payments are recorded in the cash payments journal, shown in Figure 4.5.

The overall structure of this journal is the same as that of the cash receipts journal, with one major difference: The Credits section is shown to the left of the Debits section, instead of to the right. Normally, debits are shown to the left of credits, but in a special journal, you can put the columns in any sequence.

It's more convenient to show the Credits section to the left of the Debits section in the cash payments journal because it places the Cash column on the left side of the worksheet, where it's more easily accessible. The accessibility is important because, in cash transaction journals, every transaction contains a cash entry.

Notice in Figure 4.5 that the specific ledger accounts in columns J and K are accounts payable and purchases, respectively. The reason is that they are the accounts most frequently debited when your company makes a cash payment. Typically, you use other accounts, such as salaries and telephone expenses, only once a month when checks are written to employees and to the phone company. Again, the way your company does business should determine which accounts you show as columns in the cash payments journal and which ones you show as line items in the Other Accounts column, such as column L in Figure 4.5.

Excel Tables and Dynamic Range Names

Before continuing with the topics of journals and ledgers, it's useful to take a detour into the topics of Excel tables and named ranges. The reason is that tables and ranges can help you manage your journals and ledgers (and other data groupings).

Prior to the 2007 version, Excel used what were called *lists*. A list is not a formal structure such as a pivot table or an embedded chart. It is a way of organizing data that conforms to certain Excel requirements. A list is a rectangular grouping of adjacent cells, with different records (for example, people, accounts, or transactions) in different rows, and with different fields (for example, person's first name, account balance, or transaction date) in different columns. The name of each field is in the list's first row.

There was never an Excel command to insert or build or convert or name a list. However, certain tasks such as building pivot tables and using the built-in Data Form required that basic data layout, and they still do.

Excel 2007 made a formal object of the informal list and called it a *table*. This creates some confusion with other, different structures such as pivot tables and data tables (the latter are used in so-called "What-If Analysis"), and Microsoft documentation repeatedly warns the reader about that sort of misunderstanding.

Tables in Excel 2007 and 2010 have some capabilities that lists do not:

- They have formal names: by default, `Table1`, `Table2`, and so on. You can change the default name if you want.
- Their number of rows and columns automatically grows as you add data adjacent to the rightmost column or bottommost row.
- They have optional total rows, shown at the bottom of the table, that show column statistics such as Sum or Count.
- Their columns can behave like range names.

For example, if the range A1:E6 in Figure 4.3 were an Excel table named `Table1`, you could use this formula

```
=SUM(Table1[Credit])
```

to get the total of the values in cells E2:E6. If the formula is in a cell that is part of the table, you don't need to use the table name as a qualifier. That is, again in Figure 4.3, this formula would work in a cell in or adjacent to a table in A1:E6:

```
=SUM([Credit])
```

If you have a range of data laid out like the data in Figure 4.3, you can convert it to a table in Excel 2007 or 2010. Just select a cell in the range, click the Ribbon's Insert tab, and click Table in the Tables group.

Having done so, you can show the total of the credits in the purchases journal using

```
=SUM(Table1[Credit])
```

or, if you've renamed the table, using something like this:

```
=SUM(PurchaseJournal[Credit])
```

Notice that the formula works much like using the `SUM` function with a named range. If the range E2:E6 in Figure 4.3 were named `CreditAmounts`, you could get the total of those cells with either this:

```
=SUM(E2:E6)
```

or this:

```
=SUM(CreditAmounts)
```

The basic structure of `=SUM(CreditAmounts)` is similar to the function as applied to a column in a table: `=SUM(Table1[Credit])`. But if a range name refers directly and specifically to, say, E2:E6, problems can arise. Those are discussed next.

Building Dynamic Range Names

Each of the first three chapters of this book discussed range names. You have seen how to specify a particular range of cells using a name that you provide: `Inventory_Product_Code`, for example. Those range names were static. The name always refers to the same set of cells unless you change the address that the name refers to.

Using static range names has several advantages but also some drawbacks. Suppose that you have five values in the range A1:A5. These values represent your company's revenues for the first five months of the year, and you have given the range A1:A5 the name `Revenues`. Elsewhere on the worksheet, you use the formula `=SUM(Revenues)` to display your total year-to-date revenues.

At the end of June, you enter June's revenue figure in cell A6. Now, to get the correct result for `=SUM(Revenues)`, you need to click the Formulas tab and select Name Manager in the Defined Names group, and include A6 in the `Revenues` range (prior to Excel 2007, use Insert, Name, Define).

That's a headache you don't need every month—actually, the real headache is remembering to do it.

Using the OFFSET Function in Dynamic Range Names

What you need is a way to make the name `Revenues` respond by expanding its own address when you add new values: You need a *dynamic* range name, not a static one. You can create a dynamic range name by using Excel's `OFFSET` function. When you define a name, you're not required to enter a specific worksheet address in the Refers To box. You can enter a value or a formula. For example, you could use this formula:

```
=OFFSET($A$1,0,0,COUNT($A:$A),1)
```

This formula illustrates the `OFFSET` function. It returns a reference to a range of cells and contains these arguments:

- **An anchor cell (or range of cells)**—In the example, it's one cell: $A$1. The anchor cell informs `OFFSET` which cell to use as its basis.
- **A `Rows` argument**—In the example, this is the first zero. The reference that `OFFSET` returns is shifted (or *offset*) that number of rows from the anchor cell. In this case, the reference is shifted from $A$1 by zero rows.
- **A `Columns` argument**—In the example, this is the second zero. `OFFSET` shifts the reference by that number of columns from $A$1. Again, this example shifts the reference by zero columns. So far, the `OFFSET` function is just returning a reference to its own anchor cell, $A$1.

- **A `Height` argument**—In this example, this is `COUNT($A:$A)`. Using the `COUNT` function informs `OFFSET` of how many numeric values exist in a range of cells, which is column A in this example. This is the heart of the dynamic range definition. When the number of numeric values in column A changes, it causes `COUNT` to recalculate. In turn, the `OFFSET` function recalculates and returns a reference with a different number of rows.
- **A `Width` argument**—In this example, this is the number `1`. It defines the number of columns in the range that `OFFSET` returns.

> **TIP**
> Use `COUNTA` instead of `COUNT` if your range could legitimately contain text values, not just numbers.

So this formula returns a reference that depends on the number of numeric values in column A:

```
=OFFSET($A$1,0,0,COUNT($A:$A),1)
```

Suppose that column A contains six numbers. The formula returns a reference that is offset from $A$1 by zero rows and zero columns. The reference is six rows high and one column wide. So it returns the reference A1:A6.

As soon as a seventh number is entered in column A, the `COUNT` and `OFFSET` functions combine to make the reference one row larger. The reference would then be A1:A7. The name `Revenues`, defined in this way, is not a static range name, but a dynamic one.

The dynamic range name isn't subject to the drawback to static range names mentioned at the beginning of this section. You no longer need to manually redefine the name `Revenues` when a new revenue figure is included with the existing values. Your formula `=SUM(Revenues)` automatically recalculates and returns the sum of all the values in the `Revenues` range.

> **CAUTION**
> Unfortunately, the dynamic range name comes with a drawback of its own. A value that's unintentionally added to the column causes the range to become larger. Continuing the `Revenues` example, suppose that you inadvertently entered a numeric value such as a date in column A. The `COUNT` function (and, therefore, the `OFFSET` function that includes the `COUNT`) would respond to the date's presence even if it were all the way down in cell A1048576. The `Revenues` range would contain one more row than the number of revenue values.
>
> In this particular example, that might not make much difference. But there are plenty of other situations in which you'd wind up with a serious error.

One further point: You must keep formulas that refer to the dynamic range outside of that range. Suppose that you put your `=SUM(Revenues)` formula in column A. The formula gets counted as one of the values that define the extent of the range, which means that the

`Revenues` range in the `SUM` function is helping to define itself. That's a circular reference error, and Excel won't let you get away with it unscathed—at the very least, you'll need to resolve an error message.

Using Dynamic Range Names in the Journals

The sales and the purchases journals use several dynamic range names. Each range name is sheet level. For example, there is a range named `'Purchases Journal'!Amount` and one named `'Sales Journal'!Amount`. Each journal has these names and definitions:

- `TransactionDate`—In the case of the sales journal, this range refers to the following:
  `=OFFSET('Sales Journal'!$A$1,1,0,COUNT('Sales Journal'!$A:$A),1)`
- `Account`—It's useful and convenient to make this name, as well as the names `Posted` and `Amount`, dependent on the size of the `TransactionDate` range. On the `Sales` worksheet, the name `Account` is defined as follows:
  `=OFFSET('Sales Journal'!TransactionDate,0,1)`

  The reference it returns is offset from `TransactionDate` by zero rows and one column. When you do not supply a `Height` or a `Width` argument for the `OFFSET` function, as in this example, it defaults to the `Height` and `Width` of the anchor argument. In this case, that corresponds to the `TransactionDate` range, so the `Account` reference has as many rows and columns as the `TransactionDate`.
- `Posted`—This name is defined as follows:
  `=OFFSET('Sales Journal'!TransactionDate,0,3)`

It is offset from `TransactionDate` by zero rows and three columns.

- `SJDebitsCash`—The definition is as follows:

  `=OFFSET('Sales Journal'!TransactionDate,0,4)`

The name `SJDebitsCash` uses a naming convention for the journals in the `Financial Reports.xlsm` workbook: the initials of the sheet name (here, `SJ` for sales journal), followed by either `Debits` or `Credits`, followed by the name of the account that has been debited or credited. The corresponding name in the purchases journal is `PJCreditsCash`.

The names `TransactionDate`, `Amount`, and `Posted` on the purchases journal use the sheet named `'Purchases Journal'` instead of `'Sales Journal'` before the exclamation point in the `OFFSET` function, but they are defined identically otherwise.

Choosing Between Tables and Dynamic Range Names

Both tables and dynamic range names have one particularly valuable advantage over static range names in Excel: They automatically redefine their size when you add new data. That means that if there's another part of the workbook—a chart, for example, or even just a formula—that takes its data from the named range or table, it will automatically update when the table updates or when the range is redefined.

TIP

If you use a dynamic range name as the source for a data series in an Excel chart, use its name qualified either by the name of the range's home sheet or by the name of the workbook: That is, if `Credits` is a dynamic range name, use `=SERIES(,,Sheet1!Credits,1)` or `=SERIES(,,Book1.xlsx!Credits,1)` rather than `=SERIES(,,Credits,1)`. You'll need the qualified name even if the chart is embedded in a worksheet that constitutes the name's scope.

So, how do you decide whether to use a dynamic range name or a table? It's largely a matter of personal preference, and my own is to use dynamic range names. But there's no reason that you should follow my personal preference. Instead, consider the following drawbacks.

If you have more than one column in a table, you need to specify both the table name and the column header that you want to use. For example:

```
=SUM(SalesJournal[Debits])
```

whereas if `Debits` were a dynamic range name, you could use this:

```
=SUM(Debits)
```

It's marginally easier for me to remember the name of a range than to remember the name of a table *and* the field header.

Furthermore, if I use the name of a table in the definition of a charted data series, Excel converts the table name to a worksheet reference. Thus, `=SERIES(,,Sheet1!Table3[Credits],1)` would get changed to something like `=SERIES(,,Sheet1!$D$2:$D$20,1)`.

However, if you subsequently add data to the table, the charted series definition is updated to show the new data. For example, `=SERIES(,,Sheet1!$D$2:$D$20,1)` might automatically become something like `=SERIES(,,Sheet1!$D$2:$D$25,1)`.

Dynamic range names have drawbacks, too. A dynamic range name determines the number of rows in the range by using `COUNT` or `COUNTA` to get the number of values already present, usually in a column. Therefore, if you have extraneous values in the column, say in A100 when the range you're interested in occupies A1:A20, the `COUNT` function can easily return one value too many and make the range one row too big.

The other side of that problem is missing values. If you have values in A1:A20 except for one empty cell in, say, A11, the count will be too small by one, and so will the range. This is one reason that I define names such as `Debits` as offsets from a transaction date range. There will be a transaction date for each transaction, but not necessarily a value in the Debits column for each transaction.

Using tables avoids both these problems at the cost of having to qualify the table's column name by the name of the table itself, and of losing the table name in a chart series definition.

Understanding Ledgers

Just as you can choose which special journals to maintain for your business, you can choose which ledgers to maintain. If you kept only one ledger with detailed information about all accounts, it would lose some of its value as a summary document.

Therefore, it's normal to establish some *subsidiary ledgers* that contain detailed information from the journals. You can then keep information about specific sales and specific purchases in the subsidiary ledgers, and you can transfer their summary totals to a general ledger. Because of the frequency of transactions involving sales and purchases, many businesses keep information about these transactions in an accounts receivable subsidiary ledger and an accounts payable subsidiary ledger.

Creating the General Ledger

By keeping detailed information from the journals in these subsidiary ledgers, it's easier to check the status of your individual accounts with both creditors and customers. At the same time, you can keep the general ledger from becoming cluttered with detailed information about individual customers who owe you money, and about individual creditors who expect to be paid. See Figure 4.6, which displays a general ledger's asset and liability accounts.

Figure 4.6
The general ledger should show the account, date, and journal reference for each debit and credit.

D4 =SUM('Cash Receipts Journal'!CRJDebitsCash)

	A	B	C	D	E
1	Account	Date	Reference	Debit	Credit
2	*Asset & Liability Accounts*				
3	Cash	5/31/2011	Balance	$ 24,525.00	
4		6/30/2011	Cash Receipts	$ 84,794.10	
5		6/30/2011	Cash Payments		$ 11,419.30
6		6/30/2011	Balance	$ 97,899.80	
7	Notes Receivable	5/31/2011	Balance	$ -	
8		6/12/2011	Cash Receipts	$ 6,000.00	
9		6/30/2011	Balance	$ 6,000.00	
10	Accounts Receivable	5/31/2011	Balance	$ 3,256.00	
11		6/8/2011	General: Return of books		$ 42.00
12		6/30/2011	Sales	$ 2,411.10	
13		6/30/2011	Cash Receipts		$ 1,505.10
14		6/30/2011	Balance	$ 4,120.00	
15	Unexpired Insurance	5/31/2011	Balance	$ -	
16		6/29/2011	Cash Payments	$ 990.95	
17		6/30/2011	Balance	$ 990.95	
18	Building	5/31/2011	Balance	$ 96,000.00	
19		6/12/2011	Cash Receipts		$ 24,000.00
20		6/30/2011	Balance	$ 72,000.00	

General Ledger

Every dollar entry in this ledger refers directly to either an entry in a journal or a total of the transactions in a journal. For example, the formula in cell D8 is as follows:

```
='Cash Receipts Journal'!$E$9
```

Figure 4.4 shows the cash receipts journal. Notice that the value of $6,000 in cell D8 of the general ledger in Figure 4.6 is the single entry in the cash receipts journal that represents the note accepted by Bell Books in partial payment for the third floor of its building. In contrast, the formula in cell D4 of Figure 4.6 is as follows:

```
=SUM('Cash Receipts Journal'!CRJDebitsCash)
```

Here, the name `CRJDebitsCash` is a dynamic range name that refers to this:

```
=OFFSET('Cash Receipts Journal'!TransactionDate,0,2)
```

This dynamic range does not include the sum in cell C15 in Figure 4.4. That's because the range is based on TransactionDate, which extends only through A13. OFFSET's optional Rows argument is not supplied, so the row count is taken from TransactionDate.

This example illustrates how a ledger entry summarizes all the transactions in a given category that appear individually in a journal.

So debits to the general ledger's cash account are based on the cash receipts journal. In contrast, credits to the general ledger's cash account are based on the cash payments journal. Figure 4.5 shows the cash payments journal, and column D contains the cash payments made during the month, totaling $11,419.30 (cell D15). The outflow of cash is represented in the general ledger by credits to the cash account. The formula in cell E5 of Figure 4.6 is as follows:

```
=SUM('Cash Payments Journal'!CPJCreditsCash)
```

Here, the name `CPJCreditsCash` is a dynamic range name scoped to the `Cash Payments Journal` worksheet that refers to this:

```
=OFFSET('Cash Payments Journal'!TransactionDate,0,3)
```

Consider the accounts receivable classification in Figure 4.6. It contains three amounts: `$42.00`, `$2,411.10`, and `$1,505.10`. The `$42.00` value represents the return of merchandise from a customer and is taken from the general journal.

4

This formula returns the `$2,411.10` value:

```
=SUM('Sales Journal'!SJDebitsCash)
```

The value is the sum of all sales in the sales journal, which by definition are noncash transactions. A range in the sales journal is named `SJDebitsCash` and refers to cells E2:E8 of that worksheet, shown in Figure 4.2. The range contains noncash sales that are recorded as debits to accounts receivable. (The dynamic range name `SJDebitsCash` was discussed in this chapter's section on dynamic range names in journals.)

This formula returns the `$1,505.10` value in cell E13 of Figure 4.6:

```
=SUM('Cash Receipts Journal'!CRJCreditsAR)
```

This refers to the total of the credits in accounts receivable, from the Credits section of the cash receipts journal (see Figure 4.4).

In this way, the activity in the accounts receivable account is summarized for the month. New credit sales are totaled in cell D12, and receipts for credit sales are totaled in cell E13, both in the general ledger. You might find it useful to open the `Financial Reports.xlsm` file and view each of its entries to determine its source in the journals. If you do, you will find that every value for June in the general ledger refers (either directly, or indirectly via the `SUM` function) to an entry in a journal.

Figure 4.7 shows the Revenue and Expense section of the general ledger.

Figure 4.7
All general ledger entries should be linked to the general journal or special journal transactions.

D60 {=SUM((B4:B59=DATE(2011,6,30))*(C4:C59="Balance")*D4:D59)}

	A	B	C	D	E
36	*Revenue & Expense Accounts*				
37	Sales	5/31/2011	Balance		$ -
38		6/30/2011	Sales		$ 2,411.10
39		6/30/2011	Cash Receipts		$ 289.00
40		6/30/2011	Balance		$ 2,700.10
41	Sales Returns	5/31/2011	Balance	$ -	
42		6/8/2011	General	$ 42.00	
43		6/30/2011	Balance	$ 42.00	
44	Purchases	5/31/2011	Balance	$ 8,827.00	
45		6/30/2011	Purchases	$ 6,384.06	
46		6/30/2011	Cash Payments	$ 1,653.34	
47		6/30/2011	Balance	$ 16,864.40	
48	Purchase Returns	5/31/2011	Balance		$ -
49		6/17/2011	General		$ 1,525.00
50		6/30/2011	Balance		$ 1,525.00
51	Salaries	5/31/2011	Balance	$ -	
52		6/17/2011	Cash Payments	$ 5,252.20	
53		6/30/2011	Balance	$ 5,252.20	
54	Telephone	5/31/2011	Balance	$ -	
55		6/1/2011	Cash Payments	$ 324.66	
56		6/30/2011	Balance	$ 324.66	
57	Advertising	5/31/2011	Balance	$ -	
58		6/29/2011	Cash Payments	$ 95.09	
59		6/30/2011	Balance	$ 95.09	
60				$210,698.10	$210,698.10

General Ledger

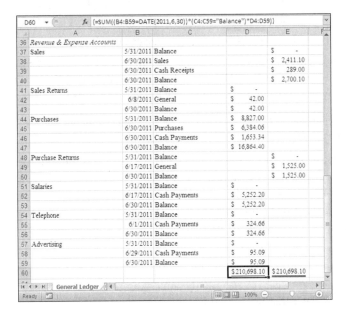

The entries in the general ledger's Revenue and Expense section follow the pattern established in its Assets and Liabilities section. That is, each entry comes from a journal and is either a specific journal entry or the total of several journal entries that belong to the same account.

The values in cells D60 and E60 of Figure 4.7, `$210,698.10`, show that the accounts are in balance. As noted previously, the double-entry method is meant to ensure that the total of the debits for a given period equals the total of the credits for the same period. Each transaction is a debit to one account and a credit to another.

Cells D60 and E60 total the debit and credit account balances in the general ledger. They are equal, which is evidence that the accounts are in balance. However, just because the two totals are equal doesn't necessarily mean that all entries are accurate. For example, compensating errors might exist. But if the two amounts were unequal, it would demonstrate that at least one error existed somewhere.

Creating Subsidiary Ledgers

Bell Books uses two subsidiary ledgers: accounts receivable and accounts payable. The purpose of these ledgers is to keep tabs on accounts that customers have with Bell Books and that Bell Books has with its suppliers. Figure 4.8 shows the accounts receivable ledger.

Neither the accounts receivable ledger nor the accounts payable ledger links to the general ledger. Each subsidiary ledger repeats some of the information in the general ledger; specifically, the accounts receivable ledger provides details about the individual accounts for Bell Books' credit customers.

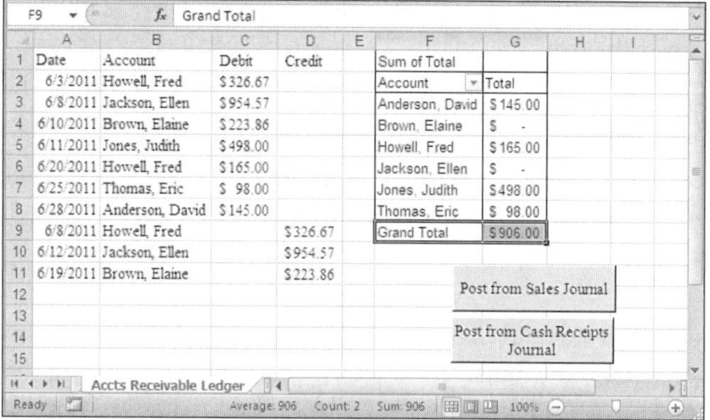

	A	B	C	D	E	F	G
1	Date	Account	Debit	Credit		Sum of Total	
2	6/3/2011	Howell, Fred	$326.67			Account	Total
3	6/8/2011	Jackson, Ellen	$954.57			Anderson, David	$ 145.00
4	6/10/2011	Brown, Elaine	$223.86			Brown, Elaine	$ -
5	6/11/2011	Jones, Judith	$498.00			Howell, Fred	$ 165.00
6	6/20/2011	Howell, Fred	$165.00			Jackson, Ellen	$ -
7	6/25/2011	Thomas, Eric	$ 98.00			Jones, Judith	$498.00
8	6/28/2011	Anderson, David	$145.00			Thomas, Eric	$ 98.00
9	6/8/2011	Howell, Fred		$326.67		Grand Total	$906.00
10	6/12/2011	Jackson, Ellen		$954.57			
11	6/19/2011	Brown, Elaine		$223.86			

Figure 4.8
The accounts receivable ledger helps track the status of individual accounts.

Two worksheet buttons appear on the accounts receivable ledger. One is labeled Post from Sales Journal. That button contains VBA code that posts information about noncash sales from the sales journal to the accounts receivable ledger. Clicking the button causes the VBA code to run. The button labeled Post from Cash Receipts Journal also contains associated VBA code that posts information from the cash receipts journal to the accounts receivable ledger. The cash receipts represent payments for credit sales that were recorded in the sales journal.

The accounts receivable ledger also contains a pivot table that provides the current balance for each of the accounts receivable.

In Figure 4.8, cell D9 contains the value `$326.67`. That value represents the payment received from Fred Howell on June 8 that was entered into the cash receipts journal (refer to cell I8 of Figure 4.4). The value `$326.67` is transferred to the general ledger (refer to cell E13 of Figure 4.6) as part of the total of the credits to accounts receivable from the cash receipts journal.

This example illustrates that amounts posted to subsidiary ledgers must be included in two ledgers: both the subsidiary ledger and the general ledger. Doing so ensures that the account's amount, as shown in the general ledger, equals the amount shown in the subsidiary ledger.

Automating the Posting Process

You can put buttons in various places in an Excel workbook; for example, you can put buttons on worksheets and user forms such as dialog boxes. By associating the button with VBA code, you can cause Excel to take the actions you want it to when the button is clicked. Here's how to create a button on a worksheet using Excel 2007 or Excel 2010:

1. Click the Developer tab and then click Insert in the Controls group.

> **TIP** If you don't see the Developer tab, establish it by clicking the File tab, choosing Excel Options, and clicking Customize Ribbon.

2. Click the Command Button icon in the ActiveX Controls section. Move the mouse pointer over the worksheet.
3. Holding down the left mouse button, drag across and down on the worksheet to indicate where you want the button to appear. Then release the mouse button.
4. The Command button is established on the worksheet. Right-click the Command button to invoke a shortcut menu. One of its items is View Code. When you are ready to provide the VBA code that is to run when the button is clicked, select the View Code item.
5. The button has a default label, `CommandButton1` if it's the first Command button on the worksheet. You can change the label in various ways, including this one: Right-click the button and select CommandButton Object, Edit from the shortcut menu. When you move your mouse pointer over the button's label, the pointer changes to an I-bar. Hold down the left mouse button and drag across the label to highlight it. Then type whatever text you want to appear on the button.
6. Deselect the button by clicking any worksheet cell.

The Post from Sales Journal button shown in Figure 4.8 is linked to the VBA procedure named `PostFromSalesToAR` in Listing 4.1, which actually performs the posting.

Listing 4.1 VBA Procedure PostFromSalesToAR

```
Option Explicit
Option Base 1

Sub PostFromSalesToAR()
Dim SalesDate As Range, Acct As Range, Posted As Range, SalesAmount As Range
Dim ThisTransaction As Integer, NextEntryRow As Long


With Sheets("Sales Journal")
    .Activate
    Set SalesDate = .Range("TransactionDate")
    Set Acct = .Range("Account")
    Set Posted = .Range("Posted")
    Set SalesAmount = .Range("SJDebitsCash")
End With
NextEntryRow = ThisWorkbook.Sheets("Accts Receivable Ledger") _
     .Range("TransactionDate").Rows.Count

For ThisTransaction = 1 To Acct.Rows.Count
     If Posted(ThisTransaction) <> Chr(252) Then
          With ThisWorkbook.Sheets("Accts Receivable Ledger")
               .Range("TransactionDate").Offset(NextEntryRow, 0).Resize(1, 1) = _
                    SalesDate(ThisTransaction)
               .Range("AccountNames").Offset(NextEntryRow, 0).Resize(1, 1) = _
                    Acct(ThisTransaction)
               .Range("Purchases").Offset(NextEntryRow, 0).Resize(1, 1) = _
                    SalesAmount(ThisTransaction)
          End With
          Posted(ThisTransaction).FormulaR1C1 = "=CHAR(252)"
          NextEntryRow = NextEntryRow + 1
```

```
        End If
    Next ThisTransaction

    With ThisWorkbook.Sheets("Accts Receivable Ledger")
        .Activate
        .PivotTables("ARSummary").PivotCache.Refresh
    End With
    End Sub
```

The first two lines of code in Listing 4.1 set two general options. `Option Explicit` requires you to explicitly declare all variables that you use in the code. If this option is not set, new variables could be declared implicitly on the fly—simply typing a variable name would create it. Because this approach makes the code much more difficult to trace and debug, it's wise to use `Option Explicit` and to explicitly declare each variable. (See the discussion of the `Dim` statements later in this section.)

The second option, `Option Base 1`, requires that the first element of all VBA arrays be element number one. Omitting this option causes Excel to treat the first element of an array as element number zero. Suppose that the first element of `MyArray` was `Fred Howell`. Using `Option Base 1`, you would refer to this value as `MyArray(1)`. Without Option Base 1, you would refer to it as `MyArray(0)`. If you prefer to start counting at one instead of at zero, use `Option Base 1` in your VBA code.

4

The next statement in Listing 4.1, `Sub PostFromSalesToAR( )`, classifies and names the procedure. VBA has two types of procedures: functions and subroutines. The keyword `Sub` identifies the procedure as a subroutine. VBA procedures always have a set of parentheses following the name. If the parentheses enclose a variable name or names, those variables are being passed as arguments to the subroutine. (The topic of *arguments* is lengthy and complicated. For now, just be aware that arguments help provide values of variables to the procedures that use them.) In this case, no variables are being passed to the subroutine.

The next two statements are `Dim` (short for *dimension*) statements. Using `Option Explicit` requires the code to explicitly declare all variables. The `Dim` statements declare the existence and types of several variables. The variable named `ThisTransaction`, for example, is declared as type `Integer`. This means that the variable cannot take on a numeric value that has a fractional component, such as `3.1416`, and cannot take on a text value such as "Ellen".

The four variables that are declared as type `Range` will later refer specifically to worksheet ranges. After the `Dim` statement declares the variables, the `Set` statements assign them to ranges. In this case, the variables are simply conveniences: The code can refer to the variable instead of to the name of the range in the worksheet where it exists and to the workbook that contains the worksheet.

Consider the next statement in Listing 4.1:

```
With Sheets("Sales Journal")
```

The statement starts what's called a `With` block. That's a set of statements that pertain to the object named in the `With` statement. In this case, the next five statements all have to do with the sheet named Sales Journal. It's a sort of shorthand; instead of repeating the name of the worksheet in each of the five statements, the code encloses them inside a With . . . End With structure.

Here's the first statement in the With block:

```
.Activate
```

This statement causes Excel to make the sheet named Sales Journal the active worksheet. The Sales Journal worksheet, of course, contains the sales transactions that will be posted. Without the With block, the statement would have had to be this:

```
Sheets("Sales Journal").Activate
```

This probably doesn't seem like much of a savings, but the code can do the same thing with the following four statements, which assign the four Range variables to named ranges:

```
    Set SalesDate = .Range("TransactionDate")
    Set Acct = .Range("Account")
    Set Posted = .Range("Posted")
    Set SalesAmount = .Range("SJDebitsCash")
   End With
```

These statements cause the variable SalesDate to stand in for the range named TransactionDate in the sales journal, Acct to stand in for the range named Account, and so on. Then the end of the With block is indicated.

When the range variables have been set, the code determines the next available row in the AcctsReceivable sheet to post a transaction. It does so by counting the number of rows that are presently in the AcctsReceivable range:

```
NextEntryRow = ThisWorkbook.Sheets("Accts Receivable Ledger") _
    .Range("TransactionDate").Rows.Count
```

NextEntryRow will be used as an offset, so we can be sure not to overwrite what is at present the final row of data on the Accts Receivable Ledgers worksheet.

The statement names three objects that are separated by dots. In VBA, this is termed *dot notation* and denotes a hierarchy: An object that follows the dot belongs to an object that precedes the dot. This was implicit in the With structure just discussed.

The statement refers to a range named TransactionDate. That range belongs to a sheet named Accts Receivable Ledger. In turn, that sheet belongs to the ThisWorkbook object—that is, the workbook containing the VBA code that's executing.

The TransactionDate range has a Rows property, which returns a collection of the rows that belong to the TransactionDate range. That collection of rows itself has properties, one of which is the Count property. The Count property returns the number of objects in a collection. As used here, it returns the number of rows in the TransactionDate range found on the AcctsReceivable sheet that is in the workbook containing the VBA code.

The number of rows in the range is assigned to the variable NextEntryRow. That variable is used later in the code as an argument to the Offset function, and it determines which row the next transaction will be posted to.

Now the meat of the procedure begins. Consider this statement in Listing 4.1:

```
For ThisTransaction = 1 To Acct.Rows.Count
```

It starts a loop that executes once for each row in the range named `Account`, which is represented by the `Acct` variable. The approach is similar to that used to find the next entry row: `Acct.Rows.Count` returns the number of rows in the range represented by the `Acct` variable. The loop steps through the sales journal row by row, looking for transactions that should be posted to the accounts receivable ledger.

The `For` loop starts at `1` and ends at `Acct.Rows.Count`; therefore, it executes as many times as there are rows in that range. The `Acct` variable represents the range named `Account` on the `Sales Journal` worksheet. So the loop executes once for each row in that range.

The first statement inside the loop is as follows:

```
If Posted(ThisTransaction) <> Chr(252) Then
```

This statement causes the statements that follow it to execute if its condition is satisfied, but to be skipped otherwise. The condition is that a particular value does not equal the ANSI character associated with the number `252`. (Using the Wingdings font, that's a check mark.) The particular value that's tested is the element in the `Posted` range that corresponds to the current value of `ThisTransaction`. The `Posted` variable refers to the range named `Posted` in the sales journal. Notice how it's declared in the second line of the procedure.

In brief, the first time that the loop executes, `ThisTransaction` has a value of `1`. Excel examines the first value in `Posted` to see if it equals `Chr(252)`: that is, to see if it appears on the worksheet as a check mark. If that value is not a check mark, subsequent statements are executed because the transaction has not yet been posted; otherwise, the transaction has already been posted and the subsequent statements (up to `End If`) are skipped.

4

> **NOTE** The VBA code discussed here uses the `Chr` function, whereas the `CHAR` function is used on an Excel worksheet. VBA has its own set of functions, as does Excel. VBA's `Chr` function is equivalent to Excel's `CHAR` function.

On the other hand, if the current transaction has not yet been posted—if the result of `Chr(252)` is not found in the current element of the `Posted` range—the statements that follow the `If` should be executed, up to the `End If` statement. Executing those statements results in the posting of the transaction to accounts receivable.

More on Dot Notation

Next, the code begins another `With` block:

```
With ThisWorkbook.Sheets("Accts Receivable Ledger")
```

Inside the `With` blocks are references to objects (such as a worksheet), methods (such as a worksheet's `Activate` method), and properties (such as a cell's `Font` property). Some of the references are preceded by a dot (for example, `.Range`), with nothing immediately preceding that dot. Anything with nothing but a dot preceding it is taken to belong to whatever object is named in the `With` statement. In this case, all objects, methods, and properties referred to inside the `With` block belong to the sheet named `Accts Receivable Ledger`, which, in turn, belongs to `ThisWorkbook`.

Inside the block, several statements use ranges belonging to the `Accts Receivable Ledger` sheet. If the `With` block weren't used, the code would need to repeatedly qualify those ranges by referring to the sheet where it's found, as well as the workbook where the sheet is found. But because the `With` block is used, the code needs to refer to that sheet only once: in the `With` statement.

Each statement inside this `With` block accomplishes some task in the posting of a transaction from the sales journal to the accounts receivable ledger. For example, consider the first statement inside the `With` block:

```
.Range("TransactionDate").Offset(NextEntryRow, 0).Resize(1, 1) = _
    SalesDate(ThisTransaction)
```

Notice the following aspects of the statement:

- Because of the `With` statement, the fragment `.Range("TransactionDate")` is taken to belong to the sheet named `AcctsReceivable` in `ThisWorkbook`.
- The `Offset` fragment describes a range that is offset from the `TransactionDate` range by `NextEntryRow` rows and by zero columns. The first time through the loop, `NextEntryRow` equals the number of rows in the `TransactionDate` range. (Refer to the assignment statement that precedes the `For` loop.) So the offset to the `TransactionDate` range refers to one row below it and in the same column.
- The `Resize` fragment temporarily defines the size of the range as containing one row and one column: thus, one cell.
- This cell is set equal to the value in the `Sales Journal` sheet, referred to by the variable `SalesDate`, for the current value of `ThisTransaction`, which is the transaction being posted. That is, the date of the current transaction is placed in the `TransactionDate` range in the `Accts Receivable Ledger` worksheet.

This process is repeated in the remainder of the `With` block so that the account name and purchase amount are also posted.

The `End With` statement terminates the `With` block. Then a check mark is placed in the `Posted` range of the `Sales` worksheet by means of this statement:

```
Posted(ThisTransaction).FormulaR1C1 = "=CHAR(252)"
```

The variable that controls the offset to the ranges on the `Accts Receivable Ledger` worksheet is incremented. Therefore, the next time the loop executes, the sales date, account, and amount are placed one row farther down:

```
NextEntryRow = NextEntryRow + 1
```

Then the `If` block is terminated with an `End If`. (This marks the end of the statements that are executed if a transaction in the sales journal has not yet been posted.) The final statement in the loop is this:

```
Next ThisTransaction
```

Control returns to the beginning of the loop if the value of `ThisTransaction` does not yet exceed `Accts.Rows.Count`. When the loop has executed once for each row in the range named `Account` in the `Sales` worksheet, the loop ends.

After the final instance of the loop has completed, another `With` block is started for the ledger sheet. The `Accts Receivable Ledger` sheet is activated, and its pivot table is refreshed. The purpose of refreshing the data in the pivot table is to cause the table to incorporate the transactions that have just been posted to the ledger:

```
With ThisWorkbook.Sheets("AcctsReceivable")
    .Activate
    .PivotTables("ARSummary").PivotCache.Refresh
End With
```

Using Pivot Tables to Summarize Individual Accounts Receivable

The purpose of the pivot table is to summarize the current status of all the individual accounts receivable. Figure 4.8 shows the data posted from the sales journal and the cash receipts journal. Notice, for example, that Fred Howell has made two purchases, one for \$326.67 and one for \$165.00, and accounts receivable has been debited for those two transactions. Howell has made payment for the first transaction but not for the second. And the pivot table shows that Howell still owes \$165.00 for the second transaction.

This is managed by creating a calculated field named `Total` inside the pivot table, using that field as the pivot table's data field, and using `Account` as the row field. More specifically, the following steps are taken. (You need to take them only once, when you first add the pivot table to the worksheet.)

1. Click the Formulas tab and then select Define Name from the Defined Names group.
2. Type `DataRange` in the Name box. In the Refers To box, type `=OFFSET(TransactionDate,0,0,ROWS(TransactionDate),5)` and click OK.
3. Select cell F1. Click the Insert tab and select PivotTable from the Tables group.
4. The Create PivotTable dialog box appears. In its Table/Range box, type `DataRange`. Make sure that the Location box contains a reference to cell F1. Click OK.
5. A pivot table schematic appears on the worksheet, the pivot table field list appears, and the Ribbon displays the pivot table options groups. Drag Account from the field list to the Drop Row Fields Here area on the worksheet.
6. On the Ribbon, click Formulas in the Tools group and then click Calculated Field in the drop-down menu.
7. In the Name box, type `Total`.
8. In the formula box, type `= Debit - Credit` and click OK.

9. If the new, calculated `Total` field does not automatically appear in the pivot table's data area, drag it there from the Field list.
10. Close the Field list by clicking its Close box.

The result of this maneuvering is a pivot table with one row for each account. Associated with each account in the table is a calculated field, named `Total` in this example. That field expresses the difference between an account's debits and its credits, thus summarizing the information in the `Purchases` and `Payments` ranges on the `AcctsReceivable` worksheet.

> **TIP**
>
> Each sheet in Financial Reports.xlsm contains a sheet-level range named `TransactionDate`. In some circumstances, it's necessary to qualify a reference to `TransactionDate` with the name of the sheet. But if you have, for example, the `Accts Receivable Ledger` sheet active when you name the range in step 2, you don't need to qualify the range name with the name of the sheet. Excel assumes that you mean the instance of the range that belongs to the active sheet.

Pivot tables do not respond immediately to changes in their underlying data sources, regardless of whether the source is a worksheet range or an external data source. In this respect, pivot tables are different from worksheet formulas, defined names, and charted data series, which *do* recalculate immediately when their source changes.

If a change occurs to a pivot table's data source, it's necessary to refresh the pivot table, and that's the purpose of this VBA statement:

```
.PivotTables("ARSummary").PivotCache.Refresh
```

After the pivot table has been refreshed, the subroutine ends with the `End Sub` statement.

You can write this VBA code in slightly more efficient ways. For example, you could create more variables that refer to worksheet ranges in the `Accts Receivable Ledger` worksheet as well as in the `Sales` worksheet. However, the structure was chosen to illustrate a variety of VBA capabilities, including the `With and If` statements, the `Offset` and `Resize` methods, and the automated redefinition of range addresses.

These VBA subroutines and their associated buttons are replicated for the accounts payable ledger (see Figure 4.9).

Figure 4.9
The accounts payable ledger details information about open accounts with the company's suppliers.

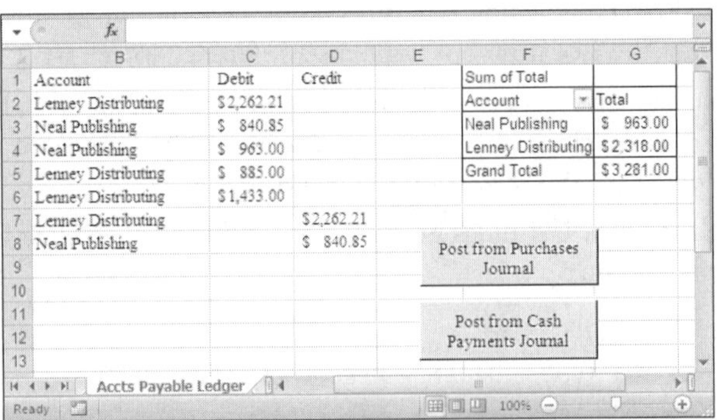

The main difference in the VBA code that posts to the accounts payable ledger is that the code accesses the purchases journal instead of the sales journal. The code that manages postings from the cash payments and cash receipts journals is also similar to the code for the purchases and sales journals; the principal difference consists of which journals are accessed.

Getting a Current Liabilities Balance

Now that a structure for journals and ledgers has been defined, it's straightforward to move amounts for liabilities into the balance sheet (see Figure 4.10).

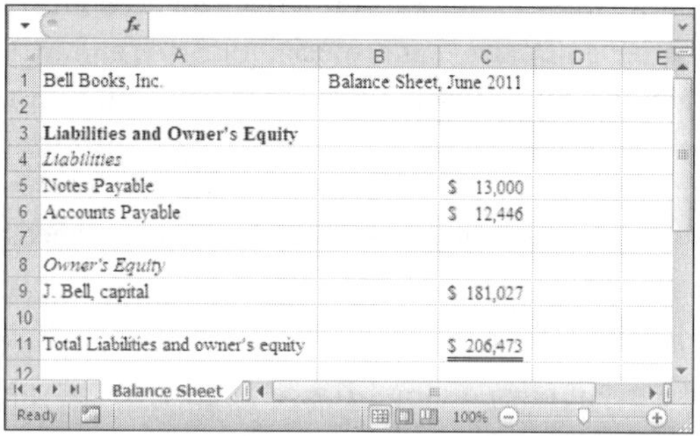

	A	B	C	D	E
1	Bell Books, Inc.	Balance Sheet, June 2011			
2					
3	**Liabilities and Owner's Equity**				
4	*Liabilities*				
5	Notes Payable		$ 13,000		
6	Accounts Payable		$ 12,446		
7					
8	*Owner's Equity*				
9	J. Bell, capital		$ 181,027		
10					
11	Total Liabilities and owner's equity		$ 206,473		

Figure 4.10
The balance sheet for Bell Books, June 2011 (liabilities and owner's equity) links directly to the general ledger's asset and liability accounts.

Notes payable, accounts payable, and owner's equity on the balance sheet are linked to their general ledger balances.

Although this example illustrates only two types of liabilities, accounts payable and notes payable, other types of liabilities exist that you might need to include in your ledger accounts:

- **Taxes payable**—You often need to estimate the taxes due on both income and salaries. You should consult an accountant or tax lawyer to determine the percentage rates to apply against your estimated income and estimated salaries. With these amounts, you can establish journal and ledger accounts that contain the proper estimates.
- **Salaries payable**—Often you pay employees' salaries before closing your books for a given accounting period. When that occurs, the days that elapse after payment is made and before the books are closed usually result in the accrual of salary amounts. You need to pay those accruals after closing the books. Journal and ledger accounts that accumulate these salaries help you keep track of these liabilities.
- **Interest payable**—Depending on whether a note is discounted, you might want to account for interest on the note on a periodic basis instead of on the date that the note is actually paid. An interest payable account allows you to accrue this liability over time.
- **Unearned revenue**—Sometimes a customer pays you for a product or service that won't be delivered until after the books are closed. In that case, the revenue represents

both an asset in the cash account and a liability (until delivery has occurred), which you can account for with an unearned revenue account.

- **Long-term debt**—If you have taken out a loan whose payable date is longer than a year from the date that the books are closed, you should keep this amount separate from the Current Liabilities section of the balance sheet. Its amount would be listed in a separate account, perhaps named `Long-Term Debt`, and listed in the Long-Term Liabilities section of the balance sheet.

Summary

This chapter has shown how you can use Excel to create an account structure in a workbook that contains both a general journal and special journals, and in a workbook that contains both a general ledger and subsidiary ledgers. As they occur, transactions are entered into the journals in chronological order. The transactions are then posted to the appropriate accounts in the ledger workbook. This accounts for the bulk of the work involved in creating both the Assets and the Liabilities sections of a balance sheet.

You also learned in this chapter some VBA techniques for automating the process of posting from journals to their associated ledger accounts and how to use Excel's pivot table facility to determine the current outstanding balance of an account. Those techniques, such as structuring a procedure and using `With` blocks, apply to many coding problems, not just posting from journals to ledgers.

Chapter 5, "Working Capital and Cash Flow Analysis," discusses an important technique for determining your company's financial position. Although the accrual method of accounting is, for most companies, the most accurate way to match revenue and expenses to determine profit, it tends to obscure the way the company handles its most liquid asset, cash. You will learn techniques for tracking the flow of cash and working capital in Chapter 5.

Working Capital and Cash Flow Analysis

5

IN THIS CHAPTER

Because cash is the most liquid of all assets, many managers are particularly interested in how much cash is available to a business at any given time. Because the flow of cash into and out of a business is mainly a matter of *investing* (purchasing assets) and *disinvesting* (disposing of assets), an analysis of cash flows can help measure management's performance.

This chapter describes the process of accounting for and analyzing cash flows. Although it doesn't replace them, the cash flow statement is a useful adjunct to income statements and balance sheets. Using tools that are available to you in the form of different functions and links, you'll see how to use Excel to convert the information in a balance sheet and income statement to a cash flow statement.

To set the stage, the next section discusses how costs are timed.

Matching Costs and Revenues

Several other chapters in this book mention the *matching principle*, which is the notion that revenue should be matched with whatever expenses or assets produce that revenue.

The matching principle leads inevitably to the *accrual method* of accounting. If you obtain the annual registration for a truck in January and use that truck to deliver products to your customers for 12 months, you have paid for an item in January that helps you produce revenue all year long.

If you record the entire amount of the expense in January, you overstate your costs and understate your profitability for that month. You also understate your costs and overstate your profitability for the remaining 11 months.

Largely for this reason, the accrual method evolved. Using the accrual method, you would accrue 1/12 of the expense of the truck registration during each month of the year. Doing so enables you to measure your expenses against your revenues more accurately throughout the year.

Similarly, suppose that you sell a product to a customer on a credit basis. You might receive periodic payments for the product over several months, or you might receive payment in a lump sum sometime after the sale. Again, if you wait to record that income until you have received full payment, you misestimate your profit until the customer finishes paying you.

Some small businesses and sole proprietorships use an alternative to accrual, called the *cash method* of accounting. They find it more convenient to record expenses and revenues as of the date that the transaction takes place. In small businesses, the additional accuracy of the accrual method might not be worth the added effort. An accrual basis is more complicated than a cash basis and requires more effort to maintain, but it is often a more accurate method for reporting purposes.

The main distinction between the two methods is that if you distribute the recording of revenues and expenses over the full time period when you earned and used them, you are using the accrual method. If you record their totals during the time period when you received or made payment, you are using the cash method. As an example of the cash method of accounting, consider Figure 5.1.

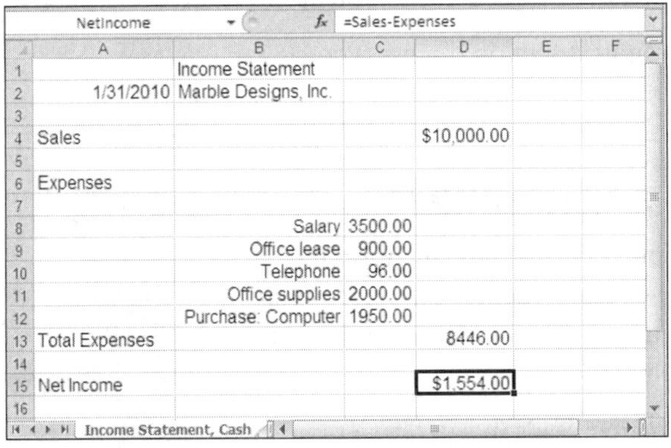

NetIncome =Sales-Expenses

	A	B	C	D	E	F
1		Income Statement				
2	1/31/2010	Marble Designs, Inc.				
3						
4	Sales			$10,000.00		
5						
6	Expenses					
7						
8		Salary	3500.00			
9		Office lease	900.00			
10		Telephone	96.00			
11		Office supplies	2000.00			
12		Purchase: Computer	1950.00			
13	Total Expenses			8446.00		
14						
15	Net Income			$1,554.00		
16						

Income Statement, Cash

Figure 5.1
The cash basis understates income when costs are not associated with revenue that they help generate.

Suppose that Jean Marble starts a new firm, Marble Designs, in January. At the end of the first month of operations, she has made $10,000 in sales and paid various operating expenses: her salary, the office lease, phone costs, office supplies, and a computer. She was able to save 20% of the cost of office supplies by making a bulk purchase that she estimates will last the entire year. Recording all of these as expenses during the current period results in net income for the month of $1,554.

Contrast this result with Figure 5.2.

Using the accrual method, Marble Designs records 1/12 of the cost of the office supplies during January. This is a reasonable decision because the supplies are expected to last a full

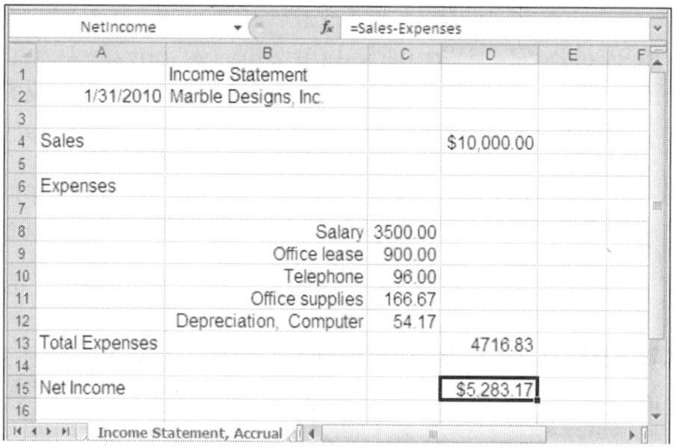

Figure 5.2
Marble Designs' income statement: The accrual basis more accurately estimates income.

NetIncome | f_x =Sales-Expenses

	A	B	C	D
1		Income Statement		
2	1/31/2010	Marble Designs, Inc.		
3				
4	Sales			$10,000.00
5				
6	Expenses			
7				
8		Salary	3500.00	
9		Office lease	900.00	
10		Telephone	96.00	
11		Office supplies	166.67	
12		Depreciation, Computer	54.17	
13	Total Expenses			4716.83
14				
15	Net Income			$5,283.17
16				

Income Statement, Accrual

year. Marble also records 1/36 of the cost of the computer as depreciation. The assumption is that the computer's useful life is three years and that its eventual salvage or residual value will be zero. The net income for January is now $5,283, which is 3.4 times the net income recorded under the cash method.

The net income of $5,283 is a much more realistic estimate for January than $1,554. Both the office supplies and the computer will contribute to the creation of revenue for much longer than one month. In contrast, the benefits of the salary, lease, and phone expenses pertain to that month only, so it is appropriate to record the entire expense for January.

But this analysis says nothing about how much cash Marble Designs has in the bank. Suppose that the company must pay off a major loan in the near future. The income statement does not necessarily show whether Marble Designs will be able to make that payment.

> **NOTE** Notice that both Figure 5.1 and Figure 5.2 use the same formula, `=Sales - Expenses`, to calculate Net Income, but the results are different. This occurs because the scopes of the range names Sales and Expenses are local—that is, they are sheet-level names. For example, in Figure 5.1, the name Expenses refers to cell D13 in the worksheet named `Income Statement, Cash`, which contains the value `8446.00`. In Figure 5.2, the name Expenses also refers to cell D13, but on the worksheet named `Income Statement, Accrual`. That cell contains the value `4716.83`, so the formula for Net Income returns a different result than in Figure 5.1. You set a range name's scope either to the full workbook or to a particular worksheet when you define the name.

5

Broadening the Definition: Cash Versus Working Capital

So far, we have discussed funds in terms of cash only. A broader and more useful way of looking at the availability of funds involves the concept of *working capital.*

How does your company create income? If you manufacture a product, you use funds to purchase inventory, produce goods with that inventory, convert those goods into accounts receivable by selling them, and convert accounts receivable into cash when you take payment. If you are a merchandising firm, the process is basically the same, although you probably purchase finished goods instead of producing them.

Each of the components in this process is a current asset, such as an asset that you can convert into cash in a relatively short period (usually, but not necessarily, one year) in the course of your normal business operations. Inventory and accounts receivable, for example, are not as liquid as cash, but your business expects to convert both to cash before too long.

Current liabilities, on the other hand, are obligations that you must meet during the same relatively short time period that defines your current assets. Notes payable, accounts payable, and salaries are examples of current liabilities.

Determining the Amount of Working Capital

Working capital is the result of subtracting current liabilities from current assets. It is a measure of a company's solvency, its capacity to make large purchases and take advantage of bulk discounts, and its ability to attract customers by offering advantageous credit terms.

There are several steps needed to go from a listing of transactions to an analysis of working capital. But if you want, you can find the amount of working capital in one step by subtracting current liabilities from current assets. You can also get those figures by looking at a balance sheet such as the one shown in Figure 5.3.

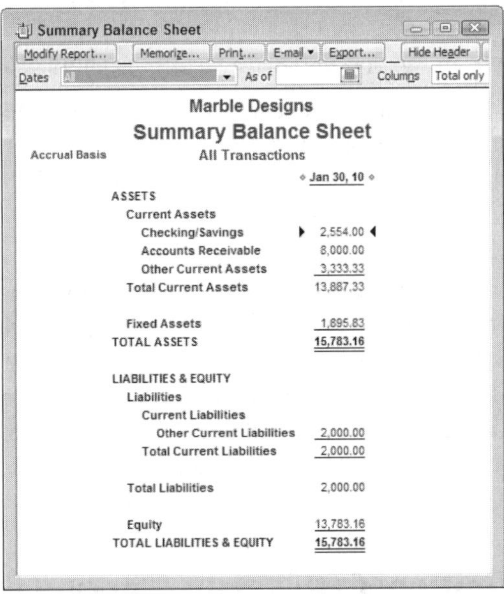

Marble Designs
Summary Balance Sheet
Accrual Basis — All Transactions

	Jan 30, 10
ASSETS	
Current Assets	
Checking/Savings	2,554.00
Accounts Receivable	8,000.00
Other Current Assets	3,333.33
Total Current Assets	13,887.33
Fixed Assets	1,895.83
TOTAL ASSETS	15,783.16
LIABILITIES & EQUITY	
Liabilities	
Current Liabilities	
Other Current Liabilities	2,000.00
Total Current Liabilities	2,000.00
Total Liabilities	2,000.00
Equity	13,783.16
TOTAL LIABILITIES & EQUITY	15,783.16

Figure 5.3
A detailed balance sheet for Marble Designs.

If Marble keeps her books using an application such as QuickBooks, she can call for a balance sheet that the software automatically prepares. She sees that she has $13,887.33 in current assets and $2,000.00 in current liabilities at the end of January, and therefore $11,887.33 in working capital.

Assuming that you use an accounting software package to keep your books, that subtraction is the best way to figure your working capital routinely. There's no reason to calculate it from scratch month after month. However, you should go through the exercise at least once to get a feel for what's involved and for what the analysis is telling you. (Besides, no one enters all financial transactions with perfect accuracy, and running the numbers from scratch once in a while can help you identify errors.)

The remainder of this section steps you through the process of using Excel to get from a listing of transactions to Marble Designs' working capital.

CASE STUDY: MARBLE DESIGNS' WORKING CAPITAL

To complicate the activities of Marble Designs in January 2010 with one additional transaction, assume that the company purchases $2,000 worth of inventory on January 1. The inventory is purchased on credit, and Marble Designs uses $500 of the inventory during January to deliver products to customers.

Accounting for the Cash Transactions

Figure 5.4 shows the cash transactions that occur during January. Because they are all cash transactions, they do not include the inventory purchased on credit.

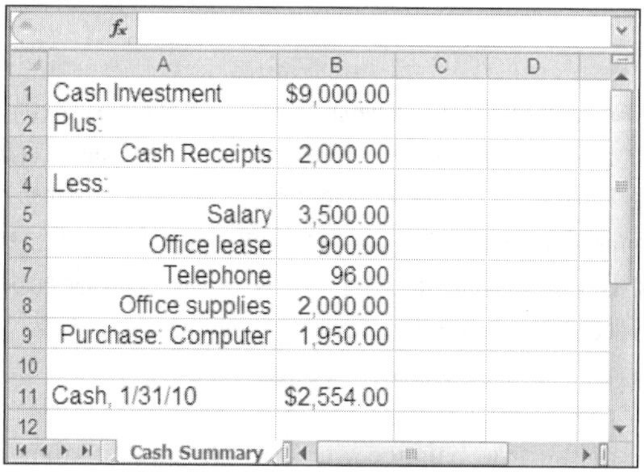

	A	B	C	D
1	Cash Investment	$9,000.00		
2	Plus:			
3	Cash Receipts	2,000.00		
4	Less:			
5	Salary	3,500.00		
6	Office lease	900.00		
7	Telephone	96.00		
8	Office supplies	2,000.00		
9	Purchase: Computer	1,950.00		
10				
11	Cash, 1/31/10	$2,554.00		
12				

Cash Summary

Figure 5.4
The cash transactions undertaken by Marble Designs during January 2010 affect its working capital but do not fully define it.

Jean Marble establishes capital for her new firm by investing $9,000 at the outset. Of the $10,000 in sales that she makes during the first month, she receives cash payment of $2,000: Her cash account is now $11,000. From that $11,000, she makes cash payment for the following:

- $3,500 for her salary
- $900 for the monthly office lease
- $96 for the telephone line
- $2,000 for office supplies
- $1,950 for a computer and peripheral equipment

5

Getting an Adjusted Trial Balance

Figure 5.5 shows these transactions in a format that helps Marble move to a trial balance and then to an adjusted trial balance, and subsequently to an income statement and balance sheet.

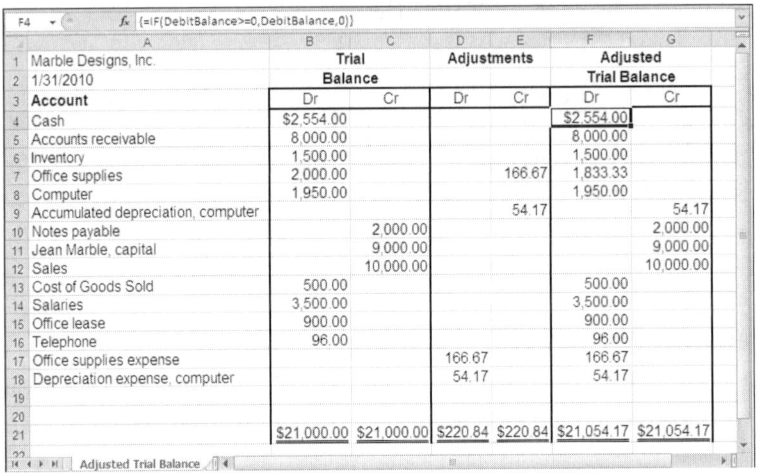

Figure 5.5
Marble Designs' trial balance, adjustments, and adjusted trial balance begin to focus on the company's working capital.

F4 {=IF(DebitBalance>=0,DebitBalance,0)}

	A	B	C	D	E	F	G
1	Marble Designs, Inc.	Trial		Adjustments		Adjusted	
2	1/31/2010	Balance				Trial Balance	
3	**Account**	Dr	Cr	Dr	Cr	Dr	Cr
4	Cash	$2,554.00				$2,554.00	
5	Accounts receivable	8,000.00				8,000.00	
6	Inventory	1,500.00				1,500.00	
7	Office supplies	2,000.00			166.67	1,833.33	
8	Computer	1,950.00				1,950.00	
9	Accumulated depreciation, computer				54.17		54.17
10	Notes payable		2,000.00				2,000.00
11	Jean Marble, capital		9,000.00				9,000.00
12	Sales		10,000.00				10,000.00
13	Cost of Goods Sold	500.00				500.00	
14	Salaries	3,500.00				3,500.00	
15	Office lease	900.00				900.00	
16	Telephone	96.00				96.00	
17	Office supplies expense			166.67		166.67	
18	Depreciation expense, computer			54.17		54.17	
19							
20							
21		$21,000.00	$21,000.00	$220.84	$220.84	$21,054.17	$21,054.17

Adjusted Trial Balance

TIP

Figure 5.5 shows its six totals with double-underlines. Excel provides a special format for double-underlined totals as well as for single-underlined subtotals. Select the cell or cells whose values you want to underline. Select the Home tab on the Ribbon, click the Format drop-down in the Cells group, and select Format Cells from the drop-down menu. (If you are using earlier versions of Excel, select Format, Cells.) Click the Font tab and select Single Accounting or Double Accounting from the Underline combo box. Select OK to return to the worksheet.

On the left or debit side of the trial balance are the ending cash balance of $2,554, the accounts receivable of $8,000 (recall that sales of $10,000 were made and $2,000 in cash payments were received), the ending $1,500 inventory purchased with the $2,000 loan, and the office supplies, computer, salary, lease, and telephone service paid for with cash. You'll also find the $500 worth of inventory used and shown as Cost of Goods Sold.

On the right or credit side of the trial balance are Marble's initial $9,000 capital investment, the $10,000 in sales, and the $2,000 borrowed to purchase the inventory.

In the Adjustments section, shown in columns D and E, the adjustments to the trial balance include $54.17 in depreciation on the computer during the first of 36 months of its useful life, and the $166.67 worth of supplies prorated during the first month. The $54.17 in depreciation is found with this formula:

```
=SLN(B8,0,36)
```

SLN( ) is the Excel function that returns straight-line depreciation. This particular entry computes the monthly depreciation on the value in cell B8 ($1,950), assuming that its eventual salvage value will be $0 and that its useful life is 36 months.

➜ You will learn more about Excel's depreciation functions in Chapter 16, "Fixed Assets."

> **NOTE** Couldn't you just divide $1,950 by 36 to get the $54.17 straight-line monthly depreciation? Sure. But by using the SLN( ) function, you make it explicit both that you are calculating depreciation and that you assume 36 months of useful life and a zero salvage value. A year from now, reviewing your income statement, you might appreciate that your calculation was unambiguous.

The conventions used by accounting state that a decrease in an asset account is recorded as a credit. The Office Supplies account is an asset account. So when office supplies are consumed, the amount used is recorded as a credit.

Those same conventions record an increase to an expense account as a debit. The Office Supplies Expense account is, obviously, an expense account. The value of Office Supplies consumed during the month is $166.67: the value of $2,000 in cell B7 divided by 12. Therefore, $166.67 is recorded as a credit to Office Supplies and as a debit to Office Supplies Expense.

Similarly, the Accumulated Depreciation, Computer account is an asset account; therefore, the loss of value to the computer after one month of use, $54.17, is recorded there as a credit. The offsetting $54.17 debit is recorded in the Depreciation Expense account.

> **NOTE** It would be possible to record the monthly depreciation directly in the Computer asset account as a credit, reflecting its monthly reduction in value due to depreciation. It's typical, though, to record the depreciation in a separate account so that the asset's original value and its ongoing depreciation can be kept distinct. Used in this way, an accumulated depreciation account is termed a *contra-asset* account. It is used in conjunction with the asset account to offset the asset's original value on the balance sheet.

These adjustments are combined with the trial balance to arrive at the debit amounts in the adjusted trial balance. The worksheet accomplishes this by means of this array formula in cells F4:F18:

```
=IF(DebitBalance>=0,DebitBalance,0)
```

(Recall that you enter an array formula using Ctrl+Shift+Enter, not simply Enter.)

In the array formula, DebitBalance is the name of another formula, which is defined as follows:

```
=(TrialDebits-TrialCredits)+(AdjustDebits-AdjustCredits)
```

The formula for `DebitBalance` uses four named ranges (the cell references are to the worksheet shown in Figure 5.5):

- `TrialDebits` refers to B4:B18, the debit amounts in the trial balance.
- `TrialCredits` refers to C4:C18, the credit amounts in the trial balance.
- `AdjustDebits` refers to D4:D18, the debit amounts in the adjustments.
- `AdjustCredits` refers to E4:E18, the credit amounts in the adjustments.

After naming those four ranges, take these steps to define the formula named `DebitBalance`:

1. Select the Formulas tab on the Ribbon and then click Define Name in the Defined Names group. In earlier Excel versions, choose Insert, Name, Define.
2. Type DebitBalance in the Name box. In earlier versions, use the Names in Workbook box.
3. In the Refers To box, type this formula:
   ```
   =(TrialDebits-TrialCredits)+(AdjustDebits-AdjustCredits)
   ```
4. Click OK.

For each of the fourth through eighteenth rows shown in Figure 5.5, the formula subtracts any amounts in the Credit column of the trial balance from any amounts in its Debit column. It then adds any adjusting debits and subtracts any adjusting credits. The result is the debit balance—thus the name of the formula.

As noted earlier in this section, `DebitBalance` is used in this formula, array-entered with Ctrl+Shift+Enter in cells F4:F18 in Figure 5.5:

```
=IF(DebitBalance>=0,DebitBalance,0)
```

5

To illustrate the array formula's effect, consider cell F7, the adjusted trial balance for the Office Supplies account. The trial balance provides a debit amount of `$2,000` and no credit amount. The adjustments include no debit amount but a credit amount of `166.67`. So the named formula `DebitBalance` returns (2000 – 0) + (0 – 166.67), or `1,833.33`. Because that value is greater than zero, the condition in the array formula in cell F7 is satisfied and returns the value `1,833.33`.

Before you continue, you might want to be sure that you understand why no nonzero value appears in cells F9:F12.

Cells G4:G18 contain this array formula:

```
=IF(CreditBalance>=0,CreditBalance,0)
```

It's similar to the array formula in cells F4:F18. The sole difference is that it relies on a different named formula, `CreditBalance`. Using the procedure described earlier to define the `DebitBalance` formula, `CreditBalance` is defined as follows:

```
=(TrialCredits-TrialDebits)+(AdjustCredits-AdjustDebits)
```

Notice that the formula reverses the relationship between debits and credits used in `DebitBalance`. Its purpose is to combine trial and adjusting credits and debits so that if credits exceed debits, the formula returns a positive value. Then the array formula in G4:G18 returns only those values that are greater than or equal to zero.

You might have noticed that these various formulas call for Excel to return a zero amount if a condition is not met. For example, the array formulas in F4:F18 and G4:G18 return a `DebitBalance` or `CreditBalance` amount when the balances equal or exceed zero but a zero when they do not. The figure does not show these zero amounts, primarily to avoid visual clutter.

TIP

You can suppress the display of any zero amounts in a worksheet. Click the File tab and then click Options, near the bottom of the navigation bar. Click Advanced in the Excel Options window and scroll down to the Display for This Worksheet area. Clear the Show a Zero in Cells That Have Zero Value check box. In earlier versions of Excel, select Options from the Tools menu, select the View tab, and clear the Zero Values check box.

Structuring the Income Statement

With the cells in the Adjusted Trial Balance section completed, their revenue and expense information is carried over from the adjusted trial balance to the income statement and balance sheet (see Figure 5.6).

For the income statement, information on revenues and expenses is needed. The debit amounts are obtained by means of this formula in C4:C18:

```
=IF(OR(AcctType="Revenues",AcctType="Expenses",AcctType="COGS"),
     AdjustedDebits,0)
```

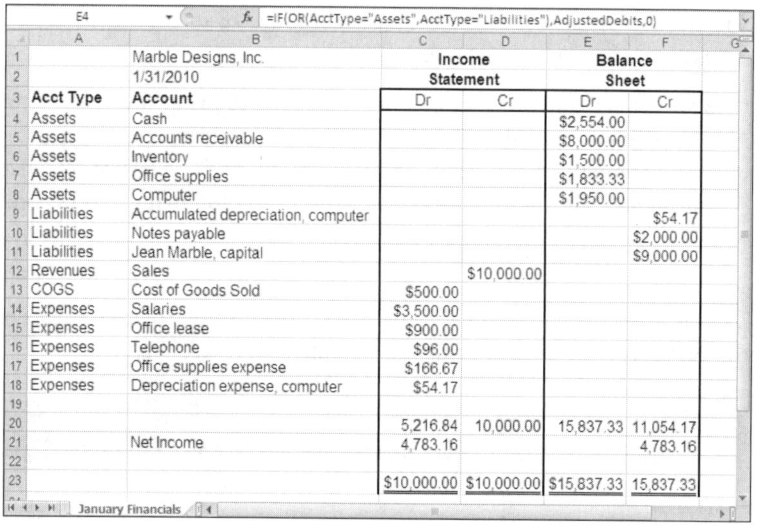

Figure 5.6
Marble Designs' income statement and balance sheet enable you to determine net income.

E4 =IF(OR(AcctType="Assets",AcctType="Liabilities"),AdjustedDebits,0)

	A	B	C	D	E	F
1		Marble Designs, Inc.	Income		Balance	
2		1/31/2010	Statement		Sheet	
3	**Acct Type**	**Account**	Dr	Cr	Dr	Cr
4	Assets	Cash			$2,554.00	
5	Assets	Accounts receivable			$8,000.00	
6	Assets	Inventory			$1,500.00	
7	Assets	Office supplies			$1,833.33	
8	Assets	Computer			$1,950.00	
9	Liabilities	Accumulated depreciation, computer				$54.17
10	Liabilities	Notes payable				$2,000.00
11	Liabilities	Jean Marble, capital				$9,000.00
12	Revenues	Sales		$10,000.00		
13	COGS	Cost of Goods Sold	$500.00			
14	Expenses	Salaries	$3,500.00			
15	Expenses	Office lease	$900.00			
16	Expenses	Telephone	$96.00			
17	Expenses	Office supplies expense	$166.67			
18	Expenses	Depreciation expense, computer	$54.17			
19						
20			5,216.84	10,000.00	15,837.33	11,054.17
21		Net Income	4,783.16			4,783.16
22						
23			$10,000.00	$10,000.00	$15,837.33	15,837.33

January Financials

The formula uses two range names:

- `AdjustedDebits`, a workbook-level name, refers to the range that occupies cells F4:F18 in Figure 5.5
- The range named `AcctType` occupies cells A4:A18 in Figure 5.6 and contains values that identify the type of account: revenue, expense, asset, COGS or liability.

By testing the values in `AcctType`, the formula can limit the amounts brought into the income statement to debits from a revenue, expense, or COGS account.

TIP

The formulas used in Figure 5.5, in the Adjusted Trial Balance range, are array formulas and *must* be entered using the keyboard combination Ctrl+Shift+Enter to work properly. The formulas used in columns C:F in Figure 5.6 are standard Excel formulas, not array formulas. You could begin by selecting C4 and entering its formula as usual; then copy and paste it into C5:C18.

But you could also enter the formula used in each cell of the C4:C18 range in Figure 5.6 by selecting that full range, typing the formula, and finishing with Ctrl+Enter instead of just Enter. Doing this places the same formula in each selected cell. The formulas return different results due to the effect of the implicit intersection. The same is true of rows 4 through 18 in columns D, E and F.

➜ See Chapter 11, "Examining a Business Case: Investment," for a discussion of the use of implicit intersections in Excel formulas.

Similarly, the credit amounts in the income statement are obtained by means of this formula in cells D4:D18:

```
=IF(OR(AcctType="Revenues",AcctType="Expenses",AcctType="COGS"),
     AdjustedCredits,0)
```

The `AdjustedCredits` range occupies cells G4:G18 in Figure 5.5 Like `AdjustedDebits`, `AdjustedCredits` is a workbook-level name.

One additional amount, Net Income, is needed to bring the income statement into balance. Net Income is included in the Debit column and represents the difference between the income statement's total credits and its total debits. The figure returned is `$4,783.17`. As a check, notice that this amount is the result of the following expression:

$10,000.00 – $500.00 – $4,716.83 = $4,783.17

That is, sales revenue less COGS less total operating expenses equals net income. Including the Net Income brings the income statement into balance.

NOTE

Recall that COGS equals beginning inventory (here, $0) plus purchases ($2,000) minus ending inventory ($1,500).

Structuring the Balance Sheet

Finally, the Debit and Credit columns of the balance sheet are obtained by formulas similar to those used for the income statement. This formula returns the debit amounts in E4:E18 of Figure 5.6:

```
=IF(OR(AcctType="Assets",AcctType="Liabilities"),AdjustedDebits,0)
```

This formula returns the credit amounts in cells F4:F18:

```
=IF(OR(AcctType="Assets",AcctType="Liabilities"),AdjustedCredits,0)
```

Now Marble is in a position to calculate her working capital. Recall that working capital is defined as the difference between current assets and current liabilities. As of January 31, 2010, Marble's *current* assets are as follows:

$2,554.00 (cash)

$8,000.00 (accounts receivable)

$1,500.00 (ending inventory)

$1,833.33 (office supplies, a prepaid expense)

This adds up to $13,887.33. Marble's current liabilities include only the $2,000 note payable—neither depreciation on a fixed asset nor paid-in capital is regarded as a current liability. Therefore, her working capital is $11,887.33, or $13,887.33 – $2,000.

> NOTE
> Notice that the computer asset is not involved in determining working capital. This is because the computer is not a current asset, one that can quickly be converted to cash in the normal course of business operations.

5

Determining Changes in Working Capital

From a management perspective, it is important to understand how the amount of working capital changes over time. A comparative balance sheet is useful for this purpose. Figure 5.7 shows an income statement and a balance sheet for Marble Designs, in a somewhat different format than the one used in Figure 5.6.

The balance sheet section of Figure 5.7 lists Marble Designs' assets and liabilities. On January 1, 2010, when the firm began operation, it had no liabilities and $9,000 in assets, consisting entirely of cash. Its working capital was, therefore, $9,000. By the end of the month, the sum of the firm's assets, as shown in cell F11, was $15,783 (which was, of course, also the sum of its liabilities and owner's equity in cell F19.

However, not all these assets and liabilities are *current*. The current assets as of January 31, 2010, include cash, accounts receivable, inventory, and office supplies, which total $13,887.33. The sole current liability is the note for the purchase of the beginning inventory, for $2,000. The difference between the total of the current assets and the current liability is $11,887.33, which agrees with the amount arrived at using the information in Figure 5.6.

Figure 5.7
An income statement and comparative balance sheet can clarify how your financial position changes over time.

F22 =SUM(CurrentAssets)-CurrentLiabilities

	A	B	C	D	E	F
1		Income Statement		Changes to Balance Sheet, 1/1 - 1/31		
2	1/31/2010			**Assets**		
3	**Revenues**				1/1/2010	1/31/2010
4	Sales		$10,000.00	Cash	$9,000.00	$2,554.00
5	Less Cost of Goods Sold			Accounts Receivable		$8,000.00
6	Beginning Inventory	0.00		Inventory		$1,500.00
7	Purchases	2,000.00		Office Supplies		$1,833.33
8	Ending inventory	1,500.00	500.00	Computer		$1,950.00
9				Accumulated depreciation		(54.17)
10	Gross profit		9,500.00			
11					$9,000.00	$15,783.17
12	**Operating Expenses**					
13	Salaries		3,500.00	**Liabilities and Owner's Equity**		
14	Office Lease		900.00			
15	Telephone		96.00	Notes payable		2,000.00
16	Office supplies		166.67	Jean Marble, equity	9,000.00	13,783.17
17	Depreciation, Computer		54.17			
18						
19	Net income		$4,783.17		$9,000.00	$15,783.17
20						
21						
22				Working capital	9,000.00	11,887.33

Comparative Balance Sheet

So the change in working capital from the beginning to the end of the month is $11,887.33 —$9,000.00, or $2,887.33.

You can calculate changes in working capital in several different ways. It's useful to look at the three discussed here, both to understand working capital from different perspectives and because you might want to calculate working capital in the context of different worksheet layouts.

Using Transactions to Calculate Changes to Working Capital

Figure 5.8 shows one way to calculate working capital, using information about individual transactions.

5

During January, the sale of products for more than they cost increased working capital: The gross profit was $9,500. Placing $2,000 worth of materials in inventory also increased working capital. (The $500 in COGS is represented in the gross profit calculation.) These are both current assets, totaling $11,500.

Figure 5.8
It's laborious to determine changes in working capital by examining individual transactions.

B19 =IncreasesToWC-DecreasesInWC

	A	B
1	Effect of transactions on working capital, 1/1/2010 - 1/31/2010	
2		
3	Increases	
4	Gross profit ($10,000 Sales - $500 COGS)	$9,500.00
5	Addition to inventory	2,000.00
6		
7	Total increases	11,500.00
8		
9	Decreases	
10	Note payable for purchase to inventory	2,000.00
11	Purchase of computer from cash	1,950.00
12	Payment of salary from cash	3,500.00
13	Payment of lease from cash	900.00
14	Payment of phone bill from cash	96.00
15	Use of office supplies	166.67
16		
17	Total decreases	8,612.67
18		
19	Net increase (decrease) in working capital	$2,887.33

Transactions & Working Capital

Acquiring a loan of $2,000, the note payable that was used to purchase the inventory, decreased working capital. Working capital was also decreased by the payment of cash for the computer, various operating expenses, and the use of office supplies. These are all current liabilities, totaling $8,612.67.

The net effect of the increase of $11,500 in working capital and the decrease of $8,612.67 in working capital is $2,887.33. During the month of January, Marble Designs increased its working capital by this amount. Note that this is the same figure as was determined by the analysis in Figure 5.7 ($11,887.33 – $9,000).

Normally, you would not determine changes in working capital by examining each transaction that occurred in a given period; there are quicker ways. In addition, many transactions occur that affect current assets and current liabilities to the same degree and so have no net effect on working capital.

For example, when you collect payment for a product or service, the transaction has no effect on working capital. Doing so merely increases one current asset (cash) and decreases another current asset (accounts receivable) by identical amounts. When you write a check for an account payable, you decrease both a current asset account (cash) and a current liability account (accounts payable) by equal amounts. There is no net effect on the amount of working capital.

Therefore, the example shown in Figure 5.8 could have ignored the transaction involved when Marble Designs acquired $2,000 in inventory. This transaction increased a current asset, inventory, and increased a current liability, notes payable, by identical amounts.

In general, transactions that involve a current asset account and a current liability account *do* affect individual working capital accounts, but they *do not* have a net effect on the amount of working capital.

Examining Changes to Current Assets and Liabilities

Because working capital is the difference between total current assets and total current liabilities, the *change* in working capital is the combined effect of *changes* in current liabilities and in current assets. Figure 5.9 shows how you can quickly determine the change in working capital by examining changes to the accounts that make up the current assets and liabilities.

As it happens, the only current asset that declines during January is the Cash account. All other current asset accounts increase in value. One current liability account, Notes Payable, increases by $2,000.00. You can then determine the change in working capital by subtracting the net increase in current liabilities from the net increase in current assets: $4,887.33 – $2,000.00 = $2,887.33.

Checking the Sources and Uses of Working Capital

Another means of determining changes in working capital is to compare its sources with its uses. Recall that transactions involving only current asset and current liability accounts have

Figure 5.9
Determine changes in working capital by comparing changes in current assets and in current liabilities.

WorkingCapitalDelta fx =CurrentAssetDelta-CurrentLiabilityDelta

	A	B	C	D
1	Changes in components of working capital			
2				
3	*Current assets*	1/1/2010	1/31/2010	Increase (decrease)
4				in working capital
5				
6	Cash	$9,000.00	$2,554.00	($6,446.00)
7	Accounts receivable		8,000.00	$8,000.00
8	Inventory		1,500.00	$1,500.00
9	Short-term prepayments		1,833.33	$1,833.33
10				
11	*Total current assets*	9,000.00	13,887.33	$4,887.33
12				
13	*Current liabilities*			
14				
15	Notes payable		2,000.00	$2,000.00
16				
17	*Total current liabilities*		2,000.00	$2,000.00
18				
19	Working capital	$9,000.00	$11,887.33	$2,887.33

Comparative Working Capital

no net effect on working capital. The same is true of transactions that involve only noncurrent accounts. For example, when Marble records $54.17 as the month's depreciation on the computer, she credits Accumulated Depreciation, a noncurrent asset account, and debits Depreciaton Expense, an expense account, with no net effect on working capital.

However, a transaction that involves a current account and a noncurrent account does affect the amount of working capital. Suppose that Marble invested an additional $1,000 in her business, recording it in both the capital account (noncurrent) and the cash account (a current asset). This transaction would increase working capital by $1,000.

Therefore, when determining changes to working capital, it can be convenient to limit the analysis to transactions that affect only current accounts and noncurrent accounts. Figure 5.10 gives an example.

In this case, the sources of working capital consist solely of net income. What is depreciation doing there? Recall that depreciation is a noncash expense that, for the purposes of the income statement, acts as an offset to gross profit in the calculation of net income. However, no funds change hands as a result of recording depreciation. Therefore, when you use net income to calculate your sources of working capital, it is necessary to add depreciation back—in other words, to reverse the effect of subtracting it in the calculation of net income.

Figure 5.10
Another way to determine changes in working capital is to examine current and noncurrent accounts.

B10 fx =SourcesOfWC-UsesOfWC

	A	B	C	D	E
1	*Sources*				
2	Net income	$4,783.16			
3	Depreciation	54.17			
4	Total sources	4,837.33			
5					
6	*Uses*				
7	Computer purchase	1,950.00			
8	Total uses	1,950.00			
9					
10	Increase in working capital	$2,887.33			

Sources and Uses

The cash portion of net income, a noncurrent account, is deposited in the cash account, a current asset. Therefore, in combination with the act of adding depreciation back, it can be used to calculate the change in working capital. You can verify the data by comparing the net income shown in cell B2 of Figure 5.10 with that shown in cell C19 of Figure 5.7.

The sole use of working capital shown in Figure 5.10 is to purchase the computer. It is also used to determine the change in working capital. Funds from the cash account, a current asset, were used to purchase equipment, a noncurrent asset.

The difference between the total sources of working capital and the total uses of working capital is, once again, $2,887.33, just as was found by means of the analyses in Figures 5.7 to 5.9.

Analyzing Cash Flow

For various reasons, you might want to determine how a company uses its cash assets. The choice to use cash to acquire an asset, to meet a liability, or to retire a debt is a process of investment and disinvestment, and a manager always has choices to make, some smart and some maladroit. It's important to keep track of how well a company's management is making these choices.

Furthermore, as useful as the accrual method of accounting is in matching revenues with expenses, it tends to obscure how cash flows through a firm. One of the purposes of cash flow analysis is to highlight differences between, say, net income and the actual acquisition of cash. For example, accounts receivable is one component of net income, but it will not show up as cash until the check clears. A company might have a healthy net income, but if its customers do not pay it on a timely basis, it might have difficulty meeting its obligations. Cash flow analysis can illuminate problems—even impending problems such as that one.

To illustrate this process, consider what might transpire in Marble Designs' financial structure over the period of a year.

CASE STUDY: MARBLE DESIGNS (CONTINUED)

During the 12 months following the analyses shown in Figures 5.1 to 5.10, Marble Designs enjoys successful operations and records the following transactions:

- Makes $90,000 in sales to customers, using $24,500 in inventory to deliver on those sales. As of January 31, 2011, $5,500 remains in accounts receivable, so $84,500 has been received in payment.
- Uses cash to purchase $25,000 in materials to replenish its inventory.
- Collects the $8,000 that remained in accounts receivable at the end of January 2010.
- Pays $53,951 in cash to cover operating expenses.
- Purchases a new computer in July for $2,320 in cash.
- Buys $2,000 in additional office supplies.

- Purchases office space in a new building for $30,000. Before construction of the building is complete, decides against occupying the space and sells it for $35,000, making a $5,000 nonoperating profit.
- Retires the $2,000 note acquired during January 2010 and obtains a new note for $3,000.
- Depreciates the two computers, for a total of $1,037 from January 31, 2010, through January 31, 2011.

Some of these transactions are cash, some are transactions that pertain to normal operations, and some affect current assets and liabilities. Others are noncash, nonoperating, and long term. To determine their effect on Marble Designs' cash flow, it is necessary to disaggregate them.

NOTE This is a relatively simple situation to analyze. Because it is illustrative, it omits many of the transactions that you would normally take into account. For example, it assumes that Marble Designs is an S-corporation and therefore its earnings are taxed on the shareholders' personal returns.

As a benchmark against which the following analysis will be compared, Figure 5.11 shows the actual cash transactions that occurred as a result of Marble Designs' activities during the 12-month period.

Again, though, the information in Figure 5.11 is simply a benchmark used as a check on the cash flow analysis. You would almost never attempt to do a cash flow analysis using actual cash receipts and payments over any lengthy period of time because it would be too time consuming and is a less informative method of analysis.

5

Figure 5.11
Marble Designs' cash positions can be tracked by examining individual cash transactions.

D15 =CurrentBalance-PriorBalance

	A	B	C	D
1	**Cash transaction summary, 1/31/10 - 1/31/11**	**Deposits**	**Withdrawals**	**Balance**
2	Beginning cash balance			$2,554.00
3	Plus cash deposits from revenues	84,500.00		
4	Less purchases to inventory		25,000.00	
5	Plus payment of 1/31/10 accounts receivable	8,000.00		
6				
7	Less cash expenses		53,951.00	
8	Less purchase of new computer		2,320.00	
9	Less purchase of new supplies		2,000.00	
10	Plus gain on sale of office	5,000.00		
11	Less retirement of old note		2,000.00	
12	Plus acquisition of new note	3,000.00		
13	Ending cash balance			$17,783.00
14				
15	Increase in cash balance			$15,229.00

Cash Transaction Summary

Developing the Basic Information

Instead of beginning with a checkbook register, start with the standard financial reports: the income statement and balance sheet. Figure 5.12 shows the income statement for the period January 31, 2010, through January 31, 2011, for Marble Designs, as well as a comparative balance sheet showing assets, liabilities, and equity at the beginning and end of that period.

Figure 5.12
The income statement and balance sheet provide starting points for a cash flow analysis.

F22 =SUM(CurrentAssetsJan2011)-CurrentLiabilitiesJan2011

	A	B	C	D	E	F
1		Income Statement		Changes to Balance Sheet, 1/31/10 - 1/31/11		
2	1/31/2011				Assets	
3					1/31/2010	1/31/2011
4	**Revenues**					
5	Sales		$90,000.00	Cash	$2,554.00	$17,783.00
6	Beginning inventory	1,500.00		Accounts Receivable	$8,000.00	5,500.00
7	Purchases	25,000.00		Inventory	1,500.00	2,000.00
8	Ending inventory	2,000.00		Office Supplies	1,833.33	1,833.33
9	Less Cost of Goods Sold		24,500.00	Computer	1,950.00	1,950.00
10				Computer		2,320.00
11	Gross profit		65,500.00	Accumulated depreciation	(54.17)	(1,090.83)
12					$15,783.17	$30,295.50
13	**Operating Expenses**					
14	Salaries		42,000.00	**Liabilities and Owner's Equity**		
15	Office Lease		10,800.00			
16	Telephone		1,151.00	Notes payable	2,000.00	3,000.00
17	Office supplies		2,000.00	Jean Martin, equity	13,783.17	27,295.50
18	Depreciation, Computers		1,036.67			
19						
20	Gain on sale of office		5,000.00		$15,783.17	$30,295.50
21						
22	Net income		$13,512.33	Working capital	$11,887.33	$24,116.33
23						

Financial Statements

The income statement shows $1,500 worth of materials in inventory at the beginning of the period, an additional $25,000 purchased during the period, and $2,000 remaining at the end. Therefore, $24,500 in materials was used in the completion of $90,000 in sales for the period, resulting in a gross profit of $65,500.

Against that gross profit, various operating expenses were incurred: salaries, the cost of the office lease, and the telephone expense. The $1,833 in office supplies that remained at the end of January 31, 2010, was consumed: This was a prepaid expense because Marble purchased the entire stock of supplies at the beginning of January 2010. Another $2,000 was purchased during the period covered by the income statement.

The depreciation on the computers also appears in the income statement. However, this is a noncash expense. The formula used in cell C18 of Figure 5.12 is as follows:

```
=SLN(1950,0,3)+SLN(2320,0,3)/2
```

This formula uses Excel's straight-line depreciation function, whose arguments are `Cost`, `Salvage Value`, and `Life`. The cost is simply the item's initial cost, its salvage value is the item's value at the end of its useful life (here, Marble estimates that the value will be zero), and its life is the number of periods that will expire before the item reaches its salvage value. The function returns the amount of depreciation that occurs during one period of the item's useful life. So this fragment returns `$650`, the amount of depreciation in the value of the first computer purchased, during one year of its assumed three-year life:

```
SLN(1950,0,3)
```

The second computer was purchased for $2,320 in July 2010, which was halfway through the period covered by the income statement. Therefore, the depreciation on that computer during the second half of the year, $386.67, is returned by this fragment:

```
SLN(2320,0,3)/2
```

Together, the $650 in depreciation over 12 months for the first computer and the $386.67 in depreciation over six months for the second computer result in a total equipment depreciation of $1,036.67.

5

> **NOTE** Expenditures that add to business assets, such as the purchase of the computer, are *capital expenditures*. They are recorded in asset accounts, which is why the cost of the computers does not appear in the income statement. Expenditures for repairs, maintenance, fuel, and so on are *revenue expenditures* and do appear in the income statement.

It's important to keep in mind that this depreciation does not constitute a cash expense such as a salary check or the payment of a monthly telephone bill. As noted previously, no funds change hands when you record depreciation: It is merely a means of apportioning, or accruing, an earlier use of capital to a period in which the item contributes to the creation of revenue.

Finally, the $5,000 profit from the acquisition (for $30,000) and subsequent sale (for $35,000) of the office space is recorded and added to obtain the total net income. Note that this $5,000 is nonoperating income—that is, it is profit created from an activity, the purchase and sale of property, that is not a part of Marble Designs' normal operations.

The balance sheet in Figure 5.12 repeats from Figure 5.7, in column E, Marble Designs' assets, liabilities, and equity at the end of January 31, 2010. Column F also shows these figures as of January 31, 2011. The transactions that occurred during the 12-month period resulted in a healthy increase in cash and minor changes to the remaining asset and liability categories. These entries are taken from ledger accounts; the exception is the owner's equity figure of `$27,295.50`. The owner's equity in cell F17 of Figure 5.12 is calculated as follows:

```
=E17+C22
```

That is, this the prior equity figure of `$13,783.17` in cell E17, plus the net income of `$13,512.33` for the period in cell C22.

Summarizing the Sources and Uses of Working Capital

Figure 5.13 shows the changes in working capital that occurred during the year, determined by analyzing the effect of noncurrent accounts. Sources of working capital include operations, the nonoperating profit realized from the purchase and sale of the office space, and a new short-term note.

> **NOTE** It can be easy to confuse the concept of working capital itself, the result of subtracting current liabilities from current assets, with an analysis of how working capital is created and used, which is the subject of the present section. As you work through this analysis, keep in mind that sources and uses of working capital involve noncurrent assets and liabilities.

Note three points about this analysis of sources and uses of working capital:

- You can *calculate* overall cash flow by determining the net change in the Cash account, but to *analyze* cash flow, you need to examine all the changes in the balance sheet accounts—including working capital. The details and the overall effect of changes in

Figure 5.13
Analyzing the sources and uses of working capital is often a useful indicator of how well a business is managing its resources.

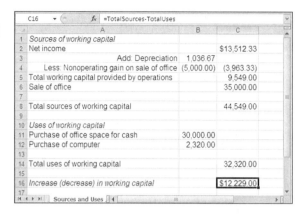

C16 f_x =TotalSources-TotalUses

	A	B	C
1	*Sources of working capital*		
2	Net income		$13,512.33
3	Add: Depreciation	1,036.67	
4	Less: Nonoperating gain on sale of office	(5,000.00)	(3,963.33)
5	Total working capital provided by operations		9,549.00
6	Sale of office		35,000.00
7			
8	Total sources of working capital		44,549.00
9			
10	*Uses of working capital*		
11	Purchase of office space for cash	30,000.00	
12	Purchase of computer	2,320.00	
13			
14	Total uses of working capital		32,320.00
15			
16	*Increase (decrease) in working capital*		$12,229.00
17			

Sources and Uses

working capital usually differ from those of cash transactions. Both the working capital and the cash impacts are important in understanding a company's financial position.

- Changes in working capital are not the same as changes in cash. In this case, cash increases during the accounting period by $15,229, whereas working capital increases by $12,229.
- The profit on the purchase and sale of the office space appears to have no effect on the increase in working capital. In fact, however, it does: The profit of $5,000 has already been included in net income. Figure 5.13 subtracts that profit from net income to provide a more accurate picture of operations as a source of working capital. Furthermore, the transaction is shown under both sources and uses, to show how capital has been generated and used, not simply to calculate the increase or the decrease over time.

Identifying Cash Flows Due to Operating Activities

The next step in analyzing cash flows is to focus on cash generated by and used in operations. Figure 5.14 shows this step.

Generally, three sources or uses of cash arise from operating activities:

- **Cash receipts from customers**—You can easily determine this amount by combining the value for sales (net of any discounts that might have been provided to customers) with changes in accounts receivable. That is, add accounts receivable at the end of the period to the sales figure and then subtract accounts receivable at the beginning of the period. The logic is that if accounts receivable has declined during the period, you have collected more in cash than you have accrued in accounts receivable; if it has increased, you have accrued more in receivables than you have collected in cash.
- **Cash outlays for purchases**—From the standpoint of operating activities, there is one use of cash for purchases: inventory. Therefore, to summarize cash flow for operating purchases, add the cost of goods sold during the period to the ending inventory level, and subtract the beginning inventory level.

  In addition, you might have purchased inventory with a note or account payable to the suppliers of your inventory materials. In this case, you add any decrease in these pay-

Figure 5.14
Determine cash flows from operating activities.

B23 fx =TotalCashReceipts-TotalCashPurchases-TotalCashExpenses

	A	B	C	D	E
1	*Cash receipts*				
2	Sales	$90,000.00			
3	Accounts Receivable, 1/31/2011	5,500.00			
4	Accounts Receivable, 1/31/2010	8,000.00			
5	Change in Accounts Receivable	-2,500.00			
6	Total receipts	92,500.00			
7					
8	*Cash purchases*				
9	Cost of Goods Sold	24,500.00			
10	Inventory, 1/31/2011	2,000.00			
11	Inventory, 1/31/2010	1,500.00			
12	Change in Inventory	500.00			
13	Cash payments for purchases	25,000.00			
14					
15	*Expenses*				
16	Operating expenses	54,987.67			
17	Depreciation	1,036.67			
18	Notes Payable, 1/31/2011	3,000.00			
19	Notes Payable, 1/31/2010	2,000.00			
20	Change in Notes Payable	1,000.00			
21	Cash payments for expenses	54,951.00			
22					
23	*Cash provided by operations*	12,549.00			

Cash Flow, Operations

ables (because you used cash to decrease them) or subtract any increase in these payables (because you used credit, not cash, to acquire the materials).

- **Cash outlays for expenses**—These are available from the operating expenses portion of the income statement. Combine the total operating expenses with any changes in prepayments and accrued liabilities such as employee salaries earned, but as yet unpaid, at the end of the period.

5

In the case of Marble Designs, applying these calculations as shown in Figure 5.14 indicates that sales, increased by a reduction of $2,500 in accounts receivable, results in cash receipts of $92,500. Cost of goods sold, increased by the $500 change in inventory level, results in $25,000 in cash purchases. Total operating expenses also were (a) reduced by $1,036.67 in depreciation, a noncash, long-term prepayment, and (b) increased by a change in the amount of notes payable, converted to cash and used to acquire office supplies.

Subtracting cash payments for purchases and for expenses from total receipts results in $12,549.00, the amount of cash provided by operations.

This completes the process of converting information contained in the income statement, receipts, and outlays represented as accruals into a cash basis, represented as actual cash receipts and outlays occurring during the period in question.

Combining Cash from Operations with Cash from Nonoperating Transactions

The final step in developing the cash flow analysis is to combine the cash amounts used for normal operations with the cash transactions that apply to nonoperating activities. Figure 5.15 provides this summary.

Cash receipts, in this case, consist of cash from operations and cash received from selling the office space. Cash outlays consist of the purchase of the new computer and the office

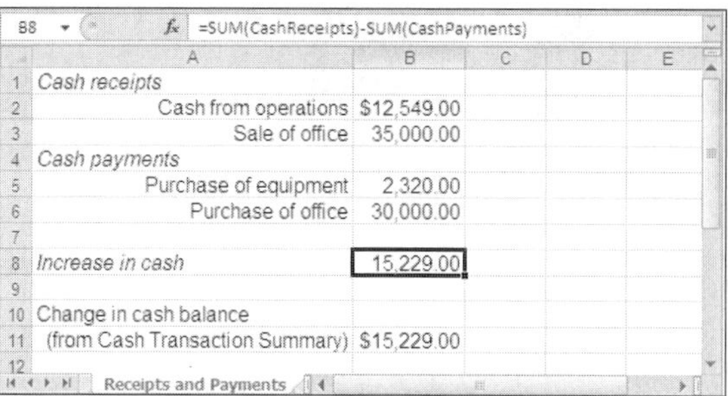

	A	B	C	D	E
1	*Cash receipts*				
2	Cash from operations	$12,549.00			
3	Sale of office	35,000.00			
4	*Cash payments*				
5	Purchase of equipment	2,320.00			
6	Purchase of office	30,000.00			
7					
8	*Increase in cash*	15,229.00			
9					
10	Change in cash balance				
11	(from Cash Transaction Summary)	$15,229.00			
12					

B8 =SUM(CashReceipts)-SUM(CashPayments)

Receipts and Payments

Figure 5.15
Marble Designs' cash flow statement, January 31, 2010, through January 31, 2011.

space. The difference between the two, $15,229, represents the amount of cash Marble Designs generated during the 12-month period; this figure should agree with the difference in the cash account between January 31, 2010, and January 31, 2011. Refer back to Figure 5.11: The difference between the ending balance of $17,783 and the beginning balance of $2,554 is $15,229, which agrees with the results of the cash flow analysis.

In reality, cash flow analysis is a much more complicated task than the relatively simple example provided here. It includes many more transactions than were included in this example: The effect of taxes must be taken into account, accrued liabilities complicate the process, and such transactions as the issuance of stock, dividends, and long-term bonds affect the identification and calculation of cash flows. However, the example illustrates the basic principles and overall process of converting balance sheets and income statements into information about how a company creates and uses its cash resources.

Summary

In this chapter, you saw how to calculate working capital, analyze its sources and uses, and move beyond the information in the balance sheet and income statement. Working capital is an important gauge of a company's financial health, and it can be hidden by the accrual basis used by other analyses.

This chapter also described how to analyze the flow of cash into, through, and out of a company as a result of its transactions. Because cash is the most liquid form of working capital, it is an important component of many financial ratios used by investors and potential creditors; you will learn more about these in Chapter 7, "Ratio Analysis." Cash flow analysis is also an important means of understanding the difference between such items as net income and actual receipts.

Furthermore, the ways that a company uses its working capital and, in particular, its cash are a good indicator of how well it manages its assets overall. This highlights and summarizes the investments and disinvestments the company's management makes every day. Highlighted, those choices can give you insight into the way management handles its responsibilities. People who know how to create these analyses stand a much better chance of protecting their investments before management folds the company's tents.

Statement Analysis

6

IN THIS CHAPTER

Chapters 1 to 4 discussed the structure and purpose of income statements and balance sheets and how to use them for reporting purposes. This chapter, in conjunction with Chapter 7, "Ratio Analysis," describes how to use the information in income statements and balance sheets to improve your insight into business operations.

No dollar amount in a financial report stands on its own—let alone the report itself. The knowledge that a company's total operating expenses during 2001 were $250 million is not, by itself, very informative. To understand the meaning of that number, you need to know other figures, such as gross profit and operating income. Similarly, a balance sheet is fundamental to evaluating the financial condition of a company, but it does not speak to questions such as these:

- Is the company's value increasing or decreasing over time?
- How well does the company's management use its resources to create value?
- How do the company's assets, liabilities, and equity change over time?

Statement analysis and ratio analysis give you context to make judgments such as these. *Statement analysis* helps complete the picture of a company's operations, strategies, and policies. *Ratio analysis* helps fill in the details of why a company's value is increasing or decreasing.

Fundamentally, statement analysis examines the relationships among items on an income statement or a balance sheet and how they change over time. Ratio analysis focuses on certain relationships between individual numbers on a financial report.

At its heart, statement analysis depends on *common-sizing*, which converts the raw numbers to a common unit of measurement.

Understanding a Report by Means of Common-Sizing

A *common-sized report*, which is sometimes referred to as a *normalized report*, typically expresses every dollar category as a percentage of some other dollar category. This enables you to compare, for example, last year's results with those from a prior year, one company with another, or a company with an industry composite.

It's conventional to common-size an income statement by dividing each dollar figure by the total sales for the period covered by the statement. Doing so converts each dollar figure—cost of goods sold, operating income, income taxes, operating expenses, and so on—to its percentage in terms of total sales.

The rationale for common-sizing in terms of total sales is that most of a company's activities depend on its revenues. For example, the more goods the company sells, the greater its cost of goods sold. In a well-managed firm, greater revenues result in greater profits. Even though plenty of exceptions exist, a higher level of sales tends to cause a higher level of salaries. Because total sales impact so many of the items in an income statement, a common-sized statement is usually based on total sales.

Using Common-Sized Income Statements

Figures 6.1 and 6.2 show examples of a dollar-denominated income statement and the same statement common-sized by total sales.

Figure 6.1
This income statement uses the regular dollar metric: It is not common-sized.

OpInc | fx =GrossProfit-OpEx

	A	B	C
1	Daniell Labs		
2	Income Statement for the year ending 12/31/2010		
3			
4	*Sales*		$524,201
5	Less: Returns	2,534	
6	Less: Discounts	1,463	
7	Net sales		520,204
8	*COGS*		
9	Inventory 1/1/10	77,743	
10	Purchases	283,145	
11	Inventory 12/31/10	72,905	
12	COGS	287,983	
13	Gross profit		232,221
14			
15	*Operating Expenses*		
16	Communications	4,547	
17	Lease	29,744	
18	Interest, notes payable	11,300	
19	Depreciation	4,182	
20	Salaries	158,148	
21	Total operating expenses		207,921
22			
23	*Operating income*		$24,300

To convert the income statement shown in Figure 6.1 to a common-sized income statement based on total sales, follow these steps:

1. Select the worksheet range containing the entire statement. In Figure 6.1, this range is A1:C23.
2. Click the Home tab on the Ribbon and then click the Copy button in the Clipboard group. In earlier versions of Excel, choose Edit, Copy.
3. Activate a blank worksheet to make sure that you won't overwrite any important data.
4. While you're still on the Home tab, click the Paste drop-down and then select Paste Special. In earlier versions, choose Edit, Paste Special.
5. In the Paste Special dialog box, click Values in the Paste area and then select OK. This converts any formulas in the original income statement to values in the new worksheet. The reason for converting formulas to values is discussed shortly.
6. Switch back to the original income statement. Select the cell that contains the value of total sales. In Figure 6.1, that's cell C4.
7. Click the Copy icon in the Clipboard group(in earlier versions, choose Edit, Copy) and switch back to the new worksheet.
8. Select the worksheet range containing the numbers in the entire statement. In Figure 6.2, the range is B4:C23.

Figure 6.2
This income statement has been common-sized on the basis of sales, which is cell C4 in Figure 6.1.

OpInc | fx 4.63562641047995%

	A	B	C
1	Daniell Labs		
2	Income Statement for the year ending 12/31/2010		
3			
4	*Sales*		100.0%
5	Less: Returns	0.5%	
6	Less: Discounts	0.3%	
7	Net sales		99.2%
8	COGS		
9	Inventory 1/1/10	14.8%	
10	Purchases	54.0%	
11	Inventory 12/31/10	13.9%	
12	COGS	54.9%	
13	Gross profit		44.3%
14			
15	*Operating Expenses*		
16	Communications	0.9%	
17	Lease	5.7%	
18	Interest, notes payable	2.2%	
19	Depreciation	0.8%	
20	Salaries	30.2%	
21	Total operating expenses		39.7%
22			
23	*Operating income*		4.6%

9. Click the Paste drop-down on the Home tab's Clipboard group and select Paste Special from the drop-down menu. In earlier versions, choose Edit, Paste Special.
10. In the Paste Special dialog box, click Values in the Paste area. Then click Divide in the Operation area and click OK.
11. While the full range is still selected, click the Percent button in the Home tab's Number group. In earlier versions, if you have the Format toolbar open, just click the

Percent button. Otherwise, choose Cells from the Format menu. In the Format Cells dialog box, click the Number tab. Select Percentage in the Category list box, adjust the number of Decimal Places, and click OK.

> TIP
>
> You might want to clear any cells in the range B1:C23 that now contain zero values. (The Skip Blanks option in the Paste Special dialog box refers to blanks in the range you are copying from, not in the range that you are copying to.) Or, perhaps better, you can click the File tab and then click Options. Click Advanced; then, in the Display Options for This Worksheet area, clear the Show a Zero in Cells That Have Zero Value check box. Clearing the cells removes the zero values from the worksheet; clearing the Zero Values check box just prevents them from showing.
>
> In earlier versions of Excel, select Tools, Options, select the View tab, and clear the Zero Values check box.

> NOTE
>
> Step 5 recommends that you convert formulas on the income statement to values because the subsequent Divide operation in step 10 does not necessarily work as intended on a formula. For example, cell C7 in Figure 6.1 contains this formula:
>
> ```
> =C4-B5-B6
> ```
>
> The Divide operation in Paste Special converts each of those three cells to a fractional value. When the formula is also divided by Sales, this expression results:
>
> ```
> =(C4-B5-B6)/524201
> ```
>
> Cells C4, B5, and B6 now contain fractional values as a result of dividing them by Sales, and each cell has a value less than or equal to `1`. Therefore, the formula would return `0.0`% instead of the desired and correct value of `99.2`%.

Although the common-sized income statement in Figure 6.2 doesn't add information to the raw dollar income statement, it helps you answer some questions about how the company generates profits. For example, it's easy to see that the greatest cost incurred by Daniell Labs is its cost of goods sold (COGS), at 54.9% of sales in cell B12. Although it's by no means unusual to find COGS to be approximately 50% of total sales, this alerts you that COGS is a good candidate for management attention in the search for greater profits.

Furthermore, if you have developed a feel for what a percentage of total sales *should* be in your business, the common-sized income statement makes it very easy to identify categories of income and expenses that are out of line.

Using Common-Sized Balance Sheets

You can do the same sort of analysis using a balance sheet. Figure 6.3 shows Daniell Labs' balance sheet, both in raw-dollar format and common-sized by total assets.

The steps to go from a balance sheet that's denominated in dollars to a common-sized balance sheet are largely the same as those for the income statement. The difference is that you divide by total assets instead of total sales.

Again, the use of component percentages in the common-sized balance sheet begins to answer some questions about how the company does business. You can immediately determine the relative importance of various assets and liabilities.

For example, Figure 6.3 immediately makes it clear that a very large percentage—more than 70%—of the company's assets is in its inventory. This knowledge would probably cause you to focus on the firm's inventory-management procedures. In a case such as this, when you begin to analyze specific ratios, you might start with a careful look at the firm's inventory turns ratios.

Figure 6.3
Balance sheets, as well as income statements, are often more informative when they have been common-sized.

LiabilitiesAndEquity | fx =Liabilities+Equity

	A	B	C	D	E
1	Daniell Labs				
2	Balance Sheet for the year ending 12/31/2010				
3				Percentage of	
4		Dollars		Total Assets	
5	Cash		$9,554		9.44%
6	Accounts receivable		6,432		6.35%
7	Inventory		72,905		72.00%
8	Equipment		16,543		16.34%
9	Less: accumulated depreciation	4,182		4.13%	
10	Total assets		**101,252**		**100.00%**
11					
12	Liabilities				
13	Notes payable	12,409		12.26%	
14	Accounts payable	51,243		50.61%	
15	Total liabilities		63,652		62.86%
16					
17	Owner's equity				
18	Capital		37,600		37.14%
19	Total liabilities and owner's equity		**$101,252**		**100.00%**

➔Refer to Chapter 7 for more information about how to analyze specific ratios.

The situation would be quite different if Daniell Labs' inventory represented only 40% of its total assets. The point is that by looking at the component percentages in a common-sized financial report, you can direct your attention immediately to sources of existing and impending problems.

Examining a common-sized balance sheet often gives you insight into a company's procedures for raising capital. By comparing the component percentages for short-term liabilities such as Accounts Payable, long-term liabilities such as Notes Payable, and Retained Earnings, you can determine how the company focuses its efforts to obtain resources. A relatively large component percentage for long-term Notes Payable, for example, would indicate a reliance on debt financing, and therefore on financial leverage. On the other hand, a relatively large component percentage for Retained Earnings would suggest that a company relies on operating income to provide its resources.

Using Comparative Financial Statements

The advantages of using common-sizing become more apparent in comparative financial statements, which display results side by side over time or across companies. Figure 6.4 shows a comparative income statement for Daniell Labs.

Figure 6.4
Comparative income statements, especially when common-sized, make it easier to assess year-to-year performance.

I25 f_x =OpInc2011/TotalSales2011

	A	B	C	D	E	F	G	H	I
1	Daniell Labs Comparative Income Statement								
2									
3		Raw Dollars				Common-sized by sales			
4		2010		2011		2010		2011	
5	*Sales*		$524,201		$583,478		100.0%		100.0%
6	Less: Returns	2,534		2,663		0.5%		0.5%	
7	Less: Discounts	1,463		1,588		0.3%		0.3%	
8	Net sales		520,204		579,227		99.2%		99.3%
9	*COGS*								
10	Inventory 1/1	77,743		72,905		14.8%		12.5%	
11	Purchases	283,145		292,896		54.0%		50.2%	
12	Inventory 12/31	72,905		77,589		13.9%		13.3%	
13	COGS	287,983		288,212		54.9%		49.4%	
14	Gross profit		232,221		291,015		44.3%		49.9%
15									
16	*Operating Expenses*								
17	Communications	4,547		4,320		0.9%		0.7%	
18	Lease	29,744		29,744		5.7%		5.1%	
19	Interest, notes payable	11,300		10,780		2.2%		1.8%	
20	Depreciation	4,182		4,182		0.8%		0.7%	
21									
22	Salaries	158,148		194,390		30.2%		33.3%	
23	Total operating expenses		207,921		243,416		39.7%		41.7%
24									
25	*Operating income*		$24,300		$47,599		4.6%		8.2%

In Figure 6.4, the annual income statement for 2010 appears in columns B and C, and in columns D and E for 2011. Focusing on only the firm's ending inventory dollar amounts in cells B12 and D12, you can tell that the amount of inventory has increased from the end of 2010 to the end of 2011. Initially, this tends to confirm your suspicion (from viewing the common-sized balance sheet in Figure 6.3) that Daniell Labs needs to tighten its inventory-management procedures.

However, the common-sized income statements in columns F through I present a different picture. At the end of 2010, inventory amounted to 13.9% of total sales, whereas at the end of 2011, it amounts to 13.3% of total sales. Although you might not regard 0.6% as a sizable difference, at least the ending inventory levels are moving in the right direction *when viewed in terms of total sales*. As sales increase (as they do from 2010 to 2011), you normally expect that inventory levels will increase because management must allow for more contingencies in customers' requirements. However, Figure 6.4 shows that, relative to total sales, inventory levels decreased from 2010 to 2011. Inventory might still require further management attention, but some evidence suggests that management has been taking steps to keep it under control.

Figure 6.4 also makes it apparent that Daniell Labs has been managing its profit levels more efficiently in 2011 than in 2010. Notice (from cells F13 and H13) that, as component percentages, the COGS decreased during the two-year period, even though the raw dollar amounts increased slightly (compare cell B13 to cell D13). The decrease in the COGS percentage occurs because, although the dollars spent were virtually identical, the amount of total sales increased.

This finding points to one of two conclusions: Either Daniell Labs has increased its unit sales price while holding its unit COGS constant, or its production costs have fallen. Perhaps the company has obtained more favorable pricing from its suppliers, reduced its labor costs, or taken some other steps to increase its productivity. Any of these could help Daniell Labs hold its unit sales price constant while its unit COGS decreases.

This effect also shows up in the company's gross profit margins (cells G14 and I14), which increase by 5.6% of sales from 2010 to 2011. You can attribute nearly the entire increase to the change in the COGS percentage. And the greater gross profit margin flows down to the company's operating income, which increases by 3.6% from 2010 to 2011.

The difference between the 5.6% growth in the gross profit margin and the 3.6% growth in operating income is due to the fact that, as *component percentages*, operating expenses rose slightly while COGS dropped. This effect emphasizes the importance of examining both the raw dollar statements and the common-sized statements.

The combined effect of increased sales and an unchanged COGS would not be apparent if you looked at only the common-sized statements. By examining the raw dollar statements as well, you can tell what happened to the basis (total sales) of the component percentages. Doing so helps you better understand the context for changes in component costs.

On the basis of the comparative income statements, you might conclude that business is proceeding nicely for Daniell Labs. However, Figure 6.5 presents a different picture.

Figure 6.5
Daniell Labs' comparative balance sheets for 2010 and 2011 show some erosion in the company's worth.

G20 fx =LiabilitiesAndEquity/TotalAssets

	A	B	C	D	E	F	G	H	I
1	Daniell Labs Comparative Balance Sheet								
2									
3		Raw Dollars				Common-sized (Total Assets)			
4		2010		2011		2010		2011	
5		12/31/2010		12/31/2011		12/31/2010		12/31/2011	
6	Cash		$9,554		$4,697		9%		5%
7	Accounts receivable		6,432		7,143		6%		7%
8	Inventory		72,905		77,589		72%		79%
9	Equipment		16,543		16,543		16%		17%
10	Less: accumulated depreciation	4,182		8,364		4%		9%	
11	Total assets		101,252		97,608		100%		100%
12									
13	Liabilities								
14	Notes payable	12,409		6,733		12%		7%	
15	Accounts payable	51,243		68,946		51%		71%	
16	Total liabilities		63,652		75,679		63%		78%
17									
18	Owner's equity								
19	Capital		37,600		21,929		37%		22%
20	Total liabilities and owner's equity		$101,252		$97,608		100%		100%

From 2010 to 2011, Total Assets (in dollars) declined slightly, and Owner's Equity significantly declined (in dollars and as a percent of Total Assets). At the same time, Accounts Payable increased. The Equipment asset declined in value when you factor in the depreciation. These effects show up in both the raw dollar figures and the common-sized balance sheet.

In view of the fact that operating income increased during the same period (see Figure 6.4), you should dig more deeply into the numbers, as described in Chapter 5, "Working Capital and Cash Flow Analysis." When income increases and valuation declines, it's important to determine how the company has been using its assets.

Using Dollar and Percent Changes in Statement Analysis

The prior section discussed how to evaluate an income statement and a balance sheet in terms of component percentages. For example, you can measure operating income or operating expenses as a percent of total sales. This analysis might show that operating income increases from 4.6% of total sales in 2010 to 8.2% of total sales in 2011.

Another way of viewing changes over time in income statements and balance sheets is by means of dollar changes and percentage changes (see Figure 6.6). To express changes over time in terms of dollars, you consolidate two reports into one by showing, for each category, the difference in dollars between the two. Or you might decide to consolidate the information by dividing each category in one report by the same category in the other: for example, measuring inventory dollars in 2011 as a function of inventory dollars in 2010. This method expresses changes over time as percentages.

Figure 6.6
With comparative balance sheets and income statements, you can better focus on changes over time by calculating year-to-year differences.

I16 =Capital2011-Capital2010

	A	B	C	D	E	F	G	H	I
1	Daniell Labs Comparative Balance Sheet: Dollar Changes							2009 to	2010 to
2								2010	2011
3	**Assets**	12/31/2009		12/31/2010		12/31/2011			
4	Cash		$1,620		$9,554		$4,697	$7,934	-$4,857
5	Accounts receivable		2,298		6,432		7,143	4,134	711
6	Inventory		20,965		72,905		77,589	51,940	4,684
7	Equipment		16,543		12,361		8,179	-4,182	-4,182
8	Total assets		41,426		101,252		97,608	59,826	-3,644
9									
10	Liabilities								
11	Notes payable			12,409		6,733		12,409	-5,676
12	Accounts payable	31,263		51,243		68,946		19,980	17,703
13	Total liabilities		31,263		63,652		75,679	32,389	$12,027
14									
15	Owner's equity								
16	Capital		10,163		37,600		21,929	27,437	-15,671
17	Total liabilities and owner's equity		$41,426		$101,252		$97,608	$59,826	-$3,644

Assessing the Financial Statements

It's nearly always satisfying for an owner to view changes in dollar amounts, such as those shown in Cash and Accounts Receivable from 2009 to 2010 in Figure 6.6. Column H, which contains the difference in each classification from the end of the first year to the end of the second, shows that the company's assets increased dramatically during that period.

It's true that a major portion of the increase in assets was paid for by means of the acquisition of debt (Notes Payable and Accounts Payable), but it's also true that the amount of the increase in assets is larger than the increase in debt.

Furthermore, including information about 2009 helps to put the changes from 2010 to 2011 (refer to Figure 6.5) in a slightly longer perspective. Viewed in the context of the large increases in assets and equity that occurred in 2010, the decreases in assets and increases in liabilities that occurred in 2011 (see column I of Figure 6.6) do not appear as threatening.

But you can get an even better understanding of Daniell Labs' business operations by examining percentage changes in addition to dollar changes (see Figure 6.7).

Figure 6.7
You can obtain further perspective on changes in financial position with ratios that represent percentage of change.

H11 =(D11-B11)/B11

	B	C	D	E	F	G	H	I	J	K	L
1	Sheet: Dollar Changes						2009 to	2010 to			
2							2010	2011			
3	12/31/2009		12/31/2010		12/31/2011						
4		$1,620		$9,554		$4,697	489.8%	-50.8%			
5		2,298		6,432		7,143	179.9%	11.1%			
6		20,965		72,905		77,589	247.7%	6.4%			
7		16,543		12,361		8,179	-25.3%	-33.8%			
8		41,426		101,252		97,608					
9											
10											
11			12,409		6,733		#DIV/0!	-45.7%			
12	31,263		51,243		68,946		[illegible]	[illegible]			
13		31,263		63,652		75,679	[illegible]	[illegible]			
14											
15											
16		10,163		37,600		21,929	270.0%	-41.7%			
17		$41,426		$101,252		$97,608	144.4%	-3.6%			

The formula or function used is dividing by zero or empty cells.

In Figure 6.7, the year-to-year changes in each statement classification are shown as percentages, instead of dollar amounts, in columns H and I. The percents are *not* simple ratios, such as Total Assets for 2010 divided by Total Assets for 2009. Instead, they are the difference between a comparison year's amount and a base year's amount, divided by the base year's amount. For example, the formula in cell H5 of Figure 6.7 is as follows:

```
=(E5-C5)/C5
```

This represents the difference between 2010's Accounts Receivable and 2009's 'Accounts Receivable, expressed as a percentage of 2009's 'Accounts Receivable.

Notice that each year's balance sheet information occupies two columns, but the information on percentage changes occupies one column for each pair of years. This means that once you have entered the following formula

```
=(E5-C5)/C5
```

into cell H5, you cannot simply copy and paste it into cell I5 to get the analogous percentage change from 2010 to 2011. If you did so, the relative references in the formula would show up in I5 as the following and would return the Excel error value `#DIV/0!` because cell D5 is empty:

```
=(F5-D5)/D5
```


TIP

To overcome this relative referencing problem, copy the formula to the cell that will adjust the references properly. In this case, you could copy cell H5 to cell J5 so that the references would adjust to this:

```
=(G5-E5)/E5
```

Then use either Edit, Cut and Edit, Paste, or use your mouse pointer to drag and drop the formula in J5 back into I5. This is just a matter of first using Copy and Paste to adjust the references properly and then using Cut and Paste to adjust the formula's location.

Handling Error Values

Also in Figure 6.7, notice the Excel error value `#DIV/0!` in cell H11. Its formula is this:

```
=(D11-B11)/B11
```

Because cell B11 is a zero value (there is no amount for Notes Payable in 2009), the formula results in an error due to the attempt to divide by zero. You can avoid this type of error by using Excel's `IF` statement. For example, you might enter this formula in H11:

```
=IF(B11<>0,(D11-B11)/B11,"")
```

This formula causes Excel to examine the value in cell B11 first. If it does not equal zero, the cell then displays the appropriate percentage change. If B11 does equal zero, the cell displays nothing, as indicated by the null string defined by the pair of empty quotation marks.

If you're an experienced Excel user and are comfortable with, and perhaps still using, versions earlier than Excel 2002, the additional error information shown in Figure 6.7 might look unfamiliar to you. For example, in Excel 2002 and subsequent versions, when you induce an error value such as `#DIV/0!`, `#NUM!`, or `#REF!`, Excel inserts a triangle in the cell's upper-left corner, similar to a comment indicator in a cell's upper-right corner.

If you then select that cell, Excel displays a control next to the error value. The control has an icon of an exclamation point on a traffic caution sign. Moving your screen pointer over the icon causes a drop-down arrow to appear. If you leave the screen pointer there for a couple of seconds, you will also see a ScreenTip that explains the error. In Figure 6.7, that tip says, `The formula or function used is dividing by zero or empty cells.`

If you click the drop-down arrow, you see a menu of actions that you can take. The list of menu items varies with the type of error value that has occurred. In the case of division by zero, the menu items include these:

- **Help on This Error**—Click this item to see Help documentation that explains the error value and how to correct it.
- **Show Calculation Steps**—Clicking this item invokes the Audit Formula dialog box; this box is also available by clicking the Formulas tab and choosing Evaluate Formula in the Formula Auditing group. In earlier versions, choose Tools, Formula Auditing, Evaluate Formula.
- **Ignore Error**—This item removes the error indicator from the cell and the warning icon next to it. You can change your mind later by clicking the File tab, choosing Excel Options, clicking Formulas, and then pressing the Reset Ignored Errors button in the Error Checking area. In earlier versions, you would choose Tools, Options, click the Error Checking tab, and click the Reset Ignored Errors button.
- **Edit in Formula Bar**—This item just activates the formula bar so that you can change the formula, presumably to avoid an error value.
- **Error Checking Options**—Use this item to display the dialog box that you usually display by clicking the File tab, choosing Options, clicking Formulas, and scrolling

down to the Error Checking area. In earlier versions, choose Tools, Options, and click the Error Checking tab.

- **Show Formula Auditing Toolbar**—This toolbar, also available by choosing View, Toolbars, is not available in versions of Excel subsequent to Excel 2003. The toolbar has buttons that help you determine what's going on with a formula. Suppose that C5 is the active cell. If you click the Auditing toolbar's Trace Dependents button, it displays arrows that point from cell C5 to any cells containing formulas that refer to cell C5. (This option does not appear in Excel 2007 or 2010, due to the absence of task-oriented toolbars.)

Evaluating Percentage Changes

To return to the perspective that percentage changes can provide, notice that in cells H7 and I7 of Figure 6.6 the raw dollar changes from year to year are constant.

This is because Daniell Labs is using straight-line depreciation on its equipment, and this method results in a constant depreciation figure from period to period. Therefore, the book value of the firm's equipment declines by a constant $4,182 during each year.

➜See Chapter 16,"Fixed Assets," for a full discussion of depreciation methods in Excel.

However, cells H7 and I7 of Figure 6.7 show that the decrease in the value of the equipment is accelerating from year to year, from a loss of 25% during 2009—2010 to a loss of 34% during 2010—2011. The reason for this is that each percentage difference uses a different base. As the size of that base decreases from $16,543 in 2009 (see cell C7 of Figure 6.6) to $12,361 in 2010 as shown in cell E7), the formula's denominator decreases, and the size of the ratio increases because its numerator remains constant.

In this case, the difference between a loss in value of –25% to –34% is not drastic, especially considering the associated and relatively small raw dollar differences.

If a very large decrease in equipment valuation occurred, you might want to check into the depreciation methods being used. The company might employ an aggressive, accelerated depreciation method, which would tend to reduce its taxable income sharply while the equipment was still fairly new.

On the other hand, a steep decrease in equipment valuation might suggest that the company has sold or written off a significant portion of its equipment. Did it do so in the normal course of operations because the equipment had become obsolete? In that case, was the equipment replaced? At a lower cost? Or did the company sell the equipment to raise needed cash?

Examining period-to-period changes in balance sheets and income statements, measured both in dollar amounts and as percentage changes, can provide you with useful information about how a company manages its operations and its financial position.

Common-Sizing and Comparative Analyses in Other Applications

Accounting applications such as QuickBooks make it easy to create a common-sized financial statement, as well as comparative statements. For example, Figure 6.8 shows a common-sized income statement for Daniell Laboratories.

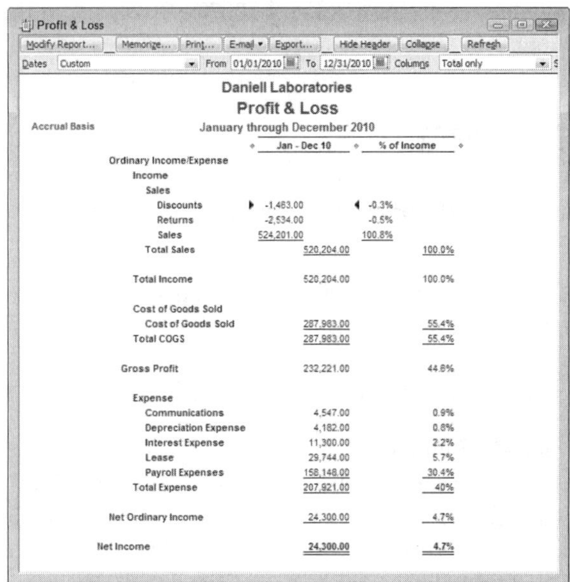

Profit & Loss

Modify Report... | Memorize... | Print... | E-mail | Export... | Hide Header | Collapse | Refresh

Dates: Custom | From 01/01/2010 | To 12/31/2010 | Columns: Total only

Daniell Laboratories

Profit & Loss

Accrual Basis — January through December 2010

	Jan - Dec 10		% of Income	
Ordinary Income/Expense				
Income				
Sales				
Discounts	-1,463.00		-0.3%	
Returns	-2,534.00		-0.5%	
Sales	524,201.00		100.8%	
Total Sales		520,204.00		100.0%
Total Income		520,204.00		100.0%
Cost of Goods Sold				
Cost of Goods Sold		287,983.00		55.4%
Total COGS		287,983.00		55.4%
Gross Profit		232,221.00		44.6%
Expense				
Communications		4,547.00		0.9%
Depreciation Expense		4,182.00		0.8%
Interest Expense		11,300.00		2.2%
Lease		29,744.00		5.7%
Payroll Expenses		158,148.00		30.4%
Total Expense		207,921.00		40%
Net Ordinary Income		24,300.00		4.7%
Net Income		24,300.00		4.7%

Figure 6.8
Click Modify Report to common-size a QuickBooks income statement by Total Income.

If you're using QuickBooks to common-size an income statement, all you have to do is call for a Profit & Loss in the Reports menu (Company & Financial sub-menu), click Modify Report, and select the % Income check box. That's quicker and easier than doing the common-sizing from scratch, as you must in Excel.

However, there's a price, and the price is lack of flexibility. For example, if you choose to common-size an income statement in QuickBooks, you can't choose to do so on the basis of total sales. The closest you can come is Total Income, which QuickBooks defines as net of discounts and returns.

In this case, it is a small thing—compare Figure 6.8 to Figure 6.2 to see the size of the difference. But if you want to exert more control over the analysis, consider piping the data from your accounting application into Excel.

Working in Excel with a Profit & Loss from QuickBooks

In the example shown in Figure 6.8, you can click the Export button. One of your options is to export the report to a new Excel workbook. Once you do so, you see a worksheet that looks like the one in Figure 6.9.

Figure 6.9
The percentages can now be easily recalculated to match those shown in Figure 6.2.

I6 =ROUND(IF(G10=0, 0, G6/G10),5)

	A B C D E F	G	H	I
1				
2		Jan - Dec 10		% of Income
3	Ordinary Income/Expense			
4	Income			
5	Sales			
6	Discounts	-1,463.00		-0.28%
7	Returns	-2,534.00		-0.49%
8	Sales	524,201.00		100.0%
9	Total Sales	520,204.00		100.0%
10	Total Income	520,204.00		100.0%
11	Cost of Goods Sold			
12	Cost of Goods Sold	287,983.00		55.36%
13	Total COGS	287,983.00		55.36%
14	Gross Profit	232,221.00		44.64%
15	Expense			
16	Communications	4,547.00		0.87%
17	Depreciation Expense	4,182.00		0.8%
18	Interest Expense	11,300.00		2.17%
19	Lease	29,744.00		5.72%
20	Payroll Expenses	158,148.00		30.4%
21	Total Expense	207,921.00		39.97%
22	Net Ordinary Income	24,300.00		4.67%
23	Net Income	24,300.00		4.67%

Fortunately, QuickBooks uses formulas to calculate the percentages you see in column I, so it's just a matter of changing the formulas to use total sales instead of total income as the denominator.

Here's the formula in cell I6:

```
=ROUND(IF(G10=0,0,G6/G10),5)
```

Working from the inside out, the formula does the following:

- Tests to see if the value in G10 is `0`. If it is, return `0`; otherwise, return the result of dividing the value in G6 by the value in G10. This test avoids the problems raised by trying to divide by zero.
- Rounds the result to 5 decimal places. You see only two decimal places on the worksheet because the cells are formatted to show 2-decimal percentages.

All the formulas in column I conform to that pattern; all that changes are the row numbers in the numerators. So, to convert the common-sizing basis from cell G10 to cell G8, total sales, just three steps are needed:

1. Select column I.
2. On Excel's Home tab, click the Find & Select button in the Editing group. Select Replace from the drop-down menu.
3. Enter `G10` in the Find What box, and enter G8 in the Replace With box. Click Replace All, and then click Close.

This sequence of steps replaces all references to G10 in column I's formulas with references to G8. For example, this formula

```
=ROUND(IF(G10=0,0,G6/G10),5)
```

becomes this

```
=ROUND(IF(G8=0,0,G6/G8),5)
```

and all the percentages become based on total sales, as in Figure 6.2, instead of total income.

Working in Excel with a QuickBooks Balance Sheet

Similar considerations apply when you want to get a comparative financial statement out of QuickBooks and into Excel. This section shows you how to do so using a QuickBooks balance sheet.

Figure 6.10 shows a balance sheet as prepared in QuickBooks for Daniell Laboratories. It's a comparative balance sheet for 2010 and 2011.

The comparative balance sheet shown in Figure 6.10 is standard; it is normal to show later periods to the left of earlier periods. Notice the Export button: You can export any QuickBooks financial report to an Excel workbook.

Once again, it's easier to get the comparative balance sheet in QuickBooks, but in this case there's not much to edit once you have it in Excel.

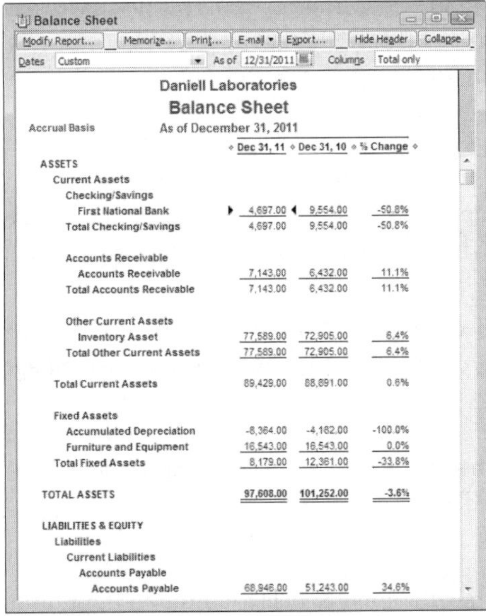

Daniell Laboratories
Balance Sheet
Accrual Basis — As of December 31, 2011

	Dec 31, 11	Dec 31, 10	% Change
ASSETS			
Current Assets			
Checking/Savings			
First National Bank	4,697.00	9,554.00	-50.8%
Total Checking/Savings	4,697.00	9,554.00	-50.8%
Accounts Receivable			
Accounts Receivable	7,143.00	6,432.00	11.1%
Total Accounts Receivable	7,143.00	6,432.00	11.1%
Other Current Assets			
Inventory Asset	77,589.00	72,905.00	6.4%
Total Other Current Assets	77,589.00	72,905.00	6.4%
Total Current Assets	89,429.00	88,891.00	0.6%
Fixed Assets			
Accumulated Depreciation	-8,364.00	-4,182.00	-100.0%
Furniture and Equipment	16,543.00	16,543.00	0.0%
Total Fixed Assets	8,179.00	12,361.00	-33.8%
TOTAL ASSETS	97,608.00	101,252.00	-3.6%
LIABILITIES & EQUITY			
Liabilities			
Current Liabilities			
Accounts Payable			
Accounts Payable	68,946.00	51,243.00	34.6%

Figure 6.10
Notice that the periods—here, years—are shown with the most recent in the left column.

> **TIP** If you're going to get at least one financial statement from an accounting package, it's best to get all of them from that package, particularly if your intent is to analyze them further in Excel. If you get all the necessary statements from the same software and company file, you know that you're working with numbers that come from the same data set.

To get the comparative balance sheet in QuickBooks shown in Figure 6.10, take these steps:

1. Open a balance sheet from QuickBooks Report menu, using the Company & Financial submenu.
2. If necessary, select the effective date for the report from the As Of box.
3. Click Modify Report. Select the Previous Year check box and its subsidiary % Change check box.
4. Click OK.

Once exported to an Excel workbook, the comparative balance sheet looks like the one shown in Figure 6.11.

The formulas that QuickBooks uses to calculate period-to-period change are idiosyncratic. For example, here's the one used in cell J9 of Figure 6.11:

```
=ROUND(IF(F9=0, IF(H9=0, 0, SIGN(-H9)), IF(H9=0, SIGN(F9), (F9-H9)/H9)),5)
```

Figure 6.11
The exported statement largely reflects the appearance of the QuickBooks native report.

J6 =ROUND(IF(F6=0, IF(H6=0, 0, SIGN(-H6)), IF(H6=0, SIGN(F6), (F6-H6)/H6)),5)

	A–E	F	H	J
1				
2		Dec 31, 11	Dec 31, 10	% Change
3	ASSETS			
4	Current Assets			
5	Checking/Savings			
6	First National Bank	4,697.00	9,554.00	-50.84%
7	Total Checking/Savings	4,697.00	9,554.00	-50.84%
8	Accounts Receivable			
9	Accounts Receivable	7,143.00	6,432.00	11.05%
10	Total Accounts Receivable	7,143.00	6,432.00	11.05%
11	Other Current Assets			
12	Inventory Asset	77,589.00	72,905.00	6.43%
13	Total Other Current Assets	77,589.00	72,905.00	6.43%
14	Total Current Assets	89,429.00	88,891.00	0.61%
15	Fixed Assets			
16	Accumulated Depreciation	-8,364.00	-4,182.00	100.0%
17	Furniture and Equipment	16,543.00	16,543.00	0.0%
18	Total Fixed Assets	8,179.00	12,361.00	-33.83%
19	TOTAL ASSETS	97,608.00	101,252.00	-3.6%
20	LIABILITIES & EQUITY			
21	Liabilities			
22	Current Liabilities			
23	Accounts Payable			
24	Accounts Payable	68,946.00	51,243.00	34.55%

CAUTION

I'm not inclined to go into all the reasons that the formula just given is ill-conceived. (I will point out that as written, the formula treats an account that grows from $0 to *any* positive value as a 100% increase, which is, as noted, ill-conceived.)

With this in mind, you might simply replace the formula in cell J6 with this formula:

```
=(F6-H6)/H6
```

Copy and paste this formula into the report's remaining rows.

6

If the value in a divisor is `0`, you get a `#DIV/0!` error from Excel. You can then deal with the error value any way you wish, including just deleting the formula. That's a lot more sensible than redefining mathematics to make the result of dividing by zero equal to 100%.

Common-Sizing for Variance Analysis

In the context of finance and accounting, the term *variance analysis* means the examination of differences between one set of numbers and another. For example, if your company's actual total salaries during the first quarter differ from its budgeted first-quarter salaries, a variance exists between the budget and the actual results. (Don't confuse this usage with the variance analysis used in statistics, which has a very different purpose.)

Common-sizing can help you perform variance analysis more quickly and easily. Speed and facility in variance analysis are particularly important because companies often spend an enormous amount of time and effort examining the differences between their plans and their actual results and between prior and current results. Consider the following case study on travel agency New Way Tours.

CASE STUDY: NEW WAY TOURS

New Way Tours is a small business with three full-time and two part-time employees. It specializes in planning and arranging ski vacations; therefore, its business is highly seasonal, with the majority of its revenues occurring during the winter months.

New Way's owner, Gena Anderson, has prepared an operating budget for 2011, based on past information about revenues and operating expenses during the most recent five-year period (see Figure 6.12).

Figure 6.12 shows New Way's anticipated gross profit for each month in 2011, based on average monthly results from 2006 through 2010. The gross profit is the revenues minus the sales discounts and any purchases that its customers later cancel.

6

Figure 6.12
New Way Tours' operating budget for 2011.

	A	B	C	D	E	F	G	H	I	J	K	L	M
1		Jan	Feb	Mar	Apr	May	Jun	Jul	Aug	Sep	Oct	Nov	Dec
2	Gross profit	42589	53765	38846	15214	20512	21213	20674	12698	11854	12779	55155	52702
3	Salaries	20000	20000	20000	17500	17500	17500	17500	17500	17500	17500	20000	20000
4	Payroll taxes	5040	5040	5040	4410	4410	4410	4410	4410	4410	4410	5040	5040
5	Lease	1000	1000	1000	1000	1000	1000	1000	1000	1000	1000	1000	1000
6	Phone	500	500	500	500	500	500	500	500	500	500	500	500
7	Supplies	300	300	300	300	300	300	300	300	300	300	300	300
8	Insurance	500	500	500	500	500	500	500	500	500	500	500	500
9	Total OpEx	27340	27340	27340	24210	24210	24210	24210	24210	24210	24210	27340	27340
10	EBITDA	15249	26425	11506	-8996	-3698	-2997	-3536	-11512	-12356	-11431	27815	25362
11													
12	Gross profit	100%	100%	100%	100%	100%	100%	100%	100%	100%	100%	100%	100%
13	Salaries	47%	37%	51%	115%	85%	82%	85%	138%	148%	137%	36%	38%
14	Payroll taxes	12%	9%	13%	29%	21%	21%	21%	35%	37%	35%	9%	10%
15	Lease	2%	2%	3%	7%	5%	5%	5%	8%	8%	8%	2%	2%
16	Phone	1%	1%	1%	3%	2%	2%	2%	4%	4%	4%	1%	1%
17	Supplies	1%	1%	1%	2%	1%	1%	1%	2%	3%	2%	1%	1%
18	Insurance	1%	1%	1%	3%	2%	2%	2%	4%	4%	4%	1%	1%
19	Total OpEx	64%	51%	70%	159%	118%	114%	117%	191%	204%	189%	50%	52%
20	EBITDA	36%	49%	30%	-59%	-18%	-14%	-17%	-91%	-104%	-89%	50%	48%
21													

Operating Budget

TIP

Notice cells B1:M1 in Figure 6.12, which show the names of the months of the year in abbreviated form. Excel provides these names as a custom list; other predefined custom lists include months of the year (spelled out in full) and days of the week (abbreviated and spelled out). You can fill a range of cells with these values by typing, for example, `Jan` in one cell and then using AutoFill by dragging the cell's fill handle right or left, or up or down.

In Excel 2007 and 2010, you can define your own custom lists by clicking the File tab and selecting Excel Options. Click Advanced and scroll down to the General area, and then click the Edit Custom Lists button. In versions earlier than Excel 2007, choose Tools, Options and click the Custom Lists tab. This is a handy way to save a chart of accounts in the Excel application itself, not just in a particular workbook.

Figure 6.12 also shows the operating expenses, which are abbreviated as `OpEx` in cells A9 and A19, for each month. The major operating expense is Salaries, which is higher leading up to the winter months and varies with the number of hours worked by Anderson's two part-time employees. Payroll tax dollars vary with the monthly salaries. The cost of New Way's lease and insurance is expected to be constant throughout the year. Telephone expenses and office supplies are difficult to estimate on a monthly basis; however, they are small enough that making a constant monthly estimate is a reasonable approach.

Row 9 shows the total of the monthly operating expenses, and row 10 shows the anticipated Earnings Before Interest, Taxes, Depreciation, and Amortization (EBITDA)—the result of subtracting the operating expenses from the gross profit.

Rows 12 to 20 show the budget, common-sized by gross profit: Each entry in B12:M20 is the classification's percentage of that month's forecasted gross profit. Anderson can use this common-sized information in isolation. For example, New Way receives much of its revenue during the winter, and Anderson expects to lose money during the warmer months. In fact, from April through October, the total budgeted operating expenses are greater than 100% of gross profit. Anderson has decided that it is more important to keep three experienced employees year-round than to reduce the staff further during her business's slow months.

But it is the process of comparing the budgeted information with the actual results that helps to bring matters into focus (see Figure 6.13).

Figure 6.13 shows New Way Tours' actual financial results for the first two quarters of 2011. The planned, monthly EBITDA from Figure 6.12 is also shown, in row 11. January was a disastrous month. Besides a gross profit that is nearly $10,000 less than projected in the budget, Anderson has paid more than $7,500 more in salaries than budgeted, in a failed attempt to increase revenues for the month. February was better, but the subsequent four months continue the pattern that began in January.

Anderson can perform this variance analysis by checking the common-sized EBITDA values in rows 21 and 22 of Figure 6.13. For January through June, EBITDA as a percentage of gross profit is less than budgeted, and if business does not turn around during the second

Figure 6.13
New Way Tours' actual financial results for 2011 are much worse than its budget anticipated.

	A	B	C	D	E	F	G
1		Jan	Feb	Mar	Apr	May	Jun
2	Gross profit	32,845	46,208	21,710	12,607	18,938	18,268
3	Salaries	27,520	22,701	25,984	22,618	16,761	16,783
4	Payroll taxes	6,935	5,721	6,548	5,700	4,224	4,229
5	Lease	1,000	1,000	1,000	1,000	1,000	1,000
6	Phone	562	737	608	678	486	259
7	Supplies	142	263	132	299	106	158
8	Insurance	500	500	500	500	500	500
9	Total OpEx	36,659	30,922	34,772	30,795	23,077	22,929
10	EBITDA: Actual	-3,814	15,286	-13,062	-18,188	-4,139	-4,661
11	EBITDA: Plan	15,249	26,425	11,506	-8,996	-3,698	-2,997
12							
13	Gross profit	100%	100%	100%	100%	100%	100%
14	Salaries	84%	49%	120%	179%	89%	92%
15	Payroll taxes	21%	12%	30%	45%	22%	23%
16	Lease	3%	2%	5%	8%	5%	5%
17	Phone	2%	2%	3%	5%	3%	1%
18	Supplies	0%	1%	1%	2%	1%	1%
19	Insurance	2%	1%	2%	4%	3%	3%
20	Total OpEx	112%	67%	160%	244%	122%	126%
21	EBITDA: Actual	-12%	33%	-60%	-144%	-22%	-26%
22	EBITDA: Plan	46%	57%	53%	-71%	-20%	-16%

half of the year, New Way Tours will lose money for the year. Anderson will need to find a way to either increase gross profits or decrease her operating expenses. Another way to view the actual results for the first six months of 2011, in the context of the 2011 budget, is to subtract the budgeted gross profit dollars from the actual gross profit dollars; you can do the same for budgeted and actual operating expenses. Anderson can also calculate the ratio of the actual-to-budgeted figures. This analysis appears in Figure 6.14, which shows the differences between the planned figures and the year-to-date actual results for 2011.

Figure 6.14
Variances between budgets and actual results, expressed both in dollar amounts and as ratios, often help point to problems in a company's operations.

	A	B	C	D	E	F	G
1		Jan	Feb	Mar	Apr	May	Jun
2	Gross profit	-9,744	-7,557	-17,136	-2,607	-1,574	-2,945
3	Salaries	7,520	2,701	5,984	5,118	-739	-717
4	Payroll taxes	1,895	681	1,508	1,290	-186	-181
5	Lease	0	0	0	0	0	0
6	Phone	62	237	108	178	-14	-241
7	Supplies	-158	-37	-168	-1	-194	-142
8	Insurance	0	0	0	0	0	0
9	Total OpEx	9,319	3,582	7,432	6,585	-1,133	-1,281
10	EBITDA	-19,063	-11,139	-24,568	-9,192	-441	-1,664
11							
12	Gross profit	77%	86%	56%	83%	92%	86%
13	Salaries	138%	114%	130%	129%	96%	96%
14	Payroll taxes	138%	114%	130%	129%	96%	96%
15	Lease	100%	100%	100%	100%	100%	100%
16	Phone	112%	147%	122%	136%	97%	52%
17	Supplies	47%	88%	44%	100%	35%	53%
18	Insurance	100%	100%	100%	100%	100%	100%
19	Total OpEx	134%	113%	127%	127%	95%	95%
20	EBITDA	-25%	58%	-114%	202%	112%	156%

Notice that, for each month, the planned versus actual dollar differences for gross profit are negative, and for operating expenses, they are generally positive. (The formulas subtract the budgeted figures from the actual figures.) These dollar differences help Anderson understand how much money is being lost. The ratios, which are actuals divided by budgeted figures, put the losses into a percentage context. For example, the actual gross profit during January is 77% of the budgeted figure, and the actual salaries paid for January are 138% of the budgeted amount.

Ratio to Ratio Comparisons

These variance analyses, useful as they are, do not present the full picture. For example, because the gross profit varies from month to month, Anderson cannot directly compare the actual-to-budget ratios for January with the actual-to-budget ratios for February: The basis differs across months. One way to make direct comparisons is to take ratios of the ratios (see Figure 6.15).

Figure 6.15
New Way Tours' variance ratios for the first half of 2011 create the percentages on a common basis.

B2 =' Variance, Actual vs. Plan'!B13/'Operating Budget'!B12

	A	B	C	D	E	F	G
1		Jan	Feb	Mar	Apr	May	Jun
2	Gross profit	100%	100%	100%	100%	100%	100%
3							
4	Salaries	178%	132%	232%	156%	104%	111%
5	Payroll taxes	178%	132%	232%	156%	104%	111%
6	Lease	130%	116%	179%	121%	108%	116%
7	Phone	146%	172%	218%	164%	105%	60%
8	Supplies	61%	102%	79%	120%	38%	61%
9	Insurance	130%	116%	179%	121%	108%	116%
10							
11	Total OpEx	174%	132%	228%	154%	103%	110%
12							
13	EBITDA	130%	116%	179%	121%	108%	116%

The formula for the value of 178% in cell B4 of Figure 6.15 is as follows:

```
='Variance, Actual vs. Plan'!B14/'Operating Budget'!B13
```

NOTE

Notice in the preceding formula that the cell references B14 and B13 are preceded by the names of the sheets that contain those cells.

Under some conditions, Excel encloses the sheet name in single quotes when it is used in a reference or in a defined name. These conditions include the presence of at least one space in the sheet name, one of the special characters such as % that is allowed in the sheet names, and when the sheet names begin with a numeral.

In the preceding formula, both sheet names contain spaces, so Excel inserts the single quotation marks around each in the formula.

The numerator of this ratio is the percentage of January's actual gross profit accounted for by January's actual salaries paid. The denominator is the percentage of January's budgeted gross profit accounted for by January's budgeted salaries. Therefore, for the month of January, the actual salary expense ratio was 78% greater than the budgeted salary expense ratio.

This analysis places the variance for expenses into the context of the shifting gross profit figures, which are equalized by taking the ratio of the ratios. Notice that the ratio of the actual gross profit percentage to the budgeted gross profit percentage is, in each month, 100%. Thus, Anderson can tell that, regardless of the actual monthly gross profit, her firm's actual expense levels are running well ahead of its budgeted expense levels.

The case study on New Way Tours discussed one basic kind of variance analysis: actuals to budget. This sort of analysis is the one performed most frequently, but other useful types of variance analysis exist.

For example, you might analyze the differences between your year-to-date actuals and your current estimate. A *current estimate* is a type of budget. During the year, you revise and update your budget for the current year to take into account changes in the assumptions that you used to build your initial budget. It's useful, then, to do variance analysis on the year-to-date actuals with the current estimate.

It's also helpful to do variance analysis on year-to-date actuals with the actuals from the prior year. Yet another form of variance analysis involves a different sort of common-sizing: expressing a statement's data in terms of headcount.

Common-Sizing by Headcount

Headcount refers to the number of people who are on the payroll at any given time. Particularly if you are in the midst of a downsizing (or, euphemistically, "rightsizing") situation, it's useful to common-size on the basis of headcount. Doing so does not result in the type of information shown by earlier figures in this chapter, in which the result was a percentage of revenue or assets. Common-sizing on the basis of headcount usually results in some number of dollars per employee (see Figure 6.16).

Figure 6.16
New Way Tours' actual results for 2011, common-sized by headcount, express operating expenses as dollars spent per employee.

B14 =GrossProfit/Headcount

	A	B	C	D	E	F	G
1		Jan	Feb	Mar	Apr	May	Jun
2	Headcount	5	5	5	5	3	3
3	Gross profit	32,845	46,208	21,710	12,607	18,938	18,268
4	Salaries	27,520	22,701	25,984	22,618	16,761	16,783
5	Payroll taxes	6,935	5,721	6,548	5,700	4,224	4,229
6	Lease	1,000	1,000	1,000	1,000	1,000	1,000
7	Phone	562	737	608	678	486	259
8	Supplies	142	263	132	299	106	158
9	Insurance	500	500	500	500	500	500
10	Total OpEx	36,659	30,922	34,772	30,795	23,077	22,929
11	EBITDA: Actual	-3,814	15,286	-13,062	-18,188	-4,139	-4,661
12	EBITDA: Plan	15,249	26,425	11,506	-8,996	-3,698	-2,997
13							
14	Gross profit	6,569	9,242	4,342	2,521	6,313	6,089
15	Salaries	5,504	4,540	5,197	4,524	5,587	5,594
16	Payroll taxes	1,387	1,144	1,310	1,140	1,408	1,410
17	Lease	200	200	200	200	333	333
18	Phone	112	147	122	136	162	86
19	Supplies	28	53	26	60	35	53
20	Insurance	100	100	100	100	167	167
21	Total OpEx	7,332	6,184	6,954	6,159	7,692	7,643
22	EBITDA: Actual	-763	3,057	-2,612	-3,638	-1,380	-1,554
23	EBITDA: Plan	3,050	5,285	2,301	-1,799	-1,233	-999
24							

Headcount Analysis

Rows 14 to 23 of Figure 6.16 show the actual results for January through June, found in rows 3 to 12, divided by the number of employees on payroll for each month (headcount, as shown in row 2). This range shows that the fixed expenses, such as those for the office lease and insurance, vary on a per-employee basis as the headcount changes. Other expenses, particularly salaries and payroll taxes, remain fairly stable as headcount changes.

If gross profit and an operating income figure, such as EBITDA, are *not* sensitive to headcount, but such major-expense classifications as salaries *are* sensitive, there can be a compelling business reason to reduce the number of employees. For example, if New Way Tours can expect roughly the same level of revenue, regardless of its headcount, Anderson should give serious thought to reducing the number of employees.

Keep in mind that taking this action can have unintended consequences. For example, it might be that even though increasing headcount doesn't increase gross profit, decreasing headcount below some minimum level will result in poor customer service. Sooner or later, this is guaranteed to reduce gross profit.

On the other hand, if headcount is directly related to gross profit, there might be an argument for increasing headcount, particularly if the business uses some method of direct sales. The trick is to increase the number of productive salespeople and hold steady the number of staff who contribute only to expenses, not to gross profit. This process is tricky because, in most cases, the greater the gross profit, the larger the number of staff required to support after-sale processes.

However, suppose that Anderson believes she can convert the responsibilities of three of her current full-time staff from both sales and staff functions to sales only. She also considers hiring one additional salesperson. She believes that if these employees are free to perform a sales role only instead of both revenue-producing activities and support activities, each salesperson can generate an average of $13,138 in gross profit per month (for a total of $52,552 for January through April) instead of January's figure of $6,569. The remaining employees will devote 100% of their time to performing support activities. Figure 6.17 shows this projection.

Anderson obtains the dollar figures for Gross Profit, in row 4 of Figure 6.17, by multiplying the Sales headcount in row 3 by her assumed gross profit level of $13,138 per salesperson. She also assumes that her average salary per employee will be $5,450. Restated, these assumptions are as follows:

6

- Both total gross profit and average gross profit are sensitive to the number of sales employees.
- Total salary expense is sensitive to the total number of employees, but average salary expense is constant.

The result, if Anderson's assumptions pay off, is that she can actually *increase* total headcount and cause New Way Tours' EBITDA to turn positive, even during its traditionally money-losing summer months. The assumptions involved are optimistic—particularly the

Figure 6.17
New Way Tours' 2011 projections, common-sized by new headcount.

B5 fx =5450*(B2+B3)

	A	B	C	D	E	F	G
1		Jan	Feb	Mar	Apr	May	Jun
2	Headcount (staff)	2	2	2	2	1	1
3	Headcount (sales)	4	4	4	4	3	3
4	Gross profit	52,552	52,552	52,552	52,552	39,414	39,414
5	Salaries	32,700	32,700	32,700	32,700	21,800	21,800
6	Payroll taxes	8,240	8,240	8,240	8,240	5,494	5,494
7	Lease	1,000	1,000	1,000	1,000	1,000	1,000
8	Phone	562	737	608	678	486	259
9	Supplies	142	263	132	299	106	158
10	Insurance	500	500	500	500	500	500
11	Total OpEx	43,144	43,440	43,180	43,417	29,386	29,211
12	EBITDA: Projected	9,408	9,112	9,372	9,135	10,028	10,203
13	EBITDA: Budget	15,249	26,425	11,506	-8,996	-3,698	-2,997
14							
15	Gross profit	8,759	8,759	8,759	8,759	9,854	9,854
16	Salaries	5,450	5,450	5,450	5,450	5,450	5,450
17	Payroll taxes	1,373	1,373	1,373	1,373	1,373	1,373
18	Lease	167	167	167	167	250	250
19	Phone	94	123	101	113	122	65
20	Supplies	24	44	22	50	27	40
21	Insurance	83	83	83	83	125	125
22	Total OpEx	7,191	7,240	7,197	7,236	7,346	7,303
23	EBITDA: Projected	1,568	1,519	1,562	1,522	2,507	2,551
24	EBITDA: Budget	2,542	4,404	1,918	-1,499	-925	-749

notion that making some employees full-time salespeople will double the per-employee gross profit. However, even if the per-employee increase in gross profit were only 50%, the results would increase the profit in good months and reduce the loss in bad months.

NOTE

This type of headcount analysis is closely related to the concept of *leverage*, which is discussed in greater detail in Chapter 14, "Planning Profits." The common ground between leverage and common-sizing on the basis of headcount is that you seek to keep certain costs constant as variable revenues increase.

In large corporations, common-size analysis on the basis of headcount is done frequently and is especially tricky. Often one division reduces its headcount to decrease its expenses, hoping that revenues will not suffer. It can also happen that the employees who leave that division find employment in another division of the same corporation: usually, one that is not currently under pressure to reduce its expenses.

The net result is that, although one division might improve its profitability through a reduction in expenses, another division's profitability suffers because of an increase in expenses. Then the corporation, as a whole, has probably not improved its profitability. However, it has managed to disrupt people's lives and probably increase costs, such as those for training, that do not directly produce revenue.

Therefore, when divisions report that they have reduced headcount and, consequently, increased their profitability, they also need to estimate the effect on the corporation as a whole.

Summary

In this chapter, you saw some of the basic techniques of statement analysis, including variance analysis and common-sizing, according to bases such as revenues, total assets, and headcount.

These techniques are global—that is, the results can direct your attention to obstacles to your company's profitability, but they do not provide you as much specific information as you might want. Chapter 7 discusses the particular ratios that you often calculate to obtain highly targeted information about your company's profitability and overall financial condition.

Ratio Analysis

7

In previous chapters, you read about different indicators of a company's financial condition. Values such as current assets, inventory levels, sales, and accounts receivable help you understand how much money a company has, how much it owes, and how profitable it is.

These numbers can be useful if you know the company fairly well. For example, assume that you work for a company that has $2 million worth of materials in its finished goods inventory. You probably know whether that's an acceptable figure, whether it's so low that the company will have difficulty delivering the products that it sells, or whether it is so high that the company might need to slow its production rate. Because you are familiar with the company, its operations, and its distribution channels, you have a context to help interpret that $2 million figure.

But if you aren't familiar with the company, $2 million is just a number: It has no context to help you interpret it. Knowing that the company has $2 million worth of finished goods in stock tells you nothing about whether the company is doing well, doing poorly, or functioning as usual.

However, if you also happen to know the amount of the company's current assets and current liabilities, you could quickly create a useful insight into the company's current financial situation. The following formula, called the *quick ratio*, would tell you how liquid the company is in the short term:

IN THIS CHAPTER

```
(Current Assets - Inventory)/(Current Liabilities)
```

If the company's current assets are $4 million and its current liabilities are $1 million, the formula would return the following:

```
($4 million - $2 million)/($1 million) = 2
```

The company's quick ratio is 2.0. This means the company's quickly accessible assets are twice the value of its short-term liabilities and the company is liquid.

> **NOTE** Although inventory is part of current assets, it can take longer to convert inventory to cash than to other current assets. Therefore, this formula subtracts the value of inventory to quantify quickly accessible assets. See this chapter's section on the quick ratio for more information.

But if the company's current assets are $2.5 million, the formula would return the following:

```
($2.5 million - $2 million)/($1 million) = 0.5
```

The company's quickly accessible assets are only half its short-term liabilities. If the company needed to cover its liabilities in a hurry, it wouldn't be able to do so.

As a prospective investor, you would probably have a different attitude toward the company depending on whether the quick ratio were 2.0 or 0.5. If the value were 2.0, you would be more confident that your investment would produce a return. As a prospective stockholder, you would be more confident of receiving a dividend check if the value were 2.0. As the company's CEO, you would have a meeting with the production and sales managers if the value were 0.5, and the meeting would probably be a testy one.

The value of the quick ratio does not depend solely on how well the company is managing its assets and liabilities. The ratio's value also depends on other issues, such as how well the company's business sector is doing in the present economy. And companies in growth industries often have smaller quick ratios than companies in mature industries. Too much cash on hand can mean that the company isn't using its assets effectively.

Your evaluation of the quick ratio would take these issues into account. You would also want to know how that ratio has behaved in the past: If the ratio has been consistently increasing, your confidence in the company's management and its financial structure might be greater than if it has been sliding for some time.

Ratios such as the quick ratio can help depict a company's financial status, and relationships among ratios can help you locate sources of concern in the way a company is run.

This chapter describes some of the most important ratios, such as those that are frequently published in financial reports and in commercially available data sources. This chapter also helps you interpret them to determine a company's profit outlook.

Interpreting Industry Averages and Trends

You can learn a good deal by evaluating a ratio that describes a particular company in terms of the industry average on that ratio. But that can also be misleading. Consider one commonly reported indicator, the price/earnings (P/E) ratio (equivalently, the E/P ratio).

Suppose you know, from examining stock exchange tables in the newspaper, online, or from some other source, that the P/E is 10 for a communications firm in which you have some interest. This means that stock in the company presently sells for 10 times its earnings per share. Perhaps you also know from information obtained from a commercial service that the average P/E for the telecommunications industry is 15. At first glance, 10 looks like a good P/E, compared to the industry average: Holding earnings constant, it is only two-thirds as expensive as other such stocks.

And 10 might be a good P/E ratio. However, this comparison can mislead you in various ways, as the next section illustrates.

Comparing Ratios Within Industries

During the 1980s and 1990s, the telecommunications industry changed quickly and dramatically. Companies that once provided little more than basic telephone service aggressively entered new fields such as data communications, wireless communications, cable TV, financial and other business services, and electronic advertising.

These firms also entered into partnerships with companies such as software developers and firms that provide the programming that you see on television, in theaters, and on your cell phone. For a time, e-business, in general, and dot-coms, in particular, spread faster than bad news.

Some of these efforts bore fruit in the form of higher earnings, and some resulted in drastic losses for the firms involved. It might be that the communications firm with a P/E of 10 has refrained from investing in newer opportunities. Therefore, a larger portion of its revenues is available in the form of earnings than is the case with a telephone company that has aggressively invested in alternatives to its historic revenue base. Higher earnings tend to lower the P/E ratio.

The fact that a firm has a P/E that is lower than its industry average is not clear evidence that it is better managed than the other companies in that industry group. In fact, to continue the present example, you might find that this company is managed ineptly if other communications firms do very well with their investment and partnering strategies. It's also possible that other investors have more and better information than you do, and this information caused them to push the price down.

The point is that industry groups are gross classifications. Just because a company is categorized in the "telecommunications industry" does not mean that its business strategies, product mix, and investments align with those of other companies in its category. (An infamous market research study from the mid-1980s classified the motion picture industry as "information services.") Before you put much faith in the comparison of a financial ratio such as P/E with its industry average, you should be sure that the company's management and operations are, in fact, similar to those of other firms in its classification.

But even if you are confident that you are making a sensible comparison, the question of accounting procedures arises. As discussed in Chapter 1, "Working with Income

Statements," there are ground rules that all companies are required to follow in computing their revenues, costs, expenses, earnings, and so on. Sometimes companies play fast and loose with those rules. Even in the vast majority of cases in which companies act scrupulously, the rules leave room for choice and operate differently in different situations.

For example, Chapter 5, "Working Capital and Cash Flow Analysis," briefly discussed the effect that depreciation has on net income: You subtract depreciation, along with other expenses, from your gross profit to arrive at a net income figure. As you will see in Chapter 16, "Fixed Assets," there are a variety of ways to compute depreciation, and these different methods usually return different figures. Different ways of figuring depreciation expense therefore result in different estimates of earnings. (On the other hand, companies in a particular industry group tend to use the same depreciation procedures even when variation is permitted.)

You also saw in Chapter 3, "Valuing Inventories for the Balance Sheet," that there are different ways of valuing inventories. The cost of goods sold (COGS) is subtracted from sales to arrive at a figure for gross profit. COGS is often determined by this formula:

```
Cost of Goods Sold = Beginning Inventory + Inventory Purchases - Ending
  Inventory
```

So the method a firm uses to value its inventory affects its COGS, its gross profit, and, therefore, the determination of its earnings.

In short, a financial ratio might not be commensurate among companies that are in the same line of business because legitimate differences in accounting methods can cause different values for the same ratio.

Analyzing Ratios Vertically and Horizontally

Comparing one company's ratio with that of an entire business sector is often termed *vertical analysis*. Another approach, called *horizontal analysis*, tracks financial ratios over time. Access to several years' worth of information on, for example, the P/E reported by a given company enables you to determine whether its P/E has been increasing, decreasing, or remaining stable.

Evaluating Horizontal Analysis

Horizontal analysis minimizes some of the problems associated with vertical analysis that are discussed in the prior section. When you focus on the changes to a ratio reported by one company over time, you have less reason to be concerned about the effect of different accounting methods on the comparisons. Although a company might alter some of its methods from time to time, it is required to report any material changes in those methods. Therefore, it's easier to tell whether a substantial change in a financial ratio from one year to the next has been caused by a modification in accounting methods or by a change in the way a company does business.

The major weakness of a strictly horizontal analysis is that it provides no information about a *standard* for a given ratio. Suppose you know that a retailer's inventory turns ratio has increased steadily from 8 turns per year to 10 per year over a five-year period. On its face, this is a cheery finding that indicates the company has been moving goods through its retail outlets faster over time. But if other, similar retailers average 15 turns per year, then although this company is improving, it might not yet be managing its inventory as well as it should. A strictly horizontal analysis would not give you this information.

Neither a vertical nor a horizontal analysis of financial ratios is good enough by itself. Doing both types of analysis can be better than doing just one and is certainly better than doing neither, but you can still be misled. It's best not to think of financial ratios as absolute, objective measures of a company's performance, but as clues: pointers to questions that you would want to ask about a company's financial structure and business strategies.

To return to an earlier example, suppose that a company reports a quick ratio of 0.8. It might not make much difference whether the ratio has been steadily improving from 0.1 over a period of time or that other, directly comparable companies report quick ratios that average 0.5. What does matter is that the company has greater current liabilities than it does current assets minus inventory. Knowing this puts you in a position to ask *why* that situation exists. The answers to that question might position you to take corrective action as a manager or to make a more informed decision as a creditor or investor.

Depending on Reported Figures

As you've seen in recent years, some decision makers are capable of arranging the misstatement of earnings and costs and of hiding debts and assets where auditors have difficulty finding them—sometimes even with the auditors' complicity. But as you have also seen, structures such as special-purpose entities, the so-called Raptors that Enron executives used to stash losses and debt off the balance sheet, can't stand forever.

Nor can the credit default swaps. (Credit default swaps are contracts that act something like insurance if the insured instrument, often a bond, defaults on its obligations.) Their sellers did not maintain sufficient reserves—which would have been required under standard insurance regulations and procedures—and their holders, such as AIG and Lehman Brothers, in consequence suffered liquidity crises.

An analysis of Enron's quick ratio did not prevent the collapse of the seventh-largest company in the United States or an old and admired accounting firm such as Arthur Andersen. It also did not prevent AIG from posting a $62 billion quarterly loss. But the self-styled "smartest guys in the room" can't keep a house of cards up forever. As the whistleblower testified, "Accounting just doesn't get that creative." Eventually, the numbers tell the story. Something somewhere is so out of whack that it shows up in the usual indicators such as the ratios discussed in this chapter. And then you might start thinking about them as the smartest guys in the cell.

Getting a Basis for Ratios

The remainder of this chapter discusses specific financial ratios, both their calculations and what questions a ratio's value might prompt you to ask. By way of example, Figures 7.1 and 7.2 show

Figure 7.1
This income statement for Orinoco Books contains defined names, such as Sales and Net_Income, used to compute financial ratios.

Net_Income | =Pretax_Income-Taxes

	A–C	D	E	F	G	H
1	Orinoco Books			Income Statement		
2	Sales	Q1	Q2	Q3	Q4	Total 2010
3	Sales	$2,652,077	$1,860,290	$1,498,534	$3,134,388	$9,145,289
4	Cost of sales	$1,432,744	$978,673	$1,107,254	$3,103,300	$6,621,971
5						
6	Gross profit	$1,219,333	$881,617	$391,280	$31,088	$2,523,318
7	Expenses					
8	Operating expenses	$756,796	$533,991	$496,472	$432,676	$2,219,935
9	Interest	$18,232	$17,112	$19,227	$19,211	$73,781
10	Depreciation	$32,500	$33,958	$33,958	$33,958	$134,374
11	Amortization	$1,500	$1,500	$1,500	$1,500	$6,000
12	Total expenses	$809,028	$586,561	$551,157	$487,345	$2,434,090
13	Operating income	$410,305	$295,056	($159,877)	($456,257)	$89,228
14	Other income and expenses					
15	Sale of assets	$87,500	$15,000	$2,000	$398,600	$503,100
16	Other	$15,000	$65,000	$98,000	$202,000	$380,000
17	Subtotal	$102,500	$80,000	$100,000	$600,600	$883,100
18	Pretax income	$512,805	$375,056	($59,877)	$144,343	$972,328
19	Taxes @ 30%	$153,842	$112,517	($17,963)	$43,303	$291,698
20	Net income	$358,964	$262,539	($41,914)	$101,040	$680,630

Income Statement

Figure 7.2
The continuation of the income statement data for Orinoco Books breaks out categories such as Interest, which is used to calculate the times interest earned ratio.

End_Retained_Earnings | =ROUND(Net_Income+Start_Retained_Earnings-Dividends,0)

	A–C	D	E	F	G	H
20	Net income	$358,964	$262,539	($41,914)	$101,040	$680,630
21						
22	Retained earnings-start of period	$1,400,000	$1,758,964	$2,021,503	$1,979,589	$2,030,629
23						
24	Dividends paid	$0	$0	$0	$50,000	$50,000
25						
26	Retained earnings-end of period	$1,758,964	$2,021,503	$1,979,589	$2,030,629	$2,661,259
27						
28	Supporting Information					
29		Q1	Q2	Q3	Q4	Total 2010
30	Cost of sales					
31	Labor	$447,484	$289,067	$228,637	$528,479	$1,493,667
32	Materials	$745,835	$544,763	$723,374	$867,984	$2,881,956
33	Other costs	$239,425	$144,843	$155,243	$1,706,837	$2,246,348
34						
35	Depreciation					
36	Buildings (30 year)	$12,500	$12,083	$12,083	$12,083	$48,749
37	Equipment (10 year)	$20,000	$21,875	$21,875	$21,875	$85,625
38						
39	Interest					
40	Long-Term @ 10.00%	$1,875	$1,875	$1,875	$1,875	$7,500
41	Short-Term @ 10.00%	$16,357	$15,237	$17,352	$17,336	$66,281

Income Statement

Figure 7.3
The figures in the Assets section of the balance sheet are important for determining profitability ratios.

Current_Assets | =Cash+Accounts_Receivable+Inventory+Other_Current_Assets

	A–B	C	D	E	F	G
1	Orinoco Books			Balance Sheet		
2	Current Assets	2009	Q1 2010	Q2 2010	Q3 2010	Q4 2010
3	Cash and cash equivalents	$502,081	$32,089	$292,901	$406,715	($276,911)
4	Accounts receivable	$401,075	$657,581	$493,151	$427,397	$660,855
5	Inventory	$451,109	$630,411	$590,959	$575,178	$1,186,002
6	Other current assets	$61,047	$60,000	$45,090	$76,320	$50,000
7	Total Current Assets	$1,415,311	$1,380,081	$1,422,101	$1,485,610	$1,619,946
8	Fixed Assets					
9	Land	$100,000	$112,500	$125,000	$137,500	$150,000
10	Buildings	$1,500,000	$1,450,000	$1,450,000	$1,450,000	$1,450,000
11	Equipment	$800,000	$875,000	$875,000	$875,000	$875,000
12	Subtotal	$2,400,000	$2,437,500	$2,450,000	$2,462,500	$2,475,000
13	Less cumulative depreciation	$400,000	$432,500	$466,458	$500,416	$534,374
14	Total Fixed Assets	$2,000,000	$2,005,000	$1,983,542	$1,962,084	$1,940,626
15	Other and Intangible Assets					
16	Other assets	$25,000	$33,000	$120,000	$5,000	$23,000
17	Trademark	$50,000	$50,000	$50,000	$50,000	$50,000
18	Less cumulative amortization	$20,000	$21,500	$23,000	$24,500	$26,000
19	Total Assets	$3,470,311	$3,446,581	$3,552,643	$3,478,194	$3,607,572

Balance Sheet

Figure 7.4
The figures in the Liabilities and Stockholders' Equity section of the balance sheet are used to compute liquidity ratios.

Stockholders_Equity | =Capital_Stock+Paidin_Capital+Retained_Earnings

	A	B	C	D	E	F	G
19	Total Assets		$3,470,311	$3,446,581	$3,552,643	$3,478,194	$3,607,572
20							
21							
22	LIABILITIES AND STOCKHOLDERS' EQUITY						
23	Current Liabilities		2009	Q1 2010	Q2 2010	Q3 2010	Q4 2010
24		Accounts payable	$575,000	$300,345	$310,294	$326,551	$315,626
25		Notes payable	$125,000	$75,000	$75,000	$75,000	$75,000
26		Current portion of long-term debt	$100,000	$100,000	$100,000	$100,000	$100,000
27		Income taxes	$26,495	$116,178	$82,030	($53,183)	$11,860
28		Accrued expenses	$86,880	$88,474	$103,964	$91,991	$114,382
29		Other current liabilities	$16,772	$13,852	$11,457	$12,896	$13,128
30		Total Current Liabilities	$930,147	$693,849	$682,745	$553,255	$629,996
31	Non-Current Liabilities						
32		Long-term debt	$747,296	$554,267	$509,473	$594,062	$593,443
33		Deferred income	$132,704	$134,612	$117,076	$111,867	$117,690
34		Deferred income taxes	$37,101	$37,664	$30,487	$35,220	$31,443
35		Other long-term liabilities	$73,063	$117,225	$41,359	$54,201	$54,371
36		Total Liabilities	$1,920,311	$1,537,617	$1,381,140	$1,348,605	$1,426,943
37	Stockholders' Equity						
38		Capital stock issued	$100,000	$100,000	$100,000	$100,000	$100,000
39		Additional paid in capital	$50,000	$50,000	$50,000	$50,000	$50,000
40		Retained earnings	$1,400,000	$1,758,964	$2,021,503	$1,979,589	$2,030,629
41		Total Equity	$1,550,000	$1,908,964	$2,171,503	$2,129,589	$2,180,629
42		Total Liabilities and Equity	$3,470,311	$3,446,581	$3,552,643	$3,478,194	$3,607,572

Balance Sheet

an income statement for a book publisher, Orinoco Books. Figures 7.3 and 7.4 show the company's balance sheet.

The data shown in Figures 7.1 to 7.4 is used to compute each of the ratios discussed in the next several sections.

This chapter discusses the 12 important financial ratios listed in Table 7.1. These ratios are usually thought of as belonging to four basic categories: profitability ratios, liquidity ratios, activity ratios, and leverage ratios.

Table 7.1 Ratios That Provide Insights into a Company's Finances and Management Practices

Category	Ratio
Profitability ratios	Earnings per share
	Gross profit margin
	Net profit margin
	Return on assets
	Return on equity
Liquidity ratios	Current ratio
	Quick ratio
Activity ratios	Average collection period
	Inventory turnover
Leverage ratios	Debt ratio
	Equity ratio
	Times interest earned

Analyzing Profitability Ratios

If you are thinking of investing money in a company, you should analyze its profitability. If the company intends to pay dividends to its stockholders, those dividends must come out of its profits. If the company wants to increase its worth in the marketplace by improving its product line, it needs capital to fund the improvements. The company's profits are an important source of capital.

A company has plenty of uses for its profits beyond dividends and product development. A prospective investor needs to look hard at a company's profit and loss reports to learn how the company's management is putting the funds to use. There are several different but related means of evaluating a company's profitability.

Finding and Evaluating Earnings Per Share

If you're investing for income, you might consider buying shares in a company to obtain a steady return in the form of regular dividend payments. If you're investing for growth, you might buy the stock to profit by owning it as the market value of its shares increases. Both of these objectives might be met by the same investment. In practice, however, they often are not. Companies frequently face a choice between distributing income in the form of dividends and retaining that income to invest in research, new products, and expanded operations. The hope is that retaining income to invest in the company will increase its earnings in the future, making the company more profitable and increasing the market value of its stock.

In either case, *earnings per share* (EPS) is an important measure of the company's income. Its basic formula is shown here:

```
EPS = (Income Available for Common Stock)/(Shares of Common Stock Outstanding)
```

EPS is usually a poor candidate for vertical analysis because different companies always have different numbers of shares of stock outstanding, and sometimes the differences are large. EPS *might* be a good candidate for horizontal analysis if you have access to information about the company's income and shares outstanding. With both these items, you can control for major fluctuations in shares outstanding that occur over time. This sort of control is important because it's not unusual for a company to purchase its own stock on the open market to reduce the number of outstanding shares. When this occurs, it increases the value of the EPS ratio, perhaps making the stock appear a more attractive investment.

Suppose that Orinoco Books has 1,000 shares outstanding. Figure 7.5 shows Orinoco's EPS at the end of each quarter in 2010.

Note that the EPS is in decline through the year, with one particularly bad third quarter. In this example, the number of shares outstanding is constant throughout the year, so the EPS changes are due solely to changes in net income. The major impact to net income is the very small value of gross profit during the fourth quarter (see cell G6 in Figure 7.1). In turn, that gross profit is due to the relatively large cost of sales during that quarter. The cost of sales is the sum of cells G31:G33, as shown in Figure 7.2.

	C	D	E	F	G
1		Q1	Q2	Q3	Q4
2					
3	Net Income	$358,964	$262,539	$(41,914)	$101,040
4	Shares of common stock outstanding	1,000	1,000	1,000	1,000
5	EPS	$ 359	$ 263	$ (42)	$ 101

Figure 7.5
EPS ratios during 2007 vary as net income drops.

Cell G33 in Figure 7.2 shows one very large "Other cost" of $1,706,837 during the fourth quarter. As a prospective shareholder, you want to know the reason for this cost, if it will be recouped in the future, and if it will repeat. Any extraordinarily large cost such as this will certainly impact the market value of the company's stock. It might interfere with the company's future ability to pay any dividends that you expect to receive.

Many companies issue at least two different kinds of stock: *common* and *preferred*. Preferred stock is issued under different conditions than common stock and is often callable at the company's discretion. It pays dividends at a different rate per share—usually a higher rate. Preferred stock might not carry voting privileges, and it often has priority on liquidated assets if the company goes out of business.

Calculating EPS for a company that has issued preferred stock complicates things, but just a little. Because the company pays dividends on preferred stock before any distribution to shareholders of common stock, you must first subtract these dividends from net income:

```
EPS = (Net Income - Preferred Dividends)/Shares of Common Stock Outstanding
```

Determining Gross Profit Margin

The gross profit margin is a basic ratio that measures, for a manufacturing firm, the value that the market places on the company's nonmanufacturing activities. For a firm that resells products, the ratio measures the value placed by the market on the activities that enhance those products.

Its formula is as follows:

```
Gross Profit Margin = (Sales - Cost of Goods Sold)/Sales
```

Figure 7.6 shows Orinoco Books' gross profit margin.

	A	D	E	F	G
1		Q1	Q2	Q3	Q4
2					
3	Sales	$2,652,077	$1,860,290	$1,498,534	$3,134,388
4	Cost of Sales	$1,432,744	$ 978,673	$1,107,254	$3,103,300
5	Gross Profit Margin	46%	47%	26%	1%

Figure 7.6
The fourth quarter's gross profit margin is low due to its large cost of sales.

7

The worksheets that contain Orinoco Books' income statement and balance sheet have several defined names (see Figures 7.1 to 7.4). The name `Sales` refers to the range D3:H3 on the income statement in Figure 7.1. The name `Cost_Of_Sales` refers to the range D4:H4, also shown on the income statement in Figure 7.1. In turn, `Cost_Of_Sales` is the sum of rows 31 to 33 in Figure 7.2. These rows, in columns D through H, contain the cost of labor, materials, and other costs (usually taken to mean factory overhead) involved in the production of goods for sale. In other words, in this example the `Cost_Of_Sales` is the COGS.

The formulas used to calculate the gross profit margins in Figure 7.6 are as follows. The sales values for the four quarters, shown in cells D3:G3, are obtained by selecting that range, typing the following formula, and then finishing with Ctrl+Enter:

```
=Sales
```

There are two points to consider about the formula just described that picks up the sales values from the income statement. One has to do with the mechanics of entering the formulas, using Ctrl+Enter. The second point concerns the importance of the columns in which you enter the formula.

Distinguishing Ctrl+Enter from Ctrl+Shift+Enter

When you select a range of cells and enter a formula (or even a static value) using Ctrl+Enter instead of just Enter, that formula is entered into each of the cells in the selected range. This may seem like an array formula, but it is not. A true array formula, entered with Ctrl+Shift+Enter, places just one formula in all the selected cells and treats the entire selection as one cell. The true array formula may display different values in the cells it occupies, but it's still one formula. (In fact, you cannot delete or otherwise change a cell that's occupied by an array formula: you have to change all its cells at once.)

Using Ctrl+Enter also places one formula in all the selected cells. However, in that case, Excel treats each cell as a separate, independent instance of the formula. For example, you can edit just one cell in the selection if you used Ctrl+Enter to enter the formula.

Implicit Intersections on Different Worksheets

The name `Sales` refers to D3:H3 in Figure 7.1. In Figure 7.6, the range that returns the sales figures occupies columns D through G. Note that column H on the income statement, which contains annual totals, is omitted because the focus here is on the quarterly results. This means that the formula takes advantage of the implicit intersection: Whatever is in column D in the named range is returned to column D in the formula's range. The same is true for columns E through G. If you entered the formula in a column not used by the defined name (that is, any column to the left of column D or to the right of column H), you would get the `"#VALUE!"` error.

This example shows that the use of the implicit intersection is not limited to the worksheet where the named range exists. However, if (as here) you use it on a different worksheet, the name must be scoped to the workbook, or you must qualify the named range with the name of the sheet that it's scoped to. In this example. `Sales` is a workbook-level name and so needs no qualifier. If it were a sheet-level name, and if its scope were the Income Statement worksheet, the formula would have to be as follows:

```
='Income Statement'!Sales
```

The same approach is used to get the Cost of Sales in cells D4:G4 of Figure 7.6. You select cell range D4:G4, enter the following formula in the formula bar, and then press Ctrl+Enter:

```
=Cost_Of_Sales
```

Finally, you obtain the gross profit margin in cells D5:G5 of Figure 7.6 by selecting that range, typing the following formula in the formula bar and then pressing Ctrl+Enter:

```
=(Sales-Cost_Of_Sales)/Sales
```

Impact of COGS on Gross Profit Margin

COGS is an important component of the gross profit margin. It is usually calculated as the sum of the cost of materials the company purchases, the labor involved in the manufacture of finished goods, and the associated overhead.

The gross profit margin depends heavily on the type of business in which a company is engaged. A service business such as a financial services institution or a laundry company typically has little or no COGS. A manufacturing, wholesaling, or retailing company typically has a large COGS and a gross profit margin that varies from 20% to 40%.

The gross profit margin measures the amount that customers are willing to pay for a company's product, over and above the company's cost for that product. As mentioned previously, this is the value that the company adds to the products it obtains from its suppliers. This margin can depend on the value of the company's name, for example, or the attractiveness of additional services, such as warranties, that the company provides. The gross profit margin also depends heavily on the ability of the sales force to persuade its customers of the value added by the company.

This added value is created by activities that cost money to undertake and that are paid for by the gross profit on sales. If customers don't place enough value on whatever the company adds to its products, there won't be enough gross profit to pay for the associated costs. Therefore, the calculation of the gross profit margin helps to highlight the effectiveness of the company's sales strategies and sales management.

Determining Net Profit Margin

The net profit margin narrows the focus on profitability and highlights not just the company's sales efforts but also its ability to keep operating costs down, relative to sales. This formula is generally used to determine the net profit margin:

```
Net Profit Margin = Earnings After Taxes / Sales
```

Figure 7.7 shows the calculation of Orinoco Books' net profit margin.

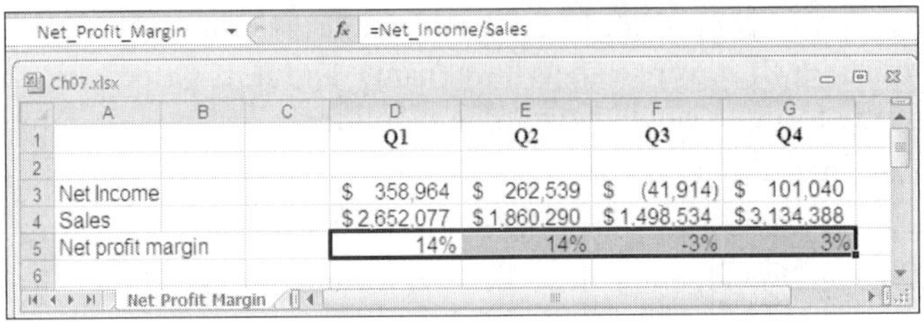

Net_Profit_Margin	fx =Net_Income/Sales			
	Q1	Q2	Q3	Q4
Net Income	$ 358,964	$ 262,539	$ (41,914)	$ 101,040
Sales	$ 2,652,077	$ 1,860,290	$ 1,498,534	$ 3,134,388
Net profit margin	14%	14%	-3%	3%

Figure 7.7 The net profit margin, in contrast to the gross profit margin, takes expenses into account.

The quarterly earnings after taxes is returned by this formula, again entered with Ctrl+Enter in the range D3:G3:

```
=Net_Income
```

The name `Net_Income` is defined as the range D20:H20 on Orinoco Books' income statement (refer to Figure 7.1). As in the gross profit margin calculation, the following figure returns sales figures in the range D4:G4:

```
=Sales
```

The following formula returns the net profit margin for each quarter in the range D5:G5:

```
=Net_Income/Sales
```

Why does the net profit margin decrease so much from the first to the fourth quarters? The principal culprit is, once again, the cost of sales. Notice that the materials expense is $745,835 in the first quarter, as shown in cell D32 of Figure 7.2. Sales decreased by 30% from the first to the second quarter, and by 20% from the second to the third quarter. Even so, the company's production operations consumed a relatively large amount of materials during the fourth quarter.

→ Chapter 6, "Statement Analysis," described the use of common-sized statements to make comparisons that are more informed. In the present example, common-sized quarterly statements would help identify Orinoco's problem areas.

Another place to look when you see a discrepancy between gross profit margin and net profit margin is operating expenses. When the two margins co-vary closely, it suggests that management is doing a good job of reducing operating expenses when sales fall and of increasing them, when necessary, to support production and sales in better times.

Determining the Return on Assets

One of management's most important responsibilities is to create a profit by effectively using its resources. The *return on assets* (ROA) ratio measures the effectiveness of resource usage. You can measure this ratio in several ways; one useful method is the following:

```
Return on Assets = (Gross Profit - Operating Expense) / Total Assets
```

This formula returns the percentage earnings for a company in terms of its total assets. The better the job management does in managing its assets—the resources available to it—to bring about profits, the greater this percentage will be.

Figure 7.8 shows the return on total assets for Orinoco Books.

Figure 7.8
The return on total assets is usually computed on an annualized basis.

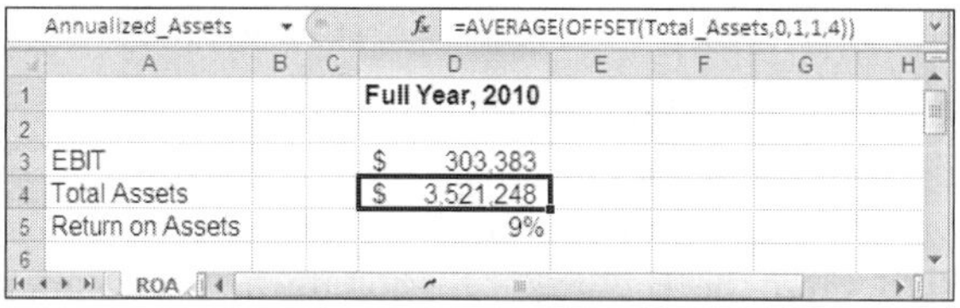

Annualized_Assets | =AVERAGE(OFFSET(Total_Assets,0,1,1,4))

	A	B	C	D	E	F	G	H
1				Full Year, 2010				
2								
3	EBIT			$ 303,383				
4	Total Assets			$ 3,521,248				
5	Return on Assets			9%				
6								

ROA

Earnings Before Interest and Taxes (EBIT) is shown in cell D3 of Figure 7.8. The following formula is used to obtain the figure:

```
=(Income_2010 Gross_Profit) - (Income_2010 Operating_Expenses)
```

This formula uses three range names: `Income_2010`, `Gross_Profit`, and `Operating_Expenses`:

- `Income_2010` refers to the annual total column in the income statement—specifically, the range H3:H26.
- `Gross_Profit` refers to D6:H6 on the income statement.
- `Operating_ Expenses` refers to D8:H8.

Refer to Figure 7.1 to view all three of these ranges.

The formula uses the *intersection operator*, a blank space, between `Income_2010` and `Gross_Profit` to specify the cell where these two ranges intersect; in Figure 7.1, that's cell H6. Similarly, it uses the intersection operator to specify the cell where `Income_2010` intersects `Operating_Expenses` (see cell H8 in Figure 7.1). The formula for EBIT then subtracts the annual operating expenses from the annual gross profit to return the value of `$303,383` shown in Figure 7.8.

NOTE

You could have typed fewer characters to get the same result:

```
='Income Statement'!H6 -'Income Statement'!H8
```

However, if you looked at that a few months later, you would not have any idea what you had in mind when you entered it. You would have to backtrack to the original cells, as well as their row and column labels, to determine what the formula is up to.

In contrast, as the formula is entered

```
=(Income_2010 Gross_Profit) - (Income_2010 Operating_Expenses)
```

you can immediately tell that it's intended to subtract 2010's operating expenses from 2010's gross profit.

It's normal to calculate the return on total assets on an annual basis instead of a quarterly basis. For this reason, the range named `Income_2010` is used to show the EBIT for the full year. The total assets portion of the formula—its denominator—is usually computed by taking an average of the company's total assets for the period in question.

The formula for total assets, cell D4 in Figure 7.8, is shown here:

```
=AVERAGE(OFFSET(Total_Assets,0,1,1,4))
```

Orinoco Books' balance sheet defines the range `Total_Assets` as referring to cells C19:G19 (refer to Figure 7.3). The first cell in this range, C19, contains the value of total assets for the prior year, 2009. Because this cell must be ignored when calculating the company's average quarterly total assets for the current year, 2010, Excel's `OFFSET` function is used.

This `OFFSET` specifies a range *within* `Total_Assets` (first argument) that is offset by 0 rows (second argument) and 1 column (third argument). In other words, the offset range is right-shifted from `Total_Assets` by one column, to ignore its first cell (C19). The function also specifies that the offset range is one row high (fourth argument) and four columns wide (fifth argument). Therefore, the `OFFSET` function, as used here, returns the range D19:G19.

Enclosing the `OFFSET` function and its arguments within the `AVERAGE` function returns the average of the values within the offset range, D19:G19.

Finally, the return on total assets in Figure 7.8 is calculated by this formula:

```
=D3/D4
```

In other words, this is EBIT divided by the average of the quarterly total assets.

Determining the Return on Equity

Another profitability measure related to ROA is *return on equity* (ROE), which measures management's effectiveness in maximizing the return to holders of common stock. The formula for ROE is as follows:

```
Return on Equity = (Net Income - Preferred Dividends) / (Average Common
  Stockholders' Equity)
```

Here, the average common stockholders' equity is the average of the equity at the end of the prior year and at the end of the current year.

Figure 7.9 displays Orinoco Books' ROE.

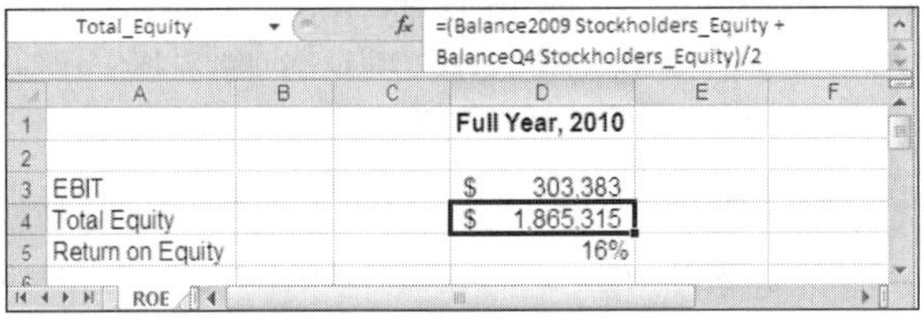

Figure 7.9
Compare ROE with ROA to infer how a company obtains the funds used to acquire assets.

Total_Equity | fx =(Balance2009 Stockholders_Equity + BalanceQ4 Stockholders_Equity)/2

	A	B	C	D	E	F
1				Full Year, 2010		
2						
3	EBIT			$ 303,383		
4	Total Equity			$ 1,865,315		
5	Return on Equity			16%		

ROE

The principal difference between the formula for ROA and for ROE is the use of equity instead of total assets in the denominator. The stockholders' equity figures are obtained by this formula:

```
=(Balance2009 Stockholders_Equity + BalanceQ4 Stockholders_Equity)/2
```

This formula uses intersection operators to return the values at the beginning and end of the period, as shown in cells C41 and G41 of the balance sheet in Figure 7.4. For example, the blank space in `Balance2009 Stockholders_Equity` specifies the cell where the range named `Balance2009` and the range named `Stockholders_Equity` intersect.

Here, the technique of comparing ratios again comes into play. By examining the difference between ROA and ROE, you can gain insight into how the company is funding its operations.

Assets are acquired through two major sources: creditors (through borrowing) and stockholders (through retained earnings and capital contributions). Together, the retained earnings and capital contributions determine the company's equity. When the value of the company's assets exceeds the value of its equity, you can expect that the difference is made up by some form of financial leverage, such as debt financing.

In the example used in this chapter, Orinoco Books' ROA is 9% and its ROE is 16%. Because the larger of the two ratios is ROE, you can determine that Orinoco Books is using debt financing. In addition, as the balance sheet in Figure 7.4 shows, at the end of 2010, Orinoco Books has $75,000 in Notes Payable and $693,443 in Long-Term Debt ($100,000 of which is current).

Analyzing Leverage Ratios

In the context of business analysis, the term *financial leverage* means the purchase of assets with borrowed money. For example, suppose that your company retails office supplies. When you receive an order for business cards, you pay one of your suppliers 50% of the revenue to print them for you. This amount is a variable cost: The more you sell, the greater your cost.

➜ See Chapter 14, "Planning Profits," to learn more about financial leveraging of assets.

But if you purchase the necessary printing equipment, you could make the business cards yourself. Doing this would turn a variable cost into a largely fixed cost: No matter how many cards you sell, the cost of printing them is fixed at however much you paid for the printing equipment (apart from consumables such as ink and paper stock). The more cards you sell, the greater your profit margin. This effect is termed *operating leverage*.

If you borrow money to acquire the printing equipment, you are using another type of leverage, termed *financial leverage*. The equipment cost is still fixed at the amount you must pay at regular intervals to retire the loan. Again, the more cards you sell, the greater your profit margin. However, if you do not sell enough cards to cover the loan payment, your firm will have less revenue to cover other costs of doing business. In that case, it might be difficult to find funds either to make the loan payments or to cover your other expenses. In addition, your credit rating might fall, making it more costly for you to borrow money in the future.

Leverage is a financial tool that accelerates changes in income, both positive and negative. A company's creditors and investors are interested in how much leverage has been used to acquire assets. From the standpoint of creditors, a high degree of leverage represents risk because the company might not be able to repay a loan. From the investors' standpoint, if the ROA, which was discussed earlier in the chapter, is less than the cost of borrowing money to acquire assets, the investment is unattractive. The investor could obtain a better return in different ways—one way would be to loan funds rather than invest them in the company.

The next sections discuss two ratios that help you measure leverage——the debt ratio and the equity ratio.

Determining the Debt Ratio

The debt ratio shows what percentage of assets has been acquired through borrowing. It is defined by this formula:

```
Debt Ratio = Total Debt / Total Assets
```

Figure 7.10 shows the debt ratio calculated for Orinoco Books.

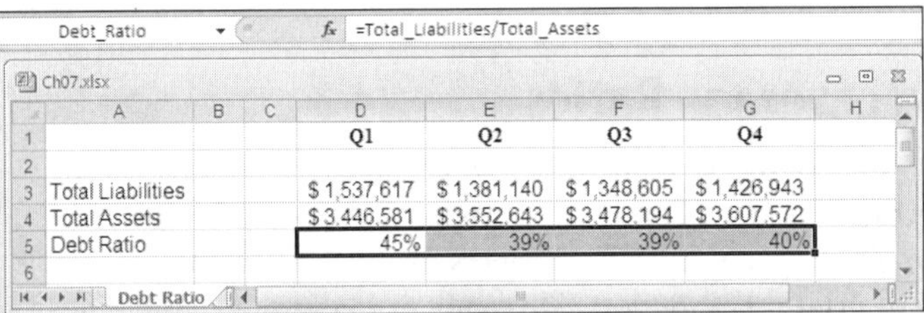

Debt_Ratio =Total_Liabilities/Total_Assets

Ch07.xlsx

	A	B	C	D	E	F	G	H
1				Q1	Q2	Q3	Q4	
2								
3	Total Liabilities			$ 1,537,617	$ 1,381,140	$ 1,348,605	$ 1,426,943	
4	Total Assets			$ 3,446,581	$ 3,552,643	$ 3,478,194	$ 3,607,572	
5	Debt Ratio			45%	39%	39%	40%	
6								

Debt Ratio

Figure 7.10
The debt ratio indicates the company's use of financial leverage.

The term *total debt*, in this context, is synonymous with the term *total liabilities*. The formula used in the range D3:G3 of Figure 7.10 to return the total debt is as follows:

```
=Total_Liabilities
```

The range D4:G4 in Figure 7.10 returns the company's total assets for each quarter in similar fashion, and the range D5:G5 simply divides the total debt by the total assets as shown in the formula bar.

In the "Determining the Return on Equity" section covered earlier in this chapter, the comparison of the ROA to the ROE suggested that Orinoco Books relies on debt financing. It might be a healthy sign, then, that the company's debt ratio has fallen during 2010. A multiyear analysis of return ratios might be useful. As the ROA decreases, the net income available to make payments on debt also decreases. If this has been happening, Orinoco Books should probably retire some of its short-term debt and the current portion of its long-term debt as soon as possible.

Determining the Equity Ratio

The *equity ratio* is the complement of the debt ratio. This is the portion of the company's assets financed by stockholders, shown in the following formula:

```
Equity Ratio = Stockholders_Equity / Total_Assets
```

In Figures 7.10 and 7.11, the equity ratio and debt ratio in each quarter total 100%. This is generally true for all companies because assets are acquired either through debt or through *equity*, which is investment plus retained earnings.

Figure 7.11
The equity ratio indicates the degree to which assets are acquired via capital contributions and retained earnings.

Equity_Ratio =Stockholders_Equity/Total_Assets

Ch07.xlsx

	A	B	C	D	E	F	G	H
1				Q1	Q2	Q3	Q4	
2								
3	Stockholders' Equity			$ 1,908,964	$ 2,171,503	$ 2,129,589	$ 2,180,629	
4	Total Assets			$ 3,446,581	$ 3,552,643	$ 3,478,194	$ 3,607,572	
5	Equity Ratio			55%	61%	61%	60%	
6								

Equity Ratio

It is usually easier to acquire assets through debt than to acquire them through equity. For example, you might need many investors to make up the amount of capital you need, but you might be able to borrow it all from just one creditor.

The topic of priority is also a consideration. By law, if a firm ceases operations, its creditors have the first claim on its assets to help repay the borrowed funds. Therefore, an investor's risk is somewhat higher than that of a creditor, and the effect is that stockholders tend to demand a greater return on their investment than a creditor does on its loan. The stockholders' demand for a return can take the form of dividend requirements or ROA, each of which tends to increase the market value of the stock.

But there is no "always" in financial planning. Because investors usually require a higher return on their investment than do creditors, it might seem that debt is the preferred method of raising funds to acquire assets. However, potential creditors look at ratios such as the ROA and the debt ratio. A high debt ratio (or, conversely, a low equity ratio) means that existing creditors have supplied a large portion of the company's assets and that there is relatively little stockholder's equity to help spread the risk.

Determining the Times Interest Earned Ratio

Creditors frequently use the *times interest earned ratio* to evaluate the risk involved in loaning money to a company. This ratio is the number of times in a given period that a company earns enough income to cover its interest payments. A ratio of 5, for example, would mean that during an accounting period the company earns five times the amount of interest payments it must make during that period.

The usual formula is as follows:

```
Times Interest Earned = EBIT / Total Interest Payments
```

Again, EBIT stands for Earnings Before Interest and Taxes. Figure 7.12 shows the times interest earned ratio for Orinoco Books.

The formula used in the range D3:G3 of Figure 7.12 is as follows:

```
=Net_Income+Interest+Taxes
```

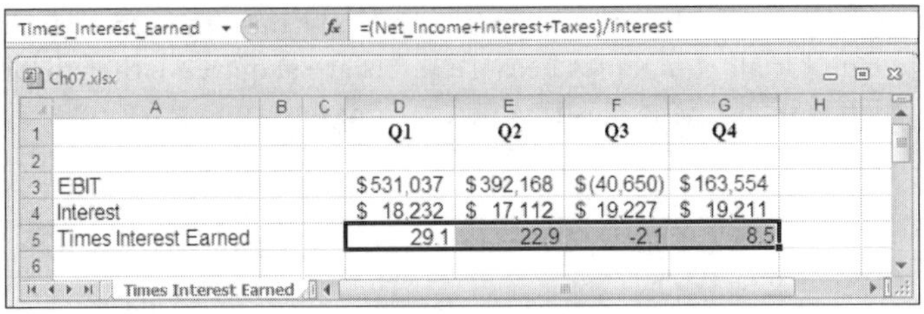

Figure 7.12
The times interest earned ratio measures a company's ability to meet the cost of debt.

Times_Interest_Earned · fx =(Net_Income+Interest+Taxes)/Interest

Ch07.xlsx

	A	B	C	D	E	F	G	H
1				Q1	Q2	Q3	Q4	
2								
3	EBIT			$531,037	$392,168	$(40,650)	$163,554	
4	Interest			$ 18,232	$ 17,112	$ 19,227	$ 19,211	
5	Times Interest Earned			29.1	22.9	-2.1	8.5	
6								

Times Interest Earned

This is a slightly different formula for EBIT than is used in Figures 7.8 and 7.9. There, EBIT was calculated for a full year by subtracting operating expenses from gross profit. Here, EBIT is calculated for each quarter by adding interest and taxes back to net income.

This formula is used to return the interest amount in the range D4:G4:

```
=Interest
```

The formula uses the defined name *Interest*, which refers to the range D9:H9 on Orinoco Books' income statement (refer to Figure 7.1).

In reality, the times interest earned ratio seldom exceeds 10. A value of `29.1` such as that calculated in cell D5 in Figure 7.12 is *very* high, although certainly not unheard of during a particularly good quarter. A value of `8.5` such as in cell G5 of Figure 7.12 would usually be considered strong but within the normal range.

Notice that this is a measure of how deeply interest charges cut into a company's income. For example, a ratio of 1 means the company earns just enough income, after meeting costs such as operating expenses and costs of sales, to cover only its interest charges. This means there will be no income remaining to pay income taxes, meet dividend requirements, or retain earnings for future investments. (Of course, in this case, it is likely there will be no income tax liability.)

Analyzing Liquidity Ratios

Creditors place great emphasis on the issue of *liquidity*, or a company's ability to meet its debts as they come due. As discussed in previous chapters, a company might have a substantial amount in total assets, but if those assets are difficult to convert to cash, it's possible that the company might not be able to pay its creditors on schedule.

The next sections discuss two useful measures of a company's liquidity, the current ratio and the quick ratio.

Determining the Current Ratio

The *current ratio* compares a company's current assets (those that can be converted to cash during the current accounting period) to its current liabilities (those liabilities coming due during the same period). The usual formula is the following:

```
Current Ratio = Current Assets / Current Liabilities
```

Figure 7.13 shows the current ratio during each quarter for Orinoco Books.

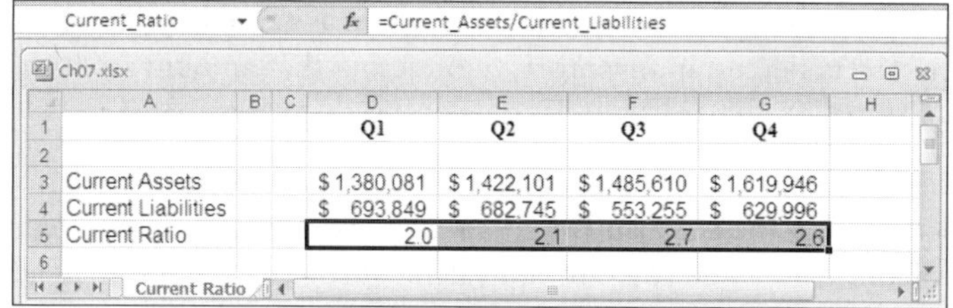

Current_Ratio | =Current_Assets/Current_Liabilities

Ch07.xlsx

	A	D	E	F	G
1		Q1	Q2	Q3	Q4
2					
3	Current Assets	$ 1,380,081	$ 1,422,101	$ 1,485,610	$ 1,619,946
4	Current Liabilities	$ 693,849	$ 682,745	$ 553,255	$ 629,996
5	Current Ratio	2.0	2.1	2.7	2.6

Current Ratio

Figure 7.13
The current ratio measures the company's ability to repay the principal amounts of its current liabilities.

The ranges D3:G3 and D4:G4 in Figure 7.13 refer to ranges named `Current_Assets`, which are cells D7:G7 on the balance sheet in Figure 7.3 and `Current_Liabilities`, which are cells D30:G30 on the balance sheet in Figure 7.4. The current ratio is the current assets divided by the current liabilities. The current ratio values in Figure 7.13, ranging from `2.0` to `2.7`, indicate that the company is able to meet its liabilities as they come due.

The current ratio is closely related to the concept of working capital, which was discussed in detail in Chapter 5. *Working capital* is the difference between current assets and current liabilities.

Is a high current ratio good or bad? From the creditor's standpoint, a high current ratio means that the company is well placed to pay back its loans. But keep in mind the nature of the current assets: They consist mainly of inventory, cash, and cash equivalents. Cash does not contribute meaningfully to the creation of operating income. Therefore, from the standpoint of stockholders and management, a current ratio that is very high (say, 4 or more) often means that the company's assets are not being used to its best advantage.

Determining the Quick Ratio

The *quick ratio*, which is sometimes referred to as the *acid test ratio*, is a variant of the current ratio. The quick ratio takes into account that although inventory is a current asset, it is not as liquid as cash or accounts receivable. Cash is completely liquid, and accounts receivable can normally be converted to cash fairly quickly by pressing for collection from the customer. On the other hand, inventory can't be converted to cash except by selling it. The quick ratio determines the relationship between quickly accessible current assets and current liabilities:

```
Quick Ratio = (Current Assets - Inventory) / Current Liabilities
```

Figure 7.14 shows the quarterly quick ratios for Orinoco Books.

Quick_Ratio | =(Current_Assets-Inventory)/Current_Liabilities

Ch07.xlsx

	A	D	E	F	G
1		Q1	Q2	Q3	Q4
2					
3	Current Assets	$ 1,380,081	$ 1,422,101	$ 1,485,610	$ 1,619,946
4	Inventory	$ 630,411	$ 590,959	$ 575,178	$ 1,186,002
5	Current Liabilities	$ 693,849	$ 682,745	$ 553,255	$ 629,996
6	Quick Ratio	1.1	1.2	1.6	0.7

Quick Ratio

Figure 7.14
The quick ratio shows whether a company can meet its liabilities from quickly accessible assets.

The rather low quick ratio for the fourth quarter is caused by the relatively large portion of current assets tied up in inventory. Subtracting that amount from the total current assets results in a smaller numerator and a quick ratio that's less than 1.0.

In practice, a quick ratio of 1.0 is normally considered adequate, with this caveat: The credit periods that the company offers its customers and those granted to the company by its own creditors must be roughly equivalent. If revenues will stay in accounts receivable for as long as 90 days, but accounts payable are due within 30 days, a quick ratio of 1.0 means that accounts receivable cannot be converted to cash quickly enough to meet accounts payable.

A company can manipulate the values of its current and quick ratios by taking certain steps toward the end of an accounting period, such as a fiscal year. For example, it might wait until the start of the next period to purchase more inventory, which will help maintain a higher quick ratio during the current period. As a potential creditor, you might want to examine the company's current and quick ratios on a quarterly basis for at least a full year.

Both a current and a quick ratio can mislead you if the inventory figure does not represent the current replacement cost of the materials in inventory. As you saw in the discussion of inventories in Chapter 3, there are various methods of valuing inventory. The LIFO method, in particular, can result in an inventory valuation that is much different from the inventory's current replacement value; this is because it assumes that the most recently acquired inventory is also the most recently sold.

For example, if your actual costs of materials are falling, the LIFO method could result in an overvaluation of the existing inventory. This would tend to inflate the current ratio and to underestimate the quick ratio if you calculate it by subtracting inventory from current assets instead of summing cash and cash equivalents.

Analyzing Activity Ratios

Activity ratios can give you insight into how well a company manages its operating and sales activities. The primary goal of these activities is to produce income through effective use of the company's resources. Two ways to measure this effectiveness are the average collection period and the inventory turnover rate.

Determining the Average Collection Period

You can obtain a general estimate of the length of time it takes to receive payment for goods or services by calculating the average collection period. One formula for this ratio is as follows:

```
Average Collection Period = Accounts Receivable / (Credit Sales/Days)
```

Here, `Days` is the number of days in the period for which accounts receivable and credit sales accumulate. For an example based on Orinoco Books financials, see Figure 7.15.

The formula in the range D3:G3 of Figure 7.15, quarterly accounts receivable for 2010, is as follows:

```
=Accounts_Receivable
```

The `Accounts_Receivable` name refers to the range C4:G4 on the balance sheet (see Figure 7.3).

For the range D4:G4 in Figure 7.15 that is labeled `Credit Sales`, the formula is as follows:

```
=Sales
```

The assumption here is that all sales are credit sales. The number of days in each quarter is entered in D5:G5 and used as the denominator of the formula that returns Credit Sales per Day. For cell D6, that formula is as follows:

```
=Sales/D5
```

Figure 7.15
The average collection period is an indicator of how well a company manages its accounts receivable.

Average_Collection_Period | =Accounts_Receivable/Credit_Sales_per_Day

Ch07.xlsx

	A	B	C	D	E	F	G
1				Q1	Q2	Q3	Q4
2							
3	Accounts Receivable			$ 657,581	$ 493,151	$ 427,397	$ 660,855
4	Credit Sales			$ 2,652,077	$ 1,860,290	$ 1,498,534	$ 3,134,388
5	Days in Period			90	91	92	92
6	Credit Sales per Day			$ 29,468	$ 20,443	$ 16,288	$ 34,069
7	Average Collection Period			22.3	24.1	26.2	19.4

Average Collection Period

Thus, D6 contains the average amount of credit sales on any day during the first quarter. The range D6:G6 is given the name `Credit_Sales_Per_Day`. Then the range D7:G7 is the ratio of `Accounts_Receivable` to `Credit_Sales_Per_Day`. This ratio measures the average number of days that any given sale remains in accounts receivable.

You can interpret the average collection period in terms of the company's credit policies. For example, if the company's stated policy is that payment is to be received within two weeks, an average collection period of 30 days indicates that collections are lagging. Collection procedures might need to be reviewed, or one particularly large account might be responsible for most of the collections in arrears. It's also possible that someone needs to tighten up the qualifying procedures that the sales force uses.

NOTE The calculation of the average collection period assumes that credit sales are distributed evenly during any given period. To the degree that the credit sales cluster at the end of the period, the average collection period will return an inflated figure. If you obtain a result that appears too long or too short, be sure to check whether the sales dates occur evenly throughout the period in question. If they don't, you should take that into account when you evaluate the average collection period.

Regardless of the cause, if the average collection period is too long, it means that the company is losing profit. The company is slow in converting cash due from customers into new assets that can be used to generate new income.

Determining Inventory Turnover

Most companies do not want to have too large an inventory. Merchandise that remains in inventory too long ties up the company's assets in idle stock, often incurs carrying charges for the storage of the goods, and can become obsolete while sitting on the shelf.

Just In Time inventory procedures attempt to make inventory purchases no sooner than absolutely required to fulfill sales. That's an unrealistic ideal, but by calculating the inventory turnover rate, you can estimate how well a company is approaching it.

The formula for the inventory turnover ratio is the following:

```
Inventory Turnover = Cost of Goods Sold / Average Inventory
```

Here, the Average Inventory figure refers to the value of the inventory on any given day during the period when the Cost of Goods Sold is calculated. Figure 7.16 shows the quarterly inventory turnover rate for Orinoco Books.

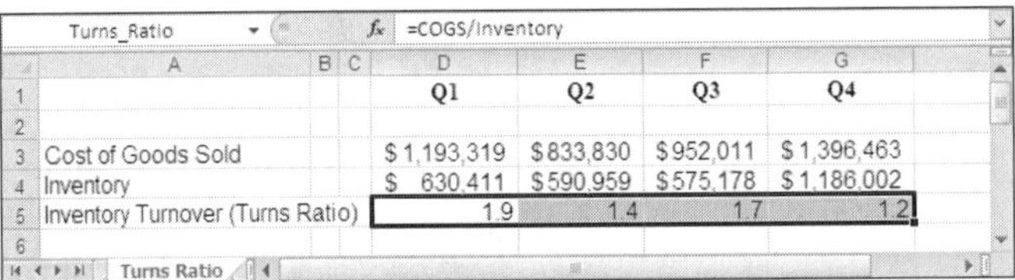

Turns_Ratio | =COGS/Inventory

	A	B	C	D	E	F	G
1				Q1	Q2	Q3	Q4
2							
3	Cost of Goods Sold			$ 1,193,319	$833,830	$952,011	$ 1,396,463
4	Inventory			$ 630,411	$590,959	$575,178	$ 1,186,002
5	Inventory Turnover (Turns Ratio)			1.9	1.4	1.7	1.2
6							

Turns Ratio

Figure 7.16
The higher an inventory turnover rate is, the more closely a company conforms to Just in Time procedures.

Figure 7.16 suggests that this company's inventory is completely replaced once or twice a year.

You can determine an acceptable inventory turnover rate only if you have knowledge of a company's business sector. If you are in the business of wholesaling fresh produce, for example, you might need an annual turnover rate in the 50s. A much lower rate would mean that you were losing too much inventory to spoilage. But if you sell computing equipment, you could probably afford an annual turnover rate of 3 or 4 because hardware does not spoil, nor does it become technologically obsolete more often than every few months.

Summary

This chapter described some of the financial ratios that are important in understanding how, and how well, a company conducts its business. Variations exist for virtually every ratio discussed here, and some ratios weren't covered, but their principal forms follow the formulas illustrated.

Only occasionally can you calculate one of these indicators and gain immediate insight into a business operation. More frequently, you need to know the company's industry because the marketplace places different demands on different lines of business. Furthermore, you can usually understand one ratio by considering it in the context of another ratio. (The debt ratio and the ROA together constitute a good example of one ratio providing the context for another.)

Keep in mind that it's important to evaluate a financial ratio in terms of its trend over time, a standard such as an industry average, and other ratios that describe the company's operations and financial structure.

Budgeting and Planning Cycle

8

So far, this book has focused on events that have already occurred. The income, balance sheet, and cash flow statements provide a picture of a company's past performance. But understanding what has already happened isn't much help if you can't use it to plan for the future. This chapter provides an overview of financial planning and budgeting and discusses how forecasts and projections, based on a company's recent history, form the foundation for planning.

Textbooks describe the elements of good business planning, including mission statements, business strategies, financial objectives, and marketing tactics. The process of financial planning involves much more detail than these few concepts suggest. But they underscore that the foundation of good financial planning is good business planning. It's impossible to build meaningful financial plans without knowing what you want your business to accomplish and how you want it to get there.

IN THIS CHAPTER

Creating Pro Forma Financial Statements

The goal of financial planning is to understand and project your financial future. You use financial projections to compare and evaluate business plans, to estimate future financing needs, and to establish internal operating budgets. Creating pro forma financial statements is a standard way to forecast a company's financial future.

Pro forma statements build on the financial tools and concepts you already know about, such as income statements, balance sheets, and cash flow analysis. Many approaches exist for developing pro forma statements, ranging from back-of-the-envelope estimates to extensive computerized models that attempt to forecast and take account of future economic conditions. Regardless of the approach, the goal is the same: to develop realistic and useful financial projections.

As you develop a pro forma statement, keep these three drivers in mind:

- **Known relationships and trends**—Sales commissions might normally have been 5% of revenue. Keep them there in your projections unless you have reason to believe they'll change.
- **Information regarding future changes**—A competitor might be preparing to release a new product. Bear that in mind when you estimate future market shares for your own offerings.
- **Your business goals**—You might intend to reduce expenses by 10 percent through staff attrition and layoffs. Think through what the unintended consequences of the cost reductions might be.

You can choose among several approaches to develop your pro forma financial statements. The three drivers just described imply *horizontal* approaches—they focus on changes over time. Another class of *vertical* approaches focuses on industry groups.

For example, you might want to determine whether your cost of goods sold (COGS), as a percentage of net sales, is similar to that of other companies in your industry. Successful companies within an industry group often have similar relationships between key indicators. It can be useful to compare the relationship between, say, COGS and net sales at your company with the industry average. It would be discouraging to find that your cost-to-sales ratio is high compared to the industry average; that knowledge would probably prompt you to take action to lower costs.

➜See Chapter 6, "Statement Analysis," for information on common-sizing, a technique that can help you do this sort of analysis.

The values of key ratios within different industry groups are commercially available. You can calculate some of them yourself by accessing the financial reports of publically traded companies that are often publicized on the Internet. The difficulty is that it might be misleading to compare your company to an industry average.

Suppose that you work for a local telephone company. If you compare your company's results to the industry averages for telecommunications firms, you will be comparing your results to those of cable TV firms, cellular communications firms, long-distance providers, companies that offer high-speed dedicated connections, and so on. Their financial structures might well be very different from yours, so any comparison could mislead you. A vertical analysis can be enlightening, but it must be prepared with great care.

In contrast, a horizontal approach uses your own historic data as the point of comparison. In effect, your company acts as its own control group. Although it requires every bit as much care as a vertical approach, a horizontal analysis is relatively straightforward and can be an effective way to project financial results. The next section illustrates a horizontal analysis, based on projections that use Percentage of Sales.

Forecasting by Percentage of Sales

The Percentage of Sales forecasting approach is based on the concept that many business activities, such as incurring certain expenses, acquiring assets, and assuming liabilities, are directly tied to sales dollars. Without sales, a business would neither incur selling expenses nor generate accounts receivable. An increase in sales should result in additional cash in the bank, greater variable costs, higher income taxes, additional administrative expenses, and so on. Sales is a key driver of most other indicators; therefore, it can be useful to base the projection of other indicators on the projection of sales.

The Percentage of Sales forecasting method entails several general steps:

1. Analyze historical trends and financial relationships. For example, over several years, variable costs might have averaged 47% of total sales. A preliminary analysis would at least take a glance at whether that ratio has been rising, falling, or remaining roughly constant during that period.
2. Forecast the key driver, sales, through the next planning horizon—one year, for example. There are many ways to generate that forecast. A good one to *avoid* is having sales managers estimate their team's sales, unless you can be sure they're not doing so just by fiddling with their own quotas.
3. Estimate future expenses and balances based on their historical relationships to sales. If you project that sales will increase by 3% during the next year, it would be reasonable to project that sales commissions will also increase by 3%.
4. Prepare the pro forma financial statement using the projected sales and expenses.

CASE STUDY: CUMMINS PRINTING

Cummins Printing is a small business that specializes in custom print runs of office stationery, annual reports, and catalogs. It has been in existence for three years, since Jim Cummins incorporated the company and acquired its assets partly through a bank loan and partly through funding that he supplied. Cummins Printing is preparing pro formas for 2012. It does so both to estimate its annual expenses and financial results for the next year and to guide an operating decision it must make early in the year.

The first step is to review a company's existing financial statements for trends, patterns, and relationships. The statement and ratio analysis tools discussed in Part I, "Analyzing Financial Statements," make up the platform for the pro forma view. For example, Figures 8.1 and 8.2 display the 2009 to 2011 income and balance sheet statements for Cummins Printing.

8

Figure 8.1
Cummins Printing income statement for 2009 to 2011.

	A		B	C	D
1	Cummins Printing				
2	Income Statement for the year ended:		12/31/2009	12/31/2010	12/31/2011
3	**Sales**		$498,541	$367,450	$389,864
4	Cost of Goods Sold				
5	Inventory, 1/1		$116,081	$85,919	$112,969
6	Purchases		$115,372	$147,970	$187,540
7	Available for sale		$231,453	$233,889	$300,509
8	Inventory, 12/31		$85,919	$112,969	$129,125
9		Cost of goods sold	$145,534	$120,920	$171,384
10	Gross profit		$353,007	$246,530	$218,480
11					
12	**Expenses**				
13		Advertising	$6,166	$5,915	$6,770
14		Office lease	$8,750	$9,110	$9,544
15		Insurance	$3,906	$3,754	$4,010
16		Office supplies	$2,110	$2,680	$3,862
17		Salaries	$62,378	$72,924	$94,347
18		Communications	$3,708	$5,507	$7,014
19		Travel	$1,070	$6,310	$8,733
20		Depreciation	$4,192	$4,192	$4,192
21	Operating expenses		$92,280	$110,392	$138,472
22	Operating income		$260,727	$136,138	$80,008
23	Taxes		$65,182	$34,035	$20,002
24	Net income		$195,545	$102,104	$60,006

Figure 8.2
Cummins Printing balance sheet for 2009 to 2011.

	A	B	C	D	E
1	Cummins Printing	Balance Sheet for the year ended:	12/31/2009	12/31/2010	12/31/2011
2	**ASSETS**				
3	**Current Assets**	Cash	$282,289	$272,787	$281,278
4		Accounts receivable	$66,567	$158,054	$163,422
5		Inventory	$85,919	$112,969	$129,125
6		*Total Current Assets*	$434,775	$543,810	$573,825
7	**Fixed Assets**	Equipment	$62,903	$62,903	$62,903
8		Less-accumulated depreciation	$4,192	$8,384	$12,576
9		*Total Fixed Assets*	$58,711	$54,519	$50,327
10					
11		*Total assets*	$493,486	$598,329	$624,152
12					
13	**LIABILITIES AND STOCKHOLDERS' EQUITY**				
14	**Current Liabilities**	Accounts payable	$169,856	$203,742	$183,592
15		Notes payable	$62,903	$62,903	$62,903
16		Income taxes	$65,182	$34,035	$20,002
17		*Total liabilities*	$297,941	$300,680	$266,497
18	**Stockholders' Equity**	Retained earnings	$195,545	$297,649	$357,655
19					
20					
21		*Total liabilities and Stockholders' Equity*	$493,486	$598,329	$624,152

Identifying Financial Trends

Now Cummins needs to identify the financial trends, patterns, and relationships that flow from these worksheets. Many different tools and indicators are available, but the key for budget planning is to focus on what drives the business. Growth in revenues and an increase in working capital are two examples of these drivers. Cummins focuses on growth in revenue as the business's key driver and uses percentage of sales as its principal indicator. Figure 8.3 displays the income statements from Figure 8.1, along with a breakdown of components by sales. Each statement component is expressed both in terms of raw dollars and as a percentage of sales. The assumption is that as sales dollars vary, other components such as inventory and most operating expenses should vary accordingly.

Figure 8.3

Cummins expresses statement components as a percentage of sales as the first step in creating a pro forma.

	A	B	C	D	E	F	G
1	Cummins Printing					Percentage of Sales	
2	Income Statement for the year ended:	12/31/2009	12/31/2010	12/31/2011		3-year average	2011 only
3	**Sales**	$498,541	$367,450	$389,864		100.00%	100.00%
4	Cost of Goods Sold						
5	Inventory, 1/1	$116,081	$85,919	$112,969		25.21%	28.98%
6	Purchases	$115,372	$147,970	$187,540		37.17%	48.10%
7	Available for sale	$231,453	$233,889	$300,509		62.39%	77.08%
8	Inventory, 12/31	$85,919	$112,969	$129,125		27.03%	33.12%
9	Cost of goods sold	$145,534	$120,920	$171,384		35.35%	43.96%
10	Gross profit	$353,007	$246,530	$218,480		64.65%	56.04%
11							
12	**Expenses**						
13	Advertising	$6,166	$5,915	$6,770		1.53%	1.74%
14	Office lease	$8,750	$9,110	$9,544		2.23%	2.45%
15	Insurance	$3,906	$3,754	$4,010		0.94%	1.03%
16	Office supplies	$2,110	$2,680	$3,862		0.71%	0.99%
17	Salaries	$62,378	$72,924	$94,347		18.85%	24.20%
18	Communications	$3,708	$5,507	$7,014		1.35%	1.80%
19	Travel	$1,070	$6,310	$8,733		1.39%	2.24%
20	Depreciation	$4,192	$4,192	$4,192		1.02%	1.08%
21	Operating expenses	$92,280	$110,392	$138,472		28.02%	35.52%
22	Operating income	$260,727	$136,138	$80,008		36.62%	20.52%
23	Taxes	$65,182	$34,035	$20,002		9.16%	5.13%
24	Net income	$195,545	$102,104	$60,006		27.47%	15.39%

With so few data points (only three years' worth of information on sales), it's not a good idea to project sales growth on the basis of prior data alone. For example, if you use an approach based on time snapshots, such as Excel's Moving Average tool, or a regression-based method such as Excel's `TREND` function or a chart trendline, you will get an answer, but you shouldn't base any important decisions on that evidence alone—certainly not with just three data points.

How can you tell what to believe? When you prepare an analysis that projects earlier results into the future—such as next year's sales revenues—you assume that the future will in some way resemble the past. If you have many data points in the analysis, the assumption has much more justification than if you have only a handful. You can examine the baseline of the data and perhaps note that sales revenue in a prior year does a good job of predicting the revenue in a subsequent year. But with a short baseline, such as three years, you can obtain an apparently reliable trend that turns out to be completely misleading.

➜See Chapter 15, "Making Investment Decisions Under Uncertain Conditions," which has much more to say about the issue of statistical reliability.

NOTE

There are two general ways in which a trend that seems reliable can turn out to be unreliable. One is *generalizability*. Suppose that your three-year baseline happened to come at the top of a business cycle. Your data does not extend far enough into the past to be truly representative. Although it may have held reliably steady for three years, your baseline provides no clue that your revenues are about to fall off a cliff.

The other issue is *statistical reliability*. When you have only a few data points, a confidence interval around a projection can be so wide that the projection is revealed to be little more than a shot in the dark.

In the situation shown in Figures 8.1 to 8.3, you should try to get additional evidence—for example:

- Do other indicators, such as local or national economic forecasts, suggest that your revenues will continue as before?
- Is your competition gearing up or scaling back? Are they taking steps to snatch away your customers?
- Are changes occurring in your business's technology? If so, do they work for you or against you? When will they begin to take effect in the marketplace?
- What changes in business conditions are your existing customers facing? Do these changes suggest that they will continue to buy? And will they continue to buy from you?
- Are you preparing to discontinue an existing product line or to introduce a new one? Do you have credible evidence that your customers will take to the new product?
- What is the market trend for your product? Is demand declining or accelerating?

The answers to questions such as these, combined with the actual results from earlier years, lead Cummins Printing to the reasonable assumption that the growth in revenues for 2012 will be slightly weaker than that experienced during 2011. In particular, Cummins concludes that sales growth will continue but slow down due to the short-term nature of some of the Federal government's financial stimulus legislation of 2009. However, Cummins has arranged a new advertising campaign that it hopes will diversify the available market. Cummins projects that the 2012 revenue will be $411,696, a 5.6 percent increase over 2011.

Forecasting Based on Recent History

The next step is to forecast expenses based on their historical Percentage of Sales and applied to the projected 2012 revenue. Figure 8.4 displays this forecast.

The components that are expected to vary with net sales are shown as a percentage in column B, carried over from column G of Figure 8.3. Other components either are calculated from the projections for 2012 (such as gross profit) or are derived from the end of the previous period (such as beginning inventory, lease payments, and depreciation).

The forecast is fine as far as it goes, but a disturbing trend emerges from the 2009 to 2011 income statements shown in Figure 8.3. Cummins Printing makes most of its revenues through custom print runs, which often require special paper stock. During the three years of its existence, Cummins has purchased stock for special uses in quantities larger than needed for a particular order. The quantity purchases reduced the variable costs because larger purchases involved better discounts from suppliers. Cummins also hopes that customers will make subsequent orders that will require using the rest of that stock purchase.

Unfortunately, this hasn't happened yet. Cummins Printing's inventory of paper goods has steadily increased over the three-year period (see Figure 8.3, cells B8:D8), as the sales dollars have declined (see Figure 8.3, B3:D3). Figure 8.4 indicates that unless changes

Figure 8.4
Applying historical percentages to projected sales results in a pro forma budget for 2012.

=C22-C23

	A	B	C
1	Projected Sales, 2012	$ 411,696	
2		2011 percentage	2012 projections
3	**Sales**	100.00%	$ 411,696
4	Cost of Goods Sold		
5	Inventory, 1/1		$ 129,125
6	Purchases	48.10%	$ 198,042
7	Available for sale		$ 327,167
8	Inventory, 12/31	33.12%	$ 136,356
9	Cost of goods sold		$ 190,811
10	Gross profit		$ 220,885
11			
12	**Expenses**		
13	Advertising	1.74%	$ 7,149
14	Office lease		$ 9,900
15	Insurance	1.03%	$ 4,235
16	Office supplies	0.99%	$ 4,078
17	Salaries	24.20%	$ 99,630
18	Communications	1.80%	$ 7,407
19	Travel	2.24%	$ 9,222
20	Depreciation		$ 4,192
21	Operating expenses		$ 145,813
22	Operating income		$ 75,072
23	Taxes		$ 18,768
24	Net income		$ 56,304

are made, inventory at the end of 2012 will be $136,356 (33.12% of the projected sales, $411,696).

Analyzing Impact of New Procedures

What impact would a change in purchasing procedures have on Cummins Printing's pro forma income statement and balance sheet for 2012?

Cummins knows that a significant proportion of its sales depends on the custom work done for its customers. As much as 40% of its business has been due to Cummins' willingness to acquire the stock required for special jobs, to purchase stock in bulk, and to use some of the unit cost savings to provide a gentle reduction in the prices it charges its customers.

Cummins assumes that at some point its existing customers will repeat their orders, enabling the company to work down the special inventory it has acquired. In the meantime, one option is to curtail inventory buys, slowing the increase in its inventory levels until new orders come in. Cummins needs to attract new customers. But if Cummins curtails new purchases to its inventory, the custom production runs for new customers might take too long or cost too much. Therefore, the process of working down the existing inventory to a more manageable level is likely to cause the level of new sales to decrease. Is this a sensible business decision?

Cummins explores the effect of reducing its purchase of stock by 50% during 2012, from the pro forma figure of $198,042 to $99,021. Looking at a pessimistic outcome, Cummins assumes that the company will lose the entire 40% of its business that has come from those special jobs. This would bring the sales figure down to $247,018, which is 60% of the 2012 sales projection in cell B1 of Figure 8.4 (also see cell B1 of Figure 8.5).

Figure 8.5
The 2012 pro forma income statement, based on curtailing inventory purchases and resulting in lower net sales.

	A	B	C
1	Modified Sales Projection, 2012	$ 247,018	
2		2011 percentage	2012 projections
3	**Sales**	100.00%	$ 247,018
4	Cost of Goods Sold		
5	Inventory, 1/1		$ 129,125
6	Purchases	48.10%	$ 99,021
7	Available for sale		$ 228,146
8	Inventory, 12/31	33.12%	$ 81,814
9	Cost of goods sold		$ 146,333
10	Gross profit		$ 100,685
11			
12	**Expenses**		
13	Advertising	1.74%	$ 4,289
14	Office lease		$ 9,900
15	Insurance	1.03%	$ 2,541
16	Office supplies	0.99%	$ 2,447
17	Salaries	24.20%	$ 59,778
18	Communications	1.80%	$ 4,444
19	Travel	2.24%	$ 5,533
20	Depreciation		$ 4,192
21	Operating expenses		$ 93,125
22	Operating income		$ 7,560
23	Taxes		$ 1,890
24	Net income		$ 5,670

Most of Cummins's expenses decrease proportionately with net sales. The exceptions are the office lease and equipment depreciation, which would not normally be expected to vary with net sales. The projected outcome is shown in Figures 8.5 (the pro forma income statement) and Figure 8.6 (the pro forma balance sheet).

If stock purchases are cut in half, and if net sales consequently falls by 40%, net income will fall by $50,663, or 90%: As a percentage, that's a huge financial impact for any business. To reduce salaries in accordance with the reduction in net sales by 40%, one employee would have to be laid off: a major human factor for a small business.

All in all, the costs are just too great to justify the improvement in the inventory situation. This is what you would expect when an operational decision exerts such a powerful influence on the way a company does business with its customers.

Figure 8.6
The 2012 pro forma balance sheet in column F reflects the effect of reduced sales on the company's worth.

	A	B	C	D	E	F
1	Cummins Printing	Balance Sheet for year ended:	12/31/2009	12/31/2010	12/31/2011	12/31/2012
2	**ASSETS**					
3	**Current Assets**	Cash	$282,289	$272,787	$281,278	$358,801
4		Accounts receivable	$66,567	$158,054	$163,422	$122,164
5		Inventory	$85,919	$112,969	$129,125	$74,605
6		*Total Current Assets*	$434,775	$543,810	$573,825	$555,570
7	**Fixed Assets**	Equipment	$62,903	$62,903	$62,903	$62,903
8		Less-accumulated depreciation	$4,192	$8,384	$12,576	$16,768
9		*Total Fixed Assets*	$58,711	$54,519	$50,327	$46,135
10						
11		*Total assets*	$493,486	$598,329	$624,152	$601,705
12						
13	**LIABILITIES AND STOCKHOLDERS' EQUITY**					
14	**Current Liabilities**	Accounts payable	$169,856	$203,742	$183,592	$106,075
15		Notes payable	$62,903	$62,903	$62,903	$62,903
16		Income taxes	$65,182	$34,035	$20,002	$18,768
17		*Total liabilities*	$297,941	$300,680	$266,497	$187,746
18	**Stockholders' Equity**	Retained earnings	$195,545	$297,649	$357,655	$413,959
19						
20		*Total liabilities and Stockholders*	$493,486	$598,329	$624,152	$601,705

Using Excel to Manage the Analysis

Excel makes the analysis particularly easy—much easier than the business decision itself might be. The effort is in setting up the worksheet that contains the historic data for the income statement and balance sheet. After that's done, calculating the percentages is easy and simple. For example, to create the `100%` value that was shown in cell G3 of Figure 8.3, you would enter this formula:

```
=D3/$D$3
```

Then copy that formula and paste it into G5:G10 and G13:G24. The absolute reference $D$3 ensures that the denominator in the formula is always the value in cell D3, whereas the numerator in the formula changes according to where the formula is pasted. For example, the formula as pasted into cell G6 changes to `D6/$D$3`.

> **TIP**
> The F4 key gives you a convenient way to convert one reference style to another. Suppose that you want to use the contents of cell D3 as part of a formula in a different cell. If you specify cell D3 by using the mouse to point at the cell, Excel uses the relative reference style (that is, no dollar signs) by default. To convert the relative reference D3 to the absolute reference style $D$3, just highlight that portion of the formula in the Formula box and press F4. Pressing F4 repeatedly cycles the reference through mixed reference styles as well: D3, $D$3, D$3, $D3, and then back to D3. This is much more convenient than using the mouse or arrow keys to locate where the $ sign should be placed.

To calculate the values shown in column F of Figure 8.3, enter this formula in cell F3:

```
=(B3+C3+D3)/($B$3+$C$3+$D$3)
```

Then copy and paste it into F5:F10 and F13:F24. You can calculate the percentage in a couple of different ways. This formula just given assigns greater weight to a year in which, for example, the advertising expense is high relative to net sales.

Another version of this formula is shown here:

```
=AVERAGE(B3/$B$3,C3/$C$3,D3/$D$3)
```

This version of the formula assigns equal weight to each of the three years involved. You choose which version to use by deciding whether you want the average to emphasize or reduce the effect of an unusual value.

> **TIP**
> Yet another version of the equal-weight formula is `=AVERAGE(B5:D5/$B$3:$D$3)`, array entered. Compared to a conventional formula, an array formula requires a little more care when you're entering it or editing it. But you might find it easier to understand what's going on when you see it in the worksheet.

After these formulas are set up, checking the effect of a change in net sales on such variables as expenses, net income, and owner's equity is just a matter of changing the value of net sales. Because the remaining categories in the income statement and balance sheet depend heavily on net sales, Excel's adjustments track the changes you make to net sales.

8

Performing Sensitivity Analysis

After you have created your pro forma statements in Excel, you can use them to analyze and compare different financial scenarios. Evaluating possible changes in your projected financial statements might help you identify future risks or opportunities. The Cummins case study illustrates what might happen if sales declined by 40%. It does so by assuming that most costs would follow changes in net sales.

It makes good sense to examine the assumption itself—that is, it helps to know how sensitive various costs are to changes in net sales (or any other driver). You might want to understand the effect on net income of lowering your COGS by 10%, and then by 20%. Or you might ask whether you could stay in business if one of your vendors raised its prices by 20%, or by 30%.

NOTE

Excel provides the Scenario Manager to help you keep track of different assumptions in your pro formas.

➜ Chapter 13, "Creating a Sensitivity Analysis for a Business Case," discusses the Scenario Manager in some depth.

For a single change to a pro forma, it's usually quicker to simply make a change to the critical cell instead of taking the time to deal with a more cumbersome (but effective) tool such as the Scenario Manager. Nevertheless, taking the time to distinguish different assumptions using the Scenario Manager is often worth the extra effort.

For example, cell C6 in Figure 8.4 shows projected purchases to inventory. The formula is as follows:

```
=ROUND(B6*$B$1,0)
```

This equals $198,042. If you changed the formula to this:

```
=ROUND(B6*$B$1*1.2,0)
```

it would show the effect on projected purchases to inventory if the vendor raised prices by 20%. The purchases would increase to $237,650, and the added costs would reduce net income from $56,304 to $26,597.

That's good to know, but this adjustment can tell you much more. Another way of viewing the change in net income is to note that an increase in the cost of purchases to inventory results in a decrease of more than 52% in net income (1 – $26,597/$56,304). This means that your net income, which is driven by the cost of goods available for sale, is at the mercy of your vendors' pricing.

The impact can be much apparent if you make increases in vendor pricing explicit. One way to do so is by way of different scenarios, using the Scenario Manager to keep track of them.

Moving from the Pro Forma to the Budget

A pro forma statement can be translated into financial budgets for the upcoming year. The pro forma statement is the forecast. Budgets are used to plan, coordinate, and control a company's operations. The budgeting time period is a matter of judgment. A business might develop annual, quarterly, or monthly budgets depending on such factors as its information needs, its sales cycle (for example, seasonal peaks and valleys versus a steady trend), its operational methods, and its financial structure.

Suppose that Cummins Printing wants to create a quarterly operating budget for 2012, based on its pro forma income statement for that year. Figure 8.7 shows the quarterly budget.

Figure 8.7
The 2012 quarterly operating budget for Cummins Printing, created from its pro forma.

	A	B	C	D	E	F
2		for 2012	Q1	Q2	Q3	Q4
3	**Sales**	$411,696	$82,339	$164,678	$102,924	$61,754
4	Cost of Goods Sold					
5	Inventory, 1/1	129,125	129,125	130,571	133,464	135,271
6	Purchases	198,042	39,608	79,217	49,511	29,706
7	Available for sale	327,167	168,733	209,788	182,974	164,978
8	Inventory, 12/31	136,355	130,571	133,464	135,271	136,356
9	Cost of goods sold	190,811	38,162	76,324	47,703	28,622
10	Gross profit	220,885	44,177	88,354	55,221	33,133
11	**Expenses**					
12	Advertising	7,149	1,430	2,860	1,787	1,072
13	Office lease	9,900	1,980	3,960	2,475	1,485
14	Insurance	4,235	847	1,694	1,059	635
15	Office supplies	4,078	816	1,631	1,020	612
16	Salaries	99,630	19,926	39,852	24,908	14,945
17	Communications	7,407	1,481	2,963	1,852	1,111
18	Travel	9,222	1,844	3,689	2,306	1,383
19	Depreciation	4,192	1,048	1,048	1,048	1,048
20	Operating expenses	145,813	29,372	57,696	36,453	22,291
21	Operating income	75,072	14,805	30,657	18,768	10,842
22	Taxes	18,768	3,701	7,664	4,692	2,710
23	Net income	$56,304	$11,104	$22,993	$14,076	$8,131

Projecting Quarterly Sales

The quarterly budget follows the assumption in the pro forma that the main driver of expenses is the company's net sales. As it happens, revenues for this firm are moderately seasonal. Historically, 20% of its sales have occurred during the first quarter, 40% during the second quarter, 25% during the third quarter, and 15% during the fourth quarter. To allocate the annual projected net sales of $411,696 to each quarter, make the following entries:

In cell C3:

```
=.2*B3
```

In cell D3:

```
=.4*B3
```

In cell E3:

```
=.25*B3
```

In cell F3:

```
=.15*B3
```

These formulas distribute the total projected sales on a quarterly basis, based on sales percents for each quarter in prior years.

Again, keep in mind that the Scenario Manager helps you keep track of the effects of different sets of projections.

Estimating Inventory Levels

To briefly review the process of accounting for inventory, you begin with the inventory level at the end of the previous period. New purchases to inventory are added, the COGS is subtracted, and the result is the inventory value at the end of the period. (In some situations it's easier and just as accurate to subtract the ending inventory from the goods available for sale, to arrive at COGS.)

To estimate inventory purchases during each quarter, Cummins uses both the total projected purchases for the year and the net sales for the quarter. The formula in cell C6 of Figure 8.7, inventory purchases during the first quarter, is as follows:

```
=$B6*C$3/$B$3
```

The formula represents the amount of anticipated inventory purchases for the year (cell B6), prorated according to the ratio of sales for the quarter (cell C3) to sales for the year (cell B3). Due to the use of mixed references in the formula, copying and pasting from C6 into D6:F6 adjusts the reference to the quarterly net sales from C3 to D3 for the second quarter, to E3 for the third quarter, and to F3 for the fourth quarter; the formula in cell F6 winds up as this:

```
=$B6*F$3/$B$3
```

As a check, notice that the sum of the quarterly inventory purchases in C6:F6 equals the total projected for 2012, shown in cell B6.

The inventory available for sale during each quarter, shown in row 7, is the sum of the inventory at the beginning of the quarter plus purchases during that quarter.

The projection for inventory at the end of the quarter equals the amount that is available for sale minus COGS, and COGS is a function of net sales. For example, the formula in cell C9 is as follows:

```
=$B9*C$3/$B$3
```

The formula represents the projected COGS for all of 2012 in B9 multiplied by the ratio of projected sales for the first quarter in C3 to the projected sales for the year in B3.

Then the end-of-quarter inventory (cell C8) is projected by means of this formula:

```
=C7-C9
```

This is the projected cost of goods available for sale during the first quarter, in C7, minus the projected first-quarter COGS in C9.

The gross profit is estimated by subtracting the COGS from the net sales. For example, the gross profit for the first quarter is estimated by this formula:

```
=C3-C9
```

Expenses for each quarter are estimated, as are the inventory projections, by prorating the annual expense by the ratio of the quarter's net sales to the annual net sales. For example, the first quarter's advertising expense is estimated with this formula:

```
=$B12*C$3/$B$3
```

Again, due to the use of the mixed references, this formula can be copied and pasted into the range C15:C19, and the cell precedents will adjust accordingly. Rows 13 and 14, which represent the cost of the office lease and the insurance that the company carries, are *not* assumed to vary with net sales. Instead, they are estimated on the basis of the most recent information available at the end of the previous period.

NOTE

This book recommends using named ranges in formulas wherever possible. This chapter's discussion of using relative, mixed, and absolute cell addresses in the formula-building process might seem to conflict with the use of range names.

In situations such as the one discussed here—when you want to fill a large range with related formulas—it's more effective to use relative, mixed, and absolute addresses before building the names. The reason is that addresses respond beautifully to Excel's AutoFill feature, whereas the use of names in conjunction with AutoFill (even names that use relative addresses) is often awkward.

Total expenses are obtained in row 20 by summing each quarter's expense categories, and taxes are estimated in row 22 at 25% of operating income (gross profit less expenses). Net income is the gross profit less the total expenses, less taxes.

Distributing Operations

Now suppose that Cummins Printing wants to distribute its quarterly operations more evenly. The quarterly net sales will continue to be seasonal. But Cummins might be able to get useful estimates of orders that will be placed during the second through fourth quarters—from established customers, Cummins might even get commitments. In that case, Cummins might be able to balance the quarterly workload more evenly, with consequent savings in overtime salary payments during the busy second quarter.

Cummins estimates that overtime payments during the year are roughly $10,000. Figure 8.8 shows the effect of distributing the workload evenly across quarters. The resulting changes are in cells G20:G23.

Figure 8.8
2012 quarterly operating budget for Cummins Printing, with workload adjustments to allocate salary costs evenly.

	A	B	C	D	E	F	G
1	Cummins Printing	Total		Quarterly projections			Modified
2		for 2012	Q1	Q2	Q3	Q4	2012 Totals
3	**Sales**	$411,696	$82,339	$164,678	$102,924	$61,754	$411,696
4	Cost of Goods Sold						
5	Inventory, Start of period	129,125	129,125	140,474	113,660	115,469	129,125
6	Purchases	198,042	49,511	49,511	49,511	49,511	198,042
7	Available for sale	327,167	178,636	189,984	163,171	164,979	327,167
8	Inventory, End of period	136,355	140,474	113,660	115,469	136,358	136,355
9	Cost of goods sold	190,811	38,162	76,324	47,702	28,621	190,811
10	Gross profit	220,885	44,177	88,354	55,222	33,133	220,885
11	**Expenses**						
12	Advertising	7,149	1,430	2,860	1,787	1,072	7,149
13	Office lease	9,900	1,980	3,960	2,475	1,485	9,900
14	Insurance	4,235	847	1,694	1,059	635	4,235
15	Office supplies	4,078	816	1,631	1,020	612	4,078
16	Salaries	99,630	22,500	22,500	22,500	22,500	90,000
17	Communications	7,407	1,481	2,963	1,852	1,111	7,407
18	Travel	9,222	1,844	3,689	2,306	1,383	9,222
19	Depreciation	4,192	1,048	1,048	1,048	1,048	4,192
20	Operating expenses	145,813	31,946	40,344	34,046	29,847	136,183
21	Operating income	75,072	12,231	48,010	21,176	3,287	84,702
22	Taxes	18,768	3,058	12,003	5,294	822	21,176
23	Net income	$56,304	$9,173	$36,008	$15,882	$2,465	$63,527

First, notice in Figure 8.8 that the purchases to inventory have been distributed evenly across the four quarters (cells C6:F6). This is due to the assumption that the workload will be constant, so the need for additional inventory will be more balanced over time.

Second, the projection of annual salaries has been reduced from $99,630 to $90,000. Compare cells B16 and G16 in Figure 8.8.) This represents the anticipated savings in overtime payments. Additionally, the quarterly salary payments are constant across quarters in Figure 8.8. This is done by changing the formula in cell C16 from this, in Figure 8.7:

```
=$B16*C$3/$B$3
```

to this, in Figure 8.8:

```
=$G16/4
```

This assigns 25% of the annual salary estimate in G16 to the first quarter. The formula is copied and pasted into cells D16:F16.

The effects of these adjustments are as follows:

- The annual net income increases by $7,223, due to the combination of savings in overtime salary payments and the resulting increase in taxes.
- The net income becomes more variable across quarters. This is because the gross profit for any quarter remains the same, but some quarterly expenses are reduced—and, in the case of the second quarter, the expenses are reduced dramatically, by about 30%.

NOTE Most of the calculations for the modified 2012 totals, shown in column G, are simply the sum of the quarterly amounts. The inventory calculations are different: Starting inventory is taken from the first quarter starting inventory, and the ending inventory is taken from the end of the fourth quarter. The cost of goods available for sale is the sum of the beginning inventory and purchases. And the COGS is the cost of goods available for sale minus the ending inventory.

Other Ways to Distribute Net Income

So far this example illustrates how an operating budget can help you plan and schedule your expenses to increase your profitability. Simply reducing expenses by balancing the workload more evenly can have a substantial effect on net income.

It might also be useful to distribute the net income differently than by using percentage of net sales as the only driver. Suppose that Cummins Printing has a large loan payment coming due at the end of the second quarter. By balancing the workload more evenly, net income through the end of the second quarter is increased from 61% of annual net income to 71% of annual net income. Cummins Printing might need that additional income earlier in the year to help meet the loan payment.

You can realize other benefits by reworking a pro forma as an operating budget. For example, if a business projects that its revenue will increase by 10% during the next year, it might want to develop targets for each product line on a quarterly or even monthly basis. The entire increase might occur during the month of December—particularly for a retailer. If so, there would be significant impacts on the business—for example, December's cash balances, inventory levels, and staffing levels. Budgeting is the process of translating the pro forma statements into plans that help you manage your business and optimize your profits.

By comparing your actual results to the budget projections, you can tell whether you're likely to reach your business goals and financial forecasts. Budget comparisons help you focus on areas of opportunity and concern. If vendor costs increase sharply, you might want to search for a different supplier. If you see an increase in demand for a product, you might raise the sales price or alter inventory schedules. Thus, budgets can serve as real-time flags for your operational and financial decisions.

Fitting the Budget to the Business Plan

For large companies, the planning cycle is extensive. Top management establishes multiyear business plans. Next, managers create operational plans to attain the strategic goals. Pro forma financial statements are then created to quantify and evaluate the plans. Finally, budgets are developed from the pro forma statements.

Three types of budgets are commonly used:

- **Operating budgets** track projected revenues and expenses to help make sure that the projected net income level is achieved.
- **Cash budgets** project cash receipts and disbursements over a period of time. Cash budgets help determine whether it might be necessary to seek outside investment or some other form of external financing.
- **Capital budgets** detail the planned capital (or additions to fixed assets) projects during a designated period.

There are many pitfalls in the budgeting process. One trap is to spend too much time considering the effects of different scenarios that involve minuscule differences. Doing so can be cumbersome and adds little to the analysis. Another trap is to allow budgeting concerns to supersede business goals. Budgeting is a means, not an end. It's important to keep budgeting in perspective; used properly, budgets can give a business a means of planning, coordinating, and monitoring its operations. Done improperly, budgeting can waste time and distract your attention from the bottom line.

Business plans and pro forma statements are particularly valuable when a project requires planning beyond a 12-month horizon. The company might reasonably ask whether it should continue to invest its resources in a particular division, or it might need to know the anticipated revenue for a product over the next five years. The long-range forecast often impacts operational and financial plans well past the current year. Financial plans should extend over the most meaningful planning horizon for your business.

Summary

In this chapter, you saw how to use historical information to project future revenues and expenses by means of the Percentage of Sales method. This process enables you to create pro forma income statements and balance sheets. Pro formas, in turn, help you examine the likely effects on your operations and profits if conditions change or if you modify some aspect of your revenues and expenses.

Operating budgets, which help you plan and manage the way you conduct your business, flow naturally from pro forma statements. You can use budgets to break down your operations and finances into meaningful time periods such as months and quarters. This gives you additional insight into how changes, whether planned or thrust on you, might affect your financial picture.

The key to the entire process is the quality of your projections. Chapter 9 describes how to use Excel to generate the most accurate forecasts possible.

Forecasting and Projections

9

IN THIS CHAPTER

In business, you often use forecasting to project sales, a process which involves estimating future revenues based on past history. This puts you in a position to make estimates of other resources, such as cost allocations and staffing, that you need to support the revenue stream.

The term *forecasting*, as used here, is the result of looking back at that historic data to investigate how what happened previously determined what happened subsequently. In other words, the process of forecasting takes account of past and current conditions, and uses that information to project what's likely to happen next.

This might sound a bit like reading Tarot cards, but it's not. For example, economists, physical scientists, and computer engineers have employed these models for decades to forecast (with varying degrees of success) everything from sunspots and the size of skipjack tuna catches to the number of duplicated database queries.

Forecasts that are exactly correct are either very lucky or trivial. Real-world systems always have some element of randomness, and no forecasting technique can predict something that occurs on an entirely random basis. However, if there are components in historic data that vary in a way you can depend on, you can use forecasting techniques to make reasonably accurate projections—projections that are better than blind guesses. And that increased accuracy is what reduces your business's operational risk.

Unfortunately, businesses often make an offhand effort at a revenue forecast and ignore other ways to use forecasts in their planning. Using Excel, you forecast many other variables, as long as you have a reasonable baseline to create a forecast. For example:

- If your business depends on high-bandwidth telecommunications, you might want to forecast the resources required to keep your users connected to remote computing facilities.
- If you manage a particular product line, you might want to forecast the number of units that you can expect to sell. This kind of forecast can help you determine the resources necessary to support activities such as installation, warehousing, and maintenance.
- If you manage customer service, it can be important to forecast the number of new customers you expect. The forecast may lead you to consider changing your staffing levels to meet changing needs.

In this chapter, you will examine the fundamentals of creating a useful forecast. You will also read about different methods of using baseline data to create forecasts, advantages and drawbacks associated with forecasts, and how to choose a forecasting method.

Making Sure You Have a Useful Baseline

A *baseline* is a set of numeric observations made over time and maintained in chronological order. Examples of baselines are

- Monthly revenue totals for the past four years
- Daily hospital patient census for the past six months
- Average annual liquor consumption since 1970
- Number of calls to customer service per hour for the past week

In short, a baseline consists of a set of quantities measured over time. From the standpoint of forecasting, baselines have four important technical characteristics:

1. A baseline is ordered from the earliest observation to the most recent. This is a fairly simple, even obvious requirement to meet, but you must meet it.
2. All the time periods in the baseline are equally long. You should not mix daily observations with, for example, the average of three days' observations. In practice, you can ignore minor skips. February and March have different numbers of days, but the two- or three-day difference is usually ignored for baselines that use monthly summaries. The very use of monthly summaries implies that such minor differences are not a matter of concern.
3. The observations come from the same point within each time period. For example, suppose you're monitoring freeway traffic, hoping to forecast when you will have to add new lanes. The conditions that you're measuring are very different on Friday at 5:00 p.m. than on Tuesday at 11:00 a.m. For consistency in the meaning of the baseline, you should stick to a particular time and day.

4. Missing data is not allowed. Even one missing observation can throw off the forecasting equations. If a small fraction of your time series is missing, try replacing that data by estimating it.

NOTE In forecasting, the terms *baseline* and *time series* are often used interchangeably. However, a baseline is formally a time series that precedes a forecast. You will find both terms used in this chapter.

TIP A reasonable and quick way to estimate missing data in a baseline is to take the average of the observations immediately before and after one that's missing. For example, if the value for cell A5 is missing, you could enter this into cell A5:

```
=AVERAGE(A4,A6)
```

But don't overdo it. If you find that you're estimating even 10%of your data, you probably need to find a more complete source of information.

If your baseline has these four characteristics, your chances of getting a useful forecast are much better. However, there's nothing like a good, long baseline—more on that starting in the next section.

Many of Excel's tools, including those that have to do with forecasting, require you to arrange your baseline observations vertically in columns. That is, if the first observation in the baseline is in cell A2, the next observation is in cell A3, not B2.

For consistency, the examples in this chapter use baselines in columns rather than rows. For example, if you have your measurements in a worksheet range where rows represent years and columns represent months, it's best to rearrange the numbers into a single column, with the earliest at the top. That orientation makes it easier to use the analysis tools that Excel provides.

NOTE The limitations imposed by the 256-column structure have largely gone away since Excel 2003. Excel gives you 16,384 columns starting with the 2007 release.

In addition to arranging for the baseline, you need to choose a method of creating a forecast. Excel provides three basic approaches to forecasting: moving averages, regression, and smoothing. This chapter also describes a fourth approach: Box-Jenkins. The publisher's website makes Excel workbooks discussed in this book available for download. One of the workbooks, `ARIMA.xls`, contains a VBA module that enables you to perform the identification phase of Box-Jenkins forecasting.

Moving Average Forecasts

Moving averages are easy to use, but sometimes they are too simple to provide a useful forecast. Using this approach, the forecast at any period is just the average of the most recent observations in the baseline. For example, if you choose a three-month moving average, the forecast for May would be the average of the observations for February, March, and April. If you choose to take a four-month moving average, then the forecast for May would be the average of January, February, March, and April.

This method is easy to compute, and it responds well to recent changes in the time series. Many time series respond more strongly to recent events than to events that occurred long ago. For example, suppose that you are forecasting the sales volume of a mature product, one that has averaged nice, stable sales of 1,000 units per month for several years. If your company suddenly and significantly downsizes its sales force, the units sold per month would probably decline, at least for a few months.

Continuing that example, if you were using the average sales volume for the past four months as your forecast for the next month, the forecast would probably overestimate the actual result. But if you used the average of only the past two months, your forecast would respond more quickly to the effect of downsizing the sales force. The two-month moving average forecast would lag behind the actual results for only a month or two. Figure 9.1 gives a visual example of this effect, where the vertical axis represents sales volume and the horizontal axis represents months.

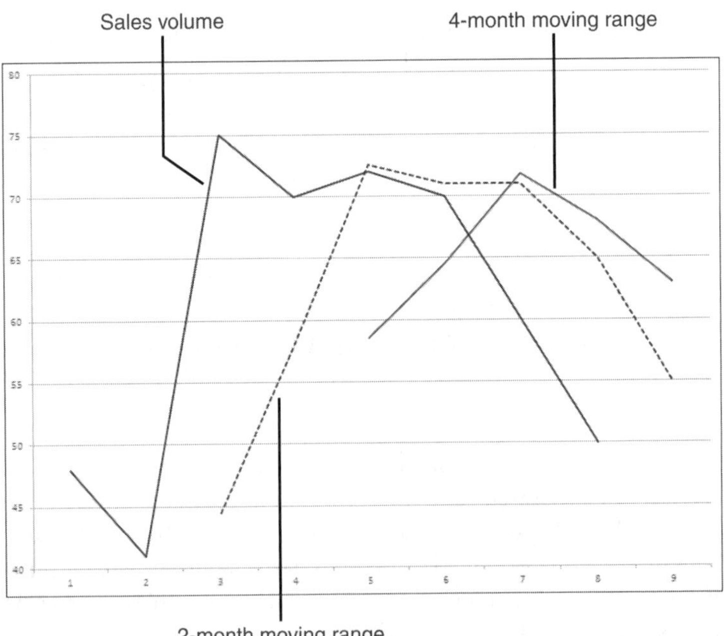

Figure 9.1
The two-month moving average for sales volume tracks the actual sales more closely than does the four-month moving average.

The effect depicted in Figure 9.1 occurs because, with a two-month moving average, the two most recent months are each responsible for one-half of the forecast's value. With a four-month average, the four most recent months are each responsible for only one fourth of the forecast value.

Therefore, the fewer and the more recent the observations involved in a moving average, the greater the influence each has on the value of the moving average and the more quickly the average responds to changes in the level of the baseline.

In Figure 9.1, also notice that there are two fewer four-month averages than two-month averages. This occurs because two more months must elapse before you can get a four-month average than a two-month average.

You don't want to use a shorter moving average just because it's shorter and reacts more quickly to the baseline. If you base your moving average forecast on just two observations, it can become trivial (and if you use just one observation in the average, it *is* trivial). In particular, the moving average won't depict an underlying trend in the data any better than the baseline itself does.

Knowing how many observations to include in a moving average is equal parts experience and knowledge of the data series in question. You need to balance the greater responsiveness of a shorter moving average against the greater volatility of that average.

One highly unusual data point in a three-component average can make a forecast look silly. And the fewer the components, the less the moving average responds to signal and the more to noise. There's no good general rule to use here: You have to use your judgment guided by your knowledge of the time series you're working with.

CASE STUDY: CUSTOMER SERVICE

You manage the customer service group for a software-development firm. You receive an email from one of your support staff that says she is getting more phone calls from customers who are having a problem with one of your newer applications. You request her to track these calls over a two-week period and report back to you.

The report that you receive has the daily number of calls that she has received concerning this product. You enter the data into an Excel worksheet, laid out as shown in cells A2:A11 of Figure 9.2. To see whether there is any trend in the data, you create a moving average from the number of phone calls, as shown in cells B5:B12 of Figure 9.2.

Figure 9.2
Moving average forecasts always lose some data at the beginning of the baseline period.

B5 =AVERAGE(A2:A4)

	A	B	C	D
1	Actual calls	Forecast calls		
2	10			
3	11			
4	10			
5	12	10.33		
6	13	11.00		
7	13	11.67		
8	13	12.67		
9	10	13.00		
10	16	12.00		
11	17	13.00		
12		14.33		

9

TIP

If you calculate moving averages using formulas like the one shown in Figure 9.2, Excel's Error Checking feature (available since Excel 2002) might flag them as possibly erroneous. This occurs because the formulas omit reference to adjacent cells that contain values. You can prevent the error indicator from appearing by clicking the File tab and then clicking the Excel Options button. Select Formulas in the list box, and find the Error Checking Rules area. Clear the Formulas Which Omit Cells in a Region check box. If you are using a version prior to Excel 2007, select Tools, Options, and click the Error Checking tab. Then clear the Formula Omits Cells in Region check box.

Or, if you want to clear the error indicator after the fact, you can select all the cells that contain the indicator, move your mouse pointer over the warning icon to display the menu drop-down, click the drop-down to display the shortcut menu, and click Ignore Error.

You decide to use a three-day moving average: a shorter moving average might bounce around too much to depict any trend well, and a much longer moving average might obscure a trend. One way to create a moving average in Excel is to enter the formula directly. To get the three-day moving average for the number of phone calls, as shown in Figure 9.2, you enter

```
=AVERAGE(A2:A4)
```

into cell B5. Next, AutoFill or copy and paste that formula into B6:B12. The moving average does seem to be trending up, and you might decide to bring the situation to the attention of your company's product testing group.

NOTE

To use AutoFill, use your mouse pointer to drag the fill handle of a selected cell or range vertically or horizontally. The fill handle is the small square in the lower-right corner of the selection.

Creating Forecasts with the Moving Average Add-In

Another way to create a moving average is to use the Analysis ToolPak. You reach this utility by following these steps:

1. With a worksheet active, click the File tab. Click Excel Options, and then choose Add-Ins from the list box. Select Excel Add-Ins in the Manage drop-down, and click Go. In a version prior to Excel 2007, choose Tools, Add-Ins.
2. Excel displays a dialog box with the available add-ins. Click the box labeled Analysis ToolPak and then choose OK. You will now see a new Analysis group on the Ribbon's Data tab. Earlier Excel versions show a Data Analysis option at the bottom of the Tools menu. (If you don't see the ToolPak in the dialog box, you will have to run Office Setup and install it from the CD.)
3. If necessary, activate a worksheet that contains your baseline data.

4. Click the Data tab and then click Data Analysis in the Analysis group. In earlier Excel versions, choose Tools, Data Analysis.
5. Excel displays a dialog box containing the available data analysis tools. Scroll down the list box until you see Moving Average. Select that tool and then click OK.
6. Excel displays the Moving Average dialog box that prompts you for the Input Range, Interval, and Output Range, as shown in Figure 9.3.

Figure 9.3
The Moving Average dialog box enables you to define an interval consisting of the observations that go into each average.

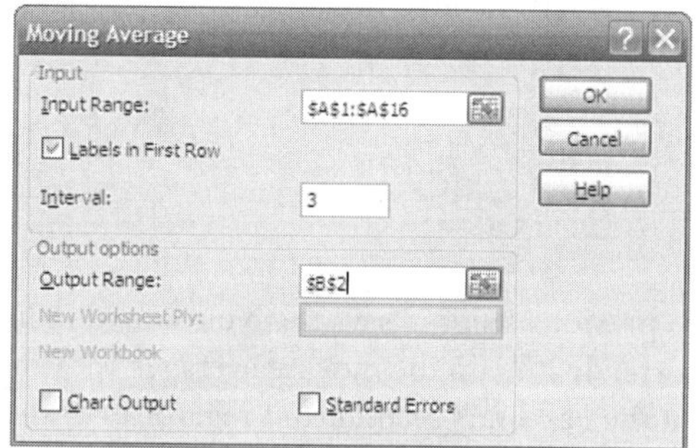

7. Click in the Input Range edit box, and either select your baseline data or type its reference.
8. Click in the Interval edit box, and enter the number of periods that you want to include in each moving average.
9. Click in the Output Range edit box, and enter the address of the cell (or just click the cell) where you want the output to start.
10. Click OK.

Excel fills in the formulas for the moving average on your behalf. The moving averages begin with some `#N/A` error values. There are as many `#N/A` values as the interval you specified, minus one (as you'll see in the next section, this is one `#N/A` too few). The error values come about because there's not enough data to calculate averages for those first few observations: for example, you can't calculate a three-month moving average on two months' worth of data. Figure 9.4 shows the results of using the moving average add-in on the same data as used in Figure 9.1, with a three-period interval.

Dealing with the Layout of Excel's Moving Averages

It's standard to regard a moving average forecast as a forecast for the first period immediately following the last observation in the average. For example, suppose that you create a three-month moving average of sales revenues and that the final three observations in your baseline are for January, February, and March. The average of those three observations is usually regarded as the moving average forecast for April: the first period immediately following the last observation.

However, Excel's Moving Average add-in (and, as you will see in the next section, its Moving Average trendline) does not properly line up the forecasts with the baseline values.

Figure 9.4
A three-interval moving average cannot calculate an average for the first two intervals.

B4 | fx =AVERAGE(A2:A4)

	A	B	C	D
1	Sales volume			
2	68	#N/A		
3	60	#N/A		
4	74	67.33		
5	63	65.67		
6	52	63.00		
7	34	49.67		
8	27	37.67		
9	38	33.00		
10	41	35.33		
11	75	51.33		
12	70	62.00		
13	72	72.33		
14	70	70.67		
15	60	67.33		
16	64	64.67		

Notice that step 9, in the previous section, says that you should indicate where you want the output to start. To correctly line up the moving averages with the baseline figures, you should start the output in the baseline's second row, regardless of the number of intervals you specify for the moving average.

If you start the output range in the same row as the one where the baseline starts, you'll wind up with the final moving average in the same row as the end of the baseline. For example, compare Figure 9.2, where the moving averages were created by entering formulas directly on the worksheet, and Figure 9.4, which was created by the Moving Average add-in. Notice that each moving average in Figure 9.4 is in the same row as one of the baseline values that makes up that average. This implies that 67.33, the first moving average that is computed, is the forecast for the third period.

But it's illogical to regard a number as a forecast for a period that was used to calculate the forecast. The standard interpretation would be that 67.33 is the forecast for the fourth period, not for the third period.

This isn't just a matter of being finicky. When you make a forecast, you often want to follow it up by charting the baseline and the forecasts against the baseline's dates. If you don't get the forecasts and dates paired up accurately on the worksheet, the chart won't display them accurately either.

If you chart the output by selecting the Chart Output check box in the Moving Average dialog box, the chart positions the moving averages incorrectly, regardless of where you place the output range. The Moving Average add-in pairs the final forecast with the final baseline observation. So doing locates all the forecasts one position too early on the chart. To handle this problem, edit the chart's forecast series by clicking it and, in the formula bar, change the series' first row to the row that precedes it. For example, change this:

```
=SERIES("Forecast",,'Sales Forecast'!$B$3:$B$25,2)
```

to this:

```
=SERIES("Forecast",,'Sales Forecast'!$B$2:$B$25,2)
```

Creating Moving Average Forecasts with Excel's Charts

You can trade speed for information by creating a chart that uses your baseline data to show a moving average trendline. This method is usually a little faster than using the Moving Average add-in. Furthermore, if you did not install the Analysis ToolPak when you installed Excel, you will need to do so before you can invoke the Moving Average add-in.

The trade-off is that neither the worksheet nor the chart will show the actual numeric values of the moving average. It also suffers from the defect already noted in the prior section: The forecast is displayed one time period too early. In this case, there is no workaround because you can't shift the location of a chart's trendline.

If you decide that you can live with these trade-offs, you can create a moving average trendline by following these steps in Excel 2007 and 2010 (if you are using a version prior to Excel 2007, skip to the next list):

1. Select the baseline data.
2. Click the Ribbon's Insert tab, and then click the Line button in the Charts group.
3. Click the Line with Markers button. A new line chart appears, embedded in the active worksheet.
4. Select the chart. Notice that three Chart Tools tabs appear on the Ribbon. Click the Layout tab.
5. Click the Trendline drop-down in the Analysis group, and select the More Trendline Options item from the drop-down list.
6. In the Format Trendline dialog box, click the Moving Average option in the Trend/Regression Type area.
7. Enter `3` in the Period box.
8. Click Close to view the moving average trendline, as shown in Figure 9.5.

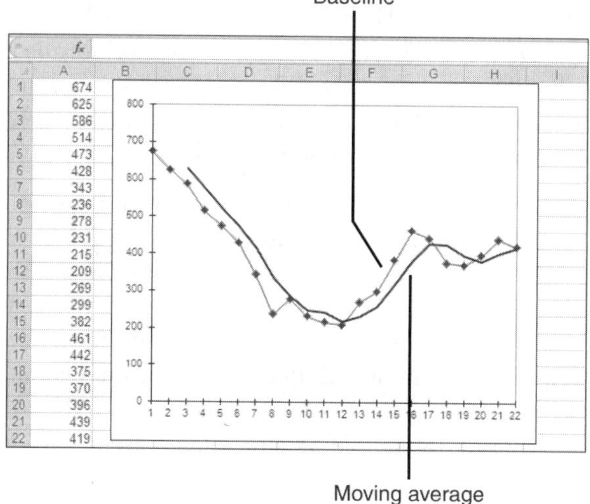

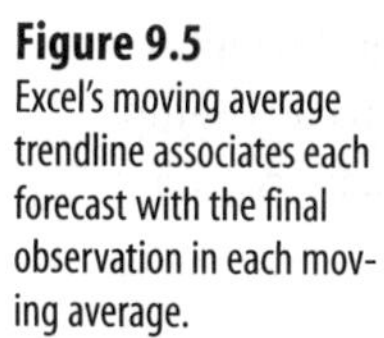

Figure 9.5
Excel's moving average trendline associates each forecast with the final observation in each moving average.

Here are the steps to use when working with versions prior to Excel 2007:

1. Select your baseline data.
2. Begin the Chart Wizard, either by clicking the button on the Standard or Chart toolbar or by selecting Insert, Chart.
3. In step 1 of the Chart Wizard, select Line Chart. Then select a Line Chart subtype that includes both lines and markers. Click Next.
4. In step 2, verify the data range address and orientation (rows or columns). Click Next.
5. In step 3, set options such as Legend, Chart Title, and Axis Titles to the values that you want. Click Next.
6. In step 4, select a location for the chart. Click Finish.
7. Click on the data series in the chart to select it, and select Chart, Add Trendline.
8. On the Type tab, click the Moving Average box, and either type the periods you want in the edit box or use the spinner to change the number of periods. The period is the number of observations to include in any given moving average.
9. Click OK. When you are finished, you will see the moving average trendline on the chart, along with the actual observations, as shown in Figure 9.5.

The first few moving averages on the trendline are missing, for the same reason that the Moving Average add-in returns `#N/A` for the first few moving averages. A moving average consisting of three prior observations can't be calculated until the third period has been observed.

Notice that the moving average trendline in Figure 9.5 displays the first moving average, based on three baseline observations, at the same point on the x-axis as it displays the third data point. Because you can't correct the trendline's location, you might prefer to calculate the moving averages yourself and display them in a chart as a standard data series.

Forecasting with Excel's Regression Functions

A simple moving average is a quick-and-dirty way to get a feel for the general trend of a time series, but you're likely to want more than that. If you worked through the examples for moving average forecasts, you probably noticed that they don't give you a projection more than one period beyond the final point in your baseline.

For example, suppose you're calculating a three-month moving average on a baseline that ends with March, April, and May. Your final three-month average forecasts a value for June. If you move one month further out, into July, you have only the actuals for April and May on which to base the July forecast, and that changes the nature of the moving average from a three-month to a two-month moving average. In turn, the moving average becomes more volatile and more sensitive to a one-month fluctuation. So, although mathematically you can generate another moving average, you lose information and the two-month average isn't truly commensurate with the preceding three-month averages.

You can get a projection further into the future by using one of Excel's regression functions. Each of these methods estimates the relationship between the actual observations and some other variable, and results in an equation that you can use to make forecasts. That other variable is often a measure of *when* the observation was made. It could be the numeric position of each observation in the time series, or it could be the date when you made the observation.

NOTE

One regression approach, *autoregression*, estimates the relationship between observations in the time series and earlier observations in the same time series. See the "Understanding ARIMA Basics" section later in this chapter to learn more about autoregression.

Making Linear Forecasts: The TREND Function

The TREND worksheet function is the easiest way to create a regression forecast. Suppose that your baseline observations are in cells A1:A10, and indicators such as day of the month are in cells B1:B10, as in Figure 9.6. Select the range C1:C10 and array-enter the following formula:

```
=TREND(A1:A10,B1:B10)
```

to get the results shown in Figure 9.6.

NOTE

Reminder: To array-enter a formula, use Ctrl+Shift+Enter.

Figure 9.6
The TREND function forecasts a series of observations on the basis of some other variable.

fx {=TREND(A1:A10,B1:B10)}

	A	B	C	D
1	10	1	9.75	
2	11	2	10.36	
3	10	3	10.97	
4	12	4	11.58	
5	13	5	12.19	
6	13	6	12.81	
7	13	7	13.42	
8	10	8	14.03	
9	16	9	14.64	
10	17	10	15.25	
11				

There are several points to notice about this forecasting method:

- The same array formula returns each result in cells C1:C10. Even though it covers 10 cells, it's one single formula. Hidden within the array formula is a more complex expression. In this example, the actual, expanded formula is

Cell C1: = `9.13 + .61 * 1`

Cell C2: = `9.13 + .61 * 2`

Cell C3: = `9.13 + .61 * 3`

and so on. The value `9.13` is the *intercept* of the forecast line: that is, the value of the forecast at time zero. The value `.61` is the *slope* of the forecast line.

9

> **NOTE** The *slope* is the change in the value of the forecast for each change in the date of the observations. Back in algebra class, your teacher probably called this the "rise over the run."

- Because the same intercept and the same slope together create each forecast value, the forecast doesn't reflect changes in the time series as they occur. For example, the series jumps between the eighth observation (`10`) and the ninth observation (`16`). The intercept and slope take account of this shift, but it affects *all* the forecast values. The jump affects the forecast at time 2, even though time 2 is six observations before the shift actually occurs. Contrast this outcome with a moving average that responds to a shift only afterward, and only temporarily.
- In this example, `TREND` computes the forecast based on the relationship between the actual observations and the numbers 1 through 10, which could be the first 10 days of the month or the first 10 months of the year. Excel terms the first argument to the `TREND` function the *known y's*, and the second argument the *known x's*.

> **NOTE** If you supply only the first argument, the known y's, to `TREND()`, Excel assumes that the known x's are a series beginning with 1 and ending with the number of known-y values that you specify. Assuming that the numbers 1 through 20 are in cells B1:B20, these two formulas are equivalent:
>
> ```
> =TREND(A1:A20)
> =TREND(A1:A20,B1:B20)
> ```

The regression approaches to forecasting let you make projections beyond the end of the baseline. The regression forecast shown in Figure 9.6 goes only as far as the final actual observation. In practice, you normally want to forecast at least through the value of the next (and, so far, unobserved) point in the baseline. Here is how to do that using `TREND`.

Using the same worksheet data as in Figure 9.6, enter the number `11` in cell B11, and in cell C11, enter

```
=TREND(A1:A10,B1:B10,B11)
```

NOTE

Earlier in this section, examples of the `TREND` function stated that the formulas should be array-entered. There are several reasons to array-enter formulas, and one is that a single formula that returns an array of results must be array-entered. The earlier examples returned an array of results. The current example returns one value only and the formula can be entered normally. However, you may recall that previous chapters discussed single-cell formulas that must be array-entered. For just one example, see Figure 3.5.

The example shown in Figure 9.7 uses an additional argument to the `TREND` function. The first argument, the range A1:A10, defines the baseline observations, which are the known y's, as before. The second argument, the range B1:B10, defines the times when the baseline observations were made, which are the known x's, also as before. The value `11` in cell B11 is a *new x* that defines the time period to associate with the projection that `TREND` displays in the cell where it is entered.

Figure 9.7
The TREND function forecasts beyond the end of the baseline by means of its new x's argument.

fx =TREND(A1:A10,B1:B10,B11)

	A	B	C	D
1	10	1	9.75	
2	11	2	10.36	
3	10	3	10.97	
4	12	4	11.58	
5	13	5	12.19	
6	13	6	12.81	
7	13	7	13.42	
8	10	8	14.03	
9	16	9	14.64	
10	17	10	15.25	
11		11	15.87	

In effect, the formula says, "Given the relationship between the y-values in cells A1:A10 and the x-values in cells B1:B10, what y-value would result from a new x-value of `11`?" Excel returns the value `15.87`, which is a projection of the observed data into the as-yet-unrecorded 11th time point.

TIP

You can forecast to dates later than just the next time point by entering a larger value into cell B11. Suppose that the observations in cells A1:A10 were monthly sales volume for January through October 2007. Then the number `24` in cell B11 would specify the 24th month: December 2008. The `TREND` function would return `23.8`. This is the projected sales volume for December 2008, which is based on actual observations from January through October 2007.

You can project to more than one new time point at once. For example, enter the numbers `11` through `24` in cells B11:B24. Then select cells C11:C24 and array-enter

```
=TREND(A1:A10,B1:B10,B11:B24)
```

In cells C11:C24, Excel returns its forecast for the 11th through 24th time points. It bases the forecast on the relationship between the baseline observations in cells A1:A10 and the baseline time points 1 through 10 in cells B1:B10.

NOTE

Note that you have to array-enter the formula because, in this case, it returns an array of values.

CAUTION

Stretching a regression forecast out too far can be seriously misleading. The prior example showed how to forecast 14 future data points on the basis of a 10 point baseline. That was done simply to demonstrate the function's syntax, not to recommend that you do so. Stretch any forecast too far and it's likely to snap back at you.

Making Nonlinear Forecasts: The GROWTH Function

The TREND function creates forecasts based on a *linear* relationship between the observation and the time that the observation was made. Suppose you chart the data as a line chart with the observations' magnitude on the vertical axis and time on the horizontal axis. If the relationship is a linear one, the line on the chart is relatively straight, trending up or down, or it may be horizontal. This is your first and often best clue that the relationship is linear and that TREND is probably the best regression-forecasting tool.

However, if the line has a clear upward or downward curve to it, then the relationship between observations and time periods may well be *nonlinear*. There are many kinds of data that change over time in a nonlinear way. Some examples of this data include new product sales, population growth, payments on debt principal, and per-unit profit margin. In some cases where the relationship is nonlinear, Excel's GROWTH function can give you a better picture of the pattern than can the TREND function.

CASE STUDY: BOOK SALES

The purchasing manager of a large online book retailer has just requested that a new banner be placed on the website's home page. The banner advertises a novel that is receiving excellent reviews. The manager suspects that she'll have to order additional copies earlier than she normally would. To avoid being caught short, the manager starts to track daily orders for the book and records the sales shown in Figure 9.8.

Figure 9.8 shows how both the actual data and the forecasts appear in a standard line chart. Because the line for the actuals curves upward, the manager decides to forecast using the GROWTH function. As with TREND, the manager can generate forecasts by simply providing

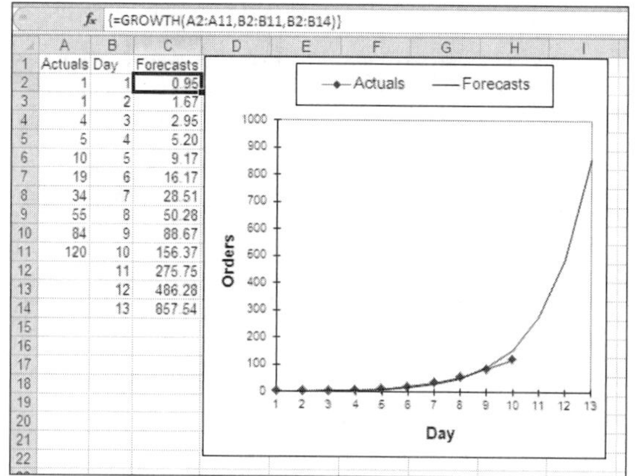

{=GROWTH(A2:A11,B2:B11,B2:B14)}

Actuals	Day	Forecasts
1	1	0.95
1	2	1.67
4	3	2.95
5	4	5.20
10	5	9.17
19	6	16.17
34	7	28.51
55	8	50.28
84	9	88.67
120	10	156.37
	11	275.75
	12	486.28
	13	857.54

Figure 9.8
The GROWTH function can be useful in forecasting nonlinear baselines.

new x-values. To forecast into days 11 to 13, enter those numbers into cells B12:B14, and array-enter the following `GROWTH` function into cells C2:C14:

```
=GROWTH(A2:A11,B2:B11,B2:B14)
```

Cells C12:C14 contain numbers of orders that are forecast for the next three days, if the current nonlinear growth pattern continues. It's smart to temper such optimistic forecasts with some sense of reality, though. When this sort of forecast projects orders that exceed the total of site hits, it's probably time to back off the forecast.

In cases that display this sort of explosive growth, you might find it more convenient to deal with the logarithms of the observations instead of the observations themselves. For example, you can show the exponential growth as a straight line by using a log scale for the chart's vertical axis. Figure 9.9 shows how the book club data appears in a line chart where the scale of the vertical axis is in log units.

What if the manager used `TREND` instead of `GROWTH` on the book club data? `TREND` returns linear values: values that plot a straight line. In Figure 9.10, notice that the `TREND` series in col-

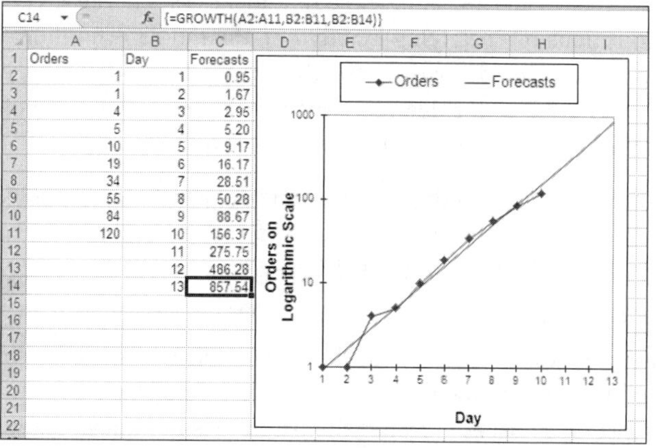

C14 {=GROWTH(A2:A11,B2:B11,B2:B14)}

Orders	Day	Forecasts
1	1	0.95
1	2	1.67
4	3	2.95
5	4	5.20
10	5	9.17
19	6	16.17
34	7	28.51
55	8	50.28
84	9	88.67
120	10	156.37
	11	275.75
	12	486.28
	13	857.54

Figure 9.9
The logarithmic chart of exponential growth in book sales can be easier to interpret than the standard line chart.

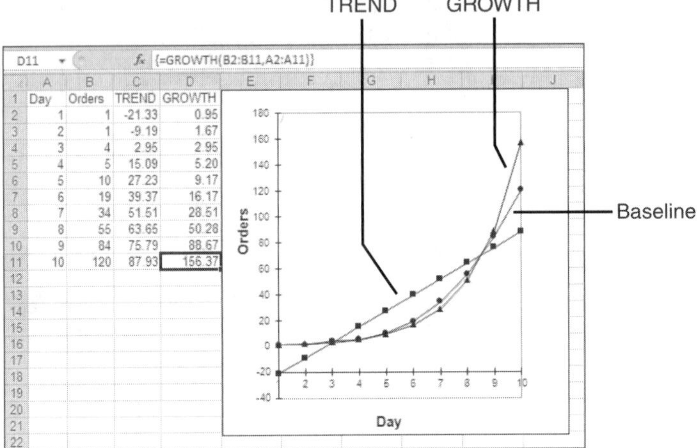

Day	Orders	TREND	GROWTH
1	1	-21.33	0.95
2	1	-9.19	1.67
3	4	2.95	2.95
4	5	15.09	5.20
5	10	27.23	9.17
6	19	39.37	16.17
7	34	51.51	28.51
8	55	63.65	50.28
9	84	75.79	88.67
10	120	87.93	156.37

Figure 9.10 Modeling with GROWTH( ) can be more convenient than modeling with TREND( ) when baselines are nonlinear.

umn C describes that straight line on the chart. Figure 9.10 also shows the baseline and the results of the GROWTH function. You can see that the values projected by the GROWTH function are much closer to the ones actually observed, and the GROWTH line is a much better representation of the first 10 actual observations than is the TREND line. Therefore, working with this baseline, you are likely to forecast subsequent data more accurately by using GROWTH than by using TREND. By using GROWTH, you acknowledge that the baseline is nonlinear.

Nevertheless, there is nothing magical about GROWTH: It's simply a convenient way to return specifically logarithmic results, which describe just one type of nonlinear relationship. Natural logarithms do not describe all nonlinear series. For example, you might want to project a quadratic trend by squaring its results, like this:

```
=TREND(B2:B11,A2:A11)^2
```

To see how dramatically this quadratic trend differs from the one returned by GROWTH, enter it on a worksheet just as TREND and GROWTH are entered in the worksheet shown in Figure 9.10, and then chart all three.

You should consider using TREND in these nonlinear cases because you can maintain control over your projections by specifying exactly *how* the model is nonlinear. Although TREND always returns values that describe a straight line on an XY (Scatter) chart, using it with other worksheet functions (or operators such as the exponentiation operator, as in the previous formula) can bring about the type of result you're after.

To shed a little more light on the relationship between TREND and GROWTH, Figure 9.11 shows an example of how to use the TREND function to return results identical to the GROWTH function. The array formula used in cells C2:C14 is

```
=EXP(TREND(LN(B2:B11),A2:A11,A2:A14))
```

Note that these values are identical to the ones returned by GROWTH shown previously in Figure 9.8 and would describe the same curve on a line chart. In many cases, you will want to use TREND instead of GROWTH, even if the baseline is nonlinear. GROWTH is a useful shortcut

Figure 9.11
Use the TREND function in place of the GROWTH function to handle relationships of any type.

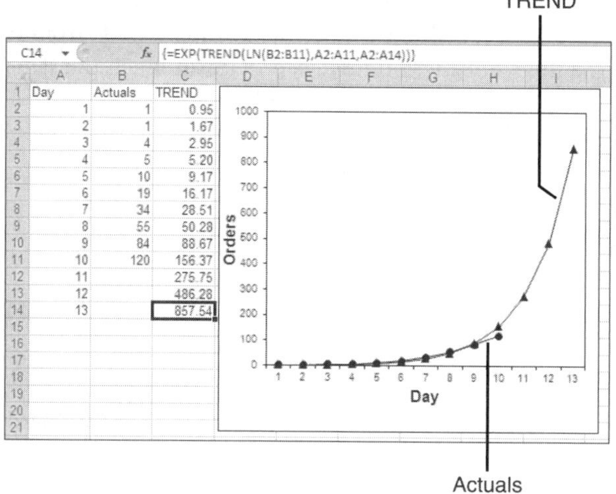

Day	Actuals	TREND
1	1	0.95
2	1	1.67
3	4	2.95
4	5	5.20
5	10	9.17
6	19	16.17
7	34	28.51
8	55	50.28
9	84	88.67
10	120	156.37
11		275.75
12		486.28
13		857.54

for using TREND in combination with logarithms (the LN function) and the base of the natural logarithms (the EXP function) when you have data that natural logarithms fit well.

It helps to keep these points in mind:

- When you chart a variable, the pattern of the data points often suggests a straight line. Then using the TREND function with no frills is likely the best way to forecast future values.
- If the charted data points suggest a curved line, one possibility is that the GROWTH function will provide your best forecast. Compare the results of using GROWTH on your baseline with the baseline itself. If the fit is good, you should consider using GROWTH to forecast from the baseline.
- If the charted data points suggest a curved line but GROWTH doesn't provide a good approximation, experiment with one of the chart trendlines that Excel provides. These are discussed in the next section.

Creating Regression Forecasts with Excel's Charts

There are plenty of reasons to make extensive use of Excel's charts when you're building a forecast. It always helps to visualize the data. Furthermore, some of the regression techniques you use in forecasting are extremely sensitive to outliers—that is, data points that are unusually far from the regression trendline. It's much easier to tell if outliers have an effect on your forecasts if you put the data on a chart.

> **NOTE** The reason for that extreme sensitivity to outliers is found in one of the building blocks of regression analysis: the use of *least squares*. A regression equation minimizes the sum of the squared deviations between each actual observation and the associated, predicted one. This means that an outlier's impact on the analysis is a function not just of its distance from its predicted value, but of the square of that distance.

At times, you just want to view a regression forecast on a chart without calculating the forecast values in worksheet cells. You do so by creating a chart from the baseline values in the worksheet. You then add a trendline to the chart, in much the same way that you add a moving average trendline to a chart. Figure 9.12 displays baseline data and a chart with the baseline, trendline, and forecasts.

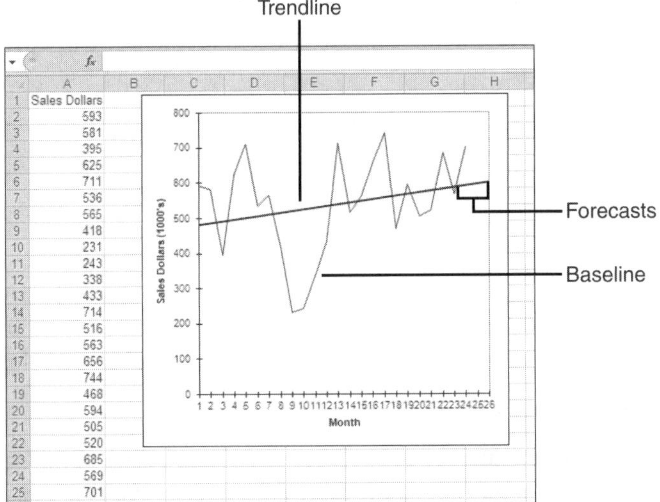

Figure 9.12
Create regression-based forecasts directly on a chart by means of trendlines.

To create the chart shown in Figure 9.12,start by selecting cells A2:A25, click the Ribbon's Insert tab and then select one of the 2D line chart types from the Line drop-down. In versions of Excel prior to 2007, click the Chart Wizard button and follow its steps to create a line chart.

Click the chart to open it for editing, click the data series on the chart to select it, and complete these steps:

1. Click the Ribbon's Layout tab, which appears when you open the chart. In earlier versions of Excel, choose Chart, Add Trendline.
2. In the Analysis area, click the Trendline drop-down and then select More Trendline Options from the drop-down list.
3. Select Linear under Trend/Regression Type.
4. If necessary, click the Options tab.
5. In the Forecast Group box, enter the number of Forward forecast periods you want.
6. If you want, select the Display Equation on Chart check box. Doing so places the forecast equation (intercept and slope) as text on the chart. Excel's placement of the equation may obscure the chart's data or trendline, or the equation may not be fully visible. You can move the equation by clicking it and then dragging it to a new location.
7. Click Close.

Unlike a moving averages trendline, a linear trendline can return forecast values, and, if specified, it displays them on the chart.

Forecasting with Excel's Smoothing Functions

Smoothing is a way to get your forecast to respond quickly to events that occur during the baseline period. Regression approaches such as TREND and GROWTH create forecasts by applying the same formula to each baseline point. Therefore, it becomes quite complex to get a quick response to a shift in the level of the baseline without backcasting to points before the shift occurred. Smoothing is a useful way to deal with this problem. It resembles the moving average approach in some ways, but improves on it by building in a self-correction mechanism.

Projecting with Smoothing

The fundamental idea behind the smoothing approach is that each new forecast is obtained in part by moving the *next* forecast in a direction that would have improved the *prior* forecast. Here's the basic equation:

F[t+1] = F[t] + a × e[t]

where:

t is the time period, such as Month 1, Month 2, and so on.

F[t] is the forecast at time t, and F[t+1] is the forecast at the time period immediately following time t.

a is the *smoothing constant.*

e[t] is the error: the difference between the forecast for time t and the actual observation at time t.

In a sense, a smoothing forecast is self-correcting. In words, the formula just given states that each new forecast is the sum of the prior forecast, plus a correction factor that moves the new forecast in the direction that would have made the prior forecast more accurate. Later in this chapter, in the section titled Choosing a Smoothing Constant, you will see how to select a smoothing constant.

Consider the example shown in Figure 9.13.

Notice that the level of the baseline increases dramatically at time 8. This is known as a *step function* or *step change*. Smoothing is useful when there are large differences between levels of data in the time series. The linear trendline does not do a good job of reflecting the step increase that occurs between time 7 and time 8. It overestimates the level of the series through time 7, and it underestimates the series from time 8 on. But the smoothing forecast tracks the actual baseline fairly closely.

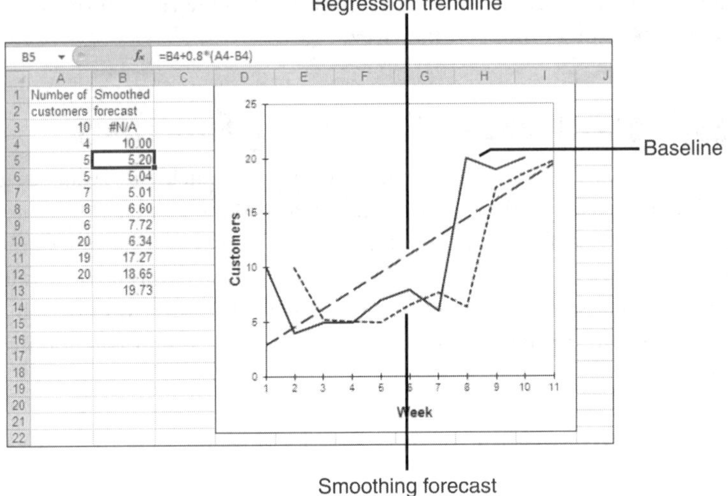

Figure 9.13
The linear trendline forecast misses the baseline's step change, but the smoothing forecast tracks it.

Using the Exponential Smoothing Add-In

The forecasting methods that are collectively known as *smoothing* handle the step-function effect (as well as seasonality) much better than do regression methods. Excel provides one such method directly with the Exponential Smoothing tool in the Analysis ToolPak.

The Exponential Smoothing tool creates forecasts that are identical to the one shown in Figure 9.13. It uses an apparently different but algebraically equivalent formula to calculate each forecast. Each component—prior observation and prior forecast—in each forecast is multiplied by a factor that represents the component's contribution to the current forecast.

To get the Exponential Smoothing tool, first load the Analysis ToolPak if you have not already done so (see this chapter's section titled Creating Forecasts with the Moving Average Add-In). Once the Analysis ToolPak is installed, you can begin working with the Exponential Smoothing tool by clicking the Data tab on the Ribbon and then clicking Data Analysis in the Analysis group. In Excel versions before 2007, choose Tools, Data Analysis.

CASE STUDY: SKI RACKS

Suppose that you operate a car-rental agency in the Rocky Mountain region. As winter approaches, you start to track customer requests for vehicles that have ski racks. (You don't worry about the snowboarders because they just toss their boards into the trunk.) After a few days of monitoring these requests, an early winter storm passes through the area. As expected, the number of requests per day increases substantially. On the tenth day, you would like to know how many cars equipped with ski racks you should have on hand on the eleventh day.

You enter the data for the first 10 days in cells A2:A11 of a worksheet and a column header in cell A1. Then you start Excel's Exponential Smoothing add-in (see Figure 9.14).

NOTE

The *damping factor* in the Smoothing dialog box and the *smoothing constant* mentioned in the prior section are related as follows:

```
1 - smoothing constant = damping factor
```

Therefore, knowing the damping factor means that you also know the smoothing constant, and vice versa. Excel chooses to ask you for the damping factor. Most references discuss smoothing in terms of the smoothing constant rather than the damping factor.

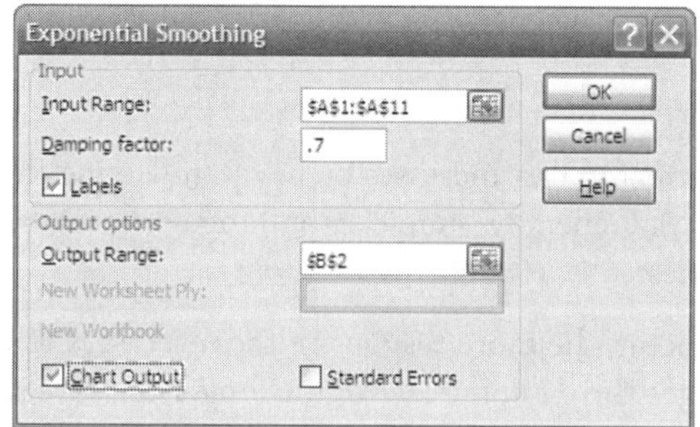

Figure 9.14
The Exponential Smoothing dialog box asks you for a damping factor rather than a smoothing constant.

You use cells A1:A11 as the Input Range, select the Labels check box, use cell B2 as the Output Range, and use 0.7 as the Damping Factor. Excel returns the results shown in Figure 9.15.

TIP

To forecast one time period beyond the end of the baseline, enter one extra row in the Smoothing dialog box's Input Range edit box.

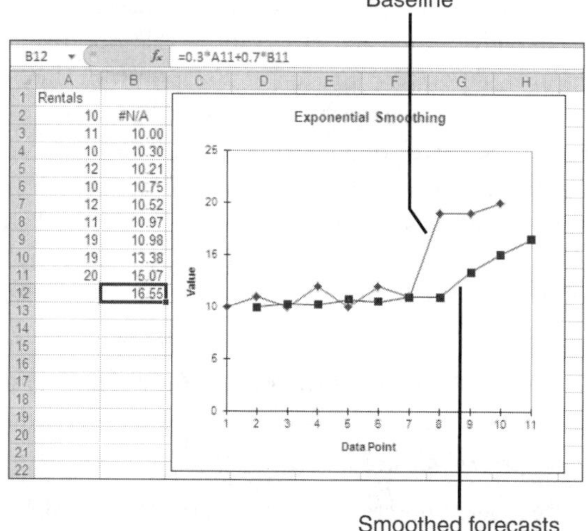

Figure 9.15
Car rental data with smoothed forecasts; notice the lag in the forecasts.

According to the smoothed forecast, the best estimate of the required number of cars with ski racks on day 11 is 16 or 17. This estimate reflects both the overall level of the baseline data and the increase in requests that occurred on the eighth day. The actual number needed on the eleventh day could drop by several units, as a result of anything from a change in weather conditions to an increase in airline fares. The smoothed forecast strikes a good balance between the recent surge in requests and the average number of requests for the entire 10-day period.

9

NOTE

Even if you select the Labels check box in the Smoothing dialog box, Excel does not show the label in the resulting chart.

Notice in Figure 9.15 that the forecast increases on day 9, reflecting the increase in the baseline that occurs on day 8. Generally, simple smoothing approaches lag one step behind occurrences in the time series.

The smaller the damping factor, the more responsive the forecast is to recent observations. On the other hand, the larger the damping factor, the longer the forecasts will lag behind recent observations. This is useful if recent observations reflect random occurrences that do not alter the overall level of the time series for long.

Choosing a Smoothing Constant

You should avoid using a damping factor smaller than 0.7. If exponential smoothing appears to work *significantly* better with a larger smoothing constant, it is likely due to a substantial amount of autocorrelation in the time series. If so, you need to deal with it by means of a forecasting technique other than simple smoothing.

Autocorrelation is an important concept in forecasting. It quantifies a dependency between observations that occur at a given time and observations that occur some number of time periods earlier. For example, if you pair up each observation with the observation that immediately precedes it, you can calculate the correlation between the two sets of data that result from the pairings. If the correlation is strong—say, 0.5 or greater—then there is a substantial amount of autocorrelation in the time series. The *autocorrelation*—the dependable relationship between earlier observations and later ones—is at the heart of an autoregression forecast. However, a baseline time series with much autocorrelation does not lend itself well to the smoothing approach to forecasting.

TIP

You can use Excel's CORREL function to test for autocorrelation. If your baseline is in A1:A10, you might use

```
=CORREL(A1:A9,A2:A10)
```

to estimate the autocorrelation between each observation and its immediate predecessor. If the autocorrelation is strong, then the magnitude of each observation depends largely on the value of the observation that immediately preceded it.

Another kind of autocorrelation has to do with seasonality in the series. In a time series that consists of months in a year, the observation in each February might be dependent on the prior February, March on the prior March, and so on. In such cases, you should use seasonal smoothing, which is discussed in the next section. You might also use a Box-Jenkins model, which is discussed later in this chapter.

Given that the amount of autocorrelation in your baseline is not too great, you might use Solver to help you arrive at the optimal smoothing constant. The idea is to calculate the degree of error in the forecasts using one smoothing constant and then direct Solver to minimize that error value by changing the smoothing constant. To do so, take these steps (based on Figure 9.15):

1. Install Solver from Office Setup, if necessary, and then make it available. Click the File tab, click Excel Options, click Add-Ins, and finally click Go at the bottom of the dialog box. In versions of Excel prior to 2007, make Solver available by clicking Tools, Add-Ins.
2. In cell B15, enter this formula:
   `=SQRT(SUMXMY2(A3:A11,B3:B11)/9)`
3. Give some other cell the name `SmoothingConstant` and enter the value `0.3` into that cell.
4. Give another cell the name `DampingFactor` and enter the formula
   `=1-SmoothingConstant.`
5. In cell B4, enter the formula `=SmoothingConstant*A3+DampingFactor*B3`, and copy and paste it into cells B5:B12. Leave the range B2:B3 as it is in Figure 9.15.
6. Click the Ribbon's Data tab, and click Solver in the Data Analysis group. (In earlier versions of Excel, choose Tools, Solver.)
7. Set Target Cell to B15 and click the Min option button.
8. Set Changing Cells to SmoothingConstant. Click Solve.

The formula in cell B15 calculates what's sometimes termed the *root mean square error*. It uses the `SUMXMY2` worksheet function to return the sum of the squared differences between, in this case, the actual observations and the smoothed forecasts: these are the squared errors. The formula then divides by the number of forecasts and takes the square root of the result. The root mean square error is one standard way of measuring the degree of error in forecasts.

When you invoke Solver as just described, it tries other values of the smoothing constant until it finds the one that minimizes the root mean square error—that is, the one that provides the most accurate smoothed forecasts. You use Solver here instead of Goal Seek because you are not seeking a specific value but a minimum.

Making Smoothed Forecasts Handle Seasonal Data

If you want to forecast sales, you almost certainly need to account for seasonal trends. Sales data and related time series are frequently seasonal. For example, sales may spike at the beginning of the year and then return to a lower level until the next year.

This effect can be due to the nature of the product: The demand for parkas is lower during spring and summer than during fall and winter. It can also be due to fiscal years: Buyers might increase their purchases at the point in the fiscal year when cash accounts are flush. In cases like these, the simple regression and simple smoothing methods are usually unable to forecast the seasonal trend.

When a time series displays a seasonal trend, it's usually necessary to modify the smoothing formula. Instead of forecasting just on the basis of the prior observation, a seasonal forecast works on the basis of two components:

- **A trend component**, which represents any upward or downward drift in the baseline.
- **A seasonal component**, which represents any upward or downward movements in the level of the baseline that occur at regular intervals.

The seasonal smoothing process takes place in two phases:

1. **Initialization phase**—Quantifies the magnitude of the trend and seasonal components
2. **Forecasting phase**—Makes the projections based on those components

Consider the time series in Figure 9.16.

The series in Figure 9.16 is seasonal. It trends up each August and down again each November. A forecast that used simple exponential smoothing would have some undesirable lag because a current forecast is based on the prior observation and the prior forecast. Therefore, a forecast of the surge in the series' value that occurs each August would lag by a month each year. Figure 9.16 also shows the forecast based on the time series by means of simple exponential smoothing.

Seasonal smoothing takes account of this regularity in the data by looking back at the pattern in prior years. The current forecasts then reflect the prior pattern. This minimizes the lag from the prior observation to the current forecast. Figure 9.17 shows the same baseline

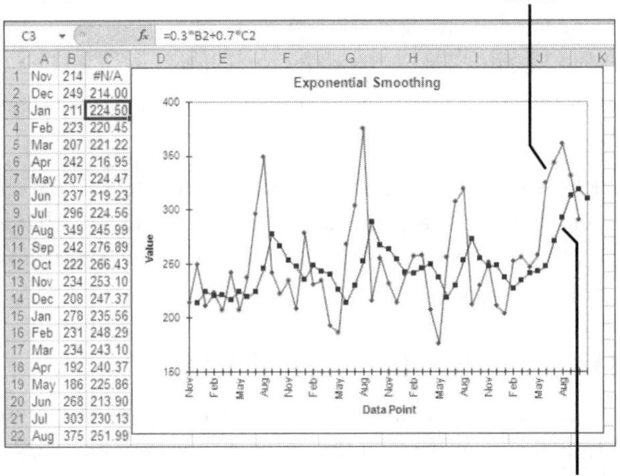

	A	B	C
1	Nov	214	#N/A
2	Dec	249	214.00
3	Jan	211	224.50
4	Feb	223	220.45
5	Mar	207	221.22
6	Apr	242	216.95
7	May	207	224.47
8	Jun	237	219.23
9	Jul	296	224.56
10	Aug	349	245.99
11	Sep	242	276.89
12	Oct	222	266.43
13	Nov	234	253.10
14	Dec	208	247.37
15	Jan	278	235.56
16	Feb	231	248.29
17	Mar	234	243.10
18	Apr	192	240.37
19	May	186	225.86
20	Jun	268	213.90
21	Jul	303	230.13
22	Aug	375	251.99

Figure 9.16
Sales data from baselines greater than one year in length often have a seasonal component.

as in Figure 9.16, along with a seasonally smoothed forecast. There is still some lag, but not as much as with simple smoothing. Furthermore, because each forecast depends in part on an observation from a prior year, it is possible to extend the forecast further into the future than it is with simple smoothing.

> **NOTE** This kind of analysis can be useful to a business even if it never prepares a formal forecast. Just knowing about seasonality in revenues, costs, or profits helps you to make operational decisions that are more effective. Knowing the degree of change caused by the seasonality makes these decisions more effective still.

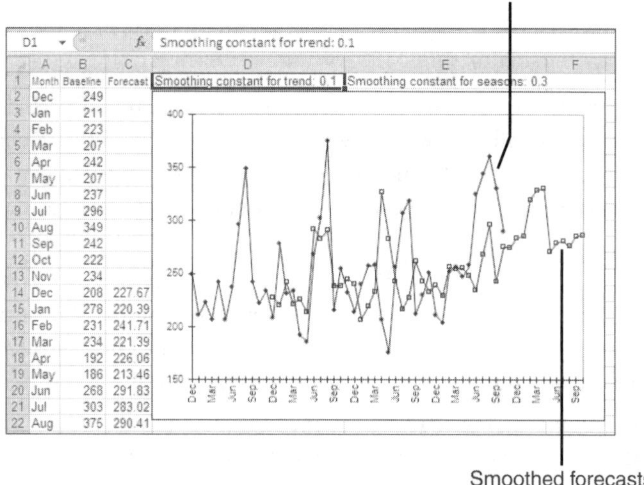

Figure 9.17
Seasonality can sometimes let you forecast further into the future than can a one-step-ahead forecast.

Two smoothing constants are necessary for seasonal smoothing: one for any trend there may be in the series, and one for the seasonal component. You can use Solver, as shown in the prior section, to help you find the best values for the constants. Just include both constants as the changing cells in Solver.

The website for this book contains a folder with a file named `Smooth.xls`. The file contains a module, also named `Smooth`. The module contains a VBA procedure, `SeasonalSmooth`. `SeasonalSmooth` provides seasonally smoothed forecasts from a baseline of observations. To run the `SeasonalSmooth` code, have a worksheet with your baseline open. The baseline should occupy a single column. Then follow these steps:

1. Open `Smooth.xls` and click the Ribbon's Developer tab. Then click the Macros button in the Code area.
2. In the Macro Name list box, select `Smooth.xls!SeasonalSmooth`.
3. Click Run.

> **NOTE** Chapter 18, "Exporting Business Data From Excel," describes how to put the Developer tab on the Ribbon. See the section in that chapter titled Getting at VBA.

If you're using a version of Excel prior to 2007, these are the steps:

1. Open `Smooth.xls`, and switch back to the worksheet that contains your baseline observations.
2. Select Smooth from the Data menu.

When you run that macro, a dialog box similar to the Exponential Smoothing dialog box appears on your screen, giving you the opportunity to identify these items:

- An input range—your baseline—found on your worksheet in a single column.
- The number of periods in each season. For example, if your input data consists of one observation for each month in the year, then the number of periods in each season (spring, summer, fall, and winter) would be 3. If your input data consists of one observation for each week in the month, then the number of periods in each season would be 4, if you consider that a month is a season, or 12, if you consider that a quarter is a season.
- The number of seasons per calendar block. A *calendar block* is the period of time during which a seasonal cycle becomes complete. For example, if you are concerned with quarterly cycles, then the calendar block will likely be one year. If you are concerned with weekly cycles, then the calendar block might be one month.
- The two smoothing constants: one for the trend and one for the seasons. Both constants should be set to a fractional value between 0 and 1.

CASE STUDY: CURBSIDE PICKUPS

A municipality makes special curbside pickups of its residents' green waste such as lawn and brush clippings. It has been doing so every other month for two and one-half years. To budget the next year of the program properly, it forecasts the tonnage that it expects to pick up based based on the first 30 months that the program has been in place.

You enter the baseline data into cells A2:A16 of a worksheet and a column header into cell A1. Then start the seasonal smoothing add-in as described in the prior section (see Figure 9.18).

You complete the entries in the Seasonal Smoothing dialog box as follows:

1. Enter `A2:A16` into the Baseline Range box, either by dragging through the range on the worksheet or by typing the reference directly into the edit box.
2. Enter `1` into the Periods per Season box. Because there is only one pickup scheduled every other month, each observation constitutes one season.

Figure 9.18
Because the pickups occur every other month, there is one period per season and six seasons per year.

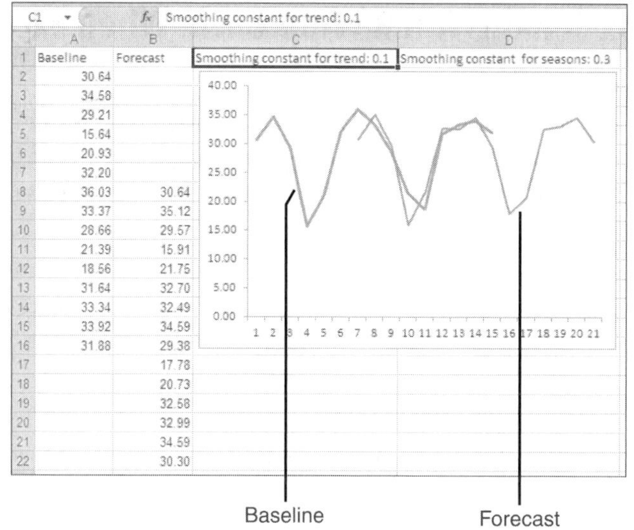

	A	B
1	Baseline	Forecast
2	30.64	
3	34.58	
4	29.21	
5	15.64	
6	20.93	
7	32.20	
8	36.03	30.64
9	33.37	35.12
10	28.66	29.57
11	21.39	15.91
12	18.56	21.75
13	31.64	32.70
14	33.34	32.49
15	33.92	34.59
16	31.88	29.38
17		17.78
18		20.73
19		32.58
20		32.99
21		34.59
22		30.30

3. Enter `6` into the Seasons per Block box. You expect annual seasonality in the amount of waste picked up, and there are six two-month seasons per year.
4. Enter `.1` as the trend smoothing constant and `.3` as the seasonal smoothing constant.

> **TIP**
> In practice, you might use Solver as discussed earlier in this chapter to vary these constants so as to minimize the root mean square error.

After you click OK, a new worksheet is opened and the baseline and forecast values are written along with the smoothing constants you used (see Figure 9.19). At this point, you can chart both the baseline and the forecast using the data as laid out in Figure 9.19.

1. Select the range A1:B22.
2. Click the Ribbon's Insert tab, and click Line in the Charts group.
3. Click the first of the 2D line chart options. You'll get a chart much like the one in Figure 9.19.

Figure 9.19
The seasonal smoothing approach takes into account both the prior observation and the prior season.

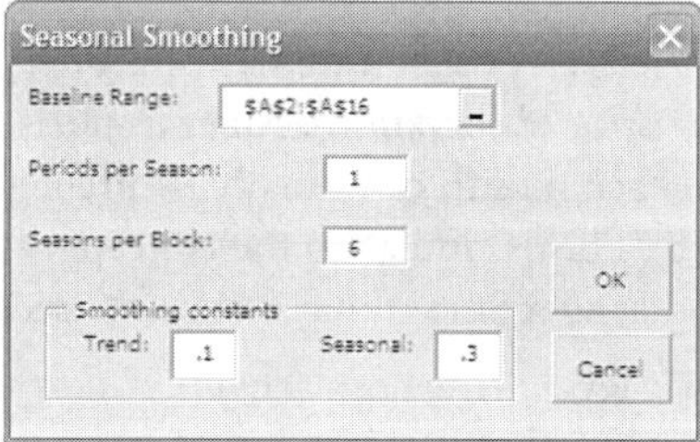

Using the Box-Jenkins ARIMA Approach: When Excel's Built-In Functions Won't Do

Box-Jenkins methods, often called *ARIMA* (for AutoRegressive Integrated Moving Average) models, have much broader scope than a simple moving average or regression or smoothing forecasts. They can often remove most of the drawbacks of the approaches discussed previously. But they are based on and use those approaches.

Box-Jenkins methods are also much more complex—well beyond the scope of this book to cover in detail. This chapter discusses only the preliminary phase of these methods: the identification phase. Completing the identification phase helps you to decide whether to make your forecast using a program written specifically for Box-Jenkins or whether you can choose a regression or smoothing approach that Excel supports directly.

The publisher's website for this book includes a workbook with VBA code that will assist you in determining whether a Box-Jenkins model is necessary to forecast your time series properly.

Understanding ARIMA Basics

Suppose that you have a baseline of observations that you want to use to make a forecast. Excel provides little in the way of guidance on whether you should use a regression approach such as `TREND` or `GROWTH`, or a smoothing approach such as the Exponential Smoothing add-in, to create forecasts from your baseline. Many people choose one or the other on an *ad hoc* basis because they might be more familiar with one approach than with another, or they might want to save time by forecasting with a chart trendline, or they might just flip a coin.

Box-Jenkins models provide you with a quantitative basis for deciding between regression and smoothing—and, carried to their conclusion, they can apply both regression and smoothing simultaneously to create the best forecast. The process does this by examining the patterns of correlations in the baseline and returning information to you that suggests whether a regression approach (in ARIMA, autoregressive) or a smoothing approach (in ARIMA, moving average), or a combination, is optimal.

The Box-Jenkins identification phase, covered in this section, is a formal rather than *ad hoc* means of choosing an approach to forecasting. The identification phase uses these aspects of a time series:

- **An autoregressive component**—Each observation depends on a prior observation (not necessarily the immediately prior observation). An example is revenue from leases, in which the amount of revenue each month can usually be predicted by the amount of revenue from the prior month. This is similar to the concept of autocorrelation, described previously in the "Choosing a Smoothing Constant" section.
- **A trend component**—The series level drifts regularly up or down over time. An example is unit sales of a new product that is gaining market acceptance. Eventually,

the unit sales figures will become constant and the trend will disappear, but during the early phases, there is often a clear, sometimes explosive trend.

- **A moving average component**—In the Box-Jenkins context, this means that the series experiences random shocks over time. The effect of these shocks may linger in the level of the series long after the shock has occurred.

These three components may exist separately or in combination in any time series. There are autoregressive (AR) models, moving average (MA) models, and autoregressive moving average (ARMA) models. In some cases, such as those with trend in the raw series, it's necessary to work with the differences between one observation and the next. Then, before forecasting, the observations have to be undifferenced or *integrated*. Then an *I* becomes part of the model: ARI models, IMA models, and ARIMA models. Furthermore, there may be seasonality in the series, leading to (for example) a series that has both a regular and a seasonal AR component, as well as a regular and a seasonal MA component.

With all these models from which to choose, how do you select the one that best fits your time series and is thus the best one to use for forecasting? ARIMA jargon refers to this as the *identification* phase. Early in the analysis, charts called *correlograms* are created. These correlograms help identify what sort of forecasting model, if any, you should use.

Charting the Correlograms

A VBA module can be found in the file named `ARIMA.xls` on the publisher's website. This module contains a macro named `ARIMA` that creates correlograms for your time series. By examining the correlograms, you can determine whether you should use one of the complete Box-Jenkins computer programs to complete the analysis or whether you can use an Excel regression function or the Exponential Smoothing add-in. There are many programs available that perform complete Box-Jenkins analyses; the more familiar ones include R, SAS, and SPSS.

To run the `ARIMA` macro, have a worksheet open that contains your baseline in a single column. Then take these steps:

1. Open `ARIMA.xls` and switch back to the worksheet that contains your baseline observations.
2. Click the Ribbon's Developer tab. Then click the Macros button in the Code area.
3. In the Macro Name/Reference list box, select ARIMA.
4. Select Run.

If you're using an Excel version prior to 2007, simply open `ARIMA.xls` and select ARIMA from the Data menu.

The ARIMA code displays a dialog box where you enter the address of your baseline data, whether to compute first differences, and how many lags you want to view for the autocorrelations. The remainder of this section describes the choices you have in the dialog box and how to interpret the procedure's output.

You should not use Box-Jenkins models with fewer than 50 observations in the time series. It takes at least this many observations to model the data with any accuracy. In practice, you usually want well over 100 observations before starting the forecast process.

TIP

This recommendation is not limited to Box-Jenkins forecasts: It could and should be used for most forecasts based on any regression method. Before you place much faith in a regression forecast, use the worksheet function `LINEST` or `LOGEST` to determine the standard error of estimate for the regression. (This is the value returned in the second column of the array's third row.) If the standard error is large relative to the precision that you need to have confidence in a forecast, it is probably best to obtain a longer baseline before you proceed with a forecast.

In other words, before you decide to employ these methods with any real baseline data, be sure that you have enough data points to make the task worth your time.

Starting with Correlograms to Identify a Model

A *correlogram* displays correlation coefficients in graphic form, one for each lag in a time series. Figure 9.20 shows a correlogram for lags 1 to 20.

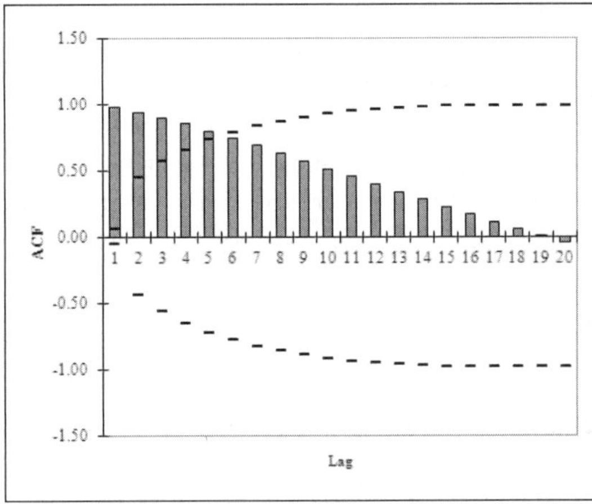

Figure 9.20
The correlogram for ACFs for lags 1 to 20: This could be either an AR or an ARMA process.

The ACF is the *autocorrelation function* and is a type of correlation coefficient, similar to the autocorrelations discussed earlier in the "Choosing a Smoothing Constant" section of this chapter. The dashed lines show two standard errors of the ACFs. An ACF that extends above an upper dashed line or one that extends below a lower dashed line—thus, over two standard errors from zero—is usually considered statistically significant. Here, the ACFs gradually tail off. This pattern in the ACFs is typical of an AR model.

The lags simply identify which pairs of data points are used in the ACF. For example, consider the ACF at lag 1 in Figure 9.20. It is the autocorrelation between the second through twentieth observations, and the first through nineteenth observations.

That is, observation number 1 is paired with observation number 2, 2 with 3, 3 with 4 and so on. The series consisting of observations 2 to 20 lags one step behind the observations 1 to 19. Similarly, the ACF at lag 2 is based on observations 3 to 20, paired with observations 1 to 18. The second set lags two steps behind the first set (see Figure 9.21).

> **NOTE**
>
> When a baseline has trend—that is, when it has a pronounced upward or downward slope—it is often necessary to *difference* the observations. First-differencing usually removes the trend in the baseline, making it stationary—that is, roughly horizontal. (Subsequently undifferencing the differenced observations is termed *integrating*, the *I* in *ARIMA*.) The ACFs of a stationary baseline can be interpreted; the ACFs of an undifferenced baseline that has a trend are ambiguous: You don't know how to attribute them in identifying a model.
>
> The ARIMA code's dialog box has a check box for first-differencing. If your baseline has a pronounced slope, select the check box. ARIMA will then difference your baseline, in most cases removing the trend and making the ACFs interpretable.

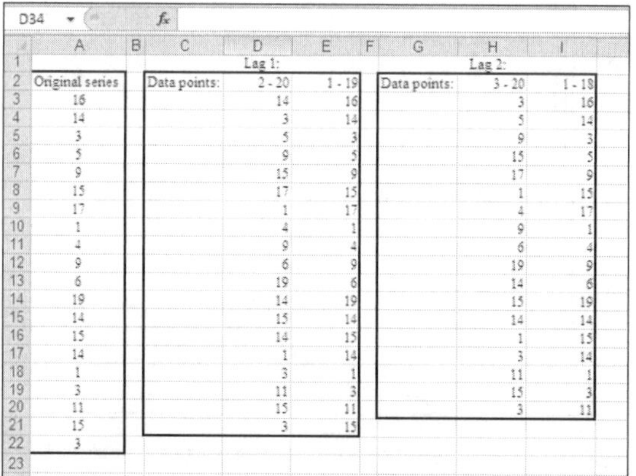

D34 fx

	A	B	C	D	E	F	G	H	I
1				Lag 1:				Lag 2:	
2	Original series		Data points:	2 - 20	1 - 19		Data points:	3 - 20	1 - 18
3	16			14	16			3	16
4	14			3	14			5	14
5	3			5	3			9	3
6	5			9	5			15	5
7	9			15	9			17	9
8	15			17	15			1	15
9	17			1	17			4	17
10	1			4	1			9	1
11	4			9	4			6	4
12	9			6	9			19	9
13	6			19	6			14	6
14	19			14	19			15	19
15	14			15	14			14	14
16	15			14	15			1	15
17	14			1	14			3	14
18	1			3	1			11	1
19	3			11	3			15	3
20	11			15	11			3	11
21	15			3	15				
22	3								
23									

Figure 9.21
Lags measure the distances between different subsets of a time series.

Identifying Other Box-Jenkins Models

To identify a particular Box-Jenkins model, you need to examine two correlograms: one for the ACF at different lags and one for the partial autocorrelation function (PACF) at the same lags.

A PACF is conceptually similar to a partial correlation coefficient, which is the relationship between two variables after the effect of another variable or variables has been removed. For example, a partial correlation coefficient might measure the relationship between revenue and profit margin, after the effects of number of salespeople and advertising costs have been statistically removed from the relationship.

Similarly, a PACF at lag 4 would measure the relationship between, say, cells A5:A20 and A1:A16, after the effects of the intervening series have been removed.

Each Box-Jenkins model (AR, MA, ARMA, and so on) has a distinctive signature in the pattern of the ACFs and PACFs in their correlograms. Figure 9.20 shows the ACF of an autoregressive series. It is characterized by either a gradual decline in the ACFs, as shown in Figure 9.20, or a single spike in the PACF.

For a baseline that displays this pattern of ACFs and PACFs, you could use an Excel regression technique and regress the baseline onto itself, according to the location of the PACF's spike. For example, suppose that the spike were at lag 1. In that case, your known y's would begin at the second observation in the baseline and would end at the end of the baseline. Your known x's would begin at the start of the baseline and end at its next-to-last observation.

Figure 9.22 shows the ACFs for a moving average process, and Figure 9.23 shows its PACFs.

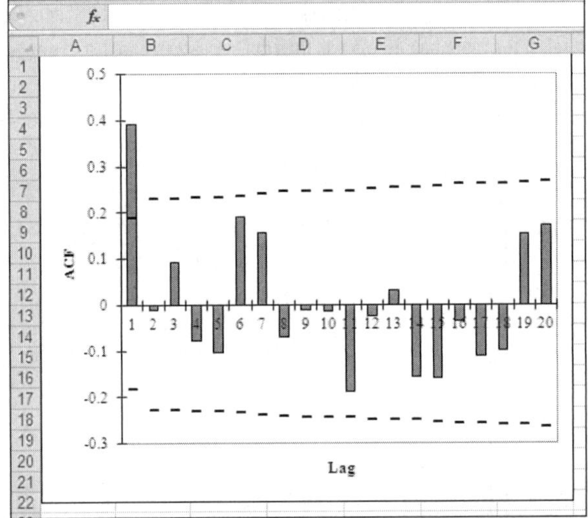

Figure 9.22
ACFs of a moving average process: Notice the single spike at lag 1.

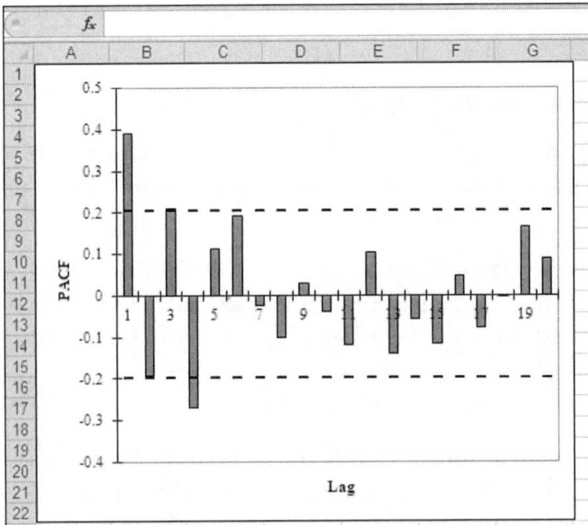

Figure 9.23
PACFs of a moving average process: Notice the gradual decline in the absolute magnitude of the PACFs.

Notice the large, statistically significant ACF value at lag 1 in Figure 9.22. A value such as this is often termed a *spike*. It is the only significant ACF in the correlogram.

Also notice that, among the first six PACF values in Figure 9.23, three are statistically significant and two just miss significance. This suggests that the PACFs are gradually dying out—in contrast to the single spike in the ACF correlogram in Figure 9.22.

This pattern—single spike in the ACF, gradual decline in the PACF—is characteristic of an MA process. If the ACF's spike is at lag 1, you can use Excel's Exponential Smoothing add-in with some confidence that it's the right tool. If the single spike occurs at some other lag, you should use an application that provides specifically Box-Jenkins forecasting.

Figures 9.24 and 9.25 show the ACFs and the PACFs in the correlograms for a mixed process, one with both autoregressive and moving average (ARMA) components.

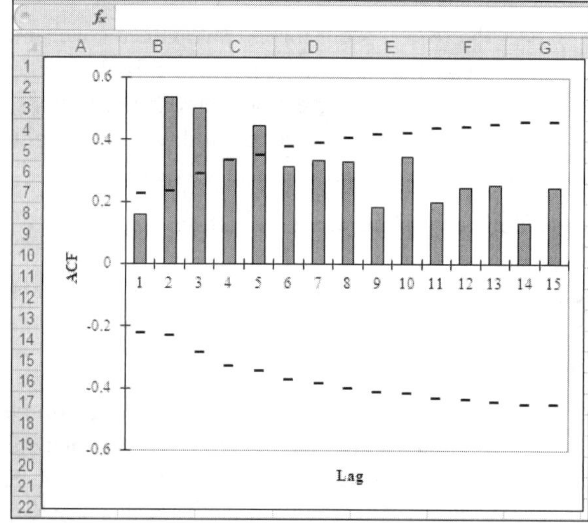

Figure 9.24
ACFs of an autoregressive moving average process gradually decline.

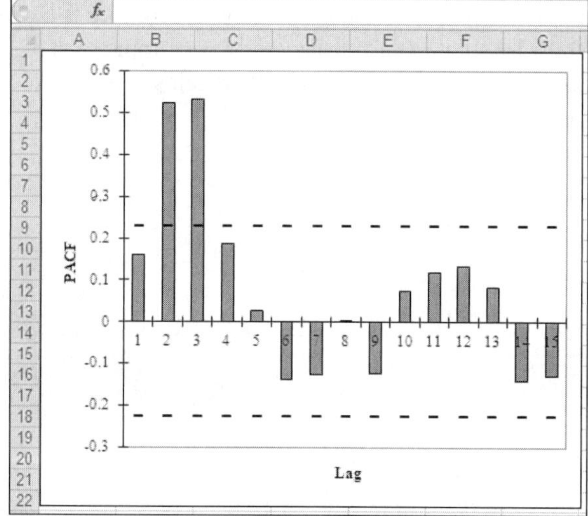

Figure 9.25
The absolute values of the PACFs of an autoregressive moving average, like its ACFs, gradually decline.

Notice the gradual decline in the ACFs in Figure 9.24, as well as in the PACF in Figure 9.25. This pattern in the correlograms is typical of a mixed ARMA process. To forecast properly from this baseline, you would need to use an application that performs Box-Jenkins forecasting.

If your baselines show any patterns similar to these when you run the Box-Jenkins add-in, you should consult a text that specifically covers Box-Jenkins models and use one of the standard statistical programs that offer Box-Jenkins options. You are likely to get a much more accurate forecast of your data if you do so than if you use simple moving averages, regression, or exponential smoothing without a quantitative rationale for choosing a method.

Summary

Forecasting can be tricky. To create a good forecast, you need a well-measured, well-defined baseline of data. You should use the suggestions made in this chapter to choose the most appropriate approach (moving average, regression, smoothing, or Box-Jenkins). At times, your baseline might not suggest an appropriate method, and you might need to wait for a longer baseline before you can be confident of your forecast.

Even if you feel you've done everything right, conditions have a way of changing unexpectedly, making your careful forecast look like a blind guess. Be sure to regard your forecasts with a healthy dose of skepticism. The more variables you have to work with, the more ways there are to view the future. Changes in one forecast can tip you off to the possibility that another forecast is about to change.

The methods described in this chapter are accurate ways to help you build your business plan. They can help you answer questions such as whether to anticipate an increase or a decrease in demand, whether price levels are rising or falling, and, perhaps more important, to what degree.

Because discussion of the underlying theory of these approaches is beyond the scope of this book, you should consider studying a text devoted to the topic such as *Time Series Analysis, Forecasting, and Control* by G. E. P. Box and G. M. Jenkins if you make many forecasts in the course of your work.

Measuring Quality

10

Product quality is an important part of profitability. Other things being equal, a product with a reputation for high quality tends to sell more units than a product that's known to have poor quality. A product with good quality gets fewer customer complaints, fewer free service calls, and fewer warranty repairs. Poor product quality goes directly to the bottom line in the form of lost profit.

It's also true that the quality of *operations* drives profit margins. When a customer service representative spends too much time chatting with one customer, that means another customer is on hold, looking for a competitor's phone number. When invoices are wrong or illegible, there's usually a delay in receipts. When the purchasing department orders unnecessary parts from a supplier, there is an unnecessary increase in inventory levels and in carrying costs. When the quality of goods purchased is *too* high, the cost of the goods is probably also too high: Zero-defect manufacturing is very expensive.

You can stay on top of all these processes using Excel. The only other item you need is a source of data. This chapter describes how to use Excel to help you keep track and maintain control.

In this chapter, you learn to create and interpret statistical process-control charts for both variables and attributes, create sampling plans to help you determine whether shipments of goods are acceptable, and decide whether a tested sample's defects are representative of those in its population.

IN THIS CHAPTER

Monitoring Quality Through Statistical Process Control

The idea behind statistical process control (SPC) is that over a period of time, you can take measurements on a process and determine whether that process is going out of control. Examples of process measurements include the following:

- Number of defective units in a manufacturing run
- Average number of defects in a unit
- Average diameter of a part that must meet a precise specification
- Average number of errors in invoices
- Average length of time that customers remain on hold
- Average available capacity of a data communications circuit

You can make process measurements on virtually any process that your company uses.

The key phrases here are "over time," "average," and "out of control." *Over time* means that SPC depends on repeated and regular measurement of the process—daily, perhaps, or hourly or weekly. You choose how often to measure the process, and that depends on how closely you want to monitor it.

For example, if it's a continuous process that's critical to your company's success, you might decide to monitor it hourly. This could happen if, for example, you were in the business of manufacturing ceramic tiles, and the color of the glaze as it leaves the kilns is an important standard to your customers. You try not to shut down the kilns if you can help it (it's costly to get them hot again after a shutdown) so you want to know as soon as possible if something's going wrong—if the system is going out of control—and that implies continuous quality checks.

Using Averages from Samples

Average has two implications for SPC. First, it means that SPC often depends on sampling and measuring several units at any given time. Suppose that you decide to monitor errors in the invoices that your accounting department prepares. It would be too expensive to check every invoice for errors. But if you examine only one invoice per day, you probably won't get a good estimate of how accurate the invoices are overall.

In cases such as these—and that's most of them—SPC takes a random sample from the process and uses the average of that sample as an estimate of the process quality for that time period. For example, you might decide to sample 16 invoices daily and to use the average number of errors in that sample as the error estimate for that day.

In other cases, you might use a 100% sample, and then you would monitor every instance of the process. For example, this could occur in a manufacturing environment if you use a procedure that tests every unit as soon as assembly is complete.

The second implication of SPC averaging is the calculation of the typical value of the process. The periodic measurements that you take combine to form an overall value. For example, you might find that over a several-week period, you produce an average of 1 tile in 500 that has defective glazing. This long-term average forms a central point, the process's average level, and your periodic measurements vary around that level—some higher, some lower.

Out of control means that SPC uses information not only about the average level of a process, but also about how the process varies around that average level. Suppose that you run the customer service department for a financial services company and 20 people answer your phones to take orders from your customers. You arrange to monitor the call length of 16 randomly sampled calls per day, and you learn that the average call lasts two minutes and five seconds.

That figure of 125 seconds for the average phone call seems about right—until you notice that 12 calls took less than a minute, and four calls took more than six minutes each. You might decide that you need to learn why some calls take so long. (Are some of them personal calls? Is a representative putting callers on hold to look up something that he should vc have known? Or is it just that the longer calls are about more complicated matters?) You would not have known about the variations if you had looked at only the average call length. You also need to look at how far the measurements depart from the average.

When you have this information, you're in a better position to decide if the unusual measurements are just natural, random variation, or if they are warning you that the process is going out of control.

Using X-and-S Charts for Variables

SPC typically uses charts to depict the data graphically, as shown in Figure 10.1.

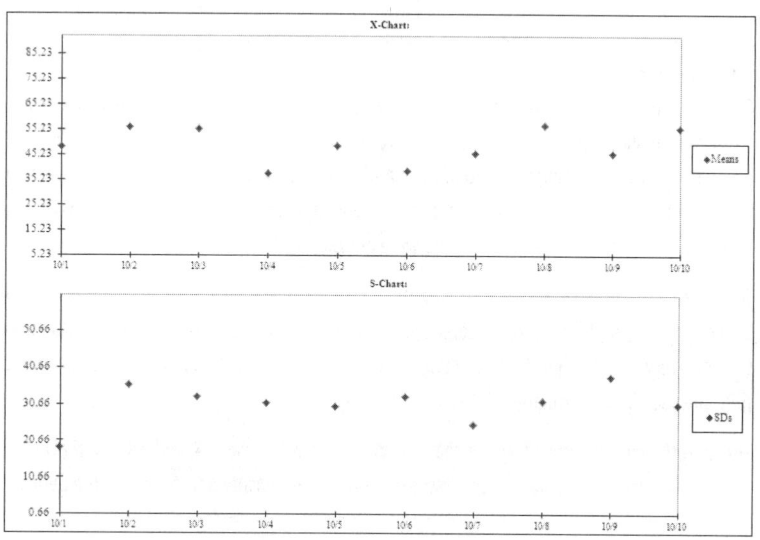

Figure 10.1
These SPC X-and-S charts summarize the actual observations, but you need control limits as context before you can interpret them properly.

Figure 10.1 shows two charts: one for the process average (the X-chart) and one for the process standard deviation (the S-chart).

NOTE

A *standard deviation* is a measure of how much individual scores vary around an average. Conceptually, it is similar to the range between the highest score and the lowest score. It's more useful than the range, though. The *range* tells you only the difference between the two most extreme observations. The standard deviation takes all the scores into account in measuring how much variability there is in the group of scores.

If you're not familiar with standard deviations, just keep in mind that a standard deviation, like a range, is a measure of variability, of how much individual observations tend *not* to cluster. This book explains standard deviations more fully in Chapter 15, "Making Investment Decisions Under Uncertain Conditions."

Many SPC charts look like the ones shown in Figure 10.1. They have these characteristics:

- The horizontal axis of both an X-chart and an S-chart always shows the time (which hour, which day, which week, and so on) that measurements were taken.
- The X-chart's vertical axis always represents the average measurement of a sample on a particular date or time.
- The S-chart's vertical axis always represents the standard deviation of the sample on a particular date or time.

They are known as X-and-S charts because the statistical symbol for a sample average is $\overline{X}$, and the statistical symbol for a sample standard deviation is *s*.

What About X-and-R Charts?

One alternative to X-and-S charts is the X-and-R chart, which substitutes the *range* of measures—the largest measure minus the smallest measure—for the standard deviation as an estimate of the variability in the process. The principal rationale for using the range instead of the standard deviation is that in the early 20th century, when these techniques were developed, calculating a standard deviation was tedious and error prone, whereas calculating a range was quick and easy. Even electronic hand calculators were decades in the future.

Tools such as Excel make it a snap to calculate a standard deviation, but some traditionalists prefer the range as a measure of process variability. Its main defect, of course, is that the size of the range depends entirely on two observations. Change every measure but the maximum and the minimum, and the range remains constant. In contrast, all observations are used in the calculation of the standard deviation.

This chapter does not cover X-and-R charts. It does discuss the use of X-and-MR (for *moving range*) charts. That's because X-and-MR charts are required for processes that have one measure only for each time period.

> **NOTE** You might have seen charts like the ones shown in this chapter referred to as Deming or Shewhart charts, after the people who developed the technique. Many variations exist in the way these charts are created. But regardless of the name—SPC or Deming or Shewhart—the basic approaches described here are standard.

Figure 10.2 adds three refinements to the charts in Figure 10.1.

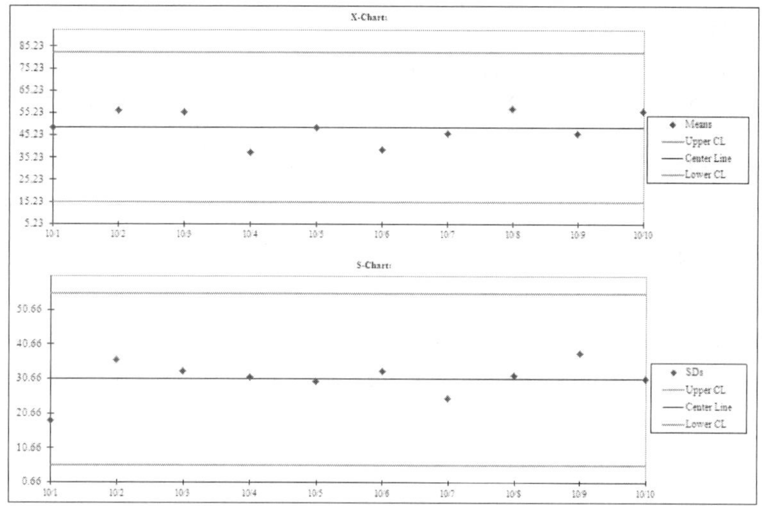

Figure 10.2
X-and-S charts with Center Line and Upper and Lower Control Limits, which put the observed values into context.

The charts in Figure 10.2 have three horizontal lines, generally referred to by their acronyms:

- The upper control limit (UCL)
- The center line (CL)
- The lower control limit (LCL)

These horizontal lines can help you understand the nature of the process you are studying. For example:

- If even just a couple of points are either above the UCL or below the LCL, something is probably wrong with the process.
- If an extended sequence of points exists between the CL and the UCL, or between the CL and the LCL, something might be wrong with the process.
- If an extended sequence of points is trending up toward the UCL or down toward the LCL, something might be going wrong with the process.

You can see how useful this sort of information can be. It alerts you not only to the possibility that the process is out of control, but also to the time or date when it started going out of control. Perhaps something unusual always occurs during a staff change, such as at the end of a shift. Maybe it occurs during a change from daylight saving time to standard time, which might interfere with people's sleep for a few days. It might be associated with drops in ambient temperature that cause the heating system to kick in, introducing dust into a delicate manufacturing environment.

Whatever the cause, if you know that a problem has occurred and when it occurred, you are well on your way to identifying it.

Concerning the CL

The CL is a double-average. In an X-chart that uses each point to represent a particular day, for example, the observations for a given day are averaged to get the chart's point for that day. Then the averages for all the days are averaged to get the overall average: This overall average is the CL for the X-chart. You create the CL for an S-chart in the same way, except that you start by calculating each day's standard deviation and then average those standard deviations to get the CL for the S-chart.

Concerning the UCL and LCL

The UCL and the LCL are a little more complicated than the CL. A UCL is usually three standard deviations above the CL, and an LCL is usually three standard deviations below the CL.

It's actually more complicated than that. The standard deviations are really standard errors, and the gamma distribution gets involved. Unless you're really interested, don't worry about it. Instead, remember that programs such as the SPC add-in that accompanies this book at www.quepublishing.com do all those calculations for you.

> NOTE
>
> Although in many cases it is obviously impossible to actually *observe* a value below zero, such as a diameter of –5 centimeters, SPC calculations sometimes result in a negative LCL value. Some texts replace a negative LCL with a zero value. To make it clear that UCLs and LCLs are equidistant from the CL, the figures in this book allow for a negative LCL.

Because of the way standard deviations behave, it's known that in the long run, only 0.3% of the charted observations occur above the UCL or below the LCL *unless something unexpected is going on.*

So in the normal course of events, you would expect to see about one observation in 370 that is outside either control limit, either above the UCL or below the LCL. If you do find more than 1 in 370 outside the limits, it suggests that something might have happened to the process. You can expect to get one observation in 370 outside either the UCL or LCL, just by chance, even though the process is in control.

Understanding the Terminology

In this chapter and in the much broader context of statistical process control in general, you'll see the terms *standard deviation*, *standard error*, and *sigma*. These terms tend to be used interchangeably, and it's accurate to do so, even though there's a difference.

If you take a sample of, say, 10 observations, you can calculate a standard deviation from the sample, and that 's the value plotted on an S-chart. If you take 10 samples, calculate the mean of each sample, and then calculate the standard deviation *of those means*, that's called the *standard error of the mean*. It's a standard deviation, but it's a special sort of standard deviation, calculated on means rather than on raw, individual observations. Therefore, it's given a different name. This standard error is used to determine the location of the X-chart's UCL and LCL.

Partly to avoid getting tangled up in this distinction, the term *sigma* is often used to stand in for either the standard deviation or the standard error—so the UCL is sometimes called the *three sigma limit*. The lowercase Greek letter σ, or *sigma*, is used by statisticians to represent the standard deviation of a population.

Interpreting the Control Limits

It's easy, and often correct, to conclude that several observations occurring outside a control limit are "bad" because consistency is usually a desirable trait for a process. More broadly, though, it means that something unusual has occurred. For example, suppose that you found an observation *below* the LCL on an S-chart. This means that the variability among the individual observations made at that time is very low. Is that bad?

It's hard to tell; it depends on the nature of the process. It could mean that something changed in the way the observations are measured. Or it could mean that all the observations were made on one machine, or on one person, or on any other process component, when the other samples were taken from multiple components. Or it could be 1 of the 370 cases that you expect, just by chance, to exceed a control limit.

Whatever the cause, the outcome might or might not be "bad." The main point is that something unusual has occurred that probably deserves closer study.

Manufacturing

Suppose your company manufactures light emitting diodes (LEDs), and you are monitoring the LEDs' energy efficiency as they come off the production line. Too many LEDs are manufactured on a given day to test each of them, so you decide to test a random sample of eight LEDs from each day's production run. You measure the LEDs' energy efficiency in lumens per watt, and over a 10-day period, you obtain the results shown in Figure 10.3.

In Figure 10.3, all appears to be fine. All the points are between the UCL and the LCL on both the X-chart and the S-chart, there are no long runs above or below the CL, and there's no trend showing up in the values.

On the other hand, suppose that your SPC charts looked like those in Figure 10.4.

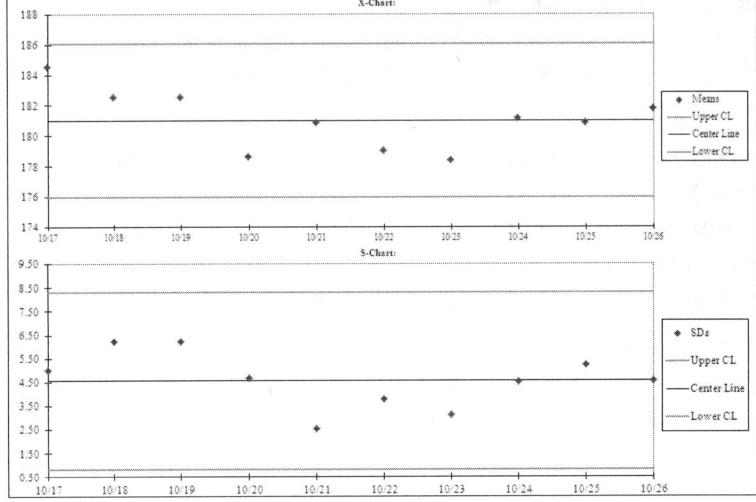

Figure 10.3
The X-and-S charts for LED energy efficiency point to a process that is in control.

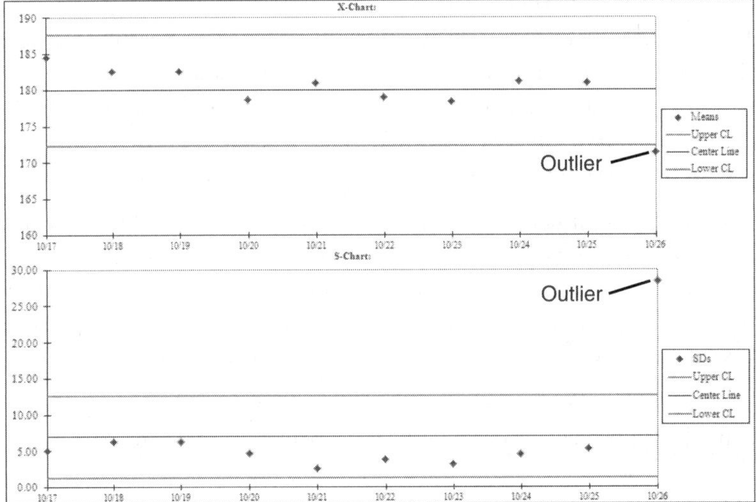

Figure 10.4
The X-and-S charts with outliers suggest a problem with the process on 10/26.

In Figure 10.4, the average energy efficiency for LEDs manufactured on 10/26 is below the LCL on the X-chart, and the standard deviation for the LEDs' energy efficiency on 10/26 is well above the UCL on the S-chart. These two points are known as *outliers* because they lie outside the charts' control limits.

What does this mean to you? Because the 10/26 average energy efficiency dropped, there must be one or more LEDs on 10/26 that have relatively low energy efficiency. The standard

deviation on 10/26 is relatively high because the capacity of at least one LED wa
day's average measured energy efficiency. Therefore, the variability in energy eff
those LEDs is relatively large.

Two possibilities arise:

- Something unusual was going on with the production process on 10/26.
- The average of the observations on 10/26 was 1 of the 370 expected, by chance, to diverge so far from the overall process average.

Although this could be a chance finding, there is some reason to look into the production conditions on 10/26.

Table 10.1 shows the observations used to create the charts in Figure 10.4. Notice that the fourth measurement on 10/26 (in bold) is well below the level of all the other measurements. That lowers the average and raises the standard deviation for that day.

Table 10.1 Data for Figure 10.4: LED Energy Efficiency (Lumens per Watt)

LED:	1	2	3	4	5	6	7	8
Date								
17-Oct	182	190	176	187	191	186	181	183
18-Oct	190	180	177	185	191	178	174	185
19-Oct	192	185	184	187	177	176	174	185
20-Oct	174	189	178	177	176	181	176	178
21-Oct	182	176	180	181	184	179	182	183
22-Oct	174	184	183	183	177	176	178	177
23-Oct	175	184	177	175	180	178	181	177
24-Oct	179	179	175	183	176	186	187	184
25-Oct	177	180	191	184	184	176	176	179
26-Oct	177	180	188	**102**	176	184	186	178

Why is it necessary to look at both the X-chart and the S-chart? Consider Figure 10.5.

There is nothing unusual about the X-chart, but the standard deviation on 10/26 is well above its UCL. Table 10.2 shows the data for Figure 10.5.

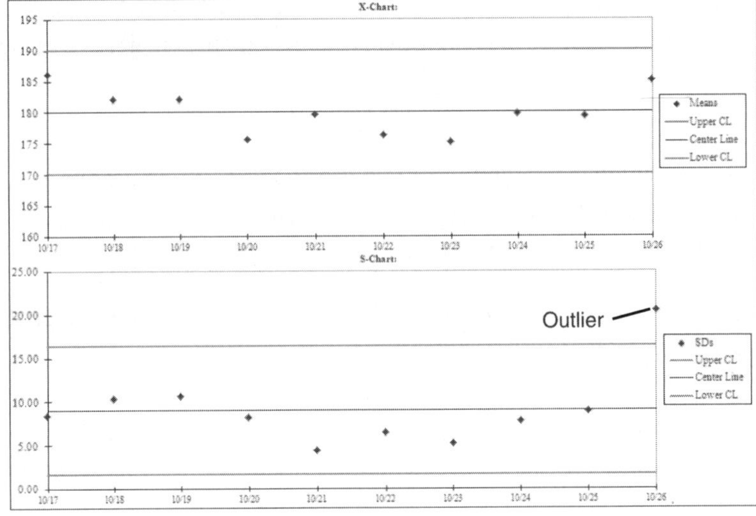

Figure 10.5
The X-and-S charts, with an outlier on the S-chart only, together suggest that there are compensating problems.

Table 10.2 Data for Figure 10.5: LED Energy Efficiency (Lumens per Watt)

LED:	1	2	3	4	5	6	7	8
Date								
17-Oct	181	196	172	190	196	189	180	184
18-Oct	195	177	174	186	196	174	168	186
19-Oct	198	187	184	190	172	171	168	186
20-Oct	168	194	174	173	171	179	171	174
21-Oct	182	171	178	180	184	176	181	184
22-Oct	168	185	184	182	173	171	174	173
23-Oct	169	184	173	170	179	175	179	172
24-Oct	176	176	169	184	171	187	190	185
25-Oct	172	178	196	185	185	171	171	176
26-Oct	**144**	192	196	187	170	**213**	192	186

Notice that the first and sixth measurements on 10/26 (in bold) are, respectively, well below and well above the average for the day. In the average observation for that day, the two measurements have little joint effect: one pulls the average up, the other pulls it back down. But they increase the variability around the mean—one much higher and one much lower—and, therefore, increase the standard deviation for that day. This is evidence that something unusual went on in the production process, resulting in less consistency in the LEDs' energy efficiency. Again, you might want to examine the process for that day.

Even if neither the X-chart nor the S-chart contains outliers, you might find a trend that causes you to examine a process. Consider Figure 10.6.

Here, the daily average energy efficiency of the LEDs is declining gradually but consistently. It's possible that the operating specification of some device or the quality of some raw material is progressively degrading.

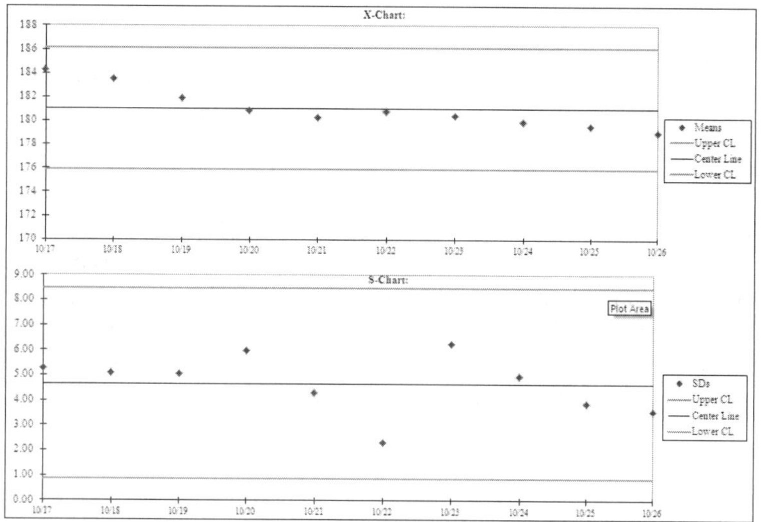

Figure 10.6
When X-and-S charts display a trend, it suggests problems in the process, even if there are no outliers.

Using P-Charts for Dichotomies

Sometimes it's necessary to measure a unit more broadly than by focusing on a single variable such as the energy efficiency of an LED. An LED can be unacceptable in many ways—for example, the color of the emitted light is wrong, or its current or heat management is defective.

If you were monitoring the quality of invoices produced by an accounting department, you might not be interested in exactly why an invoice is unacceptable—just that it is. In this kind of case, you might want your measurement to be a dichotomy, such as acceptable versus unacceptable. Other terms used in quality control are *conforming* versus *nonconforming*.

An SPC chart for this kind of analysis is based on the fraction of a sample that is unacceptable. For example, if you find that five invoices in a sample of 50 are unacceptable, the fraction nonconforming is 0.1. This is the value that is shown on the chart. In quality control, the chart is usually termed a P-chart (for *proportion*) and is analogous to an X-chart.

No S-chart is used when the measurement is a dichotomy. This is because the standard deviation for a dichotomy is completely represented by the fraction itself and is defined as follows:

s = SQRT(p × [1 – p])

Here, *p* is the fraction and *SQRT* stands for the square root. For example, if the fraction is .2, its standard deviation is as follows:

SQRT(.2 × [1 – .2]) = SQRT (.2 × .8) = SQRT(.16) = .4

Because knowing the fraction means that you automatically know the standard deviation, it is usual to create only the P-chart in this kind of analysis.

> **NOTE** The standard deviation's maximum value is .25, when the proportion is .5. The closer that the proportion comes to 0 or 1, the smaller the standard deviation.

But like an X-chart, a P-chart also has a UCL, an LCL, and a CL. The CL is the overall average fraction nonconforming for the process, just as the CL on an X-chart is the overall average of the process measurement. The UCL and LCL are based on the overall fraction nonconforming: They represent three standard errors or sigmas above and below the CL. These standard errors are calculated from the fraction nonconforming for the process, and they take the sample size into account. (See Figure 10.7.)

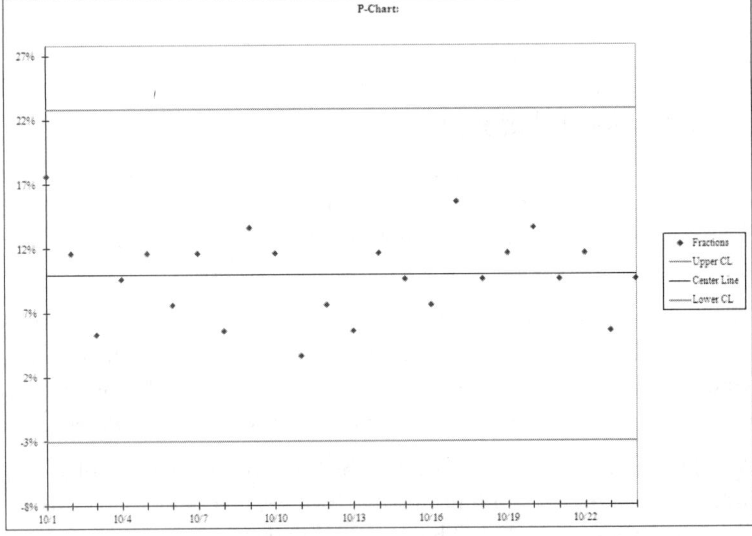

Figure 10.7
P-charts for conforming/nonconforming are not normally accompanied by an S-chart.

For example, if the overall fraction nonconforming is .2 and the size of each sample is 50, the UCL is as follows:

.2 + 3 × SQRT(.2 × [1 – .2] / 50) = .37

This is the LCL:

.2 - 3 × SQRT(.2 × [1 – .2] / 50) = .03

With P-charts, it's better to maintain a constant size for each sample, if possible, to keep the level of the UCL and LCL constant for all samples. For example, assume that the CL is .2 and the fraction nonconforming in the first sample is .1. If the first sample has 20 observations, the UCL is as follows:

.2 + 3 × SQRT(.1 × [1 – .1] / 20) = .40

If the next sample has 10 observations, again with a fraction nonconforming of .1, the UCL is this:

.2 + 3 × SQRT(.1 × [1 – .1] / 10) = .48

For this reason, in a P-chart, the UCL line wanders up and down (as does the LCL) if different samples are based on different sample sizes. This wandering isn't easy to explain to someone who's unfamiliar with how sample size can affect standard errors, so it's a good idea to keep the sample size constant. What's more, it looks cleaner.

If it's not possible to maintain a constant sample size, you can apply transformations to assign constant values to the UCL and LCL. For information on these transformations, see an advanced text on statistical process control.

Choosing the Sample Size

The size of the sample you take, for either an X-and-S or a P-chart, affects the accuracy of the average. The larger the sample, the better the sample's average as an estimate of the value of the population's average.

The sample size also helps determine the distance of the control limits from the center line. As discussed in the prior section, different sample sizes result in different values for the P-chart's UCL and LCL, so you usually try to make the sample sizes constant.

In an X-chart, the values of the UCL and LCL depend on the values of each sample mean. Again, the larger the sample size, the more closely the sample mean estimates the population mean. Therefore, as sample size increases, the more closely the sample means cluster around the CL. The more closely they cluster, the smaller their standard error, and therefore the closer the UCL and the LCL are to the CL.

From the point of view of the accuracy of the sample estimates, the larger the sample that you take, the better.

But it's also true that the larger the sample you take, the greater the cost of quality control. This is particularly true of destructive testing, where the test makes an item unusable. Suppose that you manufacture automobiles, and one quality test that you run is how well the front bumper stands up to a 5 mph collision. Bumper damage makes it hard to sell the cars you've tested.

Therefore, you want to take samples that are small enough to be affordable but large enough to yield accurate estimates. One useful way to define an accurate estimate is that the estimate gives you a 50% chance of detecting that a process has gone out of control.

A 50% chance might not seem too accurate, but keep in mind that you have multiple opportunities to detect the problem. Suppose that you're monitoring a process hourly. If the process goes out of control at, say, 10:15 a.m., you have an opportunity to detect it at 11:00, 12:00, 1:00, and so on. The probability that the problem will remain undetected at, say, 2:00 p.m. is .5 × .5 × .5 × .5 = .0625, or 6.25%. After only four hours, you have nearly a 94% chance to detect that the process is out of control.

The previous examples used samples of size 8 for X-and-S charts and of size 50 for a P-chart. In combination with the process standard deviation, these sample sizes defined the location of the UCL and the LCL—that is, how far the UCL and the LCL are from the center line. You can instead turn it around and begin by defining the location of the UCL and the LCL. Doing so determines the required sample size.

In effect, you ask, "How large a sample do I need if I want the UCL to be a particular distance from the CL?" You want to find a sample size that is large enough to pull the UCL down to the point that if the process shifts up or down, you'll stand a 50% chance of recognizing it.

Suppose that the overall fraction nonconforming for a process is .1. You decide that a fraction nonconforming of .25 is unacceptable. You also decide that you want to have a 50% chance of detecting that the overall fraction nonconforming has increased from .1 to .25. If the process average increases to .25, half the samples would be larger than .25 and half would be smaller. This assumes that defects are distributed symmetrically around their average—that's the usual assumption in statistical process control. In that case, you would have your desired 50% chance to detect a shift in the process average: 50% of the observations would exceed .25.

You can set the UCL, three standard deviations above the CL, to equal the fraction nonconforming that you want to detect. The size of the change to detect is .25 – .1 = .15, and you can set up this equation:

$$.25 - .1 = .15 = 3 \times \text{SQRT}([.1 \times (1 - .1) / N])$$

Here, N is the sample size. Rearranging this equation, you have this:

$$N = (3 / .15)^2 \times .1 \times (1 - .1)$$

$$N = 36$$

or, more generally:

$$N = (s / d)^2 \times p \times (1 - p)$$

Here, d is the size of the shift you want to detect, p is the fraction nonconforming, and s is the number of standard deviations above and below the CL for the UCL and LCL. Given that the UCL and LCL are three standard deviations above and below the CL, the process average is .1, and you want a 50% chance of detecting a shift from .1 to .25, you should take samples of 36 observations each. The Excel worksheet formula is as follows:

```
= (3 / .15)^2 * .1 * .9
```

NOTE

Setting the probability of detecting a shift to 50% simplifies the equation that gives the necessary sample size. If you wanted to increase that probability to, say, 80%, you would need to determine or assume the shape of the distribution of defects, make reference to the resulting theoretical distribution, and add to the equation a term that represents the units of measurement associated with an increase of 30% (that is, 80% – 50%). For detailed information, see an advanced text on statistical quality control.

Determining That a Process Is Out of Control

So far, this chapter has waffled and weaseled about whether a process is in control. It has used phrases such as "might be going out of control" and "something might be wrong with the process."

The reason for this is that the decision that a process is out of control is a completely arbitrary one. Suppose that you observe a measurement that's beyond the UCL or the LCL. That's going to happen once for every 370 samples you take from the process, and it has everything to do with the mathematical definition of a standard deviation and might have *nothing* to do with the process.

In that case, what if you observe 2 measures in 370 beyond the control limits? Is the process then out of control? No? What about three or four outliers? When do you decide the process is out of control?

It's just as well not to ask the question because the usual suspects—logic, mathematics, probability, statistics—won't help here. But don't regard this as a defect of SPC analysis. You've already suffered losses by the time a process has gone out of control, whether or not you decide that has happened. No, the great strength of SPC is to give you an early warning that not all is right. Then you can look carefully into the situation and *perhaps* decide to take action.

However, tradition offers a guide. Analysts use rules, often termed the *Western Electric rules*, to make a decision about a process. These rules involve the CL, the UCL, and the LCL. They also involve four more control limits not yet discussed in this chapter:

- The upper 1 sigma control limit. This control limit is one standard error, or *sigma*, above the CL.
- The upper 2 sigma control limit. This control limit is two standard errors above the CL.
- The lower 1 sigma and 2 sigma control limits. As with the upper 1 sigma and 2 sigma limits, these control limits are one and two standard deviations from the CL, but they are below it instead of above it.

Using this terminology, the UCL and the LCL discussed so far in this chapter are called the upper and lower 3 sigma control limits.

Those additional control limits determine whether there has been a violation of the Western Electric rules, as follows:

- One or more observations above the upper 3 sigma limit, or one or more observations below the lower 3 sigma limit, are a violation.
- At least two of three consecutive observations above the upper 2 sigma limit signal a violation. Similarly, at least two of three consecutive observations below the lower 2 sigma limit are a violation.
- At least four of five consecutive observations above the upper 1 sigma limit signal a violation, or at least four of five consecutive observations below the lower 1 sigma limit.
- Eight or more consecutive observations on either side of the CL are a violation.

10

> **NOTE** The "rules" listed above are really just recommendations in a handbook published by the Western Electric Company in 1956.

Under these decision rules, a violation of any one of the four rules defines a process as out of control. Figure 10.8 shows a 3 sigma violation.

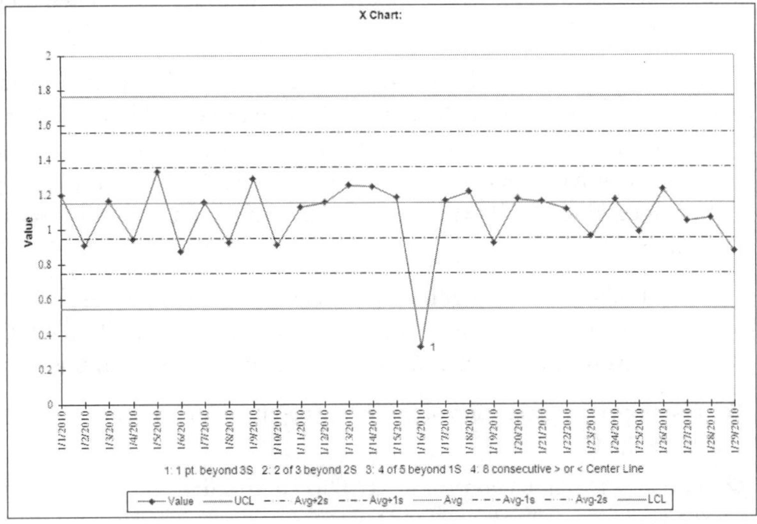

Figure 10.8
When the process returns to its original level after a violation, it is possible that an incorrect measurement caused a violation.

If a 3 sigma violation is followed by a shift in the apparent level of the process, it's easier to believe that the violation was meaningful. In contrast, if the process resumes after the violation at roughly its original level, you should suspect that a one-time event occurred—perhaps someone entered the data wrong.

Violations of the other rules are easier to believe than are 3 sigma violations. These violations have their own confirmation built in. For example, the violation shown in Figure 10.9 requires not just one, but two out of three observations beyond a 2 sigma limit.

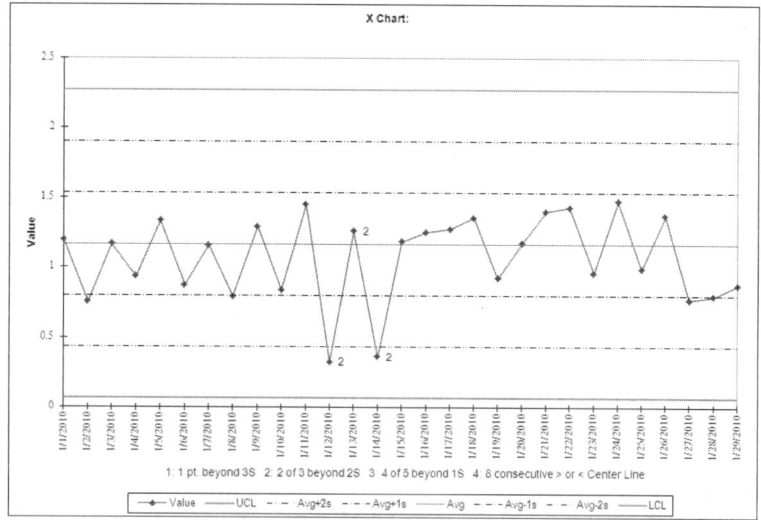

Figure 10.9
One sigma and 2 sigma violations require that the observations occur outside the same sigma limit.

Notice in Figure 10.9 the three observations labeled with the number 2. Two of them lie outside the –2 sigma limit. The third of the three points that cause the violation actually lies above the center line. Had it fallen outside the –2 sigma limit, the three observations would still have resulted in a violation. The rule calls for at least two of three consecutive observations outside a 2 sigma limit.

What if either of the two observations that are below the –2 sigma limit were to fall above the +2 sigma limit? In that case, these three observations would not cause a violation. Two of three consecutive observations must lie outside the *same* 2 sigma limit.

Violations that involve four of five consecutive observations are even more convincing, as shown in Figure 10.10.

Although a 1 sigma violation requires four of five consecutive observations to lie outside a limit, that limit is only one sigma away from the CL. So the observations do not have to be as distant from the CL, but more are needed to confirm an out-of-control situation.

Don't be misled by the wording of these rules. An observation can be farther off than a given rule calls for. For example, suppose that of five consecutive observations, three fall between the +1 sigma and the +2 sigma limits, and a fourth falls outside the +2 sigma limit. Those four discrepant observations create a 1 sigma violation. It doesn't matter how far beyond the limit in question an observation is, as long as it is beyond the limit.

Figure 10.11 shows an example of the fourth type of violation.

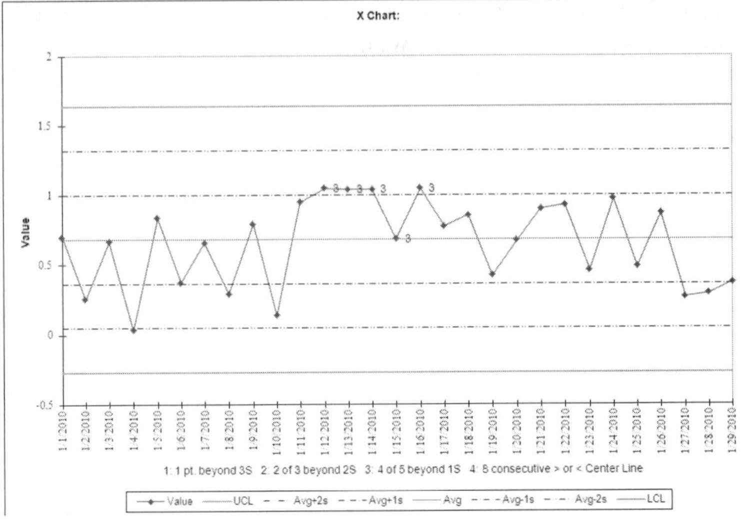

Figure 10.10
A 1 sigma violation requires more observations, but the observations can occur closer to the CL.

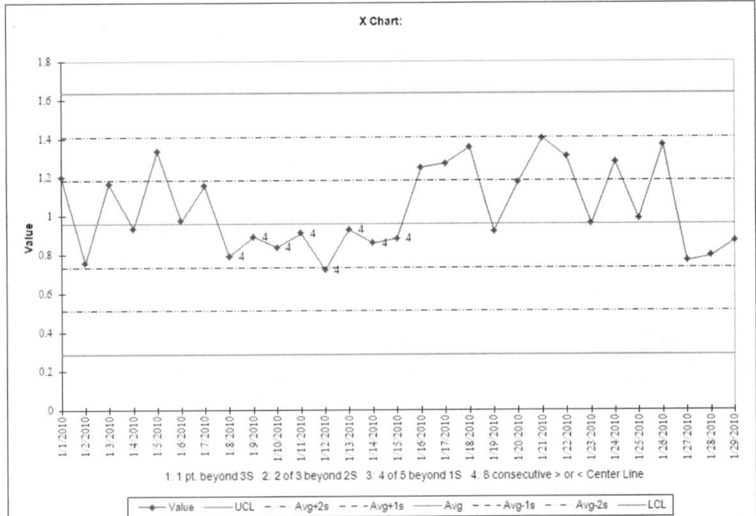

Figure 10.11
Eight consecutive points on the same side of the CL almost always signal at least a temporary process shift.

Using X-and-MR Charts for Individual Observations

You often have only one observation available for a given time point. Perhaps the process that you're measuring takes so much time or resources that you can't wait for a larger sample before starting your analysis. Or perhaps the process defines only one measure per time point: An example is budget variance analysis, in which there is only one variance per account during a given accounting period.

In this sort of case, X-and-S analysis doesn't help you because you can't calculate a standard deviation based on one observation only. The range suffers the same defect, so X-and-R charts are useless here. But you can use the *moving range* (MR) instead. The MR is defined as the absolute value of the difference between one observation and the next. So if you observe the value 23 on January 5 and the value 31 on January 6, the MR is 8: that is, the absolute value of 23 – 31.

> **TIP** Excel has a worksheet function that returns the absolute value: ABS. So `=ABS(A2-A3)` returns the absolute value of the contents of A2 minus the contents of A3.

The X-and-MR analysis estimates a standard deviation with these steps:

1. Find the value of each moving range. There are as many moving ranges as there are observations, minus 1.
2. Take the average of the moving ranges.
3. Divide the average of the moving ranges by 1.128. The result is an estimate of the variability in the data set.

Couldn't you just take the standard deviation of all the observations instead? Sure. But that method addresses the wrong kind of variability. Taking the moving range approach stresses the variability due to the difference between consecutive observations. Using the standard deviation of all the observations stresses the (squared) difference between each observation and the overall mean. In many cases, the difference between the moving range estimate and the actual standard deviation might be trivial. But when there is an actual process shift, you can expect the difference between the standard deviation and the moving range to be substantial.

Even when you have many observations available at each time point, it can be useful to average them as in X-and-S analysis and then use X-and-MR analysis on the averages, as described here. When the variability you're interested in stems from differences in consecutive observations, the moving range can be the right way to estimate that variability.

Creating SPC Charts Using Excel

SPC charts are easy to create by using the Excel add-in named `SPC.xla` at the website www.quepublishing.com. To create SPC charts, you need a worksheet that contains data laid out as in Tables 10.1 and 10.2. There should be a range of dates or times of day in one column, and a range of observations for each date or time in adjacent columns. Those two ranges should occupy the same rows.

The observations can be in one or more columns of variable measurements (such as LED energy efficiency, for X-and-S charts) or one column of percentages (such as the fraction nonconforming, for P-charts). In the case of P-charts, you use just one column for the measurements because it's easier for you to enter the fraction nonconforming than to enter several columns, each with a 1 or a 0 to indicate conforming/nonconforming.

Before you can use `SPC.xla` to create control charts, you need to load it into Excel—this is conceptually similar to loading what other applications term *plug-ins*. After you've downloaded the `SPC.xla` add-in, start Excel. Next, take these steps:

1. Click the File tab and click Options. Then select Add-Ins from the list on the left of the dialog box. Make sure that the drop-down at the bottom of the Add-Ins dialog box has Excel Add-ins selected, and then click Go. Using a version earlier than Excel 2007, choose Tools, Add-Ins.
2. In the Add-Ins dialog box, shown in Figure 10.12, click the Browse button. This enables you to find `SPC.xla` in the location you downloaded it to.

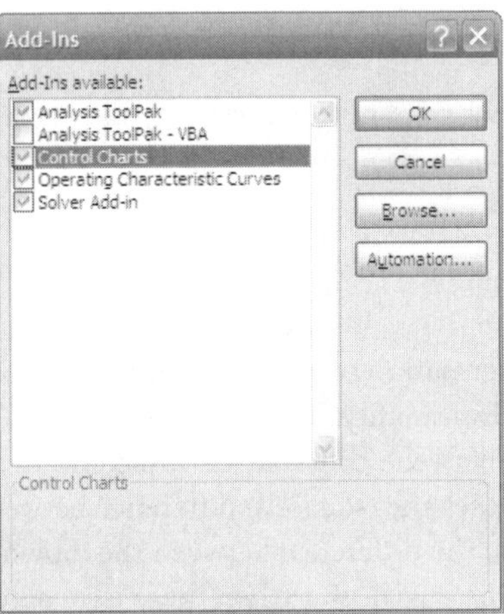

Figure 10.12 Clear a check box to keep the add-in from loading the next time you start Excel. The add-in's effects, such as custom menu items, are then removed.

10

3. When you have located `SPC.xla`, click its icon to select it and click OK. You are returned to the Add-Ins dialog box. Select the check box next to Control Charts and then click OK.
4. In Excel 2007 and 2010, the Add-Ins tab appears on the Ribbon as soon as you load an add-in such as the SPC add-in described here. Click the Add-Ins tab and notice there is now a Control Charts item in the Menu Commands group. (Add-ins that come with Microsoft Office, such as the Solver, appear on the Ribbon's Data tab after they are loaded.) Using versions of Excel prior to 2007, you will see a new item, Control Charts, in the Data menu. Regardless of your Excel version, the Control Charts item will remain accessible until you remove it, using Excel Options or using Tools, Add-Ins.

To run the Control Charts add-in, click the Ribbon's Add-Ins tab and choose select Control Charts from the Menu Commands group. In earlier versions, choose Data, Control Charts. You see a user form that prompts you to enter the range that contains the times or dates, and the range that contains the actual observations. The form is step 1 of a three-step wizard. Figure 10.13 shows the Step 1: Control Charts page of the wizard.

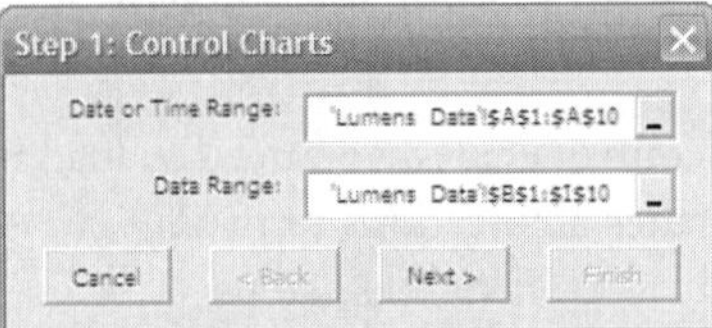

Figure 10.13 Click the Collapse Dialog button at the right of each reference edit box to collapse the user form—this can make it easier to locate the cells you want.

Click in the Date or Time Range reference edit box, and either type in the range of dates or times, or drag through that range on your worksheet. That range does not need to have actual date or time values. You can leave that range blank on the worksheet, but the Control Charts add-in requires you to identify a worksheet range.

Then click in the Data Range reference edit box and drag through that range on the worksheet so that the address appears in the edit box.

When you click the Next button in step 1, the Step 2: Control Charts page of the wizard appears, as shown in Figure 10.14.

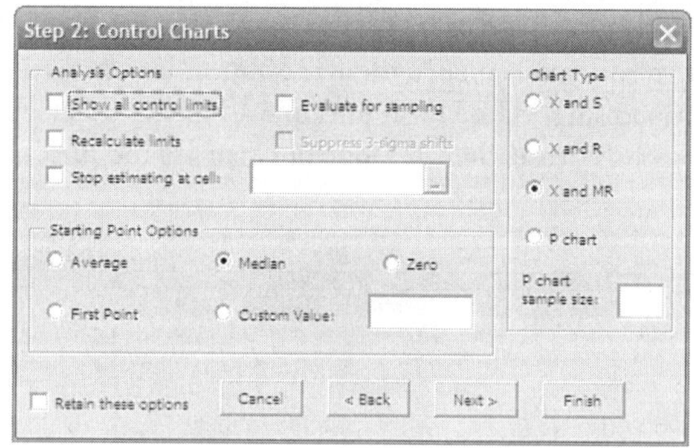

Figure 10.14
Select the Retain These Options check box if you want to use the SPC wizard several times. Your choices will be kept on the user forms.

Use step 2 to define the options you want to use. You can select X-and-S, X-and-R, X-and-MR, or P-charts. If you select a P-chart, you must also supply the sample size: the number of observations that make up each fraction in the input range.

You have several options for the X chart's starting point—that is, the first point in its center line. The custom value is often useful in process capability analysis.

The Analysis Options are not available for P-charts, but for other chart types, they have the following effects:

- **Show All Control Limits**—If you select this check box, the X-chart shows the CL, the UCL, the LCL, and the upper and lower 1 and 2 sigma limits. If you clear this check box, the X-chart shows only the CL, the UCL, and the LCL.
- **Evaluate for Sampling**——Selecting this check box causes an additional worksheet to be included in the output workbook. The worksheet assists you in calculating the minimum sample size needed to detect a shift in the process. You are asked to provide the size of the shift that you want to detect.
- **Recalculate Limits**—Some analysts like to recalculate and redraw the CL and the sigma limits in response to a shift in the level of the process. That is, when one of the Western Electric rules is violated, the CL, as well as the various control limits, can be recalculated at the point where the shift occurred. Doing this makes a difference in the probability statements that you can make about the SPC analysis, pertaining to the

nature of the data and the location and size of the shift. The option is provided for you to use if you feel that you need it. If so, select the check box.

- **Stop Estimating at Cell**—You might want SPC to stop estimating the process parameters (mainly the CL and the variability around it) before it reaches the end of the observations. This is particularly true when you have planned to intervene in a process. For example, suppose that you plan to change an important piece of equipment after Day 20. You expect that change to have an effect on the process. To measure that effect accurately, you want to stop estimating the process average and variability as of Day 20. You can arrange that by selecting the Stop Estimating at Cell check box, clicking in the associated edit box, and then clicking the cell on the worksheet that represents Day 20.

As usual with Excel wizards, you can click the Back button in step 2 to return to step 1, click Cancel to stop processing, click Finish to skip setting any other options, or click Next to go to the next step. In this case, Step 3: Control Charts is the final page of the wizard, as shown in Figure 10.15.

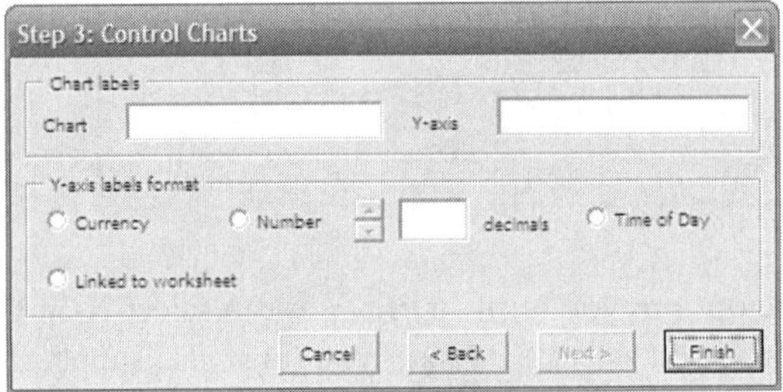

Figure 10.15
On the SPC charts shown in this chapter, the y-axis is the vertical axis.

Use this step to set a chart title, a label for the y-axis (which represents the values of your observations), and the format used by the tick labels on the y-axis. When you're done, click Finish to create your charts.

Performing Acceptance Sampling

Acceptance sampling often enables you to reduce the cost of goods that you purchase. It can also enable you to control your loss when a buyer returns products to you due to defects.

You do not want to purchase materials, whether supplies or equipment, that are faulty. Nor do you want to offer defective goods for sale. However, it's normal for the purchaser and the seller of large amounts of merchandise to negotiate an acceptable fraction of merchandise that might be defective.

Here's the reasoning. It is extremely expensive to produce any appreciable amount—one lot, say—of goods that has no defective units. To do so, the producer would have to perform 100% testing because any less would run the risk of having at least one defective product in the lot. In addition, because testing itself is not perfect, a test result of 0% defective is not a guarantee that no defects exist. Furthermore, the producer always bears the sunk cost of having manufactured the defective units.

The producer is in business to make a profit. To cover the costs of attaining 0% defects, the producer would have to raise the selling price. You, as a purchaser, might then decide to purchase the goods elsewhere. But if you demand 0% defects from another producer, that producer also has to raise the selling price to meet your requirement.

If you, as the purchaser, can tolerate some relatively small percent defective in the lots that you purchase, you might be in a position to negotiate a lower price from your suppliers.

This is the "invisible hand" at work: Adam Smith's principle that optimum values result when participants in an economic activity act in their own self-interest.

Now consider it from the producer's viewpoint. Suppose that the contract that you, the producer, enter into with your customer allows you to make shipments that contain some small percentage of defective product. In that case, you could test a *sample* of the product that you ship instead of the entire lot. Your testing costs immediately drop. Your costs drop again when you consider that you do not have to bear the cost of returned, defective goods, if you have met the customer's criterion for an acceptable shipment. This puts you in a position to gently reduce your selling price, thus retaining the customer but still making a profit.

However, the moment that you start sampling, you start dealing with probability. Suppose that the contract with your customer calls for you to ship no more than 1% defective units. You test 20 units, and you find 1 defective. How likely is it that only 1% of the units in your entire shipment are defective? Put another way, how likely is it that any shipment from your inventory will exceed the 1% limit? How large a testing sample should you take? In addition, if you start finding defects in the sample, when should you stop your tests of the sampled units and conclude that the complete lot is unacceptable?

Excel provides several functions that help you answer these questions, and the next sections explore them.

Charting the Operating Characteristic Curve

An operating characteristic curve shows how an agreement between buyer and vendor works out in theory. The curve in Figure 10.16 is an example.

The curve shows the probability that a lot will be acceptable (vertical axis) with different percents of defects (horizontal axis). Notice that, as you would expect, the lower the number of actual defects, the higher the probability that a lot will be accepted. Four factors define the curve:

- The acceptable quality level (AQL) of the supplier's goods. This is the worst percent of defects that the buyer is willing to accept *as a process average*.
- The lot tolerance percent defective (LTPD) of a given lot. This is the worst level of quality that the buyer is willing to accept *in a given shipment*.

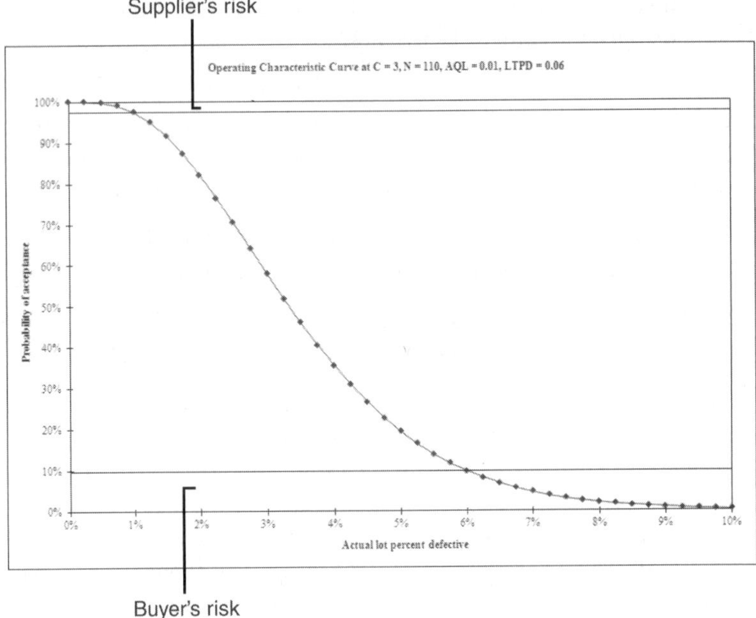

Figure 10.16
The operating characteristic curve helps you visualize the relationships among the different kinds of risk assumed by the buyer and the seller.

- The amount of risk to the supplier that a good shipment will be rejected as bad due to sampling error. The *distance between* the upper horizontal line and the 100% point in Figure 10.16 represents this degree of risk assumed by the supplier. In Figure 10.16, the supplier's risk is 3%, not 97%.
- The amount of risk to the buyer that a bad shipment will be accepted as good due to sampling error. The lower horizontal line represents this degree of risk—in Figure 10.16, 10%.

Taken together, these four factors can provide a great deal of information to the supplier and buyer:

- The operating characteristic curve itself
- The sample size necessary to keep both the supplier's risk and the buyer's risk acceptably low
- The maximum number of defects in a sample before a lot is rejected (usually termed *c*)
- The actual supplier's risk and the actual buyer's risk, at a specific sample size and a specific *c*

Figure 10.17 shows the curve for an AQL of 1%, an LTPD of 3%, and supplier's risk of 5% and buyer's risk of 10%. The upper horizontal line represents the supplier's risk: The distance between this horizontal line and the top of the vertical axis indicates the probability that a good shipment will be rejected. The lower horizontal line represents the buyer's risk: The distance between this horizontal line and the bottom of the vertical axis indicates the probability that a bad shipment will be accepted.

Also shown at the top of Figure 10.17 is *N*, the sample size needed, and *c*, the maximum number of defects that you can find in a sample before concluding that the entire lot contains too many defects. Therefore, this operating characteristic curve tells you that you should sample 390 units. As you test those units, if you find as many as eight defective units, you can stop testing and decide that the full lot contains too many defects.

NOTE

Excel offers a worksheet function, `CRITBINOM`, that returns a number similar to the *c* that this section discusses. `CRITBINOM` is discussed in detail at the end of this chapter, in the section titled Using the CRITBINOM Function. (Excel 2010 keeps CRITBINOM as a compatibility function and offers BINOM.INV as a consistency function. This book's Introduction discusses compatibility and consistency functions.) CRITBINOM is normally different from *c* because it takes into account only the supplier's risk or the buyer's risk. The procedures discussed here take both types of risk into account. Therefore, *c* is usually different from the value you would obtain if you used `CRITBINOM`.

10

The curve shown in Figure 10.17, while steeper than the curve in Figure 10.16, is not extremely steep. Generally, the larger the sample size, the better you can discriminate between an acceptable and an unacceptable lot, and the steeper the curve. Contrast Figure 10.17 with Figure 10.18, where the sample size is larger and the curve is even steeper.

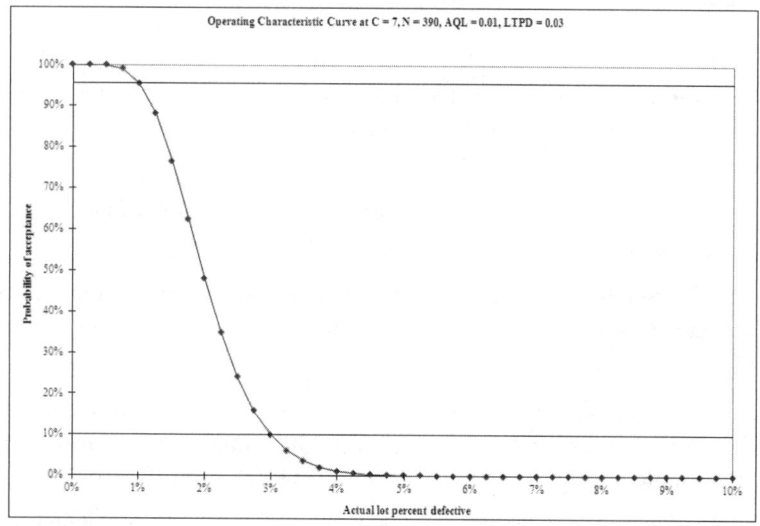

Figure 10.17
The steepness of operating characteristic curves usually depends largely on their sample sizes.

In Figure 10.17, an increase in the actual defect rate from 2% to 3% is accompanied by a drop in the probability of acceptance from about 48% to 10%.

In Figure 10.18, the increase in actual defect rate from 2% to 3% is accompanied by a drop in probability of acceptance from about 95% to 10%.

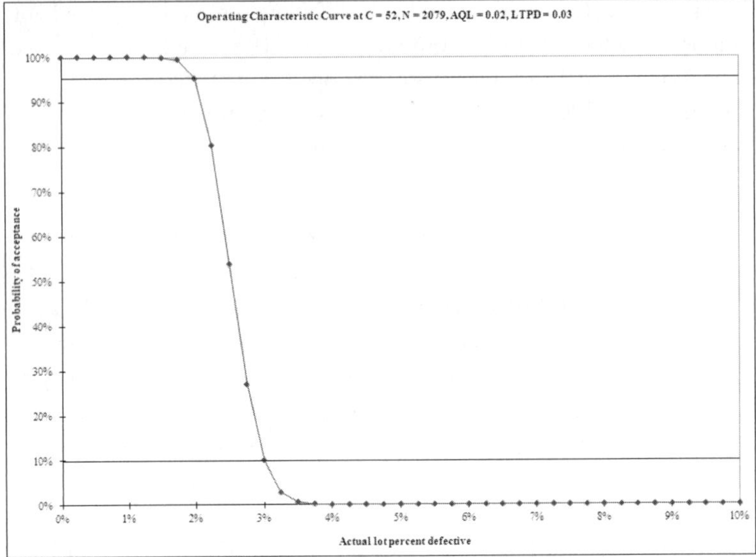

Figure 10.18
The required sample size of an operating characteristic curve depends to some degree on the value of the AQL.

What causes the increase in the required size of the sample? The operating characteristic curve in Figure 10.17 uses an AQL of 1%, whereas the curve in Figure 10.18 uses an AQL of 2%. Another add-in at the website www.quepublishing.com, `occ.xla`, created the operating characteristic curves shown in this chapter. It calculates the minimum sample size that satisfies all four criteria (AQL, LTPD, supplier's risk, and buyer's risk). The smaller the AQL, the smaller the sample required. This is because the smaller the AQL, the fewer defects there are to find. Furthermore, the smaller the AQL, the smaller the value of *c* that's required to determine whether the current lot is a bad one.

So when you increase the AQL from, say, .01 to .02, the necessary sample size increases as a result. This effect can be a dramatic one: In the case of Figures 10.17 and 10.18, the increase in sample size is from 390 to 2,079.

LTPD also influences the required sample size. Figure 10.19 shows the operating characteristic curve with the same inputs as shown in Figure 10.17, except that instead of an LTPD of 3%, it uses an LTPD of 4%.

Modifications of supplier's risk and buyer's risk have relatively small effects on sample size. Figure 10.20 shows the effect of reducing the supplier's risk from 10% to 5%, and Figure 10.21 shows the effect of reducing the buyer's risk from 10% to 5%.

If you want to lower the degree of risk, you need to increase the power of the testing to discriminate between a good lot and a bad lot. You increase that power by increasing the size of the sample. Doing so causes the curve to steepen: The steepness of the curve is a visual guide to how well the testing will discriminate between lots that meet the criteria and lots that are substandard. And, of course, the better the discrimination, the better the degree of protection for both the buyer and the supplier.

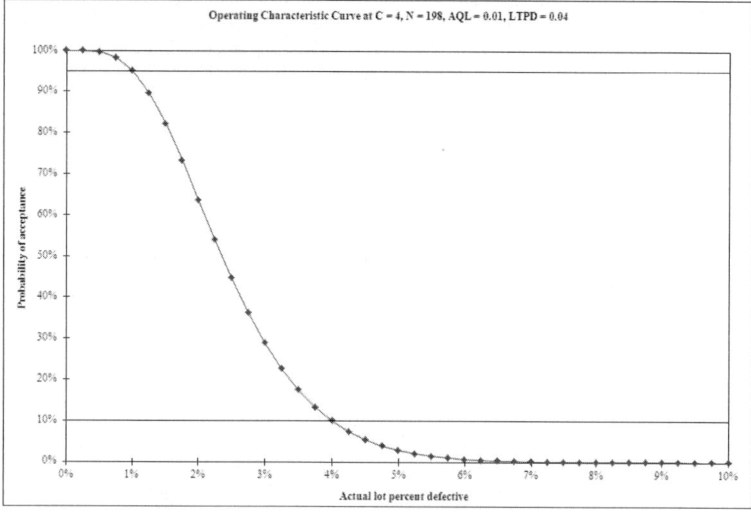

Figure 10.19
An operating characteristic curve with a smaller Lot Tolerance Percent Defective reduces the required sample size.

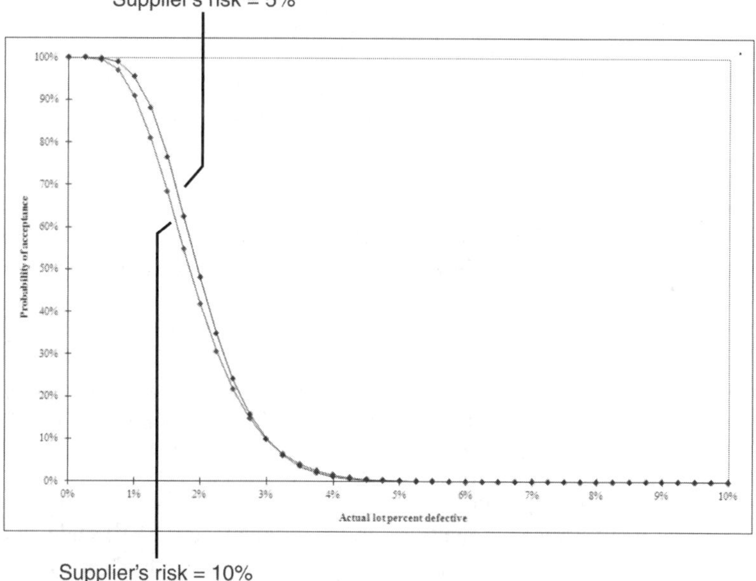

Figure 10.20
Operating characteristic curves that reduce the supplier's risk tend to shift, and gently steepen, the curve.

Again, you can generate these curves by installing and running `OCC.xla`, which you can download from www.quepublishing.com. After it's downloaded, you install it just as described earlier in this chapter, where we discussed the SPC add-in. After the `OCC.xla` add-in has been installed, a new item, OC Curves, is added to Excel's Data menu in versions through Excel 2003, and to the Menu Commands group in the Add-Ins tab in subsequent versions.

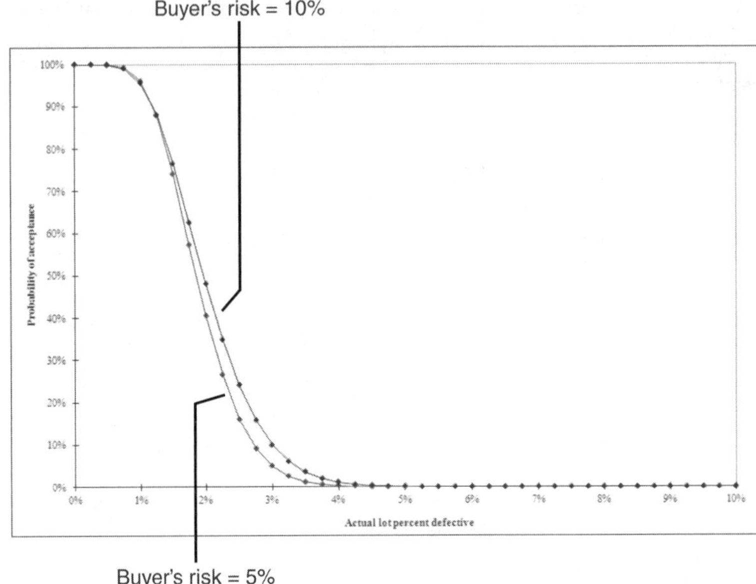

Figure 10.21
Varying the buyer's risk also shifts the curve to the right or left.

When you select OC Curves Excel displays a dialog box that prompts you to supply an AQL, an LTPD, a fraction that represents supplier's risk, and a fraction that represents buyer's risk.

After you click OK, Excel searches for the minimum sample size and *c* that satisfy the four criteria. Summary data is placed on a worksheet, and the curve is plotted on a separate chart sheet.

You can use these curves and the associated summary data in negotiations between suppliers and buyers. As a buyer, you might be willing to increase your LTPD requirement slightly to reduce the required sample size. This would save the supplier some testing costs that could be reflected in the cost of the goods.

As a supplier, you might be willing to accept a slightly increased level of risk that a good shipment will be rejected due to sampling error. Accepting this additional risk would save sampling and testing costs, and you might be able to apply these savings to another negotiating point where you need additional bargaining room.

The operating characteristic curves discussed in this section are based on a single sample from a lot. Other, more complex sampling plans include double samples, multiple samples, and sequential samples. For further information, see an advanced text on quality control.

Using Worksheet Functions for Quality Control

You can use Excel to help answer a variety of questions that occasionally arise in quality control situations. It's important to understand the nature of the tools that are available to you when such questions come up. Because statistical quality control is largely an exercise in probability—and in choosing the right tool in a given case—this chapter concludes with a discussion of some of these questions and how you can use Excel to answer them.

Sampling Units from a Finite Population

To this point, we have discussed statistical process control and acceptance sampling in terms of theoretically infinite populations. There has been no limit to the size of the population of products that has been sampled to create X-and-S charts, P-charts, or operating characteristic curves.

Things change some when you sample from a finite population. You have a finite population when you are interested in only a specific group, such as the items in a special production run, or your own company's sales staff, or customers' responses to a temporary price reduction. In each of these cases, the specially produced items, your company's sales reps, or your customers' responses constitute a population, not a sample. There aren't other items or reps or responses that you're sampling from.

When you sample from a finite population, it's usual to do so *without replacement*—that is, if you are going to sample two items, you select the first item and then select the second item without putting the first item back into the pool. Suppose that you have a population of 10 items. The chance of selecting any given item at random is 1/10, or 10%. After selecting the item, if you put it back into the pool, the chance of selecting any given item is still 10%. But if you do not return the item to the pool, the chance of selecting at random any given item as your second choice is 1/9, or 11%.

CASE STUDY: MANUFACTURING

A customer wants you to manufacture 200 coffee cups with a glazing that differs substantially from the glazing of those that you normally make. This will be a special production run; therefore, the 200 cups constitute a finite population. Your agreement with the customer allows for a 5% defect rate.

You plan to sample 20 cups, without replacement, from your production run, and to reject the run if you find unacceptable imperfections in the glazing on more than 5% of the sample. That is, you will reject the run if the sample contains 2 or more defectives. What is the probability that your full run of 200 has met the 5% criterion if you find 0 or 1 defective cup in your sample of 20?

You answer this question with Excel's `HYPGEOMDIST` function (but see the next section for information on the `HYPGEOM.DIST` function, new in Excel 2010). It takes four arguments:

- The number of "successes" in the sample. Here, that argument is `0` or `1`: the number of imperfect cups in your sample if you accept the production run.
- The sample size. Here, that argument is `20`, the number of cups you sample.

- The number of "successes" in the population. Here, that argument is `10`. If you tested all 200 cups, the 5% criterion implies that no more than 10 would be imperfect.
- The size of the population. Here, that argument is `200`, the number of special cups that you manufactured.

`HYPGEOMDIST` returns the probability that you would observe an exact number of successes, given the sample size, the successes in the population, and the population size. So if you entered this, Excel would return `.34`:

```
=HYPGEOMDIST(0,20,10,200)
```

Therefore, there's a 34% probability of finding no imperfect cups in a sample of 20 when there are exactly 10 imperfect cups in the population of 200.

In this example as described, you also need to know the probability of finding exactly one defective cup in your sample, so you enter this:

```
=HYPGEOMDIST(1,20,10,200)
```

Excel returns `.40`. Therefore, there's a 40% probability of finding exactly one imperfect cup in your sample. Together, these two probabilities add up to 74%. Given that your sample contains zero or one imperfect cups, it is more likely (74%) than not (100% – 74% = 26%) that there are 10 imperfect cups in the full production run.

> **TIP**
>
> You can use an array constant in `HYPGEOMDIST`, and similar functions, to get the sum of the function's results. Instead of entering
>
> ```
> =HYPGEOMDIST(0,20,10,200)
> ```
>
> and
>
> ```
> =HYPGEOMDIST(1,20,10,200)
> ```
>
> and summing the results, you can enter this:
>
> ```
> =SUM(HYPGEOMDIST({0,1},20,10,200))
> ```
>
> This formula executes `HYPGEOMDIST` twice: once for the first element in the array `{0,1}` and once for the second element. It then adds the results and, in this case, returns .74, or 74%.

Using HYPGEOM.DIST in Excel 2010

As is the case with several other statistical functions such as `TDIST` and `FDIST`, Excel 2010 has a new version of `HYPGEOMDIST`. The old version is still supported in 2010, but a new version has been included that is distinguished from the old version by the period in `HYPGEOM.DIST`.

The arguments are identical, except that a *cumulative* argument has been included. So this expression

```
=HYPGEOM.DIST(1,20,10,200,TRUE)
```

returns the cumulative results of these two expressions:

```
=HYPGEOM.DIST(0,20,10,200,FALSE)
```

and

```
=HYPGEOM.DIST(1,20,10,200,FALSE)
```

Using the array constant form of the old version as discussed earlier, these two expressions are equivalent:

```
=SUM(HYPGEOMDIST({0,1},20,10,200))
```

and

```
=HYPGEOM.DIST(1,20,10,200,TRUE)
```

No new functionality has been introduced with the new `HYPGEOM.DIST` function. Whether or not it adds consistency to the statistical function set, as Microsoft contends, is a subjective question for you to decide.

10

Sampling Units from a Nonfinite Population

When you monitor a nonfinite population, you are interested in a larger group than when you monitor a finite population. For example, instead of testing a special, finite production run, you might be testing your normal, ongoing, nonfinite product line. If you were testing a new invoice format, you might try it for a week before deciding to adopt it; then sampling for invoice accuracy would involve a finite population that consists of the week's worth of invoices you produced. On the other hand, if you were monitoring invoice accuracy as a normal procedure, you would probably consider your sample to be from a nonfinite population.

To make probability statements about a sample from a nonfinite population where your measure is something such as perfect/imperfect, good/bad or pass/fail, you can use Excel's `NORM.S.INV` or its `NORMSINV` function. You can also use Excel's `BINOM.DIST` consistency function, or, equivalently, its `BINOMDIST` compatibility function. An example follows in the case study of equipment rentals, but first it's helpful to discuss some distribution theory. Feel free to skip it, but if you want to know more about the ins-and-outs of choosing statistical functions, the next section may help.

Using `NORMSDIST` to Approximate `BINOMDIST`

If you are looking into a dichotomous variable such as whether a production lot is acceptable or unacceptable, you are using something called the *binomial distribution*. *Binomial* means "two names," such as acceptable vs. unacceptable, conforming vs. nonconforming, good vs. defective, and so on.

Suppose you have a large production lot, thousands of units, of merchandise that either works properly or doesn't. Therefore, you're working with a binomial distribution. Unknown to you, 10% of the units are defective. You take a sample of, say, 10 units from that lot and test each of them, finding 9 that work and 1 that doesn't. Your best estimate of the percent acceptable in the full lot is now 90%. It's not a very good estimate, based on only 10 units, but it's the best you have.

However, you can sample from that lot once, a few times, or many times. If you took many samples—say, 100—each of size 10 and charted the percent defective in each sample, that chart would look very similar to the one shown in Figure 10.22.

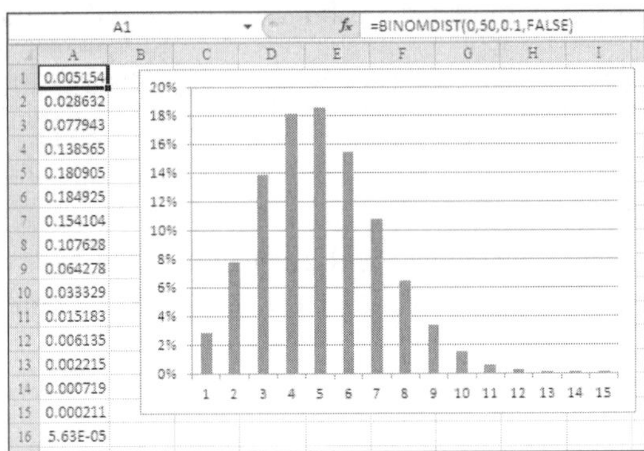

Figure 10.22
The binomial distribution's shape depends on the population percent and the sample size.

Excel has worksheet functions that tell you about any binomial distribution, including the one shown in Figure 10.22 that is based on repeated samples of size 10 and a population percent defective of 10%. For example, this formula

```
=BINOMDIST(1,50,0.1,FALSE)
```

gives you the probability of getting exactly one defective item (first argument) in a sample of 50 (second argument) when the population has a 10% defective rate (third argument). The `FALSE` argument specifies that Excel should return the probability of exactly one defective; using `TRUE` instead would return the cumulative probability of 0 or 1 defective.

Excel 2010 adds the consistency function `BINOM.DIST` to the function library. Its arguments and results are the same as the compatibility function `BINOMDIST`.

Figure 10.22 shows the probability of different numbers of defectives in a sample of 50. The chart shows the values in cells A1:A16. Notice that the curve is skewed rather than symmetric.

Figure 10.23, in contrast, shows a symmetric curve, one that is very nearly a normal or "bell" curve. But it is still built on a binomial distribution. The difference in the curves in Figures 10.22 and 10.23 is that the sample sizes in Figure 10.22 are each 50, and the sample sizes in Figure 10.23 are each 100.

What you see in Figures 10.22 and 10.23 is due to something called the *central limit theorem*. Put simply, the theorem states that regardless of the shape of the underlying distribution, the means of repeated samples from the underlying distribution will approximate the normal curve when the samples become sufficiently large. Figure 10.24 shows the shape of the underlying distribution.

So the underlying binomial distribution is as shown in Figure 10.24, with 90% good units and 10% defective. Repeated samples of 50 units each would result in the frequency dis-

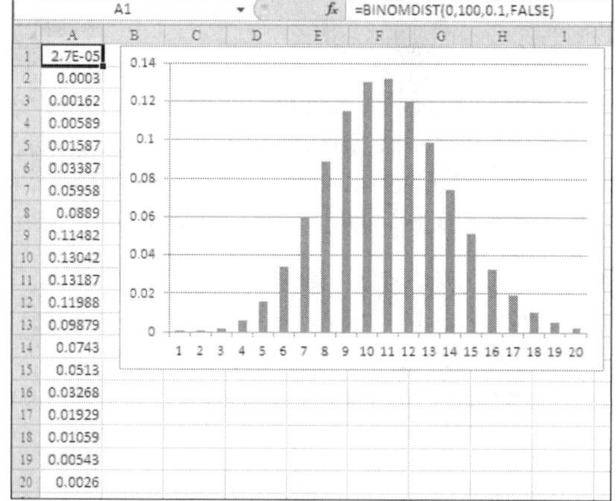

Figure 10.23
The larger the sample sizes, the more the frequency distribution resembles a normal curve.

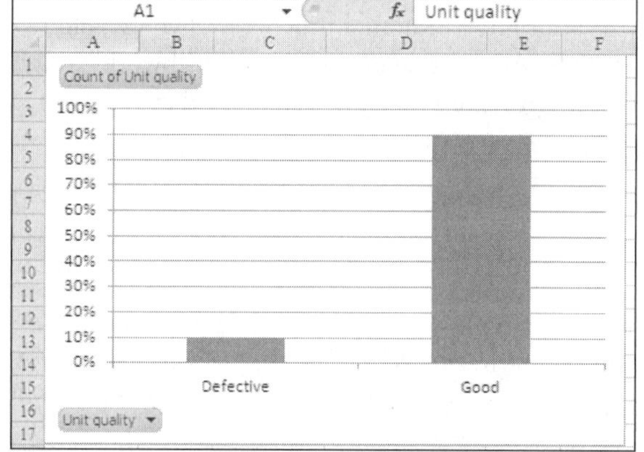

Figure 10.24
A binomial distribution has just two possible values, thus just two columns in a chart—about as far from a bell curve as it can get.

tribution shown in Figure 10.22. Samples of 100 would result in the distribution shown in Figure 10.23.

Quality testing makes use of this phenomenon. It takes samples from a production lot that are large enough that, repeated enough times, would approximate the normal curve. Then statistical tests based on that normal curve can be applied, and a decision reached about the quality in the full production lot.

Excel supports analysis based on normal distributions, of course. Instead of using `BINOMDIST`, or `BINOM.DIST` in Excel 2010, you use `NORMDIST` (or `NORM.DIST`).

For example, suppose that you take just one sample of 100 units from the production lot and find that it has three defectives. Your contract with your customer states that only 1% of the production lot may be defective. What is the likelihood that 1% or less of the full production lot is defective, when 3% of the sample is defective?

One way to answer this sort of question is discussed in the next section.

CASE STUDY: EQUIPMENT RENTALS

Suppose you are in the business of renting medical equipment such as wheelchairs, rolling tables, and gurneys to hospitals. Hospitals need more of these at some times than at others, but hospital regulators don't like to see them lined up unused in the halls, so hospitals regard renting as a good option during peak census periods. After these items have been rented some number of times, their quality deteriorates to the point that you consider them to be unusable.

You want to maintain an inventory of wheelchairs that is at least 90% acceptable; you would really prefer 95%, but the equipment gets pretty rough treatment at times. It's difficult to identify all damage from just a visual inspection, so you relax the criterion a little, from 95% to 90%. Although you have a finite number of items in your rental stock on any given day, your inventory is constantly changing due to equipment replacement. You therefore consider your population of wheelchairs to be nonfinite.

Testing the equipment is a time-consuming process, and you would like to keep the test sample as small as possible. An old rule of thumb that still works well in quality testing is to make sure both of these expressions result in a number that is 5 or greater:

$n \times p$

and

$n \times (p - 1)$

Here, n is the sample size, and p is the probability of an acceptable unit in the population. If your wheelchairs meet your criterion of 90% acceptable, p is .90. To make sure that both $n \times p$ and $n \times (p - 1)$ are equal to or greater than 5, you need n, the sample size, to be at least 50.

> **NOTE** The rule of thumb just described is due to the relationship between the binomial and the normal distributions. The sampling distribution of a binomial variable such as defective/acceptable is very close to a normal distribution when both $n \times p$ and $n \times (1 - p)$ are greater than 5. Notice that these two criteria are not both met by the samples charted in Figure 10.22, but they are both met by the samples charted in Figure 10.23.

You test the *random* sample of 50 wheelchairs, finding 2 that are defective and 48 that are acceptable, so 96% of your sample is acceptable. Given that finding, what is the probability that at least 90% of your population of wheelchairs is acceptable?

> **NOTE** The word *random* is italicized in the preceding paragraph because it's an important component of the testing process: the sample must be randomly drawn from the population. Indeed, that is the *only* assumption the test makes. By appealing to the central limit theorem, it's possible to run this sort of statistical test without assuming normality in the underlying distribution.

You decide that you want to make a correct decision about the defects in your population of wheelchairs 95% of the time that you test samples. The following Excel formula returns the criterion that you need if you are to have that amount of protection (the formula's result is known as a *critical value*):

```
=NORMSINV(.95)
```

Excel returns 1.64. This critical value is the number that your test statistic needs to exceed if you are to make a correct decision.

> **TIP** NORMSINV is easier and quicker to use than NORMINV. However, NORMINV gives you greater control over the characteristics of the underlying distribution. With NORMINV you specify the mean and standard deviation; with NORMSINV the mean is assumed to be 0.0 and the standard deviation 1.0. In Excel 2010, the equivalent functions are NORM.INV and NORM.S.INV.

Normal Distribution Functions in Excel 2010

Excel 2010 now has so many different functions that concern the normal distribution that you might find it helpful to review them here along with a description of each.

NORMDIST tells you the cumulative area under the normal curve that's to the left of the point you specify on its horizontal axis. So NORMDIST(115,100,15,TRUE) returns .8413. That is, 84.13 percent of the area under a normal curve with a mean of 100 and a standard deviation of 15 lies to the left of a value of 115.

The Excel 2010 function NORM.DIST has the same arguments and returns the same results as NORMDIST. For both versions of the function, you supply

- A point on the horizontal axis (in the earlier example, 115)
- The mean of the distribution (earlier, 100)
- The standard deviation of the distribution (earlier, 15)
- Whether to return the cumulative area to the left of the point specified or the height of the curve at that point (earlier, TRUE)

You can interpret the area under the curve to the left of the point specified as the probability of occurrence of that point or any smaller value. The height of the curve leads to (not "is," but "leads to") a measure of the probability of occurrence of that specific point.

NORMSDIST also returns the area under a normal curve to the left of a point you specify. However, it assumes one particular normal curve, the one with a mean of 0 and a standard deviation of 1. This special normal curve is sometimes called the *unit* normal curve or the *standard* normal curve—hence, the first "S" in NORMSDIST. Because the mean and standard deviation are fixed in the unit normal distribution, you do not need to supply them as you do in NORMDIST. Furthermore, NORMDIST always returns the cumulative probability, so it has no *cumulative* argument. The (nearly) equivalent function in Excel 2010 is NORM.S.DIST, which does have a *cumulative* argument. So, these two formulas return the same result:

```
=NORMSDIST(1)
```

and

```
=NORM.S.DIST(1,TRUE)
```

NORMINV is the *inverse* of the NORMDIST function. That is, you supply a value on the horizontal axis to NORMDIST, and it returns the probability, the area under the curve to the left of that point. In contrast, you supply an area, or probability, to NORMINV and it returns the associated point on the horizontal axis. The Excel 2010 equivalent of NORMINV is NORM.INV. You also need to supply the mean and standard deviation whether you are using NORMINV or NORM.INV, just as you do with NORMDIST or NORM.DIST.

NORMSINV is the inverse of NORMSDIST, just as NORMINV is the inverse of NORMDIST. If you supply a probability value to NORMSINV, it returns the associated point on the horizontal axis. Like NORMSDIST, NORMSINV works with the unit normal curve, where the mean and standard deviation are known, so you do not supply either.

The Excel 2010 equivalent of NORMSINV is NORM.S.INV. Both functions take only one argument, the probability level in which you are interested.

To get the test statistic for the wheelchair study, enter this Excel formula:

```
=(0.96-0.90)/SQRT(0.10*0.90/50)
```

It returns 1.41. The general formula is as follows:

```
= (x - p) / SQRT(p × [p - 1] / n)
```

Here, x is the percent acceptable in the sample, p is the hypothetical percent acceptable in the population, n is the sample size, and the denominator is the standard error of p.

Because your test statistic of 1.41 is less than your critical value of 1.64, you can't conclude that your inventory of wheelchairs is at least 90% acceptable. Put simply, your sample result of 96% is not far enough above your criterion of 90% for you to conclude that at least 90% of the population of wheelchairs you might own is acceptable.

The situation is that you have a favorable finding from your sample, but the statistical test you apply might not be powerful enough for you to make a confident decision about your population. You suspect that your population of wheelchairs is at least 90% acceptable, but the test statistic (1.41) isn't large enough to put you on the firmer ground implied by your choice of 1.64 as the critical value.

In cases such as these, you usually have at least two options: increase the sample size or relax the test criterion. Both options give you a more sensitive statistical test—in statistical jargon, this is called increasing statistical power. The next section provides an example of how they would work using a new sample.

> **NOTE** This is just an example. Don't let it talk you into the idea that it's okay to repeat an experiment over and over until it returns the result you hope for. In this case study, the best sequence is to get preliminary numbers as just described, not intending of making a decision based on them. Design your test with those numbers in mind, planning on a larger sample size if necessary. Then, when you do run the formal experiment, it will have enough statistical power that you can have confidence in its results.

Increasing the Sample Size

Probably the most intuitively satisfying way to increase statistical power is to use a larger sample. Not only does this result in a more sensitive statistical test, but it increases the representativeness, or *generalizability*, of your sample.

The sensitivity of the statistical test is increased because the denominator of the test statistic is reduced. In this example, with a sample of 50, you get this:

```
(0.96 - 0.90)/SQRT(0.10*0.90/50)
```

The formula returns `1.41`. If you increase the sample size to 68, the formula changes to this:

```
(0.96 - 0.90)/SQRT(0.10*0.90/68)
```

It returns `1.65`. That value is (barely) larger than `1.64`, the criterion you get from `NORMSINV(.95)` or from `NORM.S.INV(.95)`, but it's considerably larger than the calculated value of `1.41` that you get with a sample size of `50`. With 1.65 as the outcome, you could reject the hypothesis that in the population the acceptable proportion is less than 90%. That decision would come at the 95% confidence level because `NORM.S.INV(.95)` returns 1.64: your test statistic of `1.65` exceeds the test criterion of `1.64`.

10

Keep in mind that this is not merely a meaningless result of arithmetic. By increasing the sample size you tend to get a more accurate estimate of the population value—the larger the sample, the broader the basis you use to estimate the proportion acceptable in the population, and the more accurate the estimate. And the better the estimate, the more sensitive the statistical test.

Relaxing the Test Criterion

Suppose you were willing to reach an incorrect conclusion in 10% of your samples rather than the 5% that this example has assumed so far. You would use `.9` as the argument to `NORMSINV` (or `NORM.S.INV`) rather than `.95`. This formula would return `1.28`:

```
=NORMSINV(.9)
```

At a 10% error rate, your original test statistic of `1.41` would have been large enough to reject the hypothesis of a population proportion of less than 90% acceptable.

> **NOTE** The statistical technique described here is an older one, although it's still perfectly valid. You might prefer to use what's termed *logistic* analysis, which can be more sensitive. (Keep in mind that this use of the term *logistic* has nothing to do with the management of supplies and equipment.) But if you choose logistic analysis, be aware that Excel's functions do not do a straightforward job of supporting it: you must piece a logistic analysis together using the functions that Excel does supply.

Sampling Defects in Units

So far this chapter has discussed one particular attribute: whether a unit is acceptable or defective. A related measure is the number of defects in a particular unit. For example, if you were concerned with the quality of the purchase orders that your company distributes to suppliers, you might want a more detailed measure than acceptable/defective. It might be important to understand the frequency of occurrence of critical defects in the purchase orders (such as erroneous account numbers or ship-to addresses) versus minor defects such as misspelling the supplier's city.

To make inferences about numbers of defects in units, as distinct from numbers of defective units, the Excel `POISSON` function is often useful. Excel 2010 also offers the `POISSON.DIST` function, which is identical to `POISSON` as to both arguments and results.

CASE STUDY: FORMS

As the manager of the purchasing department for a large firm, you have recently put a new purchase order system in place. Since then, you have noticed an unusual number of complaints that deliveries from suppliers have been late. Following up on some of the complaints, you find that some suppliers report that the deliveries have been delayed because of errors on the purchase orders. There apparently have been problems relating to unit pricing, want-dates, model numbers, and contract references.

Because suppliers sometimes place inappropriate blame on buyers, you decide to examine a sample of purchase orders to see whether the overall rate of defects per form might be high enough to cause these delays.

You decide that an overall defect rate of .5 defects per purchase order is acceptable. If Purchase Order A is perfect and Purchase Order B has only one defect, the average rate is .5 defects per purchase order. Therefore, there should be enough good information on Order B for the supplier to be able either to fill it or to resolve the incorrect information quickly.

You also decide that you want to set a limit of 5% on the likelihood of deciding that the average defect rate is one-half of one defect per order, when, in fact, it is some other number.

You sample 10 purchase orders at random and examine them for inaccuracies. You find 12 instances of misinformation in the sample. Given this data, should you continue to believe that the average number of defects in all your purchase orders is .5?

Use Excel's `POISSON` function. Enter this formula:

```
=1-POISSON(11,5,TRUE)
```

It returns `.005`. The first argument, `11`, is 12 – 1: that is, the number of inaccuracies that you found, minus 1; it's called *degrees of freedom*. The second argument, `5`, is the number of inaccuracies that you would expect to find in 10 purchase orders if the average number of inaccuracies were .5. The third argument, `TRUE`, specifies the cumulative form of the Poisson distribution: that is, the sum of the probability for zero inaccuracies, plus the probability for one inaccuracy, and so on.

You decided beforehand that the level of protection you wanted against an incorrect decision was 5%, or .05. Because .005 is less than .05, you reject your hypothesis that there are .5 errors per form among all your purchase orders. You probably need to make sure that your staff is properly trained on your new system and that the system itself is operating as it was designed.

Using the CRITBINOM Function

It's sad but true that Excel's Help documents sometimes read as though they were written by someone who doesn't comprehend what he's writing about. A good example is the explanation of the `CRITBINOM` function, which says, `Smallest value for which the cumulative binomial distribution is greater than or equal to a criterion value.`

And what criterion value is that? The Help documentation merely says that it's `Alpha`. Left unsaid is how you choose it, what the consequences of selecting a particular value are, how it helps you interpret the result returned by `CRITBINOM`—in short, anything that suggests that any informed thought went into the writing of the Help document.

> **NOTE** The Excel 2010 equivalent of `CRITBINOM` is `BINOM.INV`. The two versions use the same arguments and return the same results. Like `NORMINV`, `NORMSINV`, `NORM.INV`, and `NORMS.INV`, you supply the probability and Excel returns the associated point on the horizontal axis.

Understanding the Distributions

Here's what a CRITBINOM value means and how you might use it. Suppose you have a production lot of manufactured goods. The lot has too many items (perhaps thousands) to test all of them for defects, so you take a sample of 100 individual units.

What you're concerned about is that the percentage of defective units in the full lot is more than a standard such as 1%. This question is similar to the issue of acceptance sampling and operating characteristic curves that is discussed earlier in this chapter, but there's a difference. Operating characteristic curves take into account two kinds of risk: the buyer's risk and the seller's risk. The situation discussed in this section, and that is addressed by `CRITBINOM`, concerns one party's risk only. In practice, that's usually the seller, but it could just as well be the buyer.

You undertake the task of checking for defects in a sample from a production lot for one of two reasons:

- You want to estimate the percentage of defective items in the full lot by counting the number of defectives in the sample.
- You want to decide whether the lot passes your standard for percentage of defects.

In the first case, you would want to check all units in your sample. That gives you an estimate of the percentage defective in the full production lot that the sample came from. In turn, that information can give you insight into issues such as the quality of your production facilities and the materials you use to manufacture your product.

In the second case, you don't necessarily want to check all the units in the sample, although you usually wind up doing so. You intend to ship the lot if your sample indicates that the lot passes muster. But it might be that by the time you've tested 10 units, you've found so many defectives that it's pointless to continue testing. In that case you decide to throw out the lot and start over.

The question is how large that number should be before you quit testing and reject the lot. The `CRITBINOM` function provides the answer. However, you have to give the function some information, including the size of the sample, the percentage of defects you hope for in the lot, and how sure you want to be of making a correct decision.

The syntax of `CRITBINOM` is as follows:

```
CRITBINOM(Number of trials, Probability of success, Alpha)
```


The first two arguments are easy. The number of trials is just the size of the sample you've taken: at the outset you intend to test each item in the sample, and each test constitutes one trial. So if you take a sample of 100 items from the production lot, `CRITBINOM`'s first argument is 100.

The second argument concerns the percentage of defective items that represents your quality standard. That is, if the full production lot meets your standard of, say, 1% defectives, then the probability of success is also 1%, when "success" means that you've found a defective item.

The third argument, `Alpha`, is where the trouble arises, and that causes people to post questions to newsgroups. Calling it *alpha* or *criterion value* isn't helpful. The third argument is the probability that the full lot contains the percentage of defective units that you've specified with the second argument, `Probability of success`. Yes, that makes the third argument the probability of another probability, and as such it is a little confusing, but read on.

Suppose that the production lot has 1,000 units and your quality standard calls for a maximum of 1% defective. Under your hypothesis that no more than 10 of the units in the lot are defective, your best estimate of the number of defectives in a sample of 100 units is 1: that is, 1%.

However, sampling error can cause more or fewer defective units than expected in the sample. You might happen to get your hands on 100 units with no defective units—or you might wind up with an unusually large number of defective units in the sample: two or three or even more, just by the luck of the draw. (Clearly, if you get more than 10 defective units in your sample, the full lot of 1,000 *must* violate your 1% standard.)

Critical Values in the Binomial Distribution

This gets us to the binomial distribution. As noted earlier, it's termed *binomial* because it's made up of things with one of two ("bi") names ("nomial"): good or bad, true or false, acceptable or defective. When you take samples of a given size from a production lot, those samples follow the binomial distribution. The number of defects in the repeated samples follows the distributions shown in Figure 10.25

Figure 10.25
The lower the percentage of defects in the full production lot, the steeper the binomial distribution.

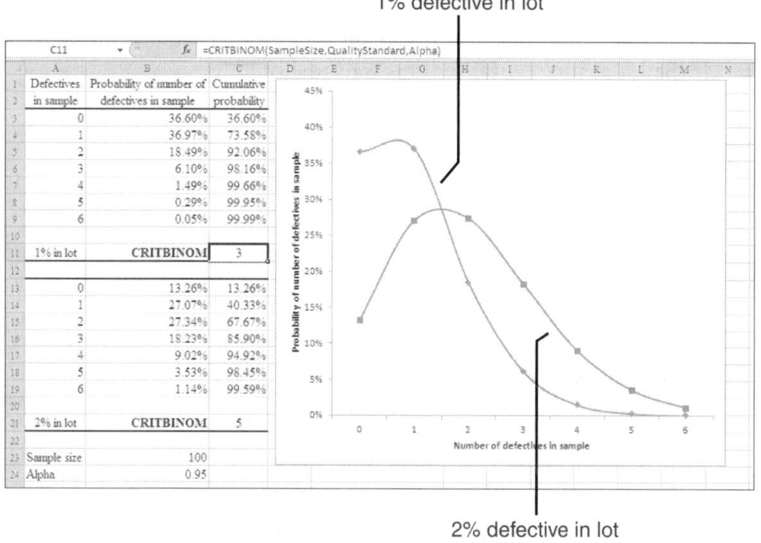

Defectives in sample	Probability of number of defectives in sample	Cumulative probability
0	36.60%	36.60%
1	36.97%	73.58%
2	18.49%	92.06%
3	6.10%	98.16%
4	1.49%	99.66%
5	0.29%	99.95%
6	0.05%	99.99%
1% in lot	**CRITBINOM**	3
0	13.26%	13.26%
1	27.07%	40.33%
2	27.34%	67.67%
3	18.23%	85.90%
4	9.02%	94.92%
5	3.53%	98.45%
6	1.14%	99.59%
2% in lot	**CRITBINOM**	5
Sample size	100	
Alpha	0.95	

TIP

Notice the curvature of the lines in the chart in Figure 10.25. That's not the standard appearance of a data series in a line chart, which usually appears more articulated. You can call for a smoother appearance by right-clicking the line and then selecting Format Data Series from the context menu. Click Line Style in the list box and then select the Smoothed Line check box.

In a version prior to Excel 2007, select the Smoothed Line check box on the Patterns tab and click OK.

Suppose that 1% of your production lot is defective and that you take samples of 100 items each from it. If your decision rule is to reject the lot if a sample contains more than three defective units, you will (incorrectly) reject the lot 1.84% of the time.

Cell C6 in Figure 10.25 shows that if you accept the lot when the sample yields as many as three defective items, you accept it for 98.16% of the samples. (It is this number, 98.16%, that is the basis for the Alpha argument in `CRITBINOM`—more on that shortly.) Given that, unknown to you, only 1% of the production lot is defective, you will have four or more defective units in your sample and therefore incorrectly reject the lot 1.84% of the time. You will have three or fewer defective units, and therefore correctly accept it, 98.16% of the time.

On the other hand, suppose that not 1% but 2% of the production lot is defective, and that you're still applying the decision rule to reject the lot if your sample contains more than three defective units. Now, instead of incorrectly rejecting the lot 1.84% of the time, you will correctly reject it for 14.1% of the samples and incorrectly accept it for 85.9% of the samples. See (See cell C16 in Figure 10.25.)

So the farther that the full production lot wanders from your quality standard of no more than 1% defective units, the greater the likelihood that you will make a correct decision to reject the lot as unacceptable. This is as it should be.

Examining a Specific Case

But how do you determine the criterion you should apply to your sample from the full lot? That's what the `CRITBINOM` function is for. Again, its syntax is

```
CRITBINOM(Number of trials, Probability of success, Alpha)
```

If you are using Excel 2010, you can instead use this:

```
BINOM.DIST(Number of trials, Probability of success, Alpha)
```

Regarding the three arguments to these functions:

- The number of trials, or sample size, is under your control, and you determine it largely by deciding how much time and energy you can afford to spend checking the sample.
- The probability of success—that is, the percentage of defects in the full production lot—is under your control only to the degree that you control the quality of your production materials and methods. But you can select a value that you want to use as a criterion for acceptance.
- You can easily specify `Alpha`, the probability that you make a correct decision to accept a lot on the basis of a sample.

If you want to correctly accept a lot using a criterion that will pass 95% of the possible samples from that lot, you set `Alpha` to 0.95. But there are still two ways to go wrong:

- Some number of possible samples will cause you to reject the lot incorrectly, because those samples have an improbably large number of defective units.
- You will accept some lots that don't meet your quality standard of, say, 1% defective. If your decision rule is to reject the lot if a sample has more than three defective units, you will *accept* a lot that contains 2% defective units 85.9% of the time. (See cell C16 in Figure 10.25.)

You can reduce the likelihood of accepting a bad lot by lowering your criterion for acceptance or by increasing the sample size. Suppose you reduce the criterion from 3 to 2, rejecting a lot if your sample has three or more defective units instead of four or more. Now you will accept a 2%-defective lot 67.67% of the time, instead of 85.9%. (See cell C15 in Figure 10.25.). But the corollary is that you will reject a *good* lot, one with 1% defective units, almost 8% of the time. Cell C5 in Figure 10.25 shows that you'll accept it 92.06% of the time and reject it 7.94% of the time.

Therefore, you have to weigh the alternatives and make decisions concerning the relative costs of rejecting a good lot and accepting a bad one. That's really your only guide to determining the value of `Alpha` that's right in your situation.

NOTE You have additional guidance when you're negotiating with a buyer, as described earlier in this chapter's section titled Performing Acceptance Sampling. The added guidance is provided by negotiations regarding the buyer's requirements.

So, suppose you select .95 as the value for `Alpha`. You're now in a position to use `CRITBINOM` or `BINOM.INV` to determine your criterion for accepting or rejecting a sample. In the example this section has discussed, you would use

```
CRITBINOM(100,.01,.95)
```

Excel responds by finding the *smallest* value in the cumulative binomial distribution that is *larger* than `Alpha`. In Figure 10.25, where `Alpha` is set to .95, the smallest value larger than 0.95 is 98.16% for a 1% lot defective rate in cell C6, or 98.45% for a 2% lot defective rate in cell C18.

In the case of a 1% lot defective rate, the number of defectives associated with a 98.16% cumulative binomial probability is 3. So, if your quality standard is 1% defective units in the production lot and you're taking a sample of 100 units from the lot, then the value of .95 for `Alpha` implies you should reject a lot if the sample has at least three defective units.

TIP No number of defective units that is an integer is associated with an alpha rate of precisely .95. Because you cannot get that exact alpha, you should decide beforehand whether to be slightly conservative and reject the lot with two or more defective units in the sample, or slightly liberal and reject with three or more.

Summary

This chapter has described how to use Excel to create X-and-S statistical control charts and P-charts to monitor the ongoing performance of systems. X-and-S charts are used for variables such as the capacity of data storage discs, the length of telephone calls, and the profit margin on daily sales. P-charts are used for attributes, such as the percent of defective units in a sample of manufactured goods, or forms that you can classify as either defective or acceptable. These statistical control charts enable you to judge the performance of a system over time.

Another topic in this chapter is that of operating characteristic curves. Studying these curves puts you in a position, as a supplier, to limit the risk that an entire shipment of goods will be rejected because the number of defective units in a sample is an overestimate of the entire shipment. As a purchaser, you can use operating characteristic curves to limit your risk of accepting an entire shipment of goods, because the number of defective units in a sample is an underestimate of the entire shipment.

This chapter has also discussed four ways to estimate overall process quality on the basis of sampling:

- The overall rate of defective items in a finite population. You can estimate this rate using the HYPGEOMDIST function.
- The overall rate of defective items in a nonfinite population. Use the NORMSINV function to make this estimate.
- The overall rate of defects per unit. Use the POISSON function to determine whether your estimate of this overall rate is accurate.
- The overall rate of defects in a production lot as estimated by a sample from that lot. Use the CRITBINOM or BINOM.INV function to determine how many defects cause you to reject the lot.

Examining a Business Case: Investment

11

IN THIS CHAPTER

Business case analysis is one of the most important activities a finance department can undertake to support a company's decision-making process. If the decision under consideration is a significant one—for example, bringing a new product on line, or discontinuing one that has reached the end of its life cycle—then a financial analysis of the resulting revenue, cost, and profit is necessary to make an informed decision.

A business case can take any of a variety of forms, depending on the question being considered and the decision that needs support. For example, a basic sort of question concerning the use of capital is, "Should we lease a copy machine or buy one?" Although this question might seem trivial, the answer depends partly on an analysis of the cost effects of purchasing versus leasing. Part of this analysis involves how the tax implications of a capital expenditure differ from those involved in an operating lease.

At a more complicated level, the management of a manufacturing company might ask, "Should we enter a new line of business?" A major decision such as this involves activities that often include the following:

- Investing capital to purchase equipment
- Hiring new staff to operate the equipment
- Acquiring market research to quantify the potential costs and revenues
- Assessing cross-elasticities among product lines

Each of these issues involves costs to evaluate during the decision-making process.

This chapter discusses data-based business planning from two viewpoints:

- Why each component is important to making a good business decision
- How the planning flows into an Excel workbook in a way that supports the eventual decision.

Developing a Business Case

Most business cases are developed by specifying increments. In other words, the business case focuses on changes—increments to revenues and to costs—over and above those involved in the normal course of business, changes that would occur only if a company adopts a proposal to materially modify its operations, products, sales, or distribution. The business case emphasizes the relevant benefits of a proposed decision such as these:

- New revenues
- Larger market share
- Lower expenses
- Product diversification

The business case also emphasizes the relevant costs of adopting a proposal:

- Incremental investment
- Additional operating expenses
- Additional taxes
- Losses to the existing line of business

A business case does not typically include the costs of doing business *as usual* because you generally regard those costs as set. You would incur them whether or not the business case is adopted. For example, the costs of doing tax accounting and of rent for corporate headquarters would not change if you decide to lease a new copier. These costs would not normally change even if you decide to extend your lines of business. Therefore, the business case attends to costs and benefits over and above the status quo.

Getting Consensus for the Plan

In the first stage of business case analysis, you should review the potential benefits and costs from a qualitative standpoint. At this point, the idea is to make sure that the business case identifies the potential costs and benefits—not necessarily to quantify them. The *stakeholders* (people on whom the business decision would have substantial impact) should take part in the review. This approach is similar to obtaining consensus from individual operating units on their annual budgets.

In large organizations, the marketing or product-management group frequently offers an idea for a new product. The proposal often defines an opportunity in terms of a customer need. The marketing group might identify this need by means of focus groups, a general awareness of the industry, or an understanding of the life cycle of current product sets—in short, any of various subjective and objective indicators that carry some degree of credibility.

Planning the Analysis

Obviously, Microsoft Excel can't create a business case for you. It *can* help you analyze the projected outcomes of a business decision, but only after you provide it with numbers to work with. Therefore, the marketing or product group's proposal at some point needs to frame its product description with several types of numeric analysis. These analyses often include the product's market potential, the competitive environment, and the means, such as distribution channels and the sales force, to bring the product to market.

The proposal usually describes the product's market potential in terms of the following:

- **Current size**—How many product units would the marketplace purchase if the product were available for sale today?
- **Growth potential**—What is the forecast for additional sales during the life cycle of the product?

The proposal makes these estimates in terms of unit sales, and the unit sales projections help form the basis for projecting new product revenue. To complete the projection, an analysis of the competitive environment translates unit sales estimates into dollars. In assessing the competitive environment, it's useful to get answers to these questions:

- **Product alternatives**—Does the competition have products that compete directly with the proposed product?
- **Pricing**—Does the competition offer a single price? Is the price tiered in some way? Can the proposed product meet that pricing, and does it need to?
- **Costs**—What level of resources does the competition commit to the production and sale of its product? Does the competition have a technological edge that holds down costs relative to yours?
- **Profitability**—If you put price pressure on the competition, is its product profitable enough that it can continue production and sales?
- **Competitive advantage**—What hurdles can the competition put in your way? These might include market presence, name recognition, brand loyalty, long-term contracts with resellers, and so on.

Each of these considerations influences your pricing plans for the product. By combining that pricing estimate with unit sales forecasts, you can create a credible projection of revenue for the product.

Specifying the Costs

To complete an initial quantitative picture, you need to give Excel information about the incremental costs associated with bringing the proposed product to market. In particular, it's useful to take these costs into account:

- **Market research—**What leads you to believe that the proposed product will generate additional revenue? Is there evidence from previous product rollouts? What about external sources of information, such as trade association data? How credible is the available evidence? How much will it cost to obtain the data?
- **Distribution channels—**What are the costs, such as reseller discounts, late penalties, and warehousing, of getting the product to your customers?
- **Promotion and advertising—**How much must you pay different media to run your advertisements? How much will it cost to produce new brochures and other product literature? Should you purchase mailing lists? What does all this imply for your web presence?
- **Rollout and implementation—**Is it necessary to travel to meet with your distributors or sales force? Should you offer special incentives to those in the distribution channel so that they will focus their efforts on selling this product? Does the distribution channel need any special training to understand the product's price structure, its market niche, and its competitive strengths and weaknesses? Should you double-compensate when a vertical market intersects a horizontal market?
- **Product cross-elasticities (any characteristics that compete with your existing products)—**Is the proposed product likely to cut into the sales of existing product lines? If so, those lines will inevitably lose some revenue. How much?
- **Objectives for market share and penetration—**Will the cost of attaining one more percentage point of market share outweigh the additional revenue? Is the cost of filling the last seat in the plane more than the price of the ticket?

Questions like these are not simply useful adjuncts to a product concept. You need the answers to quantify the projected costs and revenues that are associated with the proposed product. The estimated costs and revenues are your best rationale for deciding whether to go ahead with the product development process or to pass on the opportunity.

Showing Your Work

Besides the marketing issues, you need to quantify the operational and customer service costs that will factor in the proposed product's profit potential. These cost drivers include the following:

Technology—Is the technology needed to produce this product in hand, or do you have to buy it? How much will it cost to purchase and maintain it? If you already have the necessary production capacity, what is the opportunity cost of using it?

Systems—Are the required methods and processes in place, or must you develop them? These systems usually include sales support, product tracking, billing and collections, inventory management, and the software needed to manage them.

Implementation plans—Are the plans feasible? Are the timelines reasonable with existing staff, or do you need to do more hiring?

Training—Will your staff or customers need additional training to produce or use the proposed product? If so, should you develop the training in-house or obtain it externally? How much will the training cost? How much will it cost to deliver it? Will you need to send trainers around the country, or can you get by with webinars?

It's useful for a company to develop a formal process for business case development. When in place, formal procedures make it easier to repeat the process the next time the company considers bringing new products to market. A formal and repeatable process can help you compare a business case that's currently under consideration to earlier business cases, as well as their results. If your business cases have worked well in the past, it is reasonable to use the same procedures. However, if your previous business case development was not successful, do not expect different results if you reuse the same procedures.

You should document all research and analysis. It can be difficult to complete this step, particularly with research. Early in the planning process, research is often anecdotal, non-replicable, and soft. Enough hard data to support decisions with real confidence typically isn't available until well after the product is rolled out, and by then, the data tends not to be of much use. Documenting research data can seem futile, which is one reason it's seldom done. However, if you do not document it, it's difficult to assess your business case after the fact to determine the cause of either a bad decision or a good one.

Analysis is another matter, particularly if you use the tools that Excel provides to document and audit your work. For example, comments included in cells and scenarios can be valuable. After you've completed the analysis, comments make it easier to determine how you arrived at a decision. Listed next are a few ways to document your analysis:

- As you develop your analysis worksheets, use named constants and named ranges.
- Fill in the summary information for the workbook.
- Add comments in cells.
- Where appropriate, create scenarios that include comments, and associate the scenarios with the names of the groups that define them.

Developing the Excel Model

When you use Excel to model a business case, you synthesize concepts and methods that you have already read about in this book, including:

- Income statement formation, discussed in Chapter 1, "Working with Income Statements"
- Cash flow analysis, discussed in Chapter 5, "Working Capital and Cash Flow Analysis"
- Budget planning, discussed in Chapter 8, "Budgeting and Planning Cycle"
- Forecasting, discussed in Chapter 9, "Forecasting and Projections"

The first step in developing the model is to create a pro forma income statement. The pro forma income statement takes into account the relevant benefits and costs involved in the proposed course of action.

CASE STUDY: NEW TYPE OF E-READER

Your company has been a market leader in the manufacture of electronic book readers called e-readers for the past several years. Other firms have imitated your product with some degree of success. However, your company occupies a dominant position in the marketplace because you were the first with a quality product that included some capabilities that competitors lacked.

But success can breed complacency. For this reason, your company is asking questions: Is life too comfortable at the e-reader factory? What would happen if you offered an e-reader that incorporates new sharing permissions?

A new e-reader would not completely replace the current product. Instead, it would offer additional features for a somewhat higher price. As a result, some of your current distributors might migrate from your current product to the new e-reader device, and other distributors would carry both products.

Offering this enhanced e-reader would establish a new revenue stream for your company. Using the forecasting tools developed in Chapter 9, along with some market research, you can identify the incremental margin associated with the new product (see Figure 11.1).

Developing the Inputs

Based on the new e-reader product described in the previous case study, your marketing department has provided you with a total sales forecast for the new e-reader, as shown in row 4 of Figure 11.1. The range B4:G4 is named `TotalSales`. One way to name the range is to select it—here, cells B4:G4—and then click in the Name box, type the name in the box, and press Enter.

NOTE The *Name box* is the box with the drop-down arrow at the left end of the formula bar. If the name you choose already exists as the name of a cell or range of cells in the active workbook, typing it into the Name box and pressing Enter merely takes you to the existing range.

Figure 11.1
The added value (the incremental margin) of the new e-reader takes into account both the new product's total sales and the cost of goods sold.

IncrementalGrossProfit | fx =TotalSales-COGS

	A	B	C	D	E	F	G	H
1	Year:	1	2	3	4	5	6	
2	New E-Reader: Sales Forecast							
3				($Millions)				
4	Total sales, New E-Reader	$8	$14	$18	$28	$38	$44	
5	Cost of Goods Sold @ 50% of sales	$4	$7	$9	$14	$19	$22	
6	Incremental Gross Profit, New E-Reader	$4	$7	$9	$14	$19	$22	
7								

In Figure 11.1, row 5 shows the cost of goods sold and assumes that this cost will be 50 percent of revenue. Select B5:G5, type `=0.5*TotalSales` into the Formula box, and then press Ctrl+Enter.

> **NOTE** Entering formulas by using Ctrl+Enter is *not* the same as array-entering a formula with Ctrl+Shift+Enter. Pressing Ctrl+Enter places a *normal Excel formula* in each of the selected cells. Pressing Ctrl+Shift+Enter puts an *array formula* in the selected cells.

The formula in B5:G5 takes advantage of Excel's implicit intersection. Each column in row 5 is matched to its corresponding column in the range named `TotalSales` (that's B4:G4), and the value of `TotalSales` in that column is multiplied by 0.5.

> **TIP** A good way to think of an implicit intersection is that the intersection is *implied* by the location of a formula—that is, by the row or column where the formula is located. In this case, the intersection is implied by the column in which each instance of the formula exists and the row where the range `TotalSales` exists. This means that if cell C5 contains the formula `=.05*TotalSales`, it is referring to the value in `TotalSales` found in column C. Column C is implied by the location of the formula.

With B5:G5 still selected, you can name this range by clicking in the Name box, typing `COGS` for "cost of goods sold," and pressing Enter.

The cost of goods sold reflects only the purely variable costs of material and labor to produce the e-reader. Revenue minus the cost of goods sold is the gross profit. In this case, the incremental gross profit is the additional gross profit the company expects to derive from the new product. This line item, which is in row 6 of Figure 11.1, is linked by formulas to the beginning of the income statement, shown in Figure 11.2.

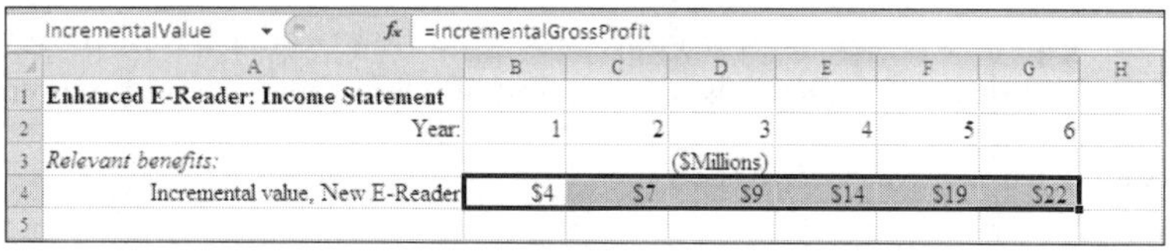

Figure 11.2
The pro forma income statement begins by identifying a relevant benefit—the incremental gross profit—of the new e-reader.

IncrementalValue | fx =IncrementalGrossProfit

	A	B	C	D	E	F	G	H
1	**Enhanced E-Reader: Income Statement**							
2	Year:	1	2	3	4	5	6	
3	*Relevant benefits:*			($Millions)				
4	Incremental value, New E-Reader	$4	$7	$9	$14	$19	$22	
5								

These steps make it easy to create the linkage between the worksheets:

1. Right-click the worksheet tab of the worksheet shown in Figure 11.1 and select Rename from the shortcut menu. Name the worksheet `Sales Forecast`.
2. Select the range B6:G6, click in the Name box, and name it `IncrementalGrossProfit`.

3. In the same workbook, activate a worksheet that will become your pro forma income statement. To do this, right-click its worksheet tab and select Rename from the shortcut menu; then name the sheet `Income Statement`.

4. To duplicate the information for the product's incremental value, as shown in Figure 11.2, select the range B4:G4 on the `Income Statement` worksheet.

5. Type the formula `=IncrementalGrossProfit` and then press Ctrl+Enter. The instances of this formula on the `Income Statement` worksheet are links to the values in `IncrementalGrossProfit` on the `Sales Forecast` worksheet. While the range is still selected, name it IncrementalValue.

Step 5 uses another instance of the implicit intersection. The formula you just entered spans columns B through G, just as the range named `IncrementalGrossProfit` does. If you entered this formula anywhere outside those six columns, you would get the `#VALUE!` error value. For example, because column S is not among `IncrementalGrossProfit`'s columns, there is nothing for the implicit intersection to intersect in column S.

TIP

As mentioned previously, the use of range names makes it easier to reuse data that you have already entered, document your work, and ensure that any changes you make in the data are reflected in dependent formulas. For example, suppose that in the future you need to adjust the sales forecast. The combination of these formulas and the named ranges lets that change flow through the workbook into formulas that depend on the sales forecast.

11

Identifying the Costs

After reviewing the product offering with the stakeholders in your organization, you identify the relevant costs:

- Some of the current distributors of the existing e-reader prefer the new features and performance enhancements. For this reason, you can expect that these distributors will stop buying the existing product and start buying the new one. An estimate of the gross margin of these lost sales is shown in Figure 11.3 in row 7, Lost value, Current Product.
- You need to get the word out about your new product. Row 8, Advertising, in Figure 11.3 quantifies the budget for an initial marketing blitz and ongoing commercials.

Figure 11.3
The relevant costs in the pro forma statement include only the costs that are directly attributable to the new product.

TotalIncrementalCosts | =SUM(B7:B11)

	A	B	C	D	E	F	G
1	**Enhanced E-Reader: Income Statement**						
2	Year:	1	2	3	4	5	6
3	*Relevant benefits:*			($Millions)			
4	Incremental value, New E-Reader	$4.0	$7.0	$9.0	$14.0	$19.0	$22.0
5							
6	Relevant costs:						
7	Lost value, Current Product	$6.0	$6.0	$6.0	$6.0	$6.0	$7.0
8	Advertising	$2.0	$1.0	$0.5	$0.5	$0.5	$0.5
9	New product management team	$1.0	$1.0	$1.0	$1.0	$1.0	$1.0
10	Market research expenses	$0.5	$0.0	$0.0	$0.0	$0.0	$0.0
11	Incremental maintenance	$0.0	$0.5	$0.5	$0.5	$0.5	$0.5
12							
13	Total costs	$9.5	$8.5	$8.0	$8.0	$8.0	$9.0

- The new e-reader's secured book-sharing capabilities mean that you need to hire a new product-management team to oversee the new e-reader's development, from its rollout through its life cycle. The amount in Figure 11.3, row 9, New product management team, is the ongoing salary cost of this group.
- The market research expenses needed to launch the product are directly related to the new e-reader and are incremental to business as usual. Row 10, Market research expenses, shows this cost.
- New equipment and software are needed to produce the new e-reader. The maintenance on the new equipment and programming will increase the total maintenance expense for the company by about $500,000 per year. Row 11, Incremental maintenance, contains this cost. Notice that the firm does not begin to incur these maintenance costs until Year 2, after the equipment has been in use for one year.

Moving to the Pro Forma

You can now assemble a pro forma income statement (see Figure 11.4) from the data you have entered so far. The relevant costs are totaled in row 13. Enter the formula `=SUM(B7:B11)` in cell B13, and then copy and paste it into C13:G13. Name the range in cells B13:G13 `TotalIncrementalCosts`. This range shows the total relevant costs that are projected for each year.

Figure 11.4
The pro forma income statement arrives at a figure for net income by taking into account depreciation and income taxes.

Depreciation | fx =SLN(CapitalCost,SalvageValue,UsefulLife)

	A	B	C	D	E	F	G
1	**Enhanced E-Reader: Income Statement**						
2	Year:	1	2	3	4	5	6
3	*Relevant benefits:*			($Millions)			
4	Incremental value, New E-Reader	$4.0	$7.0	$9.0	$14.0	$19.0	$22.0
5							
6	*Relevant costs:*						
7	Lost value, Current Product	$6.0	$6.0	$6.0	$6.0	$6.0	$7.0
8	Advertising	$2.0	$1.0	$0.5	$0.5	$0.5	$0.5
9	New product management team	$1.0	$1.0	$1.0	$1.0	$1.0	$1.0
10	Market research expenses	$0.5	$0.0	$0.0	$0.0	$0.0	$0.0
11	Incremental maintenance	$0.0	$0.5	$0.5	$0.5	$0.5	$0.5
12							
13	Total costs	$9.5	$8.5	$8.0	$8.0	$8.0	$9.0
14							
15	EBITDA	($5.5)	($1.5)	$1.0	$6.0	$11.0	$13.0
16	Less: Depreciation	$1.0	$1.0	$1.0	$1.0	$1.0	$1.0
17	Income before taxes	($6.5)	($2.5)	$0.0	$5.0	$10.0	$12.0
18	Taxes @ 36%	($2.3)	($0.9)	$0.0	$1.8	$3.6	$4.3
19	Net income	($4.2)	($1.6)	$0.0	$3.2	$6.4	$7.7
20							
21	New equipment investment	$10.0					

The total incremental costs are then subtracted from the new product's incremental value. Select the range B15:G15, enter the formula `=IncrementalValue - TotalIncrementalCosts`, and press Ctrl+Enter.

NOTE

The result of this calculation is usually referred to as *Earnings Before Interest, Taxes, Depreciation, and Amortization (EBITDA)*. As awkward as the EBITDA acronym is, it is easier to use than the full name. EBITDA represents the best estimate of a product's contribution to a company's profitability, which includes the product's revenues and the costs that are directly associated with creating those revenues. Other costs, such as interest, taxes, depreciation, and amortization, are not directly associated with the product's performance in the marketplace or the costs required to get the product to market.

For this case, the EBITDA that is shown in row 15 of Figure 11.4 estimates the earnings from the product before taking other, indirect costs into consideration. The name `EBITDA` is assigned to the worksheet range B15:G15, using the Name box to do so as the most convenient naming method.

Row 16 of Figure 11.4 contains the depreciation expense on the new production equipment. This line item is used to arrive at the pretax income figures shown in row 17. The cost of the equipment itself, which is $10 million, is shown in cell B21. Name that cell `CapitalCost`.

11

Besides the cost of the equipment, two other items are needed to calculate the annual depreciation expense: its useful life (the number of periods that you expect the equipment will contribute to revenue generation) and its salvage value (its expected value at the end of its useful life). Chapter 16, "Fixed Assets," discusses salvage value and useful life in detail.

In this example, the useful life is assumed to be 10 years, and the salvage value is set to 0. The assumption is that the equipment will depreciate a fixed amount every year for 10 years, and at that point it will have no value.

Keep in mind that you cannot use the Name box to define the name of a constant unless you store the constant in a cell. For this reason, the useful life and salvage value constants are given names by following these steps:

1. Click the Formulas tab on the Ribbon and then click Define Name in the Defined Names group. (In Excel versions earlier than 2007, choose Insert, Name, Define.)
2. Type **`UsefulLife`** in the New Name dialog box's Name box. (In earlier Excel versions, type **`UsefulLife`** in the Names in Workbook box,)
3. In the Refers To box, type `=10`.
4. Click OK. To define the next name, click Define Name again. (In earlier versions, click Add.)
5. Type **`SalvageValue`** in the Name box of the New Name dialog box. (Using earlier versions, type **`SalvageValue`** in the Names in Workbook box.)
6. In the Refers To box, type `=0`.
7. Click OK.

TIP

The preceding steps that name the salvage value and the length of the equipment's useful life cause the names to refer to actual values. If you prefer, you can make the names refer to cells where you enter the values. In this case, the values are `10` and `0`, respectively. Notice that this method was used with the `CapitalCost` name. The method you use is a matter of personal preference. Putting the values on the worksheet makes them easier to see and change. Having the names refer directly to values keeps the worksheet from looking cluttered.

The cost of the equipment, which is $10 million, will be depreciated over a 10-year period. At the end of this period, the salvage value will be `0`. Therefore, the formula for depreciation cost is `=SLN(CapitalCost,SalvageValue,UsefulLife)`, in which the `SLN` function returns straight-line depreciation. You can enter this formula in a single cell and copy it across the remaining cells. Alternatively, you can enter the formula in all six cells at once by using the Ctrl+Enter key combination.

Even though you might enter the depreciation formula with the Ctrl+Enter key combination, it is not another implicit intersection. Each of its arguments is a single, constant number, not a range of cells.

NOTE

Because the focus in this chapter is on constructing a business case, the various accelerated depreciation methods that are available are not discussed. For your own situations, keep in mind that Excel has functions that use accelerated depreciation, including sum of years' digits and declining balance. Chapter 16, "Fixed Assets," discusses these functions and their drawbacks in more detail.

You can now calculate pretax income as, in this case, EBITDA minus depreciation by completing the following steps:

1. Select cells B16:G16 and name the range `Depreciation`.
2. Select cells B17:G17. Click in the Formula box and type `=EBITDA-Depreciation`.
3. Press Ctrl+Enter.
4. While B17:G17 is still selected, name the range by clicking in the Name box and typing `PreTaxIncome`.

To calculate taxes, create a constant with the value `.36` named `TaxRate`, or give the name `TaxRate` to a cell and enter `.36` in that cell. Next, select cells B18:G18, type `=TaxRate*PreTaxIncome` in the formula box, and press Ctrl+Enter. While the range B18:G18 is still selected, go ahead and name the range `Taxes`.

NOTE

Some accountants would legitimately quarrel with the projection of a negative income tax expense. Others would (also legitimately) find it a sensible usage because early losses from a new operation can offset income from other profitable operations, thus reducing the total tax expense. To keep this example simple, the negative figure is used.

After figuring in taxes, calculate net income by subtracting taxes from income before taxes. Following the earlier examples in this section, you can do this by selecting the range B19:G19, typing the formula `=PreTaxIncome - Taxes`, and pressing Ctrl+Enter. In addition, it is a good idea to give the name `NetIncome` to the range `B19:G19`.

Row 19, Net Income, in Figure 11.4 is the result of the income statement. It shows the additional, incremental income that the company can expect from the combined revenues and costs due to offering a new product.

Preparing the Cash Flow Analysis

Keep in mind that net income is seldom identical to net cash flow. For this reason, you should estimate the amount of cash that will flow into and out of the business each year if your company decides to proceed with bringing this new product to market.

To estimate the cash flow, you need to extend the pro forma income statement so it becomes a cash flow statement. In this case, two items are needed to derive annual cash flow from the income statement: the cost of the new equipment and its depreciation. Figure 11.5 shows these modifications.

> **NOTE** To keep this example simple, factors associated with working capital requirements, such as additional inventory and accounts receivable on incremental sales, have been omitted. However, recall from Chapter 5 that it is a fairly straightforward process to add this information to your pro forma income statement.

Figure 11.5
Adding the depreciation back in and accounting for the equipment expenditure clarifies the actual cash flows for the new product.

B22 | =NetIncome+Depreciation-CapitalCost

	A	B	C	D	E	F	G
1	**Enhanced E-Reader: Cash Flow Statement**						
2	Year:	1	2	3	4	5	6
3	*Relevant benefits:*			($Millions)			
4	Incremental value, New E-Reader	$4.0	$7.0	$9.0	$14.0	$19.0	$22.0
5							
6	*Relevant costs:*						
7	Lost value, Current Product	$6.0	$6.0	$6.0	$6.0	$6.0	$7.0
8	Advertising	$2.0	$1.0	$0.5	$0.5	$0.5	$0.5
9	New product management team	$1.0	$1.0	$1.0	$1.0	$1.0	$1.0
10	Market research expenses	$0.5	$0.0	$0.0	$0.0	$0.0	$0.0
11	Incremental maintenance	$0.0	$0.5	$0.5	$0.5	$0.5	$0.5
12							
13	Total costs	$9.5	$8.5	$8.0	$8.0	$8.0	$9.0
14							
15	EBITDA	($5.5)	($1.5)	$1.0	$6.0	$11.0	$13.0
16	Less: Depreciation	$1.0	$1.0	$1.0	$1.0	$1.0	$1.0
17	Income before taxes	($6.5)	($2.5)	$0.0	$5.0	$10.0	$12.0
18	Taxes @ 36%	($2.3)	($0.9)	$0.0	$1.8	$3.6	$4.3
19	Net income	($4.2)	($1.6)	$0.0	$3.2	$6.4	$7.7
20	Plus: Depreciation	$1.0	$1.0	$1.0	$1.0	$1.0	$1.0
21	Less: New Equipment Investment	$10.0					
22	Net Cash Flow	($13.2)	($0.6)	$1.0	$4.2	$7.4	$8.7

Begin by adding the depreciation expense from row 16 back into the statement in row 20, as shown in Figure 11.5. Row 17, which contains income before taxes, subtracts depreciation from EBITDA, and now that process is reversed in row 20.

Why deal with depreciation twice? Because depreciation is not an actual cash outlay, but an accrued expense. Depreciation assigns to each time period a portion of the loss in the value of the capital investment. As an *expense*, you can use it to reduce income, for the purpose of calculating tax liabilities. As a *noncash* expense, it should not count as a cost reducing the net cash flow. Therefore, you subtract it from pretax income for the purpose of calculating taxes, and you should add it back in for the purpose of estimating actual net cash flow.

As mentioned earlier, your company needs new machinery to produce the new product. It will also be necessary to retool some of the assembly lines' production facilities that presently are dedicated to your current product. The $10 million in capital expenditures required to purchase the new equipment and accomplish the retooling is included in cell B21 of Figure 11.5.

After adding depreciation back in, the $10 million capital investment in the new machinery in row 21 is subtracted from the net income to produce the net cash flow figure for the period in row 22.

These steps extend the original pro forma income statement to make it a pro forma cash flow statement. Further analysis of this statement, including an examination of payback periods, appears in Chapter 12, "Examining Decision Criteria for a Business Case."

Summary

The topics covered in this chapter provide the basic inputs to a full business case. Chapter 12 and Chapter 13, "Creating a Sensitivity Analysis for a Business Case," explain how to analyze these inputs to determine if the business case makes financial sense. Even though the process is by no means complete, by this point you have accomplished the following:

- Identified the relevant benefits and costs of this business decision
- Estimated the dollar value of the benefits and costs and entered them in an Excel workbook
- Merged the benefits and costs to construct a pro forma income statement
- Extended the pro forma income statement to depict a pro forma cash flow statement

The result is a projection of future cash flows that would result if the company moves ahead with this business venture.

Management can use this information to decide whether to proceed with the new product based on an analysis of the cash flow's current value to the business.

In other words, if the company decides to proceed with the new product offering, it must make some investments at the outset. For example, the company needs to provide funds for retooling, anticipate the loss of revenues from the current product, support promotional activities, hire more staff, and so on.

Are the anticipated returns adequate to justify these investments? Chapter 12 discusses the additional financial concepts and indicators that assist in the decision-making process. It also demonstrates how you can use Excel to extend the pro forma cash flow model, and how you can apply valuation tools to help determine whether a decision to implement the proposal makes sense.

Examining Decision Criteria for a Business Case

12

IN THIS CHAPTER

Chapter 11, "Examining a Business Case: Investment," looked at the relevant facts surrounding a business case decision. If you worked your way through the case study, you constructed a pro forma income statement and a pro forma cash flow statement. These statements help you to describe the decision quantitatively, but that's not the end of the process.

When you evaluate an income or cash flow statement it's important to keep a criterion called the *discount factor* in mind. The term *discounting* refers to the estimation of the present value of future cash flows. For example, every dollar you own today will have a different value in the future. If you deposit $100 in a savings account that yields 5% annually, that $100 will be worth $105 in one year. Its future value one year from now is $105.

Looking into the wrong end of the telescope one year from now, you can see that $105 had a present value of $100 today.

The future and present values depend on several issues including the length of time that you hold the money and the rate of return you can obtain on the dollar. This chapter shows you how to take discounting into account in your income and cash flow statements. By doing so, you can make these statements more meaningful. That's important because your business plan is intended to project financial results into the future by several years, not just a couple of quarters.

This chapter also covers payback periods, discounted payback periods, and the concepts of future value, present value, and net present value.

Understanding Payback Periods

The *payback period* is the length of time between an initial investment and the recovery of the investment from its ongoing cash flow. For example, suppose you purchase a store for $500,000. Taking into account the income from the store, your expenses, depreciation, and taxes, it takes you 48 months to earn back the $500,000. The payback period for your investment is 48 months.

Figures 12.1 and 12.2 show the full cash flow statement from the case study begun in the previous chapter, including the discounting, payback, and other figures you will read about in this chapter.

Figure 12.1
The cash flow statement's benefits and costs summarize the relevant business case inputs.

Year fx 1

	A	B	C	D	E	F	G
1	**Enhanced E-Reader: Cash Flow Statement**						
2	Year:	1	2	3	4	5	6
3	*Relevant benefits:*			($Millions)			
4	Incremental value, New E-Reader	$4.00	$7.00	$9.00	$14.00	$19.00	$22.00
5							
6	*Relevant costs:*						
7	Lost value, Current Product	$6.00	$6.00	$6.00	$6.00	$6.00	$7.00
8	Advertising	$2.00	$1.00	$0.50	$0.50	$0.50	$0.50
9	New product management	$1.00	$1.00	$1.00	$1.00	$1.00	$1.00
10	Market research expenses	$0.50	$0.00	$0.00	$0.00	$0.00	$0.00
11	Incremental maintenance	$0.00	$0.50	$0.50	$0.50	$0.50	$0.50
12							
13	Total costs	$9.50	$8.50	$8.00	$8.00	$8.00	$9.00
14							
15	EBITDA	($5.50)	($1.50)	$1.00	$6.00	$11.00	$13.00
16	Less: Depreciation	$1.00	$1.00	$1.00	$1.00	$1.00	$1.00
17	Income before taxes	($6.50)	($2.50)	$0.00	$5.00	$10.00	$12.00
18	Less: Taxes @ 36%	($2.34)	($0.90)	$0.00	$1.80	$3.60	$4.32
19	Net income	($4.16)	($1.60)	$0.00	$3.20	$6.40	$7.68

Figure 12.2
The cash flow statement's adjustments take account of depreciation, taxes, and capital investment to arrive at net cash flows.

fx {=INDEX((Year-CumNetCashFlow/NetCashFlow),1,SUM(IF(CumNetCashFlow<=0,1,0))+1)}

	A	B	C	D	E	F	G
1	**Enhanced E-Reader: Cash Flow Statement**						
2	Year:	1	2	3	4	5	6
14							
15	EBITDA	($5.50)	($1.50)	$1.00	$6.00	$11.00	$13.00
16	Less: Depreciation	$1.00	$1.00	$1.00	$1.00	$1.00	$1.00
17	Income before taxes	($6.50)	($2.50)	$0.00	$5.00	$10.00	$12.00
18	Less: Taxes @ 36%	($2.34)	($0.90)	$0.00	$1.80	$3.60	$4.32
19	Net income	($4.16)	($1.60)	$0.00	$3.20	$6.40	$7.68
20							
21	Plus: Depreciation	$1.00	$1.00	$1.00	$1.00	$1.00	$1.00
22	Minus: Investment	$10.00	$0.00	$0.00	$0.00	$0.00	$0.00
23	Net Cash Flow	($13.16)	($0.60)	$1.00	$4.20	$7.40	$8.68
24							
25	Cumulative Net Cash Flow	($13.16)	($13.76)	($12.76)	($8.56)	($1.16)	$7.52
26							
27	Undiscounted payback period:	5.13					
28							
29	Discount Rate:	0.1					
30							
31	Discounted Cash Flow	($11.96)	($0.50)	$0.75	$2.87	$4.59	$4.90
32							
33	Cumulative Discounted Cash Flow	($11.96)	($12.46)	($11.71)	($8.84)	($4.24)	$0.65
34							
35	Discounted payback period:	5.87					

The next general step in developing the business case is to determine the payback period. To make the calculations clearer, add a row labeled Cumulative Net Cash Flow to the cash flow statement that you developed in Chapter 11. To add the row, follow these steps:

1. Select cells B2:G2. Click in the Name box, type `Year`, and press Enter.
2. Select cells B23:G23. Click in the Name box, type `NetCashFlow`, and press Enter.
3. Select cell A25, and enter the following label:
   `Cumulative Net Cash Flow`
4. Select cell B25, and enter the following formula:
   `=SUM(OFFSET(NetCashFlow,0,0,1,Year))`
5. Autofill cell B25 into C25:G25 by dragging B25's fill handle into the C25:G25 range.
6. Select the range B25:G25, click the Name box, type `CumNetCashFlow`, and press Enter.

Figure 12.2 shows the result. The formula you entered in steps 4 and 5 returns the running total of the range `NetCashFlow` for each consecutive year. Because it is a running total, it's termed a *cumulative* net cash flow.

The `OFFSET` function returns a range that is shifted some number of rows or columns from its first argument. You can also use its fourth and fifth arguments to specify the number of rows and columns occupied by the resulting range. However, those two arguments are optional. For example, `=SUM(OFFSET(A1,2,1,3,4))` returns the sum of the values in the range B3:E5, which is shifted (or *offset*) down by two rows and right by one column from A1. The optional arguments, 3 and 4, specify that the offset range contains three rows (row 3, row 4, and row 5) and four columns (columns B through E).

The range named `Year` occupies cells B2:G2 on the worksheet and contains the values `1` through `6`. As you fill row 25 with the formula that calculates cumulative net cash flow, the fifth argument of the `OFFSET` function adjusts for each successive value of `Year`, so that `1` becomes `2`, then `3`, and so on. This is another example of the implicit intersection that was discussed more fully in Chapter 11. The fifth argument to `OFFSET` specifies the number of columns in `NetCashFlow` that the `OFFSET` function will return to the `SUM` function. For example:

- In B2, the value of `Year` is `1`. So the formula `=SUM(OFFSET(NetCashFlow,0,0,1,Year))` in B25 returns the sum of the value in the first row, first column of `NetCashFlow`.
- In C2, the value of `Year` is `2`. So the formula `=SUM(OFFSET(NetCashFlow,0,0,1,Year))` in C25 returns the sum of the value in the first row, first and second columns of `NetCashFlow`.
- In D2, the value of `Year` is `3`. So the formula `=SUM(OFFSET(NetCashFlow,0,0,1,Year))` in D25 returns the sum of the value in the first row, first through third columns of `NetCashFlow`.

And so on. Because the first value of `Year` is `1`, `OFFSET` returns just the first column of `NetCashFlow` to `SUM` in B25. In C25, the formula refers to the second value of `Year`, or `2`, and `OFFSET` returns the first two columns of `NetCashFlow` to be added together by `SUM`. The result is a series of cumulative, summed values for `NetCashFlow` in row 25, Cumulative Net Cash Flow.

> TIP
>
> This book encourages you to use named ranges to help document your work in Excel. Using the `SUM` function in combination with the `OFFSET` function—`=SUM(OFFSET(NetCashFlow, 0,0,1,Year))` in step 4—is one way to use two named ranges, `NetCashFlow` and `Year`, to get the result you're after.
>
> In this case, a quicker way is to combine an absolute reference with a relative reference. To do this, enter `=SUM($B$23:B23)` in B25, and then click B25's fill handle and drag through the range C25:G25. As you do so, the absolute reference portion remains fixed and the relative reference adjusts. For example, in cell G25 you wind up with the formula `=SUM($B$23:G23)`. The trade-off is speed and convenience in entering the formulas, in exchange for clarity when you examine them later.

By examining the `CumNetCashFlow` range you can see that, sometime after five years, this project will have recouped the original investment for the company. It is at this point, represented in cell G25 in Figure 12.2, that the `CumNetCashFlow` changes from negative values to a positive value, which represents the payback period for this example. However, you cannot yet tell exactly when the payback period has ended. Instead, all you can tell so far is that the payback period ends sometime during the sixth year.

You can modify the worksheet to calculate the projected payback period exactly by array-entering this formula:

```
=INDEX((Year-CumNetCashFlow/NetCashFlow),1,SUM(IF(CumNetCashFlow<=0,1,0))+1)
```

Cell B27 is selected in Figure 12.2 so you can see the formula in the formula bar and its result in the cell. You can tell that it's been entered as an array formula because Excel has surrounded it with curly brackets.

It is a lengthy formula. Most complicated formulas are easier to understand if you break them up into segments and enter the segments on your worksheet. Figure 12.3 shows the segments of the overall formula from cell B27 and how they combine to return the payback period.

12

Row 2 in Figure 12.3 shows the number of each year in the calculation of the payback period. Row 5 contains the net cash flow, and row 7 contains the cumulative net cash flow. Each of these rows contains a named range—`Year`, `NetCashFlow`, and `CumNetCashFlow`, respectively.

> TIP
>
> If you use named ranges in formulas, you might find it easier to paste the name instead of typing it. After selecting a cell, type = (the equal sign), and then click the Formulas tab on the Ribbon. Click Use in Formula in the Defined Names group, and then click the name you want to use from the menu. In earlier versions of Excel, select Insert, Name, Paste to display any defined names. Clicking a name moves it into the Formula box.

Figure 12.3
All of these calculations are summarized in the single array formula in cell B26 of Figure 12.2.

{=SUM(IF(CumNetCashFlow<=0,1,0))}

	A	B	C	D	E	F	G
1	**Enhanced E-Reader: Cash Flow Statement**						
2	Year:	1	2	3	4	5	6
3				($Millions)			
4							
5	Net Cash Flow	($13.16)	($0.60)	$1.00	$4.20	$7.40	$8.68
6							
7	Cumulative Net Cash Flow	($13.16)	($13.76)	($12.76)	($8.56)	($1.16)	$7.52
8							
9	CumulativeNetCashFlow/NetCashFlow	1.0	22.9	-12.8	-2.0	-0.2	0.9
10							
11	Year-CumulativeNetCashFlow/NetCashFlow	0.0	-20.9	15.8	6.0	5.16	5.1
12							
13	SUM(IF(CumulativeNetCashFlow<=0,1,0))	5					

The three named ranges in Figure 12.3 are not the same ranges as those with the same names in Figures 12.1 and 12.2. In Figure 12.3, the ranges are *sheet level*, and the Name Manager would show that the names' Scope is the worksheet named `ProForma`. If you use a sheet level name outside its scope, you must qualify it with the name of its worksheet followed by an exclamation point: for example, `Sheet1!Revenues`. The reference to the sheet where they are defined, with the exclamation point as a delimiter, distinguishes them from the *book level* names used in Figures 12.1 and 12.2, which take the entire workbook as their scope. When a sheet-level name is used in formulas on the sheet where it is defined, the formulas do not need to qualify the name with that of the worksheet. You specify a name's scope as part of the process of defining the name.

Row 9 in Figure 12.3 shows the ratio of each year's cumulative net cash flow to that year's net cash flow. To enter the formula, select B9:G9, type `=CumNetCashFlow/ NetCashFlow`, and press Ctrl+Enter. This key combination enters the formula in each of the selected cells, taking advantage of the implicit intersection.

The ratio in row 9 of Figure 12.3 has a particularly useful meaning for the year during which the payback period is complete. The ratio expresses the proportion of that year during which the cumulative net cash flow has exceeded the payback of the investment.

Notice that it is not until the end of year 6 that cumulative net cash flow becomes a positive number. The ratio of the cumulative net cash flow to the net cash flow for year 6 is $7,520,000 / $8,680,000, or 0.87. If you assume that cash flows are evenly distributed throughout the year (an assumption that's violated more often than not), then the initial investment has been recouped at about 13% (1 – 0.87) of the way through year 6. In other words, when 13% of year 6 has elapsed, the cumulative net cash flow reaches zero; therefore, the amount of the initial investment has been paid back.

12

Subtracting that ratio (0.87) from the year number (6) results in 5.13. It will take about 5.13 years to pay back the initial expenses and capital investment. This calculation is shown for each of the six years in row 11 of Figure 12.3. These cells contain this formula:

```
=Year-CumNetCashFlow/NetCashFlow
```

By looking at the values in row 7, you can see where the cumulative net cash flow turns positive, but how can you get Excel to determine which of the values is the one you're looking for? Again, the payback period cannot have elapsed as long as the cumulative net cash flow is negative. Therefore, you want Excel to ignore all years before the cumulative net cash flow turns positive.

The array formula `=SUM(IF(CumNetCashFlow<=0,1,0))` assigns a `1` if the `CumNetCashFlow` is less than or equal to 0, and it assigns a `0` otherwise. It then sums the assigned numbers and returns the result, which is the number of years during which the cumulative net cash flow is less than or equal to 0. In this case, the array formula returns `5` (see cell B13 in Figure 12.3) because the cumulative net cash flow is still negative at the end of year 5. Adding 1 to this result returns the first year during which the cumulative net cash flow is greater than 0:

```
=SUM(IF(CumNetCashFlow<=0,1,0))+1
```

Finally, you are in a position to express all this with one array formula:

```
=INDEX((Year-CumNetCashFlow/NetCashFlow),1,SUM(IF(CumNetCashFlow<=0,1,0))+1)
```

You can find that formula in cell B27 of Figure 12.2.

The general syntax of the `INDEX` function is `=INDEX(ARRAY,ROW,COLUMN)`.

Here, the `ARRAY` argument is the row of six values expressed by `(Year-CumNetCashFlow/NetCashFlow)` and shown as row 11 in Figure 12.3.

The `ROW` argument is `1` because the array has only one row. The `COLUMN` argument is the result of `=SUM(IF(CumNetCashFlow<=0,1,0))+1`, which is the first year during which the cumulative net cash flow is positive, or `6`.

The result of the full array formula is `5.13`, which is the sixth column in the only row of the array of the ratios. This is shown explicitly in cell G11 of Figure 12.3 and implicitly in the formula in cell B27 of Figure 12.2.

NOTE

The approach outlined here returns the length of time required for the cumulative net cash flow to become a positive number *for the first time*. In some instances, additional investments must be made subsequent to the initial investment; these subsequent investments can cause the cumulative net cash flow to turn negative again.

Thus, the undiscounted payback period for this series of cash flows is 5.13 years.

Understanding Future Value, Present Value, and Net Present Value

This analysis so far has not taken into account the time value of money. One dollar received today is worth more than $1 received five years from today. But how much more? That would depend on how much the recipient thinks he can earn on that dollar: In other words, what's an adequate rate of return?

Calculating Future Value

A dollar received today and invested in a financial instrument that yields 10% annually will be worth $1.10 after one year. That $1.10 is the *future value* of your dollar given the time period for investment, which is one year, and the rate of return, which is 10%. After five years, the future value of the dollar will be $1.61. This value is

$1.00 × 1.1 × 1.1 × 1.1 × 1.1 × 1.1 = $1.61

or

$1.00 × 1.1 ^ 5 = $1.61

Calculating Present Value

Conversely, what is the value today of a dollar to be received five years from now? Assuming a rate of return of 10 percent, you can use the following formulas to calculate the *present value* of that future dollar:

$1.00 / 1.1 / 1.1 / 1.1 / 1.1 / 1.1 = $0.62

or

$1.00 / 1.1 ^ 5 = $0.62.

You can set up a formula in your worksheet to compute present value discount factors given a selected interest rate. You can then apply the discount factors to the period's cash flow (see Figure 12.4). To do so, follow these steps:

1. Select cell A10, and enter the label `Discount Rate`.
2. Select cell B10, and enter `0.1`.
3. With B10 selected, click in the Name box, type `DiscountRate`, and press Enter. You have now created a range named `DiscountRate`, whose value is the number (0.1) that you entered into cell B10.
4. Select cells B12:G12, and type this formula:

   ```
   =1/(1+DiscountRate)^Year
   ```

   Press Ctrl+Enter to place the formula in all six selected cells.
5. With B12:G12 still selected, click the Home tab on the Ribbon. Click the Number Format drop-down in the Number group, and then click the More Number Formats item at the bottom of the drop-down list. Select Number from the Category list box, and set the Decimal places to 2. (If you're using an earlier version of Excel, start by choosing Format, Cells.)

The result is shown in Figure 12.4.

Figure 12.4
The discounted cash flow takes account of the time value of money.

=NetCashFlow*DiscountFactors

	A	B	C	D	E	F	G
1	**Enhanced E-Reader: Cash Flow Statement**						
2	Year	1	2	3	4	5	6
3				($Millions)			
4	Net Cash Flow	-$13.16	-$0.60	$1.00	$4.20	$7.40	$8.68
5							
6	Cumulative Net Cash Flow	-$13.16	-$13.76	-$12.76	-$8.56	-$1.16	$7.52
7							
8	Undiscounted payback period:	$5.13					
9							
10	Discount Rate:	10%					
11							
12	Discount factor @ 10%	0.91	0.83	0.75	0.68	0.62	0.56
13							
14	Discounted Cash Flow	-$11.96	-$0.50	$0.75	$2.87	$4.59	$4.90

NOTE

Notice that the discount factor ranges from 0.91 at the end of the first year, to 0.83 at the end of the second year, to 0.56 at the end of the sixth year. This represents the value of a dollar that you have today at the end of one, two ... six years. For each year, the prior number 1 is divided by (1 + DiscountRate), or 1.1 raised to the number of years that have elapsed. (It can help to think of this value as *purchasing power*: as time passes, today's dollar buys less and less, as a function of the discount rate—and it can help to think of the discount rate as the effect of inflation on that dollar's value.)

Row 14 in Figure 12.4, labeled Discounted Cash Flow, is the result of multiplying row 4 (the net cash flow) by row 12 (the discount factors). This represents the discounted value of the net cash flow—that is, the value in today's dollars of future annual cash flows.

For example, the net cash flow in year 6 is $8,680,000. The discounted cash flow in year 6 is $4,900,000. This means that, under the assumption of an annual 10% rate, the funds needed to start producing the new product return $4,900,000 six years later expressed in Year 1 dollars—taking into account that you could make 10% per year in an alternative investment.

12

Calculating Net Present Value

So far, this discussion has described the discounting process as two steps—creating each year's discount factor and multiplying that discount factor by the annual net cash flow. The discussion used two steps to make what happens in the discounting process a little clearer. Excel provides a Net Present Value function, `NPV`, which enables you to perform the discounting process with just one formula. A little spadework is needed:

1. If you have already created the range name `DiscountRate` on the worksheet shown in Figure 12.2, skip to step 4. Otherwise, select cell A29 and enter the label `Discount Rate`.
2. Select cell B29, and enter `0.1`.
3. With B29 still selected, click in the Name box, type `DiscountRate`, and press Enter.
4. Enter the label `Discounted Cash Flow` into cell A31

5. Select cells B31:G31, and enter the formula:

```
=NetCashFlow/(1+DiscountRate)^Year
```

   Press Ctrl+Enter.

6. With B31:G31 still selected, click the Home tab on the Ribbon, and then click the button with the dollar symbol in the Numbers group.

The result is the discounted cash flow, which is shown in row 31 of Figure 12.2.

Row 33 in Figure 12.2, Cumulative Discounted Cash Flow, is calculated in much the same way as `CumNetCashFlow` is calculated in row 25. Row 33 shows the running total for each year of the *discounted* cash flows rather than the *undiscounted* cash flows. To obtain the cumulative discounted cash flow, select cells B33:G33 and array-enter this formula:

```
=NPV(DiscountRate,OFFSET(NetCashFlow,0,0,1,Year))
```

The outer portion of this formula, which is initiated by `NPV`, returns the net present value of its arguments: that is, the value today of a future dollar amount. The `OFFSET` component of this formula returns as many elements from the `NetCashFlow` range as are specified by the `Year` argument. For cell B33, `Year` is equal to `1`, so `OFFSET` returns the first element of `NetCashFlow`. For cell C33, `Year` is equal to `2`, so `OFFSET` returns the second element of `NetCashFlow`.

The cumulative discounted cash flow amount in the sixth year, $654,920, which is shown rounded and in millions in cell G33 of Figure 12.2, is $0.65. This is the net present value of the cumulative cash flows for the six-year period of this project. It is simply the sum of the discounted cash flows for the full six-year life of the business case.

At this point, you can also add into your worksheet a payback calculation similar to the one that you developed for the undiscounted cash flows. In cell B35 of the worksheet shown in Figure 12.2, enter the following array formula:

```
=INDEX((Year-CumDiscountedCashFlow/DiscountedCashFlow),1,
   SUM(IF(CumNetCashFlow<=0,1,0))+1)
```

> **NOTE** Notice that the payback period for the discounted cash flows is 5.87 years, instead of the payback period of 5.13 years for the undiscounted cash flows. This is as you'd expect because actual dollars being paid back are worth less the farther into the future you go. For this reason, the payback takes longer.

12

CASE STUDY: SHORTENING THE PAYBACK PERIOD

It's an unfortunate but immutable fact of business that after you have gone through careful calculations to derive payback periods based on both undiscounted and discounted cash flows, your chief financial officer says, "Smith, your analysis is close, but we have to keep the undiscounted payback to a maximum of five years. Go do it again."

The next section explains how to meet that five-year requirement.

Optimizing Costs

As you analyze the effects of costs on the payback period for offering a new e-reader product, you see that you must take several cost categories into account. Some costs such as taxes are largely beyond your company's control. Other costs such as the initial capital investment of $10 million, advertising budget, salary for the product management group, and the market research, are, to some degree, controllable.

You need a way to simultaneously modify all the controllable costs to meet the newly imposed conditions for the payback periods. This section shows how you can use Solver to accomplish this.

Other examples in this book have used Excel's Goal Seek tool to adjust one value by changing another value. Goal Seek is faster than trial-and-error in finding a particular precedent value, but it limits you to just one changing cell. Furthermore, that changing cell isn't allowed to contain a formula: It has to contain a value.

You can use Solver instead. Solver is an add-in that comes with Excel, and if you did a complete installation of Excel, it's available to you. With Solver, you can modify more than one cell at once to get to the result you're looking for. The changing cells do not need to contain values and can contain formulas, although Solver converts the formulas to values if you save Solver's solution at the end of the process. (Excel's documentation refers to "Solver" instead of "the Solver," and this book follows that usage.)

To access Solver, follow these steps if you're using a version of Excel earlier than Excel 2007:

1. Choose Tools, Add-Ins from Excel's main menu.
2. If the check box for the Solver add-in is clear, select it and then click OK. If the check box is already selected, click Cancel.
3. Excel works for a few moments loading the Solver add-in. When it has finished, Solver is a new option in the Tools menu.

If you're using Excel 2007 or 2010, follow these steps:

1. Click the File tab and then click the Options button.
2. With the Excel Options dialog box open, click the Add-Ins item in the list box.
3. Click the Manage drop-down at the bottom of the Add-Ins dialog box. Select Excel Add-Ins and click Go.
4. Continue with the second step in the preceding list.

NOTE If you cannot find the Solver add-in in the Add-Ins dialog box, try selecting Browse to find `SOLVER.XLAM`. Office 2010 stores it in `C:\Program Files\Microsoft Office\Office 14\Library`. `SOLVER.XLAM` may have inadvertently been moved to another location, or perhaps it wasn't installed. If you can't find it, you'll have to reinstall it from your installation disc. Make sure that you request the installation of Solver when you set the installation options for Excel.

Setting Solver's Inputs

You want Solver to change your controllable costs, but you need to give it some criteria to work with. For example, Solver has no way of knowing *a priori* that you must pay the product management team a positive amount of money each year. Unconstrained, Solver might suggest that you pay the product manager a negative amount of money to shorten the payback periods. Or Solver might decide to dispense with an advertising budget entirely.

Because this is unacceptable, establish some minimum values. In cell H8, as shown in Figure 12.5, enter the formula `=MIN(B8:G8)`. It returns the minimum value found in the B8:G8 range of advertising expenses.

Then copy that formula and paste it into cell H9 to get the minimum value for product management in the range B9:G9. Cells H8 and H9 will act as *constraints* on the solution that Solver reaches. The formulas return the minimum values for advertising and for product management's annual salary. Shortly, you'll specify constraints that will keep Solver from assigning negative values for salaries and other costs.

Select cell B26, which contains the undiscounted payback period. Then click the Data tab on the Ribbon and click Solver in the Analysis group. Using versions earlier than Excel 2007, choose Tools, Solver.

Complete the entries in the Solver Parameters dialog box as follows:

1. Because it was the active cell when you started Solver, the Set Objective box should contain `$B$26`. If it does not, click in that box and then click cell B26 on the worksheet.
2. Click the Value Of option button, and enter `5` in the edit box to its right. This tells Solver that you want it to modify various changing cells until the value in B26 is `5`—in this context, until the undiscounted payback period is five years.
3. Click in the By Changing Variable Cells box, and then select cells B8:G9 on the worksheet. These cells contain the annual costs for advertising and for product management's salary. Type `,` (a comma) following the G9 reference in the edit box, and click cell B10, which contains the market research cost. Type `,` (a comma) after B10 in the edit box, and click cell B21, which contains the amount of the initial investment. You have now identified the cells that Solver will change as it searches for a solution.
4. Click the Add button. In the Add Constraint dialog box, click in the Cell Reference box and then select cell H8 on the worksheet. H8 contains the minimum value of the annual advertising costs.
5. Click the down arrow next to the operator symbol, and select the `>=` operator.
6. Click in the Constraint box and enter `0`. The Add Constraint dialog box should appear as shown in Figure 12.5.
7. Select Add.
8. Repeat steps 4–7 for cells H9, B10, and B21 to establish constraints for product management's salary, the market research expense, and the initial capital investment. Let the constraints for product management and market research both be `>=0`. Use a `>=`

value of 8 for the constraint on the initial investment; although you may have to forego advertising, a product manager, and market research by means of zero costs, you cannot reduce the initial investment below $8 million.

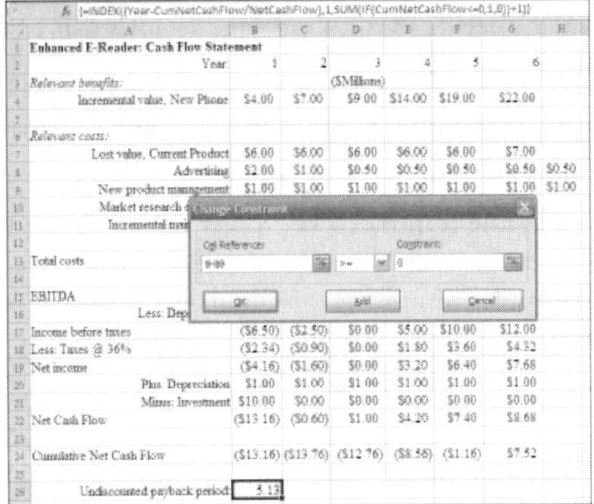

Figure 12.5
Setting this constraint on advertising expenses prevents Solver from changing them to negative values.

9. When you have finished entering cell B21 as a constraint, click OK to return to the Solver Parameters dialog box, which is shown in Figure 12.6.
10. For this problem, select GRG Nonlinear from the Select a Solving Method drop-down list.
11. Click Solve.

Solver now begins adjusting the various costs in the changing cells to reach the value 5 for the undiscounted payback period (5.0 represents the *end* of year 5 and the *beginning* of year 6). Because you specified 0 as the minimum allowable value for cells H8:H9, B10, and 8 for B21, via the Add Constraints dialog box, Solver will not attempt to establish a negative value in B8:G9 or B10 or a value less than $8 million in B21.

12

TIP

Excel 2010 has a new option in Solver that can save you some time. There is a check box on the Solver Parameters dialog box (see Figure 12.6) which, if selected, instructs Solver to prevent the values in unconstrained changing cells from falling below zero. Using this check box allows you to dispense with the constraints discussed earlier for cells B10 (Market Research, Year 1), H8 (Advertising, all years), and H9 (Product Management, all years).

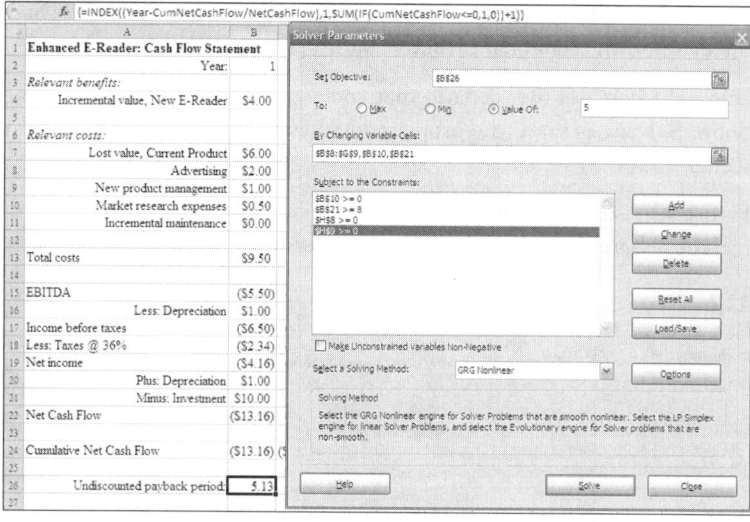

Figure 12.6
Using Solver to optimize costs involves identifying the cell that contains the objective, the changing cells, and any necessary constraints.

When Solver has reached a solution, the Solver Results dialog box appears. Occasionally, the specifications that you supply—the target value, the constraints, or even the way the formulas are set up on the worksheet—may make it impossible for Solver to reach a solution. The Solver Results dialog box lets you know whether a solution was reached. With the example data, though, Solver is able to shorten the undiscounted payback period to 5.

Holding on to Solver's Solution

Because Solver is capable of modifying a variety of cells to reach a specified result, there may be many ways to achieve the objective you want. It's useful to save the different solutions as what Excel refers to as *scenarios*. One of the scenarios that you should save contains the original values in your worksheet *before* you have Solver change them. To save the original values, click the Data tab on the Ribbon, and then select Scenario Manager from the What-If Analysis drop-down in the Data Tools group. In earlier versions choose Tools, Scenarios. Click Add, supply a name for the scenario containing the original values, and OK your way back to the worksheet.

To save Solver's solution as a scenario, click the Save Scenario button in the Solver Results dialog box. The Save Scenario dialog box appears, and you can type a descriptive name such as `Five-Year Payback` in the Scenario Name box. Click OK to return to the Solver Results dialog box. To put the inputs back in place, click the Restore Original Values option button in the Solver Results dialog box, and then click OK.

As a result of this manipulation of values and saving them in a scenario, you have an easy way of going back and forth between your original input values and the values that Solver found to bring the undiscounted payback period to 5. Just click the Data tab on the Ribbon.

Then select What-If Analysis from the Data Tools area, and select Scenario Manager from the drop-down menu. (In earlier versions, choose Tools, Scenarios.)

Select the name of the scenario that you want to view in the Scenarios list box, and click Show. Solver has saved the proper addresses and values for the changing cells into the scenario.

Figure 12.7 shows one way that Solver can change the advertising, product management, market research, and initial investment costs to shorten the undiscounted payback period.

Figure 12.7
Controllable costs are reduced to shorten the payback period.

fx {=INDEX((Year-CumNetCashFlow/NetCashFlow),1,SUM(IF(CumNetCashFlow<=0,1,0))+1)}

	A	B	C	D	E	F	G	H
1	**Enhanced E-Reader: Cash Flow Statement**							
2	Year:	1	2	3	4	5	6	
3	*Relevant benefits:*			($Millions)				
4	Incremental value, New E-Reader	$4.00	$7.00	$9.00	$14.00	$19.00	$22.00	
5								
6	*Relevant costs:*							
7	Lost value, Current Product	$6.00	$6.00	$6.00	$6.00	$6.00	$7.00	
8	Advertising	$1.86	$0.86	$0.36	$0.36	$0.36	$0.48	$0.36
9	New product management	$0.86	$0.86	$0.86	$0.86	$0.86	$0.98	$0.86
10	Market research expenses	$0.36	$0.00	$0.00	$0.00	$0.00	$0.00	
11	Incremental maintenance	$0.00	$0.50	$0.50	$0.50	$0.50	$0.50	
12								
13	Total costs	$9.07	$8.21	$7.71	$7.71	$7.71	$8.96	
14								
15	EBITDA	($5.07)	($1.21)	$1.29	$6.29	$11.29	$13.04	
16	Less: Depreciation	$0.98	$0.98	$0.98	$0.98	$0.98	$0.98	
17	Income before taxes	($6.05)	($2.19)	$0.31	$5.31	$10.31	$12.06	
18	Less: Taxes @ 36%	($2.18)	($0.79)	$0.11	$1.91	$3.71	$4.34	
19	Net income	($3.87)	($1.40)	$0.20	$3.40	$6.60	$7.72	
20	Plus: Depreciation	$0.98	$0.98	$0.98	$0.98	$0.98	$0.98	
21	Minus: Investment	$9.82	$0.00	$0.00	$0.00	$0.00	$0.00	
22	Net Cash Flow	($12.71)	($0.42)	$1.18	$4.38	$7.58	$8.70	
23								
24	Cumulative Net Cash Flow	($12.71)	($13.13)	($11.95)	($7.58)	($0.00)	$8.70	
25								
26	Undiscounted payback period:	5.00						

Notice that the cumulative net cash flow is now $0 at the end of the fifth year; therefore, the payback period is now exactly five years. The lost sales combined with the advertising, product management, and market research expenses have been reduced from a total of $9.5 million to a little less than $9.1 million during the first year. The initial investment cost has been reduced much more gently, from $10 million to $9.8 million.

You might want to modify Solver's constraints on the ongoing costs, to force more of the savings into the capital cost category. However, doing so can cause the capital cost to drop so far that you wouldn't be able to acquire the equipment. Or it may make it impossible for Solver to reach a solution that meets the required criteria. In that event, you might request additional input in setting the criteria. Or you might find that you have to report that the business case analysis suggests that the numbers do not support developing the new product.

Summary

In this chapter, you learned about payback periods, which quantify the length of time required to break even on an investment. The concepts of future value, present value, and net present value set the stage for discounted payback periods, which can vary as the value of money changes over time. You also learned how to use a powerful add-in, Solver, to optimize a variety of input values to achieve an outcome that you specify.

Each of these concepts and tools plays a part in developing a business case that conforms to your decision criteria. This chapter also described how to save different combinations of input values in scenarios so that you can revisit them and eventually select the best combination to achieve your plan's objectives.

The next chapter takes up the topic of sensitivity analysis, which enables you to quantify the magnitude of changes to the case's outcomes as you manipulate changes to its inputs.

Creating a Sensitivity Analysis for a Business Case

13

IN THIS CHAPTER

A *business case* is a snapshot of a set of assumptions about a business activity that your company is considering. Some of these assumptions can be made confidently; others are little more than educated guesses. A well-prepared business case recognizes that at least some of its inputs are bound to be inaccurate.

The business case should document the logic behind the numbers and test how sensitive its results are to variations in its input assumptions. Suppose a business case assumes, among other things, that a company can obtain a loan at 9%. According to the business case, the loan would enable the company to increase its profits by 12%. The business case should also report the expected profits for other interest rate assumptions such as 8% and 10%. By varying the input assumption (here, the interest rates), decision makers can determine how *sensitive* certain measures such as profits are to changes in assumptions. In turn, understanding that degree of sensitivity helps you understand the potential impact of making an assumption that turns out to be wrong.

Reviewing the Business Case

When you first construct a business case, you undertake a qualitative review of the potential drivers of costs and benefits. As discussed in Chapter 11, "Examining a Business Case: Investment," and Chapter 12, "Examining Decision Criteria for a Business Case," you try to quantify those drivers by attaching credible numbers to them. After you have constructed the basic framework and reviewed the results, you have an opportunity to review each of those drivers. This review enables you to judge the credibility of the assumptions that you have made about the drivers. Keep in mind that the drivers are just variables that can be anything from hard, reliable data to vague estimates.

In some cases, the accuracy of your estimate doesn't make much difference. In other cases, an apparently minor change to an estimate has a major effect on the outcome. *Sensitivity analysis* helps you calculate the importance of a particular assumption. This positions you to focus on the critical drivers and to avoid wasting time on drivers that have little effect on the outcome. It's the critical drivers that need the most attention: If it's hard to put much confidence in an estimate of a critical driver, it will also be hard to place much faith in the results of the business analysis.

Excel provides several ways to manage and manipulate these drivers. One, scenario management, helps you to manage the inputs to your business case. Using scenarios, you can alter different assumptions about decision drivers such as the discount rate or the cost of capital.

Another Excel function that gives you more insight into your business case's outcomes is `IRR`, or *internal rate of return*. And by using Excel's `Goal Seek` tool, you can get more from a sensitivity analysis.

This chapter covers each of these topics in detail.

Managing Scenarios

Chapters 11 and 12 explained how to construct a base business case. During the initial case development, you tend to be neither optimistic nor pessimistic about the initial inputs: These estimates are starting points, and they are usually just best guesses. After constructing the basic business case, it's useful to continue with a sensitivity analysis. That analysis shows you the magnitude of changes in outcomes, such as profitability, in response to changing the input assumptions.

Scenario management helps out with sensitivity analysis by enabling you to examine individual variables and assign ranges of values to them. Each combination of values results in a different view or *scenario*. You focus on each scenario and then assess the sensitivity of the outcome to changes in the underlying assumptions. Again, this helps you keep your eye on the variables that matter.

The input variables involved in the decision to produce a new e-reader, developed in Chapters 11 and 12, include the following:

- Incremental sales
- Lost sales
- Cost of goods sold for incremental sales
- Advertising expense
- New product management salaries and benefits
- Market research expense
- Capital required for new equipment

- Incremental maintenance expense
- Discount factor

A quick scan of this list shows that the two items in which you would have the least confidence are the incremental sales and the lost sales. (*Lost sales* are the purchases that customers would make in the absence of a new product. You expect that some, but not all, of these lost sales will be recovered through purchases of the new product when you introduce it.)

You normally have more confidence in your estimates of the other input variables just listed because they involve controllable costs. For example, you expect to have an accurate estimate of the factors that influence the cost of goods sold. These line items include both labor and material costs. You might control these costs by entering into long-term purchasing agreements for material and long-term wage and benefit agreements for labor. Often these agreements are already in place when you undertake the sensitivity analysis. In that case, you may not be able to control the costs, but at least you know they're not likely to vary much or jump unexpectedly.

You can also feel comfortable with your estimates of capital costs for new equipment and for retooling and of incremental maintenance. You can obtain quotes from vendors for the required equipment and arrange for the quotes to remain firm while your company evaluates the business case.

You can estimate the costs associated with hiring new product management staff fairly closely. For example, you can find out what other employers are offering new hires in product management at different experience levels, and you can check the salaries and benefits offered for similar positions within your company.

Market research is your source of information on both the new revenue and the degree of lost sales you can expect—the two drivers over which you have the least control. You might decide to spend very little on market research and just guess at the level of lost sales, or you might spend hundreds of thousands of dollars on focus groups and test marketing. Because the volume of lost sales is a critical input variable, you might use the $500,000 initially budgeted for market research as a minimum amount. You could retain the option to consider additional research expenses if you find you don't trust the preliminary research results.

Judging Research

Since finishing my own graduate work, I've read an awful lot of research—as a reviewer, as a consultant, and as a corporate suit who bought the stuff.

Judging from what's submitted to journals, the state of the art of experimental research—particularly the application of experimental methodology—is pretty dismal. Disclosures during the past few years about researchers cooking the books just makes things worse in a system that runs on trust. Medical research, if designed by national pharmaceutical corporations, tends to be stronger, but it is still dogged by serious doubts about its objectivity. Can a company with hundreds of millions of dollars in profits hanging on the findings really be trusted to report those findings without bias?

And as to market research, I'll never forget my first meeting with a national firm, headquartered in Pennsylvania, which wanted me to buy its most recent survey of the size of the telecommunications market. I asked for documentation about the accuracy of its prior surveys, and the vice president of sales said he would "hate to see our research judged that way." I'm still scratching my head over that.

When it comes to using market research, here's the moral: Trust the dealer, but cut the cards.

Advertising expenses are also under your control. Assume that, historically, sales of your product have had a strong positive correlation with the dollar level of advertising. If that is true, varying the advertising expenditures *could* have a predictable impact on sales, and sales have a corresponding impact on profitability. Of course, there is a level of advertising expenditure at which returns begin to diminish.

New sales revenue is the remaining input variable that you can't control directly and that you can't estimate as accurately as you'd like. To determine how sensitive the business case is to both underestimates and overestimates of new sales revenue, it's a good idea to create scenarios that specify different conditions, such as these:

- Incremental sales are twice the base case.
- Incremental sales are half the base case.
- Advertising expense is doubled, causing incremental sales volumes to increase by 20%.
- Advertising expense is halved, causing incremental sales volumes to decline by 30%.

NOTE These conditions, such as doubling the incremental sales and halving the advertising expenses, are just examples. In your own situation, you would probably be concerned about other variables in addition to advertising and incremental sales. Furthermore, you would want to identify a *relevant range* for each variable. Depending on the particular business case, other upper and lower limits would apply, such as plus and minus 15% of the base case's incremental sales assumption.

Saving a Scenario for the Base Case

In the previous bulleted list, the first two scenarios give you both an optimistic and a pessimistic view of the opportunity, considering large variations in incremental sales only. The last two scenarios enable you to analyze how changing the advertising plan would affect profitability.

The base case is the starting point for the sensitivity analysis (see Figure 13.1).

Use Excel's Scenario Manager to document each scenario. With the Base Case worksheet shown in Figure 13.1 open, take these steps:

1. Click the Data tab on the Ribbon. In the Data Tools area, click the What-If Analysis drop-down and select Scenario Manager from the drop-down list. In versions of Excel

Figure 13.1
The base case analysis of the decision to produce a new e-reader depicts only one possible outcome.

NetCashFlow | f_x =NetIncome+Depreciation-Investment

	A	B	C	D	E	F	G
1	**Enhanced E-Reader: Cash Flow Statement**						
2	Year:	1	2	3	4	5	6
3	*Relevant benefits:*			($Millions)			
4	Incremental value, New E-Reader	$4.0	$7.0	$9.0	$14.0	$19.0	$22.0
5							
6	*Relevant costs:*						
7	Lost value, Current Product	$6.0	$6.0	$6.0	$6.0	$6.0	$7.0
8	Advertising	$2.0	$1.0	$0.5	$0.5	$0.5	$0.5
9	New product manager	$1.0	$1.0	$1.0	$1.0	$1.0	$1.0
10	Market research expenses	$0.5	$0.0	$0.0	$0.0	$0.0	$0.0
11	Incremental maintenance	$0.0	$0.5	$0.5	$0.5	$0.5	$0.5
12							
13	Total costs	$9.5	$8.5	$8.0	$8.0	$8.0	$9.0
14							
15	EBITDA	($5.5)	($1.5)	$1.0	$6.0	$11.0	$13.0
16	Less: Depreciation	$1.0	$1.0	$1.0	$1.0	$1.0	$1.0
17	Income before taxes	($6.5)	($2.5)	$0.0	$5.0	$10.0	$12.0
18	Less: Taxes @ 36%	($2.3)	($0.9)	$0.0	$1.8	$3.6	$4.3
19	Net income	($4.2)	($1.6)	$0.0	$3.2	$6.4	$7.7
20	Plus: Depreciation	$1.0	$1.0	$1.0	$1.0	$1.0	$1.0
21	Minus: Investment	$10.0	$0.0	$0.0	$0.0	$0.0	$0.0
22	Net Cash Flow	($13.2)	($0.6)	$1.0	$4.2	$7.4	$8.7

prior to 2007, choose Tools, Scenarios. The Scenario Manager dialog box appears, as shown in Figure 13.2.

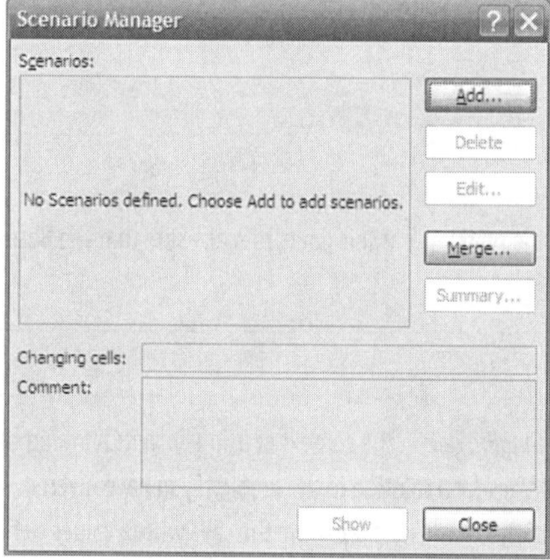

Figure 13.2
You can manipulate scenarios in several different ways by using the Scenario Manager.

2. Click Add. The Add Scenario dialog box appears (see Figure 13.3).
3. In the Scenario Name box, type Base Case. It's helpful to establish the current base case values as a scenario so that you can easily get them back.
4. Click in the Changing Cells box and enter the address of the changing cells, either by selecting the range on the worksheet or by typing the address in the edit box. In this case, the changing cells are B4:G4, the incremental values shown in Figure 13.1.

13

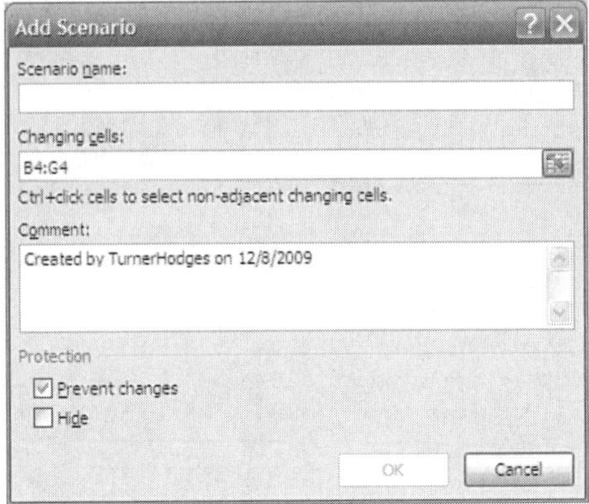

Figure 13.3
Excel provides a default comment with the current username and the current date.

5. Click OK. The Scenario Values dialog box appears (see Figure 13.4). Click OK to accept the current values.
6. The Scenario Manager dialog box reappears. Click Show to activate the worksheet and show the values for the Base Case scenario. Click Close to hide the dialog box.

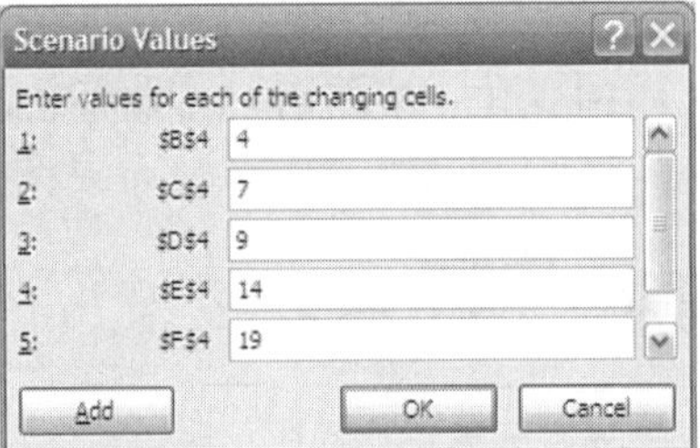

Figure 13.4
In the Scenario Values dialog box, values are saved under the scenario's name after you add the scenario to the worksheet.

TIP

It's a good idea to save the workbook at this point, to make sure that the Base Case scenario will be available later.

NOTE

Chapter 12 discussed *changing cells* in the context of using Solver. Changing cells are the cells that Solver changes as it searches for a solution to the problem you have given it. The changing cells in the Scenario Manager, mentioned earlier in step 4, are the cells whose values define a particular scenario. Although they share the name *changing cells,* their roles are not identical. Nevertheless, it often happens that the cells you tell the Solver to change are the same cells that you specify in the Scenario Manager.

Developing Alternative Scenarios

With a scenario for the base case defined, take the following steps to create the scenario under which the incremental sales are twice those of the base case.

1. Start the Scenario Manager as described in step 1 of the preceding list.
2. Click Add. The Add Scenario dialog box appears (see Figure 13.3).
3. In the Scenario Name box, enter a descriptive name for the new scenario. For this case, type **Incremental Sales Two Times Base Case**.
4. Click in the Changing Cells box.
5. Select the range B4:G4 on the worksheet, or type the address of that range into the box. These are the same changing cells that you used to establish the Base Case scenario. (Using the same changing cells in different scenarios is usually helpful, and is often the only way to create a meaningful comparison.)
6. Optionally, you can click in the Comment box and enter more information about the scenario such as its purpose or a variable that you want to monitor. That way, you'll have documented more than just the scenario name, creator, and date.
7. Select the Prevent Changes check box if you want to protect the scenario from being modified. You can also select the Hide check box to prevent the scenario's name from appearing in the Scenario Manager dialog box.

Worksheet Protection Must Be Enabled

Neither the Prevent Changes option nor the Hide option in the Scenario Manager has an effect unless the worksheet is protected. You can protect the worksheet by clicking the Ribbon's Review tab and then clicking Protect Sheet in the Changes group. (In versions of Excel prior to 2007, select Tools, Protection, Protect Sheet.) The check box labeled Protect Worksheet and Contents of Locked Cells should be selected. Scroll down in the list box that's labeled Allow All Users of This Worksheet To, make sure that the Edit Scenarios check box is cleared, and click OK. Then if you selected Prevent Changes in the Add Scenario dialog box, the Edit and the Delete buttons on the Scenario Manager dialog box become disabled. If you selected only the Hide check box on the Add Scenario dialog box, the scenario name is missing from the Scenario Manager dialog box. The Edit and Delete buttons are available only if the worksheet has another scenario that does *not* have its Prevent Changes or Hide options selected.

---

8. Click OK. The Scenario Values dialog box appears. Because this scenario doubles the sales assumptions for the base case, you would change the 4 entry in cell $B$4 to =2*4, the 7 entry in cell $C$4 to =2*7, and so on, doubling the existing value of each cell, as shown in Figure 13.5.

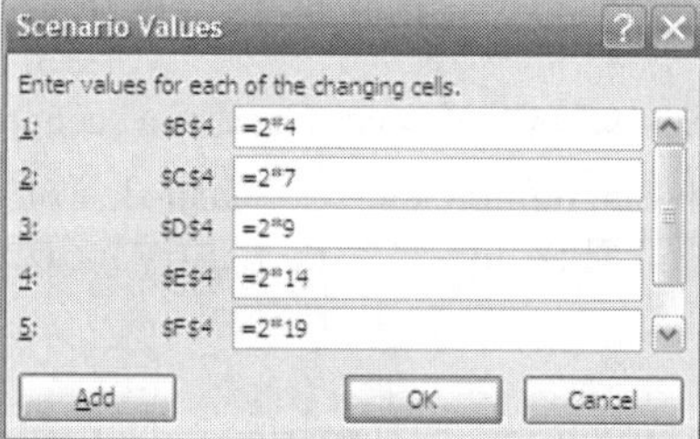

Figure 13.5
Excel converts these formulas to static values when you click the Scenario Values dialog box's OK button.

9. Click OK. The Scenario Manager dialog box reappears.
10. Click Show to activate the worksheet and show the values for the scenario highlighted in the Scenarios list box. You can also click Close to activate the worksheet with its current values.

CAUTION

If you happen to be using Excel 97, beware of hiding the only scenario on a worksheet and then protecting the worksheet. The next time you start the Scenario Manager on that worksheet, Excel 97 will crash. One workaround is to create more than one scenario on that worksheet. (Even though 1997 was a long time ago, there are still plenty of copies of Excel 97 hanging out on corporate workstations. There has been very little *functional* change to Excel since the last century. There have been plenty of cosmetic changes, but virtually no new functionality.)

In the Scenario Manager dialog box, you can also click the Edit, Merge, and Summary buttons to bring up the appropriate dialog boxes to manage your scenarios. With Merge, you can add scenarios from other worksheets or workbooks into the list of available scenarios for the active worksheet. Clicking the Summary button enables you to create a summary of the available scenarios (see Figure 13.6).

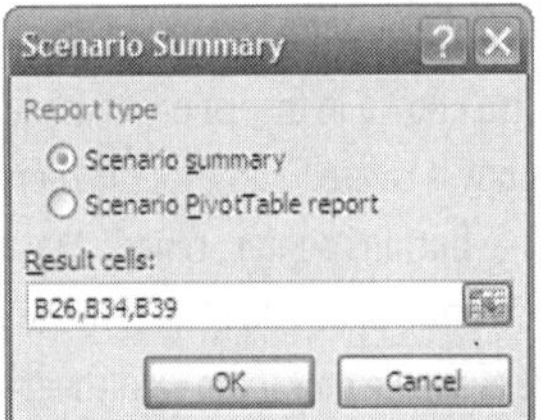

Figure 13.6
Use the Scenario Summary dialog box to summarize the results of the worksheet's scenarios.

If you took the steps just listed, you have a scenario that represents the optimistic input assumption that incremental sales will be twice those of the base case. Now create a scenario that represents a pessimistic input assumption: that incremental sales will be half those of the base case.

To do so, begin by ensuring that the worksheet shows the `Base Case` scenario's values. Next, start the Scenario Manager as described earlier, highlight Base Case in the Scenarios list box, and click Show. Then repeat the nine steps you followed for the scenario that doubled the incremental sales, but make the following changes:

- In step 3, enter **Incremental Sales Half of Base Case** as a scenario name.
- In step 8, enter a value for each Changing Cell that is half that of the Base Case scenario. Change the `4` entry for cell $B$4 to =4/2, the `7` entry for cell $C$4 to =7/2, and so on through cell $G$4.

You now have a Base Case scenario, an optimistic scenario, and a pessimistic scenario associated with the worksheet. The latter two scenarios assume that the market research was way off and that, with no additional effort, the sales of the new e-reader will be either double the Base Case values or, sadly, half the Base Case values.

Developing Scenarios That Vary Expenses

There are two more scenarios to consider—those in which you change the cost of the advertising expense. Although the optimistic and pessimistic scenarios assume that incremental sales will differ from the base case even though you use base case advertising levels, you should also assume that changing the advertising expenditure will change the level of incremental sales.

First, assume that you will double the base case advertising budget and that this additional expenditure will increase incremental sales by 20%. To create this scenario, repeat steps 1–9 shown previously, except for the following:

- In step 3, enter **Incremental Sales 120%, Advertising 200% of Base Case** as a scenario name.
- In step 5, select cells $B$4:$G$4, and then hold down the Ctrl key and select cells $B$8:$G$8. This enables you to change both the incremental sales values and the advertising budget values.
- In step 8, enter values for cells $B$4:$G$4 that are 1.2 times the Base Case values. Change the 4 entry for cell $B$4 to =4*1.2, the 7 entry for $C$4 to =7*1.2, and so on through cell $G$4. For cells $B$8:$G$8, double the advertising budget by changing the 2 value in $B$8 to =2*2, the 1 value in $C$8 to =1*2, and so on through cell $G$8.

Then assume that you will cut the Base Case scenario's advertising budget by 50%, and that this additional expenditure will decrease incremental sales by 30%. To create this scenario, repeat the nine steps, except for the following:

- In step 3, enter **Incremental Sales 70%, Advertising 50% of Base Case** as a scenario name.
- In step 5, select cells $B$4:$G$4, and then hold down the Ctrl key and select cells $B$8:$G$8. This enables you to change both the incremental sales values and the advertising budget values.
- In step 8, enter values for cells $B$4:$G$4 that are 0.7 times the Base Case values. Change the 4 entry for cell $B$4 to =4*.7, the 7 entry for cell $C$4 to =7*.7, and so on through cell $G$4. For cells $B$8:$G$8, halve the advertising budget by changing the 2 value in $B$8 to =2/2, the 1 value in cell $C$8 to =1/2, and so on through cell $G$8.

13

NOTE

You can enter static values instead of equations for the changing cell values. The instructions given in this section use equations only to emphasize the purpose of creating the scenarios: to see the effects of doubling the revenues, of halving the revenues, and so on. When you click OK to save your changes, Excel alerts you that it converts the formulas to values.

> **TIP**
> Especially if there is a range of contiguous cells involved, you might prefer to enter the new values for the changing cells directly on the worksheet. Then add a new scenario using those cells. This can be faster and more convenient than entering new values in the Scenario Values dialog box because the worksheet makes available Excel's full array of tools for editing data.

Summarizing the Scenarios

This completes the preparation of individual scenarios that reflect different input assumptions. It's useful to summarize the results of these scenarios on one worksheet. You can do this by starting the Scenario Manager and clicking the Summary button. The Scenario Summary dialog box appears (see Figure 13.6).

The Scenario Summary dialog box proposes default result cells to show in the summary. You can change that list if you want a different result set. When you click OK, Excel inserts into the active workbook a new worksheet that contains a summary of the available scenarios (see Figure 13.7).

Decision makers can now examine the Summary sheet and make a more informed judgment about the risk of funding the proposal. For example, if an undiscounted payback period of 7.5 years is thought to be too long, you might decide to repeat the sensitivity analysis with a different set of input assumptions. It may be that no set of rational assumptions results in a satisfactory outcome. In that case, you might decide that either the risk or the required investment is too great to undertake the project.

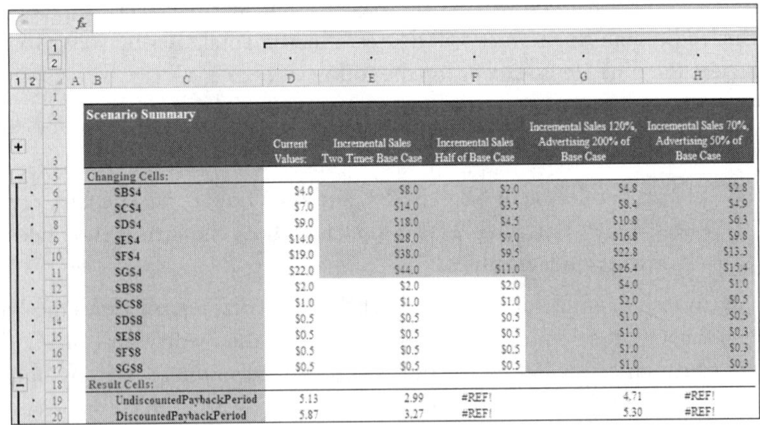

Scenario Summary	Current Values:	Incremental Sales Two Times Base Case	Incremental Sales Half of Base Case	Incremental Sales 120%, Advertising 200% of Base Case	Incremental Sales 70%, Advertising 50% of Base Case
Changing Cells:					
$B$4	$4.0	$8.0	$2.0	$4.8	$2.8
$C$4	$7.0	$14.0	$3.5	$8.4	$4.9
$D$4	$9.0	$18.0	$4.5	$10.8	$6.3
$E$4	$14.0	$28.0	$7.0	$16.8	$9.8
$F$4	$19.0	$38.0	$9.5	$22.8	$13.3
$G$4	$22.0	$44.0	$11.0	$26.4	$15.4
$B$8	$2.0	$2.0	$2.0	$4.0	$1.0
$C$8	$1.0	$1.0	$1.0	$2.0	$0.5
$D$8	$0.5	$0.5	$0.5	$1.0	$0.3
$E$8	$0.5	$0.5	$0.5	$1.0	$0.3
$F$8	$0.5	$0.5	$0.5	$1.0	$0.3
$G$8	$0.5	$0.5	$0.5	$1.0	$0.3
Result Cells:					
UndiscountedPaybackPeriod	5.13	2.99	#REF!	4.71	#REF!
DiscountedPaybackPeriod	5.87	3.27	#REF!	5.30	#REF!

Figure 13.7
Summary of the five scenarios for the sensitivity analysis.

> **TIP**
> If you're not yet convinced of the importance of naming cells and ranges in worksheets, here's another reason. Notice that Figure 13.7 shows cell addresses for the Changing Cells in the scenario summary. The Result Cells are identified by their defined names. Excel supplies the cell names in the summary worksheet if you have named them on the worksheet that contains the scenarios.

The cell names make it easy to understand what you're looking at, but the cell addresses make it inconvenient. (The Changing Cells should also have names but were left unnamed here to make this point.)

NOTE

Notice in Figure 13.7 that both the undiscounted and discounted payback periods have the #REF! error value for the scenarios whose sales are less than the Base Case scenario. In those scenarios, the cumulative net cash flow does not turn positive during the six years under consideration. Therefore, there is no index value to present to the OFFSET function that the formulas use to calculate the payback periods. The result is the #REF! error value.

Measuring Profit

So far, the sensitivity analysis has been simplified by considering only one measure of profit: payback period. There are other measures you can use, and each provides another point of view on your profit. Two of these measures, the internal rate of return and the profitability index, are discussed in the following sections.

Calculating Internal Rate of Return

Given the assumptions used in the base case, it's clear that introducing a new product will generate more than a 10% return on the funds needed to get the project going. This is easy to determine from the net present value of the project. Taking the discount rate (10%) into account, the project eventually returns a positive net present value (see cell G32 in Figure 13.8). The company would therefore create earnings beyond those available from an alternative investment.

Figure 13.8
Use various financial indicators to summarize the results of different scenarios in different ways.

	A	B	C	D	E	F	G
1	**Enhanced E-Reader: Cash Flow Statement**						
2	Year:	1	2	3	4	5	6
23							
24	Cumulative Net Cash Flow	($13.2)	($13.8)	($12.8)	($8.6)	($1.2)	$7.5
25							
26	Undiscounted payback period:	5.13					
27							
28	Discount Rate:	0.1					
29							
30	Discounted Cash Flow	($12.0)	($0.5)	$0.8	$2.9	$4.6	$4.9
31							
32	Cumulative Discounted Cash Flow	($12.0)	($12.5)	($11.7)	($8.8)	($4.2)	$0.7
33							
34	Discounted payback period:	5.87					
35							
36	Without continuing value						
37	Net present value:	$0.65					
38	Internal Rate of Return:	11.42%					
39	Profitability Index:	1.05					

But how much better than the 10% discount rate does the proposed investment perform? Asked differently, what discount rate would cause the net present value to be zero?

For example, if the net present value of the net cash flows is zero, the proposed project performs no better than the alternative investment that pays a return equivalent to the discount factor. That alternative might be less risky than gearing up to produce a new product. Other things (such as dollars earned) being equal, you would usually prefer to invest $13 million in a safer project than in a riskier project.

The *internal rate of return* tells you what discount factor would cause the discounted net cash flows to sum to zero. Excel's `IRR` function calculates the internal rate of return, and Figure 13.8 shows the result returned by `IRR` for the Base Case in cell B38.

Excel gives 11.42% as the internal rate of return for the project's base case. As compared to the discount factor of 10%, this isn't a spectacular increase, but it is useful.

In other words, if the discount factor were 11.42% instead of 10%, the net present value of the funds required to bring out a new product would be zero. `IRR` returns a value greater than the 10% assumed by the discount rate. Therefore, this business case represents a more attractive use of the funds than a 10% alternative investment.

The formula that returns the 11.42% figure in cell B38 is

```
=IRR(NetCashFlow, DiscountRate)
```

The first argument, NetCashFlow, represents the values that `IRR` uses to determine the rate of return. Notice that the result of 11.42% reflects the return on values that exist *prior* to applying the discount rate of 10%.

The second argument to `IRR`, .1 in this example, is simply an assist that you can give Excel. Excel calculates the internal rate of return by an iterative method, and it gives up (returning #NUM!) if it cannot reach a meaningful result within 20 iterations. Your guess as to what the internal rate of return might be can give IRR a head start on its iterations. This makes it a little more likely that you will get a usable result. If you do not supply the second argument, Excel uses a default value of .1—in this example, and coincidentally, identical to the discount rate used in the base case.

13

Note that at least one of the values in the first argument to `IRR` must be positive and at least one must be negative. Otherwise, `IRR` returns the #NUM! error value. In the Base Case scenario, the net cash flow conforms to this requirement: There is only one change in sign (negative to positive) in the series of cash flows—refer to Figure 13.1.

CAUTION

Use caution if the series of cash flows you use as the first argument to the `IRR` function changes sign more than once. There is one distinct internal rate of return for each change in sign in the series. In most cases where the sign changes more than once, there is only one internal rate of return that makes sense. However, if you do not supply a reasonable initial guess in the second argument, it is possible that `IRR` will iterate to something ridiculous.

Calculating Profitability Indexes

Discounted payback, net present value, and internal rate of return are indicators of the profitability of a business case and can help a company decide which projects to undertake. The company may have decision criteria specifying, for example, that a project must have a payback period of no more than five years, or that it must have an internal rate of return greater than 15%, to be considered for implementation.

Certainly, there's a limit to the amount of investment that a firm is willing or able to undertake during a given period. If a company is presented with two projects, both with net present values of $500,000, which project is the right one to select? In a case such as this, it may be useful to calculate a profitability index.

A *profitability index* is a comparison of the present value of the inflows that result from an investment to the value of the investment amount itself. The present value of the inflows is the net present value of the project, with the initial investment added back. To calculate a profitability index, two values are required: the project's net present value and its initial investment.

The worksheet shown in Figure 13.8 contains several named ranges. Two of them are

- `NetPresentValue`, which represents cell B37, the net present value of the cash flows given the discount rate
- `InitialInvestment`, which represents cell B24, the funds that would be committed to the project at the outset

The formula for the profitability index, shown in cell B39 of Figure 13.8, is

```
=(NetPresentValue + ABS(InitialInvestment))/ ABS(InitialInvestment)
```

(The `ABS` function converts a negative value to a positive value.) In words, add the project's net present value to the value of the initial investment and then divide the sum by the value of the initial investment. So doing expresses the project's value as a function of the initial investment amount: for every dollar invested at inception, the project returns $1.05.

The profitability index is useful for ranking projects that have similar internal rates of return or net present values but that require different initial investment amounts.

Estimating the Continuing Value

The impact of a decision made today often has effects that last beyond the period that the business case studies. For example, in evaluating a start-up business opportunity, you can review the financials of a forward-looking, 10-year business planning horizon, as was done in the case of the new e-reader, albeit for only six years. This is often called the *explicit forecast period*.

However, that analysis would be missing a critical element: After 10 years, the business would have some sort of value in the marketplace. This second period is often called the *post-horizon period*. How can that marketplace value be incorporated into the discounted cash flow analysis?

The concept of continuing value attempts to quantify the company's ongoing worth. It assigns a future value to the start-up opportunity. It then discounts the future value back to the present (when the decision is made) and incorporates that discounted amount into the net present value.

Not all business cases should necessarily incorporate an estimate of continuing value. For example, suppose that a computer software manufacturer announced that it would make major changes to a popular operating system three years from now. In addition, suppose that another company prepares a business case that involves improvements to application software that requires the current operating system. In that event, the business case would look at no more than three years of cash flow, and it would not incorporate continuing value estimates.

Figure 13.9 shows an estimate of continuing value in cell B41 and uses a common method of estimating continuing value: as a multiple of after-tax cash flows. The formula used for continuing value is

```
=G22/DiscountRate
```

Here, cell G22 (refer to Figure 13.1) contains the net cash flow during the final year of the Base Case scenario.

Dividing the basis of $8.7 million by the discount rate of 10% results in a continuing value of $87 million, measured as a net cash flow. In effect, this assigns a multiple of 10 to after-tax cash flows because of the value chosen for the discount rate. It is one possible answer to this question: What value would you place on a business that generates $8.7 million after taxes if your target return rate is 10%?

Figure 13.9 also shows several other values that follow from the continuing value. The cumulative net cash flow, discounted cash flow, and cumulative discounted cash flow can be

Figure 13.9 Establishing a continuing value extends your business case to the point that the product is well established.

	A	B	C	D	E	F	G
1	**Enhanced E-Reader: Cash Flow Statement**						
2	Year:	1	2	3	4	5	6
29							
30	Discounted Cash Flow	($12.0)	($0.5)	$0.8	$2.9	$4.6	$4.9
31							
32	Cumulative Discounted Cash Flow	($12.0)	($12.5)	($11.7)	($8.8)	($4.2)	$0.7
33							
34	Discounted payback period:	5.87					
35							
36	Without continuing value						
37	Net present value:	$0.65					
38	Internal Rate of Return:	11.42%					
39	Profitability Index:	1.05					
40							
41	Continuing value:	$87					
42	With continuing value						
43	Net present value:	$45.20					
44	Internal Rate of Return:	46%					
45	Profitability Index:	7.60					

13

extended to take the continuing value into account. Now you can calculate another set of indicators that include the net present value, the internal rate of return, and the profitability index (cells B43:B45 in Figure 13.9). The indicators reference the cash flows that incorporate the continuing value of the project.

It's convenient to establish two new names on the worksheet: NetCashFlowContinuingValue, which extends the NetCashFlow name to include the continuing value figure, and ContinuingValueNPV, which represents the net present value of the project under the continuing value assumption. To establish these names, do the following:

1. Select the cell that contains the continuing value figure. In Figure 13.9, this is cell B41.
2. Click in the Name box, type ContinuingValueNPV, and press Enter.
3. Click in the Name box and then select the `NetCashFlow` name. This selects the `NetCashFlow` range.
4. Hold down the Ctrl key and then click cell B41, which contains the continuing value figure. This creates a multiple selection consisting of the existing NetCashFlow range plus the cell that contains the continuing value.
5. Click in the Name box and type NetCashFlowContinuingValue.

The formulas for the indicators are the following:

For net present value, in cell B43:

```
=NPV(DiscountRate, NetCashFlowContinuingValue)
```

For internal rate of return, in cell B44:

```
=IRR(NetCashFlowContinuingValue,DiscountRate)
```

For the profitability index, in cell B45:

```
=(ContinuingValueNPV + ABS(InitialInvestment))/ABS(InitialInvestment)
```

This puts you in a position to compare profitability indicators during the period covered by the business case with indicators that assess the project beyond the business case's horizon. And using the techniques for sensitivity analysis discussed earlier in this chapter, you can compare these indicators under different sets of input assumptions.

13

CAUTION

Excel functions such as IRR are deceptively easy to use. For example, nothing is easier than presenting a series of cash flows to IRR and getting a number in return. But these functions are based on some assumptions that aren't mentioned in Excel's documentation. For example, IRR makes assumptions about the reinvestment of an investment's cash inflows; you should be sure that the assumptions are satisfied before you base an important decision on the function's result. Alternatives such as the modified internal rate of return (MIRR) are supported by Excel, but again you need to be sure that your situation conforms to their assumptions.

Varying the Discount Rate Input

One input assumption that can have a major influence on your profitability is the discount rate. Chapter 14, "Planning Profits," discusses the effects of the relationship between fixed costs and variable costs and the amount of debt financing a company uses. If a company borrows funds to obtain fixed cost assets, then the discount rate—the cost of borrowing funds—has effects on profitability that go well beyond the interest charges.

How sensitive are the financial indicators to changes in the size of the discount factor? Figures 13.10 to 13.12 recapitulate the indicators that result from the base case assumptions.

Figure 13.10
Indicators with a discount rate of 10%: This is identical to the base case.

DiscountRate | fx 0.1

	A	B	C	D	E	F	G
1	**Enhanced E-Reader: Cash Flow Statement**						
2	Year:	1	2	3	4	5	6
27							
28	Discount Rate:	0.1					
29							
30	Discounted Cash Flow	($12.0)	($0.5)	$0.8	$2.9	$4.6	$4.9
31							
32	Cumulative Discounted Cash Flow	($12.0)	($12.5)	($11.7)	($8.8)	($4.2)	$0.7
33							
34	Discounted payback period:	5.87					
35							
36	Without continuing value						
37	Net present value:	$0.65					
38	Internal Rate of Return:	11.42%					
39	Profitability Index:	1.05					
40							
41	Continuing value:	$87					
42	With continuing value						
43	Net present value:	$45.20					
44	Internal Rate of Return:	46%					
45	Profitability Index:	7.60					

13

The IRR results are the same in each figure for the Without Continuing Value analysis. This is because they are independent of the choice of discount rate: They measure the rate of return of the investment.

However, net present value uses the discount rate to adjust the value of the future cash flows back to the value of money at the present time. This quantifies how many dollars the project would generate over and above the cost of capital.

The profitability index also varies as a function of the discount rate. This is because it is a function of both the net present value of an investment and the actual dollar investment amount.

These same sensitivities hold for the indicators that include continuing value. In addition, the IRR indicator in cell B44 is sensitive to changes in the discount rate because the formula for continuing value uses the discount rate in its calculation.

Figure 13.11
Indicators with a discount rate of 5%: The business case is much more attractive than with a discount rate of 10%.

DiscountRate fx 0.05

	A	B	C	D	E	F	G
1	**Enhanced E-Reader: Cash Flow Statement**						
2	Year:	1	2	3	4	5	6
27							
28	Discount Rate:	0.05					
29							
30	Discounted Cash Flow	($12.5)	($0.5)	$0.9	$3.5	$5.8	$6.5
31							
32	Cumulative Discounted Cash Flow	($12.5)	($13.1)	($12.2)	($8.8)	($3.0)	$3.5
33							
34	Discounted payback period:	5.46					
35							
36	Without continuing value						
37	Net present value:	$3.52					
38	Internal Rate of Return:	11.42%					
39	Profitability Index:	1.27					
40							
41	Continuing value:	$174					
42	With continuing value						
43	Net present value:	$126.89					
44	Internal Rate of Return:	60%					
45	Profitability Index:	14.19					

Figure 13.12
Indicators with a discount rate of 15%: An alternative investment that returns 15% would be more attractive than the base case.

DiscountRate fx 0.15

	A	B	C	D	E	F	G
1	**Enhanced E-Reader: Cash Flow Statement**						
2	Year:	1	2	3	4	5	6
27							
28	Discount Rate:	0.15					
29							
30	Discounted Cash Flow	($11.4)	($0.5)	$0.7	$2.4	$3.7	$3.8
31							
32	Cumulative Discounted Cash Flow	($11.4)	($11.9)	($11.2)	($8.8)	($5.2)	($1.4)
33							
34	Discounted payback period:	6.37					
35							
36	Without continuing value						
37	Net present value:	($1.41)					
38	Internal Rate of Return:	11.42%					
39	Profitability Index:	0.89					
40							
41	Continuing value:	$58					
42	With continuing value						
43	Net present value:	$20.35					
44	Internal Rate of Return:	39%					
45	Profitability Index:	5.40					

The analysis depicted in Figures 13.10 to 13.12 shows you that you can be comfortable with the discount rate you have chosen for the project. A discount rate should reflect, at a minimum, a firm's weighted cost of capital. This rate can vary from year to year as a firm undergoes changes in its capital structure.

Using this minimum value as a benchmark enables you to adjust the rate upward so you can consider the relative risk of the project, over and above normal business operations. In the Base Case scenario, enhancing the current product line does not represent a substantial deviation from the firm's core business: The enhancement is simply a newer version of an existing product.

However, if the business case involved the development of a new product that is substantially different from the firm's current operations (for example, if the product were network hubs instead of e-readers), it would be wise to employ a higher discount rate than the one used for existing operations. Doing so would reflect the greater risk involved in developing an entirely new product line.

Using the Goal Seek Tool

When you carry out a sensitivity analysis, you usually try to identify the value of an input variable that is necessary to produce a specific outcome. For example, you might want to determine the level of incremental sales required for this project to break even, or the level that is required to produce a 15% internal rate of return. Rather than using the trial-and-error method of changing the sales inputs and visually inspecting the relevant outcomes, you can use Excel's Goal Seek tool.

Goal Seek is similar to Solver in that it backtracks to an input value (the Changing Cell) that satisfies a result value. Goal Seek is easier to use than Solver, however, and it often finds the optimal input value faster than does Solver. This is because Solver offers many more options than does Goal Seek and because Solver can modify more than one Changing Cell. On the other hand, there are many problems that Solver can deal with that Goal Seek can't.

You can usually use the Goal Seek tool when you want to find an input value that generates the answer you want in a formula cell. For example, to find the level of sales required to break even, the formula cell would contain the net present value, and you would want Goal Seek to cause the NPV function to return a zero value, which represents a break-even figure. In fact, Excel uses an iterative technique like Goal Seek uses to calculate IRR, which is the discount factor that sets net present value to zero.

Because Goal Seek adjusts the value in *one* cell that is a precedent to the formula cell, you need to adjust the Base Case scenario. Refer to Figure 13.1, where the relevant cells appear. You can express sales for years 2 through 6 as a function of year 1 sales:

In cell C4, enter: **=B4*3**

In cell D4, enter: **=B4*4**

In cell E4, enter: **=B4*6**

In cell F4, enter: **=B4*10**

In cell G4, enter: **=B4*20**

These changes make the values of sales in years 2 through 6 dependent on the value in cell B4. Now, even though net present value depends on sales values for all six years, you can use the single Changing Cell B4 in Goal Seek to answer a variety of questions. For example: What level of incremental sales would be required for this project to break even? To answer that question, follow these steps:

1. Select cell B37 (see Figure 13.12), which contains the NPV function.
2. Click the Ribbon's Data tab. Click the What-If Analysis drop-down in the Data Tools area, and then click Goal Seek in the drop-down list. (Using versions earlier than Excel 2007, choose Tools, Goal Seek.) The Goal Seek dialog box appears as shown in Figure 13.13.

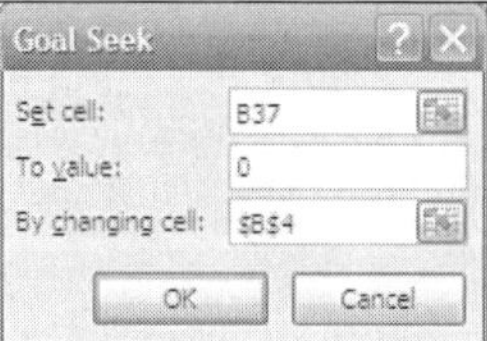

Figure 13.13
You can use Goal Seek to modify a business case's inputs and determine their effect on its results.

3. The Set Cell box should already contain the reference B37. If it does not, click in the Set Cell box and then select cell B37 on the worksheet.
4. Click in the To Value box, and enter 0 (zero).
5. Click in the By Changing Cell box, and select worksheet cell B4 (or simply type B4 in the box).
6. Click OK.

Goal Seek returns a value for year 1 sales. Because you changed the values for years 2 through 6 to formulas that depend on year 1, their values also change. The result is the incremental sales required for the project to break even—that is, to have a net present value of 0.

What level of incremental sales would be required for this project to create a 15% internal rate of return? Simply repeat steps 1 through 6 shown previously, but begin by selecting the cell that contains the IRR function, and specify in step 4 that the To value is to be .15.

13

Summary

When sensitivity scenarios are included in a business-case package, management gets a better overall feel for the project under review. The analyst who constructs the business case also has the opportunity to answer pertinent "what if" questions proactively. Sensitivity analysis provides multiple points of view on a project, and it enables the review team to focus on the business drivers that have the most significant impact on potential outcomes.

In this chapter, you have seen how to use Excel's Scenario Manager to establish and examine the effect of variations in the input assumptions of a business case, as well as how to establish upper and lower limits on the sensitivity of the business case's outputs. You have extended your understanding of profitability indicators to different ways of measuring the rate of return, and you have seen one way to solve for an input value by means of `Goal Seek`.

Chapter 14 examines the effect that changing the relationship between your fixed and variable costs, as well as the effect of borrowing, has on the profitability of your enterprise.

Planning Profits

14

IN THIS CHAPTER

The concepts of operating leverage and financial leverage are key to understanding how a company will fare in fluctuating market conditions.

A company is said to be leveraged when it incurs either fixed operating costs, referred to as *operating leverage*, or fixed capital costs, referred to as *financial leverage*.

A company's *degree of operating leverage* is the extent to which its operations involve fixed operating expenses such as the following costs:

- Fixed manufacturing costs such as equipment leases
- Fixed selling costs such as the salaries of sales support staff
- Fixed administrative costs such as the cost of maintaining an accounting department

A company's *degree of financial leverage* measures how it acquires its assets through borrowing. More specifically, financial leverage is the extent to which a company's return on assets exceeds the cost of financing those assets with debt. The company expects that the leverage acquired by borrowing will bring it earnings that exceed the fixed costs of the assets and of the sources of funds. The company expects that these added earnings will increase the amount of returns that go to shareholders.

Understanding the Effects of Leverage

In the business environment of recent years, it has been nearly impossible for a company to succeed financially without using some form of leverage. Companies commonly use leverage as a tool to help bolster their financial position and operating condition.

However, with increased leverage comes increased risk. If your company chooses to leverage itself, it must be willing to take the risk that the downside losses will be as great as its upside profits. This can occur if a company's sales volume is not large enough to cover its fixed operating expenses and the required interest payments on its debt.

You can find plenty of examples of this phenomenon in a stack of annual reports from the 1980s. Within that stack, you can find several major companies that were highly leveraged. Tracking these companies through the 1990s and the early 2000s, you would see trends depicting peaks and troughs: the positive and the negative impacts of using leverage to operate a business. Many companies were acquired via *leveraged buyouts*, in which the funds needed to make the acquisition were themselves borrowed, hence the qualifier *leveraged*.

Many of those same companies, particularly those in what was a hot trading sector, telecommunications, were later in shreds and tatters. That occurred when relatively minor operating problems cast a bright light on the companies' heavy reliance on financial leverage, as well as their efforts to conceal that reliance.

> NOTE
> And then what happened eventually in the financial sector? The credit markets began to seize up in 2008 and, despite the infusion of Troubled Assets Relief Program (TARP) funds, business activity continued at a slow pace in 2009, which was due in large measure to the difficulty of obtaining debt financing. The catalyst was the failure of derivatives such as collateralized debt obligations and credit default swaps when the housing market collapsed. However, firms such as Lehman Brothers and Bear Stearns failed because they were so highly leveraged that they could not weather even a minor downturn.

The likelihood of experiencing this sort of swing is one reason that managers, analysts, and stockholders must examine how companies use operating and financial leverage to accurately analyze a firm's overall value and financial health. These concepts also provide the background required to understand how the company conducts its business operations.

The Effect of Business Risk

Another concept that's important in this context is that of business risk. *Business risk* is the inherent uncertainty of doing business. It represents the risk that a company assumes by the nature of the products it manufactures and sells, its position in the marketplace, and its pricing structure—in short, all the fundamentals involved in the creation of profitable revenues. Assuming a higher degree of operating or financial leverage is seldom dangerous when the business risk is low. But if the business risk itself is high, increasing the degree of either type of leverage just compounds the risk.

Consider the U.S. homebuyer during the period between 2002 and 2006. Home prices were increasing dramatically at that time, and many finance companies were extending loans with virtually no qualification criteria—or were tacitly conspiring to evade the criteria.

The result was that many buyers qualified for loans that they could afford to repay only if the market value of their houses continued to appreciate. In that case, they believed that they could refinance the loans periodically, taking advantage of the hypothetical increase in value, and make a few more payments by means of the refinance.

These buyers were leveraged to the hilt. When the appreciation in house values first slowed, then stopped, then turned down, these buyers found they were unable to meet their monthly payments. As a result, many homeowners went into foreclosure or simply walked away from the loan and the property. The inherent business risk of home ownership was compounded by the financial leverage of a mortgage that the buyer could not afford.

On the other hand, there were also buyers with relatively deep pockets and an ongoing source of income sufficient to meet the monthly payments. These buyers were able to increase the leverage of a standard mortgage by taking out loans that called for interest-only payments for some period of time, with a provision for a no-penalty buyout. This meant that these buyers could get the income tax deduction for mortgage interest and put what would have been payments of the principal into other, more profitable investments. When the time came that they had to start paying principal, or that the interest rate adjusted, they had the resources to pay off the existing mortgage and take out a more traditional loan. Because the business risk of home ownership was relatively low for these buyers, the leverage was working in their favor even on the downside.

Although home ownership is a financial activity that is different from running a private sector business, the analogy is sound: Financial leverage compounds inherent risk, whether it's the risk of doing business or of owning a house.

Analyzing Operating Leverage

Operating leverage is the extent to which a company's operations involve fixed operating expenses. Managers can define the degree of operating leverage they want the company to incur based on the choices they make regarding fixed expenses. For example, they can acquire new equipment that increases automation and reduces variable labor expenses—or they can choose to maintain their variable labor expenses. Other things being equal, the more automated equipment a company acquires through capital investment, the higher its operating leverage.

CASE STUDY: SOFTWARE SALES

You own a small consulting company that sells specialty software products as one of several lines of business. When you receive an order, you burn the software to a DVD, print and affix a label, insert it into a DVD envelope, and then insert the DVD into a padded mailer. You print a mailing label and postage. Eventually, you will drop off several mailers at once at the post office.

Belatedly, you have a web developer design and establish a website for your company. An employee suggests that if you let customers order and download the software directly from your new site, you can save all the costs associated with sending out DVDs—to say nothing of the wear and tear on your car and your patience when you go to the post office.

What are the financial implications of making an operational change such as this?

Evaluating the Financial Implications of an Operational Change

You review some recent orders and find that you paid an employee an average of $5 per order to prepare each DVD for mailing. You sell the DVDs for $10 each. Your costs and profit per order are as follows:

- Variable blank DVD: $0.25
- Variable per DVD for labels, envelopes, and padded mailers: $1
- Variable burning, printing, and mailing per DVD: $5
- Total variable cost per DVD: $6.25
- Operating income per DVD: $3.75

If you can remove the cost of producing and mailing the DVDs, your total variable costs will drop from $6.25 per order to $0.00. In addition, your operating income per order will increase from $3.75 to $10.

On the other hand, to manage the sales and process the orders, you need a new computer, which costs around $1,400 including all the required peripherals. Purchasing a new computer will introduce a new, fixed cost to the sale and distribution of the software. You will have to sell 140 software units just to cover the cost of the equipment, which is the break-even point for this investment.

You should base your decision on how dependable your software orders are. Suppose you have a steady stream of around 60 orders per month—because of the stability of the flow of orders, the business risk is low. In that case, you break even on the investment in a little over two months, after which you show an additional $6.25 profit for every order. That added profit is the result of *leveraging* your capital investment.

Now suppose that your software orders are not so dependable—the business risk is a little higher. Your software is meant to provide functionality that the competition does not, but you never know when the competition will upgrade its offering and cut into your business.

If the timing of your investment coincides with a drop in orders for your software, the new computer could sit nearly idle for several months. There will be little profit to cover the cost, the break-even point will be pushed well into the future, and you will have lost the opportunity to invest the $1,400 in some other manner, such as advertising. The leverage is actually working against you.

There are other considerations to take into account, including these:

- How many of your customers prefer an actual DVD to a downloaded file?
- Will it matter if you lose the additional visibility that comes from a DVD labeled with your company name?
- How many customers will you lose who do not have the bandwidth to conveniently download a 15-megabyte file?

And so on. Business decisions are seldom clear-cut.

Operating leverage cuts both ways. This case study discusses a tiny risk, but the principles apply just as well to million-dollar decisions. A good decision can increase your profitability dramatically once you have broken even on the fixed cost. Bad timing can cut your profitability dramatically if it takes longer than anticipated to break even on the investment.

CASE STUDY: COMPARING THE DEGREE OF OPERATING LEVERAGE

For a more detailed example, consider three different paint stores. Their operations are identical except for decisions they have made regarding their variable and fixed expenses:

Your Father's Paint Store has decided to incur the lowest fixed and highest variable costs. It has little in the way of special equipment and relies heavily on the experience and knowledge of its salespeople. At this store, sales commissions are relatively high.

Paint by Numbers has decided to take on higher fixed costs than Your Father's Paint Store but to keep its variable costs lower. This store has invested a moderate amount of money in color-matching equipment that a salesperson can use to match paint samples automatically. The store's management believes that relying on the equipment allows it to hire salespeople who are somewhat less experienced and who therefore earn a bit less than in Your Father's Paint Store.

Mix 'n' Match Paints has decided on the highest fixed and lowest variable costs of the three stores. It has invested heavily in equipment that not only matches paint samples exactly, but also mixes paints automatically to produce a gallon of matching paint. Its salespeople need no special knowledge and receive lower commissions than the staff at other stores.

Evaluating Fixed Expenses

Figures 14.1, 14.2, and 14.3 display an analysis of each store's sales and Earnings Before Interest and Taxes (EBIT) for a given quantity of sales at their existing fixed costs, variable costs, and unit sales rates.

Figures 14.1 to 14.3 clarify some trends. These trends result from each store's decision about managing its variable costs and fixed costs:

- Your Father's Paint Store, which has the lowest fixed cost and the highest per-unit cost, will break even faster than Paint By Numbers and Mix 'n' Match Paints. However, once the break-even point has been met, Your Father's Paint Store's EBIT will be less than both Paint By Numbers and Mix 'n' Match Paints at any given level of production. This is because Your Father's Paint Store has the highest per-unit sales cost. No matter how many gallons of paint it sells, it incurs the same relatively high sales commission on each unit.
- Paint By Numbers, which has fixed costs between those of Your Father's Paint Store and Mix 'n' Match Paints, reaches the break-even point later than Your Father's Paint Store but earlier than Mix 'n' Match Paints. Once it reaches its break-even point, it is more profitable than Your Father's Paint Store because its unit sales cost is lower (due to lower commission rates). However, after breaking even, Paint By Numbers is less profitable in terms of EBIT than Mix 'n' Match Paints as sales increase: It pays its sales staff a higher commission than does Mix 'n' Match Paints.

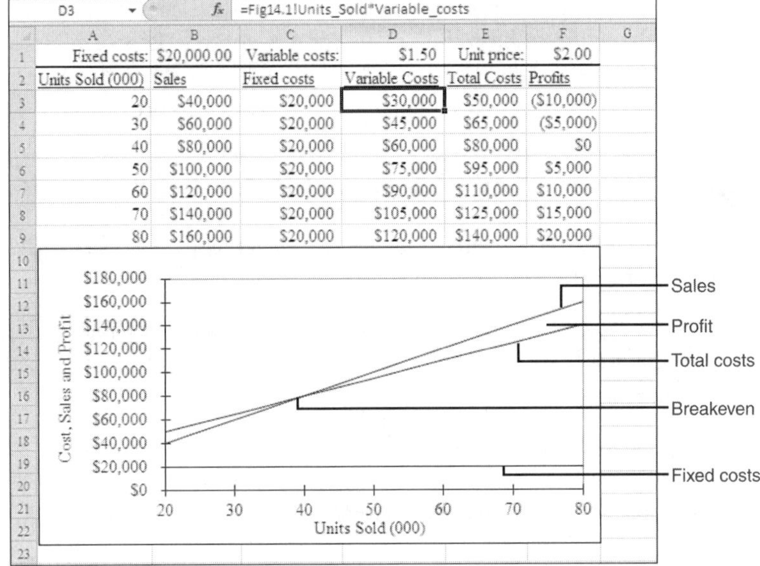

D3 =Fig14.1!Units_Sold*Variable_costs

A	B	C	D	E	F
Fixed costs:	$20,000.00	Variable costs:	$1.50	Unit price:	$2.00
Units Sold (000)	Sales	Fixed costs	Variable Costs	Total Costs	Profits
20	$40,000	$20,000	$30,000	$50,000	($10,000)
30	$60,000	$20,000	$45,000	$65,000	($5,000)
40	$80,000	$20,000	$60,000	$80,000	$0
50	$100,000	$20,000	$75,000	$95,000	$5,000
60	$120,000	$20,000	$90,000	$110,000	$10,000
70	$140,000	$20,000	$105,000	$125,000	$15,000
80	$160,000	$20,000	$120,000	$140,000	$20,000

Figure 14.1
Your Father's Paint Store breaks even quickly but has relatively low profit growth after break-even.

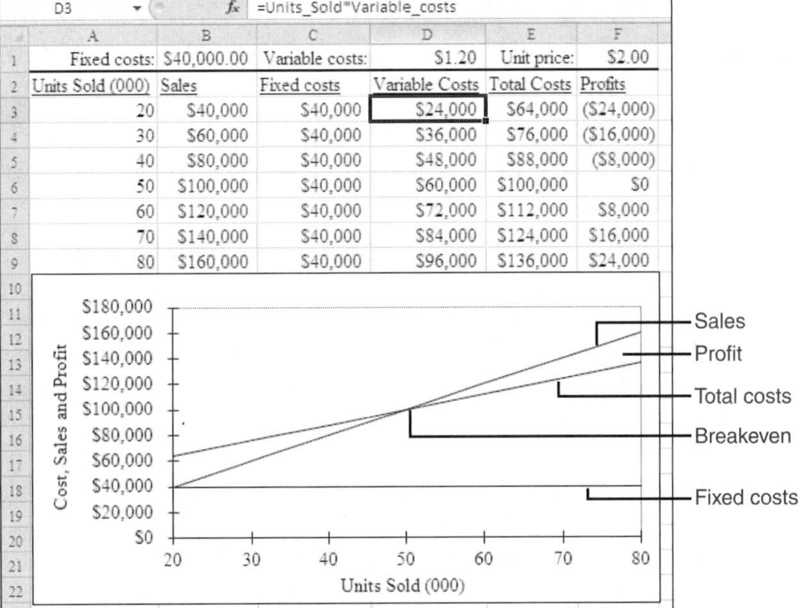

D3 =Units_Sold*Variable_costs

A	B	C	D	E	F
Fixed costs:	$40,000.00	Variable costs:	$1.20	Unit price:	$2.00
Units Sold (000)	Sales	Fixed costs	Variable Costs	Total Costs	Profits
20	$40,000	$40,000	$24,000	$64,000	($24,000)
30	$60,000	$40,000	$36,000	$76,000	($16,000)
40	$80,000	$40,000	$48,000	$88,000	($8,000)
50	$100,000	$40,000	$60,000	$100,000	$0
60	$120,000	$40,000	$72,000	$112,000	$8,000
70	$140,000	$40,000	$84,000	$124,000	$16,000
80	$160,000	$40,000	$96,000	$136,000	$24,000

Figure 14.2
Paint by Numbers breaks even more slowly, but its profitability grows faster than Your Father's Paint Store after break-even.

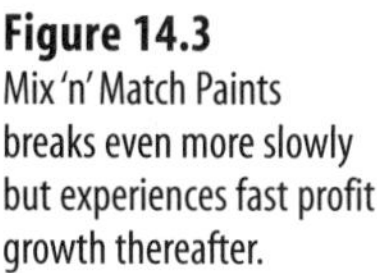

Figure 14.3
Mix 'n' Match Paints breaks even more slowly but experiences fast profit growth thereafter.

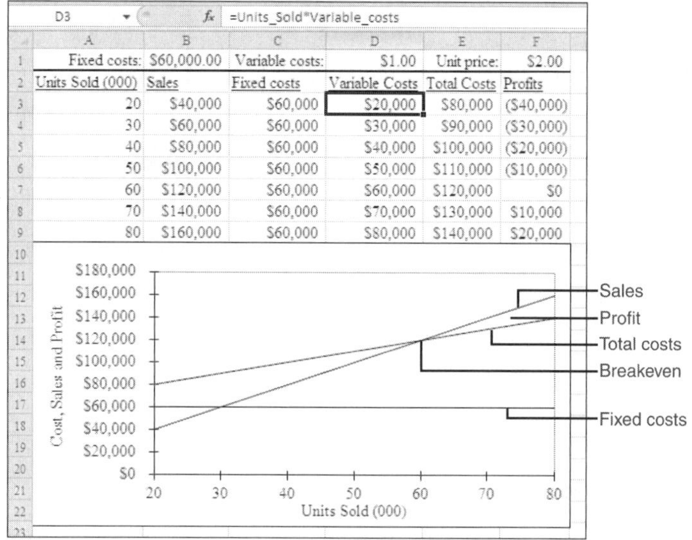

D3 =Units_Sold*Variable_costs

	A	B	C	D	E	F
1	Fixed costs:	$60,000.00	Variable costs:	$1.00	Unit price:	$2.00
2	Units Sold (000)	Sales	Fixed costs	Variable Costs	Total Costs	Profits
3	20	$40,000	$60,000	$20,000	$80,000	($40,000)
4	30	$60,000	$60,000	$30,000	$90,000	($30,000)
5	40	$80,000	$60,000	$40,000	$100,000	($20,000)
6	50	$100,000	$60,000	$50,000	$110,000	($10,000)
7	60	$120,000	$60,000	$60,000	$120,000	$0
8	70	$140,000	$60,000	$70,000	$130,000	$10,000
9	80	$160,000	$60,000	$80,000	$140,000	$20,000

- Mix 'n' Match Paints, which has the highest fixed costs and the lowest per-unit sales cost, breaks even more slowly than the other two stores. But after the break-even point has been reached, Mix 'n' Match Paints' EBIT rises faster than either Your Father's Paint Store or Paint By Numbers because of its low sales commission rates.

Figure 14.4 summarizes these trends and shows the profitability of each store across its range of units sold. The differences in profitability are due to the different operating leverage involved at each store. Spent wisely, the costs associated with automation typically push the break-even point further into the future, but the subsequent payoff can be much greater.

Another way to understand the effect of operating leverage on your company's profitability is by way of the degree of operating leverage (DOL):

DOL = Units × (Price – Variable Cost) / (Units × (Price – Variable Cost) – Fixed Cost)

Alternatively, an equivalent measure is

DOL = Contribution Margin / (Contribution Margin – Fixed Cost)

NOTE Chapter 19, "Analyzing Contributions and Margins," discusses contribution margins in some detail.

14

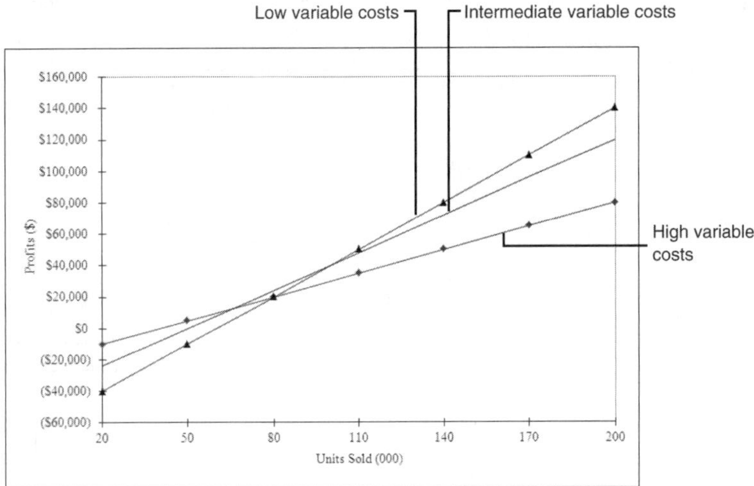

Figure 14.4
Comparison of profitability of three stores with different degrees of operating leverage.

Using the data for the three paint stores, you can calculate the DOL at the point where unit sales are 120,000 and 200,000, as shown in Figure 14.5.

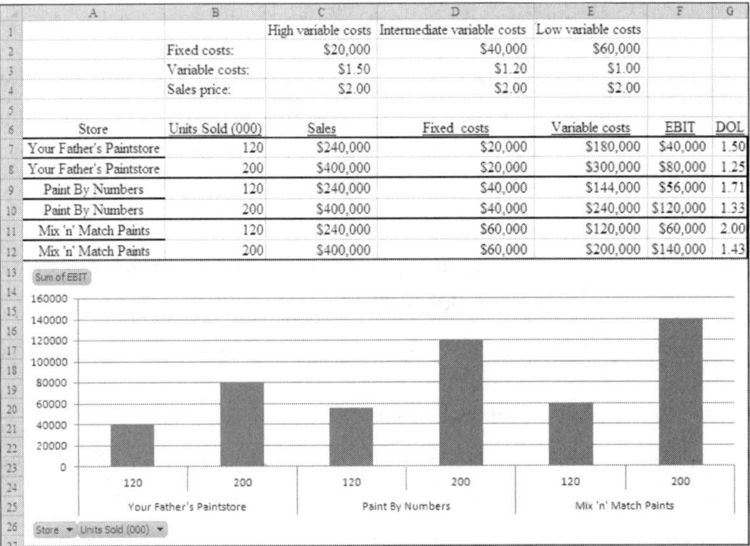

	A	B	C	D	E	F	G
1			High variable costs	Intermediate variable costs	Low variable costs		
2		Fixed costs:	$20,000	$40,000	$60,000		
3		Variable costs:	$1.50	$1.20	$1.00		
4		Sales price:	$2.00	$2.00	$2.00		
5							
6	Store	Units Sold (000)	Sales	Fixed costs	Variable costs	EBIT	DOL
7	Your Father's Paintstore	120	$240,000	$20,000	$180,000	$40,000	1.50
8	Your Father's Paintstore	200	$400,000	$20,000	$300,000	$80,000	1.25
9	Paint By Numbers	120	$240,000	$40,000	$144,000	$56,000	1.71
10	Paint By Numbers	200	$400,000	$40,000	$240,000	$120,000	1.33
11	Mix 'n' Match Paints	120	$240,000	$60,000	$120,000	$60,000	2.00
12	Mix 'n' Match Paints	200	$400,000	$60,000	$200,000	$140,000	1.43

Figure 14.5
The degree of operating leverage accelerates EBIT as unit sales increase.

NOTE

The charts shown in Figures 14.5 and 14.6 are not standard Excel charts but pivot charts, introduced in Excel for Office 2000. Like pivot tables, pivot charts make it possible to group levels of one field within another, just as different Units Sold levels are grouped within Stores in Figures 14.5 and 14.6.

This effect is equivalent to the grouping of levels of an inner field within those of an outer field in a pivot table. Traditional Excel charts do not group in quite this way, and they require the user to take extra steps to use multiple columns or rows for the axis labels.

You can base a pivot chart on a table such as the one shown in A6:G12 of Figures 14.5 and 14.6. To do this, select the range, click the Insert tab on the Ribbon, and then select PivotChart from the PivotTable drop-down.

For example, Your Father's Paint Store has a DOL of 1.5 with unit sales of 120,000:

DOL = 120,000 × ($2.00 – $1.50) / (120,000 × [$2.00 – $1.50] – $20,000)

DOL = 1.5

These calculations are the basis of the data shown in Figure 14.5. The numbers indicate that the EBIT of the companies that have the greatest operating leverage are also the most sensitive to changes in sales volume. Of course, that gets at the very definition of the term *leverage.*

Each store sells the same number of units: 120,000 or 200,000. Furthermore, each store sells the units for the same price: $2 per unit. But because the stores differ in their fixed and variable costs, they also differ in their EBIT. For Your Father's Paint Store, a 67% increase in unit sales from 120,000 to 200,000 results in a (67% × 1.5 DOL), or 100%, increase in EBIT. For Paint By Numbers, a 67% increase in unit sales results in a (67% × 1.7 DOL), or 114%, increase in EBIT. And Mix 'n' Match Paints experiences a (67% × 2.0 DOL), or 133%, increase in EBIT. The higher the DOL, the greater the EBIT as unit sales increase.

Expressed in raw dollar amounts, an increase in unit sales from 120,000 to 200,000 means an increase in profits of $40,000 for Your Father's Paint Store, $64,000 for Paint By Numbers, and $80,000 for Mix 'n' Match Paints.

However, the calculated DOL will be the same on the downside. So for every decrease in sales volume, each company's DOL will cause a decrease in EBIT corresponding to the increase in EBIT when sales volume increases (see Figure 14.6).

The DOL analysis gives managers a great deal of information for setting operating targets and planning profitability. For example, you would want to make operating leverage decisions based on your knowledge of how your sales volume fluctuates.

Figure 14.6
The degree of operating leverage accelerates loss of profit as unit sales decline.

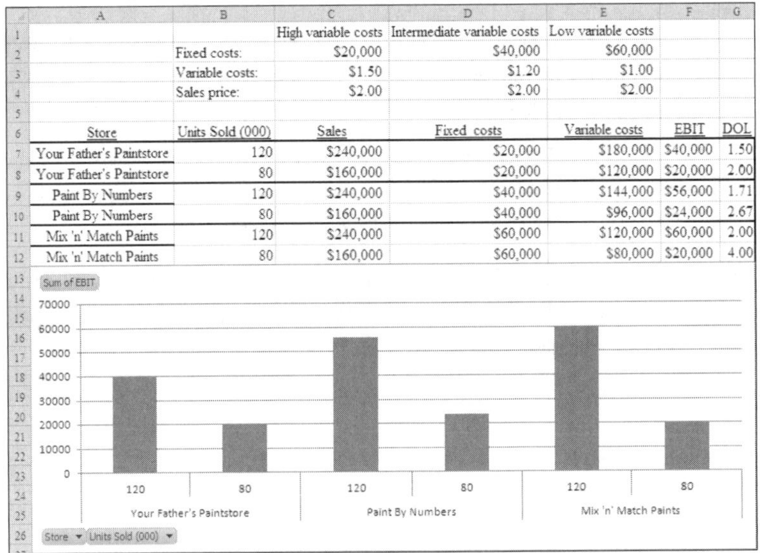

		High variable costs	Intermediate variable costs	Low variable costs		
	Fixed costs:	$20,000	$40,000	$60,000		
	Variable costs:	$1.50	$1.20	$1.00		
	Sales price:	$2.00	$2.00	$2.00		
Store	Units Sold (000)	Sales	Fixed costs	Variable costs	EBIT	DOL
Your Father's Paintstore	120	$240,000	$20,000	$180,000	$40,000	1.50
Your Father's Paintstore	80	$160,000	$20,000	$120,000	$20,000	2.00
Paint By Numbers	120	$240,000	$40,000	$144,000	$56,000	1.71
Paint By Numbers	80	$160,000	$40,000	$96,000	$24,000	2.67
Mix 'n' Match Paints	120	$240,000	$60,000	$120,000	$60,000	2.00
Mix 'n' Match Paints	80	$160,000	$60,000	$80,000	$20,000	4.00

If your company experiences large swings in sales volume throughout the year, it would be much riskier to maintain a high degree of leverage than it would be if your company had a predictable, steady stream of sales. But bear in mind that risk isn't inherently good or bad: By increasing the DOL—and, therefore, the risk—you're increasing the *size* of the possible gains or losses, not necessarily their likelihood.

CASE STUDY: COFFEE SALES

Java Man is a small business that sells specialty coffee drinks at office buildings. Each morning and afternoon, trucks arrive at the offices' front entrances, and the office employees purchase various stimulants with names such as Java du Jour. The business is profitable.

Java Man's offices are located to the north of town, where lease rates are less expensive, and the principal sales area is south of town, where the high-rise office buildings are found. This means that the trucks must drive cross-town four times each day.

The cost of transportation to and from the sales area and the power requirements of the trucks' coffee-brewing equipment are significant variable costs. Java Man could reduce the amount of driving—and, therefore, the variable costs—if it moves its own operations nearer to its sales area. However, a move would require a large, one-time expense which would draw down Java Man's cash reserves, thus increasing the company's business risk at least temporarily.

Evaluating Effect of Increasing Fixed Costs

Java Man presently has fixed costs of $10,000 per month. The lease of a new office, closer to the sales area, would cost an additional $2,200 per month. This would increase the fixed costs to $12,200 per month (see Figure 14.7).

Figure 14.7
Profit analysis for the lease of existing offices by Java Man, Inc.

`=Contribution_Margin/(Contribution_Margin-SUM(Fixed_Costs))`

	A	B	C	D	E	F
1	Units sold per month:	20,000	Unit variable costs:	$0.60		
2	Average unit sales price:	$2.20	Current fixed costs:	$10,000		
3			Contribution margin:	$202,986		
4			DOL:	2.45		
5						
6				Fixed	Variable	
7	Sales month	Units	Sales	costs	Costs	EBIT
8	January	6,582	$14,480	$10,000	$3,949	$531
9	February	11,121	$24,466	$10,000	$6,673	$7,794
10	March	14,178	$31,192	$10,000	$8,507	$12,685
11	April	13,692	$30,122	$10,000	$8,215	$11,907
12	May	11,597	$25,513	$10,000	$6,958	$8,555
13	June	9,599	$21,118	$10,000	$5,759	$5,358
14	July	9,913	$21,809	$10,000	$5,948	$5,861
15	August	10,926	$24,037	$10,000	$6,556	$7,482
16	September	14,349	$31,568	$10,000	$8,609	$12,958
17	October	12,965	$28,523	$10,000	$7,779	$10,744
18	November	6,972	$15,338	$10,000	$4,183	$1,155
19	December	4,972	$10,938	$10,000	$2,983	($2,045)
20						
21					Sum:	$82,986
22					Standard Deviation:	$4,963

Although the lease of new offices would increase the fixed costs, a careful estimate of the potential savings in gasoline and vehicle maintenance shows that Java Man could reduce the variable costs from $0.60 per unit to $0.35 per unit. Total sales are unlikely to increase as a result of the move, but the savings in variable costs could increase the annual profit from $82,986 to $88,302. This is a 6.4% growth in profit margin: In relative terms, that's a useful increase (see Figure 14.8).

But look at the change in how profits vary from month to month. From November through January, when it is much more difficult to lure office workers out into the cold to buy coffee, Java Man barely breaks even. In fact, in December 2009, the business lost money.

Figure 14.8 indicates that by converting some of the variable costs to fixed costs, Java Man increases total annual earnings but also increases the variability of the earnings from month to month. The company earns more during the spring and fall by reducing its variable costs. However, it loses more during the winter months because it must continue to meet its higher fixed costs during periods when sales are down.

This increase in cost variability is reflected in the standard deviation of the monthly earnings, which is shown in both Figures 14.7 and 14.8 directly under the annual sum of earnings. The current cost structure results in a standard deviation for earnings of $4,963, but the projected cost structure has a standard deviation for earnings of $5,738.

Figure 14.8
Profit analysis for the lease of new offices by Java Man, Inc.: Variable costs fall and degree of operating leverage increases.

=Contribution_Margin/(Contribution_Margin-SUM(Fixed_Costs))

	A	B	C	D	E	F
1	Units sold per month:	20,000	Unit variable costs:	$0.35		
2	Average unit sales price:	$2.20	Current fixed costs:	$10,000		
3	Added lease payment, new offices:	$2,200	Contribution margin:	$234,702		
4	Projected fixed costs:	$12,200	DOL:	2.66		
5						
6				Fixed	Variable	
7	Sales month	Units	Sales	costs	Costs	EBIT
8	January	6,582	$14,480	$12,200	$2,304	($23.30)
9	February	11,121	$24,466	$12,200	$3,892	$8,374
10	March	14,178	$31,192	$12,200	$4,962	$14,029
11	April	13,692	$30,122	$12,200	$4,792	$13,130
12	May	11,597	$25,513	$12,200	$4,059	$9,254
13	June	9,599	$21,118	$12,200	$3,360	$5,558
14	July	9,913	$21,809	$12,200	$3,470	$6,139
15	August	10,926	$24,037	$12,200	$3,824	$8,013
16	September	14,349	$31,568	$12,200	$5,022	$14,346
17	October	12,965	$28,523	$12,200	$4,538	$11,785
18	November	6,972	$15,338	$12,200	$2,440	$698
19	December	4,972	$10,938	$12,200	$1,740	($3,002)
20						
21					Sum:	$88,302
22					Standard Deviation:	$5,738

NOTE
To read more about the meaning and use of standard deviations, which measure the amount of variability in a set of numbers, see Chapter 15, "Making Investment Decisions Under Uncertain Conditions."

The increase in variability is also reflected in Java Man's DOL. As shown in cell D4 of Figures 14.7 and 14.8, the DOL would increase from 2.45 to 2.66 in the event of increasing fixed costs and decreasing variable costs. Both the DOL and the business risk would increase if Java Man moved its offices.

NOTE
The DOLs calculated in Figures 14.7 and 14.8 use the *contribution margin* to shorten the formulas. The contribution margin is defined as revenues minus total variable costs.

In the long run, if Java Man has plenty of money in the bank to meet unexpected expenses such as major repairs to its trucks or the trucks' coffee equipment, then the acceptance of greater fixed costs may make good financial as well as operational sense.

However, if Java Man's owners frequently take profits out of the business so that it has relatively little in the way of resources to cushion the impact of unexpected expenses, it might be unwise to add to its fixed costs. Where will the money come from to repair a truck that breaks down at the end of January?

Managers can use the DOL to plan not only their operations, as was done in the Java Man case study, but also their net income and their pricing. It's useful to perform sensitivity analysis around sales volume levels and around adjustments to both fixed and variable expenses.

For a detailed example of sensitivity analysis, see Chapter 13, "Creating a Sensitivity Analysis for a Business Case."

> **NOTE** Variability in profit levels, whether measured as EBIT, operating income, or net income, does not *necessarily* increase the level of business risk as the DOL increases. If the variability is predictable—if the timing and size of the swings can be forecast with confidence—then a company can anticipate and allow for them in its budgets.

Planning by Using the DOL

Suppose that each of the three paint stores discussed earlier in this chapter wants to capture additional market share. In January, the manager of each store might set out the store's annual operations and profit targets by means of the following assumptions:

- Each store wants to increase its sales volume from 120,000 to 200,000 units.
- Each store's research leads it to believe that to sell an additional 80,000 units, it must lower its unit sales price from $2.00 to $1.70.
- None of the three stores expects that its total fixed costs or its unit variable costs will change during the year.

Based on these assumptions, the change in net operating income for each company would be as shown in Figure 14.9.

Figure 14.9
Changes to net operating income with higher unit sales and lower sales prices.

	A	B	C	D	E	F	G	H	I
1		Unit	Unit	Total	Fixed	Unit	Total	Net	Increase
2		Sales	Price	Sales	Costs	Variable	Variable	Operating	in Net
3						Costs	Costs	Income	Income
4									
5	Your Father's	120,000	$2.00	$240,000	$20,000	$1.50	$180,000	$40,000	
6	Paintstore	200,000	$1.70	$340,000	$20,000	$1.50	$300,000	$20,000	($20,000)
7									
8	Paint By	120,000	$2.00	$240,000	$40,000	$1.20	$144,000	$56,000	
9	Numbers	200,000	$1.70	$340,000	$40,000	$1.20	$240,000	$60,000	$4,000
10									
11	Mix 'n' Match	120,000	$2.00	$240,000	$60,000	$1.00	$120,000	$60,000	
12	Paints	200,000	$1.70	$340,000	$60,000	$1.00	$200,000	$80,000	$20,000

Your Father's Paint Store immediately sees that its DOL prevents it from pursuing expansion in this way. Paint By Numbers has so little to gain that it probably should decide to stand pat. It looks like it makes sense for Mix 'n' Match Paints to expand because a reduction of 15% in its unit pricing might increase its net income by 33%.

This occurs because Mix 'n' Match Paints has a higher DOL than either of the other stores. The managers of Mix 'n' Match Paints believe that this leverage works to their advantage, but they should perform a similar analysis to test the downside.

Suppose Mix 'n' Match Paints reduces its unit sales price but its total sales remain at 120,000 instead of increasing to 200,000. In that case, the reduction in unit price would lower profits by $36,000 instead of raising them by $20,000. For this reason, companies with a high degree of leverage must be confident that their sales volumes will not fall. Otherwise, they run a significant risk of missing their profit objectives.

An analysis of the effect that leverage can have on a company's profitability is essential to a clear picture of the risk a company has decided to take on. But the DOL is only one of the indicators that a manager, shareholder, or creditor uses to measure the value and risk to a company's financial health. Another important measure is a company's degree of financial leverage.

Analyzing Financial Leverage

Financial leverage is the extent to which a company finances the acquisition of its assets by means of debt—that is, a company that borrows money to acquire assets puts financial leverage to work. This type of leverage is a critical component in the measurement of the financial health and value of a company. It helps managers, analysts, stockholders, and long- and short-term creditors distinguish between a company's level of business risk and the financial risk that the company has taken on.

Financial risk is the additional exposure, above and beyond business risk, that a company incurs by using financial leverage—that is, the debt that the company assumes by financing the acquisition of its assets.

For example, suppose that you decide to start a business that offers training classes in the design of databases and the use of database-management systems. Your business risk is defined by factors such as the desirability of the training, the number of people who might want it, the number of other companies that offer similar training classes, the market share of the database-management systems that you choose to focus on, and the quality and price of your service relative to that of your competition.

If you obtain a loan to finance the purchase of a server and workstations for your clients to use during training, you have assumed an additional financial risk beyond your business risk: the possibility that your company will be unable to repay that loan from its earnings.

Distinguishing Business from Financial Risk

It's useful to consider business and financial risk separately when you make decisions pertaining to financial leverage. One way to focus on financial risk is to analyze a company's financial structure—in particular, the way that the company has gone about financing its assets. Part of a company's overall financial structure is its capital structure. The company's capital structure is the mix of debt and equity that is used to finance the acquisition of its assets.

If you understand the nature and amount of debt that your company has assumed, you're in a much better position to make good decisions about acquiring new debt. As a creditor, it is essential to understand a borrower's capital structure to measure the risk of making a loan and to determine whether the interest rate is in line with that risk.

The assumption of additional debt changes a company's degree of financial leverage and can have either a positive or a negative effect on how creditors and stockholders regard the company.

Suppose that you can obtain a loan at 9% interest to finance the acquisition of new computer workstations. If the return on those new assets is 12%, you will have *leveraged* the loan to your benefit. But if the return on these assets turns out to be only 6%, the leverage works against you: You will pay more in interest than you will earn from the asset.

Clearly, financial leverage is an important indicator to new investors (Should I buy this stock?), to managers (Will this decision get me a promotion or a pink slip?), to current stockholders (Should I sell or hold?), and to creditors (Can they repay this loan?). Several financial leverage ratios help you analyze a company's capital structure. These ratios include the debt ratio and the times interest earned ratio.

The ratios provide managers, analysts, investors, and creditors with useful indicators of how financial leverage impacts the level of financial risk a company has assumed. The ratio information is critical for determining the stability, and even the solvency, of a company.

Determining the Debt Ratio

The debt ratio is the ratio of total debt to total assets. (Another term for the debt ratio is the *leverage factor*.) Figure 14.10 calculates the debt ratio of three companies that are identical, except for the amount of debt they have assumed.

Figure 14.10
The debt ratio is one way of measuring financial leverage.

	A	B	C	D
1		Total	Total	Debt
2		Debt	Assets	Ratio
3	Firm A	$100,000	$10,000,000	1%
4				
5	Firm B	$2,000,000	$10,000,000	20%
6				
7	Firm C	$5,000,000	$10,000,000	50%

The debt ratio measures the proportion of a company's total assets that are financed, both short term and long term, by means of creditors' funds. Managers, analysts, shareholders, and creditors use the debt ratio as one indicator of how much risk a company is carrying.

For example, a company's value is in large measure a function of the value of its assets. If a company has a high debt ratio, then a high proportion of its assets has been financed by means of debt. This implies that the company must spend a greater proportion of its earnings to pay off those debts, instead of reinvesting its earnings in the company.

On the other hand, a company with a low debt ratio has used its equity to acquire assets. This implies that it requires a smaller proportion of its earnings to retire debt, and the company can make more dollars available for reinvestment and dividends.

A company's debt ratio is also a useful indicator of how well it will weather difficult financial times. For example, if a company with a high debt ratio suffers significant earnings losses, it will be hard pressed to continue operations and simultaneously pay off its debts. But a company with a low debt ratio is in a much better position to continue operations if earnings decrease because it will not need to use a significant amount of its earnings to help retire its debt.

In Figure 14.10, Firm C has the highest debt ratio. This implies that if the company were to experience a business slowdown, the cash flow it generates may not be sufficient to meet principal and interest payments on the debt acquired. In this example, the debt ratio indicates that Firm C is at the greatest financial risk.

NOTE The equity ratio, which was discussed in Chapter 7, "Ratio Analysis," is the opposite of the debt ratio. It returns the ratio of a company's equity to its assets. The higher the equity ratio, the lower a company's financial leverage.

Determining the Times Interest Earned Ratio

Times interest earned refers to the number of times that interest payments are covered by a company's earnings. It is calculated by dividing the EBIT by interest charges—that is, the income that is available for the payment of interest, divided by the interest expense. Thus, the times interest earned ratio indicates the extent to which a company's current earnings can meet current interest payments out of net operating income or EBIT. Figure 14.11 shows possible times interest earned ratios for three companies.

Figure 14.11
The times interest earned ratio measures a company's ability to meet its interest payments.

	A	B	C	D	E
1			EBIT	Interest	Times Interest
2					Earned
3	Company A		$ 200,000	$ 30,000	6.7
4					
5	Company B		$ 200,000	$ 50,000	4.0
6					
7	Company C		$ 200,000	$ 100,000	2.0

The times interest earned ratios in Figure 14.11 indicate that Firm A, because it has relatively low debt, uses a lower proportion of its earnings to cover interest payments. Firm B covers annual interest payments four times at its current earnings level, and Firm C covers annual interest payments two times at its current earnings level.

Firm C runs a greater risk of financial difficulty than the other two companies. This is because it must cover interest payments before applying earnings to any other purpose, such as reinvestment.

Summary

Operating and financial leverage are important ingredients in determining the success or failure of most companies. Companies acquire leverage to bolster their financial position, thus increasing shareholder value. However, with increased leverage comes increased risk. Managers, analysts, shareholders, and creditors must be very clear about the implications of the risks associated with a company's operating and financial leverage to make investment decisions. Knowing these implications can help to bring their decisions in line with their desired level of risk.

Making Investment Decisions Under Uncertain Conditions

15

IN THIS CHAPTER

At times, you have access to dependable, objective information as the basis for your business decisions. For example, you might know how much you'll pay in interest for a loan to retool a manufacturing operation. Or you might know what it will cost to hire an employee who can perform a critical role for your company.

But more often, you must make a decision without access to solid information. If so, you might be able to use historical data or acquire new information that bears on your decision. The right analysis of that data can help you make probability statements about different courses of action: for example, "If we pursue Course A, the likelihood that we'll achieve an additional 10% profit is 95%. If we pursue Course B, achieving an additional 10% profit has a probability of only 45%."

Having the ability to make statements like that with confidence can be useful when you have to make a business decision that depends on uncertain information. This chapter explores the use of information about variability in data to help you make those statements. The following three concepts, and their associated Excel tools, are fundamental to this sort of decision making:

- Standard deviations
- Confidence intervals
- Regression analysis

Specialized Statistical Software

Since the early 2000's, a statistical software application called R has become increasingly popular among statisticians. R is freeware that uses a command-line interface for submitting analysis instructions.

15

However, several graphical user interfaces are available that simplify its usage. R works nicely with files that you create using Excel.

If you are contemplating using sophisticated statistical analysis on your business data, you should definitely consider using R instead of Excel. R's support for analyses such as Cox proportional hazards regression and logistic regression is much stronger than Excel's. Even though Excel can be made to perform this sort of statistical analysis, you would be reinventing the wheel to attempt it.

If your goals are more modest, though, you can save considerable time by using the functions and tools that are built into Excel to manage your statistical analyses.

Using Standard Deviations

A *standard deviation* is a measure that expresses how much the numbers in a set vary from one another. It is one important method of determining the spread of different numbers across the range of values that the numbers are able to take. For example, and as a practical matter, the age of individual human beings can range from 0 to 90. But the ages of 500 high school students spread differently across that possible range of values than do the ages of 500 college students.

Because people's ages vary, there is uncertainty about them. Because supplier prices vary, there is uncertainty about them, too. A business manager is confronted by uncertainty every day and needs to understand how to deal with it.

Suppose you are interested in analyzing the commissions that you pay salespeople who work for your firm. Of course you want to know the total amount of money in commissions that you are paying the sales force. After you have determined the total commission amount, it's natural to look into the average, or mean, commission earned by the salespeople. This is easy to obtain by dividing the number of salespeople into the total commissions paid.

The average commission is a measure of the central tendency of the individual observations—an estimate of the amount that any unspecified sales rep earns in commission. It is a point on the scale of commission payments that lies somewhere between the smallest and the largest commission payments.

In contrast, the *standard deviation* is a distance along that same scale of numbers. Like the *range*, which is the distance between the smallest and largest numbers, the standard deviation expresses a distance along a scale of numbers. Unlike the range, the standard deviation is a measure of how the individual observations vary from one another.

For example, suppose you find that the average annual sales commission is $15,000. You also find (by using functions described later in this section) that the standard deviation of these commissions is $6,000. In that case, the individual commissions vary from one another more than if you found that the standard deviation was $1,000. The *spread* of the commissions is greater when their standard deviation is $6,000 than when it is $1,000.

Why is this kind of information useful? One reason is that it immediately gives you information about the performance of your sales force. For example, it turns out that about two-thirds of the individual observations lie between one standard deviation above and one standard deviation below the mean.

In the previous example, where the average annual commission is $15,000, you might take a very different view of the performance of the sales force if the standard deviation were $1,000 than if it were $6,000. If about two-thirds of the sales force makes between $14,000 (mean – 1 standard deviation, or $15,000 – $1,000) and $16,000 (mean + 1 standard deviation, or $15,000 + $1,000), most salespeople are performing at roughly the same level, as shown in Figure 15.1.

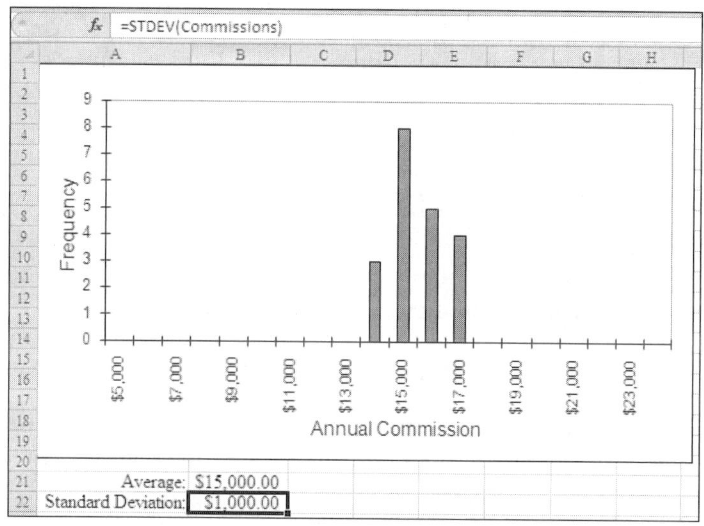

Figure 15.1
A smaller standard deviation means that the observations cluster around their average.

On the other hand, if you find that the standard deviation is $6,000, about two thirds of the sales force is earning between $9,000 (mean – 1 standard deviation, or $15,000 – $6,000) and $21,000 (mean + 1 standard deviation, or $15,000 + $6,000) in commissions, as seen in Figure 15.2. You might then conclude that most salespeople are performing very differently, and you might want to look into the reasons for those differences.

In both Figures 15.1 and 15.2, the horizontal x-axis shows different values of annual commissions. The vertical y-axis shows a count of the number of observations in each category. Notice that the observations are less spread out, left to right, in Figure 15.1 than in Figure 15.2. This is as you would expect, given the relative sizes of the standard deviations in each figure.

The formula for a standard deviation is not as intuitively obvious as is the formula for an average. The definitional form of the formula is as follows:

$$\text{Standard deviation} = \sqrt{\Sigma(X-\bar{X})^2/n}$$

Here, $\Sigma (X - \bar{X})^2$ means to subtract each number (X), from the average of the numbers ($\bar{X}$), square that difference, and then take the sum of the squared differences. The rightmost

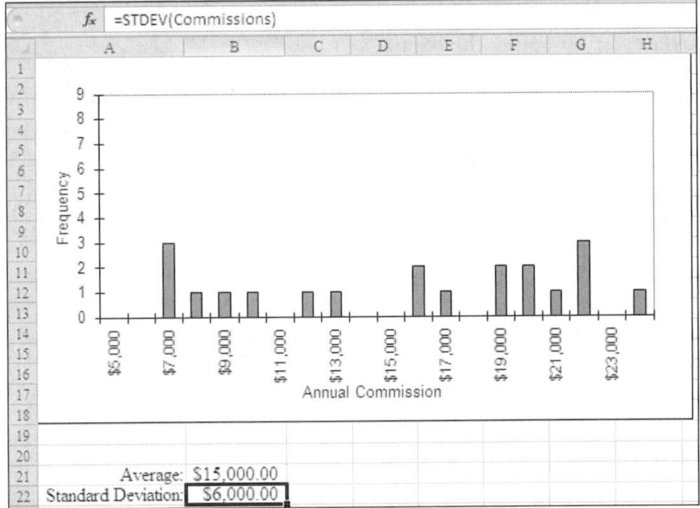

Figure 15.2 A larger standard deviation means that the observations are more dispersed around their average.

fragment of the formula, `/n`, means to divide that sum by `n`, or the number of observations. Finally, take the square root of the result of the division.

Using Excel's Standard Deviation Functions

Fortunately, Excel provides a worksheet function for the standard deviation. For example, suppose you have 20 observations in A1:A20. To get the standard deviation of these observations, use this Excel formula:

```
=STDEV(A1:A20)
```

Unfortunately, it's not quite that simple because there's more than one way to calculate a standard deviation; You use one way when your observations are a sample from a population and another when your observations *are* the population.

As previously defined, the standard deviation is properly used on a population of values. It is a *biased* statistic when you apply it to a sample. In other words, it underestimates the standard deviation of the population that the sample comes from.

Therefore, Excel provides two functions that return a standard deviation.

If you're working with a sample, you should use the `STDEV.S` function. Use `STDEV` in Excel versions prior to 2010.

If you're working with a population, use the `STDEV.P` function instead:

```
=STDEV.P(A1:A20)
```

Use `STDEVP` (without the period) for Excel versions prior to 2010.

Here, the `S` at the end of the function name is a mnemonic for Sample, and `P` at the end of the function name is a mnemonic for Population. See the Introduction for more information on differences between older functions (which Microsoft terms "compatibility functions") and new functions (which Microsoft terms "consistency functions").

Applied to a sample, the proper definitional formula is as follows:

$$\text{Standard deviation} = \sqrt{\frac{\Sigma(X-\bar{X})^2}{n-1}}$$

Notice that the denominator of the ratio is now $n - 1$: the number of observations minus 1. STDEV.S uses $n - 1$ in the denominator, whereas STDEV.P uses n in the denominator. Using $n - 1$ helps reduce the bias in this statistic. However, the adjustment has a noticeable effect only when n is relatively small. Dividing by 999 instead of by 1,000 doesn't make much difference.

CAUTION

Be careful when you use STDEV.S or STDEV.P on data whose magnitude is either very large (say, 10^5 or greater) or very small (say, 10^{-5} or smaller). With such data, rounding errors can occur in any PC application—not just Excel—because of the cumulative effect of squaring the differences between the observations and their mean. If you work with data such as this, you might rescale the numbers before using STDEV or STDEVP, and then interpret the results in terms of the rescaling.

Microsoft reports that for Excel 2010, it has improved the accuracy of functions such as STDEV.S. The improvements are primarily concerned with extremes in the input values. Nevertheless, it's wise to be a little skeptical of the results you get using extremely large or small numbers.

Finding the standard deviation of a set of numbers enables you to make precise statements about their variability. This information by itself can be useful. Suppose your company manufactures machine parts that must fall within certain physical limits, such as the maximum and minimum acceptable measurements for diameters. In that case, you need to know whether the variability of your product line's diameters is comfortably inside those limits or is likely to exceed them.

But there are many other uses for the standard deviation. Standard deviations are used heavily in the area of inferential statistics, which help you make inferences about a population on the basis of a sample. For example, opinion polls such as political preferences report something called a *margin of error*, or sometimes *sampling error*. That figure is based on the sample that was polled and is used to infer the preferences of the population that the sample came from.

Chapters 9, "Forecasting and Projections," and 10, "Measuring Quality," make extensive use of standard deviations in statistical process control and of standard errors (a type of standard deviation) in forecasting.

Understanding Confidence Intervals

In many situations, it is either too expensive or completely impossible to acquire all the information that would enable you to make a decision with absolute confidence.

Suppose you manufacture cars and want to test how well the bumpers perform in a 15 mph crash. To conclude "less than $1,000 damage" with complete confidence, you would need to test all your cars. However, you would have nothing left to sell if you did that.

15

ι this case (and in less drastic ones), the best that you can do is to use a sample to test a ..w cars instead of all of them. With the sample in hand, you can calculate a statistic that you hope is a close approximation of the value you would calculate if you had access to the entire set. You can measure the "closeness" of the approximation by means of confidence intervals.

A *confidence interval* is a bracket around a sample statistic such as the mean. It describes an interval in terms of both an upper and a lower bound, within which you can have some level of confidence that the population value exists. And when you have that objective measure—when you can quantify the degree of risk that you're running—you're much better placed to make the right decision than if you took a more subjective approach.

Using Confidence Intervals in a Market Research Situation

Your company is considering the acquisition of a new retail store, and foot traffic past the store's location is, for you, an important part of the store's market value. Each day for two weeks, you and the CFO count the number of people who walk past the location. This constitutes a 14-day sample from the population of all the possible days that you might own the store.

You calculate the average of the daily observations, which turns out to be `403`. How accurate is this average, obtained from a sample, as an estimate of the number of people who would walk past the site on *any* given day? Put differently, how well does the sample mean of 403 represent the unknown population mean—the mean of the population of passersby on all possible days, a figure that you can't observe directly?

A confidence interval around the sample mean value of `403` helps answer this question. Figure 15.3 shows the raw data and analysis.

Figure 15.3
A confidence interval around a sample mean helps you locate the mean of the population.

D7 =D5+D3

	A	B	C	D
1	Passersby		*Passersby*	
2	544			
3	468		Confidence Level(95.0%)	97.26
4	399			
5	759		Average:	403
6	526		Confidence interval lower bound:	305.74
7	212		Confidence interval upper bound:	500.26
8	256			
9	456			
10	553			
11	259			
12	469			
13	366			
14	197			
15	178			

Installing the Analysis ToolPak

To obtain this analysis, you should first check to see if the Analysis ToolPak (ATP) is installed. If you're not sure, here's how to check.

If you are using Excel 2007 or 2010, click the Data tab on the Ribbon. If you see Data Analysis in the Data tab's Analysis group, you know that the ATP is installed.

If you don't see Data Analysis on the Data tab, complete the following steps to install it:

1. Click the File tab on the Ribbon, and then click Options near the bottom of the window menu.
2. Click Add-Ins. Select Excel Add-Ins from the Manage drop-down list and then click Go.
3. If you see Analysis ToolPak in the Add-Ins dialog box, select its check box, and then click OK. You should now find the Data Analysis item in the Analysis group on the Data tab.

In Step 3 above, if you don't see Analysis ToolPak in the Add-Ins dialog box, you need to install it from the Office installation disk. To do so, reinstall Office, choosing to upgrade an existing installation. Be sure to specify the Analysis ToolPak in the Excel installation section. When you have finished with the installation routine, return to step 1 above.

If you are using a version of Excel prior to 2007, click the Tools menu. If you see that Data Analysis is an item in the Tools menu, you know the ATP is installed.

If you do not see Data Analysis in the Tools menu, you will need to install it. Click Add-Ins in the Tools menu. If you see Analysis ToolPak in the Add-Ins dialog box, select its check box and click OK. You should now find Data Analysis in the Tools menu.

If you do not see Analysis ToolPak in the Add-Ins dialog box, install it from the Office installation disc using the following steps:

1. Close Excel and load the installation disc.
2. Choose to upgrade a previous installation.
3. In the Excel section of the installation, be sure to select Analysis ToolPak. Its exact location depends on the Excel version you are using.
4. After installing the ATP from the installation disk, start Excel.
5. Select Add-Ins from the Tools menu, select the Analysis ToolPak check box, and then click OK.

Calculating a Confidence Interval

When the ATP has been installed, follow these steps to complete a confidence interval analysis:

1. Click the Data tab on the Ribbon and select Data Analysis. (If you are using a version of Excel prior to 2007, choose Tools, Data Analysis.)
2. Select Descriptive Statistics from the Analysis Tools list box, and then click OK.
3. With the flashing cursor in the Input Range edit box, select worksheet cells A1:A15 for the layout shown in Figure 15.3.
4. Select the Labels in the First Row check box and the Confidence Level for Mean check box. Make sure that the Confidence Level for Mean is set to 95%.

15

5. Click the Output Range radio button. Make sure that the flashing cursor is in the Output Range edit box, and then enter `$C$1`, either by typing it or clicking its cell.
6. Click OK.

For this set of data in Figure 15.3, the Descriptive Statistics tool returns a result of `97.26` in cell D3.

CAUTION

All the ATP's tools including Descriptive Statistics can trap you into resetting the address you enter into the Input Range (step 3). After you click the Output Range radio button in step 5, the focus reverts to the Input Range edit box. Now when you click the cell where you want the *output* to start, that cell will show up in the *input* range edit box. Before you do that, click in the Output Range edit box.

You can add this number to the mean. This number can also be subtracted from the mean to obtain a confidence interval of `305.74` to `500.26`. Assume that the result of `97.26` appears in cell D3. Then enter this formula into a blank cell:

```
=AVERAGE(A2:A15)+D3
```

This returns the confidence interval's upper bound. In another cell, enter this formula to return the confidence interval's lower bound:

```
=AVERAGE(A2:A15)-D3
```

Interpreting the Interval

What does this interval mean? If you repeated your experiment 100 times, you would have 100 two-week means and associated confidence intervals. Ninety-five of the confidence intervals would capture the population mean. In other words, the true population mean would lie between the interval's lower bound and upper bound. Five of the confidence intervals would *not* span the true population mean.

This means it is 95 to 5, almost 20 to 1, that the confidence interval you calculated is one that captures the true population mean. You move forward on the sound assumption that the number of people walking past this site on *any* given day is somewhere between 306 and 500.

It is up to you to decide if this is a precise enough estimate for your purposes. You also need to decide if the figure 403, which is your best estimate of the population mean, is large enough to make it an attractive retail location.

For example, you might take a more formal approach to this experiment and specify *beforehand* that you will consider this site if there is an average of at least 520 people who walk by it on any given day. After collecting and analyzing the information, you find that the confidence interval's upper limit is 500. Therefore, you can conclude with 95 percent assurance that this site does not meet your criterion: The confidence interval does not capture the average number of 520 that you require.

NOTE

The assumption is not documented, but the ATP assumes that the population standard deviation is unknown. Therefore, it calculates the confidence interval based on Student's t-distribution, rather than the unit normal distribution. The ATP tool multiplies the standard error of the mean by the result of the `TINV` function at 1 – (Confidence Level) and at the sample degrees of freedom. In the example shown in Figure 15.3, the standard error of the 14 observations is 45.02. `TINV(.05,13)` returns 2.16. So the ATP returns 2.16 times 45.02, or 97.26. This is the normally the correct approach, but keep in mind that you might want to take another approach if you know the population standard deviation. Using the information provided in this chapter, you can use NORM.INV instead of relying on the ATP's use of TINV.

By the way, the ATP classifies the confidence interval as a descriptive statistic when, in fact, it is an inferential statistic.

Refining Confidence Intervals

Several factors are involved in calculating a confidence interval. One is the standard deviation of the observations: You can't do much about this because it's based on the data that you observe.

Another is the confidence level that you specify in the Descriptive Statistics analysis tool. Here you can exercise some control. The greater the confidence level that you specify, the larger the confidence interval. Of course, there's a trade-off involved: You can make the interval smaller by specifying, say, 90% instead of 95% as a confidence level. But although this reduces the size of the interval, it also reduces the confidence that you can place in the estimate.

The surest way to narrow the interval yet retain an acceptable level of confidence is to increase the sample size. By taking three weeks of observations instead of two weeks, you might be able to narrow the confidence interval to between, say, 353 and 453. You might find this interval to be precise enough for your decision of whether to acquire the location.

Although increasing the sample size is your best bet to reduce the size of a confidence interval, it is not guaranteed to do so. It is possible that an increase in the sample size will cause an increase in the standard deviation. This is virtually certain to happen if the additional observations that you obtain are quite low or quite high relative to the mean of the original sample. (It would also suggest that at least one of your samples was nonrandom.)

NOTE

Many people misinterpret the meaning of a confidence interval. Suppose that you have created a 95% confidence interval. It is easy to think, "The probability is 95% that this confidence interval captures the true population mean," but that's not accurate. Either the interval captures the mean or it does not, so the probability that it captures the mean is either 1 or 0. However, out of 100 95% confidence intervals, 95 *will* capture the population mean, and it would be illogical to believe that yours is one of the 5% that fail to do so. The conclusion should be, "The probability is 95% that this is one of the many possible confidence intervals that capture the population mean." It's a subtle difference but an important one.

15

Using Regression Analysis in Decision Making

Regression analysis is a powerful tool that can help you make sense of much broader data sets than you saw discussed in the previous section. This technique is fundamental for exploring and understanding relationships among variables. When you're faced with uncertain situations, you can use it to guide decisions about everything from operations to finance and from sales commissions to marketing.

Excel provides good support for regression analysis. Fifteen worksheet functions bear directly on regression analysis, along with other capabilities, such as the following:

- The Regression tool in the ATP
- Menu items such as Edit, Fill, Series, and Linear
- Trendlines on charts that make certain regression computations more convenient (if less precise)

Regressing One Variable onto Another

Suppose you're considering an increase in your advertising budget to boost a particular product's unit sales. However, you're concerned that you won't sell enough additional units to justify the increased cost of advertising, which would depress your earnings. In this case, you're interested in the relationship between the advertising budget for each product and the unit sales of those products. Can you estimate the effect of an increase in advertising on unit sales?

Yes and no. For the "no" part of that answer, see the section titled "Avoiding Traps in Interpretation: Association Versus Causation." Here's the "yes" part:

You need access to the right data. Many—perhaps most—retail stores have point-of-sale terminals that can capture information about product sold, sales price, date, location sold, and, if the customer pays by credit card, about the customer. Operations, marketing, and finance groups have learned to mine the resulting databases for insight into how best to distribute, price, and sell their companies' products. They have learned to *do* it but not necessarily how to do it to create useful information. Read on.

Figure 15.4 shows two variables, advertising budget and unit sales, for 18 different models of a product sold by a company. The figure also shows an XY chart that summarizes the relationship between advertising budget and unit sales. Each point on the chart represents one of the 18 models and shows visually where its advertising budget and unit sales intersect.

NOTE

An *XY chart* is a specific kind of chart in Excel. It has two axes that Excel terms *value axes*. You can't create an XY pivot chart. For that matter, you can't create a Stock pivot chart or a Bubble pivot chart either.

Figure 15.4
Unit sales increase as advertising dollars increase.

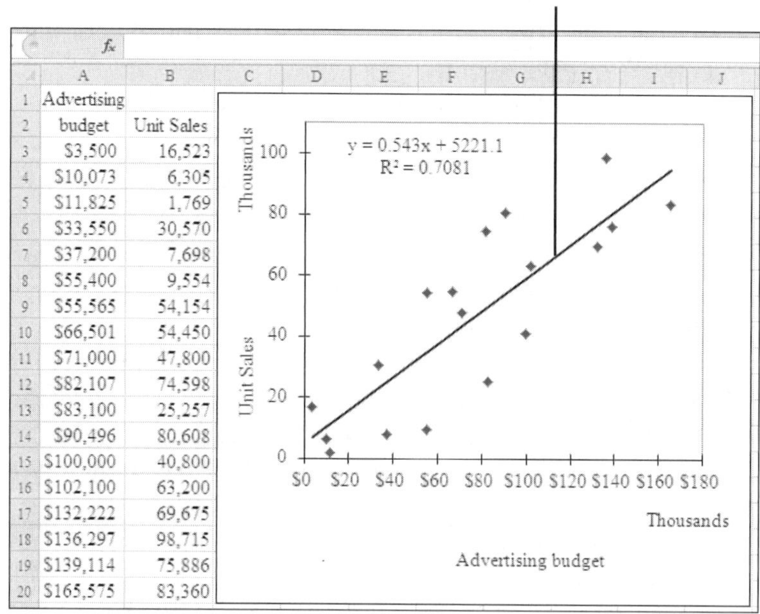

	A	B
1	Advertising	
2	budget	Unit Sales
3	$3,500	16,523
4	$10,073	6,305
5	$11,825	1,769
6	$33,550	30,570
7	$37,200	7,698
8	$55,400	9,554
9	$55,565	54,154
10	$66,501	54,450
11	$71,000	47,800
12	$82,107	74,598
13	$83,100	25,257
14	$90,496	80,608
15	$100,000	40,800
16	$102,100	63,200
17	$132,222	69,675
18	$136,297	98,715
19	$139,114	75,886
20	$165,575	83,360

Complete the following steps to create the XY chart shown in Figure 15.4 using Excel 2007 or Excel 2010:

1. Select A3:B20, as shown in Figure 15.4.
2. Click the Insert tab on the Ribbon, and then click the Scatter button in the Charts group.
3. Click the Scatter with Only Markers button to create a new, embedded chart.
4. If you want to put the chart on its own sheet, right-click the embedded chart and select Move Chart from the context menu. Select New Sheet in the Move Chart dialog box, and then click OK.
5. Click any data marker in the chart to select the charted data series.
6. Click the Layout tab on the Ribbon, which appears when you have activated a chart.
7. Click the Trendline drop-down in the Analysis group.
8. Click Linear Trendline in the Trendline drop-down list. A trendline appears on the chart.
9. Click the trendline to select it, and then click Format Selection in the Ribbon's Current Selection group.
10. In the Format Trendline dialog box, select the Display Equation on Chart and the Display R-squared Value on Chart check boxes.
11. Click Close.

To create the embedded chart shown in Figure 15.4 using an earlier version of Excel, follow these steps:

1. Select the data in A3:B20.
2. You can either select Insert, Chart or click the Chart Wizard button. Step 1 of the Chart Wizard appears.
3. In step 1 of the Chart Wizard, click the XY (Scatter) chart option in the Chart Type list box.
4. Still in step 1 of the Chart Wizard, click the first XY chart format option, which is the markers only option. Click Next.
5. In step 2 of the Chart Wizard, make sure that the Series in Columns option button is selected. In this step, you can also verify the worksheet address of the data that you want to chart. Click Next.
6. In step 3 of the Chart Wizard, add axis titles and other options if you want, and click Next.
7. Step 4 of the Chart Wizard appears. Click Finish to accept the default chart location in the active worksheet. If you prefer to put the chart on its own sheet, select the As New Sheet option button and click Finish.
8. Assume that you chose to place the chart in the active worksheet. When the chart appears in the worksheet, sizing handles should appear on its border. If you don't see the sizing handles, single-click the chart. Notice also that a Chart menu appears on the menu bar.

This example has one data series only. If the chart that you create has more than one data series, you need first to select the series you want to base a trendline on. Then take these steps:

1. Click on any of that series' markers to select the series. If you have one data series only, just make sure the chart is selected.
2. Select Chart, Add Trendline, and then click the Type tab, if necessary. For this example, select the Linear type.
3. Click the Options tab and select the Display Equation on Chart and the Display R-squared Value on Chart check boxes.
4. Click OK.

Interpreting the Trendline

From the information in Figure 15.4, you can see that as advertising dollars increase, so do unit sales. That's termed a *positive* or *direct relationship*. If one variable increases as the other falls, it is termed a *negative* or *inverse relationship*. The trendline (the straight line which, in this case, runs from the chart's lower-left corner to its upper-right corner) emphasizes that the budgets and the unit sales grow jointly.

The chart also contains this equation:

$$y = 0.543x + 5221.1$$

This is the *regression equation* for the data in the worksheet. It expresses numerically the relationship between dollars spent on advertising these products and their unit sales volume. In this equation, y stands for unit sales and x stands for advertising dollars. It gives you the best estimate of the unit sales volume, y, given any value of advertising dollars, x.

The trendline is the graphic expression of the regression equation. If you were to plug various values of x into the equation and chart them against the resulting values of y, you would see the trendline shown in Figure 15.4.

This does not mean you can predict unit sales precisely, given knowledge of advertising dollars. For example, plug the value of $55,400 advertising dollars into the equation as x, and it returns 35,302 units sold. Notice that $55,400 is one of the actual observations in Figure 15.4, but the actual number of units sold for that product is 9,554. As mentioned previously, regression gives you the best estimate (35,302 units) based on the data at hand, not a precise prediction.

> **NOTE** If you use the values in the chart's regression equation to predict a y-value, you are likely to obtain a slightly different value than if you use a worksheet function such as `TREND` or `LINEST`. This is because the values for the intercept and the slope in a chart's regression equation are rounded to fit inside the chart.

The right side of this regression equation has two terms. The number `0.543` is called the *slope*, and the number `5221.1` is called the *intercept*. The *slope* is simply a measure of the steepness of the trendline: The higher the number that represents the slope, the steeper the trendline. The slope might be a negative number, and, in that case, the trendline would run from the upper-left corner of the chart to the lower-right corner. For example, if you charted unit price against unit sales, you would likely get a trendline with a negative slope: The higher the unit price, the lower the number of unit sales.

The intercept indicates where the trendline crosses the vertical y-axis. In this case, the intercept is 5221.1. One way to interpret this number is to state, "If we spend zero dollars on advertising a product, we estimate that we will sell about 5,220 units." But see the next section, "Avoiding Traps in Interpretation: Association vs. Causation," for more on this.

Understanding the R^2 Statistic

The chart also shows a statistic called R^2, pronounced "R squared," where R stands for regression. This statistic is absolutely fundamental to regression analysis. R^2 expresses the proportion of the variance in y (here, unit sales) associated with the variance in x (here, advertising dollars).

15

NOTE

The *variance* is the square of the standard deviation. Like the standard deviation, it is a measure of the degree to which individual scores are dispersed about their mean. But while the standard deviation can be thought of as a distance, the variance can be thought of as an area: the square of a distance. It's often useful to keep this in mind when considering the relationship between variables, as in Figure 15.5. The R^2 value is sometimes referred to as *shared variance*—the variance shared between the predicted variable and the predictor variable(s).

The R^2 shown in Figure 15.4 is `.7081`, which means that about 71% of the variability in unit sales is associated with variability in advertising dollars, as shown in Figure 15.5.

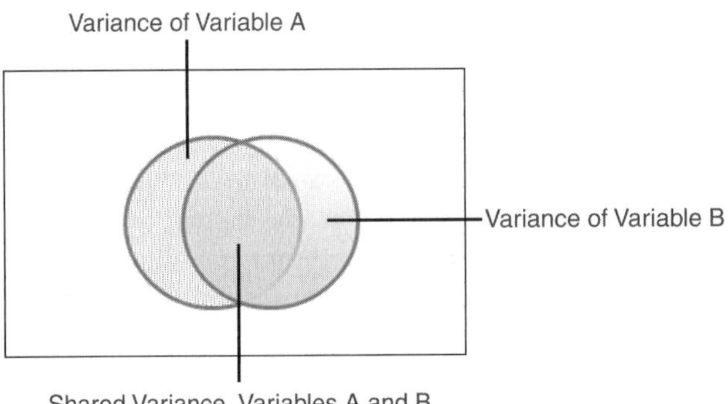

Figure 15.5
The overlapping areas indicate shared variance: Changes in the values of one variable are associated with changes in the values of the other variable.

Why R *squared*? Because R^2 is the square of the correlation coefficient, which is usually symbolized as r. If you entered the following formula on the worksheet shown in Figure 15.4, it will return `.7081`, the same as the R^2 for this data set:

```
=CORREL(A3:A20,B3:B20)^2
```

Using Excel charts and trendline options is the most visually appealing and informative way to examine the relationship between two variables. However, other worksheet functions are quicker and sometimes more convenient to use. Referring again to the data in Figure 15.4:

- This worksheet formula uses the `RSQ` function to return R^2 just as the chart trendline option does:
  `=RSQ(B3:B20,A3:A20)`
- You can get the intercept for the equation by means of this equation:
  `=INTERCEPT(B3:B20,A3:A20)`
- The slope of the regression equation is available from this equation:
  `=SLOPE(B3:B20,A3:A20)`
- If you want both the slope and intercept from one function, select a two-cell range consisting of one row and two columns, and array-enter this:

```
=LINEST(B3:B20,A3:A20)
```

Why bother with these functions when the chart trendline options are so convenient? One reason is that you might want to include the values returned by the functions in a report, or use them with other utilities such as the Scenario Manager or the Solver. In that case, the regression statistics are available from the worksheet but are more difficult to retrieve from the chart. In the section titled "Regressing One Variable onto Several Other Variables: Multiple Regression," it will become apparent that worksheet functions such as `LINEST` are more powerful than anything you can display with a trendline option. Even so, the chart trendline options are useful, quick guides to what's going on with the regression.

Avoiding Traps in Interpretation: Association Versus Causation

When you interpret the results of a regression analysis, it's important to understand that regression expresses an *association* between or among variables. This is not necessarily the same as *causation*, which means that manipulating one variable necessarily results in a change to another variable. Association is necessary for causation, but it's not sufficient.

Many (by no means all) data-mining efforts ignore this distinction. Such efforts stumble when management changes the value of some variable—say, types of households to target in a direct-mail campaign—that a data-mining project says is associated with revenues. The two variables, revenues and mailing targets, could very well be associated. However, that doesn't mean that changing the target of a direct-mail campaign will necessarily increase revenues. Putting more books in a school library won't necessarily increase student test scores, even though the two variables are related.

These points don't represent a defect in regression analysis itself: The defect, if one exists, is likely to be in how the analysis is applied. Whether you get your data from a formal, planned experiment or from a grab sample you find in a data-mining project, you probably use the same regression technique. The difference is in how the data set is established.

For example, in this chapter's example concerning advertising expenditures and unit sales, you could plug the value $200,000 into the regression equation and get 113,818 as the estimated number of units sold. That does not necessarily mean that spending $200,000 to advertise a product will result in the sale of 113,818 units (although it certainly might do so). Many reasons, other than amount of advertising budget, might account for variability in unit sales. These other reasons (for example, unit sales price) are not represented in the example's regression equation.

Furthermore, even if the relationship between variables is a causal one, regression analysis doesn't determine the direction of the causation. It is entirely plausible that as unit sales increase, the marketing department increases that product's advertising budget—so unit sales might have driven spending on advertisements instead of the other way around.

Yet another possibility is the existence of some third variable that exerts a causal influence on both sales and advertising. An upturn in either the national or the local economy is typical of this effect.

The only way to be sure of cause and effect is to conduct a formal experiment, in which you manipulate one or more input variables and measure the outcome on some result variable. You also need to arrange for a comparison that isn't subjected to the manipulation of the input variables. This helps you quantify and, thus, control for the effect of other "nuisance" variables that you either don't or can't manipulate.

The formal, experimental approach often sounds more feasible than it really is. Primary research that meets the so-called "gold standard" of an experimental group and a comparison group, with research subjects randomly assigned to groups, can be prohibitively expensive. It can be unethical, even immoral, to withhold a medical treatment from a control group when the treatment is thought to be beneficial. (This has happened in the past in pharmaceutical research, and now standards and review boards are in place to prevent its recurrence.) And true experimental research can simply be impossible, as when one wants to compare the effects of moderate alcohol consumption to the effects of abstinence. How does the researcher enforce either moderate consumption or complete abstinence?

Still, despite obstacles to its use, controlled research is the only way to ensure that comparisons are valid. Although regression is a powerful method of crunching the numbers, it can't fully make up for drawbacks in how the numbers were collected.

Regressing One Variable onto Several Other Variables: Multiple Regression

Suppose that, besides increasing advertising dollars for a product, you are considering a reduction in its unit sales price. Again, you might look to the data on all your product lines for guidance. Figure 15.6 shows, in addition to the advertising budget and unit sales, the sales price for 18 different models of a product.

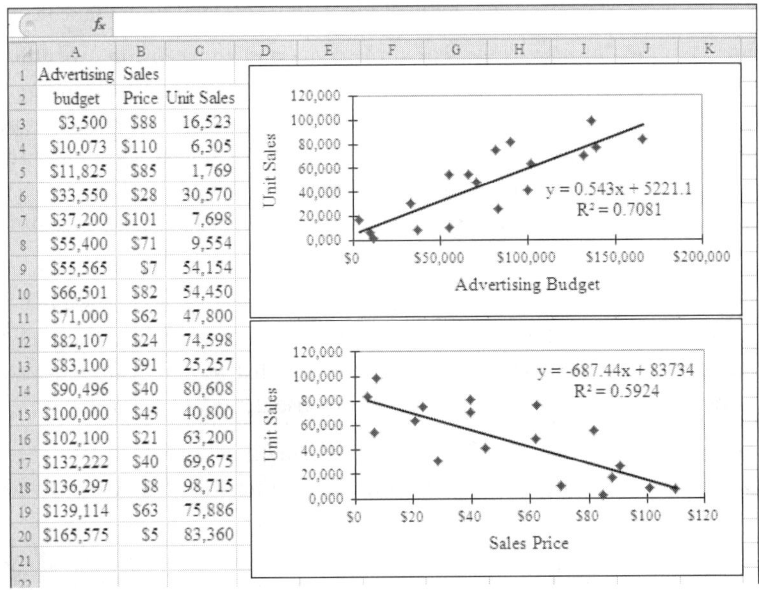

Advertising budget	Sales Price	Unit Sales
$3,500	$88	16,523
$10,073	$110	6,305
$11,825	$85	1,769
$33,550	$28	30,570
$37,200	$101	7,698
$55,400	$71	9,554
$55,565	$7	54,154
$66,501	$82	54,450
$71,000	$62	47,800
$82,107	$24	74,598
$83,100	$91	25,257
$90,496	$40	80,608
$100,000	$45	40,800
$102,100	$21	63,200
$132,222	$40	69,675
$136,297	$8	98,715
$139,114	$63	75,886
$165,575	$5	83,360

Figure 15.6
Unit sales increase as advertising dollars increase and sales price decreases.

What is the best estimate of the *combined* effect of changing both the advertising budget and the sales price on units sold? Because neither equation addresses both advertising and price simultaneously, neither chart's regression equation can answer this question.

Using the LINEST Function to Perform Multiple Regression

To answer the question posed in the previous section, use the worksheet function `LINEST`. `LINEST` is capable of analyzing the relationship between a variable such as units sold (sometimes called a *criterion* variable or *dependent* variable) on one hand and multiple variables such as advertising dollars and sales price (sometimes called *predictor* variables or *independent* variables) on the other. Figure 15.7 shows `LINEST` in this context.

Figure 15.7
The `LINEST` worksheet function returns statistics that describe the relationship between one criterion variable and one or more predictor variables.

I3 =$G$9+($E$9*B3)+($F$9*A3)

	A	B	C	D	E	F	G	H	I
1	Advertising	Sales							Derived
2	budget	Price	Unit Sales						variable:
3	$3,500	$88	16,523						6634.4009
4	$10,073	$110	6,305						1236.7804
5	$11,825	$85	1,769						10888.0683
6	$33,550	$28	30,570						39441.9600
7	$37,200	$101	7,698						14840.1943
8	$55,400	$71	9,554	LINEST(C3:C20,A3:B20,TRUE,TRUE):					32614.0957
9	$55,565	$7	54,154		-358.4634	0.3818	36842.9715		55669.9210
10	$66,501	$82	54,450		129.5278	0.0936	13164.5770		32837.3896
11	$71,000	$62	47,800		0.8068	14339.4362	#N/A		41724.2644
12	$82,107	$24	74,598		31.3176	15.0000	#N/A		59729.6358
13	$83,100	$91	25,257		1.29E+10	3.08E+09	#N/A		35948.3022
14	$90,496	$40	80,608						57053.5460
15	$100,000	$45	40,800						58889.6185
16	$102,100	$21	63,200						68402.0078
17	$132,222	$40	69,675			RSQ(C3:C20,I3:I20):	0.8068		72983.4905
18	$136,297	$8	98,715			F9/F10:	4.0799		86096.0748
19	$139,114	$63	75,886			T.DIST.RT(F9/F10,15)	0.0005		67549.2564
20	$165,575	$5	83,360			T.DIST(E9/E10,15,TRUE)	0.0072		98382.9935

The range E9:G13 contains the `LINEST` function, which, in this case, is array-entered as follows:

```
=LINEST(C3:C20,A3:B20,TRUE,TRUE)
```

> **TIP**
> Remember that to array-enter a formula, you use Ctrl+Shift+Enter instead of just Enter. So to array-enter the previous equation, select the range E9:G13, type the formula into the formula bar, hold down Ctrl and Shift, and simultaneously press Enter.

The `LINEST` function returns plenty of information about the relationships among the variables. First, it provides the best-estimate multiple-regression equation to predict units sold from the combination of advertising dollars and sales price. The equation is as follows:

```
y = 36842.9715 + (.3818 * x1) + (-358.4634 * x2)
```

15

Here, `y` represents units sold, `x1` represents advertising dollars, and `x2` represents sales price.

Notice first that there are three terms to the right of the equals sign in the equation. The first, `36842.9715`, is the intercept, just as in single-predictor regression. The second and third terms contain `.3818` and `-358.4634`. These are no longer slopes because there is only one regression line to consider, and in two dimensions one straight line can't have two different slopes. Instead, these are termed *regression coefficients*. They are coefficients that you can multiply by a value for advertising dollars and a value for sales price, to estimate units sold. You supply the advertising and the pricing values and substitute them in the equation for `x1` and `x2`. The result is an estimate of the number of units sold, given the values you supplied.

Also notice that `LINEST` returns the regression coefficients in the opposite order as the predictor variables appear on the worksheet. That is, the first coefficient (`-358.4634`) applies to the rightmost predictor variable, Sales Price (found in B3:B20). The second coefficient (`.3818`) applies to the leftmost predictor variable, Advertising Budget (found in A3:A20). This is an inconvenience in the `LINEST` function, but there is no way around it: The order in which `LINEST` returns the coefficients is always the reverse of the order of the arguments that refer to the worksheet ranges.

> **NOTE** No mathematical rationale accounts for this inconsistency. But when popular software takes a particular approach, it's stuck with it. It would be easy for the publisher to reverse the order of the coefficients returned by `LINEST`. But millions of worksheets employing `LINEST` have been created since Excel 3, when `LINEST` appeared, and Microsoft can't correct those. There are also other Excel features to consider, such as the Analysis ToolPak's Regression tool, that depend on `LINEST`.

The `LINEST` function also tells you that the value `0.8068` in the third row and first column of the `LINEST` results is the R^2 between units sold and the best combination of advertising budget and sales price. When you optimally combine sales price and advertising budget by means of the regression equation, you get a new variable that shares 80.68% of its variance with units sold.

> **NOTE** The phrase *best combination* used in the previous paragraph appears frequently in sources that describe regression analysis. The "combination" portion of the term means that the regression equation combines two or more predictor variables to create a new variable. To get that new variable, you multiply the original variables by the coefficients calculated by the regression and add the results to the intercept—just as the regression equation implies. The "best" part of the term means that the new variable has a stronger correlation with the predicted variable than any other possible linear combination of the predictors.

Figure 15.7 shows this new variable in cells I3:I20. The formula in cell I3 is as follows:

```
=$G$9+($E$9*B3)+($F$9*A3)
```

This formula is copied and pasted into cells I4:I20. Finally, the following formula is entered into cell G17:

```
=RSQ(C3:C20,I3:I20)
```

Recall that the `RSQ` function returns the R^2 between two variables: the percent of variance that they have in common. In this case, it returns `0.8068`, which is identical to the value returned in cell E11 by the `LINEST` function.

More important, `0.8068` is larger than `.7081`, which is the R^2 between units sold and advertising dollars alone. This means that by combining advertising dollars and sales price as predictor variables, you can explain an additional 10% (80.68% – 70.81%) of the variability in unit sales.

What about the second row in the `LINEST` results, cells E10:G10 in Figure 15.7? These results have to do with the statistical significance, or the dependability, of the regression coefficients. They are the standard errors of the regression coefficients and the intercept. A standard error is a kind of standard deviation. If you divide each regression coefficient by its standard error, the result is what's known as a *t-statistic*. For example, using the data shown in cells F9 and F10 of Figure 15.7:

```
=.3818/.0936
=4.0799
```

The result of the division appears in cell G18 in Figure 15.7. This means that the regression coefficient for Advertising Budget, .3818, is slightly more than four standard errors from zero. Four standard errors is a considerable distance.

> **NOTE** Without a fair amount of experience working with standard deviations and standard errors, it is difficult to know this intuitively. For now, it's okay to take the statement at face value.

Understanding the New T.DIST.RT Function

You can use either Excel's old `TDIST` function or its new `T.DIST.RT` function in Excel 2010, to help determine if you think this ratio is statistically significant. For example, you can enter this formula on the worksheet:

```
=T.DIST.RT(F9/F10,15)
```

This formula returns `.0005`. Let's consider the formula's components one by one:

- `F9/F10` is the ratio of the regression coefficient for advertising dollars to its standard error. Again, this is the t-statistic, and here its value is `4.0799`.
- `15` is the number of degrees of freedom for the t-statistic. It is the number of observations minus the number of terms in the equation. Here, there are 18 observations in

the data set (A3:C20). There are three terms in the equation (one intercept and two regression coefficients), so the degrees of freedom is 18 – 3 = 15. It is the same as the value returned by the `LINEST` function in the second column of its fourth row (see cell F12 in Figure 15.7). Other things being equal, the larger the number of degrees of freedom, the more powerful and sensitive the analysis—and, therefore, the more accurate your estimate can be.

- The `T.DIST.RT` function itself, given its t-statistic argument and its degrees of freedom argument, returns the probability of observing a ratio of the regression coefficient to its standard error as large as this one, if the regression coefficient for the population of similar products were really zero. For this data, the probability is .0005 (or 5 chances in 10,000) of getting a t-statistic greater than or equal to 4.08 if the population regression coefficient were really zero.

> **CAUTION**
>
> It is in cases such as this one that the potential for confusion in the use of Excel 2010's new function names is particularly insidious. The old `TDIST` function returned the area in the t distribution to the *right* of the calculated t-statistic, which is 4.08 in the current example. In contrast, the new `T.DIST` function returns the area in the t distribution to the *left* of the calculated t-statistic. This is the reason that this example uses `T.DIST.RT`, which does have the same effect as the old `TDIST` function, instead of `T.DIST`.

As used here, the function `T.DIST.RT` returns the area in the t distribution to the right of the t statistic. It can also be important to evaluate the t statistic in light of the area to the right of the statistic plus the area to the left of the statistic's negative value: here, the area to the right of 4.08 plus the area to the left of –4.08.

This book does not go into the amount of detail about statistical hypotheses needed to fully explain unidirectional versus bidirectional hypotheses. However, you can use this as a rule of thumb: If you expect, *before you look at the data*, a positive relationship between a predictor variable and a criterion variable, use `T.DIST.RT`, or use `1` as the third argument to the old `TDIST` function. If you don't know which to expect, a positive or a negative relationship, use `T.DIST.2T`, or use `2` as `TDIST`'s third argument. Here, it's reasonable to expect a positive relationship between advertising dollars and unit sales (the more you advertise, the more you sell), so `T.DIST.RT` is used. If you can reasonably expect that the relationship is a positive one, use `T.DIST.RT`, but if you believe that it is a negative one, use `T.DIST`: Doing so makes the statistical test more powerful.

Understanding the Statistical Significance of a Coefficient

Why do you care whether the regression coefficient is significantly different from zero? Consider the implication of a regression coefficient whose value is zero. If you multiply zero by all the values of the associated predictor variable, as you would in the regression equation, you add nothing—zero—to the predicted value of the criterion variable.

Therefore, the predictor variable would be of no use to you, and you might as well leave it out of the regression analysis.

But most people would consider 5 chances in 10,000 good evidence of a statistically significant finding. They would conclude that the regression coefficient is, in fact, nonzero and would retain the predictor variable in the equation. In the current example, they would choose to predict Unit Sales as a function of Advertising Budget. They would then go on to do a t-test on Sales Price to determine whether it also should be retained.

Dealing with Negative Coefficients

Excel's `TDIST` function requires a value greater than or equal to zero as its first argument. It returns `#NUM!` if its first argument is negative. You can get a negative ratio of the coefficient to its standard error if the coefficient itself is negative (neither a standard error nor a standard deviation can ever be negative). A negative regression coefficient can be every bit as informative as a positive one: The coefficient's sign merely indicates whether the relationship is direct (as with advertising dollars and units sold) or inverse (as with sales price and units sold).

The significance level of a regression coefficient is related to whether a *hypothesis* is directional, which you account for in `TDIST`'s third argument. However, the significance level is unrelated to the direction of the relationship between the predictor and the criterion variable. Therefore, to get around `TDIST`'s insistence on a positive value for its first argument, use Excel's `ABS` function, which returns the absolute value of a number. For example:

```
=TDIST(ABS(E9/E10),15,1)
```

Using the new functions in Excel 2010, you arrange a directional test by using `T.DIST` or `T.DIST.RT`. A bidirectional test is arranged by using `T.DIST.2T`. `T.DIST` does not insist on a positive value for its first argument.

If all this seems like a lot of work to you (array-entering `LINEST`, accounting for the order of the regression coefficients in `LINEST`'s results, noting the R^2 value, getting the degrees of freedom, getting the ratio of the coefficients to their standard errors, and using `TDIST`, `T.DIST`, or `T.DIST.RT` correctly), it should. If you want to reduce the degree of uncertainty that surrounds many business decisions, you need to do this sort of analysis—but it can be exacting and tedious.

Using Excel's Regression Add-In

Fortunately, Excel's Regression add-in provides a shortcut that returns all this information (and more) from the choices you make in just one dialog box. Figure 15.8 shows the results of running the Regression add-in on the data in Figure 15.7.

To obtain this analysis, verify that you have loaded the Analysis ToolPak. To do so, follow the instructions given earlier in this chapter in the section titled "Using Confidence Intervals in a Market Research Situation." Open a worksheet that contains the data for Figure 15.7, and follow these steps:

15

Figure 15.8
The Regression add-in automates much of the work involved in a multiple regression analysis.

B5 fx 0.806788499331942

	A	B	C	D	E	F	G
1	SUMMARY OUTPUT						
2							
3	*Regression Statistics*						
4	Multiple R	0.898214061					
5	R Square	0.806788499					
6	Adjusted R Square	0.781026966					
7	Standard Error	14339.43625					
8	Observations	18					
9							
10	ANOVA						
11		*df*	*SS*	*MS*	*F*	*Significance F*	
12	Regression	2	12878999876	6439499938	31.31756507	4.41822E-06	
13	Residual	15	3084291478	205619431.9			
14	Total	17	15963291354				
15							
16		*Coefficients*	*Standard Error*	*t Stat*	*P-value*	*Lower 95%*	*Upper 95%*
17	Intercept	36842.97148	13164.57703	2.798644529	0.013496585	8783.32251	64902.62046
18	Advertising budget	0.381775021	0.093574171	4.079918822	0.00098559	0.182326274	0.581223767
19	Sales price	-358.4634449	129.5278485	-2.767462358	0.014372093	-634.5456884	-82.38120147

1. Click the Data tab on the Ribbon and then click Data Analysis in the Analysis group. In versions prior to Excel 2007, choose Tools, Data Analysis.
2. Select Regression from the Analysis Tools list box.
3. Click OK. The dialog box shown in Figure 15.9 appears.

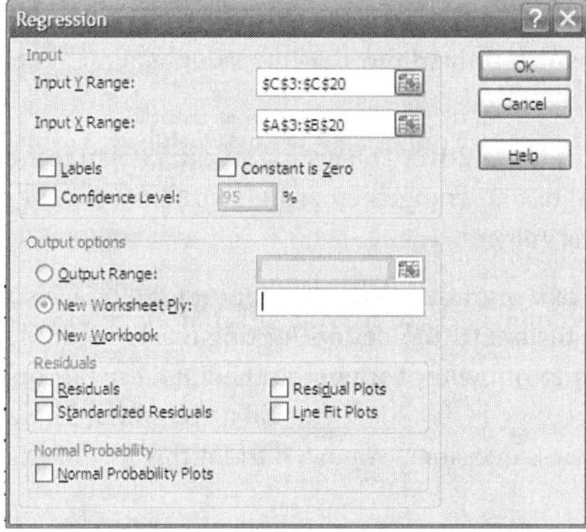

Figure 15.9
With the Regression add-in dialog box, you can specify just a few options to obtain a complete multiple-regression analysis.

4. With the flashing cursor in the Input Y Range edit box, select cells C3:C20 or type the address directly in the edit box.
5. Click in the Input X Range edit box, and select cells A3:B20 or type the address.
6. Make sure that the Confidence Level edit box contains 95 and that the New Worksheet Ply option button is selected.

NOTE There is nothing magic about these settings. Instead, they are simply the ones used to create Figure 15.8.

7. Click OK.

CAUTION

A warning included earlier in the "Using Confidence Intervals in a Market Research Situation" section of this chapter applies here. If you use the Regression tool in the Analysis ToolPak, be careful when you change the Output Options shown in Figure 15.9. Output Range is the default. Whenever you change the selected output option button, the Input Y Range edit box gets the focus. You don't want to inadvertently specify the output range for the input range.

Interpreting Regression Output

Figure 15.8 shows that the Regression output contains plenty of useful information, even though no special options such as residual analysis were used. For example, Figure 15.8's cell B5 shows the R^2 between the units sold and the combination of advertising dollars and sales price. In cell B4, it also shows the multiple R, which, as mentioned earlier, is the square root of R^2. The multiple R is a correlation coefficient, and here it is the correlation between units sold and the derived combination of the predictor variables.

The adjusted R^2, shown in cell B6, takes into account the number of observations and the number of predictor variables. In multiple-regression analysis, when the number of observations is small relative to the number of predictor variables, the R^2 tends to be biased upward. The adjusted R^2 informs you what value you would expect to obtain in another sample of data, one that would have many more observations than the current one does. Compare the actual R^2 with the adjusted R^2. By doing so, you can tell that if this example had been based on, say, 100 observations instead of just 18, the adjusted R^2 would have been only trivially different from the observed R^2.

The formula for the adjusted R^2 is as follows:

$$1 - (1 - R^2) \times ([N - 1] / [N - k - 1])$$

where N is the number of observations and `k` is the number of predictor variables.

NOTE

A discussion of the ANOVA (Analysis Of Variance) table beginning in cell A10 of Figure 15.8 is beyond the scope of this book and would add little to the object of this analysis, the regression coefficients. If you are interested in more information about ANOVA, consult an intermediate text on statistical analysis.

The third section of Figure 15.8 provides detailed information about the terms in the regression equation. The intercept and coefficients are reported, as are their standard errors, and they are identical to those returned by `LINEST`. However, the Regression tool returns them in the same order as they're shown on the worksheet. (`LINEST`'s reversal of the order of the coefficients is the source of much confusion among users. The fact that the

Regression tool returns the coefficients in worksheet order can be reason enough to prefer the tool to the worksheet function.)

The Regression tool also returns the t-statistic for the intercept and for each regression coefficient: Recall that this is the ratio of each term to its standard error. For example, cell D18 in Figure 15.8 reports the t-statistic for Advertising budget as `4.079918822`. This is the same value as shown in Figure 15.7, cell G18, which is `4.0799`. (The apparent difference between the two values is due to the different cell formats).

The P-values reported by the tool are different from those shown in Figure 15.7. There, cell G19 reports the results of the `T.DIST.RT` function for advertising dollars as `0.0005`, whereas the tool reports it as `0.00098559 in cell E18 of Figure 15.8`. The reason for the difference is in the use of `T.DIST.RT`, which specifies using a one tailed test. (See the discussion of `T.DIST`, `T.DIST.RT`, and `T.DIST.2T` earlier in this section.) The analysis in Figure 15.7 used a one-tailed, directional test because the direction of the relationship between the predictor and the criterion was known (or, at least, strongly suspected) before the data was examined.

However, the Regression tool has no way of knowing or suspecting the direction of the relationship before performing the analysis. Therefore, it is programmed to supply a two-tailed test, which is the more conservative choice. If you were to enter the following formula on the worksheet shown in Figure 15.7, it would return `0.00098559`, just as the Regression tool does:

```
=T.DIST.2T(F9/F10,15)
```

NOTE

When you use the `T.DIST` or the `T.DIST.RT` function to run a one-tailed test, it returns a smaller value than if you had used `T.DIST.2T`. The smaller the result produced by each of these functions, the greater the level of statistical significance. Therefore, a larger value is a less compelling reason to retain a predictor variable. Statisticians think of the decision to omit a variable as the more conservative, parsimonious position.

Finally, the tool reports the upper and lower limits of a 95% confidence interval around the intercept and around each coefficient. (See the section on confidence intervals earlier in this chapter for an explanation of their meaning.) Notice that none of the three confidence intervals spans zero: This is as you expect because the P-values are significant beyond the 5% level. If a P-value were .05 or greater, the 95% confidence interval for that term would span zero. In that case, you couldn't conclude at the 95% confidence level that the coefficient in the population is *not* zero.

In this case, you can conclude with 95% confidence that the intercept and regression coefficients are nonzero, that the predictor variables add information meaningfully to the regression equation, and that it's reasonable to predict unit sales from both advertising dollars and sales price.

Estimating with Multiple Regression

So far in the current example, you have found that a meaningful relationship exists between a criterion variable and a set of predictor variables, and you have obtained an equation that expresses the relationship. Now, how do you go about estimating the result of supplying a new value for one or more of the predictors? More specifically, given this regression equation, what unit sales might you hope for in a product whose advertising budget is $200,000 and whose unit sales price is $10?

> NOTE
>
> Again, keep in mind that data-mining efforts such as the one discussed in this example do not put you in a position to infer causation. They are not the result of formal experiments, but they represent convenience samples. They can point the way to possible cause-and-effect relationships, though, and that's their real value. For this reason, the previous paragraph used "hope for" instead of "expect." This is an exercise in estimation, not explanation.

The most intuitive method is simply to apply the multiple-regression equation, with the values for the predictor variables inserted. In this case, you would use the following:

```
=36842.97+(.3818*200000)+(-358.4634*10)
=109613.34
```

If you sold 109,613 units at $10 each, your revenues would be more than $1 million, which might be a good investment.

There are plenty of other tests for the quality of an investment that are discussed in the following chapters of this book:

- Chapter 11, "Examining a Business Case: Investment"
- Chapter 12, "Examining Decision Criteria for a Business Case"
- Chapter 13, "Creating a Sensitivity Analysis for a Business Case," which discusses one preliminary test you might make when you are uncertain of the investment's outcome.

Using Excel's TREND Function

A slightly easier method of applying the multiple-regression equation is to use Excel's `TREND` function. It is *much* easier to use `TREND` to predict when you want to use many predictor values. `TREND` calculates the regression equation, as does `LINEST`, but it doesn't show the regression statistics on the worksheet as `LINEST` does. Instead, `TREND` returns the values you would obtain if you entered the multiple-regression equation itself. Using the equation directly risks making typographical errors, and if you're getting the coefficients directly from `LINEST`, you need to be careful to pair the right coefficient with the right variable. `TREND` does this for you.

For example, suppose that you enter the value **`200000`** in cell A21 and the value **`10`** in cell B21 in the worksheet shown in Figure 15.6. If you then enter the following formula:

```
=TREND(C3:C20,A3:B20,A21:B21)
```

15

it returns `109613.34`. This is the result obtained earlier by entering the regression equation explicitly. In the `TREND` equation, C3:C20 is the address of the range containing the criterion variable, A3:B20 is the address of the range containing the predictor variables, and A21:B21 is the address of the range containing the new predictor variable values that you want to apply.

This might not seem much easier than entering the regression equation explicitly. However, it may be useful if you have 20 pairs of new values to test. If these new values were in A21:B40, you could array-enter this formula in a one-column-by-20-row range:

```
=TREND(C3:C20,A3:B20,A21:B40)
```

In that way, you would obtain all 20 predicted values with one array formula.

CASE STUDY: IMPROVING PROFIT MARGIN

As the product manager for a manufacturer of frames for eyeglasses, you manage a product line composed of 47 different frames. One of your primary responsibilities is to maximize the profit margin that your individual products return.

Your product line includes everything from conservatively designed frames that do little more than hold lenses in place to so-called "designer" frames that are inexpensive to manufacture but are perceived as stylish by the customer.

You have just completed a survey of the retail outlets that market your frames. The survey collected a variety of information about the products and included variables such as retail price, perceived quality of the frames, and satisfaction with the warranty terms that you offer the resellers.

Also available is data on the profit margin for each product, the total of your fixed and variable manufacturing costs, and the share of your total product line achieved by each model.

Relating Variables to Profit Margins

Each of the variables mentioned in the case study could be related in some way to your profit margin. For example:

- A higher average retail price charged by the outlets might mean that you could increase the wholesale price.
- The greater the perceived quality of the frames, the more you might be able to charge for them.
- The greater the frames' actual quality, the more it might cost to manufacture them.
- The more popular frames tend to contribute more to your overall sales—perhaps you could raise the wholesale price on those frames.
- The better the warranty terms, the more it costs you in product replacements, thus reducing your margin.
- The more it costs you to manufacture the frames, the lower your profit margin.

How can you manipulate any or all of these variables to boost profit margins? The price that you charge the retail outlets is under your control, but if you raise some prices, you run the risk that the outlets will promote the less expensive frames—or, worse, will promote frames that your competitors make.

You could modify your manufacturing operations in a way that would reduce the quality of the product and, therefore, make it less expensive to produce. But then the retail outlets might demand a price reduction.

You can't do much about the popularity of a given frame, but if it is a powerful driver of profit margin, you might decide to do nothing about the other variables: Any action you take will likely entail additional cost with no additional benefit.

You might modify the warranty terms or retool your manufacturing operation to reduce costs, but would doing so materially increase your profit margin?

The data that you have collected is shown in part in Figure 15.10.

Figure 15.10
A partial listing of the product data for the multiple-regression analysis shown in Figure 15.11.

A1 fx Profit

	A	B	C	D	E	F
1	Profit	Product	Warranty	Retail	Unit	Component
2	Margin	Quality	Terms	Price	Cost	Share
3	0.99%	1.22	1.24	$130	$35.19	2.08%
4	1.21%	1.45	1.54	$104	$80.00	1.09%
5	2.07%	1.90	1.31	$100	$23.31	2.28%
6	2.14%	2.53	1.36	$164	$80.00	1.44%
7	3.05%	3.41	2.65	$119	$80.00	1.75%
8	3.87%	1.96	1.63	$126	$68.84	1.54%
9	4.78%	2.71	1.66	$128	$80.00	0.47%
10	5.45%	1.76	1.40	$142	$30.32	2.51%
11	5.55%	2.09	2.61	$165	$80.00	2.81%
12	6.42%	1.10	2.42	$124	$32.94	0.59%
13	6.51%	3.62	3.50	$109	$28.56	0.64%
14	6.95%	3.53	1.29	$129	$78.75	1.73%
15	7.24%	2.09	2.44	$165	$38.63	1.83%
16	7.45%	1.54	2.60	$119	$48.67	0.76%
17	8.88%	2.41	2.11	$164	$40.83	0.14%
18	10.08%	3.64	2.06	$146	$80.00	3.53%
19	10.25%	2.61	1.85	$159	$80.00	2.13%
20	10.81%	2.62	2.28	$157	$80.00	3.86%
21	11.09%	3.29	4.07	$178	$80.00	1.28%
22	11.64%	1.24	1.84	$138	$31.20	4.25%

If you run the Regression tool on the data, using profit margin as the y-range and the remaining variables as the x-range, you will obtain the results shown in Figure 15.11.

Figure 15.11
The multiple-regression analysis of product data for eyeglass frames forms the basis for avoiding a useless change in pricing and operations.

	A	B	C	D	E	F	G
1	SUMMARY OUTPUT						
2							
3	*Regression Statistics*						
4	Multiple R	0.71684266					
5	R Square	0.51386340					
6	Adjusted R Square	0.45457845					
7	Standard Error	0.04694102					
8	Observations	47					
9							
10	ANOVA						
11		*df*	*SS*	*MS*	*F*	*Significance F*	
12	Regression	5	0.09549447	0.01909889	8.66768713	0.00001137	
13	Residual	41	0.09034183	0.00220346			
14	Total	46	0.18583630				
15							
16		*Coefficients*	*tandard Erro*	*t Stat*	*P-value*	*Lower 95%*	*Upper 95%*
17	Intercept	-0.11895439	0.04970656	-2.39313270	0.02136750	-0.21933887	-0.01856990
18	Product Quality	0.02980053	0.00767474	3.88293909	0.00036802	0.01430108	0.04529998
19	Warranty Terms	0.00693261	0.00889049	0.77977789	0.44000000	-0.01102212	0.02488734
20	Retail Price	0.00119016	0.00039374	3.02269683	0.00430578	0.00039498	0.00198534
21	Unit Cost	-0.00083227	0.00033930	-2.45288035	0.01851416	-0.00151751	-0.00014703
22	Component Share	0.63455512	0.59762352	1.06179743	0.29454224	-0.57237072	1.84148096

You notice first that there is variation in profit margin associated with variation in the predictor variables. The amount of variation is around 50 percent: the multiple R^2 (labeled *R Square* by the Regression tool) is .51, and the adjusted R^2 is .4546. The difference between the observed R^2 value and the adjusted value is not big enough to make you decide that you have either too many predictors or too few observations. Fifty percent is a useful amount of shared variance. It's not perfect, but at least there's a substantial amount of variation in profit margin that is associated with variation in the predictor variables.

Turning your attention to the analysis of the regression coefficients, you see that product quality, retail price, and unit cost are related significantly to profit margin at the 95% confidence level. The P-values for the t-tests of these three variables are lower than .05, and the 95% confidence intervals do not span zero, as shown in cells E18:G21 in Figure 15.11.

The coefficients for product quality and retail price are positive, so the relationships are direct: For example, the higher the retail price, the higher the profit margin. As expected, the coefficient for unit cost is negative: The higher the unit cost, the lower the profit margin.

This suggests that there might be room to raise the wholesale price that you charge your retailers, given the average retail prices that they charge. There might also be an opportunity to modify your manufacturing operations, simultaneously reducing the product quality a bit and lowering your unit production costs.

Keep in mind, though, that this data comes from a snapshot sample, not from a true experimental design in which you purposely manipulate the independent variables and note the effect of doing so on the dependent variable. The results are suggestive, and it's reasonable to hypothesize that changes in the predictors will influence the criterion variable. But without evidence from a true experiment, it's dangerous to adopt a firm conclusion that changing a predictor will *necessarily* cause a change in the criterion.

Before you undertake drastic measures such as raising prices or modifying your manufacturing operations, you should estimate the effect of doing so on the results you're getting now. Currently, for example, you have one product that has a profit margin of 10.25%. Its unit cost is $80 and its perceived quality is 2.61. What would happen if you found a way to reduce its unit cost to, say, $20 and if the perceived quality of the eyeglass frame fell from 2.61 to 1.30?

Begin by copying its predictor values shown in cells B19:F19 of Figure 15.10 to a blank range such as G19:K19. Change the unit cost in that range from $80 to $20, and change the value of perceived quality from 2.61 to 1.30. Selecting another blank cell, enter this formula:

```
=TREND(A3:A49,B3:F49,G19:K19)
```

The result is 11.84%, about 1.6% greater than 10.25%, your current profit margin for that product. This is not a dramatic increase—certainly, not one that should convince you to invest money in drastic changes to your manufacturing operations or the price you charge your retailers.

This analysis might persuade you to leave well enough alone. But if the analysis had suggested that you could bring about a 5% or 10% increase in profit margin, that might warrant a pilot test. Be sure to design that pilot test to deliberately manipulate the wholesale price and the changes to your manufacturing operations. By doing so, you could later infer real causation. Also make sure that you have a comparison group: products that are manufactured using existing procedures and wholesaled at existing prices.

Summary

In this chapter, you saw how to use information about the variability in an indicator to make decisions about investment options when you do not have perfect information available. In particular, confidence intervals can help you bracket the likely outcome by means of worst- and best-case scenarios, which give you a range within which you can make your decision.

You also saw how to use multiple-regression techniques to analyze data and to estimate the potential effect of a change in such variables as pricing, quality, and component share on an important outcome such as profit margin. Excel provides convenient and powerful tools to assist you in these analyses, but it's necessary to understand the meaning of the results so you can apply them in a way that makes sense.

Fixed Assets

16

IN THIS CHAPTER

Your company probably owns various tangible assets that it uses to help produce revenue. These assets might include buildings, land, manufacturing equipment such as dies and forms, office equipment such as computers, and transportation equipment such as trucks.

Together these assets are known as *fixed assets*. Your financial statements and reports might also refer to them as *plant and equipment* or *property, plant, and equipment*. Your company has other assets, some of which are held temporarily, some of which are intangible, and some of which will be sold to customers.

In contrast to supplies, which are consumed, your fixed assets are regarded as long lasting. In contrast to intangible assets such as name recognition, fixed assets have an objective value. And in contrast to goods that you hold for sale, such as an inventory of products that your company manufactures, fixed assets are not intended for resale.

How you choose to categorize an asset depends not only on the asset itself, but on your line of business. If your company resells computers, you would usually regard a computer component as a unit of inventory. But if your company uses computers to help sell real estate, you would regard the same computer component as a fixed asset.

Your treatment of fixed assets contributes to your company's profitability and worth in two principal ways: setting its original cost and setting its current value. This chapter explores these two processes in detail.

Determining Original Cost

If you acquire a new fixed asset—for example, a telephone system or a new building—you need to account for that asset in your books. The asset's value contributes to your company's worth on its balance sheet. Furthermore, you likely obtained the fixed asset to help you produce revenue over time, and you need to be able to match the asset's cost to the revenue it helps to produce. Therefore, it's important to value the asset accurately so you can assess your company's worth and profitability.

Among the issues involved in determining a fixed asset's original cost are which costs to include, which assets to treat as capital expenses, and whether to use the actual expenditure or its replacement value as the cost of the asset.

Determining Costs

Suppose that you purchase a new computer to help you run your business, expecting that this computer will contribute to the creation of revenue over a period of several years. Figure 16.1 shows the costs involved in acquiring the computer.

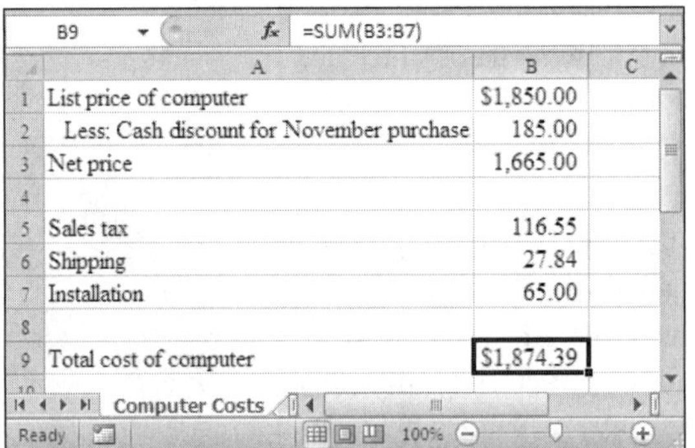

B9 =SUM(B3:B7)

	A	B
1	List price of computer	$1,850.00
2	Less: Cash discount for November purchase	185.00
3	Net price	1,665.00
4		
5	Sales tax	116.55
6	Shipping	27.84
7	Installation	65.00
8		
9	Total cost of computer	$1,874.39

Computer Costs

Figure 16.1
Fixed asset-acquisition costs involve more than just the list price of the asset.

The main portion of the expenditure is the computer's list price. But the list price does not represent the actual cost of the equipment. Suppose that the supplier is trying to clear its inventory of this particular model and offers a cash discount of 10% if a purchase is made before the end of November. You take advantage of this offer, reducing the price from $1,850 to $1,665. A sales tax of 7% applies, increasing the cost by $116.55. Shipping adds an additional $27.84, and you pay a local firm $65 to install the computer and its connection to your company's network.

> **NOTE** The rules about capitalizing and depreciating assets are complicated. It's unlikely that all the rules used in this chapter's examples are the same as all the rules that apply to your company. You should discuss these issues with your accountant; then, when you are sure you understand how the rules work in your case, you can use the techniques described in this chapter to apply them.

These additional costs are not really part of the computer itself. Shouldn't you treat them as expenses for the month of November? No. You should normally treat them as part of the cost of the fixed asset. The reason, again, is the basic principle of matching costs to revenues.

The computer will probably remain in service for several years and will contribute to the generation of your revenue during that time. The ancillary costs are necessary aspects of putting the equipment into service: You cannot use the computer to generate revenue unless you pay the sales tax on it, have it shipped to your place of business, and get it installed. Therefore, these costs should be matched to revenue generated not only this month or this year, but during the entire useful life of the equipment.

If you allocated those additional costs to expenses for the current period, you would understate your net income for that period and overstate it for subsequent periods. You should include all the costs associated with the acquisition of the equipment in its valuation and, by means of the depreciation process, you should allocate those costs against revenue through all the periods that the equipment is worth anything beyond its salvage value.

Should you apply any other costs to the computer's valuation? Possibly. It depends on whether the costs are reasonable and necessary for its use. Suppose that you told the firm installing the computer that it already has a network interface card installed, when it actually doesn't. The technician must make a special trip to obtain additional equipment and charges you extra for this trip. Your accountant might tell you that the extra charge is not a reasonable and necessary cost, and you should not include it as part of the depreciable cost of the asset.

Choosing Assets

Companies often acquire equipment that has a useful life that extends over several accounting periods but that they hesitate to treat as fixed assets. Items such as staplers, postage scales, beverage carafes, and inexpensive office decor all tend to be long lasting (*particularly* the decor) and have an objective value. But the effort the company will make to account for their depreciation usually costs more than the benefit derived from any extra accuracy due to accounting for the assets.

Therefore, it is useful to have a company policy that establishes a minimum cost (for example, $500) for an item before it is treated as a capital expense. Items that cost less are treated as current expenses, even if they are tangible, continue in use over more than one accounting period, and, in theory, represent fixed assets.

Choosing Between Actual Cost and Replacement Cost

Depending on the nature of the fixed asset, as well as the way you put it into service, you might need to use the replacement or market value of the asset to determine its cost, instead of the actual cost of acquisition. If you contribute an asset to the business as capital, this choice can become important.

Suppose that you own a house that cost you $250,000 to purchase and that, after living in it for some time, you convert it to a rental property. For your own business purposes, you might have to value the house at its current market value, which could be $175,000, $425,000, or virtually any other rational figure.

In some cases such as this, the Lower of Cost or Market principle can come into play. This principle, which can apply to inventory valuation as well as to the valuation of fixed assets, states that an item should be valued at either the price you paid for it or the current market value of an identical item—whichever is lower.

But this principle does not apply in all cases. You should check with an accountant to determine whether to use an asset's actual cost, its replacement cost, or the lower of its actual cost or its market value.

The choice of the appropriate valuation method affects both your company's worth on the balance sheet and its earnings on the income statement. Clearly, the greater the asset's valuation, the greater the company's worth. But as you depreciate the asset over its useful life, you will expense a portion of its cost during each accounting period.

The greater the cost of the asset, then, the greater the depreciation expense for any given period of time. Other things being equal, the greater the depreciation expense, the lower your taxable income and the lower your income tax liability.

Theory Versus Practice

This is fine in theory, but in practice, it can be difficult to determine either a replacement cost or the fair market value—and the two are not necessarily the same. Suppose that you want to determine the replacement cost of a personal computer two years into its useful life. Because two years have passed since you acquired the asset, the technology has changed—a computer is not a chair. It's difficult to obtain a price on a computer that is both unused and functionally equivalent to the one you own.

Even if you were able to find several replacement sources for an asset, it could be difficult to determine the market price. When you can get a product from any of several sources, those sources probably quote different prices. Deciding when to stop searching for additional pricing information, which price to adopt as an estimate of market value, whether to average several values as your estimate, and so on can take an amount of effort that isn't justified by the benefits.

Your choices for valuing an asset are also restricted by the tax laws and regulations; for this reason, you should consult an accountant or tax lawyer for advice on how to value any significant asset.

Depreciating Assets

Depreciation, in accordance with the accrual principle, influences the timing of your company's earnings by matching revenues and costs. It is the means by which a company can spread the cost of an asset over its expected useful life. In other words, *depreciation* is the allocation of prior expenditures to future time periods, to match revenues and expenses.

Understanding the Concept of Depreciation

It can be a little tricky at first to grasp the concept of depreciation. (If you feel comfortable with how depreciation works, by all means skip ahead.) Suppose that you write a check on your company's behalf to purchase a $1,000 laptop computer.

The minute the check clears the bank, that $1,000 is gone. You no longer have the cash, and it has been entirely expended during the first accounting period in which the company owns the computer. But you do have a new asset in your Fixed Assets account, worth $1,000. So the value of the company's assets remains the same as a result of the purchase.

Bit by bit, though, the computer loses value. After a month, it's no longer worth quite $1,000, if only because it's used equipment. After six months or a year, it's worth quite a bit less than you paid for it, because its technology is now somewhat out of date, and somebody has spilled Dr. Pepper on the keyboard. Nevertheless, during that time it has contributed in some way to the creation of revenue.

You spread the loss in the computer's value over time by reducing its value bit by bit, by depreciating it on your books, by subtracting some number of dollars from its asset value in your Fixed Asset account. As such, each reduction in the asset's book value is a noncash transaction: The cash is gone when you make the purchase and is replaced on your books by the value of the asset. You use depreciation to reduce the book value of the asset as an offset against the revenue that it has helped generate.

Matching Revenues to Costs

Typically, you make the full cash outlay to purchase an asset during the first year of the asset's useful life. The cash outlay itself doesn't appear in the depreciation line of an income statement. Again, depreciation does not represent a cash outlay: It's a noncash charge that you use to match the first year's expenditure with the subsequent flow of revenue.

Suppose that you match the entire cost of an asset to the earnings shown in the income statement for the year you make the purchase. Your operating income for that year would then be lower than if you spread the cost over the asset's useful life. Furthermore, the following years of the asset's useful life would get a free ride. The asset will contribute to revenue generation, but the income statements in subsequent years wouldn't reflect the associated expense.

NOTE

Although it's a fixed asset, you're not allowed to depreciate land because it's regarded as having an unlimited useful life.

When you depreciate the asset over a period of time, you associate the first year's expenditure with subsequent revenue (see Figure 16.2).

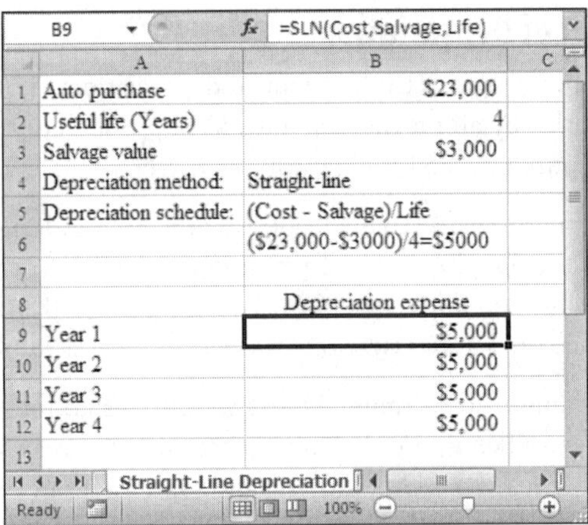

	A	B
1	Auto purchase	$23,000
2	Useful life (Years)	4
3	Salvage value	$3,000
4	Depreciation method:	Straight-line
5	Depreciation schedule:	(Cost - Salvage)/Life
6		($23,000-$3000)/4=$5000
7		
8		Depreciation expense
9	Year 1	$5,000
10	Year 2	$5,000
11	Year 3	$5,000
12	Year 4	$5,000

Figure 16.2 The straight-line method results in an equal amount of depreciation during each period.

Suppose your company purchases a van to pick up materials from your suppliers and to deliver products to your customers. Figure 16.2 shows how the vehicle might depreciate over a four-year period, which, in this example, is the asset's useful life. At the end of that period, the vehicle still has a *salvage* (also termed *residual*) value of, say, $3,000. The salvage value is subtracted from the purchase cost to obtain the amount that is to be depreciated: $20,000. The expense in each of the four years is therefore $5,000. By spreading the depreciable expense equally over the asset's useful life (instead of taking the entire expense during the first year), you can more accurately match the expense to the revenue that the vehicle will help to produce.

> **NOTE** You don't begin in all cases by subtracting the salvage value from the original cost. This is done only in the straight-line and sum-of-years'-digits methods.

If this company has earnings before interest, taxes, depreciation and amortization (EBITDA) of $100,000 annually in goods and services, the effect on pretax income would be substantial. During year 1, without depreciation, pretax income would be $100,000 – $20,000, or $80,000. During year 1, with depreciation, pretax income would be $100,000 – $5,000, or $95,000. The difference between the two calculations is $15,000, or 15% of the company's EBITDA.

Four Items Needed to Figure Annual Depreciation

Four items are needed to determine the annual amount of depreciation:

- The asset's original cost
- The asset's useful life
- The asset's salvage value (its value at the end of its useful life)
- The depreciation method itself

Two general methods are available to allocate an asset's cost over its useful life: *straight-line depreciation* and *accelerated depreciation*. Under the straight-line method, you depreciate the asset by a constant amount each year, as shown in Figure 16.2.

The second general method of depreciation, known as accelerated depreciation, is actually a family of techniques. Each accelerated technique charges more depreciation in the early years of an asset's life and less in later years. Accelerated depreciation does not enable a company to take more depreciation in total; it just alters its timing. Instead of taking, say, 20% of the total depreciation in each of five years, an accelerated method might take 40% in the first year, 20% in the second year, 10% in the third year, and so on.

The basic rationale for accelerated depreciation is the recognition that when an asset is new, it tends to operate more efficiently than after it has been in service for several accounting periods. The assumption is that when the asset operates at a high level of efficiency, its contribution to the creation of revenue is greater than after its efficiency has declined. The timing of the acquisition expense—the depreciation—should reflect the asset's contribution to revenue creation. Therefore, more depreciation should be recognized earlier, and less later, during the asset's useful life.

NOTE

A company is not required to use the same method of depreciation for tax purposes as it does for purposes such as internal planning. Many businesses use an accelerated method in figuring their taxes and use straight-line depreciation when presenting financial information in, say, a pro forma. Again, check with your accountant.

Excel offers several methods to calculate depreciation, which are shown in Figures 16.3 through 16.9 in the next sections.

Using Straight-Line Depreciation

Straight-line is the simplest way to calculate an asset's depreciation. It is the cost of the asset, less its salvage value, divided by its number of periods (usually but not necessarily the number of years) in its useful life.

Excel's `SLN` function returns the amount of depreciation taken each period using the straight-line method. It requires three arguments: the asset's cost, its salvage value, and its useful life. Figure 16.3 shows these values (in named ranges on the worksheet), and the formula used in cells B6:B10 is as follows:

```
=SLN(Cost,Salvage,Life)
```

The `SLN` function is the simplest of Excel's depreciation methods. It takes only three arguments but gives you little control over the amount of depreciation that occurs during any given accounting period. (Of course, that's because the straight-line method itself gives you no option for timing the depreciation amount: It's a constant.)

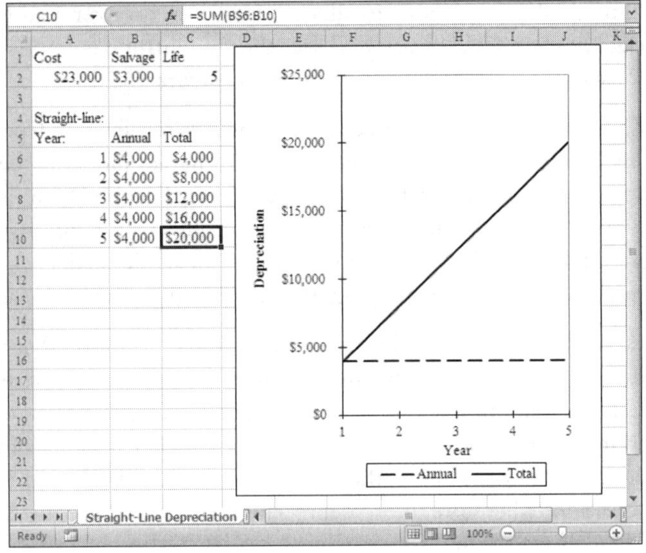

Figure 16.3
The cumulative depreciation taken over time, using straight-line depreciation, describes a straight line.

Using the Declining Balance Method

Figure 16.4 shows depreciation calculated by the *declining balance* method, one of the accelerated depreciation techniques.

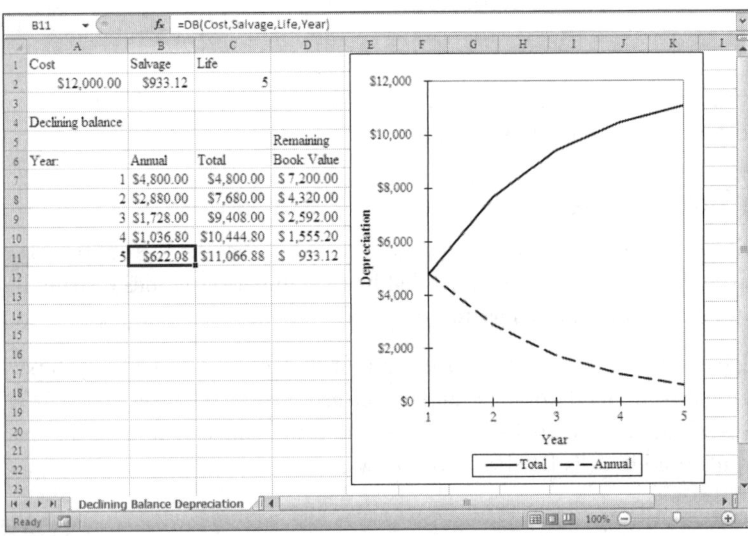

Figure 16.4
The DB function calculates depreciation based on the remaining, undepreciated value of the asset.

Excel's `DB` function returns the amount of depreciation taken each period using the declining balance method. This method calculates the depreciation each period according to the current value of the asset—that is, its remaining undepreciated value. In contrast, the straight-line method (and, as noted later in this chapter, the sum-of-years'-digits method) uses the original value of the asset minus its salvage value to return each period's depreciation. Each cell in the range B7:B11 in Figure 16.4 contains this formula:

```
=DB(Cost,Salvage,Life,Period)
```

The `DB` function requires one more argument than `SLN`. `DB`'s fourth argument is the period for which it calculates the amount of depreciation.

In the example depicted in Figure 16.4, each period is a year, and `Year` refers to the named range A7:A11. The instances of the `DB` function in cells B7:B11 in Figure 16.4 take advantage of the implicit intersection with the `Year` range to specify the `Period` argument. Examples of other depreciation functions in later figures in this chapter also use the implicit intersection to pick up the value of the `Period` argument.

➜See the case study in Chapter 11, "Examining a Business Case: Investment," for a discussion of the implicit intersection and how it is used.

Notice that a different amount of depreciation is taken during each year. The periodic depreciation is higher in the earlier periods. Declining balance, as traditionally defined, uses a depreciation rate that's double the straight-line rate.

In Figure 16.4, a straight-line calculation would depreciate the asset at a rate of 20% per year because the example gives the asset a useful life of five years. The traditional declining balance approach doubles this rate—in Figure 16.4, to 40%. The asset's cost (*not* its cost minus its salvage value, but its full cost) is $12,000, and 40% of $12,000 is $4,800, the depreciation taken during the first year. Subsequent years use the same rate, 40%, with the asset's remaining book value. But as you'll see next, the `DB` function uses 40% in this instance only because the salvage value has been chosen to force that rate.

I recommend that you *not* use the `DB` function to calculate accelerated depreciation and that you instead use either the `DDB` or `VDB` functions, discussed in their own sections later in this chapter. There are several reasons for this recommendation, as described in the following sections.

Avoiding Nonstandard Calculations

The traditional definition of declining balance depreciation in the accounting literature is that the straight-line rate is doubled and applied to the asset's as-yet-undepreciated value. (In fact, the terms "declining balance" and "double declining balance" are often used interchangeably.) But this is not how Excel's `DB` function works. Instead, it uses its `Cost`, `Salvage`, and `Life` arguments to calculate a rate. This can be confusing to someone who is using your worksheet and isn't familiar with `DB`'s idiosyncrasies.

Avoiding Rounding Errors

Excel calculates the rate to only three significant digits; beyond that degree of accuracy, it rounds the rate. This results in differences between the results of the function and the results you would obtain by calculating the depreciation via worksheet formulas.

Avoiding Sudden Acceleration

This is the formula that `DB uses`, according to Excel's Help documentation:

$$\text{Depreciation} = (\text{Cost} - \text{Accumulated Depreciation}) \times (1 - [(\text{Salvage} / \text{Cost})^{(1 / \text{Life})}])$$

If you specify that the `Salvage` value is 0, this portion of the formula:

$$(1 - [(\text{Salvage} / \text{Cost})^{(1 / \text{Life})}])$$

becomes this:

$$(1 - [(0 / \text{Cost})^{(1 / \text{Life})}])$$

To illustrate, suppose that `Life` is four periods. Then, the formula reduces to this:

$$1 - 0^{.25}$$

This equals `1`. (Recall that 0 raised to any power equals 0). Now the full formula becomes this:

$$\text{Depreciation} = (\text{Cost} - \text{Accumulated Depreciation}) \times 1$$

At the end of the first period, there is no accumulated depreciation, so the depreciation for the first period is calculated as the original cost of the asset. The full cost is depreciated in the first period.

Try it yourself, if you like. Enter something like this:

```
=DB(12000,0,5,1)
```

In theory, this returns the first period's depreciation. To get the second period's depreciation, enter this in another cell:

```
=DB(12000,0,5,2)
```

Note that the results are not what people had in mind when they coined the term *accelerated depreciation*.

If you want to look more closely at what's going on with the `DB` function, use this formula in cell B7, as shown in Figure 16.5:

```
=(2/Life)*(Cost - SUM($B$6:B6))
```

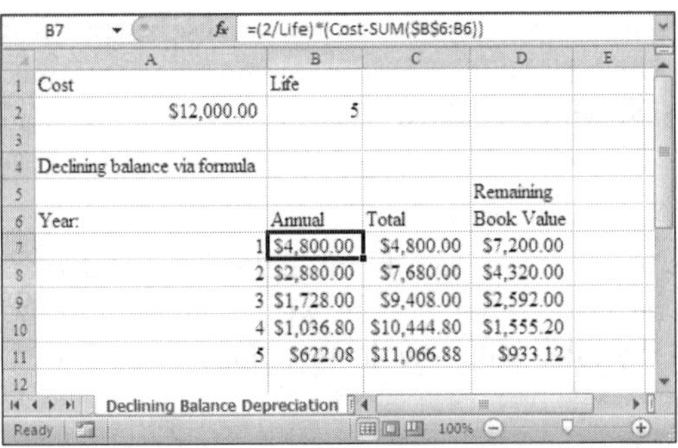

B7 =(2/Life)*(Cost-SUM($B$6:B6))

	A	B	C	D	E
1	Cost	Life			
2	$12,000.00	5			
3					
4	Declining balance via formula				
5				Remaining	
6	Year:	Annual	Total	Book Value	
7	1	$4,800.00	$4,800.00	$7,200.00	
8	2	$2,880.00	$7,680.00	$4,320.00	
9	3	$1,728.00	$9,408.00	$2,592.00	
10	4	$1,036.80	$10,444.80	$1,555.20	
11	5	$622.08	$11,066.88	$933.12	
12					

Declining Balance Depreciation

Ready 100%

Figure 16.5
The remaining book value at the end of year 5 is the same as the salvage value supplied in Figure 16.4.

The formula shows the traditional calculation for double declining balance. You can alter the acceleration of the depreciation by changing the `2` in the formula to some other number. Changing it to `1`, for example, would return the straight-line depreciation amount for the first period (only).

Copy and paste the formula into as many cells in column B as there are periods in the asset's useful life (or even further, if you want). There will be a remaining, undepreciated amount, which is the salvage value.

It's characteristic of traditional declining balance depreciation that the math never fully depreciates the asset, no matter how many periods you use. (This is, by the way, the Achilles Paradox in its purest form.) All that stops the depreciation is the minimum remaining book value—that is, the salvage value—at the end of the asset's useful life. In Figure 16.5, that's the `$933.12` figure in cell D11.

If you use the salvage value, calculated from the traditional formula just given, as the `Salvage` argument to `DB`, you can get `DB` to return the results that the traditional approach to declining balance depreciation would lead you to expect. This was done in the example shown previously in Figure 16.4.

However, if you have an independent estimate of the salvage value of an asset after a given number of years, there's a strong argument for using that estimate as the salvage value rather than calculating it using the traditional formula. (This might be what Microsoft had in mind when it coded the `DB` function.) In that case, you're better off using the `DDB` function or, better yet, the `VDB` function, both of which are discussed next.

Using the Double Declining Balance Function to Calculate Depreciation

The double declining balance (`DDB`) function also calculates accelerated depreciation, but with some differences from the `DB` function. Figure 16.6 shows how you can control declining balance depreciation calculations more effectively using the `DDB` function.

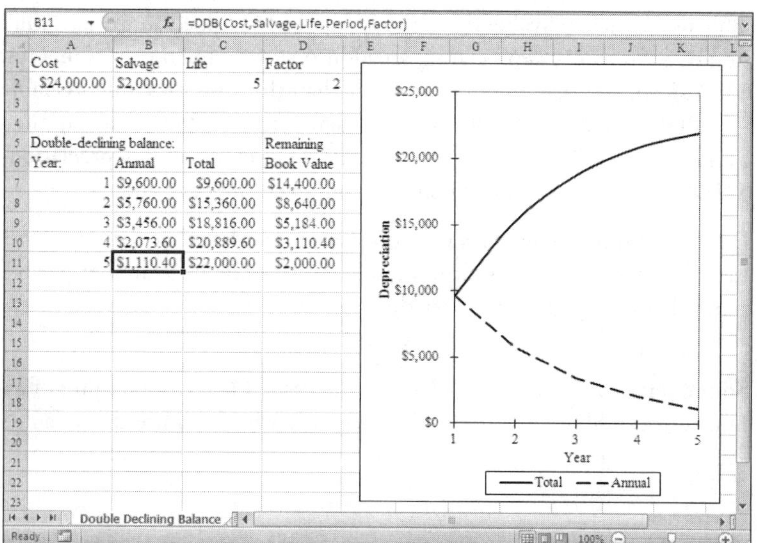

Figure 16.6
The DDB function lets you specify the depreciation rate. Compare to Figures 16.4 and 16.5.

The DDB function used for the data in Figure 16.6 is as follows:

```
=DDB(Cost,Salvage,Life,Period,Factor)
```

DDB doubles the rate that you would depreciate an asset under the straight-line method and applies that rate to the original cost minus accumulated depreciation.

Differences Between DB and DDB Functions

The two chief differences between the DB and the DDB functions are as follows:

- DDB enables you to specify a factor that multiplies the straight-line rate of depreciation. If Life is 5 and you specify 1.5 for Factor, the straight-line rate is 0.2 (that is, 1/5) and the DDB rate is 0.3 (that is, 1.5 × .2). The default value of Factor is 2—hence, *double* declining balance.
- DB uses Life and Salvage arguments together to calculate a rate of depreciation. DDB uses Salvage only to determine where to terminate depreciation. (Your accountant will not allow you to depreciate an asset beyond its assigned salvage value.)

Notice in Figure 16.6 that Life is 5 and Factor is 2. With a 5-period useful life, the straight-line method depreciates at a rate of 0.2 per period (although SLN depreciates Cost less Salvage, not Cost, as does DDB). With a value of 5 for Life and 2 for Factor, DDB depreciates at the rate of 2 × 0.2, or 0.4.

So, again in Figure 16.6, the first period's depreciation is 0.4 × $24,000, or $9,600. For the second period, the undepreciated value is $24,000 – $9,600, or $14,400; 0.4 × $14,400 is $5,760, the second period's depreciation.

This process continues until $22,000 of the original cost has been depreciated: $22,000 is the difference between the original cost and the salvage value. Notice in Figure 16.6 that through the fourth period, $20,889.60 in depreciation has been taken. The remaining undepreciated value is $24,000 –$20,889.60, or $3,110.40.

This undepreciated value times 0.4 is $1,244.16. Added to the accumulated depreciation of $20,889.60, depreciating an additional $1,244.16 results in a total depreciation of $22,133.76. But that amount is greater than the asset's total depreciable amount of $24,000 – $2,000, or $22,000. So DDB does not depreciate $1,244.16 during the fourth period, but $1,110.40 only. That $1,110.40 added to the accumulated depreciation of $20,889.60 equals $22,000, the total allowable depreciation given the Cost and Salvage values.

Excel's DDB function enables you to use a value other than 2 as its Factor argument. For example, if you did not want to double the straight-line rate per period, but instead use 1.5 times that rate, you could enter this:

```
=DDB(Cost,Salvage,Life,Year,1.5)
```

So the term *double declining balance* in the case of DDB is something of a misnomer. The function results in double declining balance only when you use the default value of 2 for the Factor argument.

You can replicate DDB explicitly with simple worksheet formulas. For any period, DDB is calculated as follows:

```
=MIN((Cost-Salvage-Accumulated Depreciation),
    (Cost-Accumulated Depreciation)*Factor/Life)
```

If you examine this formula carefully, you'll see why you should be careful about the relationship between Life and Factor in DDB (and in VDB, discussed in the next section). Suppose that both Life and Factor are set equal to 2. In that case, at the end of the first year, accumulated depreciation is still 0, and the formula reduces to this:

```
=MIN((Cost - Salvage -0),(Cost - 0)*1)
```


Therefore, the result of the formula (and of either the DDB or VDB function) is the difference between Cost and Salvage. In other words, the asset is completely depreciated at the end of the first period, no matter how many periods are in Life. The effect is the same as if you specify 0 for Salvage in the DB function (discussed in the previous section), although the reason for the effect is different.

CAUTION

In both DDB and VDB, make sure that the value you supply for Life exceeds the value you supply for Factor.

Using Variable Declining Balance Depreciation

The variable declining balance (VDB) function is the most flexible (and the most complex) of Excel's depreciation functions. VDB's general syntax is shown here:

```
=VDB(Cost,Salvage,Life,StartPeriod,EndPeriod,Factor,NoSwitch)
```

The Cost, Salvage, Life, and Factor arguments operate in the same way that they do with DDB.

The StartPeriod and EndPeriod arguments enable you to focus on a particular time span during the asset's useful life. For example, to obtain the depreciation on an asset during the first year of a five-year Life, you could use this formula:

```
=VDB(Cost,Salvage,5,0,1,Factor,NoSwitch)
```

Here, using a StartPeriod of 0 and an EndPeriod of 1 specifies a span of time from just before the beginning of the first period until the end of the first period. Neither the StartPeriod nor the EndPeriod argument requires an integer value, so you can use this, for example, to return the depreciation on the asset during the first half of the first period:

```
=VDB(Cost,Salvage,5,0,.5,Factor,NoSwitch)
```

This formula returns the *total* depreciation on the asset that occurs during the second and third periods of its 5-period life:

```
=VDB(Cost,Salvage,5,1,3,Factor,NoSwitch)
```

The NoSwitch argument is a little convoluted. Suppose that you specify a depreciation factor low enough that the asset does not fully depreciate to its salvage value during its useful life. Figure 16.7 illustrates this situation (see cell I16).

B12 f_x =VDB(Cost, Salvage, Life, Period-1, Period,Factor,NoSwitch)

	A	B	C	D	E	F	G	H	I	J	K
1	Cost	Salvage	Life	Factor	NoSwitch		Cost	Salvage	Life	Factor	NoSwitch
2	$24,000	$1,000	10	2	FALSE		$24,000	$1,000	10	2	TRUE
3											
4	Variable declining balance						Variable declining balance				
5			Remaining		"Straight-				Remaining		
6	Year	Annual	Book Value		Line"		Year	Annual	Book Value		
7	1	$4,800	$19,200		$2,300		1	$4,800	$19,200		
8	2	$3,840	$15,360		$1,707		2	$3,840	$15,360		
9	3	$3,072	$12,288		$1,536		3	$3,072	$12,288		
10	4	$2,458	$9,830		$1,404		4	$2,458	$9,830		
11	5	$1,966	$7,864		$1,311		5	$1,966	$7,864		
12	6	$1,573	$6,291		$1,258		6	$1,573	$6,291		
13	7	$1,323	$4,969		$1,242		7	$1,258	$5,033		
14	8	$1,323	$3,646		$1,215		8	$1,007	$4,027		
15	9	$1,323	$2,323		$1,161		9	$805	$3,221		
16	10	$1,323	$1,000		$1,000		10	$644	$2,577		

Variable Declining Balance

Ready 100%

Figure 16.7 Depreciation using VDB: if NoSwitch is FALSE, Excel switches to straight-line depreciation.

This formula is used to return the annual depreciation amounts shown in cells B7:B16 of Figure 16.7:

```
=VDB(Cost,Salvage,Life,Period-1,Period,Factor,FALSE)
```

The depreciation factor is 2, and the NoSwitch argument is FALSE. Setting the NoSwitch argument to FALSE means that VDB switches to straight-line depreciation if and when the straight-line depreciation for that period would be greater than the depreciation under declining balance.

Conditions That Cause a Switch to Straight-Line

Although that latter statement is correct, it's not all there is to the story. Here are the conditions under which the NoSwitch argument comes into play:

- Declining balance depreciation will not fully depreciate the asset given the combination of Life, Salvage, and Factor that you supply.
- The straight-line depreciation for the period exceeds the declining balance depreciation for the period.
- The straight-line depreciation calculated for a period is based on the remaining book value of the asset as of that period—not the original cost—minus the salvage value.

For the analysis in Figure 16.7, the VDB function switches to straight-line depreciation in Period 7, when the periodic depreciation changes to a constant $1,323. The NoSwitch argument is FALSE, so the values shown in B13:B16 are a constant, straight-line $1,323.

Notice a few points:

- The asset is not fully depreciated by the declining balance method. The remaining book value shown in cell I16 of Figure 16.7 is $2,577. To fully depreciate the asset to its salvage value, this example must result in a remaining book value of $1,000 immediately after Period 10.

- At Period 7, the declining balance method calculates depreciation as `$1,258` (cell H13). The remaining book value at the end of Period 6 is `$6,291` (both cells C12 and I12). Four periods remain after Period 6, and straight-line depreciation of the remaining book value of $6,291 is ($6,291-$1,000)/4, or $1,323. That straight-line value, $1323, is greater than the declining balance value at Period 7 of $1,258 shown in cell H13. Therefore, the `VDB` function switches to the straight-line method for cells B13:B16.
- The `VDB` argument `NoSwitch` is `FALSE` in column B, so `VDB` switches to straight-line, and the asset is fully depreciated to its salvage value (cell C16). As noted earlier, if `VDB` does not switch to straight-line depreciation, it does not depreciate the asset to its salvage value (cell I16).

Using Sum-of-Years'-Digits Depreciation

Yet another method of accelerated depreciation, sum-of-years'-digits, is shown in Figure 16.8.

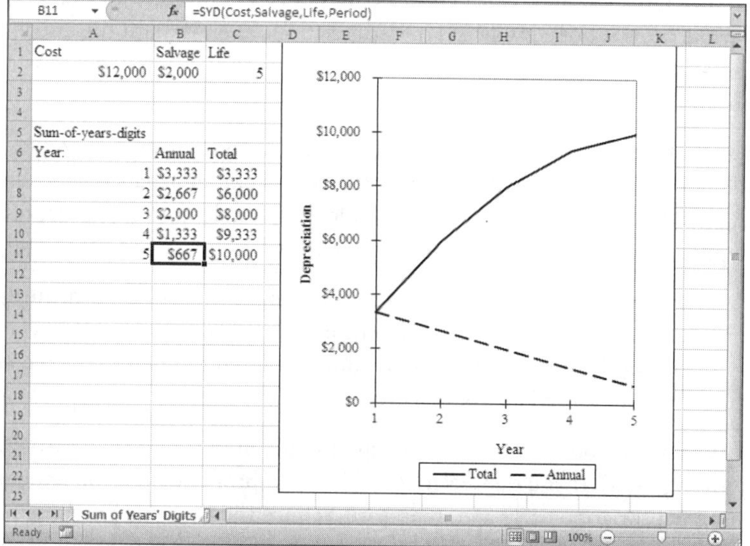

Figure 16.8
The SYD function is easy to understand but gives you little control in situations such as midyear asset purchases.

This method, which is used in Excel's `SYD` function, sums the number of years of the asset's useful life. For example, if the useful life is five years, the sum would be 1 + 2 + 3 + 4 + 5 = 15. Each year, this sum is divided into the *remaining* years of useful life.

For example, after the first year, the fraction would be 4/15; after the second year, the fraction would be 3/15, and so on. The appropriate fraction for each year is multiplied by the difference between the asset's cost and its salvage value, to compute each year's depreciation expense.

The sum-of-years'-digits method is the only approach to accelerated depreciation that fully depreciates an asset to its salvage value without ever needing recourse to straight-line depreciation, as does VDB.

So in Figure 16.8, $2,000 will be taken in depreciation during the third period. At the beginning of Period 3, three periods remain in the asset's useful life (Period 3, Period 4, and Period 5). Three remaining periods divided by the sum of the years digits is 3/15, or 20%. The difference between the cost and the salvage value is $12,000 – $2,000, or $10,000. Twenty percent of $10,000 is $2,000, the amount of depreciation assigned to the third period.

Summary

This chapter discussed the process of valuing fixed assets—usually defined as a company's property, plant, and equipment—for the purposes of determining the company's worth as well as its income for an accounting period.

An asset contributes to the creation of a company's revenue while it is in service. The principle of matching expenses to revenue over time suggests that some portion of the expense involved in acquiring the asset be attributed to the revenue created during an accounting period. This is done by means of depreciation. Even though the entire cash outlay for the asset usually occurs during the first accounting period, this expense is distributed across the useful life of the asset.

Excel offers five functions that calculate depreciation: straight-line (SLN), declining balance (DB), double declining balance (DDB), variable declining balance (VDB), and sum-of-years'-digits (SYD). The latter four methods adopt an accelerated approach, under which more depreciation is allocated early during an asset's useful life, and less is allocated later.

With all these ways to determine depreciation, how do you select the appropriate method? The tax laws allow you to use different methods depending on the type of asset you are depreciating. It's wise to check with your accountant to determine which method you should use for a particular kind of asset.

The depreciation method that you choose has an impact on the earnings that you show for a given period. If you depreciate quickly, early profits tend to be understated; you expense more depreciation early and, therefore, reduce the earnings for those periods. If you depreciate slowly, early profits tend to be overstated because you do not expense as much in earlier periods as you would if you accelerated the depreciation.

This chapter concludes Part III, "Investment Decisions." Part IV, "Sales and Marketing," begins with a discussion of how to import external data into Excel for financial analysis.

Importing Business Data into Excel

17

IN THIS CHAPTER

As you may recall, Chapter 3, "Valuing Inventories for the Balance Sheet," described how a small retail establishment named Evans Electronics keeps track of the number of units and the value of different products in its inventory. That case study mentioned that the company keeps its sales information in a true database file. Evans Electronics imports the information into Excel when it is time to close the books on an accounting period.

Isn't Evans Electronics needlessly complicating things by choosing to bring data into Excel from a database? After all, you can store data in Excel worksheets by means of structures that Excel terms *tables* or *lists*. And Excel provides many approaches to extracting data from lists, from AutoFilter to the various Lookup functions to pivot tables.

That's all true, and for a small application it probably *would* be overkill to involve a true relational database manager, one managed by Microsoft Access, SQL Server, Oracle, or some other system. But managing data isn't what Excel does best. Excel is designed and optimized to synthesize, analyze, and display data. It has some rudimentary database capabilities, and you should use them when your judgment tells you that the trade-off favors simplicity over power.

In the same way, the query language whose dialects are spoken by all standard database management systems has some rudimentary analysis tools: built-in functions such as `Sum` and `Avg`. But if your application requires a straightforward statistic such as the median, you'll want to get Excel involved. Although Access, for example, doesn't calculate the median for you, it's a *lot* better than Excel at data management. (True database management systems make you jump through hoops to calculate this simple and useful statistic.)

The point is that Excel's strengths consist of the calculation of results by means of worksheet functions and the display of data by means of charts and formatted worksheets. The strengths of a database management system consist of the efficient storage, indexing, and retrieval of data.

Perhaps more important, database management systems are designed to be multiuser applications. When you have more than one user who wants to modify the same record, and when those users want to do so simultaneously, the potential for conflicts arises. Good database management systems have the tools to handle these issues—tools that were built in when the systems were designed.

Applications such as Excel also have tools that can help resolve multiuser conflicts. But those tools were added late in the day, tacked onto the application as afterthoughts. They *can't* work as well as tools that are integral to the design of the application. They weren't intended to, and they don't.

Excel does have methods that enable you to integrate it tightly with true database management systems. If you use these methods, you can create systems that leverage the strengths of the database management system as well as those of the worksheet. This chapter covers several of the available methods, including the following:

- Open Database Connectivity (ODBC) via Microsoft Query
- Data Access Objects
- ActiveX Data Objects
- Web queries

Creating and Using ODBC Queries

ODBC is a standard that many data management systems use. If you have an ODBC-compliant data source, such as an Access or SQL Server database, you can import data from it into Excel.

But just because the standard exists and software manufacturers use it doesn't mean that all databases have the same structures. To make sure that these databases can be used in conjunction with other applications, the manufacturers provide *drivers*—in this context, a driver is software that applications such as Excel can use to establish a connection to and communication with the structures in the database, such as tables and queries. After a connection is established, the application can exchange data with the database.

> **NOTE** You can use some methods discussed in this chapter to import data into Excel from a database, or to export data from Excel into a database: ActiveX Data Objects is an example of a bidirectional method. Other methods, such as connections between Excel pivot tables and external databases, support only the transfer of data from the external source into Excel.

Preparing to Import Data

When you install Microsoft Office, the setup routine installs several drivers, including ones for Access, Oracle, dBASE, and SQL Server. Early in the process of importing data from a database into Excel, you need to identify which kind of database you intend to use. This tells Excel which driver it should use to connect with the database.

After you've identified the type of database and driver you want to use, you must provide a *query*. A query is a sequence of instructions written in a standard language called Structured Query Language, often abbreviated as SQL and pronounced either as "sequel" or as "S-Q-L." Those instructions provide information such as what tables should be opened, which fields in the tables are needed, and what criteria to apply, if any, during the retrieval of records.

Microsoft Office comes with a utility named Microsoft Query. Shortly after you start the process of importing data from a database, Microsoft Query starts to run. It helps you design the query that retrieves the records you want from the database. If you plan on importing records into Excel from an external source, you'll find it handy to have Microsoft Query available. If you didn't install Microsoft Query when you installed Office, consider adding it from the Control Panel's Add or Remove Programs or its Programs and Features routine. (Microsoft Query is found in the Office Tools section of Setup.)

After you identify the data source and create the query, the data is automatically imported into Excel. As you'll see, you need to go through this process only once for any given query. Your specifications are saved, and Excel subsequently updates the data so that you can be sure you are using the most current information in the database.

Keep in mind that importing data from a database into Excel is a two-step process: You need to identify a data source and then construct a query. The next two sections provide the details on how that's done.

Specifying Data Sources

Recall that in Chapter 3, "Valuing Inventories for the Balance Sheet," when Evans Electronics closed its books on its first accounting period, it needed to import sales data from its Access database into Excel. It did so to calculate its inventory valuation and cost of goods sold for the period. If you were the store owner, you might have taken the following steps to specify the data source:

1. With an Excel workbook open and a blank worksheet active, click the Ribbon's Data tab and click the From Other Sources drop-down in the Get External Data group. Then select From Microsoft Query from the drop-down list. In Excel versions through 2003, select Data, Import External Data, New Database Query. The Choose Data Source dialog box appears, as shown in Figure 17.1.
2. Select New Data Source from the list box and click OK. The Create New Data Source dialog box appears (see Figure 17.2).

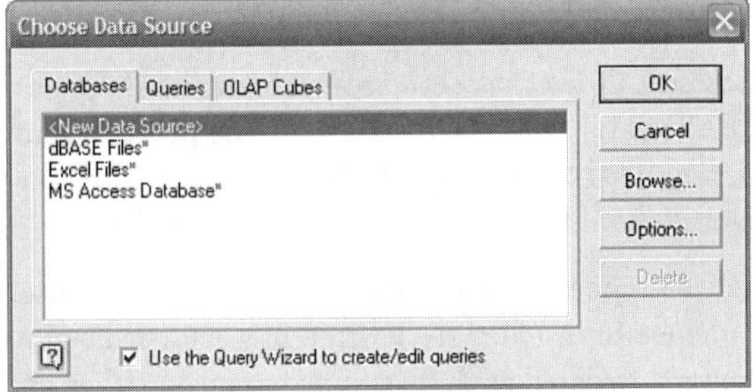

Figure 17.1
The Databases list box contains the names of installed drivers and data sources you have already specified.

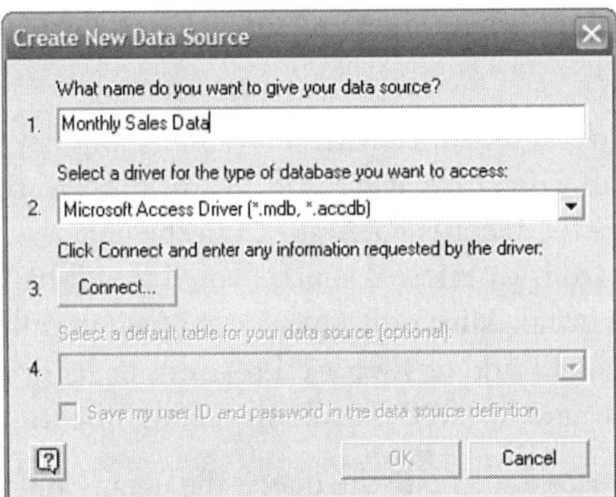

Figure 17.2
Items 2, 3, and 4 become enabled only after you make your selection for each preceding item.

3. Type a descriptive name such as `Monthly Sales Data` in the text box found in item 1. This name appears in the Choose Data Source dialog box the next time it opens.
4. Click the drop-down arrow in the combo box found in item 2. The drop-down list displays the available drivers. For this example, select Microsoft Access Driver (`*.mdb`, `*.accdb`). (Before Access 2007, Microsoft Access databases used the `.mdb` filename extension. Access 2007 and 2010 save databases with `.accdb` and `.accde` extensions, among others.)
5. Click Connect. The ODBC Microsoft Access Setup dialog box appears, as shown in Figure 17.3.
6. Click Select to open the Select Database dialog box, shown in Figure 17.4, and then browse to the database you want to use. In this example, you would browse to `Evans Electronics.mdb` and, if necessary, click its name in the Database Name list box to select it.
7. Click OK to close the Select Database dialog box, and then click OK to close the ODBC Microsoft Access Setup dialog box. You are returned to the Create New Data Source dialog box. Click OK to close it, too. You are returned to the Choose Data Source dialog box, which now shows your newly defined data source in the list box.

TIP

Suppose that the database is located on a network server and it's not convenient to store the database and Excel workbook in the same folder. In that case, it's best to use a Universal Naming Convention (UNC) address instead of a drive letter such as `H:\`. Sometimes drive letters are remapped when servers are added, and no longer point to the location they did when you specified your data source. Your network administrator can give you the UNC address for the server. It will usually have a pattern such as `\\EvansServer\UserData\Sales\`. Type that sequence followed by the database name and extension into the Database Name box, shown in Figure 17.4. A drive letter might change over time, say from `H:` to `S:`, but a UNC is much more stable.

Figure 17.3
In the case of Access, a System Database contains information about database permissions for specific users and groups.

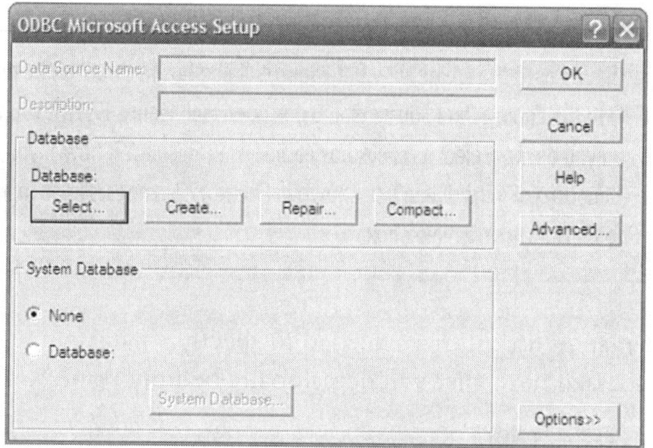

Figure 17.4
In a networked environment, it helps to put the Excel workbook in the same folder as the source database in case a drive letter gets remapped.

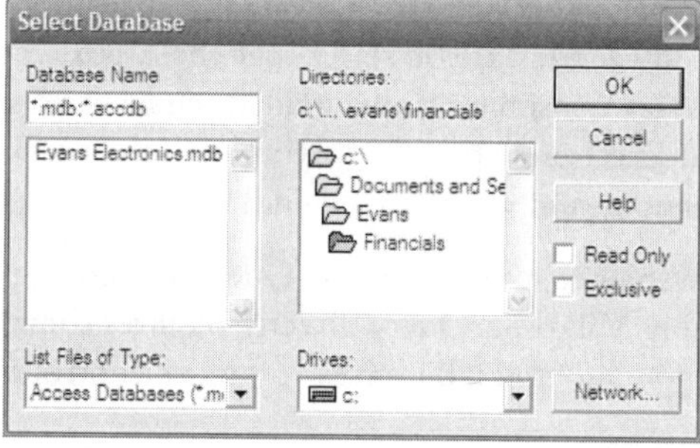

TIP

Notice the combo box in item 4 of the Create New Data Source dialog box (refer to Figure 17.2). When enabled and clicked, it displays a list of the available tables and queries. You can skip this because you will usually be selecting a table (or tables, or an existing query) in the next step.

17

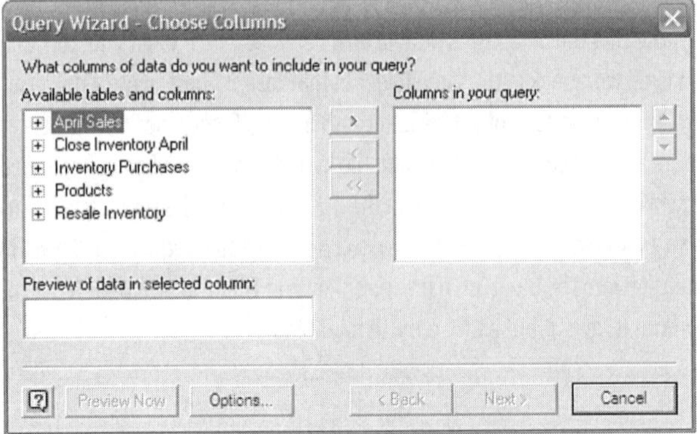

Figure 17.5
Use the Options button to specify that you want to see tables only, views (views is just another term for queries) only, or both.

17

TIP After you have closed the Create New Data Source dialog box in step 7 in the previous set of steps, you still have the Choose Data Source dialog box open (see Figure 17.1). If you want to use the Query Wizard and you did not select its check box earlier, you can select it now. If you do so, the Query Wizard—Choose Columns dialog box, shown in Figure 17.5, appears as soon as you click the OK button on the Choose Data Source dialog box.

The preceding seven steps are all that's needed to specify a data source. The steps skipped a couple of items, discussed next, that will occasionally be important.

Invoking the Query Wizard

In the Choose Data Source dialog box (see Figure 17.1) is a check box labeled Use the Query Wizard to Create/Edit Queries. If you select that check box, you will create the query by using the Query Wizard—similar to the guided sequence of steps in the Chart Wizard found in versions of Excel prior to 2007. If you leave the check box cleared, you will use Microsoft Query directly and will not be guided through the process.

The trade-off is one of convenience for power: The Query Wizard is easier to use but offers less functionality. Using Microsoft Query directly requires some experience, particularly with different ways of joining tables, but gives you more control over the process.

Arranging Insecurity

The Create New Data Source dialog box (see Figure 17.2) has a check box that enables you to save your user ID and password with the data source definition. If your database requires you to supply a user ID and password, you can avoid having to do so every time you query that data source. Just select the check box.

But bear in mind that the data source definition is just an ASCII file. Anyone who knows where to look could open the data source definition with something as simple as Notepad and learn your user ID and password. As you will see in a subsequent section in this chapter, "Working with External Data Ranges," you can save your ID and password in an encrypted format when you work with the query. So it's usually best to leave this check box cleared.

Creating Queries with the Query Wizard

The first major step in importing the external data into Excel is now complete. You have specified your data source. The second major step is to create the query to extract records from that data source. This section describes the process if you choose to follow the Query Wizard's steps. The next section, "Creating Queries with Microsoft Query," shows you how to create queries outside the comfortable confines of the Query Wizard.

Continue the data import process by following these steps:

1. Examine the Available Tables and Columns list box shown in Figure 17.5. If the box to the left of a table such as `April Sales` contains a plus sign, click it to display the columns in that table. (The Query Wizard uses the term *columns* to mean *fields*.)
2. With `April Sales` (or some other table that you choose) still selected, click the > button to move all its columns to the Columns in Your Query list box. If you don't want to include all the columns, select one of them and then click the > button to move it. Because the standard multiple-selection shortcut keys (Shift and Ctrl) do not work here, each item needs to be moved individually. Repeat this process to move any other columns you want to use in your query. Click Next.

> TIP
>
> You can preview the values in the currently selected field by clicking the Preview Now button. If you do so, keep in mind that not all values in the table appear in the Preview of Data in Selected Column box. Only unique values appear there.

3. The Query Wizard—Filter Data dialog box appears, as shown in Figure 17.6. The Query Wizard is not as powerful as Microsoft Query. The wizard enables you to filter on one column only; however, you can specify multiple conditions for that single column. In contrast, Microsoft Query does not limit the number of columns you can use as filters.
4. `April Sales`, selected in step 1 previously, contains only sales made during April. No other filtering is needed, so click Next. The next step in the wizard, the Query Wizard—Sort Order dialog box, appears, as shown in Figure 17.7.
5. It's useful to return the data to Excel sorted first by Product Name and then by Serial Number. Use the Sort By drop-down list to select Product Name, and use the first Then By drop-down list to select Serial Number. This creates a nested sort: records are sorted by Serial Number within each level of Product Name. Click Next.
6. The Query Wizard—Finish dialog box appears (see Figure 17.8), where you can choose to return the data to Excel or view the data in Microsoft Query. Click Finish.

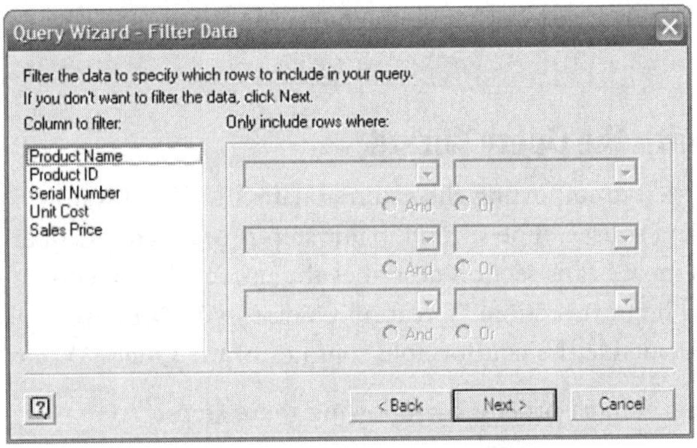

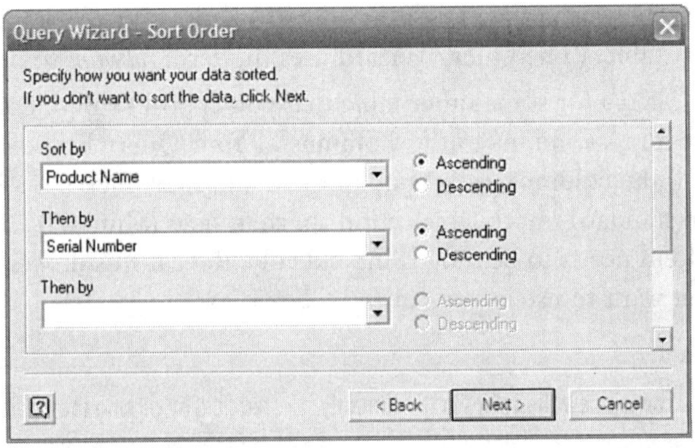

Query Wizard - Filter Data
Filter the data to specify which rows to include in your query.
If you don't want to filter the data, click Next.
Column to filter:
Only include rows where:
Product Name
Product ID
Serial Number
Unit Cost
Sales Price
And
Or
And
Or
And
Or
< Back
Next >
Cancel

Figure 17.6
To filter data is to exclude records that do not meet your selection criterion.

Query Wizard - Sort Order
Specify how you want your data sorted.
If you don't want to sort the data, click Next.
Sort by
Product Name
Ascending
Descending
Then by
Serial Number
Ascending
Descending
Then by
Ascending
Descending
< Back
Next >
Cancel

Figure 17.7
Use the vertical scrollbar at the right of the dialog box to display more sorting combo boxes.

Query Wizard - Finish
What would you like to do next?
Return Data to Microsoft Excel
View data or edit query in Microsoft Query
Save Query...
< Back
Finish
Cancel

Figure 17.8
If you save the query, you create a text file with the location of the data source and the SQL that retrieves the data.

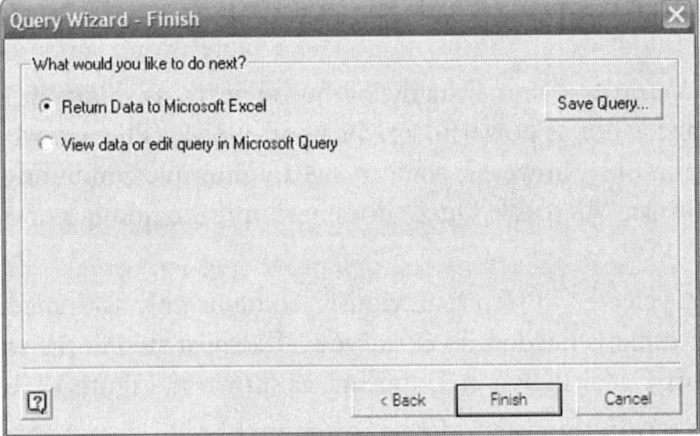

7. The Import Data dialog box appears, as shown in Figure 17.9. Use it to identify where on the active worksheet, on another existing worksheet, or on a new worksheet you want to locate the data. Click OK.

➔See the "Working with External Data Ranges" section of this chapter for information on subsequently fine-tuning the connection to the database.

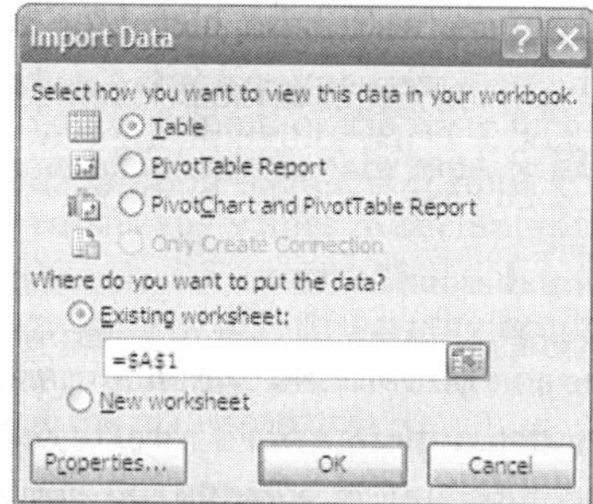

Figure 17.9
Viewing the data in a Table is the best way to diagnose a query that's not working quite right.

8. The data appears on the worksheet, as shown in Figure 17.10.

A1 Product Name

	A	B	C	D	E
1	Product Name	Product ID	Serial Number	Unit Cost	Sales Price
2	Bell DVD Drive	7708	7853	134.23	167.39
3	Bell DVD Drive	7708	344181	134.23	167.39
4	Blue Island Laser Printer	9248	235806	1020.51	1298.31
5	ChromoJet Inkjet Printer	3665	146566	632.52	774.95
6	ChromoJet Inkjet Printer	3665	336457	621.33	774.95
7	ChromoJet Inkjet Printer	3665	563523	621.33	774.95
8	ChromoJet Inkjet Printer	3665	574032	621.33	774.95
9	ChromoJet Inkjet Printer	3665	823942	632.52	774.95
10	Dado Router	4877	66202	100.36	127.02
11	Dado Router	4877	196482	95.32	127.02
12	Dado Router	4877	861710	100.36	127.02
13	Millenium PC P3	6773	139456	1820.88	2130.42
14	Millenium PC P3	6773	160082	1620.88	2130.42
15	Millenium PC P3	6773	383226	1620.88	2130.42
16	Millenium PC P3	6773	816001	1820.88	2130.42
17	Millenium PC P3	6773	876481	1820.88	2130.42

Sheet1

Ready 100%

Figure 17.10
The data appears as an Excel list or table: fields in columns, records in rows, and a header row with the field names and filter drop-downs.

Creating Queries with Microsoft Query

As you become more comfortable with the process of querying a database, you might become impatient with the Query Wizard. You might want to exercise more control over the structure of the query: after all, that's what defines which records are returned, in what order, with which fields, and so on. This section shows you how Evans Electronics returns its April sales data, bypassing the Query Wizard.

You can start Microsoft Query in several ways. One is to start from scratch: Click the Ribbon's Data tab and click the From Other Sources drop-down in the Get External Data group. Then select From Microsoft Query from the drop-down list. In versions of Excel prior to 2007, choose Data, Import External Data, New Database Query.

In the Choose Data Source dialog box (refer to Figure 17.1), clear the check box labeled Use the Query Wizard to Create/Edit Queries. Continue with the data source definition as described in the section titled "Specifying Data Sources" until you click OK on the Choose Data Source dialog box. If the check box labeled Use the Query Wizard to Create/Edit Queries is clear, Microsoft Query appears.

If you're not starting from scratch, you can use Microsoft Query to edit an existing query. Start Microsoft Query as described in the two preceding paragraphs. However, instead of selecting the New Data Source in the Choose Data Source dialog box, select the name of the saved query. Make sure the check box labeled Use the Query Wizard is clear, and then click OK.

NOTE

An existing query is often used to return data to an Excel worksheet, as shown in Figure 17.10, but the query might not have been saved so that you can see its name in the Choose Data Source dialog box. However, the worksheet range that the data occupies, termed the *external data range*, contains the query's definition, unless it has been intentionally removed. To modify the query, you can right-click in the external data range, select Table from the context menu, and then click Edit Query. Prior to Excel 2007, right-click in the external data range, and select Edit Query from the context menu.

Microsoft Query appears, as shown in Figure 17.11.

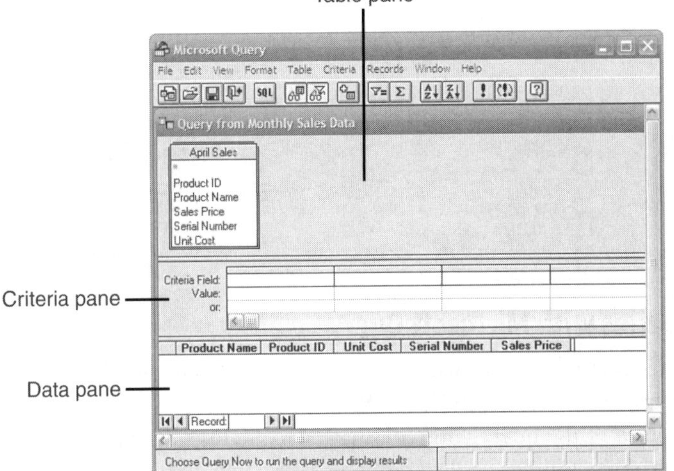

Figure 17.11
If you're creating a new query, the Add Tables dialog box appears automatically when Microsoft Query starts.

The Microsoft Query window includes three panes:

- Put tables and existing queries from the active database into the Table pane. In Figure 17.11, for example, you see `April Sales` in the Table pane.
- Specify the criteria you want to apply to the records in the Criteria pane. This pane does not appear automatically when Microsoft Query starts unless you are editing an existing query that contains criteria. To view the Criteria pane, select View, Criteria.
- Put the fields that you want the query to return into the Data pane. You can drag field names from a table into a Data pane column, double-click a field name in a table, or choose a field name from the drop-down box at the top of the Data pane.

Suppose that it's now the beginning of June and you want to return Evans Electronics' May sales data to Excel. Follow these steps:

1. If a table is visible in the Table pane, remove it by clicking on it and then choosing Table, Remove Table.
2. Select Table, Add Tables to open the Add Tables dialog box, as shown in Figure 17.12.

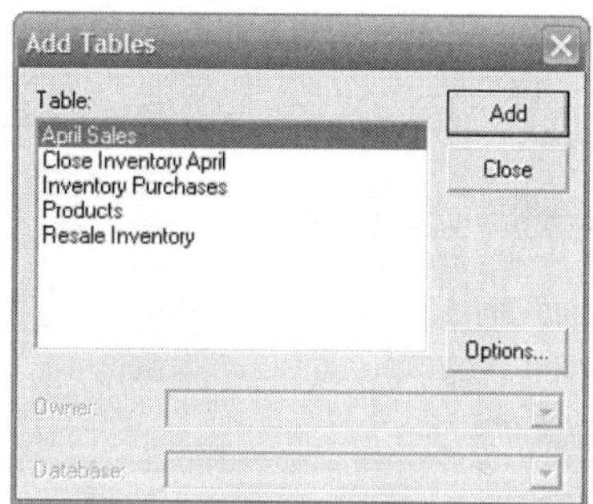

Figure 17.12
The Options button opens a window where you can refresh the list of tables or add queries to the Table list.

3. Click Resale Inventory in the Table list box, and then click Add. Click Products in the Table list box, and then click Add. Click Close. Because `Product ID` is found in both tables and is the primary key in one of the tables, Microsoft Query automatically supplies the join line. See the subsequent section "Using Joins in Microsoft Query" for more information.
4. In the Products table, double-click the `Product Name` field to move `Product Name` to the Data pane.
5. In the `Resale Inventory` table, double-click Date Sold, Product ID, Serial Number, Unit Cost, and Sales Price to move them to the Data pane.
6. If you do not see the Criteria pane, select View, Criteria. When you click in the first column of the Criteria Field row, the cell becomes a drop-down box. Click its arrow to view a list of available fields. Click `Resale Inventory.Date Sold`. It appears in the Criteria Field row as `Date Sold`, no longer qualified by its table name.
7. In the Value row below the criterion Date Sold, type `Between 5/1/2010 And 5/31/2010` and then press Enter. Notice that Microsoft Query surrounds the date values with pound signs as separators.
8. If you want, you can select Records, Query Now to see the records that Microsoft Query will return to Excel. The Microsoft Query window should now appear, as shown in Figure 17.13.
9. Select File, Return Data to Microsoft Excel. The Microsoft Query window closes and, if you're creating a new query, the Import Data dialog box opens. (Refer to Figure 17.9.)

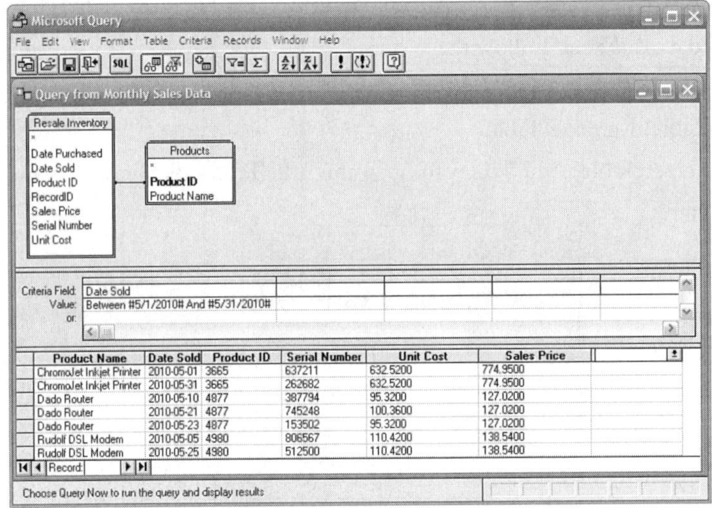

Figure 17.13
Double-click the asterisk at the top of a table to move all its fields to the Data pane.

Consider some of the other actions you might take while Microsoft Query is active. You could add other criteria by putting more field names into the Criteria Field row and appropriate expressions into the Value row. But if you use the Query Wizard, you're limited to one field as a criterion.

You can specify a sort order on one or multiple fields. Click a field name in the Data pane and then click the Sort Ascending (or the Sort Descending) button. To perform a nested sort on multiple fields, arrange the names of those fields contiguously in the Data pane. Click the leftmost field name for the sort, press Shift, and click the rightmost field name; this selects the fields simultaneously. Then click one of the Sort buttons. The records will sort with levels of a column to the right nested within levels of a column to the left. (The Query Wizard does allow you to sort on multiple fields.)

Creating Parameterized Queries in Microsoft Query

Had the owner of Evans Electronics read this book, she would not have found it necessary to create a query to return April sales records and a separate one to return records from May. She would have known that she can create a *parameterized query*, which would prompt her for the range of sales dates she wants to import from the database.

Step 7 in the previous section specified that the criterion for the `Date Sold` field should be entered as `Between 5/1/2010 And 5/31/2010`. Evans can arrange to be prompted for a new range of dates if instead she enters something similar to `Between [Enter the Starting Date] And [Enter the Ending Date]` as the criterion value.

If she does so, Evans can refresh the data whenever she wants, and she will be prompted to enter a starting date (see Figure 17.14).

After entering a starting date such as `5/1/2010` and clicking OK, Evans is prompted to enter an ending date. If she enters `5/31/2010`, the query returns from the database all records

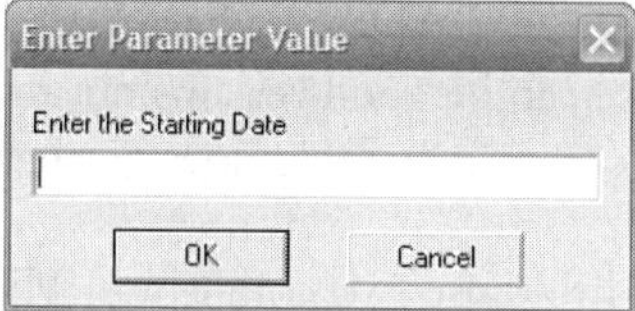

Figure 17.14
A parameterized query can be used repeatedly to return records that meet the user's changing requirements.

whose `Date Sold` field is between May 1, 2010, and May 31, 2010, inclusive. This is more efficient than creating an entirely new query for each accounting period.

The parameterized query is another example of how Microsoft Query gives you more control than the Query Wizard. You can't create a query that prompts you for criteria using the Query Wizard. You can enter something such as `[Enter a Start Date]` in the Filter Data step of the Query Wizard, but if you do, you will get an error message when you click Finish.

Using Joins in Microsoft Query

Notice the dark line that connects the `Resale Inventory` and the `Products` tables in the Table pane in Figure 17.13. It reaches from the `Product ID` field in the `Resale Inventory` table to the `Product ID` field in the `Products` table. The line is termed a *join line* because it shows how two tables are joined. It's not the purpose here to discuss relational database design in much detail, but you'll find it useful to understand a few aspects of joins.

In the Evans Electronics database, the full names of the products are stored in the Products table, along with a product ID—a unique numeric value for each product name. The product ID is also stored in the `Resale Inventory` table. Each time a sale is recorded, the product ID, instead of the product name, is recorded in the `Resale Inventory` table. Many good reasons exist for taking this approach, including data integrity and ease of data entry. By arranging the data entry procedures properly, you can choose a product name on the screen and have that choice recorded as the associated product ID.

Similarly, when it comes time to view the data in a report, you want to see the product name, not just its ID. So you join the table with the ID of the product that was sold, `Resale Inventory`, to the table that contains the product name, `Products`. You join the tables by means of the field they have in common, `Product ID`. When the query runs, it notes the value of `Product ID` in Resale Inventory, finds the corresponding Product Name in the Products table, and returns it to the screen, where you can see it, or to Excel, where you can save it.

Microsoft Query creates the join line for you if the tables meet two conditions:

- The common field (in this instance, `Product ID`) has the same name in both tables. If the fields have incompatible data types (for example, if `Product ID` is stored as text in one table but as a numeric value in the other table), Microsoft Query will draw the join line, but it won't function as intended, and you'll get an error message.
- The common field is the key field (in database jargon, a *primary key*) in one of the tables. A primary key is a field that contains no duplicate values and uniquely identifies

a particular record. Microsoft Query shows a table's primary key in boldface—see the `Products` table in Figure 17.13. (There can be good reasons not to assign a primary key to a table, and in this case the `Resale Inventory` table does not have a primary key.)

If the designer of the database does not fulfill these two conditions, Microsoft Query does not create the join line for you. You can do it yourself by clicking the common field in one table, holding down the mouse button, and dragging to the common field in the other table. When you release the mouse button, Microsoft Query draws the join line between the two fields.

Joins can have powerful effects, and they have a variety of uses beyond the rather simple one described here. Joins are, in fact, the foundation of relational database design. If you find that you frequently want to import data from a database into Excel, you will want to become familiar with the different types of joins and how to use them. A book on Microsoft Access, SQL Server, or Oracle would be a good next step. See www.InformIT.com for a range of choices, as well as articles and other resources that will help you with this topic.

Working with External Data Ranges

When you have imported data into a worksheet, as the previous section described, you have more than just the data set. A new range name is automatically defined and refers to the range of cells defined by the fields and records that were returned. That data range has properties that you can manipulate. You can access the properties before completing the import by clicking the Properties button on the Import Data dialog box (refer to Figure 17.9).

But it's usually best to look at the data before you start changing the range's properties. You can modify the properties after the data has been written to the worksheet. Select a cell in the external data range and then click the Ribbon's Data tab. Click Properties in the Connections group. To view the Connection properties, click the Connection Properties button in the Connection area of the External Data Properties dialog box. See Figure 17.15. In versions that predate Excel 2007, right-click any cell in the external data range and choose Data Range Properties from the context menu.

By setting the external data range properties, you can control how Excel responds to the refresh of data in the range. For example:

Include Row Numbers

This option returns to the worksheet each record's position in the underlying record set. That information is sometimes useful if you want to edit a record in the data source's user interface.

Adjust Column Width

Select this check box to cause column widths to autofit as new data arrives from the data source.

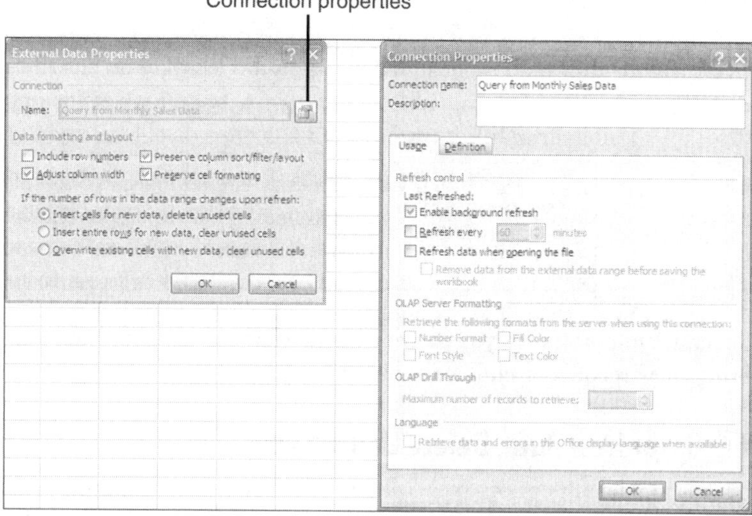

Figure 17.15
The dialog boxes shown are from Excel 2007, which uses two boxes to display the properties that appear in one box in earlier versions.

Preserve Column Sort/Filter/Layout

If this check box is clear, any data filters you have set in the table's columns are removed. The data is sorted according to the order in which it is returned from the data source.

The column layout question is a little more obscure. Suppose your external data range contains a column each for date, product sold and sales price, in that order. Now you revise the database query to include a fourth field, `Sales Territory`, and you set up the query so that territory appears to the left of date.

If the check box is selected, preserving the existing data range's layout, the territory field appears as the rightmost column of the external data range. That is, the existing column layout is preserved, and the new field is tacked on as the rightmost column.

If the check box is clear, the layout is not preserved, the order of the fields in the query governs, and in this example the territory field appears on the left, not to the right of the other columns.

Preserve Cell Formatting

This option causes formats such as fill colors, fonts, and cell borders to survive data refreshes.

The remaining three options can be important if you have data that's outside the external data range but that occupies the same rows or columns as the external data range.

Suppose that you have an external data range that looks like the one shown in Figure 17.16.

Below and to the right of the external data range are values that might stay where they are, be moved, or be overwritten depending on your selection among the next three options. If you are importing data to a report or other document containing data that should remain

Figure 17.16
Excel 2007 and 2010 retrieve data from external sources into tables instead of lists, as in prior versions of Excel.

	A	B	C
1	Product Name	Date Sold	Row 1
2	ChromoJet Inkjet Printer	4/1/10	Row 2
3	ChromoJet Inkjet Printer	4/2/10	Row 3
4	ChromoJet Inkjet Printer	4/3/10	Row 4
5	ChromoJet Inkjet Printer	4/20/10	Row 5
6	ChromoJet Inkjet Printer	4/21/10	Row 6
7	ChromoJet Inkjet Printer	5/1/10	Row 7
8	ChromoJet Inkjet Printer	5/31/10	Row 8
9	Column A	Column B	Row 9
10			

intact, it's important for you to understand what can happen when refreshing the data range brings new records or eliminates old ones.

Insert Cells for New Data, Delete Unused Cells

This is the default option. New cells are inserted as needed into the data range to accommodate additional records. If the refresh results in fewer records, cells that no longer contain data are deleted. Figures 17.17 and 17.18 show the effects of increasing and decreasing the number of records in the range.

Notice in Figure 17.17 that the values in C1:C9 remain in place. Cells were inserted into the data range's columns, pushing the values below the range down from A9:B9 into A11:B11. In Figure 17.18 you can see that the values originally in A9:B9 have been pulled up into A6:B6.

Figure 17.17
If you needed the values `Column A` and `Column B` to share a row with other values, the cell insertion would misalign them.

	A	B	C
1	Product Name	Date Sold	Row 1
2	ChromoJet Inkjet Printer	4/1/10	Row 2
3	ChromoJet Inkjet Printer	4/2/10	Row 3
4	ChromoJet Inkjet Printer	4/3/10	Row 4
5	ChromoJet Inkjet Printer	4/20/10	Row 5
6	ChromoJet Inkjet Printer	4/21/10	Row 6
7	ChromoJet Inkjet Printer	5/1/10	Row 7
8	ChromoJet Inkjet Printer	5/31/10	Row 8
9	Bell DVD Drive	4/4/10	Row 9
10	Bell DVD Drive	4/16/10	
11	Column A	Column B	
12			

Figure 17.18
The deletion of cells can also cause problems. What if you needed the values `Column A`, `Column B`, and `Row 9` to appear in the same row?

	A	B	C
1	Product Name	Date Sold	Row 1
2	ChromoJet Inkjet Printer	4/1/10	Row 2
3	ChromoJet Inkjet Printer	4/2/10	Row 3
4	ChromoJet Inkjet Printer	4/3/10	Row 4
5	ChromoJet Inkjet Printer	4/20/10	Row 5
6	Column A	Column B	Row 6
7			Row 7
8			Row 8
9			Row 9
10			

Because this option inserts and deletes cells, not entire rows, the values in C1:C9 remain where they were.

> **NOTE**
>
> The number of records returned to Excel can vary because of something that's happened in the data source (perhaps a new accounting period has begun) or something that's happened in Microsoft Query (perhaps you have changed the record selection criteria).
>
> Changing the criteria in Microsoft Query has no effect on the default option. Regardless of your selection in External Data Properties, new cells are inserted and unused cells are deleted if you change criteria in Microsoft Query and then refresh the table. Only if the change occurs *in the data source* will your choice of options discussed in this section take effect.

Insert Entire Rows for New Data. Clear Unused Cells

This option causes new records to occupy new rows, not just new cells. Notice in Figure 17.19 that two values originally in C8:C9 have been moved down to accommodate the new rows. In Figure 17.20, the cells that had been occupied by records have not been deleted (the values originally in A9:B9 are still there) but cleared instead.

Figure 17.19
Inserting entire rows to make room for new records can split ranges of cells that you want to keep contiguous.

	A	B	C
1	Product Name	Date Sold	Row 1
2	ChromoJet Inkjet Printer	4/1/10	Row 2
3	ChromoJet Inkjet Printer	4/2/10	Row 3
4	ChromoJet Inkjet Printer	4/3/10	Row 4
5	ChromoJet Inkjet Printer	4/20/10	Row 5
6	ChromoJet Inkjet Printer	4/21/10	Row 6
7	ChromoJet Inkjet Printer	5/1/10	Row 7
8	ChromoJet Inkjet Printer	5/31/10	
9	Bell DVD Drive	4/4/10	
10	Bell DVD Drive	4/16/10	Row 8
11	Column A	Column B	Row 9
12			

Figure 17.20
Clearing unused cells is the only option that is certain not to damage data outside the table.

	A	B	C
1	Product Name	Date Sold	Row 1
2	ChromoJet Inkjet Printer	4/1/10	Row 2
3	ChromoJet Inkjet Printer	4/2/10	Row 3
4	ChromoJet Inkjet Printer	4/3/10	Row 4
5	ChromoJet Inkjet Printer	4/20/10	Row 5
6			Row 6
7			Row 7
8			Row 8
9	Column A	Column B	Row 9
10			

Overwrite Existing Cells with New Data, Clear Unused Cells

Using this option, no cells or rows are inserted to accommodate additional records. The external data range simply extends down the worksheet as far as necessary, overwriting anything that was in cells below the external data range (see Figure 17.21). The result of fewer records is as shown in Figure 17.20.

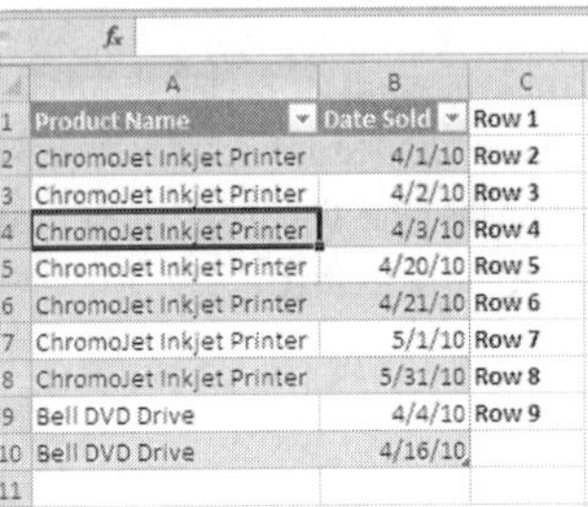

	A	B	C
1	Product Name	Date Sold	Row 1
2	ChromoJet Inkjet Printer	4/1/10	Row 2
3	ChromoJet Inkjet Printer	4/2/10	Row 3
4	ChromoJet Inkjet Printer	4/3/10	Row 4
5	ChromoJet Inkjet Printer	4/20/10	Row 5
6	ChromoJet Inkjet Printer	4/21/10	Row 6
7	ChromoJet Inkjet Printer	5/1/10	Row 7
8	ChromoJet Inkjet Printer	5/31/10	Row 8
9	Bell DVD Drive	4/4/10	Row 9
10	Bell DVD Drive	4/16/10	
11			

Figure 17.21
Notice that this option has overwritten the values `Column A` and `Column B`.

Managing Security Information

When you use Microsoft Query to import data into Excel from an external data source, one of the actions that Microsoft Query takes is to save a new text file with the extension `.dsn`. Some of the information in that text file concerns the security of the data that the query helps to transport. This section discusses how you can keep the data more secure.

The first dialog box that Microsoft Query displays is the Choose Data Source dialog box (refer to Figure 17.1). One of your options there is New Data Source.

If you select that option and click OK, you next see the Create New Data Source dialog box (refer to Figure 17.2). Notice that it has a text box labeled What Name Do You Want to Give Your Data Source? You can't continue until you have supplied a name. Assume that the name you choose is `May 2010 Data`.

When you do continue and identify the location of the data source, Microsoft Query saves a new text file with the extension `.dsn`. So if you name your query `May 2010 Data`, the new text file's name is `May 2010 Data.dsn`. Versions differ, but, by default, Office 2010 saves the `.dsn` file in `C:\Program Files\Common Files\ODBC\Data Sources`.

The `.dsn` file contains information about the data source, such as its location on the disk and the type of driver that the data source uses. You can also choose to have the `.dsn` file save a user ID and password.

In the Create New Data Source dialog box is a check box labeled Save My User ID and Password in the Data Source Definition. Suppose that the query's data source, such as a database, is password protected. When you create the query that imports data from the data source into Excel, you need to supply the password—otherwise, you can't access the data.

If you have selected the Save My User ID and Password check box, Microsoft query saves them both, along with the other information in the `.dsn` file.

Now refer to Figure 17.8 and notice that the Finish step of the Query Wizard contains a button that you can use to save the query. If you click that button, Microsoft Query creates yet another text file, this time one with the extension `.dqy`. The `.dqy` file contains the information in the `.dsn` file, plus the SQL needed to execute your query. If you chose to save the user ID and password in the `.dsn` file, you will have also saved them in the `.dqy` file. Again, versions differ, but Office 2007 and 2010, by default, save the `.dqy` file in `C:\Documents and Settings\AU\Application Data\Microsoft\Queries`. (In that path, `AU` refers to an Authorized User on the machine being used.)

Of course, it's convenient to save that information. If it's saved, you don't need to supply it each time you run the query to get updated data. But it's the rule, not the exception, that information in business databases is sensitive. The information includes employee Social Security numbers and salaries and possibly confidential medical information. If you've taken care to guard the database by means of a password, you've unguarded it by leaving the password strewn around in unprotected text files that can be read by anything from Notepad to Firefox.

NOTE If you're importing data from an Access database, these cautions apply both if you've secured the database (relatively weakly) with a database password and if you've secured it (relatively strongly) with user-level security.

This is where the external data range properties again come in handy. In versions earlier than Office 2007, two of the properties you can set are Save Query Definition and Save Password. To do so, right-click a cell in the external data range and select Data Range Properties. If you select either or both check boxes, that information is saved on the Excel worksheet *in hidden names*. If a snoop can open the workbook, he can see the data that's been returned from the database, but at least he can't tell what the password is. And saving the query definition in this way means that it doesn't need to sit out there unprotected in a `.dsn` or `.dqy` file.

NOTE Both check boxes are selected by default. This means that both a password and the query definition are saved unless you specify otherwise.

You have less control in Office 2007 and 2010. Right-click a cell in the external data range, select Table from the context menu, and then select External Data Properties. Click the Connection Properties button to the right of the Connection Name text box. You now see two dialog boxes, shown earlier in Figure 17.15.

In the Connection Properties dialog box, click the Definition tab. Select the Save Password check box to allow the password to appear in the connection string.

CAUTION

You can expect Excel to warn you about potential weakening of your security arrangements if you select the Save Password check box. The earlier cautions in this section regarding the security of the password still apply. No provision exists for saving and concealing the password in the Excel workbook, as there is via hidden names in versions prior to Excel 2007.

You may not be able to find the password in the 2007 or 2010 workbook itself, but the Definition tab has an Export Connection File button that, if pressed, creates an `.odc` (Office Database Connections) file, by default in `Documents\My Data Sources`. An `.odc` file is pure ASCII, can be opened and read with Notepad, and contains any password that you have set for the external data range. The password will also appear on the Definition tab as part of the connection string.

If it's a serious outcome for someone who's unauthorized to see the data, you should password-protect the workbook as well as the database. One way to protect an open workbook is to click the File tab (in Excel 2007, use the Office button), select Info, and click the Protect Workbook button. This appears to be quite secure, and at the time the current edition of this book was being written, password "crackers" to break into secured 2007 and 2010 workbooks were not being distributed.

NOTE

Earlier versions of Excel did a much poorer job of protecting workbooks via passwords. If you must, select File, Save As. Click the Tools button and select General Options. Supply a password to open the workbook and click OK. Confirm the password and click Save.

That is a relatively weak method because it leaves you vulnerable to password crackers that are both widely available and free. The method used to hash passwords in Excel 2003 and earlier is easily hacked. If I'm working with really sensitive data, my preference is to force the user to supply the correct password for the external data source (by declining to save it with the workbook) and to clear the external data range and resave the workbook before closing it. I do this by means of an `OnClose` event handler written in Visual Basic for Applications.

Arranging Automatic Refreshes

It's possible to waste a lot of time working with a set of data that's not current. One way to prevent this from happening is to update the data automatically. Excel refers to the process of updating the data as *refreshing* it.

You can refresh the data yourself whenever you want. Right-click any cell within the external data range and select Refresh from the shortcut menu, or left-click any cell in that range and select Refresh All in the Data tab.

> **NOTE** If you are working in versions earlier than Office 2007, you can clear the Save Query Definition check box on the External Data Range Properties dialog box. If you do so, Excel removes information about the query from the workbook, and you cannot subsequently refresh the data, either manually or automatically. You need to reestablish the query first. In Excel 2007 and 2010, right-click in the table, then select Table, Unlink From Data Source.

Using the external data range properties, you can arrange for the data to be refreshed automatically. One good way is to right-click a cell in the external data range and select Table from the context menu. Select External Data Properties and click the Connection Properties button. On the Usage tab (refer to Figure 17.15), select the Refresh Data When Opening the File check box. (In versions prior to Excel 2007, mark the Refresh Data on File Open check box on the External Data Range Properties dialog box.)

Next, save the workbook. With that check box selected, each time you open the workbook, the query will run again. This ensures that you are working with all the records in the database that meet your query's criteria at the time that you open the workbook.

If you select the Refresh Data When Opening the File check box, you automatically enable the check box labeled Remove Data from the External Data Range Before Saving the Workbook. This is a convenient way to make sure that you don't leave sensitive data behind.

You might work with a database that contains an extremely large number of records. In that case, the query can take longer than you're willing to wait to return the records to Excel. The problem is that you won't have control of Excel until the query has completed running.

If this happens to you, make sure that the Enable Background Refresh check box is selected. That way, you'll be able to continue using Excel while the query executes. The trade-off is that a background refresh often causes more time to elapse between starting the query and completing it.

Particularly if you're querying from an active database that constantly acquires new data, you might want to refresh Excel's data automatically while you have the workbook open. If so, select the Refresh Every X Minutes check box and use its spinner to set the refresh frequency.

Setting Other Data Range Options

With the records laid out as a row of field names followed immediately by rows of records, with each field occupying a different column—in other words, as an Excel list or table—they are arranged properly for input to a pivot table or a chart. That's why it's usually helpful to see the names of the fields on the worksheet. To add the field names, select the Include Field Names check box.

NOTE

Keep in mind that this applies only to versions through Excel 2003. Excel 2007 and 2010 use the term *table* instead of *list*, and include field names at the top of automatically.

Sometimes database administrators use field names that are more arcane than useful. In that case, consider supplying your own labels on the worksheet and start the external data range below them. Of course, it's your responsibility to make sure that, for example, the field that contains revenue information is the one lined up below your Revenue label.

CAUTION

Selecting the Include Row Numbers check box on the External Data Properties dialog box can be misleading. If you do decide to include row numbers, be aware that many databases start counting at Row 0.

Importing Data to Pivot Tables and Charts

If the eventual destination for imported data is a pivot table or pivot chart, you don't need to import the data into an external data range; you can bring the data directly into the pivot table.

Despite the radically different user interface introduced in Office 2007, this book has attempted to interleave instructions about both the Ribbon and the older menu structure. However, the use of external data sources to build pivot tables is so different since Excel 2007 that we have divided the discussion into two sections.

Bringing External Data into Pivot Tables Using Excel 2007 and 2010

If you're using Excel 2007 or 2010, the following steps will bring data from an external source into a pivot chart, which is accompanied by a pivot table:

1. Click the Ribbon's Insert tab. Click the PivotTable drop-down in the Tables group, and then select PivotChart from the drop-down menu. The PivotTable Wizard's first step appears, as shown in Figure 17.22.

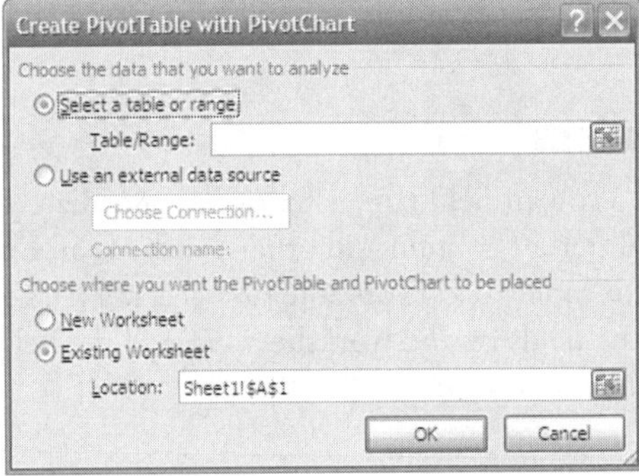

Figure 17.22
If your source data is in an existing table or range, identify it by name or by address in the Table/Range box.

2. Select the Use an External Data Source option and click the Choose Connection button. All the data connections that Excel can find are shown in the Existing Connections dialog box, as shown in Figure 17.23.

NOTE The instances of [Blank] in the Existing Connections dialog box represent each connection's description. You can supply a description by clicking the Ribbon's Data tab and then choosing Connections in the Connections group. In the Workbook Connections dialog box, click Add to add a new connection. You can also select an existing connection and then click the Properties button to supply a description for the connection. That description subsequently appears in the Existing Connections dialog box, shown in Figure 17.23. A concise, thoughtful description can help you choose which connection to use, or you might decide that you need to create a new connection, as explained earlier in this chapter in the section titled Creating and Using ODBC Queries.

Figure 17.23
The connection name appears on the pivot table dialog box after you have chosen the connection you want to use.

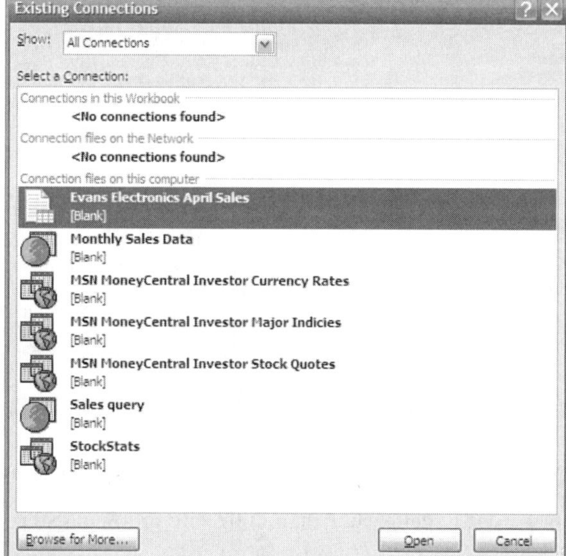

3. After selecting a connection, click Open to return to the Create PivotTable with PivotChart dialog box, and then click OK to return to the workbook—which now appears as shown in Figure 17.24.

4. To get a pivot chart that displays total sales dollars by product sold, select the check boxes for the `Product Name` field and the `Sales Price` field in the PivotTable Field List dialog box, shown in Figure 17.24. The pivot table and the pivot chart then appear, as shown in Figure 17.25.

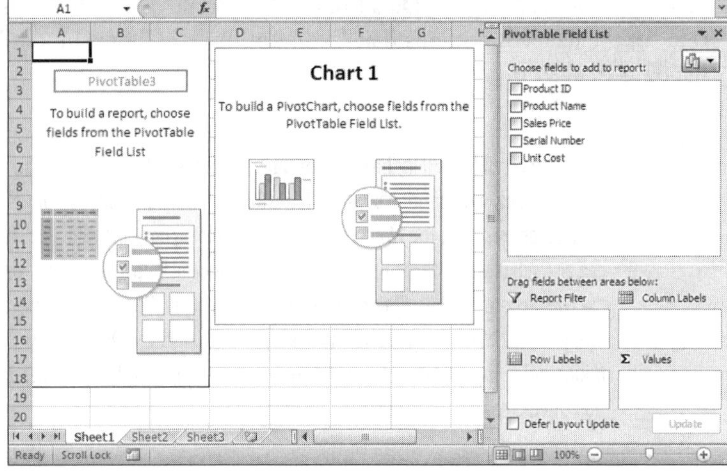

Figure 17.24 One way to create the chart is to drag the `Product Name` field into the Axis Fields area and to drag the `Sales Price` field into the Values area.

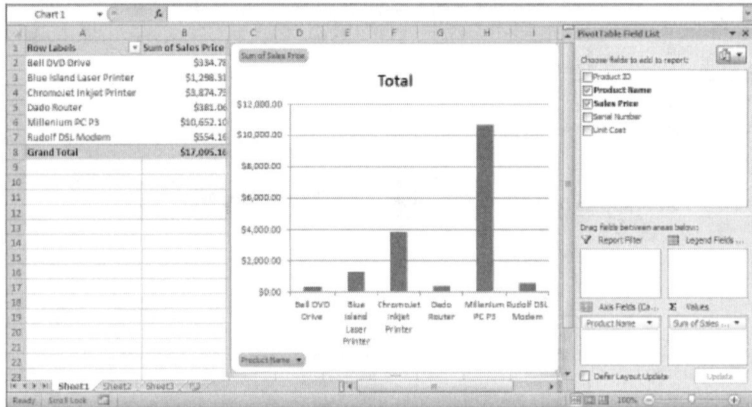

Figure 17.25 The pivot chart's default type is a Column chart, as shown.

Bringing External Data into Pivot Tables Using Versions Prior to Excel 2007

If you're using a version of Excel earlier than 2007, the following steps create your pivot chart:

1. Select Data, PivotTable and PivotChart Report. The PivotTable Wizard's first step appears, as shown in Figure 17.26.
2. Select the External Data Source option and, for this example, select PivotChart (with PivotTable). When you click Next, the wizard's second step appears, as shown in Figure 17.27.
3. When you click Get Data, the Choose Data Source dialog box appears. You saw this dialog box in Figure 17.1. In fact, the entire process from this point is identical to that illustrated in Figures 17.1 to 17.13, from defining a new data source (or using an existing source) to defining the query (or, again, using an existing query).

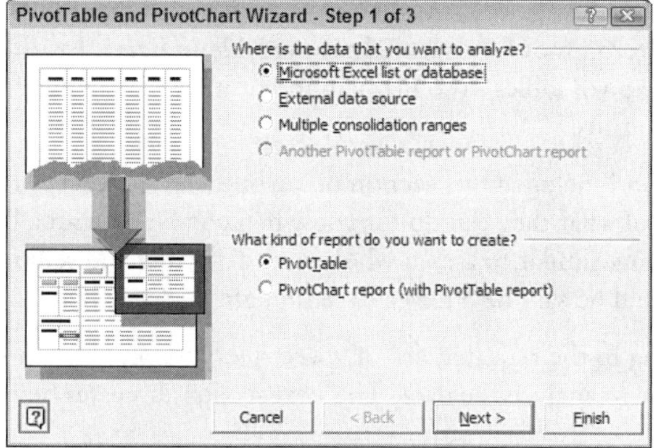

Figure 17.26
The pivot chart report must initially be accompanied by a pivot table, but you can delete the table later, if you want.

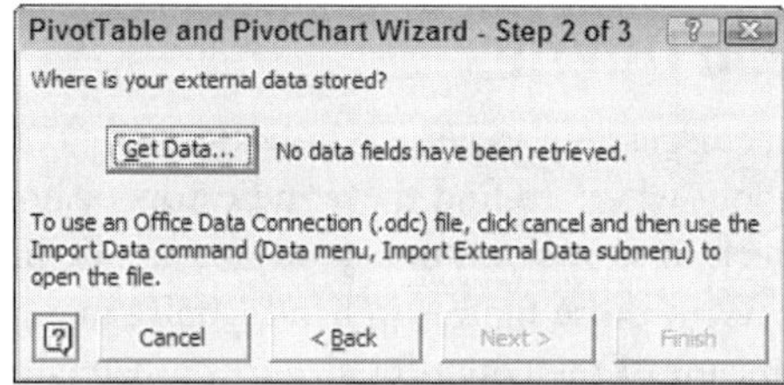

Figure 17.27
The wizard's second step has this appearance only if you use an external data source.

4. At the end of the process, you dismiss Microsoft Query by choosing File, Return Data to Microsoft Excel (or you dismiss the Query Wizard by clicking Finish). Instead of seeing the Import Data dialog box, you see the PivotTable Wizard's second step. At this point, you can click Next to get to the third step if you want to set options, or just click Finish to return to Excel.

The pivot chart appears, ready for you to locate the fields, as shown in Figure 17.28.

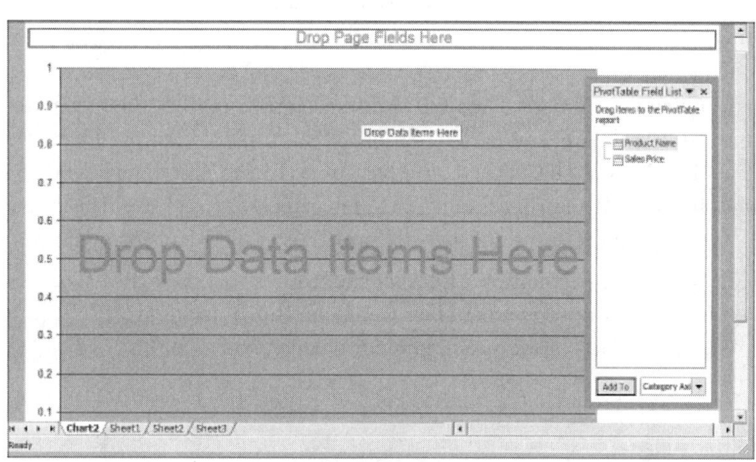

Figure 17.28
Drag the `Product Name` field into the Category Fields area, and drag the `Sales Price` field into the Data Items area.

17

I am uncomfortably aware that this book has little to say about pivot tables, which I regard as the most powerful tool for data analysis available in Excel. I wish there were more room. But you can use pivot tables in so many different ways that an entire book is really needed to do the topic justice.

The main reason I included this section on pivot tables, however brief, is to give you at least a glimpse of what they can do for you when combined with a little imagination. I showed something similar to a man who's been designing and selling software for more than 30 years, and he said he'd never have thought of doing that.

He was referring to the repeated use of a web query to populate an Excel table and then to use a pivot table to analyze the data. The next section discusses how to set up web queries using Excel.

Creating and Using Web Queries

Chapter 7, "Ratio Analysis," discusses a variety of indicators of a company's financial status. It does not go into detail about where to find those indicators or how best to get them into an Excel worksheet. This section shows you one good way to obtain financial statistics for publicly traded companies. With those figures in hand, you're in a position to compare your company with another by means of the common-sizing approach described in Chapter 6, "Statement Analysis."

A web query is a special kind of query. It obtains data not from a database, but from web pages, which are usually constructed using Hypertext Markup Language (HTML) or Extended Markup Language (XML). Web queries return data from the web page directly to your Excel worksheet.

NOTE To do this, you need Excel 2002 or a later version and a web connection. If you have those, you're ready to go. You can also create and use web queries using Excel 2000, but the process doesn't enable you to manipulate the web page you're interested in.

1. Click the Ribbon's Data tab and select From Web in the Get External Data group. (In Excel 2003 and earlier, choose Data, Import External Data, New Web Query.) The New Web Query dialog box opens to the Home page you've specified for your browser. If Internet Explorer (IE) is installed, Excel uses IE's home page even if you're using another product such as Firefox as your default browser. See Figure 17.29.
2. Type your destination's URL in the Address box and click Go, or select it from the Address drop-down list. The web page shown in Figure 17.29 contains a table with stock names, latest quote, percent change, and so on.

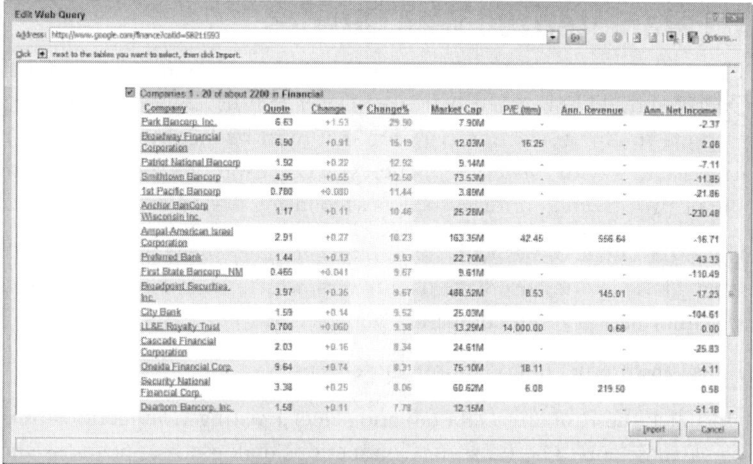

Edit Web Query

Address: http://www.google.com/finance?catid=58211593

Click next to the tables you want to select, then click Import.

Companies 1 - 20 of about 2200 in Financial

Company	Quote	Change	▼ Change%	Market Cap	P/E (ttm)	Ann. Revenue	Ann. Net Income
Park Bancorp, Inc.	6.63	+1.53	29.90	7.90M	-	-	-2.37
Broadway Financial Corporation	6.90	+0.91	15.19	12.03M	16.25	-	2.08
Patriot National Bancorp	1.92	+0.22	12.92	9.14M	-	-	-7.11
Smithtown Bancorp	4.95	+0.55	12.50	73.53M	-	-	-11.85
1st Pacific Bancorp	0.780	+0.080	11.44	3.89M	-	-	-21.86
Anchor BanCorp Wisconsin Inc.	1.17	+0.11	10.46	25.28M	-	-	-230.48
Ampal-American Israel Corporation	2.91	+0.27	10.23	163.35M	42.45	556.64	-16.71
Preferred Bank	1.44	+0.13	9.93	22.70M	-	-	-43.33
First State Bancorp., NM	0.466	+0.041	9.67	9.61M	-	-	-110.49
Broadpoint Securities, Inc.	3.97	+0.35	9.67	488.52M	8.53	145.01	-17.23
City Bank	1.59	+0.14	9.52	25.03M	-	-	-104.61
LL&E Royalty Trust	0.700	+0.060	9.38	13.29M	14,000.00	0.68	0.00
Cascade Financial Corporation	2.03	+0.16	8.34	24.61M	-	-	-25.83
Oneida Financial Corp.	9.64	+0.74	8.31	75.10M	18.11	-	4.11
Security National Financial Corp.	3.38	+0.25	8.06	60.62M	6.08	219.50	0.58
Dearborn Bancorp, Inc.	1.58	+0.11	7.78	12.15M	-	-	-51.18

Import Cancel

Figure 17.29
Use the Options button in the upper-right corner to manage data import settings.

> **NOTE** In the upper-upper- left corner of Figure 17.29, notice the square with the arrow inside it pointing right. It is termed an icon, somewhat unhelpfully, and there are as many of them visible as there are discrete tables in the web page. Their purpose is to indicate the location of the tables that you can import, and they are located at the upper-left corner of those tables. When you click one, its arrow turns into a check mark, and its background, originally a bilious yellow, turns a bilious green to indicate that it has been selected for import.

3. When you have finished selecting tables by clicking their icons, click the Import button at the bottom of the dialog box. Excel imports the data into your worksheet (see Figure 17.30).

A1 fx Companies 1 - 20 of about 2200 in Financial

	A	B	C	D	E	F	G	H
1	Companies 1 - 20 of about 2200 in Financial							
2	Company	Quote	Change	Change%	Market Cap	P/E (ttm)	Ann. Revenue	Ann. Net Income
3	Guaranty Financial Group Inc.	0.025	0.004	19.05	2.72M	-	996	78
4	Broadway Financial Corporation	6.9	0.91	15.19	12.03M	16.25	-	2.08
5	Cascade Financial Corporation	2.12	0.25	13.37	25.75M	-	-	-25.83
6	Crescent Banking Company	0.68	0.08	13.33	3.62M	-	-	-31.05
7	Patriot National Bancorp	1.92	0.22	12.92	9.14M	-	-	-7.11
8	1st Pacific Bancorp	0.78	0.08	11.44	3.89M	-	-	-21.86
9	PVF Capital Corporation	2.87	0.29	11.24	22.90M	-	-	-20.12
10	Smithtown Bancorp	4.86	0.46	10.45	72.20M	-	-	-11.85
11	Broadpoint Securities, Inc.	3.98	0.36	9.94	489.75M	8.55	145.01	-17.23
12	Ampal-American Israel Corporation	2.89	0.25	9.47	162.23M	42.16	556.64	-16.71
13	Anchor BanCorp Wisconsin Inc.	1.16	0.1	9.43	25.04M	-	-	-230.48
14	LL&E Royalty Trust	0.7	0.06	9.38	13.29M	14,000.00	0.68	0
15	Preferred Bank	1.43	0.12	9.17	22.55M	-	-	-43.33
16	Oneida Financial Corp.	9.64	0.74	8.31	75.10M	18.11	-	4.11
17	City Bank	1.57	0.12	8.28	24.75M	-	-	-104.61
18	Security National Financial Corp.	3.38	0.25	8.06	60.62M	6.08	219.5	0.58
19	Frontier Financial Corporation	3.75	0.27	7.76	1.77M	-	-	-89.74
20	Epoch Holding Corp	10.4	0.72	7.44	230.61M	30.45	31.16	5.86
21	Seacoast Banking Corporation of Florida	1.5	0.1	7.14	79.27M	-	-	-45.71
22	Ladenburg Thalmann Financial Services	0.94	0.06	6.82	157.81M	-	120.97	-20.26

Sheet1

Ready 100%

Figure 17.30
Like most external data ranges, this information updates when you right-click in it and select Refresh Data.

Using Parameterized Web Queries

The section earlier in this chapter titled "Creating Parameterized Queries in Microsoft Query" showed how you can create queries that have one or more parameters. A parameter prompts you for a selection criterion that must be met by any records it returns to Excel. It's a useful way to run a query when you don't want to change anything about it other than one or two selection criteria such as accounting period or sales region.

Microsoft Office comes with some Internet query files that have the filename extension `.iqy`. These queries also have parameters, which make them handy for returning from the web information about companies you specify.

To use an Internet query, follow these steps:

1. Click the Ribbon's Data tab and select Existing Connections in the Get External Data group. The Existing Connections dialog box appears, as shown in Figure 17.31. Using Excel versions prior to 2007, choose Data, Import External Data, Import Data to display the Select Data Source dialog box. Versions earlier than Excel 2007 offer routes to new connections by way of the New Source button in the Select Data Source dialog box.

Figure 17.31
Use the Existing Connections window to invoke any existing database or Internet queries.

2. Select either MSN MoneyCentral Investor Currency Rates or MSN MoneyCentral Investor Major Indicies (*sic*), depending on whether you're interested in currency exchanges or stock index figures. Click Open.
3. The Import Data window appears (refer to Figure 17.9). Correct the cell reference, if necessary, and click OK. The Internet query returns the data to Excel. Figure 17.32 shows an example of the stock index query results.

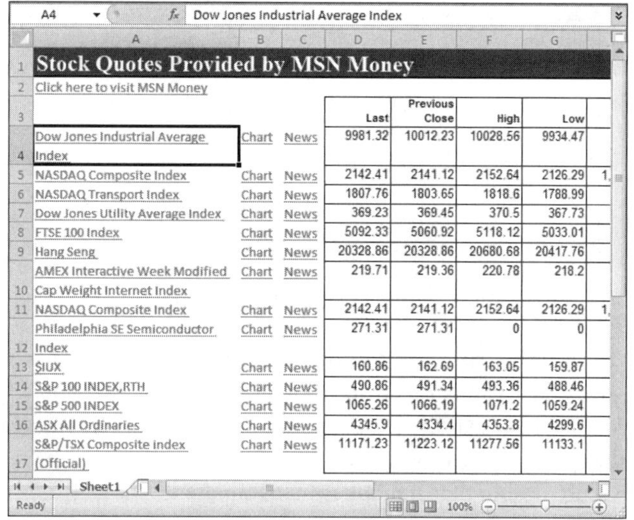

A4 | Dow Jones Industrial Average Index

	A	B	C	D	E	F	G	
1	Stock Quotes Provided by MSN Money							
2	Click here to visit MSN Money							
3				Last	Previous Close	High	Low	
4	Dow Jones Industrial Average Index	Chart	News	9981.32	10012.23	10028.56	9934.47	
5	NASDAQ Composite Index	Chart	News	2142.41	2141.12	2152.64	2126.29	1,
6	NASDAQ Transport Index	Chart	News	1807.76	1803.65	1818.6	1788.99	
7	Dow Jones Utility Average Index	Chart	News	369.23	369.45	370.5	367.73	
8	FTSE 100 Index	Chart	News	5092.33	5060.92	5118.12	5033.01	
9	Hang Seng	Chart	News	20328.86	20328.86	20680.68	20417.76	
10	AMEX Interactive Week Modified Cap Weight Internet Index	Chart	News	219.71	219.36	220.78	218.2	
11	NASDAQ Composite Index	Chart	News	2142.41	2141.12	2152.64	2126.29	1,
12	Philadelphia SE Semiconductor Index	Chart	News	271.31	271.31	0	0	
13	$IUX	Chart	News	160.86	162.69	163.05	159.87	
14	S&P 100 INDEX,RTH	Chart	News	490.86	491.34	493.36	488.46	
15	S&P 500 INDEX	Chart	News	1065.26	1066.19	1071.2	1059.24	
16	ASX All Ordinaries	Chart	News	4345.9	4334.4	4353.8	4299.6	
17	S&P/TSX Composite index (Official)	Chart	News	11171.23	11223.12	11277.56	11133.1	

Sheet1

Ready 100%

Figure 17.32
Click one of the Chart hyperlinks to see a 52-week chart of that index's performance.

NOTE

If all the Get External Data buttons are dimmed, the active cell is likely part of an existing external data range. The data might have been cleared away, but the range name and the underlying query are still in place. Click the drop-down arrow in the Name box to display any range names.

If you see one that could represent an external data range, click it to select it; click the Ribbon's Home tab and then click the Clear button in the Editing group. Select Clear All from the drop-down list. You will see a warning message that asks if you want to remove the query along with the data range. Assuming that you want to do so, click Yes. The Get External Data buttons should now be enabled.

The MSN MoneyCentral Investor Stock Quotes Internet query has some different features. Begin by entering a stock ticker symbol, such as PG for Procter Gamble, in a worksheet cell. Then click the Ribbon's Data tab and select Existing Connections in the Get External Data group. Select MSN MoneyCentral Investor Stock Quotes and click Open. You see the Import Data window. Adjust the cell reference if necessary, and click OK.

After retrieving the data, you can right-click in the data range and select Parameters to change your selection criteria. You'll see the dialog box shown in Figure 17.34.

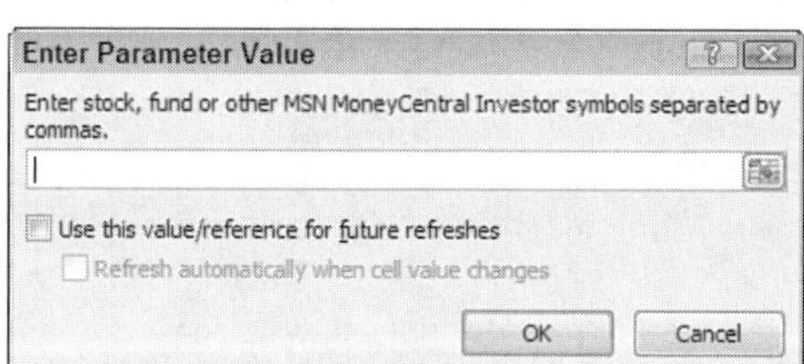

Figure 17.33
The stock ticker symbols are not case sensitive in this dialog box.

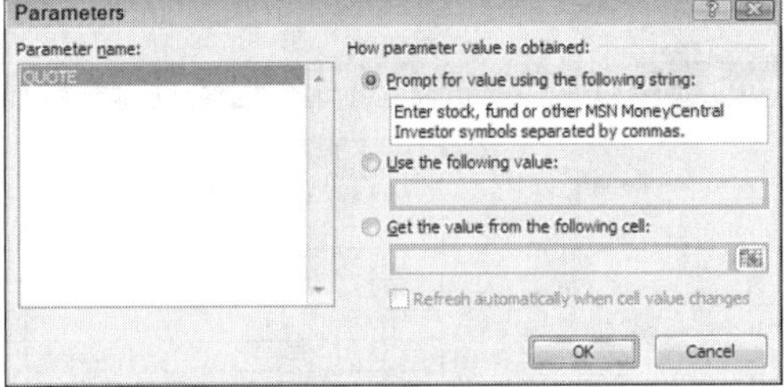

Figure 17.34
The Parameters dialog box is available only for queries that use runtime criteria.

You have three options. Your choice controls how the data is subsequently refreshed.

- **Prompt for Value Using the Following String**—This option is similar to the parameterized query that Evans Electronics created. Suppose that you select this option and type a prompt such as `Enter a Ticker Symbol`. Later, when you refresh the data, you will see that prompt and a box where you can enter a new ticker symbol. The query will be executed using that symbol as its parameter.
- **Use the Following Value**—If you select this option, its box becomes enabled, and you can type a ticker symbol into it. The query automatically returns data for that symbol.
- **Get the Value from the Following Cell**—One way to begin the web query process is by entering a stock ticker symbol in a worksheet cell. If you have done so, select this option button, click in the associated box, and then click in the worksheet cell where you entered the symbol. The query returns data for the symbol in the cell. If you also select the check box labeled Refresh Automatically When Cell Value Changes, you can bypass the Refresh Data command. Simply enter a different ticker symbol in that worksheet cell and the query automatically executes, using the new symbol as its parameter.

Summary

In this chapter you have read about several Excel and Office tools that you can use to return data from external sources, such as relational databases and websites, to Excel objects, such as worksheet tables and pivot tables. You have worked through the two step process of acquiring data via ODBC: the definition of a data source and the development of a query that specifies the data you want. Various security issues were discussed, including issues you must attend to if you want to protect an external data source from unauthorized access.

The flow of information is reversed in the next chapter, which shows you how to populate an external data source with worksheet data without leaving the Excel application.

Exporting Business Data from Excel

18

Throughout Chapter 17, "Importing Business Data into Excel" you saw various ways to get data into Excel workbooks from websites, databases and other applications. This chapter shows you how to reverse the process: to move data that you have in an Excel workbook to a database.

IN THIS CHAPTER

Using VBA to Update an External Database

The reasons you may want to move data from an Excel workbook to a database involve both user convenience and technical issues. Many people find an Excel worksheet a familiar, even intuitive work environment, but they feel at a complete loss when working directly with a database program.

Of course, many database programs present information to the user in a grid that looks similar to an Excel worksheet, with rows and columns. But in a technical sense, the tables are very different. In a database program such as Microsoft Access, the rows *always* represent records—for example, people, products, or transactions—and columns *always* represent variables—for example, a person's Social Security number, a product's name, or a transaction's income account number.

The Excel worksheet is much less rigid. Although Excel lists and tables require the same structure as a database, you might have many other uses for rows and columns; this flexibility is one reason some people are more comfortable with the worksheet.

Suppose you wanted to create a monthly calendar in Excel. It's easy enough to let the first column represent Sundays, the second Mondays, and so on. And you can let four or five rows represent the weeks in the month. Put the number of the day in each cell's upper-left corner by setting the cell's alignment format.

You can't do these things in a database because it's not primarily intended to be a display mechanism. But the attractive and functional display of information is one of Excel's great strengths.

Still, if you handle things right, you can provide a user with the comfortable and flexible Excel interface, and use that interface to move data directly into a database—for a variety of reasons the database might be the more sensible place to store the data. Arranging the data transfers requires some ability to program in Visual Basic for Applications (VBA), a BASIC dialect. Chapter 17 shows how Evans Electronics can move data from a database to Excel. This chapter demonstrates how Evans can use VBA to move data the other direction, from its Excel workbook to an Access database.

Getting at VBA

Before Evans Electronics can use VBA, it needs to establish a window where it can enter the VBA code that will perform the tasks. Using versions of Excel prior to 2007 it's not necessary to do anything special before opening Excel's Visual Basic Editor. Just choose Tools, Macro, Visual Basic Editor to open a window that has all the coding tools you need. See Figure 18.1.

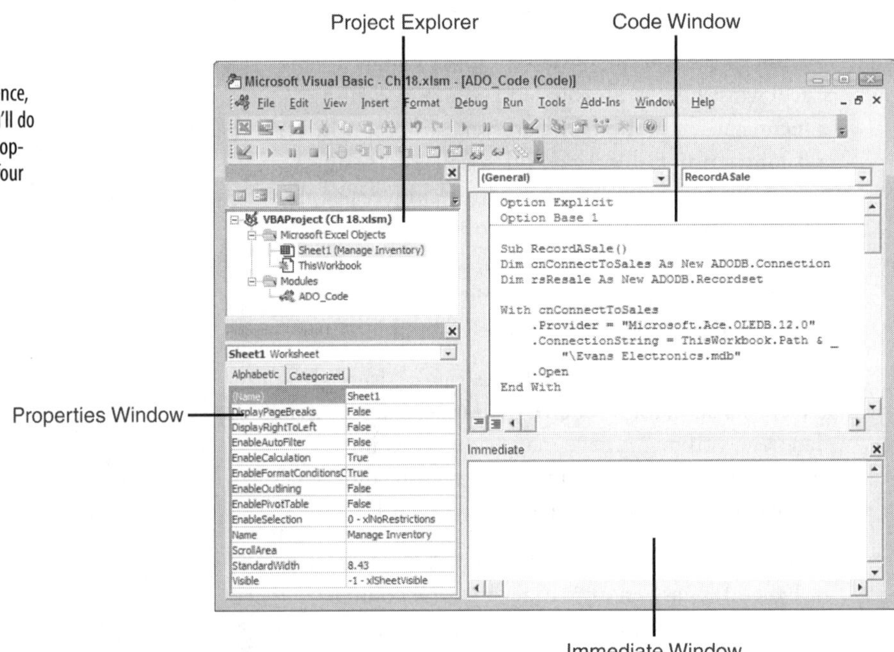

Figure 18.1
With some experience, you'll find that you'll do most of your development work in the four windows shown.

Using Excel 2007 or 2010, there's a little more work to do up front. The Ribbon has a Developer tab that you use to manage VBA code, add-ins, and controls such as check boxes and drop-downs. The Developer tab is not placed on the Ribbon by default. You can arrange for it by taking these steps:

1. Click File, Options.
2. Click Customize Ribbon in the list on the left side of the Excel Options window.
3. Find the Developer item in the Main Tabs list on the Customize the Ribbon window. Select its check box, and click OK to return to the workbook.

You will now find the Developer tab on the Ribbon. Click it, and then click the Visual Basic button in the Code group to open the window shown in Figure 18.1.

> **TIP** The keyboard combination Alt + F11 is a quick way to get to the Visual Basic Editor without using menus or the Ribbon. I find it particularly useful when I have a client on the phone who needs to do something in VBA: telling the client to press Alt + F11 is a lot faster than talking through the steps to activate the Developer tab.

Structuring the Worksheet

With access to the Visual Basic Editor established, Evans continues by creating the worksheet shown in Figure 18.2.

Evans uses cells B12:E12 to enter the sales information. Each cell in that range has been named: `Product_ID`, `Serial_Number`, `Date_Sold`, and `Sales_Price`. Evans uses the table at the top of the sheet as a reminder of the numeric Product ID that's associated with the product name.

In Chapter 3, "Valuing Inventories for the Balance Sheet," you saw that Evans uses specific identification as the method of inventory valuation and wants to uniquely identify a particular item sold. Therefore, the company needs to supply both the Product ID number and the serial number. Suppose that, by coincidence, both a Rudolf DSL modem and a Bell DVD drive have the same serial number. Given only the serial number, the database will not be able to reliably locate the specific item that was sold—but given the unique combination of a Product ID and a serial number, it's possible to do so.

	A	B	C	D	E
1		Product Name	Product ID		
2		ChromoJet Inkjet Printer	3665		
3		Dado Router	4877		
4		Rudolf DSL Modem	4980		
5		Millenium PC P3	6773		Record Sale Now
6		Bell DVD Drive	7708		
7		Blue Island Laser Printer	9248		
8					
9					
10		ID Number of Product Sold	Serial Number	Date Sold	Sales Price
11					
12		4980	1161	9/24/10	$ 195.00

Figure 18.2
The worksheet provides a convenient place for Evans to record data that describes a sale.

Establishing Command Buttons

After entering the information, Evans clicks the Record Sale Now button. That button is associated with the VBA code that is described shortly; clicking the button runs the code that moves the data from the worksheet to the database.

As you've probably come to expect, there are two ways to establish the button on the worksheet, depending on what version of Excel you're using. In Excel 2007 and 2010, click the Developer tab and then the Insert button in the Controls group. You'll see that there are two sets of controls: one labeled Form Controls and one labeled ActiveX Controls. Each includes a Button icon. Click one of them and then, holding down the mouse button, drag through any convenient area of the worksheet to establish an initial size and location for the button.

In Excel versions through 2003, choose View, Toolbars and then choose either Forms or Control Toolbox from the cascading menu. Again, both toolbars have command buttons. Click a command button icon and establish it on the worksheet by clicking and dragging.

The controls on the Control Toolbox are termed ActiveX controls in Excel 2007 and 2010, and the controls on the Forms toolbar are termed Form controls. Which set of controls, Form controls or ActiveX controls, should you use to get your command button?

Compared to ActiveX controls, Form controls are somewhat easier to design, largely because they have fewer properties to set. There's no functional difference from the point of view of the end user.

My tendency is to use the Forms command button if it's the only kind of control I want to put on the worksheet, just because it's quicker to set up. If I'm also going to put other controls such as combo boxes or scrollbars on the sheet, I use the ActiveX controls, partly for consistency and partly because I prefer to have a broader range of properties available.

Whichever type of command button you choose, you need to associate it with VBA code that runs when the button is clicked: there's little point in putting a command button on a worksheet if nothing happens when it's clicked. If you've used a Forms button, right-click it after you have established it on the worksheet. Select Assign Macro from the shortcut menu, and select the macro you want to run from the list of existing macros. Of course, this means that you'll have to enter the code into the Visual Basic Editor before you can associate it with the command button.

If you've used an ActiveX button, you can right-click it and select Assign Macro just as you would a Forms button. In this case, though, you'll be automatically transported to the Visual Basic Editor and confronted with an empty subroutine named `CommandButton1_Click`. Type the name of the macro that you want to run into that subroutine, and then close the Editor.

The reason that Assign Macro takes you to an empty subroutine is that ActiveX controls have default events associated with them: for example, clicking an ActiveX command button automatically fires its Click event, and choosing an item in an ActiveX combo box automatically fires its Change event. In turn, these events cause any code associated with them to run, and you can supply that code in the empty subroutine that appears when you select Assign Macro from an ActiveX control's shortcut menu.

In summary, a Forms control such as a command button can be associated directly with code that you have written. But an ActiveX control already has an On Click or an On Change subroutine associated with it, and you'll have to use that subroutine to call the code that you have written.

NOTE

As recently as the mid-1990s, Excel still came with an obscure, arcane, underpowered macro language. That language was abandoned in favor of VBA in Excel 95, and code that used to be called a "macro" became known as a "procedure," a "subroutine," or a "function." But the term "macro" had worked its way into the Excel menu structures and survives even in the radical redesign of the user interface represented by the Ribbon. It may be confusing at first, but keep in mind that when you see the term "macro" in Excel's user interface, it refers to VBA code, which uses the terms "subroutine" and "function."

Editing the Record's Values

Here is a fairly brief subroutine (or, using VBA terminology, "sub") that Evans could attach to a command button and that would sweep sales data from the worksheet into the company database.

18

Notice that the sixth statement specifies a database with the file extension `.mdb`, which indicates a Microsoft Access database created using Office 2003 or earlier. The directions given here are written so that the code can be used equally well with an Access database from Office 2007 or 2010, indicated by an `.accdb` file extension.

```
Sub RecordASale()
Dim cnConnectToSales As New ADODB.Connection
Dim rsResale As New ADODB.Recordset

With cnConnectToSales
    .Provider = "Microsoft.Ace.OLEDB.12.0"
    .ConnectionString = ThisWorkbook.Path & "\Evans Electronics.mdb"
    .Open
End With
rsResale.Open "Select * from [Resale Inventory]", cnConnectToSales, _
     adOpenForwardOnly, adLockOptimistic

With ThisWorkbook
  rsResale.Filter = "[Serial Number] = " _
     & .Names("Serial_Number").RefersToRange.Value _
     & " And [Product ID] = " _
     & .Names("Product_ID").RefersToRange.Value
  If rsResale.EOF Then
     MsgBox "Couldn't find that item in the database."
  Else
     rsResale.Fields("Date Sold") = .Names("Date_Sold").RefersToRange.Value
     rsResale.Fields("Sales Price") = .Names("Sales_Price").RefersToRange.
  Value
     rsResale.Update
```

```
    End If
  End With

  End Sub
```

Let's walk through the code:

The first line, `Sub RecordASale()`, just identifies the procedure as a subroutine and names it. Then two variables are declared with `Dim` statements: The variable named `cnConnectToSales` is declared as a connection that will be made to a database, and `rsResale` is declared as a recordset:

```
Dim cnConnectToSales As New ADODB.Connection
Dim rsResale As New ADODB.Recordset
```

> Many people who write code find it useful to begin the names of variables with short tags, usually just two characters each, that identify what the variable represents. Using these mnemonic devices helps the coder remember that `cnConnectToSales` represents a connection and that `rsResale` represents a recordset.

Notice the use of the keyword `New` in the two `Dim` statements. In VBA you often work with *object* variables, which stand in for existing objects. For example, in VBA for Excel you often declare a variable to represent an existing object such as a worksheet. After declaring the variable, you set it to represent a particular worksheet. This can make subsequent code more concise and easier to understand. These two statements show one approach:

```
Dim PayrollSheet As Worksheet
Set PayrollSheet = ThisWorkbook.Sheets("Monthly Payroll Data")
```

The first statement declares that an object variable named `PayrollSheet` exists, and the second statement sets the object variable equal to the existing worksheet object named `Monthly Payroll Data`.

In the case of a connection between Excel and a data source, however, there is often no existing connection to set the object equal to. Therefore, to establish an instance of a connection, the keyword `New` is used. When the `Dim` statement is processed, the `New` keyword causes a connection object to exist, but its characteristics have not yet been set—that happens next.

Making Database Objects Available to VBA

Before the VBA code can properly assign actual values to these variables, `cnConnectToSales` and `rsResale`, it's necessary to make an object library available to the code. Although VBA for Excel knows all about worksheets and pivot tables and cells, it's clueless about ADO connections and recordsets. Excel can find the necessary information in a library, but it's up to you to establish a reference to the library. The following steps show you how to do that:

1. Open the Visual Basic Editor from Excel as described earlier in the section titled "Getting at VBA."
2. Open a code module by choosing Insert, Module.
3. Select Tools, References. The References — VBAProject dialog box opens, as shown in Figure 18.3.

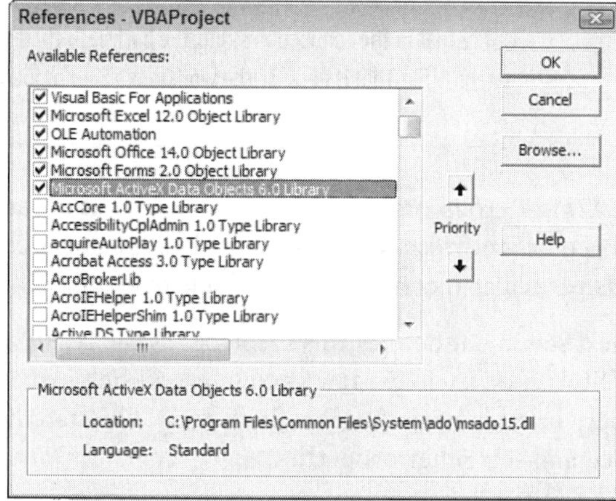

Figure 18.3
The list of references contains a variety of libraries and controls, such as the Calendar Control, that you can make available to VBA.

4. Scroll down the Available References list box until you find the item named Microsoft ActiveX Data Objects 2.7 Library or Microsoft ActiveX Data Objects 6.0 Library. (The available reference depends on the version of Office you have installed.) Make sure the check box is selected, and click OK.

The entire ActiveX Data Objects (ADO) object library is now available to your code. Here's why that's important:

In VBA for Excel, you often refer to Excel objects such as workbooks, worksheets, charts, cells, and so on. You do that so you can manipulate the objects with your VBA code—you take actions such as deleting a worksheet object, formatting a cell object, or inserting a chart object. VBA for Excel is "for Excel" because it has information about workbooks, worksheets, cells, and so on built into it.

But Excel is not a database. Therefore, VBA for Excel doesn't come with information about objects that are contained in databases, such as databases themselves, tables, and queries. Information about those database objects is contained in an object library, which is basically what ADO is. By referencing ADO using the VBA Editor, you make these database objects available to your Excel VBA code.

Using Database Objects

With those objects made available by way of the ADO object library, you can manipulate their properties and methods. In this case, the code takes these actions on the connection:

- The connection's provider is Micrsoft.Ace.OLEDB.12.0, which provides connectivity to Access, SQL Server, and other databases.
- The connection string gives the location and name of the data source.
- The connection's Open method is invoked so that data can move back and forth between Excel and the data source.

```
With cnConnectToSales
    .Provider = "Microsoft.Ace.OLEDB.12.0"
    .ConnectionString = ThisWorkbook.Path & "\Evans Electronics.mdb"
    .Open
End With
```

NOTE

Notice that in the connection string, the backslash character is supplied just prior to the name of the database file. That is because the workbook's Path property does not supply the path's final backslash.

A *recordset* is a group of records that have fields. A recordset could be a table—which, by definition, has records and fields—in a database, or it could be the results of a query that extracts particular records and their fields from one or more tables.

The next statement defines this recordset as the result of a select query, using just a snippet of SQL code to do so. It says to select all fields (that's the effect of the asterisk) from the query or table named `Resale` Inventory. The statement also specifies the connection involved and sets other properties:

```
rsResale.Open "Select * from [Resale Inventory]", cnConnectToSales, _
     adOpenForwardOnly, adLockOptimistic
```

The `adOpenForwardOnly` property tells Excel that you're going to move through the table once only, and not go back and forth to find first one record and then another. This is the most efficient way to work through the recordset. The `adLockOptimistic` property assumes that no other user will contend for access to a record while you're editing and updating it; it locks the record only when the update occurs. One alternative is `adLockPessimistic`, which locks each edited record until the update has occurred.

18

Using With Blocks

The code next establishes a `With` block:

```
With ThisWorkbook
```

In this case, the With block is built on the `ThisWorkbook` object. That means that objects such as the workbook's range names can be referred to using dot notation, without having to repeatedly mention `ThisWorkbook`. Notice the code uses the expression `.Names` several times. Because these instances follow the `With ThisWorkbook` statement, it's not necessary to qualify each instance by the object it belongs to. Without the `With ThisWorkbook` statement, the code would have to use `ThisWorkbook.Names` each time, instead of simply `.Names`.

This might seem like a trivial convenience, but consider the situation in which you want to refer to a worksheet range in your VBA code. The standard way of doing so is with syntax like this

```
Range(Cells(1,1),Cells(5,4))
```

which is pseudocode that refers to a range that begins in the first row, first column and ends in the fifth row, fourth column.

But VBA is incapable of inferring which workbook and worksheet contains the cells that you have in mind, so you have to tell it. Absent a `With` block and dot notation, you might have to write something as verbose as this:

```
Set rng = ThisWorkbook.Sheets("Sheet1").Range(ThisWorkbook.Sheets("Sheet1") _
   .Cells(1, 1), ThisWorkbook.Sheets("Sheet1").Cells(5, 4))
   [Code that depends on the defined worksheet range]
```

But using a `With` block, you can use this instead:

```
With ThisWorkbook.Sheets("Sheet1")
  Set rng = .Range(.Cells(1, 1), .Cells(5, 4))
  [Code that depends on the defined worksheet range]
End With
```

TIP

The workbook that contains the VBA code can be referred to in the code by means of the keyword `ThisWorkbook`. That's a great convenience if you want to use a property such as the workbook's path, as is done here. Among many other reasons that you might need to use `ThisWorkbook` in your code, you can rename the workbook without having to worry about changing its name in the code it contains.

Finding the Right Record

Now it's time to locate the record in the recordset that represents the item that Evans just sold. After the code has located that record, by means of its Product ID and its serial number, the code assigns values to the record's `Date Sold` field and to its `Sales Price` field. The record is located with this statement:

```
rsResale.Filter = "[Serial Number] = " _
     & .Names("Serial_Number").RefersToRange.Value _
     & " And [Product ID] = " _
     & .Names("Product_ID").RefersToRange.Value
```

18

This command uses the `Filter` method of the ADODB `recordset` object. It takes as its argument two search conditions. The first condition is that the recordset field named `[Serial Number]` must equal the value found in the worksheet range named `Serial_Number`. The second condition is that the recordset field named `[Product ID]` must equal the value found in the worksheet range named `Product_ID`.

NOTE

A means of connecting to external databases that preceded ADO, Data Access Objects (DAO), would use the `FindFirst` method instead of the `Filter` method to locate a particular record. ADO does have a `Find` (not a `FindFirst`) method, but that method can deal with only one criterion field at a time. Because the present situation requires the use of two fields, `Product ID` and `Serial Number`, to locate a specific record, ADO's `Find` can't be used. The `Filter` method of an ADO recordset does accept multiple criteria and is therefore used in this code.

Put in English instead of code: VBA tries to find a record in the `Resale Inventory` recordset that has the same Product ID as the one found in worksheet cell B12, and a serial number equal to the one in cell C12.

NOTE

The reason that the recordset field names, such as `[Serial Number]`, are enclosed in square brackets is that when you refer in VBA to a recordset field name that contains a space, you must supply those brackets. In contrast, workbook- and worksheet-level names in Excel are not allowed to contain spaces, and underscores (as in `Serial_Number`) are convenient stand-ins for spaces.

The next statement alerts the user that she has attempted to sell an item that's not recorded in the database as available for sale:

```
If rsResale.EOF Then
    MsgBox "Couldn't find that item in the database."
```

If VBA filtered for and failed to find a record that matches your specifications, the recordset's end of file (`EOF`) property has the value `True`. If at least one record remains after the filter has been applied, `EOF` is `False`.

In this instance, the code has looked in the `rsResale` recordset for a record with a particular Product ID and serial number. If Evans mistyped either value on the worksheet, VBA probably would be unable to find the record (unless Evans happened by chance to type a pair of values that do exist in the recordset). Then the `EOF` property would be `True` and a message that the item wasn't found would be displayed on the screen. This lets the user know that an error has been made somewhere, either in the `Product_ID` or `Serial_Number` range on the worksheet or when the records were originally entered in the database. In either case, the user would not continue trying to record the sale until the error was found and corrected.

Editing the Record

18

But if the record was found, `EOF` is set to `False`—that is, a record fitting the criteria was found, so you're not at the end of the file—and the code continues with the next line following the `MsgBox` statement:

```
Else
```

The `Else` statement just says that, assuming that the prior `If` condition was *not* met and the record that VBA looked for was found, the following statements are to be executed.

The next two statements are then able to modify the values of the `[Date Sold]` and `[Sales Price]` fields:

```
rsResale.Fields("[Date Sold]") = _
  .Names("Date_Sold").RefersToRange.Value
rsResale.Fields("[Sales Price]") = _
  .Names("Sales_Price").RefersToRange.Value
```

In words, locate the value in the worksheet range that's referred to by the name `Date_Sold`. Put that value in the recordset's field named `[Date Sold]`. Then locate the value in the worksheet range that's named `Sales_Price` and put it in the field named `[Sales Price]`. These values will belong to the database record that has the Product ID and serial number that VBA found, first in the worksheet and then in the recordset.

```
rsResale.Update
```

The changes to the fields' values do not fully take effect until the recordset's `Update` method is executed.

The subroutine finishes with these commands:

```
  End If
End With

End Sub
```

The `End If` statement terminates the `If` statement that checks to see if the specified record was found in the recordset. The `End With` statement terminates the `With` block that's based on the `ThisWorkbook` object. The `End Sub` statement terminates the subroutine.

In VBA, a `With` statement must be followed by an `End With` statement that marks the end of the code that uses notation such as `.Names` instead of `ThisWorkbook.Names`. And a `Sub` statement must be followed by an `End Sub` statement to mark the end of the subroutine. Similarly, when you have more than one statement that will execute should an `If` statement be `True`, you need to put those statements after the `If` and before an `End With`. In contrast—and it's not best programming practice—if there's just one thing to do after an `If`, you can put it in one statement and omit the `End If`. That is, both this:

```
If X > 10 Then Y = 5
```

and this:

```
If X > 10 Then
  Y = 5
End If
```

are syntactically correct.

The example discussed in this section is a rather simple procedure. It consists of just 19 statements, and only 7 of them actually *do* anything. But it's powerful. It enables the user to locate a record in a database and to change the values of its fields without knowing what table the record is located in, what database contains that table, where the database is located, or even that the database exists. The code knows all those things, of course, but it's all transparent to the user.

If you employed an approach such as this in your business—arranging to use Excel as the user interface, using a true database such as Access or SQL Server to store the data, writing VBA code to manage the data transfer, and making an object library available to the code—you would surely add other checks and protections in the code.

For example, you would want to provide a sequence of commands that run if the code can't find the database where you expected it would be stored. Once the code has found a record, you would probably arrange a check to make sure that the specific item has not already been sold. Or after updating the values in the fields, you might find the record again, read the values in its fields, and show the user those values in a message box to confirm that the update occurred properly.

Adding New Records to the Recordset

Now suppose that Evans wanted to use a similar approach to add records to the database. Records would be added when the store acquires new stock for sale and it must be recorded in the Resale Inventory table. The Excel worksheet might be structured much like the one shown in Figure 18.4.

The worksheet in Figure 18.4 has a command button that records a sale in the database as described in the previous section. The worksheet also has a command button that adds an

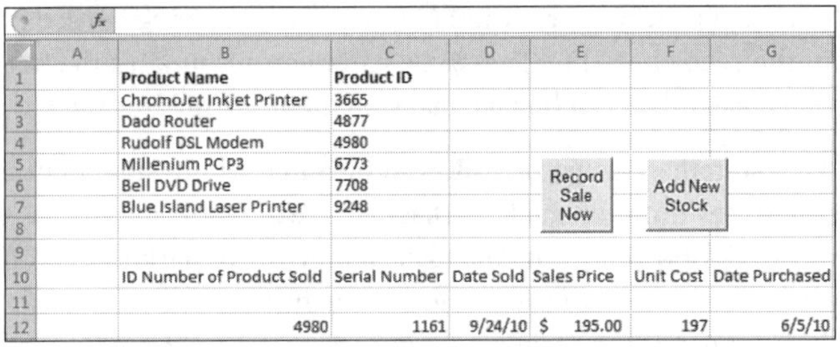

Figure 18.4
This worksheet just adds two named ranges and a command button to the worksheet shown in Figure 18.2.

	A	B	C	D	E	F	G
1		Product Name	Product ID				
2		ChromoJet Inkjet Printer	3665				
3		Dado Router	4877				
4		Rudolf DSL Modem	4980				
5		Millenium PC P3	6773		Record Sale Now	Add New Stock	
6		Bell DVD Drive	7708				
7		Blue Island Laser Printer	9248				
8							
9							
10		ID Number of Product Sold	Serial Number	Date Sold	Sales Price	Unit Cost	Date Purchased
11							
12		4980	1161	9/24/10	$ 195.00	197	6/5/10

item to the resale inventory. The act of recording a sale does not involve changing either the unit cost or the date acquired. Similarly, when Evans adds an item to inventory, the sales price and date sold are not yet known and therefore are not edited. So, in practice, it might be a good idea to put those two capabilities on separate worksheets to keep named ranges that are not involved in the data transaction off the active worksheet.

Here is the code that runs when the Add New Stock button is clicked. It also uses ADO:

```
Sub AddAnItem()
Dim cnConnectToSales As New ADODB.Connection
Dim rsResale As New ADODB.Recordset

With cnConnectToSales
    .Provider = "Microsoft.Ace.OLEDB.12.0"
    .ConnectionString = ThisWorkbook.Path & "\Evans Electronics.mdb"
    .Open
End With

rsResale.Open "Select * from [Resale Inventory]", _
    cnConnectToSales, adOpenForwardOnly, adLockOptimistic

With ThisWorkbook
  rsResale.Filter = "[Serial Number] = " _
     & .Names("Serial_Number").RefersToRange.Value _
     & " And [Product ID] = " _
     & .Names("Product_ID").RefersToRange.Value
  If Not rsResale.EOF Then
     MsgBox "Already have that item in the database."
  Else
     rsResale.AddNew
     rsResale.Fields("Serial Number") = .Names("Serial_Number") _
       .RefersToRange.Value
     rsResale.Fields("Product ID") = _
         .Names("Product_ID").RefersToRange.Value
     rsResale.Fields("Unit Cost") = _
         .Names("Unit_Cost").RefersToRange.Value
     rsResale.Fields("Date Purchased") = _
         .Names("Date_Purchased").RefersToRange.Value
     rsResale.Update
  End If
End With
```

18

TIP

If you put this subroutine in the same workbook as the RecordASale subroutine, you don't need to establish a new reference to the ADO object library. When that reference is established, it's available to all subroutines and modules in the workbook.

The AddAnItem subroutine is identical to the RecordASale subroutine in most ways. The same database and recordset variables are declared and managed in the same way. The With block has the same purpose: to establish a shortcut to the names in the workbook. The code filters the recordset for a record with a particular Product ID and serial number.

The first difference between the two subroutines comes in the If test:

```
If Not rsResale.EOF Then
    MsgBox "Already have that item in the database."
```

This time, Evans expects that the record is *not* in the database: it is just now being added to the resale inventory. So the If test gets the Not keyword added to it. If the code is not at EOF after applying the filter, there is an item in the recordset that has the same Product ID and serial number as the item that Evans is attempting to add.

In that case, you warn the user with a message box. Something is wrong, the item is already in the database, and the problem should be corrected before trying again to add the item to the database.

On the other hand, if the filter has resulted in the EOF property being True, a matching record wasn't located, and the code can go ahead and add the item to the recordset:

```
Else
    rsResale.AddNew
```

The code uses rsResale.AddNew to put a new record in the recordset. Then the appropriate fields of that new record are given values. Those values are obtained from the named ranges in the Excel workbook: Serial_Number, Product_ID, Unit_Cost, and Date_Purchased.

```
rsResale.Fields("[Serial Number]") = _
  .Names("Serial_Number").RefersToRange.Value
rsResale.Fields("[Product ID]") =
  .Names("Product_ID").RefersToRange.Value
rsResale.Fields("[Unit Cost]") =
  .Names("Unit_Cost").RefersToRange.Value
rsResale.Fields("[Date Purchased]") =
  .Names("Date_Purchased").RefersToRange.Value
```

With the values in the recordset's fields, the Update method is used to fully establish the record in the recordset:

```
rsResale.Update
```

The final three statements that end the If statement, the With statement, and the subroutine are the same as in the RecordASale subroutine.

Choosing to Use ADO

Couldn't Evans Electronics have handled all this—the recording of sales and the addition of new stock—with Access as the user interface? Sure. Someone could have created a couple of forms in Access, linked directly to the `Resale Inventory` table, that Evans could use to edit records and add new ones. VBA wouldn't be involved. ADO wouldn't be needed. Perhaps I just wasn't creative enough to come up with examples that were straightforward enough to serve as introductions to these topics, yet complicated enough to make it desirable to use ADO.

The ADO object model contains many more objects, properties, and methods than the few illustrated in the preceding sections. Using ADO, you can do the following, all from the Excel platform and without resorting to the database manager's user interface:

- Create new queries, store them in databases, and use them to return data to the worksheet
- Delete records from tables
- Use indexes to *very rapidly* find particular records in huge tables
- Perform just about any action that you might perform using the database management program

18

In many business situations, you could choose to use Excel as the user interface and, for example, an Access or SQL Server database to store the information. Suppose a user wants to review quality-control data that pertains to a manufacturing operation.

Sometimes that user must correct what he judges to be erroneous information in the database. When the factory turns out thousands of units per day, representative quality-control samples can quickly become too large to manage conveniently—or at all—in an Excel worksheet. This sort of situation virtually mandates the use of a database management system to store and retrieve the underlying records.

So why not examine that data in the database? Because then the user does not have easy access to supporting documents such as charts, reference distributions such as the normal curve and the Poisson, and tools such as Solver and Goal Seek. These are the tools and functions in Excel that enable the user to make inferences and judgments about the data: perhaps to determine that a measure in the database is so anomalous that it simply has to be wrong. That judgment suggests that information in the database should be corrected, and the active application is an ideal place to work from. Doing that directly requires the use of ADO.

Back Ends Perform Data Management

Several database management systems are commercially available; perhaps the best known are Oracle, SQL Server, and Access. The systems use different engines, the back ends that actually perform the data management.

You don't usually see the back end of the database; you normally interact with its For example, if you're an Access user, you're accustomed to seeing a database window with different tabs or dropdown items for the database's tables, queries, forms, reports, pages, and VBA modules. That's the front end. You use it for design work: putting fields in a table, joining tables with queries, placing controls on forms, creating reports, and so on. Notice that none of those tasks have to do with the actual storage and retrieval of data.

The storage and retrieval is handled by the database engine, which operates behind the scenes. It handles all sorts of things on behalf of the database developer or user: resolving conflicts caused by simultaneous attempts to change the same record, managing joins between tables, updating primary keys when new records are added, and so on.

So if a lot of users need simultaneous access to the database, or if want to be sure you're using the latest technology, or if you worry about being abandoned by Microsoft, you might want to consider using a system other than Access, such as SQL Server—and remember that ADO provides for the management of a variety of database systems, including Access and SQL Server. Keep in mind that just switching to a different system isn't necessarily a cure-all. If there's a problem, it could easily be with the way the database is designed, not with the capabilities of the database engine.

NOTE

There are more reasons to consider using a database system other than Access. One reason concerns the logging of transactions. For example, all database activity is recorded centrally using SQL Server. But if several workstations are using the same Access database, located on a shared server, the transactions are logged not in one central location, but on the individual workstations. So if a transaction corrupts the database, you don't have a feasible way to recover it, apart from resorting to a backup. But with all transactions logged centrally, you can retrace and undo the transactions until you correct the one that caused the corruption. This is yet another reason to consider using something other than Access.

Summary

This chapter focused on ADO as a method of managing a database such as an Access file from the Excel platform. Excel and Access work together quite smoothly. For example, you can copy VBA code that you have developed and written in an Excel workbook into a module in an Access database and execute the code in that context with few changes—possibly none.

But don't let that kind of tight integration cause you to forget that you can use the techniques developed in this chapter with databases other than Access. The examples of queries and of the use of ADO apply equally to any ODBC-compliant database, whether in business, scientific, educational, or other institutions.

Analyzing Contributions and Margins

19

Management accounting is concerned with the internal operations of businesses and with the drivers of business performance. Its basic tools include contribution analysis and break-even analysis, which use financial indicators such as these:

- **Contribution margin**—Usually defined as the sales revenue minus the variable costs of production
- **Unit contribution**—The margin contributed by each unit sold
- **Break-even point**—The point in the sales process at which the revenues equal the costs of production

These indicators help you make decisions about how you can

- Increase product profitability
- Manage your product sales mix
- Optimize your resources to hold your costs down and increase your profits

Your decisions often involve assumptions about a business's profitability, resources, and product mix. You can test the assumptions by considering their effect on variables such as unit contribution.

For example, suppose that you manage a product whose contribution margin last year was $1 million. If your company is to meet its targeted profit for next year, you must assume that you can increase your product's contribution margin by 10% to $1.1 million. What can you do to get an additional $100,000 profit from your product?

A good place to start is to refer to a contribution margin analysis and perhaps a unit contribution analysis. These analyses spell out the factors that tend to hold your revenues down or keep your costs

IN THIS CHAPTER

up. Examining those factors can help you determine which costs, sales prices, and volume levels you can modify to achieve your $1.1 million target.

This chapter explores the relationships among these variables. It shows you how to use Excel to identify changes that will help you meet your goals for your product.

Calculating the Contribution Margin

All firms have costs that are directly associated with their products or services. One means of understanding and controlling those costs is contribution margin analysis. The contribution margin is calculated by subtracting the variable costs required to manufacture the product from the revenue you create by selling the product.

Variable costs are those that change as production levels rise and fall. For example, the cost of raw materials is a variable cost: The more goods you manufacture, the more raw materials you need. In contrast, fixed costs are those that do not change along with differences in production levels. For example, the cost of salaried workers is a fixed cost—if that cost changes, it is not normally the result of production levels rising or falling.

CASE STUDY: PRODUCING DIGITAL VIDEO DISCS

Discography, Inc., produces custom, prerecorded DVDs for corporate communications departments. To make the DVDs, it costs Discography:

- $5 per DVD for the materials used in the DVD, including the licensing fees for the programming
- $1 per DVD for the packaging materials (the jewel box, the paper insert, the shrink wrap, and the enormous clear plastic container that's supposed to prevent you from stealing the DVD and that requires you to use the Jaws of Life to get it open)
- $0.50 per DVD for the factory employees

The total production cost is $6.50 per DVD. You would calculate the contribution margin for this product line as shown in Figure 19.1.

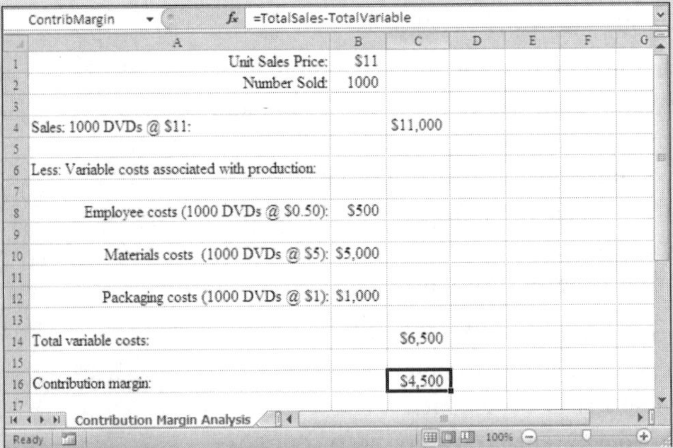

Figure 19.1
The contribution margin is defined as revenues minus variable costs.

Classifying Costs

The $6,500 required to make the production run shown in Figure 19.1 is called the *variable cost*, the cost that varies with the number of units produced. When production goes down, variable costs decrease, and when production goes up, variable costs increase.

Besides variable costs, Discography has fixed costs. Fixed costs do not vary with the level of production. For example, rent paid for a building, legal fees, and business insurance are usually the same regardless of how many DVDs Discography produces. In contrast, when Discography makes more DVDs, the total amount that it pays for materials such as blank discs increases; that is a variable cost of production.

In practice, and even when you can separate variable from fixed costs, the distinction is not quite as crisp as it is in theory. Consider, for example, the $0.50 per DVD that Discography pays its factory employees.

There are several ways that Discography can incur that cost:

- The employee is paid for each DVD produced and, as long as the current labor contract is in force, the nature and amount of the payment cannot be changed. If that's the arrangement, the payment is a variable cost: The more DVDs produced, the greater the total payments to the employees.
- The employee receives a fixed wage, regardless of the number of DVDs produced, and the $0.50 per DVD is just a long-term average—a result determined by research into the company's operations, not a contractual commitment. In this case, the employee's wage represents a fixed cost. Unless you negotiate payment terms that are based directly on production, you should not include this sort of cost in the contribution margin analysis.
- The employee is paid by the DVD, but the rate of payment changes according to how many DVDs are made. For example, for up to 1,000 DVDs made per day, you pay the employee $0.50 per DVD, but you pay $0.60 per DVD for between 1,000 and 2,000 DVDs. This is termed a semivariable cost. A semivariable cost changes along with changes in the number of units produced, but the size of that change is not precisely proportional to that of the change in the number of units.

19

NOTE

Semivariable costs are often step functions. A *step function* is one whose value changes suddenly when another variable reaches a certain threshold. In this example, when the production level reaches the threshold of 1,000 DVDs, the employee cost jumps from $0.50 per unit to $0.60 per unit.

Up to 1,000 DVDs, the ratio of total employee cost to units made is exactly $0.50. After 1,000 DVDs, the ratio is exactly $0.60. But across the full range of production (say, from 0 to 5,000 DVDs produced), the ratio is inexact: It depends on the number of DVDs that are produced above the threshold.

Estimating Semivariable Costs

Figure 19.2 shows an example of how you might account for a semivariable cost. In this case, an employee makes $0.50 for each DVD produced up to 1,000 DVDs per day, $0.60 per DVD for 1,000 to 2,000 DVDs, and so on.

H4 =IF(Number_Sold>DVDs_Made,MIN(1000,(Number_Sold-DVDs_Made))*Unit_Cost,0)

	A	B	C	D	E	F	G	H
1	Unit Sales Price:	$11						
2	Number Sold:	4510			Employee cost calculation			Employee cost
3					DVDs Made		Unit Cost	per quantity
4	Sales: 4510 DVDs @ $11:		$49,610.00		0	to 999	$0.50	$500.00
5					1000	to 1999	$0.60	$600.00
6	Less: Variable costs of production:				2000	to 2999	$0.70	$700.00
7					3000	to 3999	$0.80	$800.00
8	Employee costs (semi-variable):	$3,059.00			4000	to 4999	$0.90	$459.00
9					5000	to 5999	$1.00	$0.00
10	Materials costs (variable)	$22,550.00						
11					Materials Cost		$5	
12	Packaging costs (variable)	$4,510.00						
13					Packaging Cost		$1	
14	Total variable costs:		$30,119.00					
15								
16	Contribution margin:		$19,491.00					

Semi-variable Costs

Figure 19.2
Calculating semivariable costs in a contribution margin analysis: Employee costs are purely and proportionately variable within a quantity range, but describe a step function across ranges.

Three named ranges are used in Figure 19.2:

- `Number_Sold` refers to cell B2.
- `DVDs_Made` refers to cells E4:E9.
- `Unit_Cost` refers to cells G4:G9.

19

The implicit intersection with the ranges named `DVDs_Made` and `Unit_Cost` causes the following `IF` statement to return different values to the cells in the range H4:H9:

```
=IF(Number_Sold > DVDs_Made,MIN(1000,(Number_Sold-DVDs_Made))*Unit_Cost,0)
```

NOTE As entered in cell H6, for example, the formula just given *intersects implicitly* with the range named `DVDs_Made` at cell E6 and with the range named `Unit_Cost` at cell G6. The result is to use the values 2000 and $0.70 in the formula. The row where the formula is entered defines the row where the formula *intersects* the named range. The intersection is *implicit* because the formula does not explicitly intersect the named range: it does so implicitly by noting the row where the formula is entered.

The `IF` function takes three arguments: a condition (here, whether the units sold is greater than the units made), the value to return if the condition is true, and the value to return if the condition is false.

The `MIN` function appears in the formula because no more than 1,000 units should be counted for any level of `DVDs_Made`. In Figure 19.2, `Number_Sold` is 4,510. For the 4,000 level of `DVDs_Made`, `Number_Sold - DVDs_Made` = 510, and this amount is multiplied by the corresponding `Unit_Cost` of $0.90 to return $459.

In contrast, at the 3,000 level of `DVDs_Made`, `Number_Sold - DVDs_Made` = 1,510. But 1,510 is too many units to count: 1,000 is the maximum number of units to count for any given level. Therefore, the formula uses the `MIN` function to return the smaller of 1,000, or the difference between `Number_Sold` and `DVDs_Made`. The comparison of `Number_Sold` with `DVDs_Made` is the `IF` function's condition—the expression that's evaluated to determine whether it's `TRUE` or `FALSE`.

The smaller of those two values is multiplied by the corresponding `Unit_Cost` to return the cost of the DVDs made at that level of production. This value, calculated by the following fragment of the complete formula, is the second of the `IF` function's three arguments and is the value that's returned when the `IF` function's condition is `TRUE`:

```
MIN(1000,(Number_Sold-DVDs_Made))*Unit_Cost
```

Finally, `Number_Sold` can be less than any given level of `DVDs_Made`. In the figure example, 4,510 is less than 5,000, so no units should be counted for the 5,000 to 5,999 level. The `IF` function returns `0` in that case. The third argument to the `IF` function specifies the value to return when the `IF` function's condition is `FALSE`.

Using Unit Contribution

The analysis of contribution margin in the case study of DVD production involved total variable costs and total revenues. You can also break the information down to a per-unit and percent of sales basis. Doing so often gives you a different view of the relationship between your costs and revenues.

Producing Digital Video Discs (Continued)

19

To continue the Discography case study, consider the information summarized in Figure 19.2 from the perspective that's provided in Figure 19.3.

The detailed per-unit and percent of margin information gives you a better idea of the following:

- The product's individual contribution to total revenue
- The source of the greatest percentage of variable costs
- The relationships among the sizes of the variable costs

The detail that you obtain from this type of analysis gives you the tools you need to make decisions that maximize your profits. For example, Figure 19.3 shows that if Discography pays its employees to produce an additional 1,000 DVDs, the contribution margin goes down (39.29% at the 4,510 level, 38.84% at the 5,510 level). The company's total margin for the product line increases with more production and sales, from $19,491 to $23,540. But the unit contribution decreases.

Figure 19.3
You can derive a greater level of detail by breaking down the total cost information to a per-unit and percent of sales basis.

Unit_Percent_Margin | =Unit_Dollar_Margin/Unit_Dollar_Sales

	A	B	C	D	E
1	Unit Sales Price:	$11			
2	Number Sold:	4510		Per Unit	
3			Total	Dollars	Percent
4	**Sales: 4510 DVDs @ $11:**		$ 49,610.00	$11.00	100.00%
5					
6	Less:				
7	(DVDs at semi-variable per DVD)		$3,059.00	$0.68	6.17%
8	Materials (DVDs at $5 per DVD)		$22,550.00	$5.00	45.45%
9	Packaging costs @ $1 per DVD		$4,510.00	$1.00	9.09%
10					
11	Contribution Margin		$19,491.00	$4.32	39.29%
12					
13	Unit Sales Price:	$11			
14	Number Sold:	5510		Per Unit	
15			Total	Dollars	Percent
16	**Sales: 5510 DVDs @ $11:**		$ 60,610.00	$11.00	100.00%
17					
18	Less:				
19	(DVDs at semi-variable per DVD)		$4,010.00	$0.73	6.62%
20	Materials (DVDs at $5 per DVD)		$27,550.00	$5.00	45.45%
21	Packaging costs @ $1 per DVD		$5,510.00	$1.00	9.09%
22					
23	Contribution Margin		$23,540.00	$4.27	38.84%

Contribution per unit

Ready 100%

Increasing the Contribution Margin

Suppose that Discography wants to increase the contribution margin, expressed as a percentage of sales, from 39.29% to 45% at the 4,510 unit sales level. By analyzing the information in Figure 19.3, Discography notices that if it can lower the cost of its materials from $5 per DVD to $4.37 per DVD, it can increase the contribution margin to 45%. One way of doing so might be by using a different supplier. Lowering the cost of materials will decrease the direct material cost to 39.73% of total costs. This enables Discography to achieve its desired contribution margin of 45%.

The fastest way to perform that analysis is to use Goal Seek. Follow these steps:

1. To better document what you're doing, name a couple of cells. In the example shown in Figure 19.3, you might name cell D11 as `Unit_Dollar_Margin` and cell D4 as `Unit_Dollar_Sales`.
2. Select the cell with the contribution margin that you want to change. In Figure 19.3, that's cell E11. Make sure that it contains the necessary formula—in this case `=Unit_Dollar_Margin/Unit_Dollar_Sales`
3. Click the Data tab, and then click the What-If Analysis drop-down in the Data Tools group. Finally, select Goal Seek from the drop-down. (In versions of Excel prior to 2007, choose Tools, Goal Seek.)
4. In the To Value box, enter `0.45`. Select the By Changing Cell box and then click in cell D8, which contains the unit materials cost.
5. Click OK.

> **TIP** When you're using a dialog box as in step 4, it's usually easier to click in a cell to identify its address than to type a long defined name.

The required material cost of $4.37 per DVD then appears in D8, and the desired unit contribution margin of 45% appears in E11.

In summary, when you're in the process of making operational decisions, a contribution margin analysis can help you in several ways:

- It helps you decide what price to charge for your product. For example, if you want an additional $10 contribution margin on every unit you sell, you will have to either increase your selling price by $10, reduce your unit variable costs by $10, or arrange some combination of price increase and cost reduction that sums to $10 per unit. The contribution margin analysis makes it easy to quantify those changes.
- It helps you focus on controlling those costs that are directly related to making the product. For example, if you currently use a vendor who charges $50 per 10 units of materials, you may be able to find a vendor that charges $45 at no loss in quality. But suppose that you focused on reducing fixed costs such as office leases. Although this can be a useful activity, it usually doesn't increase your profit as you increase production.
- It helps you understand the relationships among the volume of products produced and sold, their costs, and your profits. This is especially useful in the case of semivariable costs, which are usually difficult to fully understand without doing the formal analysis.

Creating an Operating Income Statement

Once created, an Excel worksheet can make it easy to analyze contribution margin. You should first structure an operating income statement on a worksheet. The statement contains your sales, variable cost, and volume information on a total, per-unit, and percent of margin basis. This portion of the worksheet contains the values that depend on unit pricing (see Figure 19.4).

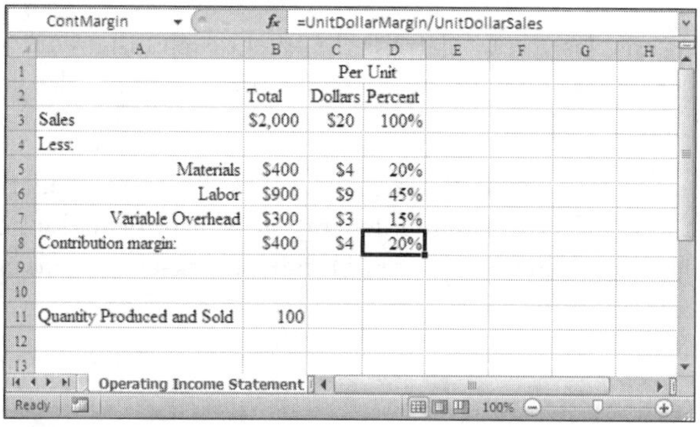

ContMargin | =UnitDollarMargin/UnitDollarSales

	A	B	C	D
1			Per Unit	
2		Total	Dollars	Percent
3	Sales	$2,000	$20	100%
4	Less:			
5	Materials	$400	$4	20%
6	Labor	$900	$9	45%
7	Variable Overhead	$300	$3	15%
8	Contribution margin:	$400	$4	20%
9				
10				
11	Quantity Produced and Sold	100		
12				
13				

Operating Income Statement

Figure 19.4
An operating income statement should detail the product's sales price, variable costs, and quantities.

The formulas used to create the information in Figure 19.4 are shown in Figure 19.5.

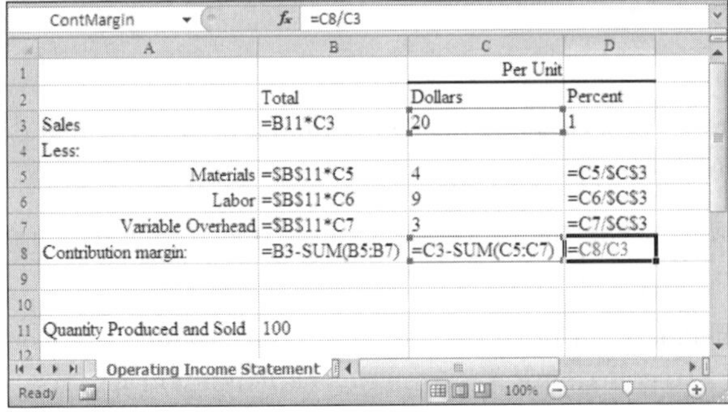

ContMargin | f_x =C8/C3

	A	B	C	D
1			Per Unit	
2		Total	Dollars	Percent
3	Sales	=B11*C3	20	1
4	Less:			
5	Materials	=$B$11*C5	4	=C5/$C$3
6	Labor	=$B$11*C6	9	=C6/$C$3
7	Variable Overhead	=$B$11*C7	3	=C7/$C$3
8	Contribution margin:	=B3-SUM(B5:B7)	=C3-SUM(C5:C7)	=C8/C3
9				
10				
11	Quantity Produced and Sold	100		

Operating Income Statement

Ready 100%

Figure 19.5
To avoid ambiguity, this figure uses cell addresses instead of cell names.

By detailing your price, cost, and quantity information separately in your operating income statement, you can easily modify selling prices, costs, and quantities to represent different assumptions. (It helps to save the values as scenarios or to save different sets of assumptions on different worksheets.) The modified values will flow through the formulas in the operating income statement and will raise or lower your calculated contribution margin.

Finding the Break-Even Point

Another way to benefit from studying a product's contribution margin is to perform a cost/volume/profit analysis. Creating this analysis is usually easy to do after you've completed your contribution analysis. This sort of analysis helps you determine the combination of production volume and sales price that maximizes your gross profits and minimizes your production costs.

One way to turn your contribution margin analysis into a cost/volume/profit analysis is to calculate the break-even point. This is the point at which total revenues equal the total of fixed and variable costs.

```
Total Revenues = Total Costs
(Unit Price x Quantity Sold) = (Fixed Costs + [Variable Costs x Quantity Made])
```

Break-even analysis enables you to plan for the level of sales that you need to cover your total costs. It also provides you with information on the level of sales you need to generate the profit you're after.

There are several ways to calculate the break-even point. Each calculation method gives you a different slant, and your choice should depend on your information requirements. The break-even calculations include break-even in units, break-even in dollars, and break-even with a specified level of profit.

Calculating Break-Even in Units

Break-even in units is the number of units you must sell at current price levels to cover fixed and variable costs. The break-even point measured in units is

```
Break-Even [units] = Total Fixed Costs / (Unit Sales Price - Unit Variable Costs)
```

Calculating the break-even point in units is most useful when managers need to analyze current or projected volume levels. You might know, for example, that with your current sales force you can expect to sell 10 units per month. By calculating break-even in units, you can determine whether your company can be profitable if you sell 10 units per month. If your company can't be profitable at that level, you might decide that you need to add sales staff.

Suppose that total fixed costs are $50, unit sales price is $20, and unit variable costs are $15. You can calculate the break-even point in units by means of this formula:

```
Break-Even [units] = $50 / ($20 - $15)
```

The result is 10. Therefore, the company needs to sell 10 units during the period when the fixed costs are incurred to break even.

Calculating Break-Even in Sales

Break-even in sales is the number of dollars of sales revenue needed to cover fixed and variable costs. There are several ways to calculate break-even in sales. Each provides the same result but uses slightly different inputs. One method is this:

```
Break-Even [sales] = (Break-Even [units] × Unit Sales Price)
```

Suppose that the number of break-even units is 10 and the unit sales price is $20. It's pretty simple to get the break-even in sales dollars of $200:

```
$200 = (10 × $20)
```

Here, you already know how many units you need to sell to break even. You just multiply that by the price of each unit.

Another formula that you can use if you haven't yet calculated break-even units is the following:

```
Break-Even [sales] = Total Fixed Costs / ([Unit Sales Price - Unit Variable
   Costs] / Unit Sales Price)
```

Here, the total of the fixed costs is $50, the unit sales price is $20, and the unit variable cost is $15. These figures result in the following:

```
$50 / ([$20 - $15] / $20)
$50 / ($5 / $20)
$50 / 0.25 = $200
```

It's easier to understand if you restate the formula in words. Find your unit contribution margin ($20 – $15 = $5) and divide by the unit sales price: $5 / $20, or 0.25. This is the *contribution margin ratio*: the proportion of unit sales price that is profit over and above your variable costs. Dividing the additional costs that you need to cover, your total fixed costs, by the contribution margin ratio results in the sales dollars needed to meet total costs.

A third approach is the following:

```
Break-Even [sales] = (Break-Even [units] × Unit Variable Cost) + Total Fixed Costs
```

Or, where break-even units is 10, unit variable cost is 15, and total fixed costs is $50:

```
(10 × $15) + $50
$150 + 50 = $200
```

This formula simply determines the total variable cost for break-even units and adds to that the total fixed cost.

In each case, you find that you need $200 in sales to break even.

Break-even as measured in sales dollars tells you how much sales revenue you need to cover your operating costs. It can give you an understanding of how aggressively you must market your product to meet your operating costs. It also gives you some indication of how efficiently you are using your resources.

TIP

In practice, it is easiest to set up one formula that involves each component as a named cell reference. The formula might be:

```
= Units * (Unit_Price - Unit_Cost) - Fixed_Costs
```

Then you can use Goal Seek to set the value of the formula to zero (the break-even point) by varying any one of the formula's precedent cells.

19

Calculating Break-Even in Sales Dollars with a Specified Level of Profit

You might also want to determine the sales revenue needed to cover fixed and variable costs and still return a profit at the level you require. Conceptually, this is similar to treating profit as a cost. You need to meet your fixed costs, and you need to meet your variable costs; you simply consider that profit is another cost category that you need to meet.

You can calculate break-even in sales dollars, with a profit, by using this formula:

```
Break-Even [sales] = Variable Costs + Fixed Costs + Expected Profit
```

Suppose that a company wants to make a $5 profit on every unit it sells. The variable cost is $15 per unit, 10 units are sold, the fixed costs total $50, and the expected profit is $5 per unit. Then the formula that provides the break-even point is

```
Break-Even [sales]
= (Unit Variable Cost × Units) + Fixed Costs + (Expected Profit × Units)
= ($15 × 10) + $50 + ($5 × 10)
= $250
```

The company's break-even point, measured in sales dollars, is $250 for 10 units, with a profit of $5 per unit. Conceptually this is a simplistic, even trivial extension to the basic break-even analysis, but it is often useful to account explicitly in the equation for a particular level of profit.

Charting the Break-Even Point

Using equations to perform a break-even analysis is one useful way to analyze the cost/volume/profit relationship. Another is to depict the break-even point graphically. Figure 19.6 displays a chart that depicts the elements of a cost/volume/profit analysis.

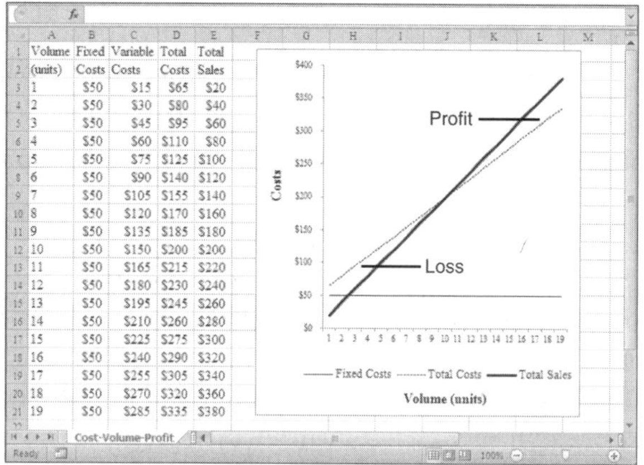

Volume (units)	Fixed Costs	Variable Costs	Total Costs	Total Sales
1	$50	$15	$65	$20
2	$50	$30	$80	$40
3	$50	$45	$95	$60
4	$50	$60	$110	$80
5	$50	$75	$125	$100
6	$50	$90	$140	$120
7	$50	$105	$155	$140
8	$50	$120	$170	$160
9	$50	$135	$185	$180
10	$50	$150	$200	$200
11	$50	$165	$215	$220
12	$50	$180	$230	$240
13	$50	$195	$245	$260
14	$50	$210	$260	$280
15	$50	$225	$275	$300
16	$50	$240	$290	$320
17	$50	$255	$305	$340
18	$50	$270	$320	$360
19	$50	$285	$335	$380

Figure 19.6
Relationships between costs, volume, and profit. Profit begins at the break-even point.

Figure 19.6 represents the relationship between total costs and total sales at different levels of production. The chart shows the sales volume at which loss, break-even, and profit occur. Below 10 units on the X-axis, the company loses money because the profit per unit has yet to make up for the fixed costs. At 10 units, there is exactly enough unit profit to cover fixed costs, and the total sales equals total costs. Above 10 units, the company increases its profit at the rate of $5 per each additional unit.

The graphic representation of a company's current cost/volume/profit relationship gives you an effective tool for determining what adjustments you need to make to volume, cost, or both to increase your profit level. Relationships among these variables can become extremely complex, especially when several products are involved. When you are dealing with a complicated situation, it is usually easier to make sense of the relationships by viewing them on a chart than by gazing at a table of raw numbers.

Convert Numeric Values to Text Values

Before putting them in a chart, the numbers shown in Figure 19.6 need a little preliminary treatment. The values in A3:A21 need to be converted from numeric values to text values. The reason is that they will be used as labels on the chart's horizontal axis. As numbers, Excel wants to treat them as a data series to be charted rather than as axis labels; as text, Excel automatically accepts them as axis labels. (You can get Excel to treat numeric values as axis labels, but that can be a little tedious if the numeric values are neither dates nor times.)

With consecutive numbers, as shown in Figure 19.6, the easiest way is to edit cell A3 so that it contains this value: `'1`.

That is, there should be an apostrophe before the numeral `1`. The apostrophe signals to Excel that what follows it is to be treated as text.

Do the same with cell A4 so that it contains `'2`. Now select A3:A4 and use A4's fill handle to drag down through cell A21. You now have the numbers `1` through `19` as text values in A3:A21.

Create the Chart Using Excel 2007 or 2010

If you're using Excel 2007 or 2010, follow these steps:

1. Select cells A1:B21. Press the Ctrl key and select cells D1:E21. You now have a multiple selection that consists of two ranges and that skips column C.
2. Click the Ribbon's Insert tab, and then click the Line chart's drop-down in the Charts group.
3. Click the Line button in the 2-D section of the drop-down. (In this case, don't select either of the stacked line chart types, which assume that the data series are additive. Also, don't select a chart type with markers: Markers just make it more difficult to see what's going on when there are several data series on the chart.)
4. A line chart with three data series appears in the active worksheet. To remove the gridlines, click any one of them to select them all; then press the Delete key.
5. Click one of the horizontal axis labels to select the horizontal axis.
6. Click the Layout tab that appears on the Ribbon when a chart is active. In the Labels area, click the Axis Titles button.
7. Click Primary Horizontal Axis Title in the Axis Titles drop-down menu. Click Title Below Axis in the shortcut menu.
8. A box containing the words `Axis Title` appears below the axis. Drag across the words and type the title you want—in this case, you might type `Volume (units)`.
9. Right-click the chart's legend and select Format Legend from the context menu. Under Legend Options, mark the Bottom option button and click Close.

Create the Chart Using Excel 2003 or Earlier

To create the chart shown in Figure 19.6 in a version earlier than Excel 2007, follow these steps:

1. With the values in A3:A21 converted to text, as described earlier, select A1:B21. Press the Ctrl key and, while you're holding it down, select D1:E21.
2. Click the Chart Wizard button on the main toolbar, or select Insert, Chart to display the Chart Wizard's first step.
3. In the Chart Wizard's first step, select Line as both the Chart type and the Chart subtype. To avoid visual clutter, choose a Chart subtype without markers. Because the break-even chart's three data series are not additive, do not choose a Stacked line subtype.
4. After choosing a subtype, click Next.

5. In the Chart Wizard's second step, check the sample chart to make sure there's nothing obviously wrong with it. If there is, click Cancel and start over. If there isn't, click Next.
6. In the Chart Wizard's third step, click the Titles tab, if necessary, and enter `Volume (units)` in the Category (X) axis box. Enter `Costs` in the Value (Y) axis box. Click the Legend tab and select the Bottom placement option. If you want to suppress gridlines, click the Gridlines tab and clear its check boxes. In this case, it's best to suppress the gridlines because the Fixed Costs describe a horizontal line. Click Next.
7. In the Chart Wizard's fourth step, select As New Sheet if you want the chart to occupy its own sheet (see Figure 19.7). If you want the chart to exist as an object on the active worksheet, select As Object In and click Finish. You can use the combo box to the right of the As Object In button to locate the chart in a different worksheet.
8. Right-click the chart's Plot Area, the rectangle that's defined by the two axes. Select Format Plot Area from the shortcut menu and then, under Area, select None. Click OK.

Figure 19.7
It's a good idea to locate the chart on the worksheet if you still have it under development.

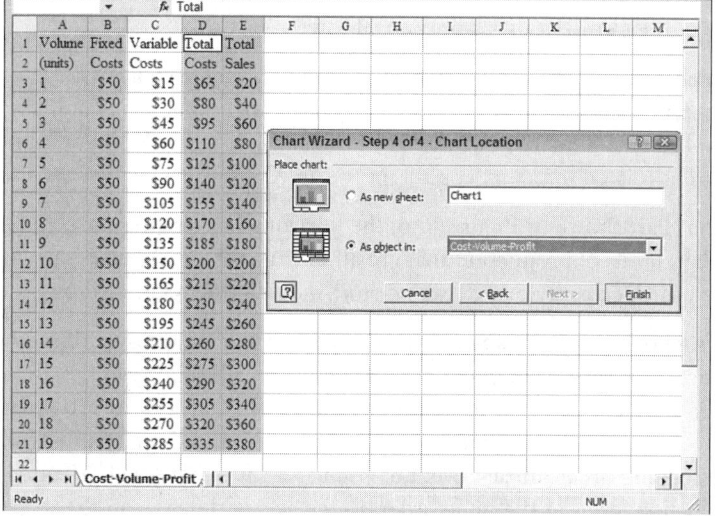

	A	B	C	D	E
1	Volume	Fixed	Variable	Total	Total
2	(units)	Costs	Costs	Costs	Sales
3	1	$50	$15	$65	$20
4	2	$50	$30	$80	$40
5	3	$50	$45	$95	$60
6	4	$50	$60	$110	$80
7	5	$50	$75	$125	$100
8	6	$50	$90	$140	$120
9	7	$50	$105	$155	$140
10	8	$50	$120	$170	$160
11	9	$50	$135	$185	$180
12	10	$50	$150	$200	$200
13	11	$50	$165	$215	$220
14	12	$50	$180	$230	$240
15	13	$50	$195	$245	$260
16	14	$50	$210	$260	$280
17	15	$50	$225	$275	$300
18	16	$50	$240	$290	$320
19	17	$50	$255	$305	$340
20	18	$50	$270	$320	$360
21	19	$50	$285	$335	$380
22					

Choosing the Chart Type

The preceding section advised you to create the break-even chart using the Line chart type. It did so because it can be more straightforward to create a Line chart that contains several data series than to use the usual alternative, the XY(Scatter) chart.

The most obvious difference between Excel chart types is their appearance: lines, dots, columns, bars, bubbles, pies, and so on. Apart from their appearance is the (occasionally obscure) issue of axis type. Excel charts have two types of axis: category and value.

19

A *category* axis or *X-axis* (Excel uses the terms interchangeably) is appropriate for qualitative variables, such as the names of products. A *value axis* or *Y-axis* (again, the terms are used interchangeably) is appropriate for quantitative variables, such as number of units produced. The category axis is usually, but not necessarily, the horizontal axis, and the value axis is usually, not always, the vertical axis.

These two types of axis have different effects on the chart's appearance and behavior. Items on a category axis are always spaced evenly. Suppose you create a Line chart showing units sold for Ford, General Motors, and Toyota. The horizontal, category axis would put each data marker equidistant from its immediate neighbors. If the middle data marker represented General Motors, it would be as far from the Ford marker as from the Toyota marker. On a category axis, distance between points conveys no special meaning.

In contrast, distance between points has meaning on a value axis. The value 4 is half as far from 2 as it is from 0. The distance between the points denotes their relative magnitude.

Most chart types in Excel have one category axis and one value axis. For example, a Column chart's horizontal axis is a category axis, and its vertical axis is a value axis. On a Bar chart, the vertical axis is a category axis, and the horizontal axis is a value axis. The Line chart shown in Figure 19.6 has a horizontal category axis.

Two chart types, the XY(Scatter) chart and the Bubble chart, have two value axes. (No 2-D chart type has two category axes.) This aspect makes them valuable for analyzing relationships between numeric, quantitative variables. For example, if you want to analyze how job tenure is related to salary, you might use an XY(Scatter) chart.

In the chart shown in Figure 19.6, the horizontal axis represents production level. The axis displays levels of production that are all one unit apart. Because they're equidistant, the Line chart's category axis doesn't distort the numeric relationships.

But suppose that you wanted to run a break-even analysis over different ranges of production. For reasons of equipment capacity and allocation, you might want to view the break-even analysis at levels of 20 to 40, 60 to 80, and 100 to 120—skipping the irrelevant ranges of 40 to 60 and 80 to 100. Your worksheet has the relevant production levels sorted in ascending order. In that event, if you use a Line chart, its horizontal axis will place the production levels in the same order on the axis as they are on the worksheet, and it will put 39 just left of 40 and 40 just left of 60. It's a category axis that ignores differences in magnitude—whether the axis labels on the worksheet are actually numeric values or text values.

This is as you want it, given the way the prior paragraph describes the situation, but it also distorts the relationship between level of production, costs, and profits. An XY(Scatter) chart would preserve the numeric relationship. Therefore, it's important to keep in mind how you want the axes to treat the charted values when you choose which type of chart to use—particularly when you're choosing between a Line chart and an XY(Scatter) chart.

NOTE

There is another reason to use an XY(Scatter) chart instead of a Line chart when you have two numeric variables. Adding any trendline other than a Moving Average to a Line chart will almost certainly return erroneous results. The trendline will be based not on the numeric values shown on the horizontal axis, but on the order in which they appear on the axis (1, 2, 3, 4, and so on). Only when the numeric values happen to match their sequential order will the trendline be correct.

Making Assumptions in Contribution Analysis

The analysis of contribution margin, break-even points, and relationships among costs, volume, and profit makes some assumptions. Before you put much trust in the results of the analysis, you should decide whether the assumptions are met, particularly those discussed in the next few sections.

Linear Relationships

Contribution margin analysis assumes that revenues and expenses are linear across the relevant range of volume. Suppose that you offer volume discounts to your customers. In that case, when you sell more goods, each additional, incremental sale generates less revenue per unit than when you sell fewer units. The revenue line would be similar to that in Figure 19.8. Notice that it is no longer straight (linear) but that it increases more slowly as volume increases (nonlinear).

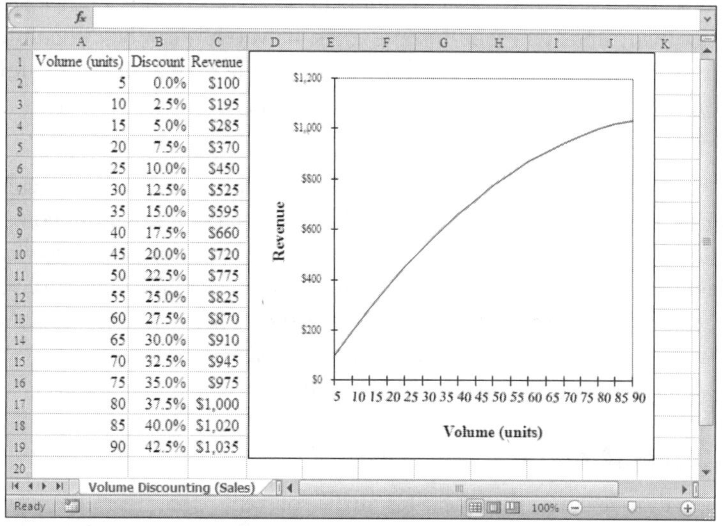

Volume (units)	Discount	Revenue
5	0.0%	$100
10	2.5%	$195
15	5.0%	$285
20	7.5%	$370
25	10.0%	$450
30	12.5%	$525
35	15.0%	$595
40	17.5%	$660
45	20.0%	$720
50	22.5%	$775
55	25.0%	$825
60	27.5%	$870
65	30.0%	$910
70	32.5%	$945
75	35.0%	$975
80	37.5%	$1,000
85	40.0%	$1,020
90	42.5%	$1,035

Figure 19.8
Volume discounts can cause nonlinear revenue growth.

Or suppose that you take advantage of volume discounts from your suppliers—in that case, the more supplies you buy, the less you pay in unit costs. The contribution margin line might be similar to that in Figure 19.9.

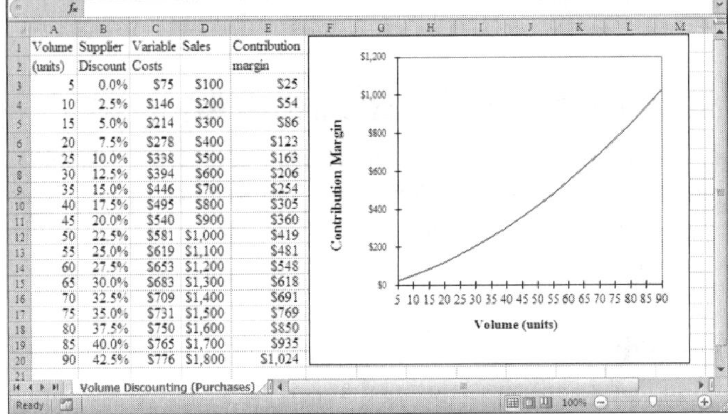

Volume (units)	Supplier Discount	Variable Costs	Sales	Contribution margin
5	0.0%	$75	$100	$25
10	2.5%	$146	$200	$54
15	5.0%	$214	$300	$86
20	7.5%	$278	$400	$123
25	10.0%	$338	$500	$163
30	12.5%	$394	$600	$206
35	15.0%	$446	$700	$254
40	17.5%	$495	$800	$305
45	20.0%	$540	$900	$360
50	22.5%	$581	$1,000	$419
55	25.0%	$619	$1,100	$481
60	27.5%	$653	$1,200	$548
65	30.0%	$683	$1,300	$618
70	32.5%	$709	$1,400	$691
75	35.0%	$731	$1,500	$769
80	37.5%	$750	$1,600	$850
85	40.0%	$765	$1,700	$935
90	42.5%	$776	$1,800	$1,024

Figure 19.9
Purchase discounts can cause nonlinear increases in the contribution margin.

Assignment of Costs

Contribution margin analysis assumes that you can accurately allocate expenses to fixed and variable cost categories, and, in most cases, you'll be able to do so. For example, up to the point that you need to acquire additional space, your monthly office lease is fixed regardless of how many units you sell. In some cases, however, it can be difficult to decide whether to treat a particular expense as fixed or variable. In particular, it can be difficult to assign an expense that bears a relationship to volume but not necessarily a direct, one-to-one relationship.

19

An example is your annual travel expenditure. Unless your sales activities are restricted to your local metro area, it is likely that the more you sell, the more you pay in airline and car rental charges. But some of those trips probably have nothing to do with incremental sales volume and everything to do with discussing an upcoming audit with your company's chief financial officer, whose office is in the next time zone. The accuracy of your analysis of contribution margin and break-even will depend on how accurately you can assign the travel and entertainment charges to the correct fixed versus variable costs category.

Constant Sales Mix

The analysis assumes that the sales mix is constant—that, from one period to the next, your total sales are based on the same percent of each product line. Note that different products usually have different cost and profit structures. If the sales mix changes so that, overall, either costs or contribution margins also change, the break-even points will vary.

Worker Productivity

The analysis assumes that worker productivity does not change (and in the early years of the current century, this has become a dangerous assumption). If, at a constant rate of pay, your workers begin to produce more product per period of time, the structure of your variable costs will change: The break-even points will come earlier, and the product's contribution margin will rise. Conversely, if your workers begin to produce less per period of time, due perhaps to illness or procedural changes, variable costs will increase and it will take longer to reach the break-even points.

Determining Sales Mix

More often than not, a company manufactures or offers for sale several product lines. If your company does so, you should consider the sales dollars and costs that are attributable to each of those product lines as you analyze the company's sales as a whole.

For example, suppose that a company sells three product lines. A side-by-side view of each of these products' price and cost information is a useful way to analyze each product's impact on the bottom line. A sample analysis is shown in Figure 19.10.

Figure 19.10
The sales mix analysis focuses on contribution margins for each type of product sold.

	A	B	C	D	E	F	G	H
1		8-oz.	Per	6-oz.	Per	4-oz.	Per	
2	Package size		Unit		Unit		Unit	Total
3	Sales (units)	10,000		15,000		20,000		
4	Sales (dollars)	$74,000	$7.40	$94,050	$6.27	$102,600	$5.13	$270,650
5								
6	Less variable costs	$37,500	$3.75	$50,850	$3.39	$60,600	$3.03	$148,950
7	(as % of Sales)	51%		54%		59%		55%
8								
9	Contribution margin	$36,500	$3.65	$43,200	$2.88	$42,000	$2.10	$121,700
10	(as % of Sales)	49%		46%		41%		45%
11								
12	Sales mix	27%		35%		38%		100%
13								
14	Break-Even	$68,932		$74,021		$83,057		$75,613
15	(Fixed costs = $34,000)							

A sales mix analysis helps you understand the relative value of the products in your current sales mix. You can determine which of your products provides the greatest contribution to your company's total sales. Suppose that your company produces an over-the-counter medicine in three different package sizes: 8 ounce, 6 ounce, and 4 ounce.

Figure 19.10 shows that the variable costs to make the 8-ounce package are 1.10 times greater than are required to make the 6-ounce package ($3.75 per unit versus $3.39 per unit) and 1.24 times greater than to make the 4-ounce package ($3.75 per unit versus $3.03 per unit). However, the contribution margin from the 8-ounce package is 1.27 times greater than from the 6-ounce package ($3.65 versus $2.88) and 1.74 times greater than from selling the 4-ounce package ($3.65 versus $2.10).

The difference in contribution margin comes about because variable costs are only 51% of the selling price for the 8-ounce package, whereas they are 54% of the selling price for the 6-ounce package and 59% of the selling price for the 4-ounce package. So even though it costs more to make the larger package, the sales price of the 8-ounce package is high enough to leave more profit after covering its variable costs than with the prices of the other sizes.

This type of analysis is a good way to determine which products you want to market most actively, which products (if any) you should discontinue, and which products to keep but at a reduced level of production. For example, if you focused sales and production efforts on the larger sizes and deemphasized the 4-ounce product, your total profit might appear, as shown in Figure 19.11.

Figure 19.11
A redistribution of product types within the sales mix can increase profitability.

Package size	8-oz.	Per Unit	6-oz.	Per Unit	4-oz.	Per Unit	Total
Sales (units)	15,000		20,000		5,000		
Sales (dollars)	$111,000	$7.40	$125,400	$6.27	$25,650	$5.13	$262,050
Less variable costs	$56,250	$3.75	$67,800	$3.39	$15,150	$3.03	$139,200
(as % of Sales)	51%		54%		59%		53%
Contribution margin	$54,750	$3.65	$57,600	$2.88	$10,500	$2.10	$122,850
(as % of Sales)	49%		46%		41%		47%
Sales mix	42%		48%		10%		100%
Break-Even	$68,932		$74,021		$83,057		$72,525
(Fixed costs = $34,000)							

In Figure 19.11, sales and production efforts have been shifted from the 4-ounce package to the 8- and 6-ounce packages. The effect has been to decrease sales of the 4-ounce package by 15,000 units and to increase sales of the 8-ounce package and 6-ounce package by 5,000 each. The total sales revenue has dropped by $8,600, but the total contribution margin has increased by $1,150.

This result is achieved by selling more of the higher-profit products and fewer of the lower-profit products. And although it is obvious that doing so will increase profit, it is useful to carry out this sort of analysis, both to quantify the potential results and to focus attention not just on the revenues, but on the contribution margins as well.

The previous analysis is a basic snapshot of the results of deemphasizing or discontinuing a product line. In addition, you should consider such issues as these:

- **The incremental costs of discontinuing a product line**—For example, the value of an existing contract to purchase the materials used.
- The **difficulty of shifting resources to a different product line**—For example, can those employees who produce one product also produce another product without additional training?

Achieving the optimum sales mix is much tougher in reality than it is in a book. Nevertheless, it's smart to monitor your sales mix closely. The wrong mix can prevent your company from being profitable. Using the tools discussed in this chapter and extending them to your actual line of business will help you achieve the optimum sales mix, both short and long term.

Summary

This chapter discussed several important tools that can help you understand how your company's profit picture is structured:

- The contribution margin analysis gives you a snapshot of how a particular product is performing, in terms of both its variable costs (which increase with each additional unit produced) and its contribution margin (sales revenue less variable costs).
- The unit contribution analysis puts you in a position to consider the profitability of a given product in greater detail.
- The break-even point in sales tells you how much revenue you must generate to cover both your products' variable costs as well as your fixed costs. This may imply that you need to lower your costs, increase your sales price, or increase the number of units sold.
- The break-even point in units tells you how many units you need to sell to cover your fixed and variable costs. You may find that you need to increase sales staff to reach the break-even point in units. This can be a complex decision when increasing staff leads to a concomitant increase in fixed costs.
- The sales mix analysis helps you understand how your product lines combine to result in a profit or loss. It can help pinpoint which products are performing best and where you may need to adjust costs to lift the performance of a given product.

Pricing and Costing

20

Whether a business operates at a loss or makes a profit depends heavily on how much it costs to produce a product and how much the business can sell it for. Costs and prices are closely related, and this chapter goes into some detail about ways to analyze that relationship.

Although neither costs nor prices are under your complete control, you can exercise some influence on both. Many methods of cost control exist, from reducing the company's payroll and lowering inventory levels to watching the travel and entertainment expenses.

Regarding prices, another difficulty arises: competition. Competitors are often intent on capturing your market share or on forcing you into a precarious position in the marketplace. They can often do so by cutting the prices they charge for products that are similar to yours. Yes, selling on the basis of features and quality and engaging in so-called "relationship selling" can mitigate the impact of a head-on assault on price structures. In the long run, though, even the most skilled sales force can't make up for a dramatic price disadvantage.

But some analytic techniques enable you to get a handle on the relationship between the costs of production and the prices you charge for your products. By understanding these relationships, you can sometimes make adjustments in the cost components without disrupting your business's operations. In turn, these adjustments sometimes have an effect on the way you price your products.

"Buy low and sell high" is a deceptively simple epigram that is both perfectly valid and utterly useless. How low is low? As the next section shows, that depends on the costs that are fixed and the costs that are variable.

IN THIS CHAPTER

Using Absorption and Contribution Costing

Two important methods of determining costs—absorption and contribution costing—can yield very different results. But there is only one major difference between the two approaches: Absorption costing allocates certain production costs between the total cost of goods sold (COGS) and the ending inventory, whereas contribution costing allocates those production costs entirely to the COGS.

The income for a period can differ depending on which method is used. The following two sections discuss the specific reasons for this difference.

Understanding Absorption Costing

You nearly always have some goods left in your inventory at the end of a period, and this can make it hard to figure your profitability. The difficulty comes about because the valuation of your inventory includes both variable and fixed costs.

CASE STUDY: QUICKDATA CABLE MODEMS

QuickData Modems is a subsidiary of a large electronics manufacturer. QuickData purchases cable modems from DataPump, another of its owner's subsidiaries. QuickData then puts its own logo on the modems and sells them at a lower price than does DataPump. QuickData keeps its total costs lower than DataPump's by offering a much more restricted product warranty.

QuickData's production process therefore consists of placing its logo on each product and preparing the product for sale—among other things, QuickData packages software along with the modem. QuickData's production costs consist of purchasing the modem from DataPump, stamping its logo on the modem, and boxing the product.

Figure 20.1 shows some basic operating data and a partial income statement for QuickData for the first quarter of 2011.

QuickData prepares 10,000 cable modems for sale during the first quarter and sells 8,000 of them for $110 each. The *variable* production cost of each modem is $38. Additionally, QuickData has a *fixed* production cost of $90,000 per quarter that it must meet, regardless of how many modems it produces—whether 1 or 100,000.

The purpose of this case study is to focus on the different effects of fixed and variable costs on the valuation of finished goods. To keep the example straightforward, it is assumed that QuickData has no beginning inventory at the start of the period. By the end of the case study, you will see how two different approaches to costing lead to two different valuations of the ending inventory—which is the beginning inventory for the next period.

Figure 20.1
Under absorption costing, some production costs are allocated to the value of the ending inventory.

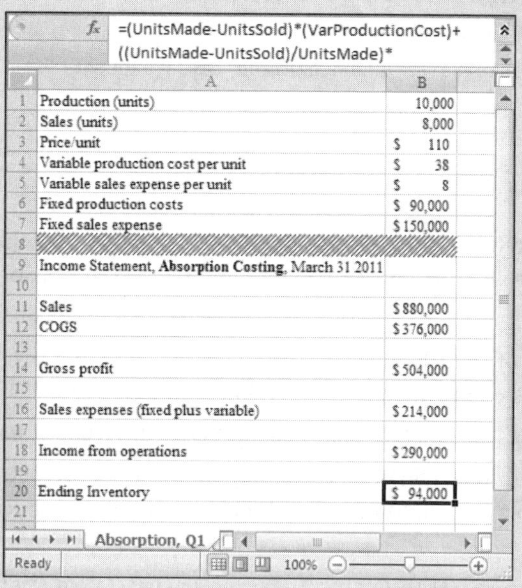

=(UnitsMade-UnitsSold)*(VarProductionCost)+ ((UnitsMade-UnitsSold)/UnitsMade)*

	A	B
1	Production (units)	10,000
2	Sales (units)	8,000
3	Price/unit	$ 110
4	Variable production cost per unit	$ 38
5	Variable sales expense per unit	$ 8
6	Fixed production costs	$ 90,000
7	Fixed sales expense	$ 150,000
8		
9	Income Statement, **Absorption Costing**, March 31 2011	
10		
11	Sales	$ 880,000
12	COGS	$ 376,000
13		
14	Gross profit	$ 504,000
15		
16	Sales expenses (fixed plus variable)	$ 214,000
17		
18	Income from operations	$ 290,000
19		
20	Ending Inventory	$ 94,000
21		

Absorption, Q1
Ready 100%

In addition to production costs, QuickData has sales expenses, both variable and fixed. The variable sales expense is $8 per modem, which includes the sales force's commission as well as a reserve for fulfilling the restricted product warranty. The fixed sales costs include such items as the printing of product brochures and the salaries paid to the sales force.

By selling 8,000 modems at $110 each during the first quarter, QuickData realizes revenue in the amount of $880,000. To arrive at its gross profit, QuickData computes its COGS as follows:

```
=Units_Sold*(Variable_Cost+(Fixed_Cost/Units_Made))
```

Using actual values, the COGS is computed like this:

```
=8000*(38+(90000/10000))
```

The result is $376,000. Notice that this is the sum of the number of units sold (8,000) times the sum of the variable production cost ($38) and the average fixed production cost of each unit that was made. It's helpful to look more closely at the components of the total COGS. Another way to express the same result is this:

```
=Units_Sold*(Variable_Cost) + Units_Sold * (Fixed_Cost/Units_Made)
```

or, using values:

```
=8000 * 38 + 8000 * (90000/10000))
```

The result of 8,000 × $38 is $304,000, the total variable production cost of the units sold.

The result of 8,000 × ($90,000/10,000) equals $72,000, which is 80% of the $90,000 in fixed production cost: the portion that can be allocated to the 8,000 modems that were sold. The sum of the variable production cost, $304,000, and the allocated fixed production cost, $72,000, is the COGS—in this case, $376,000.

The gross profit, sales minus COGS, is $504,000. The total of the fixed sales costs and the variable sales costs is calculated as follows:

```
=Units_Sold*Variable_Sales_Expense+Fixed_Sales_Expense
```

Again, using actual values produces the following:

```
=8000*8+150000
```

which returns $214,000.

The income from operations is therefore $504,00 – $214,000, or $290,000. This is the difference between the gross profit on the modems and the expenses associated with the sales process.

QuickData sells 8,000 of the 10,000 units it produces during the quarter. The remaining 2,000 units make up its ending inventory. Its value can be calculated as follows:

```
=(Units_Made-Units_Sold)*(Variable_Cost+(Fixed_Cost/Units_Made))
```

Again, this formula multiplies the units remaining in inventory (10,000 – 8,000 = 2,000) by the sum of their variable production costs and the average fixed production cost for all units made. Equivalently:

```
= (Ending_Units * Variable_Cost) + (Ending_Units*(Fixed_Cost/Units_Made))
```

The result of the first term in the formula is 2,000 × $38 or $76,000, the total variable production cost of the units remaining in inventory.

The result of the second term in the formula is 2,000 × ($90,000 / 10,000) or $18,000, which is 20% of the fixed production costs, the portion that can be allocated to the 2,000 modems that went unsold. This is the remaining 20% of the fixed production cost that was not allocated to the 8,000 modems that were sold.

The result of the full formula is $76,000 plus $18,000, or $94,000, which is the total value of QuickData's inventory at the end of the first quarter. Notice that neither the fixed nor the variable sales expense is involved in the valuation of the ending inventory: Because these 2,000 modems have not yet been sold, the expenses of selling them have not yet been incurred.

At the end of the second quarter, QuickData prepares another income statement (see Figure 20.2).

Comparing the two income statements in Figures 20.1 and 20.2, notice the following:

- The number of units sold has not changed.
- The sales price has not changed.
- Neither the fixed production cost nor the fixed sales expenses have changed.
- Neither the per-unit variable production cost nor the per-unit variable sales expense has changed.
- The number of modems produced has increased from 10,000 during the first quarter to 11,000 during the second quarter.

- The net income from operations has increased from $290,000 in the first quarter to $294,909 in the second quarter.

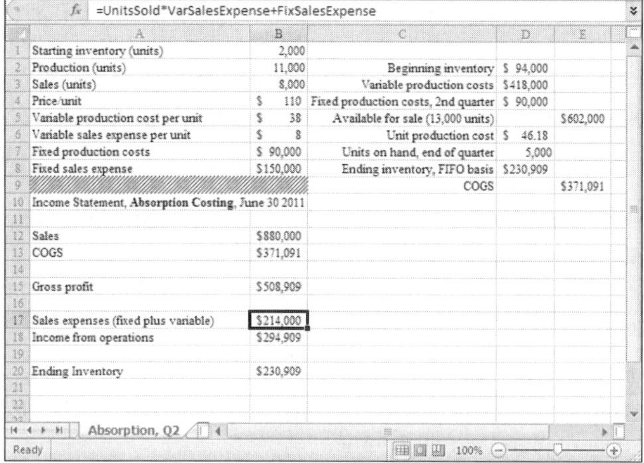

=UnitsSold*VarSalesExpense+FixSalesExpense

	A	B	C	D	E
1	Starting inventory (units)	2,000			
2	Production (units)	11,000	Beginning inventory	$ 94,000	
3	Sales (units)	8,000	Variable production costs	$418,000	
4	Price/unit	$ 110	Fixed production costs, 2nd quarter	$ 90,000	
5	Variable production cost per unit	$ 38	Available for sale (13,000 units)		$602,000
6	Variable sales expense per unit	$ 8	Unit production cost	$ 46.18	
7	Fixed production costs	$ 90,000	Units on hand, end of quarter	5,000	
8	Fixed sales expense	$150,000	Ending inventory, FIFO basis	$230,909	
9			COGS		$371,091
10	Income Statement, **Absorption Costing**, June 30 2011				
11					
12	Sales	$880,000			
13	COGS	$371,091			
14					
15	Gross profit	$508,909			
16					
17	Sales expenses (fixed plus variable)	$214,000			
18	Income from operations	$294,909			
19					
20	Ending Inventory	$230,909			
21					
22					

Absorption, Q2

Ready 100%

Figure 20.2
Absorption costing causes operating income to vary with production levels.

You might not have expected this. When the number of units sold, the selling price, and the costs and expenses are constant, as they are here, you would intuitively expect that the net income would also be constant.

Notice that the only change in the basic inputs is that the number of units produced has increased. Therefore, a different proportion of the fixed production cost is allocated to the COGS. A larger proportion of the $90,000 in fixed production cost—which does not vary as the number of units produced rises or falls—has been allocated to the ending inventory, and a smaller proportion has been allocated to the COGS. When the COGS falls, the gross profit increases, as does the net income from operations.

Pinpointing the Changes

It's a little easier to understand this effect if you bear in mind what has changed and what hasn't. In this example, the number of units sold is unchanged: 8,000 in each quarter. But more units are produced during the second quarter (11,000) than during the first quarter (10,000). Because the additional 1,000 units produced are not sold during the second quarter, the ending inventory *must* be greater, by 1,000, at the end of the second quarter than at the end of the first.

Under the absorption approach, the fixed production cost is apportioned between units sold and units in ending inventory, according to the percent of units in each category. Units sold holds steady at 8,000. Ending units grows from 2,000 at the end of the first quarter to 5,000 at the end of the second quarter.

So $72,000, or 80% of the $90,000 fixed production cost, is allocated to COGS during the first quarter. In contrast, during the second quarter, there are three sources of costs for the 8,000 units sold:

- The 2,000 units in beginning inventory, and sold during the quarter, valued at $94,000. That dollar amount represents both the variable and the fixed production costs for the first quarter that are allocated to the 2,000 units.
- Of the 11,000 produced during the second quarter, 6,000 were sold. They carry a variable production cost of 6,000 * $38, or $228,000.
- Again, of the 11,000 produced during the second quarter, 6,000 were sold. They also carry 6,000 / 11,000, or 54.55%, of $90,000 in fixed production costs. That amounts to $49,091 in the second quarter instead of the first quarter's $72,000.

The combined effects of lower variable and lower fixed production costs for the units sold during the second quarter is to reduce COGS and increase net income. The total of these COGS sources, $94,000 + $228,000 + $49,091, is $371,091. You can verify from cell B13 in Figure 20.2 that this is the second quarter COGS.

The first quarter's COGS was $376,000 (see cell B12 in Figure 20.1). So the difference between first and second quarter COGS is $4,909. That's precisely the difference between the first and second quarters' net income.

From management's perspective, this can be an unwelcome development. A manager for QuickData would want the gross profit from operations to vary as a function of sales quantities and prices, less costs and expenses. Instead, using the approach in Figures 20.1 and 20.2, net income has varied as a function of production.

For that reason, QuickData might not want to use this approach to support its decision-making process. (It is termed the *absorption* approach to costing because the fixed production costs are absorbed partly by the goods sold and partly by the goods that remain in inventory at the end of the period.) A more informative approach would be one that allows QuickData to estimate income independent of changes in the volume of products that it produces.

To get a better feel for what happens with absorption costing, consider some of the additional information shown in Figure 20.2, focusing on the range C2:E9.

The COGS is calculated using a formula that has appeared in several other chapters of this book:

```
COGS = Beginning Inventory + Production - Ending Inventory
```

The beginning inventory for the second quarter, $94,000, is the value of the first quarter's ending inventory (see cell B20 in Figure 20.1).

To that beginning inventory is added the total variable production costs of $418,000, which is returned by the following:

```
=Units_Made*Variable_Cost
```

Using actual figures, this is 11,000 × $38. The beginning inventory plus the variable production costs total $512,000. Adding the $90,000 in fixed production costs gives a total value of goods available for sale of $602,000 (see cell E5 in Figure 20.2).

The unit production cost, in cell D6, is found by adding the total variable production costs of $418,000 plus the fixed production cost of $90,000 and dividing by the number of units produced (11,000). This distributes both the variable and fixed production costs across the 11,000 units and returns $46.18 as the total cost of producing a single unit.

By multiplying the unit production cost by the ending inventory of 5,000 units, QuickData can establish a total value for its ending inventory: 5,000 units times $46.18 is $230,909. The first-in, first-out (FIFO) method is used in this method of inventory valuation. FIFO assumes that, in this case, Quarter 2's beginning inventory of 2,000 units is sold before the company starts selling the units produced during the second quarter.

➜ See Chapter 3, "Valuing Inventories for the Balance Sheet," for a discussion of the various methods of inventory valuation, including FIFO.

Arriving at COGS for the Second Quarter

Finally, QuickData can arrive at a figure for COGS during the second quarter. The figure of $371,091 in cell E9 of Figure 20.2 represents the cost of goods available for sale, $602,000, less the ending inventory of $230,909.

Notice that part of the fixed production costs of $90,000 appears in the valuation of the ending inventory. The unit production cost includes a per-unit fixed production cost and is used to value the 5,000 units that remain in inventory at the end of the quarter. In Figure 20.2, COGS is computed by subtracting the value of the ending inventory from the value of the goods available for sale during the quarter.

Computed in this way, the COGS depends partly on the valuation of the ending inventory, so it includes the portion of the fixed production costs that is not attributed to, or *absorbed by*, the ending inventory.

Another way to look at it is to explicitly calculate the percentage of fixed costs allocated to the units sold and to the ending inventory (see Figure 20.3).

Because FIFO is the valuation method used, the assumption is that the first 2,000 of the 8,000 modems sold come from the beginning inventory; its cost is $94,000 (see cell C10 in Figure 20.3).

To that $94,000, add the total variable cost of the other 6,000 modems sold: 6,000 × $38 is $228,000. The third component in the COGS is the proportion of fixed production costs that is allocated to the 6,000 newly produced modems: 6,000 / 11,000 (54.55 percent) × $90,000 is $49,091. The sum of the starting inventory, plus the variable costs of production of 6,000 modems, plus the sold goods' share of $90,000, is $371,091, which is shown in cell C15. Note that this is the same figure for COGS as appears in cell B13 of Figure 20.2.

And because the cost of the goods available for sale is $602,000, the ending inventory is $602,000 – $371,091 or $230,909, just as in cell B20 of Figure 20.2. Any way you go about calculating the COGS and the cost of the ending inventory, a portion of the fixed costs of production appears in—is absorbed by—each quantity. The portion of the fixed production cost that is attributable to either quantity depends on the ratio of the number of units sold

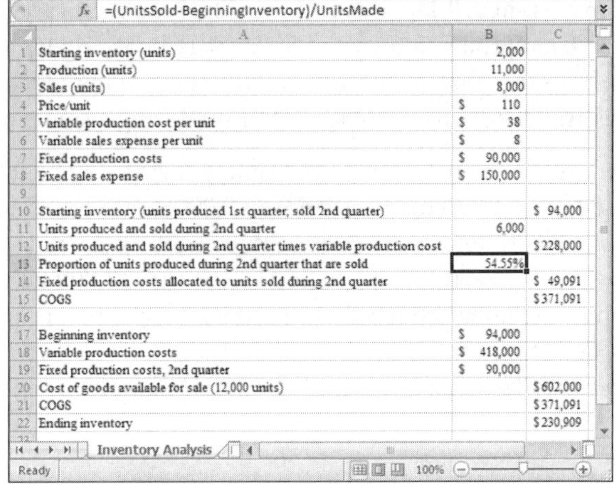

fx =(UnitsSold-BeginningInventory)/UnitsMade

	A	B	C
1	Starting inventory (units)	2,000	
2	Production (units)	11,000	
3	Sales (units)	8,000	
4	Price/unit	$ 110	
5	Variable production cost per unit	$ 38	
6	Variable sales expense per unit	$ 8	
7	Fixed production costs	$ 90,000	
8	Fixed sales expense	$ 150,000	
9			
10	Starting inventory (units produced 1st quarter, sold 2nd quarter)		$ 94,000
11	Units produced and sold during 2nd quarter	6,000	
12	Units produced and sold during 2nd quarter times variable production cost		$ 228,000
13	Proportion of units produced during 2nd quarter that are sold	54.55%	
14	Fixed production costs allocated to units sold during 2nd quarter		$ 49,091
15	COGS		$ 371,091
16			
17	Beginning inventory	$ 94,000	
18	Variable production costs	$ 418,000	
19	Fixed production costs, 2nd quarter	$ 90,000	
20	Cost of goods available for sale (12,000 units)		$ 602,000
21	COGS		$ 371,091
22	Ending inventory		$ 230,909

Inventory Analysis

Figure 20.3
With absorption costing, fixed costs are allocated according to the ratio of units sold to units produced.

to the number of units remaining in inventory at the end of the period. This is the reason that a change in units produced causes a change in net income, even though the number of units sold, the unit sales price, the variable costs and the fixed costs remain constant.

Understanding Contribution Costing

Contribution costing (also known as *variable* costing) adopts a different point of view toward the allocation of fixed production costs. Instead of allocating these costs partly to goods that are sold and partly to goods that remain in inventory, this approach allocates the entire amount of fixed production costs to COGS. Figure 20.4 shows how this works.

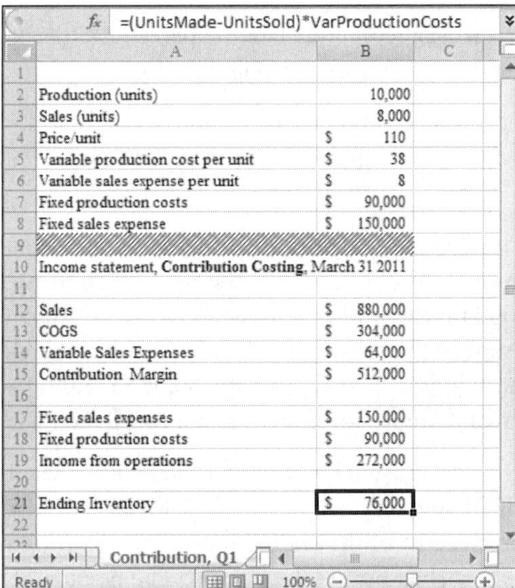

fx =(UnitsMade-UnitsSold)*VarProductionCosts

	A	B	C
1			
2	Production (units)	10,000	
3	Sales (units)	8,000	
4	Price/unit	$ 110	
5	Variable production cost per unit	$ 38	
6	Variable sales expense per unit	$ 8	
7	Fixed production costs	$ 90,000	
8	Fixed sales expense	$ 150,000	
9			
10	Income statement, **Contribution Costing**, March 31 2011		
11			
12	Sales	$ 880,000	
13	COGS	$ 304,000	
14	Variable Sales Expenses	$ 64,000	
15	Contribution Margin	$ 512,000	
16			
17	Fixed sales expenses	$ 150,000	
18	Fixed production costs	$ 90,000	
19	Income from operations	$ 272,000	
20			
21	Ending Inventory	$ 76,000	
22			

Contribution, Q1

Figure 20.4
Contribution costing allocates all fixed costs to the products that are sold.

Compare Figure 20.4 to Figure 20.1, which shows QuickData's first-quarter income statement under the absorption approach. The first major difference is in the calculation of the COGS. Using contribution costing, the COGS is as follows:

```
=Units_Sold*Variable_Costs
```

This is 8,000 × $38, or $304,000. The absorption approach included a portion of the fixed production costs in its COGS calculation.

The variable sales expense is entered into cell B14 as follows:

```
=Units_Sold* Variable_Sales_Expense
```

This returns $64,000. As discussed in Chapter 19, "Analyzing Contributions and Margins," when COGS and the variable sales expense are subtracted from the sales figure of $880,000, the result is the product's contribution margin (hence the term *contribution costing*).

Then, just as is done using the absorption approach, the fixed sales expenses are entered. But in contrast to the absorption approach, the *total* fixed production costs are entered into the computation; they are subtracted from the contribution margin to return the income from operations, in cell B19, of $272,000.

Notice that this is $18,000 less than the $290,000 income from operations reported in Figure 20.1. The reason is that in Figure 20.1, 20 percent (2,000 modems in ending inventory divided by 10,000 modems produced) of the fixed production costs were allocated to the ending inventory. Twenty percent of the $90,000 fixed production costs is $18,000. Using the contribution approach, that 20 percent is charged to income instead of to the value of the ending inventory.

Compare the income statement in Figure 20.4 with the one shown in Figure 20.5, for the second quarter of 2011.

The input information shown in Figure 20.5 is the same as in Figure 20.4. The income statements in both figures use contribution costing. However, and in contrast to absorption costing, Figures 20.4 and 20.5 show that the income from operations is the same in the second quarter as in the first quarter. This is because sales, cost, and expense data have remained constant despite the fact that production has increased from the first quarter to the second quarter.

Analyzing the Effect of Changes

This is the desirable effect of contribution costing: Changes in income are a function of changes in revenue and costs and are not due to changes in levels of production. From a management perspective, it is more informative and more efficient to analyze the effect of changes in pricing, expenses, and quantities sold on a variable that responds directly to those inputs. It is less useful to perform that analysis on a variable that also responds to production levels.

Of course, contribution costing has a consequence for the value of the ending inventory. Figure 20.4 shows that, under contribution costing, income from operations is $272,000 for the first quarter. That's $18,000 less than income from operations for the first quarter under

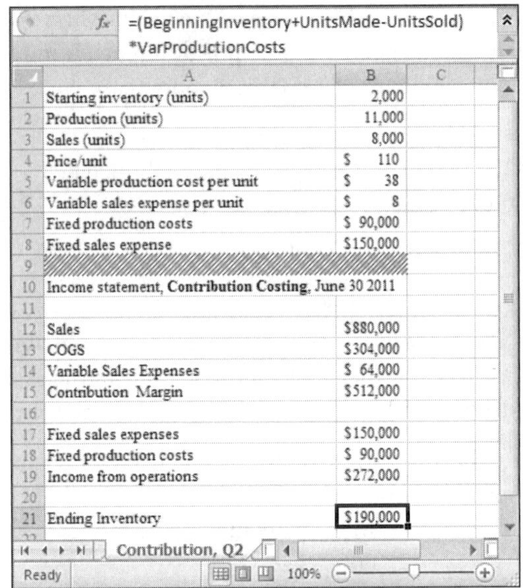

=(BeginningInventory+UnitsMade-UnitsSold)
*VarProductionCosts

	A	B	C
1	Starting inventory (units)	2,000	
2	Production (units)	11,000	
3	Sales (units)	8,000	
4	Price/unit	$ 110	
5	Variable production cost per unit	$ 38	
6	Variable sales expense per unit	$ 8	
7	Fixed production costs	$ 90,000	
8	Fixed sales expense	$150,000	
9			
10	Income statement, **Contribution Costing**, June 30 2011		
11			
12	Sales	$880,000	
13	COGS	$304,000	
14	Variable Sales Expenses	$ 64,000	
15	Contribution Margin	$512,000	
16			
17	Fixed sales expenses	$150,000	
18	Fixed production costs	$ 90,000	
19	Income from operations	$272,000	
20			
21	Ending Inventory	$190,000	

Contribution, Q2

Ready 100%

Figure 20.5
Contribution costing makes income independent of production quantities.

absorption costing. Furthermore, the value of the first quarter's ending inventory under the contribution approach is $76,000, versus $94,000 at the end of the first quarter under the absorption approach. Again, the difference is $18,000.

The $18,000 in costs that appeared in ending inventory under the absorption approach is shifted to a current-period expense under the contribution approach. This has the simultaneous effects of reducing the valuation of ending inventory and reducing the income from operations, both by $18,000.

> **NOTE** Because of the way it values inventories, the contribution approach is *not* normally used to prepare income statements and balance sheets that are used outside the company—for example, by potential creditors and investors. The contribution approach tends to undervalue inventories because it omits a portion of fixed production costs from their valuation, and it tends to understate income because it charges the full amount of fixed production costs for a period against the contribution margin.

It should be no surprise that the matching principle appears in a discussion of the relative merits of absorption costing versus contribution costing. According to this principle, costs should be matched with the revenues that they help to produce, during the period that the costs were incurred and the revenue occurred.

Absorption costing causes the costs associated with the production of products to remain with those products until they are sold. It's proper to show those costs when they have been recovered: when a product that remains in one period's ending inventory is sold during a subsequent period.

Equally, it's reasonable to argue that fixed costs of production represent the cost of being able to produce a product in the first place. Without incurring those costs, a company would be unable to produce *any* product. Therefore, these costs should not be regarded as attributable to one collection of goods but as a cost of the period in which they were incurred. In that case, these costs should be fully charged to the period, not distributed among the products that were manufactured and subsequently were either sold or held in inventory.

NOTE These are philosophical positions, though, and are moot. What matters is that absorption costing should normally be used for external reporting purposes. For internal planning purposes, in which you want to investigate the relationships among costs, volume of sales, and profitability, you are free to use any method of analysis that you and your company approve.

Applying the Contribution Approach to a Pricing Decision

How can a contribution analysis of a product line help you decide how best to set its sales price? Suppose that QuickData's income statement for the first quarter is as shown in Figure 20.6.

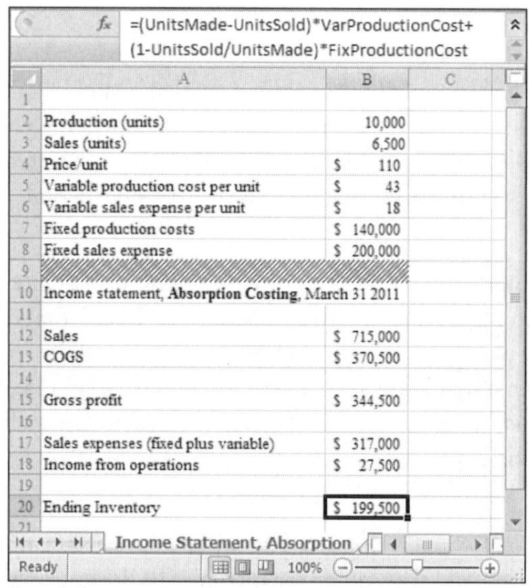

fx =(UnitsMade-UnitsSold)*VarProductionCost+(1-UnitsSold/UnitsMade)*FixProductionCost

	A	B
1		
2	Production (units)	10,000
3	Sales (units)	6,500
4	Price/unit	$ 110
5	Variable production cost per unit	$ 43
6	Variable sales expense per unit	$ 18
7	Fixed production costs	$ 140,000
8	Fixed sales expense	$ 200,000
9		
10	Income statement, **Absorption Costing**, March 31 2011	
11		
12	Sales	$ 715,000
13	COGS	$ 370,500
14		
15	Gross profit	$ 344,500
16		
17	Sales expenses (fixed plus variable)	$ 317,000
18	Income from operations	$ 27,500
19		
20	Ending Inventory	$ 199,500

Income Statement, Absorption

Figure 20.6
Absorption costing makes it difficult to arrive at cost-volume-profit decisions.

This income statement, which uses absorption costing, depicts QuickData as not doing as well as earlier figures in this chapter suggested. All of QuickData's costs and expenses have increased, and the quarter's unit sales have decreased to 6,500. As a result, the income from operations has fallen to $27,500.

QuickData's management wants to know how changes in the sales price of its modems, or changes in the quantities that it sells, might affect its net income from operations. As a first step, QuickData prepares an income statement in a contribution costing format (see Figure 20.7).

Figure 20.7
With contribution costing, the relationships among pricing, costing, and sales volumes become more clear.

fx =(UnitsMade-UnitsSold)*VarProductionCost

	A	B	C
1			
2	Production (units)	10,000	
3	Sales (units)	6,500	
4	Price/unit	$ 110	
5	Variable production cost per unit	$ 43	
6	Variable sales expense per unit	$ 18	
7	Fixed production costs	$ 140,000	
8	Fixed sales expense	$ 200,000	
9			
10	Income statement, **Contribution Costing**, March 31 2011		
11			
12	Sales	$ 715,000	
13	COGS	$ 279,500	
14	Variable sales expenses	$ 117,000	
15	Contribution margin	$ 318,500	
16			
17	Fixed production costs	$ 140,000	
18	Fixed sales expenses	$ 200,000	
19	Income from operations	$ (21,500)	
20			
21	Ending Inventory	$ 150,500	

Income Statement, Contribution

Ready 100%

The first item to notice in this contribution analysis is that QuickData's operating income from this product is actually negative. When QuickData deducts the entire amount of the fixed production costs, $140,000, from the contribution margin—instead of allocating the fixed production costs partly to the ending inventory—the net income becomes a loss of $21,500.

Using the contribution approach, QuickData's management can isolate the effect of changes in sales quantities and pricing on income from operations. Recall that, under the absorption approach, income is partly a function of production levels and costs. But when you use the contribution approach, changes in production volume have no effect on the net income attributable to the product. Therefore, if management can find the right mix of sales price and quantity sold, it can be confident that the product will remain profitable regardless of changes that might occur in the production volumes.

If QuickData's management wants to focus solely on sales price, it can use Excel's Goal Seek tool to determine its break-even point for income. To do so using the data from the worksheet shown in Figure 20.7, follow these steps:

1. Select cell B19.
2. Click the Ribbon's Data tab, click the What-If Analysis drop-down, and select Goal Seek from the drop-down list. (In Excel versions prior to Office 2007, choose Tools, Goal Seek.) The Set Cell edit box is selected by default and refers to cell B19.

3. Click in the To Value edit box, and enter `0` (zero).
4. Click in the By Changing Cell edit box, and click in cell B4 on the worksheet.
5. Click OK.

Cell B19, Income from Operations, now equals $0, and cell B4 now equals $113.31. This is the price that QuickData must charge to arrive at a break-even point if it changes nothing but the sales price (see Figure 20.8).

Figure 20.8
Break-even points are easier to find using contribution costing.

=(UnitsMade-UnitsSold)*VarProductionCost

	A	B	C
1			
2	Production (units)	$ 10,000.00	
3	Sales (units)	$ 6,500.00	
4	Price/unit	$ 113.31	
5	Variable production cost per unit	$ 43.00	
6	Variable sales expense per unit	$ 18.00	
7	Fixed production costs	$140,000.00	
8	Fixed sales expense	$200,000.00	
9			
10	Income statement, Contribution Costing, March 31 2011		
11			
12	Sales	$736,500.00	
13	Cost of goods sold	$279,500.00	
14	Variable sales expenses	$117,000.00	
15	Contribution margin	$340,000.00	
16			
17	Fixed production costs	$140,000.00	
18	Fixed sales expenses	$200,000.00	
19	Income from operations	$0.00	
20			
21	Ending Inventory	$150,500.00	

Break-even analysis

Ready 100%

NOTE

If QuickData's management wants to increase its income from operations beyond the break-even point and yet allow both price and sales quantities to fluctuate, it could use the Solver rather than the Goal Seek tool. The Solver can modify several inputs simultaneously, but Goal Seek is restricted to one input (in this example, that's sales price).

Using Contribution Analysis for New Products

Several figures in the previous section show that you calculate the contribution margin by subtracting a product's variable costs from its revenue. For example, in Figure 20.8, the contribution margin is $340,000. That's the result of subtracting the COGS ($279,500) and variable sales expenses ($117,000) from the sales figure of $736,500. This formula returns the COGS:

```
=Units_Sold*Variable_Cost
```

So you obtain the contribution margin by combining sales revenue, variable sales expenses, and variable production cost. In fact, this defines the contribution margin: It is the difference between sales revenue and variable costs and expenses. No fixed costs enter into the equation.

This method of segregating variable costs from fixed costs to determine contribution margin can be useful in other situations, such as deciding whether to bring a new offering into your product set. Suppose, for example, that DataPump, Inc., currently manufactures two kinds of data communications devices: a DSL modem and a cable modem. DataPump needs to decide whether to begin manufacturing a wireless router that would extend the reach of its cable modem to multiple stations without installing new cable.

The company makes the preliminary calculations shown in Figure 20.9, using the contribution approach.

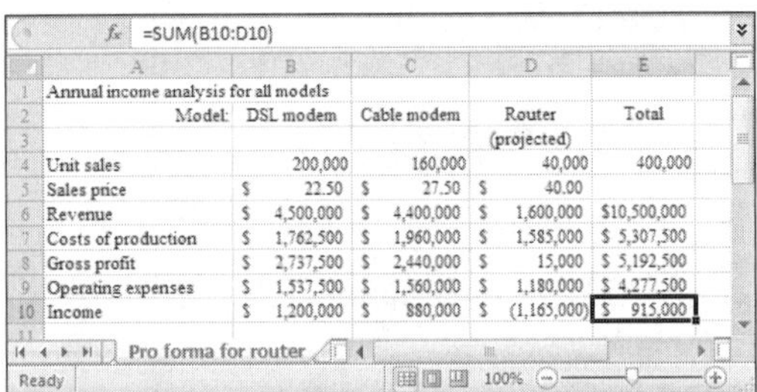

	A	B	C	D	E
1	Annual income analysis for all models				
2	Model:	DSL modem	Cable modem	Router	Total
3				(projected)	
4	Unit sales	200,000	160,000	40,000	400,000
5	Sales price	$ 22.50	$ 27.50	$ 40.00	
6	Revenue	$ 4,500,000	$ 4,400,000	$ 1,600,000	$10,500,000
7	Costs of production	$ 1,762,500	$ 1,960,000	$ 1,585,000	$ 5,307,500
8	Gross profit	$ 2,737,500	$ 2,440,000	$ 15,000	$ 5,192,500
9	Operating expenses	$ 1,537,500	$ 1,560,000	$ 1,180,000	$ 4,277,500
10	Income	$ 1,200,000	$ 880,000	$ (1,165,000)	$ 915,000

Figure 20.9
This initial view of a new product line suggests that it would lose money.

Columns B and C of Figure 20.9 show the actual revenue, cost, and expense results for the existing models. These figures indicate that the existing models have been doing reasonably well in the marketplace. But the analysis also suggests that the outlook for a new model is poor. The wireless router is not projected to be profitable at an annual sales volume of 40,000 units.

DataPump's management believes that some of the costs of producing the proposed router can be shared among all three products. Management also believes that some operating expenses can be kept to a minimum because a portion of the end-user marketplace will actively seek out the router. It appears that as time passes, more and more home users are wanting all their PCs to have high-speed connections, and the cable companies are charging a monthly fee for each attached cable modem. That's why a wireless router is a cost-effective solution. Management hopes that the market will help reduce the amount of time and money needed for the sales force to market the product effectively.

Even so, the projections for the proposed new model are not good. The projected revenue of $1.6 million is just enough to cover the costs of production, with $15,000 to spare. And when the operating expenses associated with the router are figured in, the router is projected to lose more than $1 million per year.

What if the projected sales quantity of 40,000 units is too conservative—that is, what if the router proves popular enough that DataPump can sell 50,000 or 60,000 units?

The analysis in Figure 20.9 can't answer that question. Some of the cost of production is fixed, as are some of the operating expenses. These fixed dollar amounts would not change if more units were produced and sold. On the other hand, some of the costs and expenses are variable and would increase as production and sales increased. To estimate the effect of greater sales, it's necessary to divide the costs and expenses into fixed and variable categories.

Figure 20.10 shows the first step in extending the analysis.

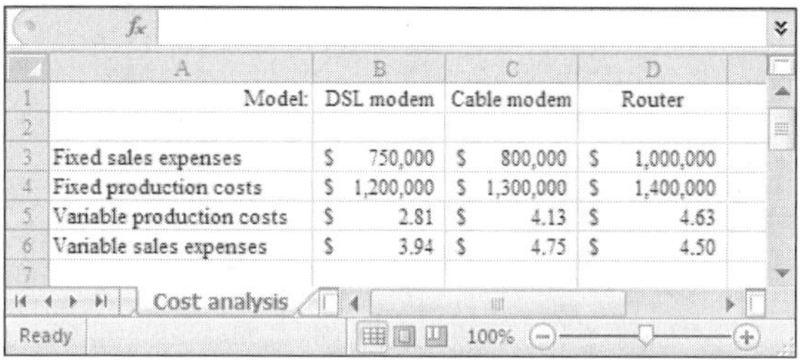

Figure 20.10
Accurate cost and expense breakdowns can be very difficult to achieve but are necessary components of pricing analysis.

	A	B	C	D
1	Model:	DSL modem	Cable modem	Router
2				
3	Fixed sales expenses	$ 750,000	$ 800,000	$ 1,000,000
4	Fixed production costs	$ 1,200,000	$ 1,300,000	$ 1,400,000
5	Variable production costs	$ 2.81	$ 4.13	$ 4.63
6	Variable sales expenses	$ 3.94	$ 4.75	$ 4.50
7				

Cost analysis

For each model, the analysis estimates four dollar amounts: fixed sales and production amounts, and variable production and sales amounts.

The keyword in the previous sentence is *estimates*. In practice, it's usually tough to determine which actual costs and expenses are fixed and which ones are variable. It can be even more difficult to allocate these dollar amounts to different products, especially when, as here, an increase in sales volume of one product (routers) might well erode the sales volume of another product (cable modems). This effect is sometimes termed *cross-elasticity* and is discussed later in this chapter, in the section titled Estimating the Effect of Cross-Elasticity.

Allocating Expenses to Product Lines

Suppose, for example, that some DataPump retailers purchase both the DSL and the cable modems for resale. The cost of sales calls made by DataPump's sales force must somehow be allocated between the two models to arrive at a variable sales expense for each. To do so with a reasonable degree of accuracy, DataPump management might analyze a sample of customer purchasing records and compare it to sales expense reports. Even so, the analyst has to use good judgment in allocating expenses to different products.

The process isn't easy but it is feasible, and this discussion assumes that the costs and expenses shown in Figure 20.10 are reasonably accurate. The next step is to use the cost analysis to create a contribution analysis (see Figure 20.11).

The amounts shown in Figure 20.11 are based on unit revenue—the sales price for one unit of each model—and on unit variable costs and expenses. Keep in mind that the definition of a contribution margin is the product's revenue, less its associated variable costs and expenses.

The situation starts to become a little clearer. Because DataPump can share some variable production costs among the three products, the incremental cost of producing each router can be kept in check. Furthermore, the variable cost of producing a cable modem is 15% of its revenue, compared to 12% of the router's revenue. However, these amounts are no more than educated guesses provided by the manufacturing department and by sales management. The decision maker must bear that in mind while interpreting the analysis.

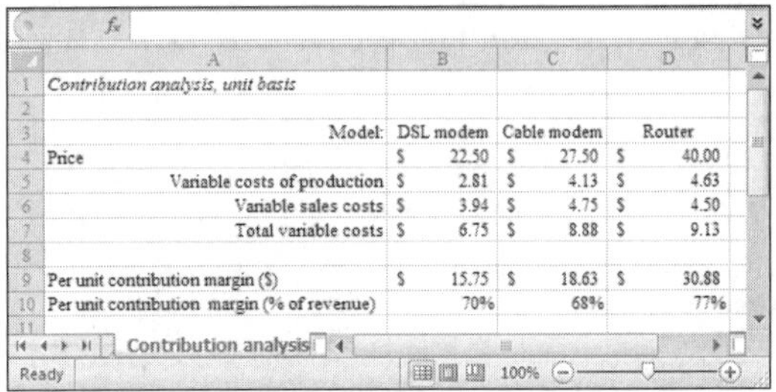

	A	B	C	D
1	*Contribution analysis, unit basis*			
2				
3	Model:	DSL modem	Cable modem	Router
4	Price	$ 22.50	$ 27.50	$ 40.00
5	Variable costs of production	$ 2.81	$ 4.13	$ 4.63
6	Variable sales costs	$ 3.94	$ 4.75	$ 4.50
7	Total variable costs	$ 6.75	$ 8.88	$ 9.13
8				
9	Per unit contribution margin ($)	$ 15.75	$ 18.63	$ 30.88
10	Per unit contribution margin (% of revenue)	70%	68%	77%

Contribution analysis

Figure 20.11
A product contribution analysis puts the new product in a different light.

Nevertheless, if the estimates are even reasonably accurate, the contribution margin for the proposed router is respectable, even impressive. Before taking fixed costs into account, the router is expected to contribute more than three quarters of its sales price to gross profit. Again, only variable costs in conjunction with sales revenue are used to arrive at the contribution margin. DataPump's management can therefore estimate which costs will rise—and by how much—as production and sales volumes increase. The remaining, fixed costs should remain stable, and DataPump can get a better picture of how adding the new router to its product set will affect its net income from operations.

Varying the Inputs

Now that you have estimated the unit contribution margins, the next step is to determine the net income under different volume assumptions (see Figure 20.12).

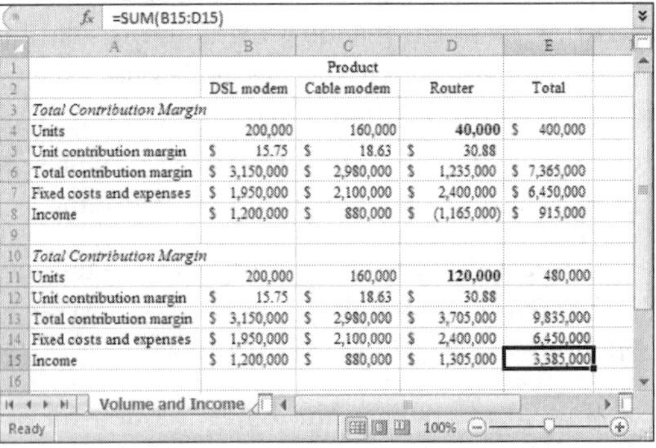

=SUM(B15:D15)

	A	B	C	D	E
1			Product		
2		DSL modem	Cable modem	Router	Total
3	*Total Contribution Margin*				
4	Units	200,000	160,000	**40,000**	$ 400,000
5	Unit contribution margin	$ 15.75	$ 18.63	$ 30.88	
6	Total contribution margin	$ 3,150,000	$ 2,980,000	$ 1,235,000	$ 7,365,000
7	Fixed costs and expenses	$ 1,950,000	$ 2,100,000	$ 2,400,000	$ 6,450,000
8	Income	$ 1,200,000	$ 880,000	$ (1,165,000)	$ 915,000
9					
10	*Total Contribution Margin*				
11	Units	200,000	160,000	**120,000**	480,000
12	Unit contribution margin	$ 15.75	$ 18.63	$ 30.88	
13	Total contribution margin	$ 3,150,000	$ 2,980,000	$ 3,705,000	9,835,000
14	Fixed costs and expenses	$ 1,950,000	$ 2,100,000	$ 2,400,000	6,450,000
15	Income	$ 1,200,000	$ 880,000	$ 1,305,000	3,385,000

Volume and Income

Figure 20.12
An aggregate contribution analysis clarifies the relationship of sales volume to operating income.

Figure 20.12 shows the effect of two different assumptions about sales volume: The range D4:D8 contains the estimated outcomes if 40,000 units (cell D4) of the proposed router are sold, and D11:D15 contains the estimates given a sales volume of 120,000 units (cell D11).

As shown previously in Figure 20.9, the new router loses $1,165,000 (cell D8 in Figure 20.12) if DataPump sells 40,000 units. This is due largely to the fixed costs and expenses that are associated with producing and selling any number of units.

However, if DataPump sells 120,000 units, it stands to increase its income by $1,305,000 (cell D15 in Figure 20.12). As DataPump sells more units, the contribution margin grows along with the sales volume. But the fixed category remains fixed and eats less into the product's contribution margin.

This analysis suggests that if DataPump can sell more than the 40,000 units initially assumed, it will begin to make money on the product (77,733 units is the break-even point).

You have probably noticed some waffling and weaseling in this discussion. That's because predicting the future is a risky undertaking. Not only does the business model involve many assumptions, but the realities of the marketplace can change during the forecast period. Here is a summary of the assumptions, both explicit and implicit, that the analysis makes:

- It's possible to distinguish fixed production costs from variable production costs.
- It's possible to distinguish fixed sales expenses from variable sales expenses.
- It's possible to allocate these costs and expenses accurately to the product lines in question.
- It's possible to estimate with reasonable accuracy the number of units that the company will actually produce and sell.
- The fixed costs and expenses remain fixed across the probable range of units produced and sold.

There is an assumption that the fixed costs and expenses are constant across a broad range of quantities. But in practice, there are usually breakpoints, such as when a company must acquire new equipment to keep pace with increased production levels.

Even though it might seem difficult to justify this set of assumptions, you will find that you generally have a good sense of how much confidence you can put in their validity and in the resulting projections.

One more major assumption remains: The introduction of the new product will have no effect on the sales of the existing products. It is necessary to test this assumption; the next section describes how to do so.

Estimating the Effect of Cross-Elasticity

When a company introduces a new product, the product often competes to some degree with products that it already produces and sells. This is termed *cross-elasticity*: the tendency of similar products to draw sales from one another instead of expanding market penetration because the products function in similar ways.

A company might want or need to introduce a new product for many reasons. The company might have to because its customers demand it, because technological advances make the new product feasible, because it must maintain the marketplace's perception of the company, or, most typically, because the competition has introduced its own version.

If the new product is so clearly superior to existing products that few customers would continue to purchase from the current product lines, it can be best to simply discontinue the existing products. But if there are real differences in function, appearance, or cost, it can also make sense to introduce a new product and continue to offer the existing lines.

What effect might the introduction of DataPump's router have both on the company's overall profitability and on the individual product lines (see Figure 20.13)?

Figure 20.13
It's useful to account for cross-elasticity when a new product competes with existing products.

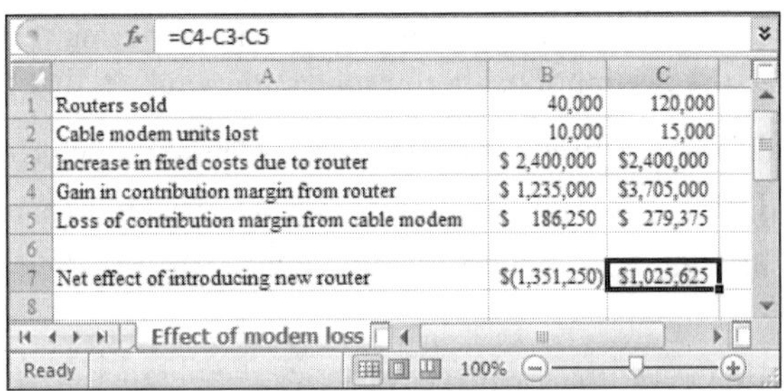
=C4-C3-C5

	A	B	C
1	Routers sold	40,000	120,000
2	Cable modem units lost	10,000	15,000
3	Increase in fixed costs due to router	$ 2,400,000	$2,400,000
4	Gain in contribution margin from router	$ 1,235,000	$3,705,000
5	Loss of contribution margin from cable modem	$ 186,250	$ 279,375
6			
7	Net effect of introducing new router	$(1,351,250)	$1,025,625
8			

The analysis in Figure 20.13 depends on DataPump's ability to estimate the sales of an existing product that would be lost to the new product. The router does not compete head to head with the cable modem, but when several PCs in a home require high-speed connections, the consumer's choice is between a modem for each PC and a router that can manage the traffic between one modem and multiple PCs.

DataPump would like to restrict the test marketing of the new product to hold down costs. One comparison between markets that would be useful is between a cable company that charges a monthly fee for each cable modem used at a given address and a company that charges one flat fee regardless of the number of cable modems installed at the address.

A market test enables DataPump to observe the effect of the product introduction in one area on the sales of its existing products. The company can then compare the outcomes in the test market to the outcomes in a control market. It should not focus solely on the test market because other influences might be at work.

For example, suppose that a cable service happened to drop its monthly rates at the same time that DataPump's market test is in progress. This might encourage some users to purchase new cable modems, but they might have no special reason to purchase a router.

In that case, the market for the cable modem might remain strong, and the effect of introducing the router could be masked. But by comparing the test market results with a comparison market, where DataPump does not introduce the router, you can isolate the effect of the router on sales of the cable modem: in other words, you can quantify the cross-elasticity of the two products.

NOTE Of course, it might not be feasible to conduct a market test. For example, DataPump might not market on a geographic basis, and thus not be able to control where its new product is sold. In that case, a typical alternative is to ask the sales force to estimate the degree of loss in the existing product that would come about as a result of the introduction of a new product. This approach is not as satisfying as conducting an empirical trial, but a carefully conducted survey of the sales force can be helpful.

Assume that DataPump has by one means or another been able to estimate how many sales of its existing cable modem it will lose to its new router. Figure 20.13 projects the financial outcomes under two scenarios: Column B describes what will happen if each of 10,000 customers purchases DataPump's router instead of at least one additional cable modem. Column C describes what will happen if 120,000 customers purchase the router: 15,000 customers purchase the router instead of the cable modem, and 105,000 new customers purchase the router. The latter 105,000 customers represent new sales, not losses from the existing product's revenue.

TIP You can also use the procedures described in Chapter 13, "Creating a Sensitivity Analysis for a Business Case," to test various outcomes under different cross-elasticity assumptions.

If DataPump's customers purchase 40,000 routers, 10,000 of them in preference to the cable modem (column B), DataPump will lose more than $1 million in income. This assumes $2.4 million in fixed costs, at a level of sales that fails to generate sufficient contribution margin ($1,235,000) to cover those costs, and at a level that reduces the contribution margin for the cable modem ($186,250).

The loss of $1,351,250 shown in cell B7 is returned by this formula:

```
=B4-B3-B5
```

This is simply the margin gained from the router, less the fixed costs due to the router, less the contribution margin lost from the cable modem.

In contrast, if DataPump sells 120,000 units of the router, suffering a loss of 15,000 units of the cable modem, it can expect to increase its net income by $1,025,625. However, in the context of the fixed costs it must take on to produce an appreciable quantity of the router, this increase in margin looks adequate, at best. On the basis of this financial analysis, it's unlikely that DataPump's management would opt to introduce the new product.

Suppose that DataPump decides that it needs to increase its net income by at least $2 million to justify the risk to its existing product line and the additional fixed costs that it would incur. DataPump can try the effect of raising the sales price of the DSL router, to increase its contribution margin (see Figure 20.14).

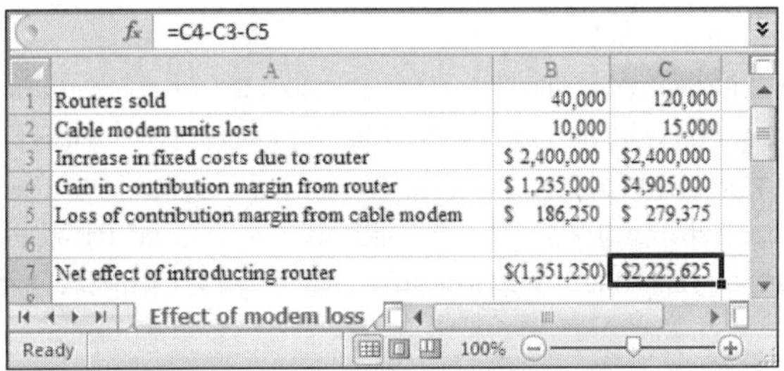

=C4-C3-C5

	A	B	C
1	Routers sold	40,000	120,000
2	Cable modem units lost	10,000	15,000
3	Increase in fixed costs due to router	$ 2,400,000	$2,400,000
4	Gain in contribution margin from router	$ 1,235,000	$4,905,000
5	Loss of contribution margin from cable modem	$ 186,250	$ 279,375
6			
7	Net effect of introducting router	$(1,351,250)	$2,225,625

Effect of modem loss

Figure 20.14
It's often necessary to revisit pricing decisions when two products or models share common characteristics.

By raising the proposed sales price of the router from $40 to $50, the net effect of introducing it is a $1.2 million increase in income. Separating the router from the cable modem by an additional $10 in sales price would certainly reduce its cross-elasticity with the existing product lines, and the number of cable modem sales lost might be less than the estimated 15,000.

However, raising the sales price would also tend to reduce the sales of the router. DataPump must be convinced that the features in the router are superior to those in its existing products by a similar margin: one that is wide enough for the new customer to justify the additional cost.

Summary

This chapter discussed the effect of the relationship between fixed costs and variable costs on your income from operations. A complex interplay exists among these costs, the price that you charge for your products, and the product quantities that you produce.

The absorption approach to costing allocates the fixed costs of production between goods that are sold and goods that remain in inventory at the end of an accounting period. This approach is used for external reporting purposes because it more accurately estimates the value of the inventory asset as well as the income earned during the period.

20

The contribution approach to costing assigns the total fixed costs of production to the goods that are sold. Although this assignment understates the value of the company's inventory asset as well as its income, it makes the income for a period insensitive to variations in levels of production (a useful effect for cost-volume-profit planning). The contribution approach is also useful for determining the potential profitability of a new product under alternative pricing structures and for assessing the impact on profitability of a product's cross-elasticity with other product lines.

Glossary

3D reference

A reference to a range that spans more than one worksheet in a workbook. A reference to the range A1:D4 is *not* a 3D reference. A reference to the range Sheet1:Sheet5!A1:D4 *is* a 3D reference. Only certain Excel functions can use 3D references; for example, `=SUM(Sheet1:Sheet5!A1:D4)` is legal, but `=MMULT(Sheet1:Sheet5! A1:D4,F1:I4)` is not.

absolute reference

Compare with *relative reference* and *mixed reference*. An absolute reference contains a dollar sign ($) before its row component and before its column component. $A$1 is an example of an absolute reference. If you enter `=$A$1` in cell C1 and then copy the formula in C1 to cell D1, the formula in both C1 and D1 will be `=$A$1`. The reference is *absolute* and will not change, regardless of where you copy it.

absorption costing

Also called full costing. A method of assigning both the variable and fixed costs of production to the goods produced on a pro rata basis, regardless of whether the goods are sold during the current period. Compare with *contribution costing*.

accelerated depreciation

Any of a variety of methods of calculating depreciation that do not necessarily assign an equal amount of depreciation to an asset during each period of its useful life. Declining balance and sum-of-years'-digits are two examples of accelerated depreciation.

acceptable quality level

Used in acceptance sampling. The lowest proportion of nondefective goods that a buyer considers an acceptable average for the supplier's production process. Compare with *lot tolerance percent defective*.

accounts payable

Amounts that a business has agreed to pay its suppliers for items purchased on credit.

accounts receivable

Amounts owed to a business for products and services purchased on credit.

accrual accounting

Recording revenue when it is earned and expenses when they are incurred. It is coincidental if this is the same period in which cash is collected from customers or paid to suppliers.

ActiveX Data Objects (ADO)

A library of database objects (such as tables and queries), methods, and properties that you can use in VBA code to manage and retrieve data from a database programmatically. It's much more flexible than Data Access Objects (q.v.), but it's not optimized for use with Microsoft Access.

actual cost

The price paid to a supplier for an asset. Compare with *replacement cost.*

adjusted trial balance

A balance of accounts, struck at the end of an accounting period, that includes adjusting entries.

adjusting entry

An entry to an account, made at the end of an accounting period, that records any account activity that is not driven by an actual business transaction. Examples include depreciation, accrued salaries, and interest due for the period.

aging approach

A method of estimating the amount in accounts receivable that might never be collected. Under this approach, open accounts are classified according to the length of time that they are past due, and a different percentage of each category is treated as doubtful. Compare with *percentage of sales.*

argument

A value or a variable that is used by a function (or, in VBA, by a procedure). For example, in the formula `=SUM(1,2,3)`, the numbers `1`, `2`, and `3` are all arguments to the `SUM` function. Excel worksheet functions can hold up to 30 arguments. But note that a reference such as A1:A1000 counts as one argument, so worksheet functions are not limited to 30 numbers as arguments.

array formula

A special kind of formula in Excel. To enter a formula as an array formula, type it as usual but, instead of pressing Enter, press Ctrl+Shift+Enter. You can tell that Excel has accepted it as an array formula if you see a pair of curly braces (`{}`) surrounding the formula in the formula bar. Do not try to enter the braces from the keyboard, because doing so would indicate a text entry to Excel. Array formulas are required in certain worksheet functions, such as `LINEST()` and `MMULT()`; in these cases, you must highlight a range of cells that corresponds to the function's requirements before you array-enter the formula. Array formulas are also required if at least one argument consists of an array when the function normally expects a single value. Array formulas that occupy one cell only are legal, and they occur frequently.

asset

Anything of value that a business owns and that contributes to its ability to make a profit.

autocorrelation function (ACF)

A measure used in ARIMA analysis of the degree to which the current observation is dependent on a prior observation. For example, if observations are recorded in the worksheet range A1:A20, you can find a close approximation to a lag-1 ACF by `=CORREL(A2:A20,A1:A19)`, and to a lag-2 ACF by `=CORREL(A3:A20,A1:A18)`.

Autoregressive Integrated Moving Average (ARIMA)

Also known as Box-Jenkins analysis. A method used in forecasting that combines the advantages of regression approaches with moving-average and smoothing approaches to forecasting. ARIMA also provides a quantitative method for determining whether a regression approach, a smoothing approach, or a combination of those two approaches works best with a given time series.

average collection period
The average length of time it takes to recover costs and earn profit on credit sales. The usual formula is accounts receivable divided by the ratio of sales made on credit to the number of days in the period. The longer the average collection period, the longer the company does not have access to its assets for reinvestment.

average cost
A method of inventory valuation that assigns a value to each unit in the inventory that is the average of the cost of all units on hand (moving average method) or that have ever been in inventory (weighted average method), regardless of when or at what specific cost they were acquired.

balance sheet
A financial statement that summarizes a business's assets in one section and its liabilities and owner's equity in the other. The totals of the two sections should equal one another—that is, they should be in balance.

block
A group of VBA statements that is initiated and terminated by certain keywords. For example, statements between an `If` statement and an `End If` statement are a block. Similarly, statements between a `With` statement and an `End With` statement are a block.

break-even point
The earliest date that the costs of an investment are fully recovered by the income it produces.

collection
In VBA, a group of objects. For example, the `Worksheets` collection consists of a group of `Worksheets`.

common-sizing
The conversion of the numbers in a financial statement from dollar amounts to another metric. You can do this in an income statement by dividing each dollar amount by net sales for the period. In this way, each entry in the statement represents a percentage of sales. You can use different divisors, such as headcount and total assets, for different analysis purposes.

confidence interval
The size of the range between an upper and a lower value such that some proportion of (usually) the averages of repeated samples from a population are expected to fall within the range. That proportion is the probability, or confidence level, associated with the interval. Therefore, a 95% confidence interval around a sample average is expected to be one of the 95 of 100 hypothetical intervals that do span the population average.

continuing value
An estimate of the total value of an investment after some specified period of time. This estimate is often based on the value of an alternative investment that would return the same cash flow as the existing investment.

contra-account
A type of ledger account established to accumulate amounts that work against other accounts. For example, a contra-revenue account, such as Sales Returns or Uncollectible Accounts, is used as an offset to Sales, to calculate Net Sales.

contribution costing
Also called variable costing. A method of assigning all the fixed costs of production to the goods sold during the current period. Compare with *absorption costing*.

contribution margin
The revenue created by the sale of a product, less the variable expenses associated with the product.

control limits
Values used in statistical process control that help define whether a process is in control. Usually, they are defined as three standard errors above and below the average value of the process.

control variable
A variable that defines the number of times a loop executes. For example, the `For` statement `For Counter = 1 to 10` causes the subsequent statements to execute 10 times. The control variable is `Counter`.

correlogram
A graph, used in ARIMA analysis, of the correlations of observations with observations that occurred earlier in the baseline. Correlograms are used in the identification phase of an ARIMA analysis to help specify a model (AR, MA, IMA, and so on) for the data.

cost of goods available for sale
The sum of the value of a period's beginning inventory plus the value of goods produced (or acquired for resale) during the period.

cost of goods sold (COGS)
Compare with *cost of goods available for sale*. COGS is the cost to a company of the acquisition and manufacture of the products that it sells. The components of COGS include the cost of raw materials, any labor costs involved in the manufacture or other preparation for sale, and any overhead associated with production. Often the most convenient way to determine the COGS is to subtract the value of the ending inventory from the cost of goods available for sale. On the income statement, the COGS is subtracted from Sales (or from Net Sales if the customer has returned goods) to find gross profit.

cost/volume/profit analysis
Analyses of the relationships among the costs paid to produce or acquire goods, the number of such goods, and the profit obtained from their sale. Particularly important in these analyses is the understanding of the relative effects of fixed and variable costs and the products' contribution margin.

credits
The right side of a T-account.

cross-elasticity
The functional similarity of different products that a business offers. Products that are cross-elastic tend to cut into one another's sales.

current assets
Cash, plus assets that a business can convert into cash, usually within one year, in the course of conducting its normal operations.

current liabilities
Debts or obligations to creditors and suppliers that a business must satisfy within the current period.

current ratio
A measure of a company's ability to meet its current liabilities from its current assets. Current assets include inventory; compare with the *quick ratio*, which subtracts inventory from current assets.

Data Access Objects (DAO)
A library of objects (and their associated methods and properties) that can be used to represent objects in databases. By making DAO available to VBA, the user can write VBA code that enables Excel to interact directly with databases, particularly Microsoft Access. Compare with *ActiveX Data Objects*.

date serial number
In Excel, each possible day is assigned a different serial number. In Excel for Windows, the system assigns serial number 1 to January 1, 1900; the serial number 2 to January 2, 1900; and so on. Optionally, you can use the 1904 date system, under which serial number 1 is assigned to January 2, 1904.

debits
The left side of a T-account.

debt ratio
The ratio of a company's total debt to its total assets. From a creditor's standpoint, the lower the debt ratio, the better.

declining balance
A method of accelerated depreciation that bases the amount of depreciation of an asset for the current period on the value of the asset at the end of the previous period. Compare with *straight-line depreciation.*

depreciation
The reduction in the value of an asset (typically, buildings and equipment) that occurs through its use in the production of revenue. This reduction in value is recognized periodically as the asset ages. Excel supports several methods of calculating depreciation, including straight-line, declining balance, and sum-of-years'-digits.

`Dim` **statement**
The typical method of declaring a VBA variable. You can use the `Dim` statement to name the variable, to declare it as a specific type such as `String` or `Integer`, to declare it as an array of values, and (if an array) to specify the bounds of its dimensions.

discount factor
The factor that determines the future value of a given present value, or the present value of a given future value.

discounted payback period
The length of time required to recover the cost of an investment, taking into account losses in the investment's value due to discounting.

double precision
A variable type. Compare with *single precision.* A VBA variable declared as a `Double` occupies 64 bits of memory and is, therefore, more precise than a single-precision variable, which occupies only 32 bits of memory.

double-entry accounting
The method of accounting under which every business transaction appears as a debit to one account and as a credit to another account.

Earnings Before Interest, Taxes, Depreciation, and Amortization (EBITDA)
Figure frequently used in financial analysis to represent a company's earnings due to its core business operations, undiluted by ancillary obligations.

earnings per share (EPS) ratio
A company's earnings (usually defined as its net income less an allowance for preferred dividends), divided by the number of shares of common stock outstanding. EPS is a measure of the attractiveness of an investment to a holder of common stock.

equity ratio
The complement of debt ratio. The ratio of a company's total equity to its total assets, and thus the portion of the company's asset base that has been acquired through investment instead of through borrowing.

event

In the Excel object model, something that happens to an object. Events and methods are closely related. VBA code might apply the `Open` method to a workbook. When that happens, the `Open` event has occurred, and other code might execute in response to and as a result of the event.

first-in, first-out (FIFO)

A method of inventory valuation that assumes that the value of the goods that were sold from inventory during the period is the value of the goods acquired earliest. Compare with *last-in, first-out (LIFO)*, and *average cost*.

fixed assets

Assets that, in contrast to consumable supplies, are long lasting and have an objective value.

fixed costs

Compare with *variable costs*. Costs of conducting operations that are the same regardless of how many product units are produced or how many services are rendered.

future value

The value at some future time of an investment made today: its original value plus whatever amount the investment earns between today and some date in the future.

general journal

Compare with *special journal*. A journal that contains, usually in chronological order, records of business transactions that do not belong in any of the special journals that a company has established. It is usually reserved for exceptional transactions, such as a one-time bonus to an employee, whereas a special journal is reserved for frequently occurring transactions such as weekly salary payments or cash sales.

general ledger

A grouping of all the accounts that pertain to the operation of a business, showing the debits and credits that apply to each account. Detailed information about very active accounts, such as cash receipts, accounts payable, and accounts receivable, are maintained in subsidiary ledgers, and their total debits and total credits are transferred to the associated account in the general ledger.

Generally Accepted Accounting Principles (GAAP)

Methods used in accounting that help ensure accurate financial reporting and that enable accurate comparisons of the results reported by one business entity with those reported by another. See *International Financial Reporting Standards*.

gross profit margin

A measure of a company's profitability before taking operating expenses into account. It is usually calculated by subtracting the cost of goods sold from sales and dividing the result by sales. This returns gross profit as a percentage of sales.

horizontal analysis

The comparison of a company's financial results with its own previous results. Compare with *vertical analysis*.

implicit intersection

The intersection of a row and a column that is implied, versus explicitly defined, by a formula. If cells A1:E1 constitute a range named `Prices`, you could enter, using the key combination Ctrl+Enter, the formula `=Prices*.06` into cells A2:E2 to return the sales tax. This formula implies that cell A2 should use the value in cell A1, cell B2 should use the value in cell B1, and so on. It implies an intersection between the Prices range and the column that contains the formula that makes reference to the `Prices range`.

income statement

A report of the changes in the financial position of a business during an accounting period. It usually consists of a summary of its revenues less the cost of goods sold, less operating expenses, less other expenses such as taxes, resulting in an estimate of earnings. Income statements used for external reporting must follow GAAP or IFRS principles and rules, but income statements used for internal planning can take any of a variety of forms that help the user focus on a particular product, operation, or business strategy.

intercept

The y-axis value of a line at the point that its value on the x-axis is zero. Combined with knowledge of the line's slope, the intercept helps to forecast an unknown y-value, given its known x-value.

internal rate of return (IRR)

A measure of the profitability of an investment based on a series of cash flows generated by the investment. IRR assumes that the cash generated can be reinvested at the same rate.

International Financial Reporting Standards (IFRS)

Accounting standards developed for use internationally, not simply in the United States, which historically used GAAP for standards and guidelines. Groups such as the Financial Accounting Standards Board have worked toward integrating the two sets of standards.

inventory profit

The profit that can be created simply by holding goods in inventory as their replacement price increases, due to changes in market conditions.

Just In Time (JIT)

An approach to inventory management that calls for goods required for production or resale to be obtained no earlier than absolutely necessary.

last-in, first-out (LIFO)

A method of inventory valuation that assumes that the value of the goods sold from inventory during the period is the value of the goods acquired most recently. Compare with *first-in, first-out (FIFO)*, and *average cost*.

liability
A debt incurred by a business; thus, a claim by a creditor against the business's assets.

long-term note payable
An obligation to a creditor that must be satisfied at some point following the end of the current accounting period.

loop
A series of VBA statements that execute repetitively. The loop can be under the control of a `For` statement, in which case the statements usually execute a fixed number of times. It can also be under the control of a `Do` statement; if so, the statements usually execute until some Boolean condition changes. Or it can be under the control of a `For Each` statement; then the statements execute once for each member of a collection, such as for each worksheet in a workbook.

lot tolerance percent defective
The lowest level of nondefective products that a buyer is willing to accept in an individual lot. Compare with acceptable quality level.

matching principle
A basic principle of accrual accounting: Revenues should be matched to the costs that helped to produce them.

method
In VBA, an action that you can perform on or apply to an object. For example, the `Range` object has the `Delete` method; you would use that method to delete a worksheet range. Compare with *event*.

mixed reference
Compare with *absolute reference* and *relative reference*. A mixed reference is a combination of an absolute and a relative reference. It has a dollar sign before either its row component or its column component, but not both. $A1 and A$1 are examples of mixed references. If you enter `=$A1` in cell C1 and copy it to cell D1, the reference does not change, but if you copy it from C1 to C2, the formula changes to `=$A2`. On the other hand, if you enter `=A$1` in cell C1 and copy it to cell D1, the reference changes to `=B$1`, but if you copy it from C1 to C2, the formula will not change.

Modified Internal Rate of Return (MIRR)
The Internal Rate of Return, modified by eliminating IRR's assumption that cash flows can be reinvested at the same rate.

moving average
A method used in forecasting in which the variation of individual observations from a long-term trend is suppressed by averaging several observations.

named range

A range of cells that is assigned a name, usually by means of the Name box or by using Define Name on the Formula tab. After you have assigned a name to a range, you can use the name in place of the range's address in formulas. This makes the structure and function of a worksheet much easier to understand. For example, suppose that cells A1:A12 are given the name `MonthlySales`. It is easier to understand the intent of the formula `=SUM(MonthlySales)` than it is to understand the intent of `=SUM(A1:A12)`.

net present value

The value of an investment as of today less its loss in value due to discounting.

net profit margin

A measure of a company's profitability after taxes and operating expenses are taken into account. After subtracting the cost of goods sold, operating expenses, and taxes from sales, the result is divided by sales. This expresses net profit—the amount available for distribution or reinvestment—as a percentage of the company's sales.

object

In VBA, a structure in a workbook, such as a worksheet, menu bar, or range. (Excel itself, the application, is also an object). Objects belong to collections; for example, the `Worksheet` collection is the collection of all the worksheets in a specific workbook. Objects have methods, properties, and events.

object variable

In VBA, a variable that stands in for an object such as a worksheet range. Object variables are assigned to the objects they represent by means of the `Set` statement.

operating characteristic curve

A curve used in acceptance sampling that provides a visual representation of the effects of quality requirements that are imposed by the buyer and by the nature of the production process.

Option Explicit

An option you can set at the beginning of a VBA module. Using this option means that you cannot use a variable name before you have declared it, usually with a `Dim` statement. If you omit this option from your VBA module, you can declare variables implicitly, by simply using their names. Because variables that are declared implicitly are, by default, `Variant` variables (which occupy a relatively large amount of memory), and because it's easy to misspell a variable's name (which would simply create a new variable), it's recommended that you use `Option Explicit` routinely.

owner's equity

The difference between a company's total assets and its total liabilities. The sum of the amounts that the owner(s) invested in the business, plus any profits that the business has retained.

passing a variable
In VBA, the process of making a variable that is available to a calling procedure (a `Sub` or a `Function`) accessible to a called procedure. The called procedure might change the value of that variable and subsequently pass the changed value back to the calling procedure. This is called passing by reference and is the default method. The alternative, passing by value, does not pass a changed value back to the calling procedure.

payback period
The time required to recover the cost of an investment from the value (usually the cash) generated by the investment.

percentage of completion
A method of determining how much revenue to recognize during any given period of a multiperiod contract, usually based on the portion of total costs that have been expended.

percentage of sales
A method of estimating many items in an income statement. Most items are driven by the dollar amount of sales in a given period, and it's often possible to establish that, for example, salaries have historically been 35% of sales. Then it is possible to estimate salaries for the upcoming period by estimating sales and calculating 35% of that estimate. The percentage of sales approach is also sometimes used to estimate the amount of past-due accounts receivable that will never be collected.

periodic inventory system
A method of inventory valuation in which inventory is counted and valued at the end of an accounting period. This method is normally used by businesses that deal in a high unit volume of products whose unit value is relatively low.

perpetual inventory system
A method of inventory valuation in which the value and the quantity on hand of each inventory unit are known and can be recorded as frequently as desired. This method is normally used by businesses that sell a relatively small number of units, each with a relatively high value.

post
To move transaction information, initially recorded chronologically in a journal, to the appropriate account in a ledger.

prepaid expenses
Amounts paid for goods and services before the expense is actually incurred. An example is an insurance policy that is purchased at the beginning of the year and that provides protection throughout the year. The expense is incurred as protection expires; the prepaid expense is the amount originally paid for the policy.

present value
The value today of an amount you will receive at some future time. For example, present value is the amount you would need to invest in a financial instrument today for that instrument to be worth $1,000 one year from today.

price/earnings (P/E) ratio
The ratio of the market price of one share of a company's stock to its per-share earnings. Generally, the lower the P/E ratio, the better the stock is as an investment. A company's earnings are usually a good measure of its value; the smaller the price you must pay for that value, the better the investment. Some prefer to invert this ratio and work with an E/P ratio instead.

pro forma
A projection or forecast based on a financial statement. A pro forma income statement, for example, might project next year's revenues, costs, and expenses.

profitability index
A measure that compares the profitability of investments that have equivalent rates of return but that require different initial investment amounts.

property
An aspect of an object. For example, a worksheet `Range` object has the `Address` property, which returns the range's reference, such as A1:C3.

query
A series of statements written in Structured Query Language that add, modify, remove, or return data from a database.

quick ratio
A company's current assets minus its inventory, divided by its current liabilities. This ratio tests a company's ability to meet its current obligations without needing to liquidate its inventory.

R-squared
A measure of how well a regression equation predicts one variable on the basis of another variable or variables. R-squared can vary from 0.0 to 1.0; the closer it is to 1.0, the better the prediction.

range
A group of cells on a worksheet, such as A1:D4. Technically, a single cell is itself a range, but in normal usage, the term *range* means more than one contiguous cell.

realization
The conversion of revenue that has been recognized to actual revenue at the point when you objectively know its amount, when you objectively know it will occur, and when the earning process is virtually complete. Compare with *recognition*.

recognition
The recording of revenue in accounting records and financial statements. Compare with *realization*.

`RefersTo` property

Whatever an Excel name represents. Most often this is the address of a worksheet range, as entered in the Refers To edit box in the Define Name dialog box. It can also be a constant value if the name represents a constant.

regression equation

An equation that you can use to predict an unknown value from known values. Excel uses the `LINEST` function to analyze the relationships among two or more variables and to return a set of coefficients that define the equation. For example, you could use `LINEST` to analyze the relationship between annual advertising expenses and revenues for each year. By applying the equation to a proposed advertising budget figure, you can predict the revenues you would expect to generate with that amount of advertising.

relative reference

Compare with *absolute reference* and *mixed reference*. A relative reference contains no dollar signs. A1:D4 is an example of a relative reference. Suppose that you enter `=SUM(A1:D4)` in cell F1. If you then copy the formula in cell F1 to cell G1, the reference adjusts to `=SUM(B1:E4)`. The reference remains *relative* to the location where the formula has been entered.

replacement cost

The cost of replacing an existing asset. This amount is sometimes used in place of actual cost as a means of valuing the asset.

return on assets (ROA)

A measure of how well a company uses its resources to create earnings. The usual formula adds net income to interest expense and divides the result by total assets. Interest expense is added back to net income because it is normally a cost of acquiring additional assets and, therefore, should not be counted against the company's performance. Compare with *return on equity (ROE)*.

return on equity (ROE)

A measure of a company's ability to create earnings, as a function of its equity. The usual formula is net income divided by stockholder equity. By comparing ROA with ROE, you can infer how a company tends to raise money: through debt financing (usually used to acquire assets) or through new investment (which contributes to equity).

revenue

The price customers pay for a business's goods and services.

Ribbon

Part of the Office user interface that was introduced in Office 2007. The Ribbon replaces the menus that were used through Office 2003. Each application in Office (that is, Excel, Word, PowerPoint, and so on) has its own Ribbon. The Excel Ribbon has tabs labeled File, Home, Insert, Page Layout, and so on. Each tab has groups of tools or options for the user to select. For example, the Cells group on the Ribbon's Home tab has an Insert control (you can insert cells, rows, columns, or a worksheet), a Delete control (to delete the same objects), and a Format control.

sales mix
The manner in which different products are combined to create a product line.

salvage value
The value of an asset at the end of its depreciable life.

scope
Either the worksheet to which a sheet-level name belongs, or the workbook to which a book-level name belongs.

seasonality
The tendency of variables such as sales to rise during certain seasons and to fall at other times of the year. For example, the sale of heavy winter apparel tends to be seasonal. Certain forecasting methods can account for and project seasonal variations in sales levels.

semivariable costs
Compare with *variable costs* and *fixed costs*. Costs of operations that do not increase on a one-to-one basis with each additional unit that is produced but increase sharply as certain production thresholds are reached.

sensitivity analysis
An analysis that examines the effects on selected results, such as revenue or earnings, of changing different inputs, such as advertising expenses or depreciation method.

`Set` **statement**
A VBA statement that causes an object such as a range of cells on a worksheet to be assigned to a VBA variable. For example: `Set CurrentRange = ActiveSheet.Range(Cells(1,1),Cells(5,5))`.

sheet-level names
A sheet-level name belongs only to the sheet where it is defined and contains the name of the sheet as a qualifier of the name. On the sheet where the sheet-level name is defined, you can use the name unqualified by its sheet name. For example, `Sheet1!Expenses` is a sheet-level name; it might be defined as `=Sheet1!A1:D4`. On `Sheet1`, you can use formulas that refer to expenses, such as `=SUM(Expenses)`. But unless `Sheet2` also contains the name `Sheet2!Expenses`, you cannot use `=SUM(Expenses)` on `Sheet2` because an unqualified sheet-level name is not accessible from another sheet, one that's outside the name's scope. Instead, on `Sheet2`, you would need to use `=SUM(Sheet1!Expenses)`. Sheet-level names enable you to define the same name, qualified by the name of its sheet, in more than one sheet in a workbook. So you might have `January!Expenses` on the sheet named `January`, `February!Expenses` on the sheet named `February`, and so on. (In Excel 2007 and 2010, you use a Scope drop-down to define a name as sheet-level; earlier versions require that you type the name of the sheet and the exclamation point to define the name.)

short-term note payable
A debt that must be satisfied during the current accounting period.

single precision
A variable type. Compare with *double precision*. A VBA variable declared as `Single` occupies 32 bits of memory. It is less precise than a double-precision variable for very large or very small numbers.

slope
The change in the level of a line on its y-axis value as a function of a change in the level of the line on its x-axis. Combined with information about the line's intercept, the slope can be used in regression methods to predict an unknown y-value, given knowledge of the associated x-value.

smoothing
A type of forecasting technique that uses, for the current forecast, a combination of the previous observation and the error involved in the previous forecast.

special journal
Analogous to a subsidiary ledger, a special journal provides a place to record frequently occurring business transactions. This allows the general journal to function as a place to record infrequently occurring transactions. In this way, you can segregate similar transactions into one location for easy reference.

standard deviation
A measure of how much different values in a set of numbers vary from their average. In a normal distribution of values, you expect to find about 68% of the values within one standard deviation on each side of the average, about 95% within two standard deviations on each side of the average, and about 99.7% of the values within three standard deviations on each side of the average.

starting inventory
The value of the goods on hand at the beginning of an accounting period, equal to the value of inventory at the end of the previous accounting period.

statistical process control (SPC)
A method of determining whether the results of a process, such as a production line, conform to their specifications. If the process is not in control, SPC can also point to the time when it began to go out of control.

straight-line depreciation
A method of calculating depreciation that divides the difference between an asset's original and final values by the number of periods in which the asset is in service.

Structured Query Language (SQL)
A language that you can use to manipulate databases, structures in databases, and the information stored there. SQL is a standard, and most database programs interpret SQL instructions in the same way. A user can embed SQL in VBA code to control a database from the Excel application.

subsidiary ledger

A representation of all the transactions that occur in a given account during an accounting period. A subsidiary ledger maintains the detail information about the account; its debit and credit totals are transferred to the associated account in the general ledger.

sum-of-years'-digits

A method of accelerated depreciation that assigns an amount of depreciation based on the number of periods (years) that an asset has been in service, factored against the asset's original value.

T-account

A format for displaying the debits and credits to an account, so called because the horizontal line under the column headings and the vertical line between the columns form a *T*.

times interest earned

The ratio of a company's earnings before interest and taxes to its total interest payments. A measure of the company's ability to meet its periodic interest payments from its earnings.

trend

In forecasting and time series analysis, the tendency of data values to increase or decrease over time. A trend might be linear, in which case it describes a straight line. Frequently occurring nonlinear trends include quadratic trends (one change of direction over the course of the time series) and cubic trends (two changes in direction over the course of the time series).

turns ratio

The number of times during a period that a company's inventory turns over completely. The usual formula is cost of goods sold divided by average inventory. Generally, the higher the turns ratio, the better. Goods that remain in inventory too long tie up the company's resources and often incur storage expenses, as well as loss of value.

unearned revenue

Revenue that must be recognized during a period because it has been received from a customer but that has not yet been earned (and, therefore, has no associated expense during the current period).

union

The combination of two different worksheet ranges so that they are treated as one. The union operator is the comma. So the formula `=SUM(A1:A5,C10:C15)` returns the sum of the values in the combination, or union, of the two ranges.

user-defined function

A function the user creates in VBA code. You can enter a user-defined function in a worksheet cell just as you enter a built-in worksheet function such as `SUM()`. In VBA, a user-defined function is identified with the keyword `Function` instead of with the keyword `Sub`. Within the body of the function's code, a value must be assigned to the function's name. When entered on the worksheet, a user-defined function can only return a value; it cannot perform other actions, such as inserting a row or formatting a range.

variable costs
Costs that increase as the number of goods produced or services rendered increases. Compare with *fixed costs*.

variable type
A variable's type defines what sorts of values it can take on. A variable's type is usually declared with VBA's `Dim` statement. If a variable is declared as `Integer`, for example, it cannot take on either the value `Fred` (which is a string) or the value `3.1416` (which has a decimal component). See `Variant`.

variance analysis
The comparison of an actual financial result with an expected result. For example, a company might have a negotiated contract with a supplier to purchase materials at a standard cost. If the actual amount of payment for the materials differs from the standard cost, the difference represents a variance. Other similar comparisons include analyzing the differences between budgeted amounts and actual expenditures. It is completely unrelated to analysis of variance, which is a statistical procedure that tests the differences between the means of two or more sets of values.

`Variant`
A type of variable in VBA. A `Variant` variable, in contrast to other variable types, can take on any value, such as an integer, a decimal value, text, or a logical value. Declaring a variable as `Variant` is also a useful way to assign the values in a worksheet range to a VBA array.

vertical analysis
The comparison of a company's financial information with that of other companies in the same industry grouping. Compare with *horizontal analysis*.

Visual Basic for Applications (VBA)
The language Microsoft provides to write procedures that Excel and other Office applications execute.

weighted average
An average of a set of numbers such that certain numbers receive a greater weight than do other numbers. The formula `=SUM(12*{1,2,3},4,5,6)/6` is a weighted average because the numbers `1`, `2`, and `3` are weighted by a factor of 12, and the numbers `4`, `5`, and `6` are not weighted.

`With` **statement and** `With` **block**
The `With` statement initiates a `With` block; the `End With` statement terminates the `With` block. Inside the block, you can refer to methods or properties of the object named in the `With` statement, yet you don't need to qualify the method or property by referring repeatedly to the object.

workbook-level names
A workbook-level name belongs to the workbook and can be used in functions or formulas in any workbook sheet. `Costs` is an example of a workbook-level name; to be a sheet-level name, it

would need to be qualified by the name of a specific sheet, as in `Sheet1!Costs`. Only one instance of a particular workbook-level name can exist in that workbook. Compare with *sheet-level names*.

working capital
The difference between current assets and current liabilities; the resources a business has on hand to support its operations.

INDEX

Symbols

A

B

C

How can we make this index more useful? Email us at indexes@quepublishing.com

S

How can we make this index more useful? Email us at indexes@quepublishing.com

W

X-Y-Z